P9-CCX-308

Major Problems in the History
of the Vietnam War

MAJOR PROBLEMS IN AMERICAN HISTORY SERIES

GENERAL EDITOR
THOMAS G. PATERSON

Major Problems in the History of the Vietnam War

DOCUMENTS AND ESSAYS

SECOND EDITION

EDITED BY
ROBERT J. McMAHON
UNIVERSITY OF FLORIDA

D. C. HEATH AND COMPANY
Lexington, Massachusetts   Toronto

Address editorial correspondence to:
D. C. Heath and Company
125 Spring Street
Lexington, MA 02173

Acquisitions Editor: James Miller
Developmental Editor: Sylvia Mallory
Production Editor: Julie Lane
Designer: Jan Shapiro
Production Coordinator: Charles Dutton
Permissions Editor: Margaret Roll

Cover photo: *Last Stand, Vietnam,* by Phillip W. Jones, 1967. United States Army Center for Military History.

Copyright © 1995 by D. C. Heath and Company.

Previous editions copyright © 1990 by D. C. Heath and Company.

All rights reserved. No part of this publication may be reproduced or transmitted in any form or by any means, electronic or mechanical, including photocopy, recording, or any information storage or retrieval system, without permission in writing from the publisher.

Published simultaneously in Canada.

Printed in the United States of America.

International Standard Book Number: 0–669–35252–7

Library of Congress Catalog Number: 94–77794

456789-QF-00 99 98

In memory of George E. Pozzetta, 1942–1994

Preface

U.S. intervention in Vietnam grew slowly in the first years after the Second World War—almost imperceptibly so to most Americans. But an ever-deepening commitment soon became evident. By the early 1950s the United States was underwriting about 80 percent of the bill for France's colonial war against Vietnamese nationalists; and following the collapse of French rule in 1954, Washington became the principal source of support for a new, struggling South Vietnamese government. By the early 1960s the United States was providing that regime with thousands of military advisers in an effort to check a renewed guerrilla insurgency. In 1965 American ground troops joined the fray, only to become bogged down in a major land war.

In the ten-year period bracketed by the introduction of American combat forces in 1965 and the collapse of the U.S.-backed Saigon regime in 1975, the Vietnam War dominated political, social, cultural, and intellectual life in the United States. Probably no issue since the Civil War has divided Americans more deeply than the Indochina conflict. Certainly few, if any, episodes in contemporary history have had a more profound impact on American society or compelled a more searching examination of America's role in the world. A complete accounting of the war's deeper costs, however, remains elusive. The passions it unleashed have not yet ebbed, nor has the nation fully absorbed or overcome its many consequences.

Indeed, the divisions opened by the Vietnam War have resurfaced in presidential campaigns since 1975. In 1992, for example, political opponents questioned Democratic presidential candidate Bill Clinton's evasion of the draft during the 1960s just as, in 1988, political opponents had questioned Republican vice-presidential candidate Dan Quayle's military record. The fact that both men avoided service in Vietnam, and that both appeared to use either subterfuge or family connections in the process, became more important in the ensuing swirl of charges and countercharges than their dramatically different positions on the conflict. Moreover, each time the United States intervened, or considered intervening, abroad during the 1970s and 1980s—whether in Iran, Lebanon, Grenada, Libya, or Central America—critics and interventionists alike drew lessons from the Vietnam experience. After the American-led coalition's victory over Iraq in the Persian Gulf War in 1991, President George Bush proclaimed triumphantly that the United States had finally overcome "the Vietnam syndrome." His assertion, however, appears to have been an expression more of wishful thinking than of careful contemplation.

The impressive outpouring of Vietnam-era reflections in the United States in recent years testifies both to the continued public preoccupation with the war and to the absence of a broad consensus on its meaning. A proliferation of movies, television series, documentaries, novels, and memoirs has competed for the public's attention with books and articles by scholars, policy analysts, military officers, civilian policymakers, and journalists. The viewpoints expressed in these diverse efforts have varied as widely as the lessons drawn. Significantly, this continuing fascination with the Vietnam years has not been confined to those with vivid memories of that turbulent time. College students, many of them born after the collapse of the Saigon regime, continue to flock to the hundreds of Vietnam War courses taught in universities both inside and outside the United States. Perhaps they are simply curious about an episode central to their parents' generation. Or perhaps they are trying to understand how and why events that reached their denouement on the battlefield two decades ago still reverberate with such force across the political and cultural landscape of contemporary America.

This volume addresses these issues and questions. It seeks to stimulate critical thinking about the Vietnam War and its long-term meaning for Americans. The essays and documents in this book, like those in the other anthologies in D. C. Heath's Major Problems in American History Series, introduce students to the main controversies and debates surrounding the subject. Because the Vietnam War represents a pivotal episode in the American national experience, the principal focus of these readings is on three America-centered questions: Why was the United States drawn into the Vietnam War? How did the nation seek to accomplish its goals in Vietnam from the 1940s to the 1970s? And what have been the lessons and consequences of the war for the United States?

The war, of course, forms a chapter not just in American history but in the history of modern Asia—and the world. Nor was the United States the only significant actor in the drama. In an effort to present students with a balanced perspective on the war and with the context necessary for understanding American decisions, I have included three chapters that deal exclusively with Vietnamese topics—and that feature Vietnamese voices. In each chapter, the essays and documents place U.S. policy in the broadest possible framework. The book's primary focus remains, nonetheless, the *American* experience in Vietnam.

Each chapter opens with a brief introduction to the topic at hand. The introduction is followed by a series of primary documents and two or three interpretive essays by historians, political scientists, participants, or other authorities. The documents reveal the flavor of the time and the range of contemporary issues and retrospective assessments. The essays present the most significant debates and controversies generated by the war. Readers are encouraged to assess evidence carefully, to weigh conflicting arguments, and to form their own opinions. Suggestions for further reading follow each chapter, providing guideposts for those interested in probing issues more deeply.

Many individuals helped in the preparation of this book. I am especially grateful to Thomas G. Paterson for first suggesting this project to me, and for his valuable suggestions at every stage. For general advice, specific recommendations, and constructive criticism on the first edition, I thank Edward P. Crapol, William J. Duiker, George C. Herring, Gary R. Hess, Richard H. Immerman, John Israel, Melvyn P. Leffler, Gary May, Kell Mitchell, Samuel L. Popkin, Donald W. Rogers, Sandra C. Taylor, and William S. Turley. I acknowledge Ted Snow's help in locating certain materials for the first edition and the expert assistance of the secretarial staff at the University of Florida's History Department. For their written reviews and helpful recommendations during the preparation of this second edition of the book, I am extremely grateful to James A. Banks, Cuyahoga Community College; David Castle, Muskingum College; John F. Guilmartin, Jr., Ohio State University; Richard H. Immerman, Temple University; Gerald Newman, Kent State University; James R. Rush, Arizona State University; David F. Schmitz, Whitman College; Robert D. Schulzinger, University of Colorado, Boulder; and Robert Weisbrot, Colby College. I have also tried to incorporate many of the numerous suggestions for improving the first volume that my students at the University of Florida have offered over the past several years. I thank D. C. Heath history editors Sylvia Mallory and James Miller for providing a marvelous combination of professionalism, enthusiasm, and support. I join them and the series editor in welcoming suggestions for future improvements in this volume.

Most of all, I am indebted to my family. My sons, Tommy and Michael, and my wife, Alison, have provided indispensable support, understanding, and encouragement.

This book is dedicated to a wonderful colleague and valued friend who passed away just as I was completing it. A Vietnam veteran, George Pozzetta died suddenly and unexpectedly in May 1994, following an operation to repair a war wound suffered twenty-five years earlier. The intelligence, integrity, and professionalism that made him such a superb colleague were exceeded only by the cheerfulness, warmth, and legendary sense of humor that made him such a pleasure to be with. I will miss him greatly.

If this volume can contribute in some small way to the current generation's understanding of how and why individuals like George Pozzetta wound up in Vietnam—and how that experience affected them—then it will have achieved its purpose. And he, more than anyone, would have been pleased.

R. J. M

Contents

C H A P T E R   6
Lyndon B. Johnson's Decisions for War
Page 207

C H A P T E R   7
U.S. Military Strategy
Page 243

CHAPTER 8
The Enemy: North Vietnam and the "Vietcong"
Page 282

CHAPTER 9
The Tet Offensive
Page 337

CHAPTER 10
The Ally: South Vietnam
Page 389

DOCUMENTS

ESSAYS

CHAPTER 11
Richard M. Nixon's Strategy for Withdrawal
Page 422

DOCUMENTS

ESSAYS

CHAPTER 12
The Antiwar Movement and Public Opinion
Page 466

DOCUMENTS

C H A P T E R 13
The Media and the War
Page 466

C H A P T E R 14
*The Paris Peace Accords of 1973
and the Fall of South Vietnam*
Page 563

C H A P T E R 15
Consequences and Lessons of the War
Page 608

Commonly Used Acronyms

ARVN	Army of the Republic of Vietnam
CIA	Central Intelligence Agency
CINCPAC	U.S. Commander in Chief, Pacific
COSVN	Central Office for South Vietnam of the Communist Party
DMZ	Demilitarized Zone
DRV	Democratic Republic of Vietnam (North Vietnam)
GVN	Government of Vietnam (South Vietnam)
ICP	Indochinese Communist Party
JCS	Joint Chiefs of Staff
MAAG	U.S. Military Assistance Advisory Group
MACV	U.S. Military Assistance Command, Vietnam
MR	Military Region
NLF	National Liberation Front
NSC	National Security Council
NVA	North Vietnamese Army
NVN	North Vietnam
PAVN	Peoples' Army of Vietnam (regular army of North Vietnam)
PLAF	Peoples' Liberation Armed Forces (regular army of the NLF, then PRG)
PRG	Provisional Revolutionary Government
RVN	Republic of Vietnam (South Vietnam)
RVNAF	Republic of Vietnam Armed Forces
SEA	Southeast Asia
SEATO	Southeast Asia Treaty Organization
SVN	South Vietnam
VC	Vietcong

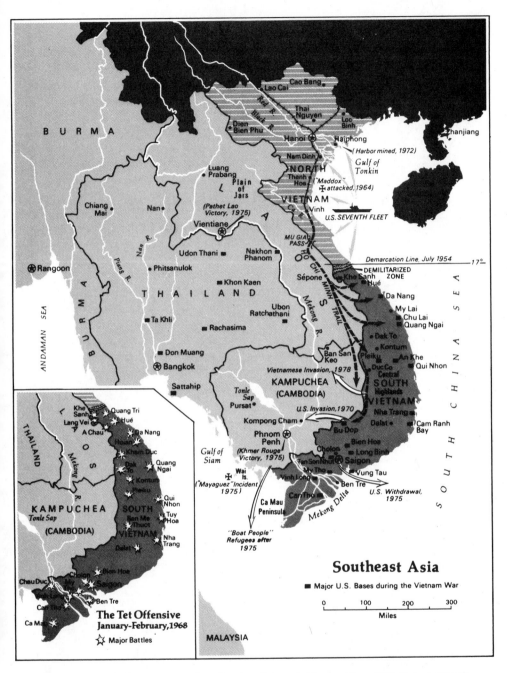

From Thomas G. Paterson, *American Foreign Policy: A History, Since 1900*, 3rd ed. (Heath, 1988), p. 559.

Major Problems in the History
of the Vietnam War

CHAPTER

1

Vietnam and America:
An Introduction

✕

America's longest war, the Vietnam conflict also was one of its most divisive. As U.S. troop levels swelled to more than half a million by the late 1960s, American society split sharply over the morality and efficacy of the war effort. The war's inconclusiveness and unpopularity spawned not only a broad-based antiwar movement but also a reexamination of America's purpose as wrenching and far-reaching as any other since the Civil War. Neither President Richard M. Nixon's decision in 1969 to begin withdrawing U.S. troops nor the fall of Saigon to the communists in April 1975 did much to resolve the debate or ease the traumas that it unleashed.

The selections in this opening chapter explore the larger boundaries of that debate by focusing on the following questions: Why did the United States intervene in Vietnam: to defend freedom and liberty or to protect imperial interests dictated by America's world position and economic needs? What did the United States seek to accomplish in Vietnam? Were its goals attainable? Who were its enemies? its allies? Can U.S. actions there be characterized as moral—or immoral? In the larger scope of U.S., Asian, and world history, how should the Vietnam War be interpreted and judged?

✕ *E S S A Y S*

In the first essay, Leslie H. Gelb, a prominent journalist and former assistant secretary of state in the Jimmy Carter administration, and Richard K. Betts of the Brookings Institution summarize and critique the various interpretations analysts have offered to explain U.S. involvement in Vietnam. They conclude that the decisionmaking system worked far better than most of its critics realize. It worked, they believe, because it achieved its stated purpose of preventing a communist victory in Vietnam until the U.S. domestic consensus shifted in 1974–1975.

In the next essay, Norman Podhoretz, the editor of *Commentary* and

1

author of numerous books about contemporary American society, insists that the United States went into Vietnam for idealistic, not selfish, reasons: to save the southern half of the Asian nation from the evils of communism. He finds vindication for the moral soundness of America's commitment in the "hideous consequences" of the U.S. defeat for the peoples of Indochina.

The final essay offers a radical perspective on the origins and consequences of the war. Gabriel Kolko of York University (Toronto) sees U.S. intervention as an essential part of Washington's overall strategy for guiding and integrating the world's political and economic system. He contends that America's defeat exposed the limitations of modern arms and armies against the force of revolutionary nationalism, making the Vietnam War one of this century's seminal events.

The System Worked

LESLIE H. GELB AND RICHARD K. BETTS

Writing history, especially history as recent and controversial as the Vietnam War, is a treacherous exercise. One picks away at the debris of evidence only to discover that it is still alive, being shaped by bitterness and bewilderment, reassurances and new testimony. Consequently answers to certain questions will forever remain elusive. Were U.S. leaders right or wrong in involving the nation in Vietnam? Did they adopt the best strategy for fighting the war? Were they genuinely seeking a compromise peace? Each succeeding generation of historians will produce its own perspective on the rights and wrongs of the war, and each perspective will be different from the others. This has happened with every other war, and it will happen with Vietnam.

What the historian can legitimately seek to do at this point is to begin to piece together the whats and whys. What were the patterns that characterized the war in Vietnam? What policy dilemmas did U.S. leaders face? Why were their choices indeed dilemmas? Why did they choose the way they did?

Four basic and recurring patterns marked what was happening in Vietnam from 1947 to 1969.

The first pattern was that of the French, the Saigon government, and their military forces. The military forces always got better, but they never got good enough. Each Vietminh or North Vietnamese offensive, whatever the immediate results, showed again and again that first the French and then the Saigon forces could not defend themselves without ever larger doses of massive American assistance. (The invasion of South Vietnam by the North Vietnamese across the demilitarized zone in 1972 was a partial exception.) These anti-Communist forces could never translate their advantages in total air superiority, dominance in mobility and firepower, and a sizable edge in manpower into victory. In fact they spent most of the time on the defensive

Leslie H. Gelb and Richard K. Betts, *The Irony of Vietnam: The System Worked* (Washington: Brookings Institution, 1979), pp. 9–26. Reprinted by permission.

until mid-1968. Something was wrong somewhere. Something always was wrong.

Military power without political cohesiveness and support is an empty shell. The non-Communist Vietnamese, to be sure, invariably had a solid strike against them: it could not be an easy task to coalesce the forces of nationalism while depending militarily on the French or the Americans. Yet the non-Communist groups never were able to submerge their own differences in a single, unified purpose and to gather support from the peasant masses. Before the end, the regime of President Nguyen Van Thieu gained in stability but seemingly not in legitimacy. Without this legitimacy—and the quest for it seemed never-ending—the anti-Communist Vietnamese perpetually required American support.

A second pattern characterized the Vietminh and later the Hanoi government. While the annual hopeful prediction was that the Communists were about to expire, their will to fight seemed undiminished and they kept coming back. When the going got rough in Vietnam, they would divert temporarily to Laos and Cambodia. One need not glorify the Communists to face this fact. The brutality of their methods of warfare matched, if not exceeded, Saigon's. And certainly Hanoi received massive doses of aid from the Soviet Union and China, although only a fraction of the aid the United States gave to France and Saigon. But something always went right for them somewhere.

The Communist leaders always had their differences, but they could put them aside in the pursuit of their goal of an independent and unified Vietnam. Although as dictatorial as their foes, if not more so, they were nevertheless able to organize and marshal their efforts effectively year after year. They were, in short, more *effectively* dictatorial than the Saigon mandarins, especially because after World War II they captured much of the banner of nationalism. The non-Communist nationalists never achieved the same degree of ideological cohesion, organizational discipline, and grass roots activism. For these reasons the Communists crept near to victory on several occasions.

Victory would have been theirs on these occasions had it not been for a third pattern—that of increasing American involvement. As U.S. involvement increased, appearing at times to raise the possibility of a Communist defeat, the Soviet Union and China would step up aid to their ally. Whenever one Vietnamese side or the other in this conflict was in danger of losing, one of the superpowers would step in to redress the balance. The war could not end as long as these outside powers wanted to keep their clients from losing.

The upshot was a fourth pattern—stalemate. From time to time negotiating initiatives were launched, serving only to emphasize that the war was basically a civil war in which neither side would risk genuine compromise. Each side tried more force. The other side would match it. The anti-Communist Vietnamese, though inefficient and corrupt, always had enough support and resiliency to hang on. The Communist Vietnamese, though battered, always possessed the determination to drive on. Death fast became a way of life in Vietnam as stalemate continued but the war got bigger.

Back in Washington, these patterns created, and were in part created by, the conflicting goals that posed a rack of interlocking policy dilemmas.

Stakes versus leverage. U.S. stakes in avoiding a Communist takeover in Vietnam were as great as the stakes of Paris and Saigon. Thus, occasional threats from Washington to "shape up or else" were never taken seriously, for leaders in Paris and Saigon realized that the United States stood to lose as much as they from withdrawal. As the stakes grew, leverage shrank. American goals and strength were therefore paradoxically a fundamental source of bargaining weakness.

Pressure versus collapse. At various times U.S. leaders believed that neither the French nor the South Vietnamese would undertake necessary reforms without hard pressure from Washington, and that pressing too hard might lead to complete collapse of the anti-Communist position. If the Americans pushed the French into granting genuine independence to Vietnam, France would have no incentive to continue the fight against communism and would withdraw. If the Americans pushed the Saigon government too hard on land reform, corruption, and the like, Saigon's administrative structure would become overburdened, its power base would be placed in jeopardy, and its ever-fragile unity might come apart. Thus the weakness of the French and the South Vietnamese was the source of their bargaining strength.

Vietnamese reform versus American performance. Truman, Eisenhower, Kennedy, and Johnson each made clear that reforms would be a precondition for further U.S. assistance. Each violated his own preconditions. The dilemma was this: if the United States performed before the French and the Saigon government reformed, they would never reform, but if the United States did not perform first and the situation further deteriorated, reforms would become academic. Thus at the end of 1964 American leaders concluded that the Saigon government was too precarious to warrant additional U.S. help but was unlikely to survive without it.

Involvement or not—a loss either way. U.S. strategists recognized over the years that greater involvement by outside powers was sure to run against the grain of Vietnamese nationalism, thereby making the war unwinnable. Eisenhower realized that getting further involved in France's colonial war was a losing proposition. Kennedy saw in 1961 that sending in American combat troops and making the American presence more visible could only transform the situation into "a white man's war," again a losing proposition. But Eisenhower, Kennedy, and the other presidents also believed that France and Saigon were certain to fail without greater U.S. involvement.

Restraint versus signals. U.S. leaders correctly calculated that increasing American involvement in Vietnam would trigger heightened domestic criticism of the war. Thus each President sought to postpone and then to downplay escalatory actions or even to conceal the significance of those actions as long as possible. But at the same time, they calculated with equal correctness that restraint for domestic political purposes would convey the wrong signal to the Vietminh, Hanoi, and their supporters. It could only be read by the Communists as a sign of U.S. weakness and ultimate irresolution.

The damned if do, damned if don't dilemma. At bottom, the presidents acted as if they were trapped no matter what they did. If they escalated to avoid defeat, they would be criticized. If they failed to escalate, they would be criticized for permitting defeat. Theirs was the most classic of all dilemmas: they were damned if they did and damned if they didn't. There seemed to be no course of action that would not risk domestic support, although until 1968 criticism for softness seemed less bearable than criticism for excessive involvement. The dilemma lay not only in balancing left-wing domestic constituencies against right-wing ones, but also in the contradictory demands of the Right. Republican rightists at various times criticized Democrats both for being the "war party" *and* for "selling out" countries to communism.

In sum, given the constant goal of a non-Communist South after the Korean War, these six U.S. dilemmas in Vietnam melded into three historically phased ones. At first, U.S. leaders realized that there was no chance of defeating the Vietminh unless France granted true independence to Vietnam, but that if France did so, it would not remain and fight the war. So the United States could not win with France and could not win without it. Then American leaders recognized that although President Ngo Dinh Diem was losing the support of the people, he nevertheless represented the only hope of future political stability. So the United States could not win with Diem and could not win without him. Later the American view was that the Saigon regime would not reform with U.S. aid and could not survive without massive U.S. involvement, and that the North Vietnamese effort seemed able to survive despite U.S. efforts. Once again, the war could neither be won with U.S. help nor without it. Why, then, did the United States continue throughout these phases to put its resources into an ever-expanding *and* never-ending war?

Nations at war and after a war, win or lose, try to scratch away at the traditions or values that hold their societies together to see what they are made of. Are they wise and just nations? Or are they foolish and aggressive? Merciless or humane? Well led or misled? Vital or decadent? Hopeful or hopeless? It is arguable whether a society should indulge in such self-scrutiny. Societies are, as Edmund Burke wrote, "delicate, intricate wholes" that are more easily damaged than improved when subjected to the glare of grand inquisitors.

But in the case of the United States and the war in Vietnam, many people have sought answers to which they are entitled, and many others are only too eager to fill in the blanks. The families and friends of those who were killed and wounded want to know whether it was worth it. This answer is clear to most by now: No. Intellectuals still want to know "Why Vietnam?" Policy analysts want to know whether the failure was conceptual and strategic (the realm of ends) or organizational and operational (the realm of means). The answers to these questions will themselves become political facts and forces, shaping the U.S. role in the world and the lives of Americans at home for years to come.

Central to this inquiry are the wide-ranging explanations of U.S. involvement given in the Vietnam War literature. Nine seem to stand out. Different authors combine them in different ways, although none presents a complete answer. The nine basic explanations are as follows:

1. The arrogance of power—idealistic imperialism. Richard Hofstadter has argued that Americans have had a misleading historical experience with warfare and that unlike the Europeans, they have not learned to live with minor setbacks and limited successes, since they have known only victory. This led to the "illusion of American omnipotence" in U.S. foreign policy.

This view holds that a driving force in American involvement in Vietnam was that the United States is a nation of enormous power and, like comparable nations in history, sought to use this power at every opportunity. To have power is to want to employ it and, eventually, is to be corrupted by it. The arrogance derived from the belief that to have power is to be able to do anything. It was also an idealistic arrogance, an imperialism more ingenuous than malevolent, a curious blend of Wilsonianism and realpolitik that sought to make the world safe for democracy even if this meant forcing Vietnam to be free. Power invokes right and justifies itself. Vietnam was there, a challenge to this power and an opportunity for its exercise, and no task was beyond accomplishment.

2. The rapacity of power: economic imperialism. This explanation, a variant of the domestic politics interpretation given below, is that special-interest groups, such as the industrial and financial elite, maneuvered the United States into war. This elite's goal was to capture export markets and natural resources at public expense for private economic gain. Gabriel Kolko's neo-Marxist analyses are the best examples of this approach.

Michael Klare, mixing the power elite model of C. Wright Mills with the economic determinism of Noam Chomsky, put the argument this way:

U.S. policy in general and U.S. intervention in Vietnam in particular were "the predictable outcome of an American drive to secure control over the economic resources of the non-Communist world." American businessmen held key posts in the executive branch. Senators, congressmen, academics, scientists, think-tankers, and the military were their hirelings. They all longed for the almighty dollar. They could not make enough "honest dollars" in the United States, so they enlisted the power of Washington to guarantee foreign markets for the export of goods and capital and access to raw materials. They hoodwinked the rest of the nation into believing that the protection of their profits was in the U.S. national interest. They needed military capability. The military-industrial complex responded with sensors, defoliants, automatic battlefields, helicopters, and the like, and tested them in the laboratory of Vietnam. Put it all together with an adversary who would do everything he could to resist, and you have a war without end.

3. Bureaucratic politics. There are several, not mutually exclusive, approaches within this view. One, a quasi-Freudian version, has it that national security bureaucrats—the professionals who make up the military services, civilians in the Defense Department, the Agency for International Development, the State Department, and the Central Intelligence Agency

(CIA)—are afflicted with the curse of machismo, the need to assert and prove manhood and toughness. This instinct compounded misunderstanding and organizational failure. The bureaucrats' career advancement and acceptability within the government depended on showing that they were not afraid to propose the use of force. Another more conspiratorial approach has it that bureaucrats purposefully misled their superiors about the situation in Vietnam and carefully constructed policy alternatives so as to circumscribe their choices, thus forcing further involvement in Vietnam.

The first approach has been set forth by Richard Barnet and James C. Thomson, Jr. According to Barnet, the national security manager quickly learns that "toughness is the most highly prized virtue." Thomson drove the point home: "Those who doubted our role in Vietnam were said to shrink from the burdens of power, the obligations of power, the uses of power, the responsibility of power. By implication such men were soft-headed and effete." Citing the lack of informed judgment on Indochina because of the "banishment of real expertise" on Asia, the "domestication of dissenters," the "effectiveness trap" whereby bureaucrats refrain from protesting for fear of losing their influence, the "curator mentality," and "bureaucratic detachment" from moral issues, Thomson observed that the conflict was bound to lead to "a steady give-in to pressures for a military solution."

Of the second approach, Stavins, Barnet, and Raskin noted:

> The deliberate inflation and distortion of issues in the advocacy process leads to what I call the bureaucratic model of reality . . . the final purpose of which is to induce the President to do something or to make him feel comfortable about something the bureaucracy has already done. . . . The shrewd adviser tailors his advice to the President's prejudices as best he knows them.

David Halberstam emphasized this bureaucratic duplicity, particularly in regard to the role of military reporting from the field in the early 1960s. A similar variant of bureaucratic politics is posed by the Committee of Concerned Asian Scholars: "The Indochina war is in large part a product of sheer institutional momentum." According to this interpretation, bureaucrats develop a stake in their solution to a problem; a change in the solution is difficult because it means a repudiation of a previous chain of decisions and is therefore an admission of personal failing in the past. As another analyst argued, the crisis managers advising the President became so involved they "would not, perhaps could not, let go." This fairly unified vision of bureaucracy contrasts with a fourth and final view of organizational determinism: bureaucratic bargaining. In this explanation the cautious approach of the State Department and the CIA gradually lost out in the councils of decision to the arguments of the professional military.

4. Domestic politics. This explanation is quite complicated, and authors argue their cases on several different levels. The magnanimous view sees American presidents fending off the Communists in Vietnam in order to save the country from another round of right-wing McCarthyism and to retain domestic support for a continuing U.S. role in the world. Chroniclers who have been close to presidents have stressed this interpretation.

Another more complex portrait was sketched by Daniel Ellsberg, who saw domestic politics as putting U.S. leaders in a bind between two conflicting imperatives: "Rule 1 . . . *Do not lose the rest of Vietnam to communist control before the next election,*" and "Rule 2 . . . *Do not commit U.S. ground troops to a land war in Asia, either.*" The former drove the presidents on and the latter constrained them. The presidential rule that "*this is a bad year for me to lose Vietnam to Communism,*" said Ellsberg, along with rules 1 and 2,

> amounts to a *recurrent* formula for calculating Presidential decisions on Vietnam realistically, given inputs on alternatives, any time from 1950 on. The mix of motives behind this judgment can vary with circumstances and Presidents, but since 1950 a variety of domestic political considerations have virtually always been present. These have been *sufficient* underpinning even in those years when . . . "strategic" concerns were not also urgent.

These constraints can also be seen as reinforced by the underlying urge, especially in Johnson's case, not to be "the first President to lose a war."

5. *Pragmatic security managers.* This interpretation is closely linked to the bureaucratic and arrogance-of-power explanations. It is the view that U.S. leaders over the years were not inspired by any particular ideology but were essentially pragmatists weighing the evidence and looking at each problem on its merits. According to this perspective, these leaders knew they were facing tough choices, and their decisions always were close ones. But having decided 51 to 49 to go ahead, they tried to sell and implement their policies 100 percent.

Pragmatists are problem-solvers, and in the words of Joseph Kraft: "The war is peculiarly the war of the Whiz Kids and their friends and supporters in the liberal, business, and academic community. It is the war of those of us who thought we could manage force, and tune violence finely."

6. *Ethnocentricity and misperception.* Some analysts emphasize the naivete and insensitivity of policymakers who did not understand the significance of cultural differences, and who therefore did not see that America's Vietnamese allies would not and could not live up to U.S. expectations. Communist revolution in the context of Vietnamese society was simplistically and falsely equated with the earlier challenges in Western Europe. Policymakers assumed that the stakes and solutions were similar, ignoring the complexity, uniqueness, and much greater foreignness of the Vietnamese setting. The United States failed in Vietnam because Americans thought they could treat it like any other Western country and were oblivious to the constraints of the traditional Vietnamese culture and character and to the reasons for the vitality of Vietnamese communism. A related view is that which stresses misunderstanding of Hanoi's and the Vietcong's motives and the miscalculation of policy based on this misperception. Better anthropology and psychology would have helped. In short, had the United States really known who it was dealing with and had it really comprehended how they viewed the war, it would not have gotten in so deeply.

7. *The slippery slope.* Tied to the pragmatic approach, the balance of power, and the arrogance of power, but attributing more to the process than to the underlying assumptions, is the explanation that holds that U.S. involvement in Vietnam is the story of the slippery slope. According to this view Vietnam was not always critical to U.S. national security; it became so over the years as each succeeding administration piled commitment on commitment. Each administration not quite knowingly slid further into the Vietnam quagmire, not really understanding the depth of the problems in Vietnam and convinced that it could win. The catchwords of this view are optimism, miscalculation, and inadvertence.

The most vocal advocate of this thesis has been Arthur M. Schlesinger, Jr., who in 1967 expressed it as follows:

> And so the policy of "one more step" lured the United States deeper and deeper into the morass. In retrospect, Vietnam is a triumph of the politics of inadvertence. We have achieved our present entanglement, not after due and deliberate consideration, but through a series of small decisions. It is not only idle but unfair to seek out guilty men. President Eisenhower, after rejecting American military intervention in 1954, set in motion the policy of support for Saigon which resulted, two Presidents later, in American military intervention in 1965. Each step in the deepening of the American commitment was reasonably regarded at the time as the last that would be necessary. Yet, in retrospect, each step led only to the next, until we find ourselves entrapped today in that nightmare of American strategists, a land war in Asia—a war which no President, including President Johnson, desired or intended. The Vietnam story is a tragedy without villains.

Schlesinger went on to say: "By continually increasing what the Pentagon calls the 'quotient of pain,' we can, according to the administration theory, force Hanoi at each new stage of widening the war to reconsider whether the war is worth the price." But "the theory that widening the war will shorten it . . . appears to be based on three convictions: first, that the war will be decided in North Vietnam; second, that the risk of Chinese or Soviet entry is negligible; and third, that military victory in some sense is possible" (at least in suppressing the resistance in the South). All these convictions, he concluded, were dangerous forms of illusion and self-deception. Marvin Kalb and Elie Abel agreed when they stated that America stumbled "step by downward step, into the longest, most costly, and most disruptive war Americans have ever fought, in the misguided belief that when things go wrong anywhere in the world the commitment of sufficient American dollars and—if need be—of American soldiers, must surely put them right."

Other writers have been less charitable. Bernard Fall, referring to Schlesinger's theory that "error creates its own reality," said that "it would not be unfair to state that the official reports on the situation from 1954 to the present depict a well-nigh unbroken series of seemingly 'unavoidable' decisions, all made with the best of intentions and for the noblest of purposes—but each gone awry at the last moment because of outside factors beyond one's control." He added, however, that "official reactions to

warnings about the surely catastrophic end results of the course upon which
the Saigon authorities—both Vietnamese and American—were embarked
fell upon both deaf and resentful ears, as differences of view between the
trained outside observers and officialdom became irreconcilable."

According to Theodore Draper:

> As a result of one miscalculation after another, we have gradually been
> drawn into making an enormous, disproportionate military and political
> investment in Vietnam. This investment—not the vital interests of the
> United States in Vietnam—has cast a spell on us. The same thing would
> happen if we should decide to put 500,000 troops in Mauritania or even
> Ruritania. Once American resources and prestige are committed on such a
> profligate scale, the "commitment" develops a life of its own and, as the
> saying goes, good money must be thrown after bad.

8. International power politics and containment—policing the world.
The desire to maintain some perceived balance of power among nations is
an explanation that is intimately related to that of pragmatism but places
more emphasis on the traditional imperatives of international relations.
According to Donald Zagoria: "For the Americans—as for the Russians and
Chinese—Vietnam has been a pawn in a global ideological and power
struggle." The United States, he said, was "intent—particularly after the
Korean War—on drawing a Cold War line in Asia."

The principal considerations in pursuing the balance-of-power goal
were seeing that "the illegal use of force" was not allowed to succeed, honoring commitments, and keeping credibility with allies and potential adversaries. The underlying judgment was that failure to stop aggression in one
place would tempt others to aggress in ever more dangerous places. As the
most powerful non-Communist nation, the United States had no choice but
to serve as the world's policeman. Intervention in Vietnam, in this view,
was not aggressive, adventurous, idealistic, or naive, but simply the
ineluctable result of the American power position in the world, the same
response that great powers have historically made to challenges from other
powers.

Kalb and Abel, for example, noted that after Lyndon Johnson won his
election, he *could* have considered changing U.S. policy. But he was determined not to lose Vietnam and thus rejected the possibility of a quiet withdrawal. "To him, that would have meant going back on the nation's pledged
commitment." Townsend Hoopes described numerous times during the
period October 1967 through March 1968 when pressures were brought to
bear on the President that might have changed U.S. policy. But the
President's reaction was that the struggle was a test of wills between
Washington and Hanoi and that the United States must not relent. Relenting
was regarded as tantamount to a resounding defeat to worldwide U.S. policy and prestige and as a green light to the Soviet Union and China to foster more Communist wars of national liberation around the world.

9. Ideological anticommunism. The analysts who offer this explanation
hold that anticommunism was the central fact of U.S. foreign policy from

at least 1947 until the end of the 1960s. After World War II, global competition between East and West began. An ideology whose very existence seemed to threaten basic American values had combined with the national force of first Russia and then China. This combination caused American leaders to see the world in "we-they" terms and to insist that peace was indivisible. Going well beyond balance-of-power considerations, every piece of territory became critical and every besieged nation a potential domino. Communism came to be seen as an infection to be quarantined rather than a force to be judiciously and appropriately balanced. Vietnam in particular became the cockpit of confrontation between the Free World and totalitarianism; it was where the action was for twenty years.

Hoopes, for example, observed that although the United States was confronted by a genuine and serious Soviet threat following World War II (and one aggravated in particular by the Korean War), unfortunately "the American response to the cold war generated its own momentum and, in doing so, led us . . . beyond the rational requirements of our national security." Anticommunism degenerated into a religious obsession despite numerous indications that the Communist bloc was no longer monolithic. U.S. aid to Vietnam continued to be based on the conviction that any Communist expansion threatened the security of the United States. The graduated escalation of the war, beginning around 1965, reflected the continuing influence of the cold war beliefs and resulted in wanton destruction grossly disproportionate to the goal sought.

Chester Cooper, in tracing the history of U.S. involvement in Vietnam since World War II, showed how the anti-Communist strain evolved through the different administrations. The residue of democratic antitotalitarian militancy of World War II, directed against fascism, carried over into cold war anticommunism.

> The issue of the "Free World vs. International Communism" made decisions about international relations seem simple and, what is more, cast a mantle of morality and righteousness over all our actions abroad. The Soviet Union and its friends, by their deeds and their words, provided the spark that launched an American crusade to save the world from Communism.

Each of these explanations provides some insight into particular issues, particular people, and the workings of bureaucratic organizations at certain times. But however these explanations are combined, they are better as answers to the question of why the United States originally became involved and committed in Vietnam than as analyses of the process of involvement, the strategy for fighting the war, and the strategy for ending it.

The most prevalent and popular combination of explanations—pragmatic security managers, domestic politics, anticommunism, and slippery slope—is misleading in three crucial respects: it sees commitment as essentially stemming from involvement, the stakes building with each successive escalation—the simple investment trap model; it does not sufficiently emphasize the constraints in fighting the war, nor does it tie these constraints in a coherent way to the strategy of gradualism; and in stressing the factor of Washington's optimism about victory, it seriously distorts official American appraisals of, and expectations about, the war. Explanations 8 and 9, which see involvement as the rational product of given premises about the international balance of power and American ideals, are closer to the mark if any are. But Vietnam, according to most observers, is a story about how the U.S. system failed because the people who ran it blundered. According to this conventional wisdom the American leaders were a collection of moderate pragmatists and cold war ideologues who were trapped by their own philosophies and their ignorance of Vietnam. Pragmatists and ideologues alike foundered, so the stories go, because neither understood that Vietnam was an endless war, a quagmire.

Both stereotypes are compelling in some ways. The pragmatic one gives comfort to those who see where the United States wound up in Vietnam and conclude that no one could have wished this result. It must have been a mistake. The ideological one offers proof to those who look at Vietnam as one more act in the American drama about communism. It was necessary to fill the bill. These general pictures of blundering and blustering are also compelling in a sense as glimpses of the organizational minds of the State Department and the armed services.

Yet the stereotypes fail. They fail because the decisionmaking system they purport to describe *did achieve its stated purpose* of preventing a Communist victory in Vietnam until the domestic balance of opinion shifted and Congress decided to reduce support to Saigon in 1974–75—that is, until the consensus, and hence the purpose, changed and the United States decided to let Vietnam go.

The system worked. The story of U.S. policy toward Vietnam is either far better or far worse than supposed. Presidents and most of those who influenced their decisions did not stumble into Vietnam unaware of the quagmire. U.S. involvement did not stem from a failure to foresee that the war would be a long and bitter struggle. Vietnam was indeed a quagmire, but most American leaders knew it. Of course, there were periods when many were genuinely optimistic. But these infrequent and short-lived periods (late 1953,1957–59,1962 and early 1963, and late 1967) were invariably followed by deep pessimism. Very few persons, to be sure, envisioned what the Vietnam situation would be like by 1968. Most realized, however, that the light at the end of the tunnel was very far away, if not unreachable. Nevertheless, the presidents persevered. Given the international compulsions to "keep our word" and "save face," domestic prohibitions against losing, and high personal stakes, U.S. leaders did "what was necessary," did it about the way they wanted to, were prepared to pay the costs each administration could foresee for itself, and plowed on with a mixture of hope and doom. They saw no acceptable alternative until 1968, when the President decided to deescalate, and again in 1974–75, when Congress decided to trim the aid cord.

[In summary, we advance three propositions.] The first proposition tells why and how the United States became involved in Vietnam. The second explains both why "winning" strategies could not be adopted and why the process of involvement was gradual. The third offers answers about expectations.

Proposition 1. U.S. involvement in Vietnam is not mainly a story of inadvertent descent into unforeseen quicksand but of why U.S. leaders considered it vital not to lose Vietnam by force to communism. They believed Vietnam to be vital, not for itself, but for what they thought its "loss" would mean internationally and domestically. Previous involvement made further involvement harder to avoid, and to this extent initial commitments were compounded. But the basic pressures, stakes, and objectives, and the judgments of Vietnam's vitalness—after the fall of China and beginning with the Korean War—were sufficient in themselves to set the course for escalation.

Proposition 2. The presidents, Congress, public opinion, and the press all both reinforced the stakes against losing and introduced constraints against winning. Until the summer of 1965 the presidents did less than those who were urging military victory recommended and rejected policies that could lead to disengagement—in effect they did what they deemed to be minimally necessary at each stage to keep Vietnam and later South Vietnam out of Communist hands. After the summer of 1965, as the war dragged on and the consensus began to dissipate, President Johnson remained a true believer and pushed for the maximum feasible, given diplomatic and domestic constraints as he saw them. Throughout, however, the presidents met the pressures of the system as brakemen, doing less than what they were being told was necessary for victory. While each President was one of the key architects of this consensus, he also was a part and a prisoner of the larger political system that fed on itself, trapping all its participants in a war they could not afford to lose and were unable to win quickly.

Proposition 3. The presidents and most of their lieutenants were not deluded by reports of progress and did not proceed on the basis of optimism about winning a near-term or even longer-term military victory. A feeling of pessimism characterized most of these men most of the time. Occasional optimism or flushes of hope that took temporary precedence over actual analysis only punctuated the general atmosphere of resignation. Policymakers recognized that the steps they were taking were inadequate to win the war and that unless Hanoi relented they would have to do more and more. In effect they chose a course of action that promised stalemate, not victory or peace. The presidents, at times, sought to escape the stalemated war through a negotiated settlement but without fully realizing (though realizing more than most of their critics) that a civil war cannot be ended by political compromise. Their strategy was to persevere in the hope that their will to continue—if not the practical effects of their actions—would cause the Communists to relent.

A Moral and Necessary Intervention

NORMAN PODHORETZ

On April 30, 1975, when the last American helicopter scurried desperately off the roof of the American Embassy in Saigon as the city fell to the invading North Vietnamese army, the Washington *Post* said that it was a day of "deliverance" for the United States. In some sense, of course, it was. For nearly fifteen years, Americans had been working, fighting, and dying in Vietnam; and from this, surely, they were delivered on April 30, 1975.

They were also delivered from something else on that fateful day—something less bloody than the war itself but in some ways no less anguished and anguishing. This was the debate over the war that had been raging with an intensity that escalated along with American involvement, bursting from time to time out of the confines of words and ideas and arguments into the demonstrations, the skirmishes, and the more violent confrontations of what had come to be called "the war at home." Overnight, it seemed, Vietnam, the great obsession of the past decade and more, disappeared from the national consciousness. The newspapers and magazines and television stations carried what were in effect obituary notices, and the debate, along with the war that had provoked it, was then hastily interred in the forensic equivalent of an unmarked grave.

But of course nothing in history ever really happens overnight. In the case of the debate over Vietnam, by the time it was buried, it had long since lost its right to be called a debate. For at least the last five years of American involvement in Vietnam, hardly any voices had been raised in defense of our continued participation in the war. The arguments all came from the other side, and for the most part they remained unanswered. Entering office in 1969, Richard Nixon, like Lyndon Johnson in the last phase of his Presidency, spoke mainly of how to get the United States out of Vietnam. Rarely did he, or anyone else in those days, attempt to justify the intervention itself. Nixon had supported the decision of John F. Kennedy's Administration to go into Vietnam; he had supported the deepening of American involvement under Johnson; and then, by resisting the temptation to withdraw immediately upon becoming President, he had taken the onus of Vietnam upon himself, turning it (in an act that many thought foolish from the point of view of his own political fortunes) into "his" war. Yet he never really made it "his" war in the sense of defending it politically and morally. There was no point, he and his people kept saying, in arguing over how and why we had got into Vietnam; the only question was how best to get out. Thus what Nixon mainly did was defend his strategy of gradual withdrawal against the demand for an immediate end to the American presence. The effect was to concede the moral and political arguments to the antiwar forces—by now a coalition that included people who

From *Why We Were in Vietnam* by Norman Podhoretz, pp. 9–15, 195–199, 210. Copyright © 1982 by Norman Podhoretz. Reprinted by permission of Georges Borchardt Inc. for the author.

had led the country into Vietnam in the first place and were eager to atone by leading it out.

Even before April 30, 1975, then, Vietnam had become perhaps the most negatively charged political symbol in American history, awaiting only the literal end of American involvement to achieve its full and final diabolization. From a narrowly political point of view, it had become to the generation that had experienced it what Munich had been to an earlier generation: the self-evident symbol of a policy that must never be followed again.

Indeed, for many people whose original support of American intervention in Vietnam had been based on memories of Munich, Vietnam not only replaced it but canceled it out. To such people the lesson of Munich had been that an expansionist totalitarian power could not be stopped by giving in to its demands and that limited resistance at an early stage was the only way to avoid full-scale war later on. Prime Minister Neville Chamberlain, returning to England from the conference in Munich at which Nazi Germany's claims over Czechoslovakia had been satisfied, triumphantly declared that he was bringing with him "peace in our time." But as almost everyone would later agree, what he had actually brought with him was the certainty of a world war to come—a war that Winston Churchill, the leading critic of the policy of appeasement consummated at Munich, would later call "unnecessary." According to Churchill, if a line had been drawn against Hitler from the beginning, he would have been forced to back away, and the sequence of events that led inexorably to the outbreak of war would have been interrupted.

Obviously, Vietnam differed in many significant ways from Central Europe in the late 1930s. But there was one great similarity that overrode these differences in the minds of many whose understanding of such matters had been shaped by the memory of Munich. "I'm not the village idiot," Dean Rusk, who was Secretary of State first under Kennedy and then under Johnson, once exploded. "I know Hitler was an Austrian and Mao is a Chinese. . . . But what is common between the two situations is the phenomenon of aggression." In other words, in Vietnam now as in Central Europe then, a totalitarian political force—Nazism then, Communism now—was attempting to expand the area under its control. A relatively limited degree of resistance then would have precluded the need for massive resistance afterward. This was the lesson of Munich, and it had already been applied successfully in Western Europe in the forties and Korea in the fifties. Surely it was applicable to Vietnam as well.

When, however, it began to become evident that, in contrast to the cases of Western Europe and Korea, the differences between Vietnam now and Central Europe then were more decisive than the similarities, the relevance of Munich began to fade, and a new set of lessons—the lessons of Vietnam—began to take hold. The legacy of Munich had been a disposition, even a great readiness, to resist, by force if necessary, the expansion of totalitarianism; the legacy of Vietnam would obversely be a reluctance, even a refusal, to resist, especially if resistance required the use of force.

For some of the older generation who rejected the tutelage of Munich in favor of the tutelage of Vietnam, the new pedagogic dispensation was generally limited to lessons of a strictly political character. When they said, or (less given to being so explicit) nodded in agreement as others said, "No More Vietnams," they had in mind a new foreign policy that would base itself on more modest expectations of American power than had prevailed in the years of Kennedy and Johnson. For them the main lesson of Vietnam was that the United States no longer should or could play the role of "policeman of the world." We had certain core interests—Western Europe, Japan, Israel—that we were, and must remain, committed to defend. But however desirable it might ideally be to undertake more than that, we lacked the power, the will, and the wisdom to carry out a more ambitious strategy with any hope of success. In this view, Vietnam represented the great cautionary argument against the "arrogance of American power."

In addition to humility about the extent of American power, Vietnam persuaded many, or perhaps most, converts from the school of Munich that humility was also required in defining the purposes for which this limited American power could and should be used. Even assuming that it might be desirable to contain the spread of Communism—and many by now had lost their former conviction that it was desirable—Vietnam showed that the United States was unable (or indeed unqualified) to go on making the effort with any hope of success. On this issue Vietnam was taken to be an irrefutable piece of evidence showing the folly of an ideologically based foreign policy in general and of an anti-Communist "crusade" in particular.

But these were only the blandest of the lessons of Vietnam. For, unlike Munich, Vietnam became the symbol of something much broader than a mistaken foreign policy. Especially for younger people who had no personal memory of the Second World War, Vietnam did not so much reverse the legacy of Munich as it succeeded to the legacy of Auschwitz. Only the most extreme elements within the antiwar movement took to spelling the name of the country as "Amerika," but many who shied away from so open an identification of the United States under Johnson with Germany under Hitler tacitly acquiesced in (if only by failing to object to) the idea that American involvement in Vietnam was an evil fully comparable to the evils done by Nazi Germany.

Sometimes the evil was taken to be the American intervention itself: an act of aggression against a people fighting to liberate themselves from a corrupt and repressive regime. Far from resisting the spread of totalitarianism, we were propping it up. We were the counterrevolutionaries, we were the imperialists, we were the enemies of freedom and self-determination.

As time went on, however, the emphasis shifted from the original "Amerikan" sin, the evil of the intervention, to the atrocities and crimes we were said to be committing in the fighting of the war itself. Within South Vietnam, the country we were allegedly trying to defend, we were uprooting villages, indiscriminately bombing and bombarding areas populated by civilians, defoliating forests and destroying crops, setting women and children on fire with napalm and other incendiary weapons, and committing random atrocities like the massacre of My Lai; and when, after 1965, we extended the war to North Vietnam, we became guilty of terror-bombing aimed at harmless civilian targets. All this added up to the great crime of genocide. Some Americans agreed with Europeans like Jean-Paul Sartre and Bertrand Russell that the United States was deliberately "wiping out a whole people and imposing the Pax Americana on an uninhabited Vietnam"; others thought that the policy was not deliberate but that (in the words of the American writer Frances FitzGerald) it "had no other military logic" and that the results were in any case "indistinguishable" from genocide.

So well and widely established did this view become, and so half-hearted and ineffective were the replies, that the word Vietnam became serviceable as a self-evident symbol of evil even outside the context of politics. (Here, for example, was how it would later seem natural for a member of the Vietnam generation to speak of himself: "Sometimes my life seems like my own personal Vietnam policy. A rap sheet so heinous that I wonder why those hooded judges of my conscience did not condemn me long ago. . . .")

But within the context of politics, the idea that the American intervention into Vietnam had been a crime led, as we would expect, to sterner lessons than those that followed from the idea that the intervention had merely been a mistake. Instead of learning humility about the extent of their power, Americans were to learn renunciation. Until we could teach ourselves to intervene on the side of good—the side of revolutionary change—the best thing we could do both for ourselves and for the rest of the world was not to intervene at all. Oppressed peoples everywhere were rising and demanding their rights, and everywhere they encountered American opposition. The lesson of Vietnam was that the United States, not the Soviet Union and certainly not Communism, represented the greatest threat to the security and well-being of the peoples of the world.

Thus it was that by April 30, 1975, the debate over Vietnam had already been settled in favor of the moral and political position of the antiwar movement. At best Vietnam had been a blunder; at worst it had been a crime. At best it exposed the folly of trying to contain the spread of Communism anywhere outside Western Europe; at worst it demonstrated that we were and always had been on the wrong side of a worldwide struggle.

That the United States was defeated in Vietnam is certain. But did that defeat truly mean what the antiwar movement seems to have persuaded everyone it meant? Do the policies that led the United States into Vietnam deserve the discredit that has been attached to them? Does the United States deserve the moral contumely that Vietnam has brought upon it in the eyes of so many people both at home and abroad? Is it true, as the German novelist Guenter Grass has said, that America "lost in Vietnam its right to appeal to morals"? The only way to answer these questions is to reopen the debate over Vietnam from which the United States was prematurely delivered in the closing years of the war. But before the political and moral issues can be properly engaged, it will be necessary to retell the story of how and why the United States went into Vietnam and how and why it was driven out. . . .

Here then we arrive at the center of the moral issue posed by the American intervention into Vietnam.

The United States sent half a million men to fight in Vietnam. More than 50,000 of them lost their lives, and many thousands more were wounded. Billions of dollars were poured into the effort, damaging the once unparalleled American economy to such an extent that the country's competitive position was grievously impaired. The domestic disruptions to which the war gave rise did perhaps even greater damage to a society previously so self-confident that it was often accused of entertaining illusions of its own omnipotence. Millions of young people growing to maturity during the war developed attitudes of such hostility toward their own country and the civilization embodied by its institutions that their willingness to defend it against external enemies in the future was left hanging in doubt.

Why did the United States undertake these burdens and make these sacrifices in blood and treasure and domestic tranquillity? What was in it for the United States? It was a question that plagued the antiwar movement from beginning to end because the answer was so hard to find. If the United States was simply acting the part of an imperialist aggressor in Vietnam, as many in the antiwar movement professed to believe, it was imperialism of a most peculiar kind. There were no raw materials to exploit in Vietnam, and there was no overriding strategic interest involved. To Franklin Roosevelt in 1941 Indochina had been important because it was close to the source of rubber and tin, but this was no longer an important consideration. Toward the end of the war, it was discovered that there was oil off the coast of Vietnam and antiwar radicals happily seized on this news as at last providing an explanation for the American presence there. But neither Kennedy nor Johnson knew about the oil, and even if they had, they would hardly have gone to war for its sake in those pre-OPEC days when oil from the Persian Gulf could be had at two dollars a barrel.

In the absence of an economic interpretation, a psychological version of the theory of imperialism was developed to answer the maddening question: *Why are we in Vietnam?* This theory held that the United States was in Vietnam because it had an urge to dominate—"to impose its national obsessions on the rest of the world," in the words of a piece in the *New York Review of Books,* one of the leading centers of antiwar agitation within the intellectual community. But if so, the psychic profits were as illusory as the economic ones, for the war was doing even deeper damage to the national self-confidence than to the national economy.

Yet another variant of the psychological interpretation, proposed by the economist Robert L. Heilbroner, was that "the fear of losing our place in the sun, of finding ourselves at bay, . . . motivates a great deal of the anti-Communism on which so much of American foreign policy seems to be founded." This was especially so in such underdeveloped countries as Vietnam, where "the rise of Communism would signal the end of capitalism as the dominant world order, and would force the acknowledgment that America no longer constituted the model on which the future of world civilization would be mainly based."

All these theories were developed out of a desperate need to find or invent selfish or self-interested motives for the American presence in Vietnam, the better to discredit it morally. In a different context, proponents of one or another of these theories—Senator Fulbright, for example—were not above trying to discredit the American presence politically by insisting that no national interest was being served by the war. This latter contention at least had the virtue of being closer to the truth than the former. For the truth was that the United States went into Vietnam for the sake not of its own direct interests in the ordinary sense but for the sake of an ideal. The intervention was a product of the Wilsonian side of the American character—the side that went to war in 1917 to "make the world safe for democracy" and that found its contemporary incarnations in the liberal internationalism of the 1940s and the liberal anti-Communism of the 1950s. One can characterize this impulse as naive; one can describe it, as Heilbroner does (and as can be done with any virtuous act), in terms that give it a subtly self-interested flavor. But there is no rationally defensible way in which it can be called immoral.

Why, then, were we in Vietnam? To say it once again: because we were trying to save the Southern half of that country from the evils of Communism. But was the war we fought to accomplish this purpose morally worse than Communism itself? Peter L. Berger, who at the time was involved with Clergy and Laymen Concerned About Vietnam (CALCAV), wrote in 1967: "All sorts of dire results might well follow a reduction or a withdrawal of the American engagement in Vietnam. Morally speaking, however, it is safe to assume that none of these could be worse than what is taking place right now." Unlike most of his fellow members of CALCAV, Berger would later repent of this statement. Writing in 1980, he would say of it: "Well, it was *not* safe to assume. . . . I was wrong and so were all those who thought as I did." For "contrary to what most members (including myself) of the antiwar movement expected, the peoples of Indochina have, since 1975, been subjected to suffering far worse than anything that was inflicted upon them by the United States and its allies."

To be sure, the "bloodbath" that had been feared by supporters of the war did not occur—not in the precise form that had been anticipated. In contrast to what they did upon taking power in Hanoi in 1954 (when they murdered some 50,000 landlords), or what they did during their brief occupation of Hue during the Tet offensive of 1968 (when they massacred 3,000 civilians), the Communists did not stage mass executions in the newly conquered South. According to Nguyen Cong Hoan, who had been an NLF [National Liberation Front] agent and then became a member of the National Assembly of the newly united Communist Vietnam before disillusionment drove him to escape in March 1977, there were more executions in the provinces than in the cities and the total number might well have reached into the tens of thousands. But as another fervent opponent of the war, the *New York Times* columnist Tom Wicker was forced to acknowledge, "what Vietnam has given us instead of a bloodbath [is] a vast tide of human misery in Southeast Asia—hundreds of thousands of homeless persons in United Nations camps, perhaps as many more dead in flight, tens of thousands of the most pitiable forcibly repatriated to Cambodia, no one knows how many adrift on the high seas or wandering the roads."

Among the refugees Wicker was talking about here were those who came to be known as "the boat people" because they "literally threw themselves upon the South China Sea in small coastal craft. . . ." Many thousands of these people were ethnic Chinese who were being driven out and forced to pay everything they had for leaky boats; tens of thousands more were Vietnamese fleeing voluntarily from what Nguyen Cong Hoan describes as "the most inhuman and oppressive regime they have ever known." The same judgment is made by Truong Nhu Tang, the former Minister of Justice in the PRG [Provisional Revolutionary Government] who fled in November 1979 in a boat loaded with forty refugees: "Never has any previous regime brought such masses of people to such desperation. Not the military dictators, not the colonialists, not even the ancient Chinese overlords."

So desperate were they to leave that they were willing to take the poor chance of survival in flight rather than remain. Says Nguyen Cong Hoan: ". . . Our people have a traditional attachment to their country. No Vietnamese would willingly leave home, homeland, and ancestors' graves. During the most oppressive French colonial rule and Japanese domination, no one escaped by boat at great risk to their lives. Yet you see that my countrymen by the thousands and from all walks of life, including a number of disillusioned Vietcongs, continue to escape from Vietnam; six out of ten never make it, and for those who are fortunate to make it, they are not allowed to land." Adds one of the disillusioned who did make it, Doan Van Toai: "Among the boat people who survived, including those who were raped by pirates and those who suffered in the refugee camps, nobody regrets his escape from the present regime."

Though they invented a new form of the Communist bloodbath, the North Vietnamese (for, to repeat, before long there were no Southerners in authority in the South, not even former members of the NLF and the PRG) were less creative in dealing with political opposition, whether real or imagined. The "re-education camps" they had always used for this purpose in the North were now extended to the South, but the result was not so much an indigenous system of Vietnamese concentration camps as an imitation of the Soviet Gulag. (*The Vietnamese Gulag,* indeed, was the name Doan Van Toai gave to the book he published about the camps in 1979.) The French journalist Jean Lacouture, who had supported the Communists during the war to the point (as he now admitted) of turning himself into a "vehicle and intermediary for a lying and criminal propaganda, [an] ingenuous spokesman for tyranny in the name of liberty," now tried to salvage his integrity by telling the truth about a re-education camp he was permitted to visit by a regime that had good reason to think him friendly. "It was," he wrote, "a prefabricated hell."

In May 1977, two full years after the Communist takeover, President Jimmy Carter—a repentant hawk, like many members of his cabinet, including his Secretary of State and his Secretary of Defense—spoke of "the intellectual and moral poverty" of the policy that had led us into Vietnam and had kept us there for so long. When Ronald Reagan, an unrepentant hawk, called the war "a noble cause" in the course of his ultimately successful campaign to replace Carter in the White House, he was accused of having made a "gaffe." Fully, painfully aware as I am that the American effort to save Vietnam from Communism was indeed beyond our intellectual and moral capabilities, I believe the story shows that Reagan's "gaffe" was closer to the truth of why we were in Vietnam and what we did there, at least until the very end, than Carter's denigration of an act of imprudent idealism whose moral soundness has been so overwhelmingly vindicated by the hideous consequences of our defeat.

The Limits of American Power

GABRIEL KOLKO

The Vietnam War was the United States' longest and most divisive war of the post-1945 epoch, and in many regards its most important conflict in the twentieth century. Obviously, the Vietnamese Communist Party's resiliency made Vietnam distinctive after 1946, but that the United States should have become embroiled with such formidable adversaries was a natural outcome of the logic and objectives of its role in the modern era. In retrospect, it is apparent that there existed two immovable forces, one of which had no conceivable option but to pursue the policy it had embarked on, and that it was far more likely for America to follow in the footsteps of the French than to learn something from their defeat. How and why it made that momentous decision and what it perceived itself to be doing reveals much about our times and the social and political framework in which contemporary history is made. For Vietnam was ultimately the major episode in a larger process of intervention which preceded and transcended it. All of the frustrations and dilemmas which emerged in Vietnam existed for Washington before 1960, and they persist to this day. The only thing that made the Vietnam War unique for the United States was that it lost completely.

The hallmark of American foreign policy after 1945 was the universality of its intense commitment to create an integrated, essentially capitalist world framework out of the chaos of World War Two and the remnants of the colonial systems. The United States was the major inheritor of the mantle of imperialism in modern history, acting not out of a desire to defend the nation against some tangible threat to its physical welfare but because it sought to create a controllable, responsive order elsewhere, one that would permit the political destinies of distant places to evolve in a manner

From *Anatomy of A War* by Gabriel Kolko, pp. 72–79, 547–551. Copyright © 1985 by Gabriel Kolko. Reprinted by permission of Pantheon Books, a Division of Random House, Inc.

beneficial to American goals and interests far surpassing the immediate needs of its domestic society. The regulation of the world was at once the luxury and the necessity it believed its power afforded, and even if its might both produced and promised far greater prosperity if successful, its inevitable costs were justified, as all earlier imperialist powers had also done, as a fulfillment of an international responsibility and mission.

This task in fact far transcended that of dealing with the USSR, which had not produced the world upheaval but was itself an outcome of the first stage of the protracted crisis of the European and colonial system that had begun in 1914, even though the United States always held Moscow culpable to a critical extent for the many obstacles it was to confront. The history of the postwar era is essentially one of the monumental American attempts—and failures—to weave together such a global order and of the essentially vast autonomous social forces and destabilizing dynamics emerging throughout the world to confound its ambitions.

Such ambitions immediately brought the United States face to face with what to this day remains its primary problem: the conflict between its inordinate desires and its finite resources, and the definition of realistic priorities. Although it took years for the limits on American power to become clear to its leaders, most of whom only partly perceived it, it has been this problem of coherent priorities, and of the means to implement them, rather than the ultimate abstract goals themselves that have divided America's leaders and set the context for debates over policy. What was most important for much of the post-1945 era was the overweening belief on the part of American leaders that regulating all the world's political and economic problems was not only desirable but also possible, given skill and power. They would not and could not concede that the economic, political, and social dynamics of a great part of the world exceeded the capacities of any one or even a group of nations to control. At stake were the large and growing strategic and economic interests in those unstable nations experiencing the greatest changes.

The interaction between a complex world, the constraints on U.S. power, and Washington's perceptions, including its illusions and ignorance, is the subject matter for most of the history of contemporary American foreign policy. The "accidental" nature of that policy after 1946 was a consequence of the intrinsic dilemmas of this ambition rather than its cause. To articulate its priorities was quite simple. Europe was, and still is, at the top of the list of America's formally defined economic, strategic, and political interests. The dilemma of priorities was that none precluded others wholly, so that America's leaders never excluded intervention in any major part of the world. In the last analysis, it was the sheer extent of its objectives, and the inevitable crises and issues which emerged when the process of intervention began, that imposed on the United States the loss of mastery over its own priorities and actions.

By the late 1940s the United States had begun to confront the basic dilemmas it was to encounter for the remainder of the century. The formulation of priorities was an integral part of its reasoning, and so was resistance to communism in whatever form it might appear anywhere in the world. Its own interests had been fully articulated, and these found expression in statements of objectives as well as in the creation of international political, military, and economic organizations and alliances the United States effectively dominated, with American-led "internationalism" becoming one of the hallmarks of its postwar efforts.

Describing the various U.S. decision makers' motives and goals is a necessary but inherently frustrating effort because American capitalism's relative ideological underdevelopment produces nuances and contradictions among men of power which often become translated into the tensions and even ambivalences of American diplomacy. But the complex problem of explaining the causes of U.S. foreign policy can never obviate a description of the real forces and considerations which lead to certain actions and to an optimizing of specific, tangible interests rather than of others. Complexity in serious causal explanations has existed since time immemorial and is intrinsic to the analytic process, yet the importance many care to assign to caprice and accident itself looks frivolous on closer examination of the historical facts and political options. There are, ultimately, main trends and forces, and these must be respected regardless of coincidental related factors.

Prevention of the expansion of communism, the "containment" doctrine, became formally enshrined no later than 1947, and in 1950 the "rollback" of communism was secretly adhered to in the famous National Security Council 68 policy. In 1947 the so-called domino theory first emerged in the form of the Truman Doctrine on Greece. Were Greece to fall, Secretary of State George C. Marshall argued in February of that year, Turkey might follow and "Soviet domination might thus extend over the entire Middle East and Asia." Later that year the same logic required the reconstruction of West Germany, lest its weakness create a vacuum of power into which communism could enter and thereby spread throughout Europe. An area was, by this calculation, no stronger than its weakest link, and the domino mode of analysis, involving interconnections and linkages in estimating the effects of major political upheavals, well before Indochina was becoming the first and probably the most durable of conventional U.S. doctrines on the process of change and power in the modern world.

Such perceptions led irresistibly to the official decision in mid-1949, when the Communists triumphed in China, to draw a line against any new communist states in Asia, even though Washington was then preoccupied with European problems. But in Indochina the interaction of European with Asian affairs was always important to American leaders, for France's growing absorption with Indochina was causing it to veto West German rearmament, and the more quickly France won and brought its troops back home to balance projected German power, the sooner it could be brought into existence. No less crucial was the future position of Japan in Asia and in the world economy should it lose access to Southeast Asian raw materials and markets.

In a word, intervening in Vietnam never generated original international political dilemmas and issues for the United States. America's leaders clarified their ideas about dominoes, the credibility of their power, or the raw materials system in the world long before their action on Indochina had more than a routine significance. It was precisely because of the repeated definitions of containment, dominoes, intervention, and linkages of seemingly discrete foreign policy questions elsewhere in the world that the United States made the irreversible decision to see the war in Vietnam through to the end. Even many of the purely military dilemmas that were to emerge in Vietnam had been raised earlier in Korea. Until well into the 1960s Vietnam was but one of many nations the United States was both involved in and committed to retaining in friendly hands, and from 1953 through 1962 it provided more military and economic aid to Turkey, South Korea, and Taiwan, about as much to Pakistan, and only somewhat less to Greece and Spain. Given its resources and goals, America was deeply involved throughout the world as a matter of routine. This fact encouraged a new intervention to the extent that it succeeded in maintaining client regimes but could also be a restraint once the demands of one nation became so great as to threaten the United States' position elsewhere.

The domino theory was to be evoked initially more than any other justification in the Southeast Asian context, and the concept embodied both strategic and economic components which American leaders never separated. "The fall of Indochina would undoubtedly lead to the fall of the other mainland states of Southeast Asia," the Joint Chiefs of Staff argued in April 1950, and with it Russia would control "Asia's war potential . . . affecting the balance of power." Not only "major sources of certain strategic materials" would be lost, but also communications routes. The State Department maintained a similar line at this time, writing off Thailand and Burma should Indochina fall. Well before the Korean conflict this became the United States' official doctrine, and the war there strengthened this commitment.

The loss of Indochina, Washington formally articulated in June 1952, "would have critical psychological, political and economic consequences. . . . the loss of any single country would probably lead to relatively swift submission to or an alignment with communism by the remaining countries of this group. Furthermore, an alignment with communism of the rest of Southeast Asia and India, and in the longer term, of the Middle East (with the probable exceptions of at least Pakistan and Turkey) would in all probability progressively follow. Such widespread alignment would endanger the stability and security of Europe." It would "render the U.S. position in the Pacific offshore island chain precarious and would seriously jeopardize fundamental U.S. security interests in the Far East." The "principal world source of natural rubber and tin, and a producer of petroleum and other strategically important commodities" would be lost in Malaya and Indonesia. The rice exports of Burma and Thailand would be taken from Malaya, Ceylon, Japan, and India. Eventually, there would be "such economic and political pressures in Japan as to make it extremely difficult to prevent Japan's eventual accommodation to communism." This was the perfect integration of all the elements of the domino theory, involving raw materials, military bases, and the commitment of the United States to protect its many spheres of influence. In principle, even while helping the French to fight for the larger cause which America saw as its own, Washington's leaders prepared for greater intervention when it became necessary to prop up the leading domino—Indochina.

There were neither private nor public illusions regarding the stakes and goals for American power. Early in 1953 the National Security Council reiterated, "The Western countries and Japan need increased supplies of raw materials and foodstuffs and growing markets for their industrial production. Their balance of payments difficulties are in considerable part the result of the failure of production of raw materials and foodstuffs in non-dollar areas to increase as rapidly as industrial production." "Why is the United States spending hundreds of millions of dollars supporting the forces of the French Union in the fight against communism?" Vice-President Richard Nixon explained publicly in December 1953. "If Indochina falls, Thailand is put in an almost impossible position. The same is true of Malaya with its rubber and tin. The same is true of Indonesia. If this whole part of Southeast Asia goes under Communist domination or Communist influence, Japan, who trades and must trade with this area in order to exist, must inevitably be oriented towards the Communist regime." Both naturally and logically, references to tin, rubber, rice, copra, iron ore, tungsten, and oil were integral to American policy considerations from the inception. As long as he was President, Eisenhower never forgot his country's dependence on the importation of raw materials and the need to control their sources. When he first made public the "falling domino" analogy, in April 1954, he also discussed the dangers of losing the region's tin, tungsten, and rubber and the risk of Japan's being forced into dependence on communist nations for its industrial life—with all that implied. Always implicit in the doctrine was the assumption that the economic riches of the neighbors of the first domino, whether Greece or Indochina, were essential, and when the United States first intervened in those hapless and relatively poor nations, it kept the surrounding region foremost in its calculations. This willingness to accept the immense overhead charges of regional domination was constantly in the minds of the men who made the decisions to intervene.

The problem with the domino theory was, of course, its intrinsic conflict with the desire to impose priorities on U.S. commitments, resources, and actions. If a chain is no stronger than its weakest link, then that link has to be protected even though its very fragility might make the undertaking that much more difficult. But so long as the United States had no realistic sense of the constraints on its power, it was ready to take greater risks. The complex interaction of America's vast goals, its perception of the nature of its power, the domino vision of challenges, and the more modest notions implicit in the concept of priorities began in 1953 to merge in what became the start of the permanent debate and crisis in American strategic and diplomatic doctrine.

Washington had by 1947 become wholly convinced that the Soviet Union was in some crucial manner guiding many of the political and social upheavals in the world that were in fact the outcome of poverty, colonialism, and oligarchies, and that it was, thereby, seriously subverting the United States' attainment of its political and economic objectives of a reformed, American-led capitalist world order. Toward the end of the Korean War, the incipient conflicts built into such a definition of the world were paralleled and aggravated by a crisis in U.S. military technology and doctrine. These two threads inevitably intertwined late in 1953 in the "New Look" debate and in the beginnings of a perpetual search for a global strategy that could everywhere synthesize America's objectives and resources.

The Korean War tested the U.S. military's overwhelming superiority of firepower and technology, along with its capacity to sustain the economic and political costs of protracted war. Given the inconclusive end of the war along the thirty-eighth parallel after three years of combat, and given the total failure of Washington's September 1950 goal of reuniting the country by force of arms, the war had fully revealed the limits of American power. The domestic political controversy it created was less decisive, but it, too, disclosed the formidable political liabilities that such dismal struggles brought to the party in power. And in fiscal 1953, with military spending at 13.8 percent of the gross national product—three times the 1950 proportion—inflation and budget deficits exposed the constraints on American economic resources. In a word, the United States had undertaken a massive effort and achieved only inconclusive results; this reality raised the issue of the credibility of its power. No less important was the fact that it had become bogged down in Asia at the very moment its main priorities and attention were focused on Europe and the Middle East. To resolve these dilemmas became an obsession in Washington, one that affected every area of the world and influenced the U.S. strategy debate for the remainder of the century.

The effort to define a "New Look" for American foreign policy, culminating in Dulles's famous January 12, 1954, speech, was stillborn, for the Soviet test of a hydrogen bomb in August 1953 decisively broke the U.S. monopoly of strategic nuclear weapons. Land war, Dulles declared, could be fought with the forces of America's allies but the United States itself would rely on its "massive retaliatory power . . . by means and at places of our choosing." It was the only "modern way of getting maximum protection at bearable cost," for limited conventional war in Korea had involved potentially unlimited costs. The dark intimation that America might destroy Peking or Moscow because of events in some distant place was the beginning of a search for a new strategy, but the internal contradictions of that view were immediately criticized in Washington. That quest did not preclude relatively minimal responses to what seemed to be small challenges, and even as the weight of military spending on the national economy was reduced substantially over the remainder of the decade and as strategic weapons became more prominent, the White House increased its reliance on covert warfare waged by the CIA—the success of which in Iran and

Guatemala greatly encouraged this relatively low-cost, often inconspicuous form of intervention. For whatever the theory, in practice the United States continued to be deeply involved in very different political contexts in every corner of the globe. Throughout the 1950s Washington never husbanded finite resources rationally to attain its primary goals, because, while it could reduce the role of military spending in the economy, it was unwilling and unable to scale down its far more decisive political definitions of the scope and location of American interests in the world.

To a remarkable extent, America's leaders perceived the nature of the contradiction but never ceased to believe that they could find a solution. The intense defense debates of the middle and late 1950s, which made the reputations of numerous articulate and immensely self-confident military intellectuals like Henry Kissinger, Maxwell Taylor, and W. W. Rostow, inconclusively contradicted and neutralized each other. But what was constant in all such theories was the need to be active rather than passive in responding to new problems and challenges, for American power both to appear and to be credible, and to seek to control and direct, rather than be subject to the dictates of, highly fluid outside forces and events. To develop a sense of mastery was the objective, but the fact that the technologies and strategies for attaining it were constantly being debated produced a perpetual dilemma.

It was in this larger context of a search for a decisive global strategy and doctrine throughout the 1950s that the emerging Vietnam issue was linked to so many other international questions. Washington always saw the challenge of Indochina as just one part of a much greater problem it confronted throughout the world: the efficacy of limited war, the danger of dominoes, the credibility of American power, the role of France in Europe, and much else. Vietnam became the conjunction of the postwar crisis of U.S. imperialism at a crucial stage of America's much greater effort to resolve its own doubts about its capacity to protect the larger international socioeconomic environment in which its interests could survive and prosper. By 1960 every preceding event required that the credibility of U.S. power be tested soon, lest all of the failures and dilemmas since 1946 undermine the very foundations of the system it was seeking to construct throughout the world. It was mainly chance that designated Vietnam as the primary arena of trial, but it was virtually preordained that America would try somewhere to attain successes—not simply one but many—to reverse the deepening pattern of postwar history. . . .

The Vietnam War was for the United States the culmination of its frustrating postwar effort to merge its arms and politics to halt and reverse the emergence of states and social systems opposed to the international order Washington sought to establish. It was not the first serious trial of either its military power or its political strategy, only the most disastrous. Despite America's many real successes in imposing its hegemony elsewhere, Vietnam exposed the ultimate constraints on its power in the modern era: its internal tensions, the contradictions between overinvolvement in one nation and its interests and ambitions elsewhere, and its material limits.

Precisely because of the unmistakable nature of the defeat after so long and divisive an effort and because of the war's impact on the United States' political structure and aspirations, this conflict takes on a significance greater than that of either of the two world wars. Both of them had only encouraged Washington's ambition to guide and integrate the world's political and economic system—a goal which was surely the most important cause of its intervention in the Vietnam conflict after 1950.

While the strategic implications of the war for the future of American military power in local conflicts was the most obvious dimension of its defeat, it had confronted these issues often since 1946. What was truly distinctive was the collapse of a national consensus on the broad contours of America's role in the world. The trauma was intense; the war ended without glory and with profound remorse for tens of millions of Americans. Successive administrations fought the war so energetically because of these earlier frustrations, of which they were especially conscious in the early 1960s, scarcely suspecting that rather than resolving them, they would only leave the nation with a far larger set of military, political, and economic dilemmas to face for the remainder of this century. But by 1975 the United States was weaker than it had been at the inception of the war in the early 1960s, a lesson hardly any advocate of new interventions could afford to ignore.

The limits of arms and armies in Vietnam were clear by Tet 1968. Although the United States possessed nominally good weapons and tactics, it lacked a military strategy capable of overcoming its enemy's abilities and appropriate to its economic resources, its global priorities, and its political constraints in Vietnam, at home, and in the rest of the world. Although its aims in South Vietnam were never to alter, it was always incapable of coping with the countless political complexities that irrevocably emerge from protracted armed conflict. America's political, military, and ideological leaders remained either oblivious or contemptuous of these until the war was essentially lost. Even today they scarcely dare confront the war's meaning as Washington continues to assert aggressively its classic postwar objectives and interests in Latin America and elsewhere. America's failure was material, of course, but it was also analytic, the result of a myopia whose importance greatly transcended bureaucratic politics or the idiosyncrasies of Presidents and their satraps. The dominating conventional wisdom of American power after 1946 had no effective means of inhibiting a system whose ambitions and needs increasingly transcended its resources for achieving them. They remained unable and unwilling to acknowledge that these objectives were intrinsically unobtainable and irrelevant to the socioeconomic forms much of the Third World is adopting to resolve its economic and human problems, and that the United States' effort to alter this pervasive reality was certain to produce conflict.

✗ FURTHER READING

David L. Anderson, ed., *Shadow on the White House: Presidents and the Vietnam War,* 1945–1975 (1993)
Loren Baritz, *Backfire* (1985)
Peter Braestrup, ed., *Vietnam as History* (1984)
Bernard Brodie, *War and Politics* (1973)
Michael Charlton and Anthony Moncrief, *Many Reasons Why* (1978)
Chester A. Cooper, *The Lost Crusade* (1970)
Phillip B. Davidson, *Vietnam at War* (1988)
Bernard Edelman, ed., *Dear America: Letters Home from Vietnam* (1985)
Daniel Ellsberg, *Papers on the War* (1972)
Gloria Emerson, *Winners and Losers* (1976)
Elizabeth Jane Errington and B. J. C. McKercher, eds., *The Vietnam War as History* (1990)
Frances FitzGerald, *Fire in the Lake* (1972)
William C. Gibbons, *The U.S. Government and the Vietnam War* (1986–1987)
James William Gibson, *The Perfect War* (1986)
David Halberstam, *The Best and the Brightest* (1972)
James Pinckney Harrison, *The Endless War* (1982)
Patrick J. Hearden, *The Tragedy of Vietnam* (1991)
———, ed., *Vietnam: Four American Perspectives* (1990)
George C. Herring, *America's Longest War* (1986)
Gary R. Hess, *Vietnam and the United States* (1990)
Hugh Higgins, *Vietnam* (1982)
Anthony James Joes, *The War for South Viet Nam* (1990)
Paul Joseph, *Cracks in the Empire: State Politics in the Vietnam War* (1981)
George McT. Kahin, *Intervention* (1986)
George McT. Kahin and John W. Lewis, *The United States in Vietnam* (1969)
Paul M. Kattenburg, *The Vietnam Trauma in American Foreign Policy, 1945–1975* (1980)
Guenther Lewy, *America in Vietnam* (1978)
Timothy J. Lomperis, *The War Everyone Lost—and Won* (1984)
Michael Maclear, *The Ten Thousand Day War* (1981)
George Donelson Moss, *Vietnam* (1990)
James S. Olson and Randy Roberts, *Where the Domino Fell* (1991)
George K. Osborn et al., eds., *Democracy, Strategy, and Vietnam* (1987)
John Clark Pratt, *Vietnam Voices* (1984)
Arthur M. Schlesinger, Jr., *The Bitter Heritage* (1966)
Anthony Short, *The Origins of the Vietnam War* (1989)
James Thomson, "How Could Vietnam Happen? An Autopsy," *Atlantic Monthly,* 221 (1968), 47–53
William S. Turley, *The Second Indochina War* (1986)
Marilyn B. Young, *The Vietnam Wars, 1945–1990* (1991)

The Development of Vietnamese Nationalism

✕

History and geography exert a powerful influence on all peoples and nations. Vietnam is no exception. American officials were often accused of approaching Vietnam with little understanding of its culture and language, and even less appreciation of its rich history—forces that, specialists now agree, contributed mightily to the war's outcome.

One of the ironic effects of the war is that it generated an explosion of new scholarship on Vietnamese history, especially in the United States. Recent historical literature has paid particular attention to the genesis of modern Vietnamese nationalism, which is the focus of the selections in this chapter. In their endeavors, scholars have sought to account for elements of continuity and discontinuity in Vietnam's long history; tried to assess the impact of French colonial rule on the social structure, economic life, and intellectual outlook within the country; and struggled to explain the emergence of a strong Communist party within the larger nationalist movement.

✕ D O C U M E N T S

The first document is a selection from the prison notes of Phan Boi Chau, still revered as one of Vietnam's great nationalists. These reflections were written in 1914 while Chau was imprisoned in China, at the request of the French, for nationalist activities. From his release in 1917 until his death in 1941, he continued to agitate for Vietnamese independence. The second document contains comments made by Nguyen Ai Quoc (more commonly known by his adopted name, Ho Chi Minh) at a National Congress of the French Socialist party, held at Tours in December 1920. After denouncing French imperialism in his native land, he approved the resolution to found the French Communist party and to join the Third International. On February 3, 1930, Ho helped to establish the Communist party of Indochina. In the next reading, he exhorts his countrymen to join the party and to forge a revolution against French rule.

During the closing months of World War II, a terrible famine that ultimately would claim between 1 and 2 million lives swept across northern Vietnam. The tragedy, which most Vietnamese blamed on the callousness of French and Japanese policies, dramatically increased the appeal of the Vietnamese communist movement throughout the country. A selection from a book by Vietnamese writer Tran Van Mai, written at the time, offers a firsthand account of the desperate conditions brought on by the famine. On September 2, 1945, Ho proclaimed an independent Democratic Republic of Vietnam; the declaration, which borrowed deliberately from the American Declaration of Independence, appears in the final document.

Phan Boi Chau's Prison Reflections, 1914

The great victory of Japan in the Russo-Japanese war [1904–05] had a tremendous impact upon us. For it was like a new and strange world opening up.

Before the time of the French Protectorate, Vietnam only knew a world with China. And when the French arrived we only knew a world with France. But the world had changed. A strange new wave as yet undreamed of had arrived.

We had been caught up in our internal affairs for so long that even if our heads were cut off and our bodies lost we still had no fear. We were that way only because we cared for our country and our conscience forced us to be so. As for a way to build independence, at that time we were still dreaming in a very thick fog.

Alas! In the middle of the nineteenth century, even though the universe was shaken by American winds and European rains, our country was still in a period of dreaming in a deep sleep. Our people were still blind and resigned to their lot. We cannot blame them, for even well-known people from the higher classes like myself were like frogs in the bottom of a well or ants at the bottom of their hole. We knew nothing about life. I think that there must be no more tragic-comic people in the world than our people.

It is only because in former times we shut our doors and stayed at home, going round and round in circles of literary knowledge, examinations and Chinese studies. To say frankly that our people were deaf and blind is no exaggeration.

Even after the French invasion our people were still deaf and blind. If we had not been awakened by the violent sound of the guns at Port Arthur, perhaps we should not yet know that there were other foreign countries besides France.

After the beginning of the Russo-Japanese hostilities, during the years of the Dragon [1904] and the Serpent [1905], the competition and struggle between the Europeans and the Asians, between the white-skinned people and the yellow-skinned people, forced us to wake up with a start. We

From Phan Boi Chau and Ho Chi Minh, *Reflections from Captivity*, David G. Marr, ed., pp. 22–23, 55–56, Ohio University Press, 1978. Reprinted by permission of the author.

became increasingly enthusiastic and intense in our commitment to our ideals. The only problem we still sought to overcome was that of obtaining weapons. . . .

When in jail, it is of course no use to lament one's pain. But there is the sorrowful fact that I have had to be separated from my brothers, without any news, with only myself to speak Vietnamese for myself to hear, thinking only of my sad destiny. I think of my failures and weep, my tears falling like torrents of rain. Truly, from the day I was born until now I have never known the taste of suffering as I know it now.

But I have arrived at this suffering because of the ambition that I have held for these last thirty years. And what has this ambition been?

It has been but a yearning to purchase my freedom even at the cost of spilling my blood, to exchange my fate of slavery for the right of self-determination.

Ah! With such an ambition I took in my own hands the supreme responsibility of speaking on behalf of my people. Is there anyone who dares say I should not have done this? Yet if such an ambition is to achieve anything great, we must rely on the toughness of our muscles, the excellence of our learning, the skill of our planning, and the careful manipulation of conditions. Instead, I wondered if at best I wasn't just a blind man leading the blind. Now I have failed simply because I am unskilled. I need complain no more.

However, I think that in this world there is no reason why a stream of water once it has flowed downward can never come up again, or why a life once set on its course cannot change. Who knows but that my failure today will not be good fortune for my people tomorrow? . . .

Let the thousands, ten thousands, even hundreds of thousands of my people who bear an ambition such as mine take heed from my failure. Let them become people who can take care of themselves. We must not wait until our finger has been cut the ninth time before we find the bandage.

I realize that I am a man who has not obtained steel weaponry worth holding on to, that on this earth I have laid down no strategy worth standing on. At most I am an empty-handed rogue with nothing to my name, weak in force and feeble in ability. Yet I am ready still to fight long-toothed tigers and sharp-clawed panthers. Those who understand my inner soul might console me by saying:

"What a brave man!"

Those who wish to look at my mistakes might well look down and say:

"What a stupid man!"

To sum up, in this world there is truly no one as stupid as I. If this be the last day of my life and if, upon my death, I still be called by such a forbidden name as "the most stupid," then this is very correct. It is impossible to call me anything else. But if I have the good fortune to survive and if, afterwards, I see tigers and panthers, then surely I will fight. May my people learn their lesson from my example.

Ho Chi Minh Deplores "Imperialist Crimes," 1920

Chairman: Comrade Indochinese Delegate, you have the floor.

Indochinese Delegate [Nguyen Ai Quoc]: Today, instead of contributing, together with you, to world revolution, I come here with deep sadness to speak as a member of the Socialist Party, against the imperialists who have committed abhorrent crimes on my native land. You all have known that French imperialism entered Indochina half a century ago. In its selfish interests, it conquered our country with bayonets. Since then we have not only been oppressed and exploited shamelessly, but also tortured and poisoned pitilessly. Plainly speaking, we have been poisoned with opium, alcohol, etc. I cannot, in some minutes, reveal all the atrocities that the predatory capitalists have inflicted on Indochina. Prisons outnumber schools and are always overcrowded with detainees. Any natives having socialist ideas are arrested and sometimes murdered without trial. Such is the so-called justice in Indochina. In that country, the Vietnamese are discriminated against, they do not enjoy safety like Europeans or those having European citizenship. We have neither freedom of press nor freedom of speech. Even freedom of assembly and freedom of association do not exist. We have no right to live in other countries or to go abroad as tourists. We are forced to live in utter ignorance and obscurity because we have no right to study. In Indochina the colonialists find all ways and means to force us to smoke opium and drink alcohol to poison and beset us. Thousands of Vietnamese have been led to a slow death or massacred to protect other people's interests.

Comrades, such is the treatment inflicted upon more than 20 million Vietnamese, that is more than half the population of France. And they are said to be under French protection! The Socialist Party must act practically to support the oppressed natives. . . .

Indochinese Delegate: On behalf of the whole of mankind, on behalf of all the Socialist Party's members, both left and right wings, we call on you! Comrades, save us!

Chairman: Through the applause of approval, the Indochinese Delegate can realize that the whole of the Socialist Party sides with you to oppose the crimes committed by the bourgeois class.

Ho's Appeal at the Founding
of the Communist Party of Indochina, 1930

Workers, peasants, soldiers, youth, and pupils!

Oppressed and exploited compatriots!

Sisters and brothers! Comrades!

Imperialist contradictions were the cause of the 1914-18 World War. After this horrible slaughter, the world was divided into two camps: One is the revolutionary camp including the oppressed colonies and the exploited working class throughout the world. The vanguard force of this camp is the Soviet Union. The other is the counterrevolutionary camp of international capitalism and imperialism whose general staff is the League of Nations.

During this World War, various nations suffered untold losses in property and human lives. The French imperialists were the hardest hit. Therefore, in order to restore the capitalist forces in France, the French imperialists have resorted to every underhand scheme to intensify their capitalist exploitation in Indochina. They set up new factories to exploit the workers with low wages. They plundered the peasants' land to establish plantations and drive them to utter poverty. They levied many heavy taxes. They imposed public loans upon our people. In short, they reduced us to wretchedness. They increased their military forces, firstly to strangle the Vietnamese revolution, secondly to prepare for a new imperialist war in the Pacific aimed at capturing new colonies, thirdly to suppress the Chinese revolution, fourthly to attack the Soviet Union because the latter helps the revolution of the oppressed nations and the exploited working class. World War II will break out. When it breaks, the French imperialists will certainly drive our people to a more horrible slaughter. If we give them a free hand to prepare for this war, suppress the Chinese revolution, and attack the Soviet Union, if we give them a free hand to stifle the Vietnamese revolution, it is tantamount to giving them a free hand to wipe our race off the earth and drown our nation in the Pacific.

However the French imperialists' barbarous oppression and ruthless exploitation have awakened our compatriots, who have all realized that revolution is the only road to life, without it they will die out piecemeal. This is the reason why the Vietnamese revolutionary movement has grown even stronger with each passing day. The workers refuse to work, the peasants demand land, the pupils strike, the traders boycott. Everywhere the masses have risen to oppose the French imperialists.

The Vietnamese revolution has made the French imperialists tremble with fear. On the one hand, they utilize the feudalists and comprador bourgeois in our country to oppress and exploit our people. On the other, they terrorize, arrest, jail, deport, and kill a great number of Vietnamese revolutionaries. If the French imperialists think that they can suppress the Vietnamese revolution by means of terrorist acts, they are utterly mistaken. Firstly, it is because the Vietnamese revolution is not isolated but enjoys the assistance of the world proletarian class in general and of the French working class in particular. Secondly, while the French imperialists are frenziedly carrying out terrorist acts, the Vietnamese Communists, formerly working separately, have now united into a single party, the Communist Party of Indochina, to lead our entire people in their revolution.

Workers, peasants, soldiers, youth, pupils!

Oppressed and exploited compatriots!

The Communist Party of Indochina is founded. It is the party of the working class. It will help the proletarian class to lead the revolution in order to struggle for all the oppressed and exploited people. From now on we must join the Party, help it and follow it in order to implement the following slogans:

1. To overthrow French imperialism, feudalism, and the reactionary Vietnamese capitalist class.
2. To make Indochina completely independent.
3. To establish a worker-peasant and soldier government.
4. To confiscate the banks and other enterprises belonging to the imperialists and put them under the control of the worker-peasant and soldier government.
5. To confiscate the whole of the plantations and property belonging to the imperialists and the Vietnamese reactionary capitalist class and distribute them to poor peasants.
6. To implement the eight-hour working day.
7. To abolish public loans and poll tax. To waive unjust taxes hitting the poor people.
8. To bring back all freedoms to the masses.
9. To carry out universal education.
10. To implement equality between man and woman.

A Vietnamese Writer Recalls the 1944–1945 Famine, 1956

Holding on to one another, crying, waiting for death

The Vietnamese people are accustomed to leading a hard working, frugal, and patient life. They believe that if they eat less, save some money, and work hard, then no matter how difficult life is for them, they can still "patch things up" and somehow manage to have at least one meal of greens and one meal of rice gruel each day. The changes in the economy of Vietnam between 1940 and 1945, however, greatly disrupted the people's livelihood, worst of all in the countryside.

In 1943 a ten-kilogram can of rice sold for only 1.00 piaster. A dozen eggs sold for only eight cents. In 1944 one had to pay 2.00 piasters a dozen.

The speculators hoarded, took advantage of their situation and their powerful influence, and very rapidly became rich. Prices of goods soared upward. Wages for labor, however, were raised very little and very slowly.

During the seasonal harvest of 1944 the wage for a harvester or a rice grinder was two meals of rice and salted cucumbers, an extra bowl of rice, and one piaster per day. A very strong laborer could earn only enough to feed himself, to say nothing of the taxes he had to pay or provision for his parents, wife, and children.

From May through September 1944 there were three typhoons in the coastal areas of Bac Viet [northern Vietnam]. In normal times this kind of catastrophe would be enough to put the population in an impossible situation. But now the disaster fell upon them during wartime and during a time

From *Before the Revolution: The Vietnamese Peasants Under the French* by Ngo Vinh Long, pp. 227–29. Copyright © 1973, 1991 Columbia University Press, New York. Reprinted with permission of the publisher.

of economic disorder. Worst of all, the French colonizers were plotting to destroy the very vitality of the population, to increase starvation in every possible way so as to be able to neutralize the traditional unyielding spirit of the Vietnamese people, and thus to rule them easily. For this reason, from September and October of 1944 onward, everybody realized that the tragedy of all times could not be avoided.

In normal times harvest season in the countryside was bustling with the activities of rice pounding and grinding. But during the seasonal harvest of the year 1944 things were completely different. The farmers went out into the fields, cried to the heavens, and moaned. People looked at each other with all hope drained from their eyes and uttered words that made it seem that they were saying farewells to one another: "There is no knowing whether we will still be alive to see each other by the time the next *chiem* harvest comes around."

The starvation began in early October. Earlier than any other year the weather was cuttingly cold. The north wind howled, and it pierced through the rags worn by the hungry and the poor. It penetrated their flesh and their bones and their weak insides. In the grey sky overhead there hung a damp layer of clouds that enveloped the hamlets and the villages. It rained continuously, day and night, and the dampness seeped into the very marrow of the hungry.

All through October and on through December the sun kept itself hidden behind the thick clouds, with but feeble rays making their way through to the tops of the drooping bamboo groves. The days and months dragged by slowly. Rain, wind, hunger, and cold seemed to slow down the wheels of time. It was so cold that people would lie in haystacks, covering themselves up with banana leaves. They were so hungry that they had to eat marsh pennywort, potato leaves, bran, banana roots, and the bark of trees. The villagers—fathers and sons, brothers and sisters, husbands and wives, all of them alike—could no longer save one another. Regardless of the time of day or night, the hungry people, over and over again, would hug each other and would moan tragically.

The Vietnamese Declaration of Independence, 1945

All men are created equal; they are endowed by their Creator with certain unalienable Rights; among these are Life, Liberty, and the pursuit of Happiness.

This immortal statement was made in the Declaration of Independence of the United States of America in 1776. In a broader sense, this means: All the peoples on the earth are equal from birth, all the peoples have a right to live, to be happy and free.

The Declaration of the French Revolution made in 1791 on the Rights of Man and the Citizen also states: "All men are born free and with equal rights, and must always remain free and have equal rights."

Those are undeniable truths.

Nevertheless, for more than eighty years, the French imperialists, abusing the standard of Liberty, Equality, and Fraternity, have violated our Fatherland and oppressed our fellow citizens. They have acted contrary to the ideals of humanity and justice.

In the field of politics, they have deprived our people of every democratic liberty.

They have enforced inhuman laws; they have set up three distinct political regimes in the North, the Center, and the South of Viet-Nam in order to wreck our national unity and prevent our people from being united.

They have built more prisons than schools. They have mercilessly slain our patriots; they have drowned our uprisings in rivers of blood.

They have fettered public opinion; they have practiced obscurantism against our people.

To weaken our race they have forced us to use opium and alcohol.

In the field of economics, they have fleeced us to the backbone, impoverished our people and devastated our land.

They have robbed us of our rice fields, our mines, our forests, and our raw materials. They have monopolized the issuing of bank notes and the export trade.

They have invented numerous unjustifiable taxes and reduced our people, especially our peasantry, to a state of extreme poverty.

They have hampered the prospering of our national bourgeoisie; they have mercilessly exploited our workers.

In the autumn of 1940, when the Japanese fascists violated Indochina's territory to establish new bases in their fight against the Allies, the French imperialists went down on their bended knees and handed over our country to them.

Thus, from that date, our people were subjected to the double yoke of the French and the Japanese. Their sufferings and miseries increased. The result was that, from the end of last year to the beginning of this year, from Quang Tri Province to the North of Viet-Nam, more than two million of our fellow citizens died from starvation. On March 9 [1945], the French troops were disarmed by the Japanese. The French colonialists either fled or surrendered, showing that not only were they incapable of "protecting" us, but that, in the span of five years, they had twice sold our country to the Japanese.

On several occasions before March 9, the Viet Minh League urged the French to ally themselves with it against the Japanese. Instead of agreeing to this proposal, the French colonialists so intensified their terrorist activities against the Viet Minh members that before fleeing they massacred a great number of our political prisoners detained at Yen Bay and Cao Bang.

Notwithstanding all this, our fellow citizens have always manifested toward the French a tolerant and humane attitude. Even after the Japanese *Putsch* of March, 1945, the Viet Minh League helped many Frenchmen to cross the frontier, rescued some of them from Japanese jails, and protected French lives and property.

From the autumn of 1940, our country had in fact ceased to be a French colony and had become a Japanese possession.

After the Japanese had surrendered to the Allies, our whole people rose to regain our national sovereignty and to found the Democratic Republic of Viet-Nam.

The truth is that we have wrested our independence from the Japanese and not from the French.

The French have fled, the Japanese have capitulated, Emperor Bao Dai has abdicated. Our people have broken the chains which for nearly a century have fettered them and have won independence for the Fatherland. Our people at the same time have overthrown the monarchic regime that has reigned supreme for dozens of centuries. In its place has been established the present Democratic Republic.

For these reasons, we, members of the Provisional Government, representing the whole Vietnamese people, declare that from now on we break off all relations of a colonial character with France; we repeal all the international obligation that France has so far subscribed to on behalf of Viet-Nam, and we abolish all the special rights the French have unlawfully acquired in our Fatherland.

The whole Vietnamese people, animated by a common purpose, are determined to fight to the bitter end against any attempt by the French colonialists to reconquer their country.

We are convinced that the Allied nations, which at Teheran and San Francisco have acknowledged the principles of self-determination and equality of nations, will not refuse to acknowledge the independence of Viet-Nam.

A people who have courageously opposed French domination for more than eighty years, a people who have fought side by side with the Allies against the fascists during these last years, such a people must be free and independent.

For these reasons, we, members of the Provisional Government of the Democratic Republic of Viet-Nam, solemnly declare to the world that Viet-Nam has the right to be a free and independent country—and in fact it is so already. The entire Vietnamese people are determined to mobilize all their physical and mental strength, to sacrifice their lives and property in order to safeguard their independence and liberty.

✗ *E S S A Y S*

In the opening essay, John T. McAlister, Jr., formerly of Princeton University, provides a brief overview of Vietnam's historical development up to the imposition of French colonial rule in the late nineteenth century. He emphasizes several persistent themes in the nation's history, including regionalism and village autonomy. Next, David G. Marr of Australian National University states that the Vietnamese revolution of 1945 cannot be understood without reference to prior changes in Vietnam's social structure and intellectual outlook. Particularly significant to later developments were ideological transformations within the intelligentsia—shifts that preceded and ultimately contributed to the success of the Vietminh. William J. Duiker, a historian at Pennsylvania State University, contends in the last selection that the key to communist success was the utilization of Vietnamese nationalism in the struggle to evict the French. His essay helps to explain how communism became the most vital element within the Vietnamese nationalist movement by the 1930s.

Vietnam: An Historical Overview

JOHN T. MCALISTER, JR.

For a people with a two-thousand-year heritage of occupation, rebellion, and a troubled search for order, the revolution launched in August 1945 represented a major landmark. It not only inaugurated a new approach to politics in Viet Nam, but also marked a millennium of freedom from Chinese occupation. Before the year 939, when the Vietnamese threw off China's direct control over their affairs, they had been ruled as a Chinese province for a thousand years. Yet the tortuous history of the country even predates Chinese control. The record goes back to 208 B.C., when the Vietnamese first appeared in official annals as a minority people in the kingdom of Nam Viet, known in Chinese history as Nan-yüeh.

Covering wide areas of present-day northern Viet Nam and southern China, the kingdom of Nam Viet was created by a renegade Chinese warlord. He had taken advantage of the decay of China's first imperial dynasty to assert his marginal power based on regional military occupation. His political creation, Nam Viet, remained autonomous for nearly a century because the power of the emerging Han dynasty was restricted to north and central China, where it was struggling to consolidate dynastic control. In the pattern that was to become familiar on China's southern periphery when its imperial regimes were weak or preoccupied internally, Nam Viet was recognized as an autonomous kingdom over which the Han retained a nominal though unenforceable sovereignty. Within the loose structure of the kingdom, the forebears of the Vietnamese were permitted their own administration. This structure consisted of fiefs governed by hereditary chiefs in the sort of feudal system that still exists among the mountain peoples of northern Viet Nam. However, after 111 B.C., when the Han dynasty was strong enough to extend its power southward and absorb Nam Viet into the Chinese empire, the Vietnamese fiefs became provinces of China.

Despite the deep imprint made on them by Chinese culture of the Han and T'ang dynasties, these early Vietnamese possessed a zeal for political autonomy. Among the numerous peoples on the southern periphery of China, only the Vietnamese adopted Chinese culture without becoming a part of the Chinese political system. Only in Viet Nam "did the [Chinese] culture outpace the [Chinese] political unit. The Vietnamese speak a Sinitic language related to Chinese; they derived their higher culture from China;

From *Vietnam: The Origins of Revolution* by John T. McAlister, Jr., pp. 17–31, 42–43, 46–47. Copyright © 1969 by the Center of International Studies, Princeton, N.J. Reprinted by permission of Alfred A. Knopf, Inc.

and they were for a long period under Chinese rule." Yet eventually they managed to establish their identity as a separate country within East Asian civilization. Indeed it may be that the adoption of Chinese culture made it possible for the Vietnamese to free themselves from political control by China. In the view of the noted scholar Henri Maspéro, Viet Nam was able to assert its autonomy because Chinese occupation, "by breaking the power of particularist institutions and local groups, and by introducing Chinese ideas and social organization, gave it a cohesion and formal structure which its neighbors lacked." Whether or not the imposition of Chinese culture was instrumental in winning the Vietnamese their autonomy, it seems certain that the way the culture was imposed provided the motivation for them to seek an end to rule by China.

Efforts to absorb the Vietnamese into the Chinese empire were carried on sporadically and haphazardly throughout a millennium of occupation. In fact it seems that the Chinese overlords were more concerned with pacifying these peripheral minority peoples than in assimilating them. As the pressure of the Chinese occupation progressively curtailed the influence of Vietnamese feudal leaders, they were afforded virtually no compensating opportunities to join the broader political and cultural world of the Chinese empire. Because the local aristocracy saw that a continuation of Chinese policy threatened to wipe them out, their hostility toward the occupation rose sharply until it culminated in a rebellion in A.D. 40. Crushed by an expedition of Chinese reinforcements, this desperate revolt by a decaying feudal regime was followed by one of the most thorough attempts to implant Chinese culture among the Vietnamese ever undertaken. Perhaps the most important result of this program was to speed the intermarriage of Vietnamese with Chinese settlers and functionaries. A new elite emerged with a commitment to Chinese language and culture that would have been difficult to obtain by coercion alone. Although this new racially mixed local elite enjoyed none of the privileges or influence of their feudal predecessors, they too were a hereditary aristocracy, but with family ties now based on Chinese customs.

The emphasis on cultural assimilation which had produced a Chinese-oriented aristocracy among the Vietnamese was not matched by efforts to absorb them into Chinese politics. Only gradually and hesitantly was this local elite allowed to participate in the Chinese provincial administration over the Vietnamese. They had to qualify for appointment by mastering the same examinations in Chinese literature and philosophy that were required of Chinese administrative officials. But, as the Han dynasty was in the decline, these administratively qualified Vietnamese demanded and were granted a status—equal to that of any qualified Chinese—which entitled them to be assigned anywhere in the empire. Mixed-blood Vietnamese were actually appointed as subprefects in two Chinese provinces. But these promising beginnings in cultural and political integration came abruptly to an end with the fall of the Han dynasty in A.D. 220.

Thereafter, China suffered several centuries of internal political disintegration. Not only did Chinese preoccupation with domestic politics reduce pressures on the Vietnamese, but it also encouraged them to seek their own political identity separate from China. Significantly, the abortive attempts to establish an autonomous Vietnamese kingdom between 542 and 602 were led by the local racially mixed aristocracy. Their short-lived kingdom was an expression of the political consciousness and skills they had acquired through Chinese culture but had been able to use only slightly within the Chinese empire. Although their flimsy kingdom was easily destroyed by the Chinese, little was done to resolve the underlying causes of the uprising. When China was once again brought under centralized control, in 618 by the T'ang dynasty, little effort was made to integrate the Vietnamese into Chinese political life. The T'ang simply used their burgeoning power to impose the most severe occupation the Vietnamese had ever known. But the power of the T'ang, like that of previous dynasties, had its limits and when it had run its course the resultant weakness in China coincided with an increasing political strength among the Vietnamese. By 939 an autonomous Vietnamese kingdom was able to defend itself against direct Chinese control.

This assertion of local strength did not mean complete independence for Viet Nam. Reimposition of Chinese rule—as was threatened during the Mongol invasion of 1285, and as occurred briefly, 1413–37, during the Ming dynasty—was always a factor in Vietnamese politics. Instead of asserting their independence of China, which would have run the risk of frequent struggles over the reintroduction of Chinese military occupation, the Vietnamese had earlier become one of China's tributary states. Until France gained control in 1885, the Vietnamese ritually acknowledged the supremacy of China and periodically sent missions bearing tribute. Moreover, these ritual ties contained a fiber of strength in the recognized prerogative of the Chinese court to invest the Vietnamese emperors with their legitimacy to rule. Rather than stimulating Chinese interference in Vietnamese affairs, this symbolic investiture contributed to stability because of the careful scrutiny given to new claimants of political legitimacy.

Once the Vietnamese had freed themselves of a millennium of Chinese domination, they struggled for another millennium with the consequences of their own autonomy. The ending of Chinese control did not mean that the Vietnamese had achieved political unity and stability. For nearly ten centuries they fought among themselves in attempting to institutionalize political power into a unified government having authority over all the Vietnamese. Significantly, the incipient dynasty that was instrumental in asserting Vietnamese autonomy from China was unable to consolidate its power in Viet Nam. Persisting feudal groups thwarted the ephemeral Ngo dynasty (A.D. 939–69) in its ambition to unify the Vietnamese. Even less durable regimes followed the Ngo as competing families sought to subdue their rivals by military force and impose their hereditary rule on the country. Not until 1009, nearly a century after Chinese rule ended, did one group prevail over its rivals and consolidate political power into a durable regime.

The leaders of the resilient Ly dynasty (1009–1225) succeeded in institutionalizing their power by stages. First they established a military administration to translate their predominant strength into territorial control over the country. But the durability of the dynasty for over two centuries undoubtedly resulted from their capacity to transform coercive force into a governmental authority widely accepted as having the legitimate use of power. This institutionalized strength was achieved by sharing power more widely and making the access to power more orderly than under military control. Specifically, a civil administration was established with recruitment based on the Chinese examination system. From this procedure a bureaucracy was created that represented those most thoroughly knowledgeable in Chinese language and culture.

Selection to the bureaucracy, or mandarinate, as the Europeans baptized this scholar-administration, was theoretically open without regard to social standing to all who could satisfy the qualifications. Since education in Chinese culture became the primary criterion for political mobility, some members of the mandarinate, called mandarins by the Europeans, did come from modest social origins. However, since only those with extensive resources could afford the leisure of long years of preparation for these examinations, the bureaucracy in fact institutionalized the power of the families with the greatest wealth and cohesion. Instead of turning their resources into military power with which to fight for dynastic succession, the Vietnamese families gradually accepted competition for political power on a more orderly basis. But despite the rigor of the examinations, power in Viet Nam was still largely hereditary.

For nearly four hundred years, between the eleventh and the fourteenth centuries, the mandarin system of bureaucracy provided relative internal order under conditions of almost constant threat of invasion by aggressive neighbors and dynastic usurpation at home. Domestic challenges to dynastic rule, often militant in character, were never sufficient to bring down the mandarin system, at least not until other factors weakened internal order. Even when the long rule of the Ly dynasty came to an end in 1225 for lack of a male heir, there was no outbreak of internal war. The Tran dynasty (1225–1400) succeeded to dynastic rule by arranging a marriage with the female heir of the Ly family, but it was by preserving the mandarinal system that they maintained the continuity of power. The Tran thus perpetuated a period of political coherence, nearly four centuries long, that was in sharp contrast to the turmoil of both earlier and later epochs.

The institutionalization of power that the mandarinal system had helped to achieve was eventually undermined by critical requirements for external defense. While the threat of invasion was a perennial dilemma, it was not until the late fourteenth century that a sustained external challenge appeared. Until then China and the other bordering states periodically attacked the Vietnamese. But in the fourteenth century, as well as in earlier periods, the main threat came from Champa, a hostile kingdom founded about A.D. 192 on Hindu cultural traditions. Champa was located just south of the Red River Delta in present-day central Viet Nam. The great Vietnamese vulnerability to spoiling attacks by Champa was reduced only after autonomy from China had been won in A.D. 939 and the forces necessary for external defense had been mobilized. By the middle of the eleventh century the Vietnamese were able to sack Champa's capital and kill its king in retaliation for a Cham invasion. As a result of such military strength the Vietnamese acquired in 1069 their first portion of Champa's territory in what was to become a steady southward expansion. Under relentless pressure the Chams were diminished by the twentieth century to a minority status in a greatly enlarged Viet Nam.

Ultimately the Vietnamese had reacted to Cham invasions by a program of territorial expansion aimed at destroying the kingdom of Champa and absorbing its domain. Yet this action was not without its political costs. They emerged when a series of Cham campaigns over a thirty-year period (1360–90) brought an unexpected military challenge to institutionalized political power in Viet Nam. The threat came not from the invaders, who were effectively repulsed, but from a trusted military leader, Le Quy Ly. He had saved the Vietnamese kingdom from destruction and occupation, yet in the process his power had gone beyond the level that could be controlled by dynastic political authority; so had his ambitions. In 1400 he overthrew the Tran dynasty, proclaimed himself Emperor Ho Quy Ly and in effect returned the country to a competition for political power through control of military force. His actions set in motion a sequence of events that increased Viet Nam's reliance on military might and made a return to institutionalized political power increasingly difficult.

After Ho Quy Ly's usurpation the resulting turmoil among the Vietnamese weakened them internally and invited the intervention of China. The former overlords came ostensibly to restore the Tran, but in fact they wished to annex the country. For two decades, 1408–28, a fierce resistance against Chinese occupation was carried on through guerrilla warfare until Le Loi—a great hero of Vietnamese history and the founder of the Le dynasty (1428–1527)—recaptured control over the country and obtained recognition of autonomy from China. Although his successors made great strides in restoring order to the war-ravaged country, their most enduring achievements were also in the field of military operations. An invasion of Champa succeeded in destroying the political viability of the rival kingdom in 1471. Severely diminished in territory, Champa lingered on for another two hundred years before the Vietnamese finally occupied and settled the whole of its territory. However, in the course of this occupation the expansiveness of Vietnamese military power merely posed more sharply the challenge to Vietnamese political ingenuity. Could the Vietnamese consolidate their gains through resilient institutions?

Southward migration (known as *Nam Tiên* in Vietnamese), following in the wake of the conquest of Champa, altered Vietnamese life fundamentally. Vietnamese territory almost doubled its original size, and the country's population, formerly concentrated in the Red River Delta, became scattered throughout areas more than six hundred miles away. The problems of increased scale produced parochial pressures too great for traditional politics to manage, and Viet Nam's central institutions gave way.

Though these institutions were modeled on those of the Chinese empire—within which the total area of Viet Nam would have been no more than a province or two—the Vietnamese, as their territory expanded, could not make these institutions work effectively. Even through military administration the Le, unlike previous dynasties, could no longer maintain territorial control over the whole country. Regionalism had become the stronger force.

By 1516 three families had emerged with a disproportionate amount of armed strength in the society while the ruling dynasty had virtually no power at all. The country fell into a state of anarchy, with rich agricultural areas being pillaged by mercenary troops hired by rival families; farming was interrupted and famine spread over the land. It seemed impossible to repeat the previously successful strategy in which the Ly dynasty (1009–1225) had achieved control over the whole country by force and then transformed military power into political institutions. With the expansion of Vietnamese territory it had become easier for more numerous and formidable military groups to develop from fertile agricultural bases; regionalism was ascendant.

In the midst of this breakdown of central authority, one of the three dominant families, the Mac, attempted in 1527 to unify the country under its dynastic control. Instead, their bid for power precipitated a fratricidal internal war that continued spasmodically until just before the French intervened in Viet Nam, almost three hundred years later. As the war became more protracted, the conflict was gradually stabilized by a partition of the country into defined territories controlled by the rival families. The beginning of this trend toward partition occurred in 1592 when the Mac were driven out of the Red River Delta by the force protecting the vestigial Le dynasty. Rather than restoring unity, the victory over the Mac merely aggravated an already strong spirit of enmity between the Trinh and the Nguyen, the two other dominant families. While they were united in opposing the Mac, these two families were divided by their desire to exercise unchallenged influence over the impotent Le rulers. They both regarded the Le as the only legitimate authority in the country, yet each accused the other of fomenting rebellion. On the outcome of this dynastic impasse rested the unity and stability of Viet Nam for more than two centuries.

Lines between the two rival families hardened as the Nguyen steadily consolidated their strength south of the Red River Delta along the strategic coastal plain. Unable to reconcile their struggle for dynastic influence and regional power, in 1620 the two adversaries confronted each other with fierce combat. This conflict persisted tenaciously for fifty years until it subsided into an armed stalemate which divided the country, north and south, into distinct areas of political-military control. The disintegration of the country into two warring states was symbolized by a wall built across the narrow waist of Viet Nam at the 18th parallel, near the town of Dong Hoi, just north of Hue. Erected by the Nguyen, the wall of Dong Hoi rose to a height of eighteen feet, extended a distance of eleven miles, and in 1672 proved strong enough to withstand a major military test from the Trinh in the north. Thereafter the country remained divided for another century on almost the same territorial basis as it is today.

Besides stimulating divisive political tendencies, territorial expansion also brought to Viet Nam an unusual geographic shape—one especially conducive to regionalism and rebellion. The striking dimensions of the territory that has resulted from relentless southward movement are its length of approximately one thousand miles and its width of only three hundred miles at its widest and about forty-five miles at its narrowest. Striking as they are, these dimensions do not reflect the fact that Viet Nam lacks geographic unity. Overall, it is an S-shaped country fragmented with mountain chains and held together by a thin coastal plain loosely connecting two deltas at extreme ends of the territory. Except for the generous extent of seacoast with frequent harbors, few natural avenues of communication span the length of the country. Isolated areas—especially those in the narrow central coastal plain, but also in the mountainous regions surrounding the deltas—have historically posed difficulties for central administration and given a haven to rebels.

In creating problems of regionalism and rebellion, the character of the terrain has been emphasized by the pattern of population settlement. If military conquest alone had been the instrument of Viet Nam's expansion, it is doubtful the Vietnamese would occupy the territory they do today. Close behind the military forces were the settlers ready to bring the land under cultivation. Yet the terrain, in addition to limiting communications, also restricted the locations in which the Vietnamese population could settle. Only land permitting the cultivation of rice under irrigation, the very foundation of the country's agricultural society, was suitable for Vietnamese migration. Such areas were extensive in the deltas located at either end of the territory; but in the approximately six hundred miles in between there were only small and frequently isolated fragments of land, snatched from the encroachment of the mountains on one side and the sea on the other. Not only was it difficult to adapt the Vietnamese style of wet rice agriculture to the surrounding mountains, but these highlands were infested with the malaria-carrying anopheles mosquito.

The overall limits these barriers imposed upon Vietnamese settlement are best seen in the curious pattern of population distribution that has emerged from southward migration. Today, roughly 30,000,000 Vietnamese are crowded into less than 20,000 of the country's approximately 128,000 square miles of territory. More than 90 per cent of the population is concentrated in less than 20 per cent of the land area, a fact which results in some of the densest population clusters anywhere in the world. Because of their rice agriculture and vulnerability to upland malaria, the Vietnamese live in the fertile lowlands. The remaining 100,000-plus square miles of plateau and mountains are sparsely populated by non-Vietnamese ethnic minorities, who are less advanced culturally than the lowlanders. Thus a major dichotomy between the upland and the lowland areas is reinforced by ethnic as well as other cultural differences.

A focus on this settlement pattern of the Vietnamese people—their reliance on irrigated rice agriculture and their history of territorial expansion—illuminates much that is complex and obscure in their past. Such a perspective sheds light on strengths and weaknesses of Vietnamese politics and society. A hypothesis of the geographer Pierre Gourou is that in a tropical country the cultivation of rice in flooded fields is what alone gives rise to the development of an advanced civilization, while at the same time limiting it both culturally and geographically. In Viet Nam these strengths and limits are best seen through the prime module of social development—the village. It was due primarily to the cohesion and flexibility of the Vietnamese village that popular migration followed upon military conquest. The village was the institution that translated the potential of the newly occupied land into the reality of productive habitation.

A system of sponsored settlement developed in which established villages sent out pioneers. They were usually young people or others without land who were eager to get new fields and create new villages. Support from the parent villages continued until the offspring were self-sufficient. Then official recognition was requested from the emperor, who bestowed a name, a communal seal, and a guardian spirit upon the new village. These imperial articles were traditionally kept in a communal house (known as the *dinh*) which was in effect the symbol of village unity: a place for religious ceremonies and public occasions and in a sense a ritual link with the rest of the country.

Through this process the Vietnamese village facilitated the southward territorial advance that simply went beyond the country's capacity to consolidate its gains through political centralization. The experience after 1500, of nearly three centuries of regionalism and disunity—trends never fully resolved before France assumed control over the country—raises several fundamental questions about traditional politics in Viet Nam. Perhaps the key question is why the village was such an effective instrument of cultural expansion while central institutions were not. The answer seems to lie in the deeply rooted autonomy of the village, which, though guaranteed by statute, had evolved through custom and practice. According to an old Vietnamese proverb, "the laws of the emperor yield to the customs of the village."

The substance behind this proverb came from the restraint village institutions imposed on the power of the central authorities. The development of these local institutions, it seems, predated those of the central administration; their origins are often traced to the period before China's occupation was overthrown. . . .

By the end of the eighteenth century a stalemate had endured for a century between the northern (Trinh) and southern (Nguyen) regimes without there having been a major military engagement. But this lack of conflict did not indicate that the sources of rebellion had been resolved. During the seventeenth and eighteenth centuries the Nguyen had continued Vietnamese expansion southward until they had occupied the Mekong Delta over the opposition of its Cambodian inhabitants. Just as this expansion was reaching its apogee, a rebellion broke out in the Nguyen territory south of Hue, in central Viet Nam. Breaking a century of stalemate, this uprising gave the northerners, the Trinh, an unexpected opportunity to extend their control over the whole of Viet Nam. Through ineptness, however, the Trinh alienated the southern rebels, known as the Tay Son, who turned on the Trinh while also fighting the Nguyen. Except for the male heir to their familial leadership, the Nguyen had been virtually eliminated by 1777, and less than a decade later, Trinh rule in the north had been defeated decisively by the Tay Son.

Although rebellion had brought disunity in the sixteenth century, it was out of this Tay Son rebellion that Viet Nam found unity in the nineteenth. At the conclusion of the Tay Son rebellion in 1802, Vietnamese territory was united from the China border to the Gulf of Siam for the first time in history. But this historic achievement was not accomplished by the Tay Son. In an epic conflict the surviving heir to the Nguyen regime capitalized on the Tay Son's preoccupation in the north to return from exile, recapture the Mekong Delta, and in 1788, seize control over the strategic region around Saigon. The heir, who later proclaimed himself Emperor Gia Long, might have been unable to consolidate these territorial gains and unify the country had it not been for the arrival of substantial military and naval reinforcements from France. Arranged by the French missionary prelate, Bishop Pigneau de Behaine, this vital aid marked the revival of a dormant interest in Viet Nam by the French church.

Opportunities for outside involvement in Viet Nam's internal conflict had existed since warfare divided the country in 1620. French interests in Viet Nam had stemmed from this earlier period in which the Nguyen regime had also been dependent on external aid. French priests had been in the country since the early seventeenth century, when the Nguyen's initial weakness against the Trinh had led them to seek sophisticated weaponry from the Portuguese. These French priests, part of a Portuguese Jesuit mission, were so successful in winning converts that they were expelled when the armed stalemate reduced the Nguyen's dependency on foreign aid. Not until the 1780's with the outbreak of the Tay Son rebellion, did France's freedom from world-wide commitments coincide with an opportunity for influence in Viet Nam. But the French revolution cut short the participation of forces raised by the influence of the French clergy at Versailles. Once again France's interest in Viet Nam subsided.

When Emperor Gia Long unified Viet Nam in 1802, the country's capacities for political centralization reached a high-water mark. Realizing that this unity had been essentially a military achievement, the new emperor tried to overcome the regionalism that had divided the country for centuries. Institutions were created to promote the political integration of the Vietnamese people, but regional and parochial identities continued to exert stronger pressures. Beneath the surface of apparent political unity the governors of the various regions held the real power while formally acknowledging the sovereignty of the emperor. Unfortunately for the future of Vietnamese politics, even this promising trend toward unification was ended with Gia Long's death, and in 1820 an authoritarian and xenophobic policy was inaugurated by his heirs.

Once again internal tensions created opportunities for outside intervention. Through the xenophobic policies of Gia Long's successors, the French
were denied the influence in Vietnamese affairs they had enjoyed during the
fight for unification and had come to expect during the period of consolidation. Not surprisingly, it was the Catholic missionaries who were the
hardest hit. Gia Long's successors saw Christianity as a threat to the
Confucian traditions upon which Vietnamese politics were founded. They
proscribed Christian missions and eventually put some of the French cler-
gymen to death. Since protection by the Far Eastern fleet for French missionaries became a significant issue in France, the Vietnamese attacks on
the church provided a convenient opportunity for Napoleon III to solidify
the tenuous domestic position of the Second Empire.

After initial setbacks, the intervention in Viet Nam launched by
Napoleon III in response to domestic religious sentiment became the spe-
cial interest of the French navy. More interested in acquiring territory than
religious converts, the navy's enthusiasm resulted in the occupation of Viet
Nam and the ethnic and culturally distinct areas of Cambodia and Laos.
These disparate countries were formed, in 1897, into a territory known
thereafter as Indochina—a name chosen as a semantic compensation for
French colonial failures in India and China at the hands of the British.

In administering their territorial acquisition, the French created a state
in which colonial administration virtually supplanted indigenous politics.
Obviously, the primary French concern was to prevent Vietnamese opposition from threatening their colonial rule. Although they could not stop
rebellion entirely, the French did neutralize it through military and administrative control. Yet the effect of these preventives was to eliminate all but
the most circumscribed and stylized political activity. In becoming the
country's incumbent government, the French suppressed the energies that
had gone into centuries of political conflict among the Vietnamese. Almost
no legitimate channels for political expression existed; the politics of the
Vietnamese became synonymous with sedition in French Indochina.
Unintentionally, however, Vietnamese political energies were enlarged by
the unexpected social consequences of colonial programs. Ultimately, when
French strength wavered in the 1940s, pent-up political energies erupted in
a revolution that no amount of French force could subdue.

The suppression of Vietnamese political life was begun by the administrative partitioning of the country, which occurred initially through the
uneven pattern of French military occupation. Viet Nam would have been
occupied all at once except for the limits on French resources imposed by
other foreign commitments; a combination of far-flung imperial ambitions
and domestic counter-pressures made the French occupation a piecemeal
affair. By the treaty of June 1862, the southernmost portion of Viet Nam,
called Cochinchina by its French occupiers, came under French control.
The central and northern parts of the country, known to the French as
Annam and Tonkin, did not become parts of the French empire until more
than twelve years after Cochinchina was occupied. Annam—the former
Chinese name for all Viet Nam and a term considered derogatory by the

Vietnamese—and Tonkin were acquired through treaties of 1884–5 with the Vietnamese government at Hue and the Chinese at Peking. The resulting fragmentation of the country was perpetuated by a colonial mythology which regarded Viet Nam not as one country but three: Annam, Tonkin, and Cochinchina. Even the name *Viêt Nam,* with which the country had been baptized by Gia Long in 1802, was outlawed and uttered only as a rallying cry of revolutionaries.

Partitioning Viet Nam into three parts aided the security of France's colonial state against countrywide uprisings. Administrative barriers were imposed to discourage the Vietnamese from unifying their potential resources against the French. Such obstacles helped to perpetuate the traditional pressures of regionalism and parochialism that had previously limited Vietnamese political unity. . . .

Besides reinforcing old—mainly regional—tensions, French colonial policies created new ones. Although colonially sponsored social change became clustered regionally, it was not planned that way. A reinforced regionalism was a by-product of changes that resulted from programs directed toward other, primarily economic, purposes. In broad outline these changes occurred from the creation of an export economy in primary products—mainly rice and rubber, but some minerals—with a protected market for French manufactured imports; from the introduction of taxation in money to finance expenditures of the colonial budget; and from the expansion of primary education. While these changes held out the promise of modernization, they were insufficient to achieve that goal; they left Viet Nam halfway between the traditional and modern worlds. Viet Nam's colonial economy was vulnerable to fluctuations in international commodity and monetary markets and did not possess the institutional structure for sustained economic growth. Moreover, it lacked a self-generating industrial sector to absorb the people drawn into the towns in hopes of gaining access to the monetary economy. . . .

Under the impact of French colonialism, Viet Nam became "a nation off balance." Social changes had been induced by colonial programs, but there was hardly a harmonious relationship between the new society and the old Viet Nam. These changes had "dislocated the traditional mode of life and produced a poorly integrated society in which a small, urban-oriented Westernized elite was largely alienated from the bulk of the village based population." Although harmony had been intermittent in traditional Viet Nam, it seems to have been a widely shared ideal, especially in the life of the villages. The basis for this harmony had been a structure of authority based on Confucian precepts and buttressed by strong patrilineal kinship ties. The social changes wrought during colonial rule were undoubtedly necessary if Viet Nam were to participate in the interdependent life of the modern world. However, too little attention was given to the effects of this process on the structure of authority or popular compliance. Since the village has been and continues to be the foundation of Vietnamese society, the deterioration of its resiliency was certain to have a strong impact on the stability of the society as a whole. Because the villages lay outside the modern sector that France was creating in the urban centers, this social instability was not apparent. French administration, commerce, and military force once provided a veneer of stability on a society halfway between the traditional and the modern world.

The Colonial Impact

DAVID G. MARR

In 1938 at least eighteen million Vietnamese were being kept in check by a mere 27,000 colonial troops. Yet a scant sixteen years later, colonial forces totaling 450,000 were unable to avoid tactical disaster at Dien Bien Phu and compulsory strategic evacuation south of the seventeenth parallel. Finally, in the years 1965–1975, various combinations of American, Republic of Vietnam, South Korean, and other allied armed forces totaling up to 1.2 million men were outfoxed, stalemated, and eventually vanquished by the National Liberation Front and the People's Army of Vietnam.

A host of explanations have been offered for this dramatic transformation in the capabilities of both sides. French and American generals have argued that massive attacks in the early stages of Vietnamese revolutionary activity could have nipped resistance in the bud. Possibly. Nevertheless, those same generals discovered that political and economic realities at home, first in Paris, then in Washington, ruled out such a Draconian solution. Other participants or observers have variously stressed the strength of primordial Vietnamese patriotism, the fury of any oppressed people lashing out at its oppressors, sophisticated communist organizing techniques, an increased Vietnamese capability to assimilate and employ modern technology, substantial international support, French and American ignorance of Vietnamese conditions, and the mass media explosion, which may have heightened revulsion in the "home" country.

None of these answers should be ignored by serious students of the struggle in Vietnam. Yet none really succeeds in explaining how, in a matter of a few years, hundreds of thousands of Vietnamese changed from seemingly docile French colonial subjects to experienced political cadres, pith-helmeted soldiers (*bo-doi*), literacy instructors, hygienists or soil technicians—all dedicated to driving out the foreigner and establishing an independent, strong, egalitarian nation. Patriotism and angry reactions to oppression may well have provided the emotional foundations, yet neither could tell Vietnamese how, when, or where to act. Organization and modern technology were certainly important, but to employ both effectively demanded some degree of conceptual transformation. Although international support was valuable, psychologically as well as materially, ultimately it was what the Vietnamese did with this backing that made the difference. As for weaknesses in enemy ranks, Vietnamese revolutionaries tried to comprehend and to exploit these wherever possible. However, they

David G. Marr, *Vietnamese Tradition on Trial, 1920–1945*, pp. 1–13, 413–416. Copyright © 1981 The Regents of the University of California. Reprinted by permission of the publisher.

also learned from painful experience that simply to wait for enemy contradictions to manifest themselves was often to leave the initiative in the hands of others.

. . . All such developments in the twentieth-century history of Vietnam must be understood within the context of fundamental changes in political and social consciousness among a significant segment of the Vietnamese populace in the period 1920–45. These changes, while not necessarily decisive, were at least one precondition for mass mobilization and successful people's war strategies from 1945 onward. To cite only one example, there was the growing conviction that one's life was not preordained, that one need not eat dirt forever, that one could join with others to force change. Victory would not occur in a blinding flash, as assumed by many earlier Vietnamese political and social movements. Yet victory was inevitable, the fruit of millions of Vietnamese perceiving their self-interests and uniting against the common enemy, foreign and domestic.

Such ideas were only the beginning of a new consciousness. What was to be the nature of that victory? Certainly it was not seen by most to be the transferring of a heavenly mandate from one ruler to another. Nor was it to be simply destruction of the colonial system. Often the objective was said to be transforming Vietnam into a "civilized" (*van minh*) nation. Although this concept meant different things to different people, it generally encompassed mastery over nature, a spirit of civic responsibility, full development of the individual's mental, physical, and moral faculties, and the ability of Vietnamese to stand proud among other peoples of the world.

These were not tasks to be accomplished overnight. Indeed, much time was spent in the early stages questioning Vietnamese capacities to do much of anything except obey fate, squabble incessantly, and scramble for petty personal gains. Beneath this severe self-criticism, even psychological flagellation, however, lurked the belief that people could change dramatically. Otherwise, why bother to publish hundreds of pamphlets and articles challenging readers to renovate themselves? At any rate, by the late 1920s both the mood of self-disparagement and the emphasis on moral rearmament were being replaced by the belief that history was moving in Vietnam's direction, and that social forces would accomplish what individual regeneration could not.

This new faith was badly shaken by the French colonial repression of 1929–32. It recovered in the Popular Front period of 1936–39. It suffered again in the Japanese-Vichy crackdowns of 1940–44. And then it burst forth as never before in the August 1945 Revolution. Through all these ups and downs a growing number of Vietnamese were learning to combine optimism and patience, moral suasion and social mobilization, theory and practice. The intelligentsia also rediscovered pride in Vietnamese culture—on a selective basis.

Without a variety of economic and social changes from precolonial to colonial times in Vietnam there would probably not have been major changes in consciousness, or, if such changes had occurred, they would have been limited to a much smaller group of people, perhaps "enlightened" members of the royal family, trusted mandarins, and a handful of foreign language interpreters, merchants, and literate Catholics. To carry this speculation a bit further, such men might have employed their newly acquired knowledge to engineer and to justify a range of institutional reforms. They might even have ended up sharing power with small new military and business elites, as happened in Thailand. But, just as in Thailand, the depth and breadth of intellectual transformation would have been far less substantial.

Vietnam never had that choice. From the 1850s Vietnam was under severe military threat. It was dismembered in the 1860s and 1870s, then swallowed completely by the French in the 1880s. By 1897 all armed resistance had been quelled. During the next five years Governor General Paul Doumer laid down the foundations and framework which were to characterize Indochina (Cambodia and Laos included) for the next four decades. These included a centralized and rather top-heavy administration, an expanded and greatly reinforced tax and corvée system, continued growth of the primary export sector by means of large land grants (often disregarding prior ownership or occupancy), near-monopoly status for French finance capital and product imports, and the construction of an impressive if not always economically viable network of railroads, roads, and canals.

Already before World War I three major changes were apparent in the lives of ordinary Vietnamese. First, the French had capacities to control and to coerce never dreamed of by previous rulers. For this reason less attention was devoted to the conciliatory political arts, to understanding local grievances, compromising, or sharing power with subordinates. It also meant that traditional village obligations to the ruler, in particular, taxes, corvée service, and military service, were no longer the subject of discreet negotiations, but could now be enforced with unprecedented efficiency. Nor was there still an open frontier beyond reach of the system, where aggrieved families could flee. It followed, too, that those Vietnamese who attached themselves to the new rulers and quickly grasped alien procedures could advance to positions of considerable wealth and self-esteem (but little real authority), without having to trouble themselves much about popular anger or any ethic of responsible government. In short, the French can be said to have strengthened some aspects of the traditional hierarchical structure to the detriment of the majority of Vietnamese, while allowing a new indigenous minority to share in the returns as long as they remained obedient and necessarily insensitive to popular grievances.

Secondly, through a policy of granting large land concessions to French companies and Vietnamese collaborators, together with the introduction of French concepts of private property and individual legal responsibility, the colonial government stimulated fundamental changes in village economic and social relations. Phrased most simply, there were now unprecedented pressures toward concentrated wealth, land alienation, and the growth of a class of landless and land-poor Vietnamese. For example, peasant families who had devoted one or more generations to clearing, tilling, and improving land now found themselves being evicted or converted into tenants, perhaps simply because they had not learned the new administrative rules as quickly as others. Small proprietors, who thought they had protected themselves legally, could still be outmaneuvered by means of usurious loans, cadastral manipulations, seizure for back taxes, or simply the duplicity of corrupt local officials. To cry out for redress in such situations was usually hopeless, and sometimes dangerous, since colonial retaliatory power was normally at the disposal of any landlord or official who kept in the good graces of his superiors.

As a corollary of this economic process, the corporate character of Vietnamese villages was gradually eroded. Communal lands—traditionally the basis of village social welfare palliatives, as well as providing modest support for local temples, schools, and routine administrative tasks—now increasingly became the private property of several well-placed families, or even came under the control of non-village members. As disparities in wealth increased, the selection of village notables, the observance of village festivals, the organizing of weddings, funerals, ceremonies to honor returning scholars and the like, became ever more the sources of contention and conspicuous consumption (both of which had always been present to some degree), and ever less the vital ritual reinforcements of community self-consciousness and solidarity. Simultaneously, richer and poorer members of clans and extended families drew further apart, the former mostly interested in special status to reflect their new wealth, the latter trying to borrow money cheaply and loosely according to outmoded lineage rationales. The ultimate breakdown of corporate ties often occurred, as one might expect, in those areas where individuals amassed enough land to leave the villages entirely. Such absentee landlords, particularly prevalent in south Vietnam, controlled the fates of hundreds or thousands of local people without ever having to meet them face to face, or, perhaps even more upsetting, showing up only at rent- or loan-collection times.

Finally, it may well be that the most important transformation of all had to do with the penetration of a cash economy into even the most isolated hamlets of Vietnam. While the implications of this change took several decades to become apparent, there is no doubt that from the turn of the century (earlier in Cochinchina) traditional multiple and personal forms of socio-economic interaction were being replaced by the single, essentially impersonal commercial exchange system. Central taxes were the cutting edge in most cases, levied on individuals rather than corporate villages as before. While several Vietnamese dynasties had experimented with taxes in cash, particularly portions of the land tax, payment in kind had always remained dominant. Now the French ordered that both the entire land tax and the even more onerous head tax be paid in silver—not the copper, zinc, or paper money recognized for other transactions, but solid silver piasters, which peasants often had to acquire solely for this purpose at marked-up rates of exchange from the money lenders or landlords. Corvée obligations could also be rendered in cash, for those who had it. On top of these payments there were diverse indirect taxes (marketing, stamp, consumer goods, transit, entrepot, navigation, etc.) as well as the government-controlled salt and liquor monopolies—all being more rigorously enforced than any comparable taxes of precolonial days. Even if a peasant continued to think of himself as essentially a subsistence farmer, he was being drawn further into the money economy by the tax system.

The preeminent economic objective of the French was to develop a modern export sector. They focused particularly on rice and mining, then later rubber as well. Taxation, monopoly, and market mechanisms soon worked relentlessly against the interests of peasants whose output had previously met the more diverse needs of an autonomous economy, but who were now non-competitive in an imperial operation controlled from Paris. Vietnamese might still need to eat something other than rice, but there were now financial disincentives in many regions to specializing in non-rice production. The same process hit traditional artisans hard, indeed wiping them out entirely if their specialty happened to compete with French imports. Peasants who derived some off-season income from making handicrafts, tools, or other simple essentials also found such opportunities drying up. Rice was now king—not just any rice, but rice in quantities and qualities suitable for export, and sent through channels dominated by non-local interests. A modicum of capital and contacts with officialdom were the two essential ingredients to success. Those who failed became part of the cheap labor pool, another essential ingredient if any company or family wished to set up a new plantation or start a new mining project.

With the outbreak of war in Europe in 1914 investments terminated abruptly. Vietnamese were pressed to help defeat the "Huns." As many as 100,000 peasants and artisans were rounded up and shipped to France to serve in labor battalions, and provided a source of some worry to the colonial authorities when they returned. Meanwhile, in Vietnam during the war, people were strongly "encouraged" to buy war bonds, in effect yet another tax. Rice exports increased. Locally produced goods were allowed temporarily to substitute for normal French imports. Larger numbers of Vietnamese were permitted to enter the bottom rungs of the colonial bureaucracy, and a modest expansion of the public school system was ordered. With that special French penchant for idealistic overstatement, Governor-General Albert Sarraut spun all of these changes into a vision of Franco-Vietnamese collaboration, complete with references to Liberty, Equality, and Fraternity. France, he said, was ready to act as "elder brother" in transmitting the full benefits of modern civilization, and to consider the possibility of native self-rule at some unspecified point in the future. After Germany was defeated, the French Government conveniently ignored these grandiloquent promises. But for many educated Vietnamese the cat had been let out of the bag. If the French needed reminding, they would be the ones to do it. If that did not work, they would try pursuing the ideal of "civilization" on their own.

In 1922, as France itself was slowly managing to pull out of a postwar depression, the Ministry of Colonies organized a grand exposition in Marseilles to try to revitalize in people's minds the French "mission" overseas and to attract new investment capital. Looked at in terms of overall twentieth-century historical trends, France had been permanently weakened by the Great War. The French people were probably more divided than ever on the colonial question. Nevertheless, viewed from the perspective of the 1920s, the response to the Marseilles exposition and other forms of colonial propaganda was nothing short of spectacular. While thousands of ordinary French citizens amused themselves by tasting strange foreign dishes, ogling native dancers, and laughing at the clothing and manners of diverse oriental potentates, potential capital investors concentrated their attention on government promises of monopoly privileges, tax shelters, cheap labor, and solid social order.

Close to three billion francs was invested in Indochina between 1924 and 1930, almost sixty per cent of the total since French arrival. Rubber cultivation, begun very modestly before the war, now was seen by investors as the new bonanza, some 700 million francs being advanced between 1925 and 1929. To provide the physical labor, somewhere between 100,000 and 200,000 Vietnamese were deceived or dragooned into the "red earth" rubber-growing region of Cochinchina during the boom years of the 1920s. Conditions were abysmal, including endemic malaria, contaminated or insufficient food and water, long hours, the docking of wages, and vicious punishments. Consequently the turnover rate due to death, escape, and nonrenewal of contracts was extraordinarily high, as indicated by the fact that the rubber plantation work force never exceeded 41,000 in any one year.

Conditions were only slightly better for the miners, of whom there were at least 50,000 during peak years, mostly in the Hon Gay pits of north Vietnam. Here the formula for profit-making included dirt-cheap labor, company stores, 12- to 14-hour shifts, physical brutality, and the absence of safety precautions. Yet French economists still complained that it was "carelessness," "lack of conscientiousness," and "delicate constitution(s)" that caused Vietnamese miners to produce at only one-quarter the rate of their French or Japanese counterparts. New coffee and tea plantations were established in the same way, and more land was cleared and drained so that more Vietnamese tenants and wage laborers could produce more rice for export. Significant expansion occurred in rice milling, distilling, sugar refining, and the production of cement, textiles, and timber. On top of this economic pyramid sat a handful of directors of prestigious French financial institutions. As of 1924, Paris and Saigon were linked by direct transoceanic cable for the first time. Direct airmail service soon followed. Indochina was now a classic colony, her economic fibers attuned to the demands of the "mother country" and the international marketplace.

With the advent of the Great Depression the bottom fell out of the rubber and rice markets. By early 1931 the Indochina economy was in serious trouble—landowners defaulting on bank loans, companies going into bankruptcy, *colons* banging on government doors demanding assistance, and uncounted thousands of Vietnamese tenants, agricultural laborers, plantation hands, miners, and factory workers thrown out of employment, roaming to and fro in search of survival. Not until 1936 did the economy begin to pick up again. Then, a mere four years later, Nazi Germany occupied

France, the Vichy-sympathizing authorities in Indochina subordinated themselves to the Japanese, and the economy underwent dislocation once again. By the winter of 1944/45, a tragic but quite predictable situation had developed, whereby hundreds of thousands of tons of rice remained in warehouses in the south (or was converted to alcohol to propel motor vehicles), while somewhere between one and two million Vietnamese people died of starvation in the north.

Looked at from the perspective of eighty years of French colonial activity, the only period when truly favorable conditions existed for full-scale capitalist economic exploitation of Indochina was from 1922 to 1929—a mere eight years. Economic fragility combined with administrative uncertainty underlay the entire colonial operation. No governor-general ever spent a term of more than five and one-half years in Indochina, and the average tenure was a scant two years and eight months. Conservative politicians spoke grandly about colonial restoration while socialists talked vaguely of provisional tutelage. Projects were begun and left uncompleted, or altered in such a way that profits survived but not the ameliorative social trimmings. This fundamental weakness of French colonialism, hardly sensed previously by even the most astute Vietnamese observers, was to become a subject of serious analysis among the new generation of intellectuals.

Vietnam has had three generations of intellectuals since 1900. Scholar-gentry or literati (*si phu*) intellectuals realized during the first decade of the twentieth century that Vietnam was being transformed whether it liked it or not. They tried desperately with whatever weapons, physical or mental, that came to hand to face up to altered conditions. By the end of World War I, however, it was obvious that they were unable to formulate either a penetrating new view of the world or a realistic program of action. Even the most sophisticated and experienced scholar-gentry members remained suspended between the Neo-Confucian classics, which they knew intimately but had come to doubt, and the ideas of Montesquieu, Rousseau, Smith, and Spencer, which they understood only vaguely but assumed to be essential to Vietnam's future. What they did manage to convey to the next generation, nevertheless, was a sense of historical crisis, a profound respect for knowledge, a commitment to action, and faith in the perfectibility of humankind.

The intelligentsia (*gioi tri thuc*) that emerged during the 1920s faced many of the same problems as the scholar-gentry, but in yet another social and economic context and with very different intellectual equipment. While not divorced from the villages and the lives of the literati, small farmers, and handicraft workers, the intelligentsia was indubitably a product of the colonial system, just as were the big landlords, tenants, miners, and plantation laborers. Young intelligentsia graduating from French and Franco-Vietnamese schools in increasing numbers generally sought employment as clerks, interpreters, primary teachers, or journalists. As career aspirations exceeded colonial possibilities, there was considerable disenchantment and unrest. To assume a correlation between job frustration and anticolonial attitudes among the intelligentsia would be risky, however. There were well-employed Vietnamese who ended up opposing the French, just as there were thwarted journalists who joined the colonial police or signed on as overseers for landlords, mine supervisors, and plantation administrators.

Unlike the scholar-gentry, the intelligentsia understood the neo-Confucian classics only vaguely but were impatient to digest two millennia of European learning in a matter of a few years. The great advantage, and simultaneously the primary weakness, of these young men and women was that they stood unsteadily between two worlds and tried hard to envisage a third. Most of them had either grown up in villages or had meaningful rural kinship ties. Their parents still believed in ghosts, arranged marriages, and strict social harmony. However, in school, and increasingly through extracurricular means, they learned of cameras, germs, atoms, galaxies, free love, class struggle, and biological evolution. Many found the advice of their elders to ignore the obvious contradictions between old and new and to concentrate on passing examinations and securing a clerkship morally and intellectually repulsive. They wanted to look further, to explain the contradictions, and to fashion a new consciousness for themselves and for the Vietnamese people at large. Often they used the image of discovering a conceptual "lodestone" (*kim chi nam*) that would guide everyone to a brighter future. Although the enthusiasm, aggressive curiosity, and iconoclasm of the intelligentsia were themselves repulsive to many other Vietnamese, social and economic changes were so profound that the latter often felt impotent, incapable of reasserting authority. Youth seized the day.

This was only the beginning, however. One of the most difficult tasks facing the intelligentsia was to distinguish universal insights from the particularities of either European or Vietnamese experience. The traditional Vietnamese preference had been to draw a line between cultured East Asians and the many barbarian peoples, Europeans included, who did not comprehend the way of the universe and hence behaved improperly. Well into the twentieth century some Vietnamese continued to seek comfort in this model of reality, even while being forced to admit that "Eastern spirit" no longer had any claim to universality. At the other extreme, many early products of French colonial schools tended to assume that to be European was civilized and to be Asian barbarian. Yet those who tried simply to imitate Europeans found that they were neither accepted as such by French *colons* nor emulated by the mass of Vietnamese.

The spectacle of China disintegrating into warlordism, of Japan trying to outfox the Western imperialists at their own game, and of the Vietnamese "emperor" on annual salary from the French, made Neo-Confucianism look pathetic. Buddhism and Taoism were seen to be more attractive in such chaotic times, yet only a small minority of the intelligentsia went beyond general knowledge of these philosophies to firm, sustained adherence. On the other side of the world, the spectacle of Europe tearing itself to pieces in World War I undercut those Vietnamese who advocated radical Westernization. If Verdun and the Somme lay at the end of the path of assimilation, then better not try.

During the 1920s Vietnamese writers started to reach beyond the East-versus-West paradigm. They eagerly sought information from anywhere, in the hope that it would help to explain and resolve their own dilemmas. Of particular interest were social upheavals in China, postwar unrest in Europe, the ongoing revolution in Russia, and non-violent resistance in India. Increasingly writers became convinced that there was no qualitative distinction between Europeans and Vietnamese. A vast reservoir of knowledge and techniques was available to anyone in the world. It might often appear to bear a particular national stamp, but that was superficial, capable of being isolated and eliminated. In place of idealized philosophical and cultural systems, Vietnamese writers moved increasingly to historical process as a central explanation of reality. The key question then became one of assessing Vietnam's place in this universal process, and determining how to improve it.

In politics this same historical quest led many Vietnamese writers to conclude that it was not enough to simply exhort people to be patriotic, to unite, and to help save the country. Writers were now poignantly aware of other peoples in the world who presumably loved their homeland and their mother tongue as deeply as did the Vietnamese their own, who even possessed a similar tradition of resisting foreign domination, yet ultimately were completely vanquished and absorbed. Clearly some ethnic groups survived and others did not. Understanding why and how became a major preoccupation. Again, Vietnamese came to the conclusion that much knowledge in the world bore no moral stamp but was available to the evil as well as the good, to colonials and anticolonials, to reactionaries, conservatives, liberals, and radical revolutionaries alike.

The next step was to relate new knowledge and techniques to specific Vietnamese conditions. This proved to be more difficult. First of all, the intelligentsia had to learn a great deal about Vietnam, past and present, that was either unavailable in the colonial schools or had previously been considered irrelevant by young men and women trying first to understand the outside world. Nor was it easy for members of the intelligentsia to move around the country collecting information. The colonial authorities imposed physical restrictions. And a young intellectual in Western dress, speaking with a different accent and having no local relatives, might have to spend months simply gaining the confidence of a few people. When it came time to publish, writers discovered a curious fact about colonial censorship: the authorities were often more charitable toward the printing of esoteric foreign information and theories than they were toward independent data on the Vietnamese experience. Many an article was blanked out precisely at the point where it shifted from foreign generalities to Vietnamese colonial particulars.

Vietnamese intellectuals overseas took the lead in discussing specific political and social developments inside the colony. Ho Chi Minh was the most notable example, but he was followed by scores of other Vietnamese residing for one period of time or another in France, the Soviet Union, and China. While they obviously could not conduct on-the-spot investigations, they did talk intensively with overseas Vietnamese from other provinces and social backgrounds. Publishing was less of a problem than smuggling copies home. Ironically, while most writers in Saigon, Hanoi, or Hue were still grappling with universals, whether in history, philosophy, the social sciences, medicine, or mathematics, writers in Paris, Moscow or Canton were trying to analyze the Bank of Indochina, the conditions of Vietnamese peasants, miners, and plantation workers, or the causes of high infant mortality. Distance from events provided the perspective for sorting the momentous from the trivial, the politically relevant from the intellectually curious.

Eventually, however, this work would have to be carried on inside the country. In the late 1920s a few authors in Saigon and Hue were able to append a bit of specific Vietnamese data to otherwise general discussions of historical evolution, religion, nationalism, and imperialism. In the early 1930s novelists and short-story writers took the lead, describing the lives of Vietnamese functionaries, landlords, intellectuals, shopkeepers, and peasants according to conceptual and stylistic criteria that had not existed in the country several decades earlier. By the late 1930s they had been joined by critical essayists, and the emphasis increasingly was on the lives of poor peasants, tenants, proletarians, beggars, and prostitutes. Collectively these publications amounted to a penetrating indictment of both Vietnamese traditional society and the colonial system.

Preoccupation with the negative could prove self-defeating, however. By the early 1940s many discussions of current conditions were naturalistic caricatures rather than realistic exposés. Sensing an impasse, other writers shifted to selective revitalization of the Vietnamese past and to assertions of a bright future. Vietnam was now seen by even the most radical intelligentsia to possess a history to some degree unique, incapable of being understood simply by reference to universal laws. As might be expected, particular attention was given to military heroes, administrative innovators, and literary giants. Popular culture was mined for evidence of an underlying strength and wisdom among the Vietnamese masses transcending the historical dialectic.

These changes coincided with momentous political developments, including the collapse of the Popular Front (1939), the establishment of the Japanese-Vichy alliance (1940), and the formation of the Communist-led Viet Minh (1941). As a group, the Vietnamese intelligentsia was badly divided on how to respond to these events. Some saw the Japanese as liberators; others hoped for Vietnamese self-rule within a French Union; still others joined the Viet Minh and worked for an allied victory and international recognition of Vietnam's independence. Probably the only thing the intelligentsia shared by 1942–44 was a feeling that the urban milieu of office bureaus, elite societies, coffee shops, and amusement parlors was very constraining, perhaps unreal. The new focus was the Vietnamese village, whether for purposes of preserving its alleged communal character, for suggesting institutional reforms, or for convincing the peasants to seize control of their own destiny.

In 1944–45 members of the intelligentsia joined the Viet Minh by the thousands. Their skills as writers, speakers, teachers, and administrators proved extremely valuable, perhaps essential. They were also competent to ferret out information and to digest and distill it for broad political and military intelligence purposes. The same ability was put to use when learning how to utilize captured materiel, or when devising new equipment and techniques appropriate to primitive conditions. However, intelligentsia linking up with the Viet Minh soon discovered that they were regarded as neither the political nor the intellectual vanguard of society. Those roles were held by the Indochinese Communist Party. Although in 1944 most members of the ICP were probably still of intelligentsia background, the Party took its worker-peasant vision very seriously. The upheavals of 1945 provided a perfect opportunity to identify and enroll thousands of suitable members from these classes.

Members of the ICP, intellectuals or otherwise, had already learned through bitter experience that to will victory, or to analyze the road to victory, was not the same as to achieve victory. They had been forced into agonizing personal choices, endured considerable deprivation, tested a variety of concepts in practice, and tried to reformulate everything in terms meaningful to the majority of their unlettered (but not necessarily ignorant) countrymen. What they wanted from any intelligentsia recruit of 1945 was a willingness to accept group discipline, to concern himself more with means than with ends, and to help the Viet Minh to establish a common frame of reference between the elite and the masses, modernity and tradition, universal and particular. The era of the educated cadre, as distinct from the alienated explorer, had begun.

In the early 1920s Vietnam's young intelligentsia had had a talismanic approach to knowledge. It was to be their invincible weapon to gain independence, freedom, and "civilization." Twenty years later, however, many intelligentsia realized that new ideas might promote or impede change; they might produce unintended as well as intended and dysfunctional as well as functional consequences. Few ideas were inherently good or bad, and even fewer remained as originally conceived. To try to force the "right" ideas in the wrong historical conditions might prove disastrous, yet to wait for the right conditions might be equally dangerous. What was needed was a complex interweaving of ends and means, strategy and circumstance, conscious formulation and spontaneous action. . . .

Between that day in 1925, when several hundred spectators heard a French judge sentence Phan Boi Chau to life imprisonment, and the day in 1945, when a huge crowd listened to Ho Chi Minh proclaim independence, Vietnam underwent a profound transformation. In the mid-1920s, the colonial government had reason to believe that it had found a viable formula for the long-term, peaceful exploitation of Indochina. Only a smattering of Vietnamese dared to disagree openly. The vast majority accepted that change would have to come either by French fiat or by heavenly intervention, not by the actions of ordinary subjects.

Twenty years later, conditions were dramatically different. The French had been forced to drown several Vietnamese uprisings in blood. They had seen the colonial economy completely disrupted. They had been humiliated by the Germans in Europe and incarcerated by the Japanese in Indochina. Even to begin to reassert sovereignty in Indochina, the French were forced to go hat in hand to the Americans, British, and Chinese. Determined to regain pride in themselves, preoccupied by intra-Allied diplomacy, they failed to take accurate measure of Ho Chi Minh, of the new Democratic Republic of Vietnam, or—most importantly—of the political and social revolution sweeping the country. General Leclerc sensed a difficult struggle when he ordered his armored columns to push Vietnamese forces out of Saigon in October 1945. He had no inkling, however, that the end of the road lay at Dien Bien Phu, the ultimate French humiliation. Vietnamese had proven themselves energetic citizens rather than passive subjects.

Neither the August 1945 Revolution nor Dien Bien Phu can be understood without reference to prior changes in social structure and intellectual outlook. The traditional Vietnamese elite had become a pathetic shadow of its former self. Rural life had been altered fundamentally by the decline of the subsistence farmer, the spread of landlordism, the gutting of customary welfare palliatives, and the necessity for ever more family members to seek employment far beyond village boundaries. More than ever before, the tax system took from the poor and gave to the rich.

In place of informal village schools and the classical examination system stood a bewildering variety of French and Franco-Vietnamese educational programs. Fewer than ten percent of the population was able to read in any language, yet this did not prevent a vigorous *quoc ngu* publishing effort from getting under way by the late 1920s. Surprisingly, even workers and peasants gained access to the printed word. [Conservative intellectual] Pham Quynh had reason to be worried when he overheard rickshaw pullers discussing the Phan Boi Chau trial on the basis of press reports. Chanh Thi, the disgruntled teenage peasant in search of a job, became a Communist Party member in part due to his being able to read about the Nghe-Tinh soviets in a heavily censored Hue newspaper. And, like most other literate Vietnamese, he transmitted his discoveries orally to a wider circle of compatriots.

At the heart of the literate constituency was the intelligentsia, perhaps 10,000 in number. Looking at photographs of these self-conscious young men and women in white linen suits and starched frocks it is easy to dismiss the entire group as Westernized misfits. Perusing French-language publications they still appear as rather faddish, over-eager students of Left Bank ideological currents. Only when one reads the profusion of Vietnamese-language materials can they be seen to be grappling with real problems which affected not just themselves but their less-educated countrymen as well. The act of writing in Vietnamese forced members of the intelligentsia to go beyond simple imitation, to experiment culturally, to overcome conceptual problems never dreamt of by their Western mentors. It also linked them to the spoken language, and hence to the intricate world of the Vietnamese village. By the early 1940s, many intellectuals were convinced that the future of Vietnam lay not in the cities but among the 95 per-cent of the population living in the countryside. The Viet Minh offered intellectuals a timely vehicle for working with peasants, whether as propa-ganda cadres, military officers, or literacy instructors.

Although the Vietnamese intelligentsia was fascinated by new ideas, eager to expose them to critical debate, to test them in varying contexts, it never defined itself primarily in cerebral terms or allowed a mood of detached scholasticism to prevail. Understanding reality was not enough. One also needed to discover the means to alter reality. In the process of ascertaining what is, one was never to lose sight of what ought to be.

Ideology was seen to provide the essential connection between objec-tive analysis and ethical vision. Confucianism had fulfilled this function until defeat and colonization at the hands of the French rendered its world view unconvincing. At best it survived as a set of moral platitudes. Buddhism offered a subtle alternative to Confucianism, yet it was extremely difficult to reconcile with growing intellectual commitment to science and progress. Social Darwinism appeared to explain a great deal about the contemporary world, to the point where Vietnamese became con-vinced that they must struggle ruthlessly in order to escape extinction. At the individual and intragroup levels, nonetheless, very few were prepared to concede that might makes right. They continued to believe that evil conduct brings retribution, and that any true ideology had to defend right and attack wrong.

Marxism possessed scientific credentials equal to Social Darwinism plus a firm moral stance. It was also more timely, reaching Vietnamese intellectuals in the wake of the Russian Revolution and the Great Depression. Even conservatives could be found employing Marxist peri-odization and social categories. Many flocked to Marxism as a new reli-gion, to the point of participating heatedly in international sectarian disputes. Still others focused on Leninist organizational theory and prac-tice. By the early 1940s, whatever their political affiliations, writers were far more concerned with relating foreign models to specific Vietnamese conditions than with proving their global philosophical credentials. For Marxists, the crucial problem was to relate Vietnamese history and culture to group decisions about revolutionary strategy and tactics.

The colonial repression of September 1939 made most intelligentsia activities of the Popular Front period illegal. As had been the case a decade earlier, Vietnamese intellectuals were forced to choose between clamming up, modifying their public positions, or going underground; this time, how-ever, the psychological shock was less profound and the individual read-justments more coherent. Also, the presence of Japanese troops in Indochina and of Allied forces in Kwangsi and Yunnan raised anticolonial stakes to the highest point in fifty years. Members of the Indochinese Communist Party, the Vietnam Nationalist Party, the Dai Viet, Cao Dai, and Hoa Hao each sensed that their moment in history had arrived. The Vichy French, appreciating their vulnerability, offered significant new educational and employment opportunities to those Vietnamese willing to eschew anti-colonialism. These wartime developments, combined with the inevitable effects of age, growing family responsibilities, and personality differences, led to the demise of the intelligentsia in the early 1940s.

In 1941 the Indochinese Communist Party was in complete disarray, its members dead, incarcerated, demoralized, or surviving precariously in the forests and swamps. Organizationally it appeared to possess less potential than any of the other groups mentioned above. Yet, only four years later the ICP had devised and implemented a plan to seize power, establish a government, sustain popular enthusiasm, and mobilize millions of people to undertake a wide variety of onerous, often dangerous tasks. Subsequently the ICP was able to stymie all efforts by rival forces, foreign or domestic, to reverse these momentous historical events.

Fortune favored the ICP in several respects. Most notably, the Tokyo-Vichy détente seriously weakened those Vietnamese groups which looked to either the Japanese or the French for political advancement. By the same token, it allowed the ICP to mount violent attacks against French colonial rule without being accused of unfaithfulness to the Allied cause. Communist parties in Malaya, Indonesia, and the Philippines were not so lucky. Important, too, was that Ho Chi Minh returned to Vietnam after thirty years, bringing with him impeccable credentials as an international revolutionary, unrivaled knowledge of world affairs, and a first-hand assessment of national united-front efforts in China.

Neither good fortune nor wise leadership would have counted for much, however, without the ideological transformations that preceded the formation of the Viet Minh and helped the ICP to take the historical initiative. Members of the intelligentsia had long before rejected the mood of bewilderment and pessimism which had characterized their elders. Instead, they possessed an infectious spirit of optimism and cultural pride. From an earlier naive acceptance of all things Western, they moved on to critical investigation and attempts at selective acculturation. Intelligentsia concepts of struggle and progress reached Vietnamese villagers in the 1930s, leading some to look at current conditions in a very different light. The fact that the colonial economy was in turmoil and rural society severely disrupted facilitated this process. When Vietnamese intellectuals and peasants came together in 1945 to uphold national independence and create a new society, there remained significant areas of misunderstanding and disagreement. Yet, there was sufficient consensus to mobilize millions to defeat the French.

Except for Ho Chi Minh, all ranking ICP leaders of the early 1940s had been members of the new intelligentsia. Many took prominent roles in the animated debates of the 1930s and drew heavily on the rhetoric of the Popular Front period in persuading people to join the Viet Minh. They defended the rights of the poor, encouraged women to participate in political struggle, stressed the importance of mass literacy, promised democratic freedoms, and portrayed the contemporary world in terms of a decisive confrontation between good and evil. To these themes were now added selective glorification of the Vietnamese past, praise of particular Vietnamese customs, and the claim that nothing could stand in the way of Vietnamese willpower asserted collectively.

The August 1945 Revolution was the sort of mass voluntarist surge of power that anticolonialists had dreamt of for decades. Even today, participants become excited as they recall the mood and events of 1945. For those who were in their teens or early twenties, it represented the formative experience of their lives, fostering a deep sense of solidarity and readiness to sacrifice; older Vietnamese saw the August Revolution as justification for previous agonies, capping three generations of struggle against unbelievable odds. Nothing that occurred subsequently, not even Dien Bien Phu or the rout of Republic of Vietnam forces in 1975, managed to capture the popular imagination in this way.

Communism and Nationalism

WILLIAM J. DUIKER

With the formation of the Vietminh League at the party's Eighth Plenum in 1941 the communist movement entered its sixteenth year of active existence. During that period it had endured a number of major setbacks which would undoubtedly have annihilated an organization of lesser skill and determination. But despite the attempts of the French to eliminate it, it had become a major political force in Vietnam, and certainly the most dynamic and effective organization within the Vietnamese nationalist movement.

Who were these men, and what drew them to communism? We have at this point relatively few sources of information on the backgrounds of the communist party leadership, but such evidence as is available demonstrates that the leadership of the communist movement in the interwar years was composed primarily of intellectuals. While there were undoubtedly workers and peasants in the movement—and particularly in the party's mass associations—few seem to have become professional revolutionaries, and even fewer reached a position of leadership in the party.

From their background it is fairly clear that the founding generation of the communist movement was made up of basically modern men— Vietnamese who had been exposed to Western culture and political ideology. Most of the party's leadership had at one time or another been educated in the Franco-Vietnamese school system and many had received a degree and entered such careers as teaching and journalism. As such, they had become members of the emerging middle class, and were of the same general social stratum as the young Vietnamese who formed the nucleus of the urban nationalist parties that arose in Vietnam after World War I. Why some of these educated young Vietnamese became revolutionaries while others were satisfied to expend their energies in moderate reformism is not an easy question to answer. From the evidence available, however, it

Reprinted from William J. Duiker, *The Rise of Nationalism in Vietnam, 1900–1941*. Copyright © 1976 by Cornell University Press. Used by permission of the publisher, Cornell University Press.

appears that moderates tended to come from the relatively affluent section of the bourgeoisie. They were somewhat more likely to have gone to the prestigious schools in the Franco-Vietnamese system and on to France for their higher education, and they were more likely to have joined such lucrative vocations as law, commerce, and medicine, than those who became members of radical parties. It would probably be wrong to view the founding members of the communist movement as totally deprived of opportunities to rise within the system. Many of the leaders of the movement, by their education and background, could have expected to achieve reasonable success in a number of careers open to them—in teaching, government, or journalism. Yet it is probably true that, as John T. McAlister states in his study, *Vietnam: The Origins of Revolution,* many young Vietnamese were drawn to revolution by a sense of being denied access to the status in society they deserved. Many of the careers to which these young men would have aspired were relatively low-paying and did not open the doors to either wealth or political power.

Yet it is not really enough to say that many became revolutionaries simply because reality did not accord with their personal aspirations, for in many cases, they seem to have become radicalized before entering the job market. It is interesting to note that of the top leadership of the communist movement during this period, the vast majority for whom we have biographical information came from scholar-gentry backgrounds. And, where we have information, it often appears that members of their immediate family were active in, or least in sympathy with, the nationalist or protonational organizations opposed to French rule—the Can Vuong, Phan Boi Chau's Exodus to the East, or the Hanoi Free School. If this is the case for the bulk of the early communist leadership, then it is likely that many acquired their resentment of French rule and their activist proclivities from their families even before entering the larger society. From this point of view, the leaders of the communist movement in the 1920s and 1930s can be viewed as direct heirs of the Phan Boi Chau scholar-patriot generation. They were a generation removed, to be sure, and more modern in their outlook and in their solutions, but essentially carried on the tradition of resistance established by their elders.

Eventually the communist movement became more than just the home of the offspring of scholar-gentry families, of course, but it is wise to keep in mind how small and how socially limited the party leadership was in its early years. The Comintern was critical of the petit bourgeois character of the League, and in the 1920s and early 1930s had emphasized the need to build up worker participation in the movement. There is not much indication, however, that this had much effect, at least prior to World War II. Party work in rural areas was similarly plagued with problems. The movement had begun to make inroads among the peasantry in some areas, notably in Annam and in parts of the Mekong delta, but Comintern distrust of the peasantry prevented the communists from following up immediately on the experience in Nghe-Tinh and it could hardly be said that before the anti-Japanese war the ICP had deep roots in the villages.

This early failure to broaden the base of the movement is not the only limitation of the party in the prewar period. Like its predecessors, it suffered from adventurism and factionalism, particularly in the early years. To a degree, such problems were the consequence of inadequate communications, ambiguous Comintern directives, and the zealous activities of the French Sûreté-Général. In retrospect, it is striking to observe how little regional sentiment surfaced in the first decade of the communist movement. In this respect the party had gone beyond its predecessors.

Whatever their early weaknesses, the uniqueness of the communists in the history of Vietnamese nationalism was that, unlike their rivals, they were able to eliminate or minimize obstacles to the ultimate seizure of power. For by the late 1930s, the ICP had begun to formulate a positive strategy which would eventually carry it to victory in the postwar period. And in the process many of the old errors would be eliminated. Some of the major elements of that strategy had already been laid out—by Lenin's theory of a nationalist alliance designed to ally all progressive and anti-imperialist forces in a colonial or semicolonial area in opposition to imperialist control; and by Mao Tse-tung's application of Marxist-Leninist strategy to a specifically Asian setting, involving the deliberate use of the peasantry as a major force in the revolution, and the adoption of guerrilla tactics in an attempt to utilize the strength of the rural population to surround the cities peopled by the bourgeoisie and controlled by the colonial power. The strategy began to become apparent in the years immediately prior to World War II, with the Bac Son uprising and the establishment of the Vietminh front. The new emphasis, the establishment of guerrilla bases along the border, reflected a shift away from the cities and the orthodox, Stalinist-style urban insurrection.

But perhaps the major significance of the formation of the Vietminh League was its solidification of the party's determination to utilize the role of nationalism in the struggle to evict the French. As the brief biographies of . . . countless communist figures . . . seem to show, communism in Vietnam was born out of the nationalist movement. Communist leaders commonly started their revolutionary careers as members of more manifestly nationalist groups—the VNQDD, the Youth Party, the Tam Tam Xa, or the Revolutionary Party—and then turned to Marxist-Leninist doctrine because it seemed like the most effective way to achieve independence.

Communism and nationalism were not always so easily matched, of course. Zealous party members occasionally puristically rejected the emotional appeals of patriotism. Slogans calling for national independence and self-determination, which appealed to the urban bourgeoisie, often had little meaning in rural communities, where a sense of nationalism was only beginning to emerge. On the other hand, as the communists found out in 1930–1931, policies that could win the support of the rural poor risked alienating the middle class in the towns. The challenge for the communists was to tailor their message to the particular target group—national concerns in the cities, economic issues in the rural areas—without destroying the effectiveness of the front as a whole. And, with the formation of the

Vietminh, the party had taken a major step towards achieving their goal of building a mass-based movement of national proportions. It had reached the apex of a period of self-education. It was now prepared to commence the struggle to grasp political power in Vietnam. . . .

A relatively mature consciousness of nationalism existed in Vietnam at the beginning of World War II. But the roots of modern nationalism are clearly discernible, well before the beginning of the present century, in Vietnam's historically strong sense of ethnic awareness, an awareness that was tempered by her age-old struggle to resist conquest from the north. Western colonialism, then, did not "create" a sense of separate national or ethnic identity in Vietnam as it did in other societies in Asia; it merely channeled Vietnam's traditional self-awareness along more modern lines.

The protonationalism of the precolonial period met its end in the protracted but undirected struggle against the French in the late nineteenth century. The failure of the Can Vuong illustrated the basic weakness of the traditionalist approach in the face of an invading force endowed with modern weapons, and the next generation of Vietnamese patriots was quick to interpret the French conquest as a sign that the old ways would not work against the new enemy. That Confucian figures such as Phan Boi Chau and Phan Chu Trinh concluded so rapidly that tradition had ceased to have relevance is indicative of the degree to which the Vietnamese gave precedence to national survival over cultural purity. The image of the new society they spun in their dreams was perhaps superficial and naive, but theirs was a sincere attempt to bring Vietnam abreast of the modern world; they took the first step toward modern nationalist movement in Vietnam.

The weakness of the scholar-patriots was inadvertent, but nonetheless fatal. Lacking experience, they did not see all the implications of the changes taking place in the world, and their techniques and actions were heavily laden with traditionalist assumptions and attitudes. Their simple slogans and isolated feats of derring-do were no match for the sophisticated colonial administration. Clearly it took more to build a modern nationalist movement in Vietnam.

The generation that grew to maturity in the wake of World War I was highly conscious of the weakness of its predecessor. With this generation Vietnamese nationalism moved into the cities. Exposed from childhood to French culture, these modern patriots deliberately brought a new Western flavor to Vietnamese nationalism and were often openly contemptuous of traditional institutions. The urbanization of Vietnamese nationalism did not represent a complete break with the past, however. Many of the leading elements in the new nationalist parties which sprang up in Saigon, Hanoi, and Hue were direct offspring of the scholar-patriots and the Can Vuong, and they felt strongly an emotional responsibility to follow the examples of their elders.

The movement into the cities was a necessary phase in the evolution of nationalism in Vietnam, for only urban Vietnamese were truly conscious of the nature of the Western challenge and were capable of devising a strategy to cope with it. But urbanization created a number of new problems.

Nationalist activities in urban areas were relatively easily controlled by the authorities, and clandestine operations were more difficult to carry on than in the countryside. Also, the diversity of the urban class structure exposed the resistance movement to the possibility of increased fractionalization and a lack of unity so necessary to the success of their efforts. Intellectuals, of course, are habitually prone to ideological theorizing and the urban nationalist movement seemed to spend more time in inner controversy than in opposing the colonial regime.

Most important, perhaps, the movement into the cities isolated the nationalists intellectually as well as physically from the traditional roots of Vietnamese society in the village. The modern urban Vietnamese, in absorbing Western values and habits, and in seeking a Western vocation, and perhaps even in speaking a Western language in preference to his own, became an alien force in the countryside, where traditional forms still retained considerable vitality. Although members of the scholar-patriot generation were by their education and, frequently, their family background, distinct from the average peasant, they generally had been raised in the village, had absorbed the traditional Sino-Vietnamese heritage, and, in a word, could speak the villager's language. The modern nationalist, by contrast, often grew up in the city, went through the Franco-Vietnamese school system, and frequently spent several years working or studying in Paris. In the process he lost his link with the villagers, who often viewed him with considerable suspicion. The break in communication, of course, frequently worked both ways, for urban nationalists had little comprehension of the problems of peasants, and the urbanite's concern for constitutional democracy and individual liberty, and his desire for more exposure to Western culture, often had little meaning outside the confines of Saigon and Hanoi.

In abandoning Confucianism as a symbol of Vietnamese nationalism, urban nationalists lost the vital emotional link with the village that a religion could provide. Where urban movements elsewhere in South and Southeast Asia maintained the essential link between elites and peasants by relying heavily on an indigenous religious tradition such as Hinduism, Islam, or Buddhism, Vietnamese intellectuals could go to the peasant only with the still alien values of Western science and democracy. The urbanization of Vietnamese nationalism, then, solved some old problems, but created some uncomfortable new ones, and risked putting modern nationalism in a position of permanent weakness. There were few indications that by the beginning of the Pacific War in 1940 the nationalist movement as a whole was on the road to finding a solution.

Out of this social milieu the Vietnamese communist movement arose. . . . Communism in Vietnam began as one answer to the "national" problem, and it was seen as such by much of its early membership, including Ho Chi Minh. As a primarily urban movement it was subject to the problems created by the urbanization of Vietnamese nationalism. Indeed, by the time a formal party was created in 1930, the urban orientation of the movement was deliberately encouraged by Comintern strategy devised in Moscow.

During these formative years, the communist movement did relatively well in competing with pure nationalist organizations for support among the workers and urban petty bourgeoisie. If they suffered to a degree for their dependence on a foreign ideology, they made up for this disadvantage by their determination and ability. By the late 1930s they had become the most vital force in Vietnamese nationalism. The striking success of the communists among educated Vietnamese was somewhat unusual in Southeast Asia and deserves further comment. One advantage for the Indochinese Communist Party perhaps, was the colonial tie with France. A large number of Vietnamese intellectuals received their education (and their Marxist beliefs) in Paris, and it is likely that the attraction of the French intellectual to Marxism rubbed off on many French-trained Vietnamese.

Another advantage of Marxism in Vietnam lay in its attractiveness to intellectuals who were in the midst of an identity crisis. As has been observed earlier, nationalists in Vietnam could not build their movement around native religious symbols because Confucianism, closely linked with the reactionary court, never took hold as a symbol of Vietnamese identity within the nationalist movement. The decline of Confucianism in the cities left an emotional and intellectual void in the minds of patriotic intellectuals, and many obviously found Marxist doctrine an attractive modern alternative to the discredited Sino-Vietnamese tradition. As an intricate and sophisticated philosophy, with a universal dogma and a comprehensive explanation of history that was optimistic, scientific, impregnated with moral fervor, and staunchly anti-imperialist, Marxism could be accepted without great difficulty as a modern equivalent of Confucianism.

Still, without a broader base than the urban areas could provide, Vietnamese communism was in the same leaky boat as its nationalist rivals, and it was first and foremost the communists who made the effort to transform nationalism into a mass phenomenon. The experience of the Nghe-Tinh soviets showed, albeit briefly, the potential force of the peasant, but the destruction of the Central Vietnamese apparatus and the emergence into leadership of Stalin School graduates trained in Moscow nipped the early indications of a rural strategy in the bud. By the late 1930s, however, changes were in the wind. The Popular Front showed that the party could work with all classes. The Comintern showed less interest in Indochina and allowed the Indochinese Communist Party greater freedom to design its own strategy. By 1938, two young Communists, Vo Nguyen Giap and Truong Chinh, had written a study of the peasant question which, though unspecific about the peasant's role in the Vietnamese revolution, called him an "invincible force" and intimated that the party should pay more attention to his problems. Then, in 1939–1940, the Indochinese Communist Party was driven from the cities and a new strategy was discovered at Bac Son. In 1941 the leadership caught up with events and at the Eighth Plenum at Pac Bo, put the final touches on the new strategy.

As the Pacific War began, then, the communists had begun the process of building a mass movement for national liberation on the basis of an alliance between the peasantry and the urban intellectuals. The fusing of intellectuals and peasants, if effective, would combine the leadership ability of the former with the tempestuous force of rural discontent. If the Vietminh could successfully attain the pose of an essentially nationalist movement, if it could become the most effective force opposed to French rule in Vietnam, with a finger on the pulse of the discontents of all major strata of Vietnamese society, it would be able to establish itself in the minds of millions of Vietnamese as the legitimate heir to French rule in Vietnam, and the new recipient of the Mandate of Heaven.

Victory would not be rapid or easy, as Ho Chi Minh continually reminded his colleagues. It would take discipline, organization, patience, and willingness to sacrifice. Whether the communists would be able to sustain their momentum after the war was a question only the future could decide, for new times would call for new solutions, new policies. Would the peasant follow the communists? Would the party be able to convince the peasant that it was the heir to the Heavenly Mandate? Would it be able to reconcile the sometimes conflicting demands of city and country, of national self-determination and social reform, in a hard, bitter struggle against its rivals as well as against the French?

In 1941, there were no answers to these questions. Yet the potential for growth was there. The party was small, but it was dedicated and its members were steeled in adversity; their revolutionary zeal was undeniable. And, of course, they were blessed with a leader of singular capacity, for over two decades Ho Chi Minh had shown a striking ability to steer the party from the shoals of factionalism, regionalism, and adventurism. In 1941, the movement, the man, and the moment converged. The communists stood on the brink of grasping victory. They had demonstrated that they alone possessed the understanding, and that indefinable sense of will so necessary to the achievement of victory in human affairs.

X *F U R T H E R   R E A D I N G*

Joseph Buttinger, *The Smaller Dragon: A Political History of Vietnam* (1958)
———, *Vietnam: A Dragon Embattled* (1967)
John Cady, *The Roots of French Imperialism in Asia* (1954)
Gerard Chailland, *The Peasants of North Vietnam* (1970)
Hoang Van Chi, *From Colonialism to Communism* (1971)
William J. Duiker, *The Communist Road to Power in Vietnam* (1981)
———, *The Comintern and Vietnamese Communism* (1975)
———, *Vietnam: Nation in Revolution* (1983)
Thomas E. Ennis, *French Policy and Developments in Indochina* (1956)
Thomas L. Hodgkin, *Vietnam: The Revolutionary Path* (1981)
Neil Jamieson, *Understanding Vietnam* (1993)
Huynh Kim Khanh, "The Vietnamese August Revolution Reinterpreted," *Journal of Asian Studies,* 30 (1971), 761–82
Jean Lacouture, *Ho Chi Minh* (1968)
Ngo Vinh Long, *Before the Revolution: The Vietnamese Peasants Under the French* (1973)
John T. McAlister and Paul Mus, *The Vietnamese and Their Revolution* (1970)

David G. Marr, *Vietnamese Anti-Colonialism* (1971)
Martin Murray, *The Development of Capitalism in Colonial Indochina* (1980)
Ken Post, *Revolution, Socialism and Nationalism in Viet Nam* (vols. 1–3) (1989)
Charles Robequain, *The Economic Development of French Indochina* (1944)
Hue-Tam Ho Tai, *Radicalism and the Origins of the Vietnamese Revolution* (1992)
Virginia Thompson, *French Indochina* (1937)
Stein Tonnesson, *The Vietnamese Revolution of 1945* (1991)
Robert F. Turner, *Vietnamese Communism* (1975)
Walter F. Vella, ed., *Aspects of Vietnamese History* (1973)
Nguyen Khac Vien, ed., *Tradition and Revolution in Vietnam* (1974)

CHAPTER

3

The Roots of the American

Commitment

During World War II, President Franklin D. Roosevelt advanced a series of proposals aimed at liberalizing colonial rule and preparing dependent peoples for self-government. He often singled out French rule in Indochina as a particularly grievous example of colonial exploitation, and he advocated a trusteeship system for the postwar period. Yet shortly before his death in April 1945, Roosevelt had begun to retreat from his anticolonial stance. The determination of France and other imperial powers to retain their overseas possessions, and America's need to work with its European allies on a broad range of postwar diplomatic initiatives, forced a modification in the president's plans. FDR consequently did not challenge France's initial efforts to regain sovereignty in Indochina.

The establishment of the independent Republic of Vietnam in the wake of the Japanese surrender, and the subsequent outbreak of hostilities between French and Vietminh forces in November 1946, posed daunting policy dilemmas for the administration of Harry S Truman. Initially reluctant to support either side in the colonial struggle openly, the United States maintained a policy of official neutrality throughout the late 1940s. Washington finally abandoned that policy in 1950 and began to supply the French with substantial military and economic assistance.

Most scholars agree that the decision to aid the French in 1950 marks the initial U.S. commitment in Vietnam. But they have offered widely divergent explanations for that decision. Was the American commitment prompted by a growing appreciation of the economic importance of Southeast Asia to the United States? Or were strategic considerations stemming from America's perceived national security needs a more significant influence on American policymakers? To what extent might political, ideological, bureaucratic, or psychological factors have also played a role in the Truman administration's decision to support the French? Historians have agreed that broad global forces—and especially the intensifying Cold War between the United States and the Soviet Union—exerted a powerful pull on the U.S.

gravitation toward the French in Indochina. They continue to disagree, however, about the precise nature of that impact. This chapter explores these issues.

✗ D O C U M E N T S

The first document presents Secretary of State George C. Marshall's cable of May 1947 to the U.S. embassy in France, in which Marshall expresses American frustration with French policy in Indochina. In the second document, the State Department reviews and evaluates U.S. policy toward Indochina, emphasizing the need to strike a balance between Vietnamese aspirations and French interests. On March 8, 1949, the Elysée Agreement established the State of Vietnam and the kingdoms of Laos and Cambodia as associated states within the French union. The third document is a public statement of American support for that agreement.

The next two readings comprise the State Department's recommendation of February 1, 1950, to provide military aid to the French in Indochina and the recommendation of the National Security Council in its Policy Paper No. 64. Secretary of State Dean Acheson's announcement that American assistance would be forthcoming is featured in the sixth document. In the concluding documentary selection, taken from a press interview, Ho Chi Minh angrily denounces that decision and calls U.S. assistance imperialist intervention.

George C. Marshall on the Indochina Dispute, 1947

We becoming increasingly concerned by slow progress toward settlement Indochina dispute. We fully appreciate French are making effort reach satisfactory settlement and hope visit Commissioner Bollaert to Indochina will produce concrete results. The following considerations, however, are submitted for your use any conversations you may have with French authorities at appropriate time this subject. We recognize it might not be desirable make such approach to newly constituted government in first days its reorganization, but nevertheless feel early appropriate opportunity might be found inform French Gov of our concern in this matter.

Key our position is our awareness that in respect developments affecting position Western democratic powers in southern Asia, we essentially in same boat as French, also as British and Dutch. We cannot conceive setbacks to long-range interests France which would not also be setbacks our own. Conversely we should regard close association France and members French Union as not only to advantage peoples concerned, but indirectly our own.

In our view, southern Asia in critical phase its history with seven new nations in process achieving or struggling independence or autonomy. These nations include quarter inhabitants world and their future course, owing sheer weight populations, resources they command, and strategic location, will be momentous factor world stability. Following relaxation European controls, internal racial, religious and national differences could plunge new nations into violent discord, or already apparent anti-Western Pan-Asiatic tendencies could become dominant political force, or Communists could capture control. We consider as best safeguard against these eventualities a continued close association between newly-autonomous peoples and powers which have long been responsible their welfare. In particular we recognize Vietnamese will for indefinite period require French material and technical assistance and enlightened political guidance which can be provided only by nation steeped like France in democratic tradition and confirmed in respect human liberties and worth individual.

We equally convinced, however, such association must be voluntary to be lasting and achieve results, and that protraction present situation Indochina can only destroy basis voluntary cooperation, leave legacy permanent bitterness, and irrevocably alienate Vietnamese from France and those values represented by France and other Western democracies.

While fully appreciating difficulties French position this conflict, we feel there is danger in any arrangement which might provide Vietnamese opportunity compare unfavorably their own position and that of other peoples southern Asia who have made tremendous strides toward autonomy since war.

While we are still ready and willing to do anything we can which might be considered helpful, French will understand we not attempting come forward with any solution our own or intervene in situation. However, they will also understand we inescapably concerned with situation Far East generally, upon which developments Indochina likely have profound effect.

Plain fact is that Western democratic system is on defensive in almost all emergent nations southern Asia and, because identified by peoples these nations with what they have considered former denial their rights, is particularly vulnerable to attacks by demagogic leaders political movements of either ultra-nationalist or Communist nature which promise redress and revenge past so-called wrongs and inequalities. Signs development anti-Western Asiatic consciousness already multiplying, of which Inter-Asian Conf an example. Unanimity support for Vietnamese among other Asiatic countries very striking, even leading to moves Burma, India, and Malaya send volunteer forces their assistance. Vietnam cause proving rallying-cry for all anti-Western forces and playing in hands Communists all areas. We fear continuation conflict may jeopardize position all Western democratic powers in southern Asia and lead to very eventualities of which we most apprehensive.

We confident French fully aware dangers inherent in situation and therefore venture express renewed hope they will be most generous attempt find early solution which, by recognizing legitimate desires Vietnamese, will restore peace and deprive anti-democratic forces of powerful weapon.

For your info, evidence that French Communists are being directed accelerate their agitation French colonies even extent lose much popular support France may be indication Kremlin prepared sacrifice temporary gains with 40 million French to long range colonial strategy with 600 million dependent people, which lends great urgency foregoing views. . . . Dept much concerned lest French efforts find "true representatives Vietnam" with whom negotiate result creation impotent puppet Govt along lines Cochinchina regime, or that restoration Baodai may be attempted, implying democracies reduced resort monarchy as weapon against Communism. You may refer these further views if nature your conversations French appears warrant.

Statement of U.S. Policy Toward Indochina, 1948

Objectives

The immediate objective of US policy in Indochina is to assist in a solution of the present impasse which will be mutually satisfactory to the French and the Vietnamese peoples, which will result in the termination of the present hostilities, and which will be within the framework of US security.

Our long-term objectives are: (1) to eliminate so far as possible Communist influence in Indochina and to see installed a self-governing nationalist state which will be friendly to the US and which, commensurate with the capacity of the peoples involved, will be patterned upon our conception of a democratic state as opposed to the totalitarian state which would evolve inevitably from Communist domination; (2) to foster the association of the peoples of Indochina with the western powers, particularly with France with whose customs, language and laws they are familiar, to the end that those peoples will prefer freely to cooperate with the western powers culturally, economically and politically; (3) to raise the standard of living so that the peoples of Indochina will be less receptive to totalitarian influences and will have an incentive to work productively and thus contribute to a better balanced world economy; and (4) to prevent undue Chinese penetration and subsequent influence in Indochina so that the peoples of Indochina will not be hampered in their natural developments by the pressure of an alien people and alien interests.

Policy Issues

To attain our immediate objective, we should continue to press the French to accommodate the basic aspirations of the Vietnamese: (1) unity of Cochinchina, Annam, and Tonkin, (2) complete internal autonomy, and (3) the right to choose freely regarding participation in the French Union. We have recognized French sovereignty over Indochina but have maintained that such recognition does not imply any commitment on our part to assist France to exert its authority over the Indochinese peoples. Since V-J day, the majority people of the area, the Vietnamese, have stubbornly resisted the reestablishment of French authority, a struggle in which we have tried to maintain insofar as possible a position of non-support of either party.

While the nationalist movement in Vietnam (Cochinchina, Annam, and Tonkin) is strong, and though the great majority of the Vietnamese are not fundamentally Communist, the most active element in the resistance of the local peoples to the French has been a Communist group headed by Ho Chi Minh. This group has successfully extended its influence to include practically all armed forces now fighting the French, thus in effect capturing control of the nationalist movement.

The French on two occasions during 1946 attempted to resolve the problem by negotiation with the government established and dominated by Ho Chi Minh. The general agreements reached were not, however, successfully implemented and widescale fighting subsequently broke out. Since early in 1947, the French have employed about 115,000 troops in Indochina, with little result, since the countryside except in Laos and Cambodia remains under the firm control of the Ho Chi Minh government. A series of French-established puppet governments have tended to enhance the prestige of Ho's government and to call into question, on the part of the Vietnamese, the sincerity of French intentions to accord an independent status to Vietnam.

Political.   We have regarded these hostilities in a colonial area as detrimental not only to our own long-term interests which require as a minimum a stable Southeast Asia but also detrimental to the interests of France, since the hatred engendered by continuing hostilities may render impossible peaceful collaboration and cooperation of the French and the Vietnamese peoples. This hatred of the Vietnamese people toward the French is keeping alive anti-western feeling among oriental peoples, to the advantage of the USSR and the detriment of the US.

We have not urged the French to negotiate with Ho Chi Minh, even though he probably is now supported by a considerable majority of the Vietnamese people, because of his record as a Communist and the Communist background of many of the influential figures in and about his government.

Postwar French governments have never understood, or have chosen to underestimate, the strength of the nationalist movement with which they must deal in Indochina. It remains possible that the nationalist movement can be subverted from Communist control but this will require granting to a non-Communist group of nationalists at least the same concessions demanded by Ho Chi Minh. The failure of French governments to deal successfully with the Indochinese question has been due, in large measure, to the overwhelming internal issues facing France and the French Union, and to foreign policy considerations in Europe. These factors have combined with the slim parliamentary majorities of postwar governments in France to militate against the bold moves necessary to divert allegiance of the Vietnamese nationalists to non-Communist leadership.

In accord with our policy of regarding with favor the efforts of dependent peoples to attain their legitimate political aspirations, we have been anxious to see the French accord to the Vietnamese the largest possible degree of political and economic independence consistent with legitimate French interests. We have therefore declined to permit the export to the

French in Indochina of arms and munitions for the prosecution of the war against the Vietnamese. This policy has been limited in its effect as we have allowed the free export of arms to France, such exports thereby being available for re-shipment to Indochina or for releasing stocks from reserves to be forwarded to Indochina. . . .

Policy Evaluation

The objectives of US policy towards Indochina have not been realized. Three years after the termination of war a friendly ally, France, is fighting a desperate and apparently losing struggle in Indochina. The economic drain of this warfare on French recovery, while difficult to estimate, is unquestionably large. The Communist control in the nationalist movement has been increased during this period. US influence in Indochina and Southeast Asia has suffered as a result.

The objectives of US policy can only be attained by such French action as will satisfy the nationalist aspirations of the peoples of Indochina. We have repeatedly pointed out to the French the desirability of their giving such satisfaction and thus terminating the present open conflict. Our greatest difficulty in talking with the French and in stressing what should and what should not be done has been our inability to suggest any practicable solution of the Indochina problem, as we are all too well aware of the unpleasant fact that Communist Ho Chi Minh is the strongest and perhaps the ablest figure in Indochina and that any suggested solution which excludes him is an expedient of uncertain outcome. We are naturally hesitant to press the French too strongly or to become deeply involved so long as we are not in a position to suggest a solution or until we are prepared to accept the onus of intervention. The above considerations are further complicated by the fact that we have an immediate interest in maintaining in power a friendly French government, to assist in the furtherance of our aims in Europe. This immediate and vital interest has in consequence taken precedence over active steps looking toward the realization of our objectives in Indochina.

We are prepared, however, to support the French in every way possible in the establishment of a truly nationalist government in Indochina which, by giving satisfaction to the aspirations of the peoples of Indochina, will serve as a rallying point for the nationalists and will weaken the Communist elements. By such support and by active participation in a peaceful and constructive solution in Indochina we stand to regain influence and prestige.

Some solution must be found which will strike a balance between the aspirations of the peoples of Indochina and the interests to the French. Solution by French military reconquest of Indochina is not desirable. Neither would the complete withdrawal of the French from Indochina effect a solution. The first alternative would delay indefinitely the attainment of our objectives, as we would share inevitably in the hatred engendered by an attempted military reconquest and the denial of aspirations for self-government. The second solution would be equally unfortunate as in all likelihood Indochina would then be taken over by the militant Communist group. At best, there might follow a transition period, marked by chaos and terroristic activities, creating a political vacuum into which the Chinese inevitably would be drawn or would push. The absence of stabilization in China will continue to have an important influence upon the objective of a permanent and peaceable solution in Indochina.

We have not been particularly successful in our information and education program in orienting the Vietnamese toward the western democracies and the US. The program has been hampered by the failure of the French to understand that such informational activities as we conduct in Indochina are not inimical to their own long-term interests and by administrative and financial considerations which have prevented the development to the maximum extent of contacts with the Vietnamese. An increased effort should be made to explain democratic institutions, especially American institutions and American policy, to the Indochinese by direct personal contact, by the distribution of information about the US, and the encouraging of educational exchange.

The United States Praises the Elysée Agreements, 1949

The formation of the new unified state of Vietnam and the recent announcement by Bao Dai that the future constitution will be decided by the Vietnamese people are welcome developments which should serve to hasten the reestablishment of peace in that country and the attainment of Vietnam's rightful place in the family of nations.

The United States Government hopes that the agreements of March 8 between President Auriol and Bao Dai, who is making sincere efforts to unite all truly nationalist elements within Vietnam, will form the basis for the progressive realization of the legitimate aspirations of the Vietnamese people.

The State Department Recommends Military Aid to the French, 1950

The Problem

Should the United States provide military aid in Indochina and, if so, how much and in what way.

Assumption

A. There will not be an effective split between the USSR and Communist China within the next three years.

B. The USSR will not declare war on any Southeast Asian country within the next three years.

C. Communist China will not declare war on any Southeast Asian country within the next three years.

D.   The USSR will endeavor to bring about the fall of Southeast Asian governments which are opposed to Communism by using all devices short of war, making use of Communist China and indigenous communists in this endeavor.

Facts Bearing on the Problem

1. When the Mutual Defense Assistance Act of 1949 was being written, the question of providing military aid to Southeast Asia was examined and it was decided not to include specific countries in that area, other than the Republic of the Philippines.

2. The attitude of the Congress toward the provision of military and economic aid to foreign countries recently has stiffened due to both economy and to policy considerations.

3. At the same time, the Congress has shown considerable dissatisfaction with policies which are alleged to have contributed to the Communist success in China and which are involved in the current United States' approach toward the question of Formosa.

4. Section 303 of the Mutual Defense Assistance Act of 1949 makes available to the President the sum of $75 million for use, at the President's discretion, in the general area of China to advance the purposes and policies of the United Nations.

5. Section 303 funds are unrestricted in their use.

6. The British Commonwealth Conference recently held at Colombo recognized that no SEA [Southeast Asia] regional military pact now exists due to divergent interest and that such an arrangement was now unlikely.

7. Communism has made important advances in the Far East during the past year.

8. Opposition to Communism in Indochina is actively being carried on by the three legally-constituted governments of Vietnam, Cambodia and Laos.

9. Communist-oriented forces in Indochina are being aided by Red China and the USSR.

Discussion

1. Indochina has common border with China and Burma, thus making it subject to invasion by Red China.

2. Its population is some 27 million concentrated in the delta regions of the Mekong and Red Rivers. Of the total population, Chinese account for between 600,000 and a million, concentrated largely in the cities.

3. Indochina has an agricultural economy based principally on rice of which it is an exporter. World War II and its aftermath seriously disrupted the national economy. The country presently has an annual trade deficit of about $85 million.

4. There are three subdivisions of Indochina: Vietnam, Laos, and Cambodia. An agreement was signed March 8, 1949, between France and

Vietnam which provides for the latter to become an Associated State within the French Union. Ratification of the Agreement, followed by the recognition of Vietnam by the West, is expected in the near future. French policy aims at making Laos and Cambodia Associated States within the French Union at the same time.

5. Governmental stability is poor in Indochina. In Vietnam, less than one-third of the country is controlled by the legal government with the French in control of the major cities; in Cambodia and Laos, the French maintain order but unrest is endemic. Before World War II Indochina was made up of four French Protectorates (Tonkin, Annam, Laos and Cambodia) and the colony of Cochinchina. It was occupied after the war by Chinese troops in the north (Tonkin) and by British and later French in the south. In 1946 a (nationalist coalition) government headed by the Moscow-trained Communist agent Ho Chi Minh consented to the return to the north (Tonkin) of the French upon promises of independence within the French Union. French negotiations with Ho were broken off following the massacre of many foreigners in Tonkin and Cochinchina in December 1946 by Ho's forces. Hostilities have continued to date.

6. The French are irrevocably committed in Indochina and have sponsored Bao Dai as a move aimed at achieving non-Communist political stability. It was a case of backing Bao Dai or accepting the Communist government of Ho Chi Minh. This latter alternative was impossible not only because it would obviously make their position in Indochina untenable but would also open the door to complete Communist domination of Southeast Asia. Such a communist advance would have severe repercussions in the non-communist world.

7. Military operations in Indochina represented a franc drain on the French Treasury of the equivalent of approximately $475 million in 1949. This constitutes nearly half of the current French Military Budget.

8. Ho Chi Minh, a Moscow-trained Communist, controls the Viet Minh movement which is in conflict with the government of Bao Dai for control of Vietnam. Ho actually exercises control of varying degree over more than two-thirds of Vietnam territory and his "government" maintains agents in Thailand, Burma and India. This communist "government" has been recognized by Communist China and the USSR.

9. Most Indochinese, both the supporters of Bao Dai and those of Ho Chi Minh, regard independence from the French as their primary objective. Protection from Chinese Communist imperialism has been considered, up to now, a secondary issue.

10. Unavoidably, the United States is, together with France, committed in Indochina. That is, failure of the French Bao Dai "experiment" would mean the communization of Indochina. It is Bao Dai (or a similar anticommunist successor) or Ho Chi Minh (or a similar communist successor); there is no other alternative. The choice confronting the United States is to support the French in Indochina or face the extension of Communism over the remainder of the continental area of Southeast Asia and, possibly, farther westward. We then would be obliged to make staggering investments

in those areas and in that part of Southeast Asia remaining outside Communist domination or withdraw to a much-contracted Pacific line. It would seem a case of "Penny wise, Pound foolish" to deny support to the French in Indochina.

11. The US plans on extending recognition to the newly-created states of Vietnam, Laos and Cambodia, following French legislative action which is expected in early February 1950.

12. Another approach to the problem is to apply the practical test of probability of success. In the present case we know from the complex circumstances involved that the French are going to make literally every possible effort to prevent the victory of Communism in Indochina. Briefly, then, we would be backing a determined protagonist in this venture. Added to this is the fact that French military leaders such as General Cherrière are soberly confident that, in the absence of an invasion in mass from Red China, they (the French) can be successful in their support of the anti-Communist governments in Indochina.

13. Still another approach to the problem is to recall that the United States has undertaken to provide substantial aid to France in Europe. Failure to support French policy in Indochina would have the effect of contributing toward the defeat of our aims in Europe.

Conclusions

A. Significant developments have taken place in Indochina since the Mutual Defense Assistance Act of 1949 was drawn up, these changes warranting a reexamination of the question of military aid.

B. The whole of Southeast Asia is in danger of falling under Communist domination.

C. The countries and areas of Southeast Asia are not at present in a position to form a regional organization for self-defense nor are they capable of defending themselves against military aggressive Communism, without the aid of the great powers. Despite their lack of military strength, however, there is a will on the part of the legal governments of Indochina toward nationalism and a will to resist whatever aims at destroying that nationalism.

D. The French native and colonial troops presently in Indochina are engaged in military operations aimed at denying the expansion southward of Communism from Red China and of destroying its power in Indochina.

E. In the critical areas of Indochina France needs aid in its support of the legally-constituted anti-Communist states.

Recommendations

1. The United States should furnish military aid in support of the anti-Communist nationalist governments of Indochina, this aid to be tailored to meet deficiencies toward which the United States can make a unique contribution, not including United States troops.

2. This aid should be financed out of funds made available by Section 303 of the Mutual Defense Assistance Act of 1949.

National Security Council Paper No. 64, 1950

The Position of the United States with Respect to Indochina

The Problem

1. To undertake a determination of all practicable United States measures to protect its security in Indochina and to prevent the expansion of communist aggression in that area.

Analysis

2. It is recognized that the threat of communist aggression against Indochina is only one phase of anticipated communist plans to seize all of Southeast Asia. It is understood that Burma is weak internally and could be invaded without strong opposition or even that the Government of Burma could be subverted. However, Indochina is the area most immediately threatened. It is also the only area adjacent to communist China which contains a large European army, which along with native troops is now in armed conflict with the forces of communist aggression. A decision to contain communist expansion at the border of Indochina must be considered as a part of a wider study to prevent communist aggression into other parts of Southeast Asia.

3. A large segment of the Indochinese nationalist movement was seized in 1945 by Ho Chi Minh, a Vietnamese who under various aliases has served as a communist agent for thirty years. He has attracted non-communist as well as communist elements to his support. In 1946, he attempted, but failed to secure French agreement to his recognition as the head of a government of Vietnam. Since then he has directed a guerrilla army in raids against French installations and lines of communication. French forces which have been attempting to restore law and order found themselves pitted against a determined adversary who manufactures effective arms locally, who received supplies of arms from outside sources, who maintained no capital or permanent headquarters and who was, and is able, to disrupt and harass almost any area within Vietnam (Tonkin, Annam and Cochinchina) at will.

4. The United States has, since the Japanese surrender, pointed out to the French Government that the legitimate nationalist aspirations of the people of Indochina must be satisfied, and that a return to the prewar colonial rule is not possible. The Department of State has pointed out to the French Government that it was and is necessary to establish and support governments in Indochina particularly in Vietnam, under leaders who are

capable of attracting to their causes the non-communist nationalist followers who had drifted to the Ho Chi Minh communist movement in the
absence of any non-communist nationalist movement around which to plan
their aspirations.

5. In an effort to establish stability by political means, where military
measures had been unsuccessful, i.e., by attracting non-communist nationalists, now followers of Ho Chi Minh, to the support of anti-communist
nationalist leaders, the French Government entered into agreements with
the governments of the Kingdoms of Laos and Cambodia to elevate their
status from protectorates to that of independent states within the French
Union. The State of Vietnam was formed, with similar status, out of the former French protectorates of Tonkin, Annam and the former French Colony
of Cochinchina. Each state received an increased degree of autonomy and
sovereignty. Further steps towards independence were indicated by the
French. The agreements were ratified by the French Government on 2
February 1950.

6. The Governments of Vietnam, Laos and Cambodia were officially
recognized by the United States and the United Kingdom on February 7,
1950. Other Western powers have, or are committed to do likewise. The
United States has consistently brought to the attention of non-communist
Asian countries the danger of communist aggression which threatens them
if communist expansion in Indochina is unchecked. As this danger becomes
more evident it is expected to overcome the reluctance that they have had
to recognize and support the three new states. We are therefore continuing
to press those countries to recognize the new states. On January 18, 1950,
the Chinese Communist Government announced its recognition of the Ho
Chi Minh movement as the legal Government of Vietnam, while on January
30, 1950, the Soviet Government, while maintaining diplomatic relations
with France, similarly announced its recognition.

7. The newly formed States of Vietnam, Laos and Cambodia do not as
yet have sufficient political stability nor military power to prevent the infiltration into their areas of Ho Chi Minh's forces. The French Armed Forces,
while apparently effectively utilized at the present time, can do little more
than to maintain the *status quo*. Their strength of some 140,000 does, however, represent an army in being and the only military bulwark in that area
against the further expansion of communist aggression from either internal
or external forces.

8. The presence of Chinese Communist troops along the border of
Indochina makes it possible for arms, material and troops to move freely
from Communist China to the northern Tonkin area now controlled by Ho
Chi Minh. There is already evidence of movement of arms.

9. In the present state of affairs, it is doubtful that the combined native
Indochinese and French troops can successfully contain Ho's forces should
they be strengthened by either Chinese Communist troops crossing the border, or Communist-supplied arms and material in quantity from outside
Indochina strengthening Ho's forces.

Conclusions

10. It is important to United States security interests that all practicable measures be taken to prevent further communist expansion in Southeast Asia. Indochina is a key area of Southeast Asia and is under immediate threat.

11. The neighboring countries of Thailand and Burma could be expected to fall under Communist domination if Indochina were controlled by a Communist-dominated government. The balance of Southeast Asia would then be in grave hazard.

12. Accordingly, the Departments of State and Defense should prepare as a matter of priority a program of all practicable measures designed to protect United States security interests in Indochina.

Dean Acheson Urges Aid for Indochina, 1950

The [French] Foreign Minister [Robert Schuman] and I have just had an exchange of views on the situation in Indochina and are in general agreement both as to the urgency of the situation in that area and as to the necessity for remedial action. We have noted the fact that the problem of meeting the threat to the security of Viet Nam, Cambodia, and Laos which now enjoy independence within the French union is primarily the responsibility of France and the Governments and peoples of Indochina. The United States recognizes that the solution of the Indochina problem depends both upon the restoration of security and upon the development of genuine nationalism and that United States assistance can and should contribute to these major objectives.

The United States Government, convinced that neither national independence nor democratic evolution exist[s] in any area dominated by Soviet imperialism, considers the situation to be such as to warrant its according economic aid and military equipment to the associated states of Indochina and to France in order to assist them in restoring stability and permitting these states to pursue their peaceful and democratic development.

Ho Chi Minh Denounces U.S. Intervention, 1950

Question: What is, Mr. President, the present situation of the U.S. imperialists' interventionist policy in Indochina?

Answer: The U.S. imperialists have of late openly interfered in Indochina's affairs. It is with their money and weapons and their instructions that the French colonialists have been waging war in Viet-Nam, Cambodia, and Laos.

However, the U.S. imperialists are intensifying their plot to discard the French colonialists so as to gain complete control over Indochina. That is why they do their utmost to redouble their direct intervention in every field—military, political, and economic. It is also for this reason that the contradictions between them and the French colonialists become sharper and sharper.

Question: What influence does this intervention exert on the Indochinese people?

Answer: The U.S. imperialists supply their henchmen with armaments to massacre the Indochinese people. They dump their goods in Indochina to prevent the development of local handicrafts. Their pornographic culture contaminates the youth in areas placed under their control. They follow the policy of buying up, deluding, and dividing our people. They drag some bad elements into becoming their tools and use them to invade our country.

Question: What measure shall we take against them?

Answer: To gain independence, we, the Indochinese people, must defeat the French colonialists, our number-one enemy. At the same time, we will struggle against the U.S. interventionists. The deeper their interference, the more powerful are our solidarity and our struggle. We will expose their maneuvers before all our people, especially those living in areas under their control. We will expose all those who serve as lackeys for the U.S. imperialists to coerce, deceive, and divide our people.

The close solidarity between the peoples of Viet-Nam, Cambodia, and Laos constitutes a force capable of defeating the French colonialists and the U.S. interventionists. The U.S. imperialists failed in China, they will fail in Indochina.

We are still laboring under great difficulties but victory will certainly be ours.

X

E S S A Y S

In the first essay, Patrick J. Hearden of Purdue University links U.S. involvement in Indochina to America's larger economic goals for the postwar world. Those goals encompassed, in his view, not just narrow U.S. commercial ambitions in Southeast Asia but the much broader needs of the world capitalist system as a whole. Hearden argues that the Truman administration's preoccupation with the economic revival of Japan played a decisive role in the U.S. commitment to the French.

Robert J. McMahon of the University of Florida also emphasizes the economic factors that tied Indochina to broader U.S. foreign-policy objectives. But material considerations cannot be viewed in isolation from strategic imperatives, McMahon emphasizes. He contends that it is the combination of economic calculations and national security fears, in conjunction with a set of powerful political and psychological pressures, that best explains the initial U.S. commitment to the French.

An Economic Perspective on U.S. Involvement

PATRICK J. HEARDEN

Even before the United States formally entered World War II, American leaders began making plans for the creation of a peaceful and prosperous international order after hostilities ceased. President Franklin D. Roosevelt and his State Department advisers hoped to establish a liberal capitalist world system based upon the principle of equal commercial opportunity. Confident that the United States would emerge from the conflict with a preponderance of military and economic power, they aimed to promote an open door policy that would give all industrial countries equal access to raw materials and commodity markets around the globe. American leaders realized that Great Britain would no longer be able to rule the world in the interest of free trade, and they believed that the United States should be prepared to fill the power vacuum. They hoped that, just as the last century had belonged to England, an Allied victory over the Axis would mark the dawn of an American century. In short, they envisioned the establishment of a Pax Americana that would replace the Pax Britannica and thereby sustain the capitalist epoch.

But the nightmare of a depression haunted American leaders when they contemplated the nature of the postwar world. Following the stock market crash on Wall Street in 1929, the United States had plunged into a decade of depression. Businessmen shut down plants and laid off workers because of a lack of demand for consumer goods, and as unemployment increased and household spending declined, more companies closed their doors. President Roosevelt launched his New Deal program to counteract the vicious circle, but economic recovery did not come until the onset of World War II. When the shooting started in Europe in 1939, American factories began receiving orders for a vast array of weapons and munitions from both the United States government and the Allied nations. The stimulus of military spending continued turning the wheels of industry and creating jobs for those without work, and in 1942 Roosevelt boasted that "Dr. Win-the-War" had replaced "Dr. New Deal." Though pleased about the wartime prosperity, Roosevelt and his advisers realized that the New Deal had failed to overcome the Great Depression. Thus they feared that, when the demand for military hardware declined at the end of the war, the twin problems of overproduction and unemployment would return to plague the United States.

Top government officials and corporate executives who participated in the decision-making process understood that there were two different ways of avoiding a postwar depression in the United States. Either they could plan the American economy so that domestic production would match the requirements of the home market, or they could obtain foreign markets to absorb the surplus output of the farms and factories in the United States.

From *The Tragedy of Vietnam* by Patrick J. Hearden, pp. 24–43. Copyright © 1991 by HarperCollins Publishers, Inc. Reprinted by permission.

American policymakers rejected the option of centralized economic planning to create an internal balance between supply and demand because they believed that excessive governmental controls would destroy the essentials of free enterprise. Fearing that an extension of New Deal regulations would undermine entrepreneurial freedom by taking management decisions out of private hands, American leaders chose the alternative of overseas commercial expansion to solve the problem of domestic overproduction. In other words, they looked to new frontiers in the markets of the world in hopes of preserving capitalism in the United States.

President Roosevelt and his State Department advisers also hoped to promote world peace by liberalizing international commerce. During the Great Depression, many manufacturing nations had erected high tariff walls around both their internal and colonial markets. The consequent decline in the volume of world trade had a particularly harmful impact on countries that did not have enough natural resources to sustain themselves in economic isolation. Germany and Japan, after being denied access to essential foodstuffs and raw materials, led a group of these "have-not-nations" in an attempt to redivide the world in order to satisfy their material needs. Although American policymakers assumed that the Allies would defeat the Axis drive to partition the planet into exclusive spheres of influences, they feared that a resumption of economic nationalism in the postwar era would sow the seeds for yet another global conflict. They were therefore intent on establishing a liberal international trading system after the war so that "have-not nations" like Germany and Japan could achieve prosperity by engaging in peaceful commerce rather than military conquest.

During their postwar planning sessions between 1941 and 1945, State Department officials drafted blueprints for the creation of a peaceful and prosperous international capitalist utopia. They carefully advanced a multi-dimensional economic program embracing the following five key points: (1) the extension of American loans to underwrite the economic reconstruction of industrial countries that had been devastated by the long military ordeal; (2) the reintegration of Germany into the global economy; (3) the limitation of armaments to permit small countries to devote their sparse resources to economic rehabilitation rather than military preparation; (4) the reduction of American tariffs to allow foreign countries to increase their exports to the United States and thereby earn dollars that they could use to purchase American products; and (5) the modification of the European imperial preference systems to give all nations equal access to raw materials and commodity markets in colonial areas such as British Malaya, Dutch Indonesia, and French Indochina.

The architects of the new world order spent much of their time in the State Department discussing the dangers of colonialism. Adolf Berle, Leo Pasvolsky, and others pointed out that the continuation of colonial monopolies in the postwar period would not only undermine American economic interests but that imperial preferences might even provoke dynamic "have-not nations" into taking aggressive actions that would culminate in World War III. These State Department experts also noted that continued colonial exploitation might stimulate a wave of revolutionary upheavals throughout the Third World. They were particularly worried that the imperial policies of the British, Dutch, and French in the Far East would give rise to a strong anticolonial movement under the banner of Asia for the Asians. Many Oriental nationalists, noncommunist as well as communist, were talking about the need for a united Asian crusade to end European rule in the Far East. American diplomats feared that such a Pan Asiatic movement would threaten the economic interests of the United States along with the other industrial countries around the world.

Disturbed by such dismal prospects, the postwar planners in the Department of State sponsored an ambitious trusteeship scheme to solve the troublesome problem of colonialism. They proposed that all dependent areas should be administered by either a single trustee country or a group of trustees acting under the auspices of the United Nations. These trustees would be responsible for helping the colonial peoples under their guardianship attain political maturity. By progressively introducing measures of self-government in dependent regions, the trustees were to prepare their wards for eventual independence. The State Department plan also called upon the trustee nations to promote economic development in colonial areas for the benefit of both the native populations and the rest of the world. The trustees would therefore be required to open the territories under their tutelage to the trade and investments of all countries regardless of their size. Under Secretary Sumner Welles stressed this point when he told his subordinates in the State Department that the issue of equal access to natural resources and commodity markets was "the keystone of the whole structure of trusteeship for dependent areas."

President Roosevelt gave the trusteeship proposal strong support. He liked to point out that during the last four decades the United States had been preparing the Philippine Islands for self-government, and he frequently suggested that the American treatment of the Philippines should serve as a model for the European powers to emulate. Roosevelt believed that colonial peoples should go through an interim period of international guardianship until they were ready for independence. He thought that the training period might be as short as a decade or so for advanced areas like Indochina and as long as a century or more for backward regions like Borneo. Although he was a gradualist with regard to the decolonization question, Roosevelt emphasized the need for the European powers to fix definite timetables for granting independence to their wards. He insisted that dependent peoples should not be held in tutelage after they were able to stand on their own feet. In a nutshell, Roosevelt regarded the trusteeship interval as a transitional stage along the road from the colonialism of the past to the self-determinism of the future.

President Roosevelt and his counselors in the State Department also planned to establish an international security system based upon the Big Four police powers. After disarming their Axis enemies at the end of the war, the United States, Great Britain, Soviet Russia, and China were to cooperate with each other in maintaining world peace. Although China was weak and divided, American leaders insisted that the disorganized Asian giant must be included in the Big Four. They hoped that China would eventually become an important trading partner and military ally of the United States. They also figured that China would be a valuable political associate that would support American positions in the United Nations. Their grand strategy called for Russia and Britain to shoulder most of the burden for keeping peace in Europe while the United States would assume primary responsibility for maintaining security in the Western Hemisphere and the Pacific Ocean. Realizing the need for distant naval and air bases, American policymakers decided that the United States would have to maintain complete control of the islands taken from Japan during the sweep across the Pacific.

At first State Department planners did not think that France would play a major strategic role in the postwar world. Although the French had a huge army on the European continent when World War II began, they surrendered to Germany within six weeks after Hitler launched his blitzkrieg against the western front. Then they quickly began collaborating with both the Germans in Europe and the Japanese in Indochina. As a result, American diplomats regarded France as a third-rate power. They not only viewed the French with contempt because of their anemic war record, but they also blamed them for having caused an arms race in Europe. The United States had tried to get France to enter into an arms limitation agreement after World War I, but the French wanted to maintain military superiority on the continent, and many smaller European countries followed the French in building up their military forces. Recalling that Hitler had used the French refusal to disarm as an excuse for rearming Germany, American policymakers reasoned that France should be disarmed when the current conflict ended.

In addition, neither President Roosevelt nor his State Department advisers thought that the French had any claim to regain their Indochina empire. It is true that in an effort to encourage the French to resist their Nazi oppressors, American officials made public pronouncements favoring the return of all French colonies in the postwar period. In their private conversations, however, they made it quite clear that French Indochina should be administered by an international trusteeship. Sumner Welles lectured his colleagues in August 1942 that France had no inherent right to exploit Indochina. "There is a great moral question involved here," he observed, "and it is a question that will shape and color the history of the world after this war is over." President Roosevelt agreed. He told Secretary of State Cordell Hull in January 1944 that Indochina should not go back to France after the war. "France has had the country—thirty million inhabitants—for nearly one hundred years, and the people are worse off than they were at the beginning," Roosevelt complained. "France has milked it for one hundred years. The people of Indochina are entitled to something better than that."

American leaders hoped that their Russian allies would support their plans for the postwar era. After crossing through Eastern Europe, the

German Wehrmacht had penetrated deep into the Soviet Union. Millions of Russians were dying in defense of their homeland, and the Nazi armies were destroying thousands of Soviet factories. Seeking to reduce Russian fears about a future German invasion, American officials indicated that the United States would participate in policing the postwar world. They also thought that they might be able to win Soviet cooperation in Eastern Europe by offering American loans for Russian economic reconstruction. But the apprehension grew in Washington that the Russians would attempt to dominate the countries of Eastern Europe in order to satisfy their security needs. As they became increasingly concerned about the likelihood of Soviet expansion on the European continent if both Germany and France were disarmed, American leaders began thinking that France should resume her traditional position as a principal European power. By November 1944, they concluded that it would be necessary to rearm France with American weapons.

After reversing himself with regard to the issue of French militarism, President Roosevelt also began changing his mind about the question of French colonialism. Roosevelt wanted to postpone making a final decision concerning Indochina until the peace settlement following the war, but after the Yalta Conference in February 1945, there was growing evidence that the Soviet Union aimed to dominate Poland and other countries in Eastern Europe. In a discussion with the American ambassador in Paris on March 13, General Charles de Gaulle pointed to the Russian menace to Europe in an attempt to blackmail the United States into supporting the restoration of the French empire in Indochina. "The Russians are advancing apace," de Gaulle warned. "When Germany falls they will be upon us. If the public here comes to realize that you are against us in Indochina there will be terrific disappointment and nobody knows to what that will lead. We do not want to become Communist; we do not want to fall into the Russian orbit, but I hope that you do not push us into it." On the next day, Roosevelt told one of his close advisers that he would agree to let the French retain their colonies in Indochina with the proviso that independence would be the ultimate goal.

Although Roosevelt died a month later and Harry S Truman entered the White House, there was no sharp break in American policy toward Indochina. The State Department assumed the difficult task of attempting to reconcile American objectives in Europe and Asia. On the one hand, American diplomats thought that the United States should allow the French to keep their Indochina empire in order to maintain France as a military ally in the event of future Russian aggression in Europe. On the other hand, they believed that the United States should urge the French to grant local autonomy in their Southeast Asian possessions in order to prevent bloodshed in Vietnam. The State Department adopted these views on April 30 in a key policy paper that held that the United States should not oppose the restoration of French authority in Vietnam, Laos, and Cambodia but that American officials should seek assurance of French intentions to establish self-government in Indochina. A few days later, at the first meeting in San

Francisco to create the United Nations, Secretary of State Edward R. Stettinius told the French ambassador that the United States had never questioned the sovereignty of his country in Indochina.

The French were eager to reestablish control over their Indochina colonies. Although Germany had delivered a sharp blow to their national pride by defeating and occupying their country, the French did not simply want to reassert their imperial authority because of a psychological need to compensate for the humiliation they had suffered at the hands of Hitler. Cosmopolitan French leaders were prompted by rational calculations rather than emotional feelings. The influential directors of the Bank of Indochina, hoping to safeguard their huge investments, demanded protection for French economic interests in the Orient. Concerned about maintaining the cohesion of their overseas empire as a whole, policymakers in Paris subscribed to the "tenpin theory," which held that if one French colony won its independence nationalism would be encouraged elsewhere in the French empire. If the first tenpin tumbled, it would strike others, and they in turn could bring down the whole stand. More specifically, should Vietnam fall to the forces of nationalism, the French might lose not only their economically less important colonies in Southeast Asia (Cambodia and Laos) but also their more valuable possessions in North Africa (Morocco, Tunisia, and Algeria).

The French received quiet assistance from the United States when they decided to send an expeditionary force to Vietnam. Two weeks after Japan surrendered in August 1945, the State Department informed the American embassy in India that the United States had no thought of opposing the reestablishment of French control over Indochina. But the American government did not merely acquiesce in the French effort to reconquer Vietnam. Although the State Department published a statement declaring that the United States would not participate in the forceful imposition of French authority in Indochina, American policymakers acted in ways that ran counter to their public posture of neutrality. The United States permitted the French to keep without payment the Lend-Lease equipment that had been given to General de Gaulle before Japan capitulated and to use these military supplies in Indochina after removing all the American insignia. The United States also provided a large number of ships for the transportation of French troops and American weapons to Vietnam.

While the American government attempted to conceal these actions, Great Britain openly supported the French campaign to recolonize Indochina. The Allied powers had agreed, at the Potsdam Conference in July 1945, that after the war the responsibility for disarming and repatriating the Japanese troops in French Indochina would go to the British in the region south of the sixteenth parallel and to the Chinese in the area north of that parallel. The first British troops arrived in Saigon on September 12, and a small detachment of French soldiers accompanied them. General Douglas D. Gracey, the commander of the British forces, promptly ordered the Vietnamese inhabitants of Saigon to turn over their weapons. When the

Vietminh called a general strike in protest on September 17, General Gracey responded by proclaiming martial law, suspending all Vietnamese newspapers, and banning demonstrations of any kind. Gracey also released from prison and armed 1,400 French soldiers who had been interned by the Japanese after their March coup. The French troops immediately took over the public buildings in Saigon and stormed down the streets looking for Vietnamese to beat.

The brutal French rampage set the stage in southern Vietnam for the outbreak of a war for national liberation. The Vietminh called a general strike on September 24, and it was soon difficult to get food and supplies into Saigon. With insufficient British and French troops to restore order and expand his control beyond Saigon, General Gracey decided to use the Japanese soldiers he had been sent to disarm. Gracey threatened to treat Japanese officers as war criminals if they refused to order their men to help subdue the Vietminh. When the first military units arrived from France on October 5, they joined with the British and Japanese in cracking the blockade around Saigon and then in driving through the Mekong delta. The Vietminh retreated into the highlands and resorted to guerrilla tactics. The Japanese, after suffering heavy casualties in the intense fighting, were gradually disarmed and replaced by reinforcements from France. As their numbers grew, the French were able to administer the larger cities and provincial towns in southern Vietnam. But they could not prevent the Vietminh guerrillas from controlling the surrounding countryside.

In northern Vietnam, by contrast, the Vietminh exercised firm control of urban as well as rural areas. The government established by Ho Chi Minh in Hanoi following the revolution in August 1945 enjoyed widespread public support. Even Catholic priests backed the Vietminh regime after Ho initiated a reformist rather than a communist program. Besides allowing native landlords who had not collaborated with the foreign enemies to keep their large holdings, the Vietminh wiped out the salt monopoly, abolished the forced labor system, reduced land taxes, legalized unions, and instituted an eight-hour day. Gambling and prostitution were banned, the use of opium and alcohol was prohibited, and free classes were set up to teach the illiterate masses how to read and write. In addition to introducing these social and economic reforms, the Vietminh established a system of universal suffrage to bring more people into the political process. All men and women over eighteen years of age were given the right to vote on both the local and national level.

However, Vietminh efforts to implement this liberal program in northern Vietnam were suddenly disrupted on September 9 when the first Chinese forces arrived in Hanoi to disarm the Japanese. General Lu Han, a warlord from southern China, led between 125,000 and 150,000 troops into famine-stricken Tonkin. Swarming down from China like a ravenous horde of human locusts, these soldiers plundered and looted everything in their path. Their officers were even more destructive. Establishing a new exchange rate between the Chinese dollar and the Vietnamese piaster, General Lu Han made Chinese money worth three times more in Hanoi than at home. The Chinese then began using their overvalued currency to buy local businesses and property at little cost to themselves. Unlike the British in the south, Lu Han had no intention of helping the French regain control of northern Vietnam. Instead, he was willing to let the Vietminh govern Tonkin while his army gouged the whole region. Lu Han and his cohorts in southern China viewed the occupation of northern Vietnam as an opportunity to impose their own long-range program of economic exploitation in Indochina.

But the Nationalist government in China, headed by Generalissimo Chiang Kai-shek, had different ideas. Uninterested in controlling any part of Indochina on a permanent basis, Chiang viewed the Chinese occupation of northern Vietnam as a chance to extract political concessions from France. The Generalissimo succeeded in working out a deal with the French on the last day of February 1946. The French agreed to relinquish their old imperial right of extraterritoriality in China, and in return Chiang agreed to allow French troops to replace Chinese forces in Tonkin. A week later, on March 6, Ho Chi Minh signed an ambiguous treaty with the French. Ho agreed to permit 15,000 French soldiers to land peaceably in northern Vietnam but with the understanding that they would be gradually withdrawn during the next five years. The French agreed to recognize the Democratic Republic of Vietnam as a free state but only on the condition that it would remain part of the French Union. Finally, both parties agreed that there would be a referendum in Cochinchina to determine whether it would be reunited with the rest of Vietnam or remain a separate state in the French Union.

Ho Chi Minh signed this unpalatable treaty because he feared the Chinese more than the French. Chiang was determined to make his own agreement with France operative, and he therefore pressured Ho to allow the return of French troops into northern Vietnam. Not wanting to risk war with both France and China at the same time, Ho decided to compromise with the French in order to get the Chinese out of his country. Many of his colleagues charged him with making a bad deal, but Ho answered his critics with a lesson in geopolitics. "You fools!" he lectured. "Don't you realize what it means if the Chinese remain? Don't you remember your history? The last time the Chinese came, they stayed a thousand years. The French are foreigners. They are weak. Colonialism is dying. The white man is finished in Asia. But if the Chinese stay now, they will never go. As for me, I prefer to sniff French shit for five years than eat Chinese shit for the rest of my life."

But the French had no intention of abiding by the provisions of their treaty with Ho Chi Minh. The French refused to hold a plebiscite in Cochinchina because they realized that the vast majority of the peasants would vote for reunification with the rest of Vietnam. The French also rejected a Vietminh request for a cease-fire in southern Vietnam. In the spring of 1946, therefore, Ho traveled to France to try to work out a permanent settlement. But he could not find a middle ground. The French were not interested in making peace if it meant that they would lose any part of their Indochina empire, and Ho was not willing to make peace if it meant that he would have to sacrifice the independence of his country. Ho left France empty-handed after months of fruitless negotiations, and when he arrived home in the autumn of 1946 he found both sides preparing for a military showdown. While the French were building up their troop strength in Vietnam, General Vo Nguyen Giap had increased the size of his regular army from 30,000 to 60,000 men. The clash soon came. Using heavy naval guns, the French shelled Vietminh forces in the port of Haiphong on November 23, and when the Vietminh attacked French troops in Hanoi on December 19, a general war erupted.

After he had ignored repeated pleas from Ho Chi Minh for American support for Vietnamese independence, President Truman decided to assist France as full-scale fighting commenced in Tonkin. He and his advisers in the State Department chose not to exert pressure on Paris to make concessions that might end the bloodletting in Indochina for fear that France would refuse to help check the spread of Russian influence in Europe. Their Europe-first mentality was reinforced by their increasing concern about the communist leadership of the Vietminh. But while American policymakers preferred French colonialism over Vietnamese communism, they did not want to be charged with sponsoring Western imperialism in the Far East. Thus they tried to camouflage American aid for the French military campaign in Vietnam by channeling most of it indirectly through metropolitan France. The United States sent France huge amounts of money and large quantities of weapons ostensibly for French economic reconstruction and European strategic protection. But American officials realized that the French were using a considerable portion of this military and financial assistance to sustain their war effort in Indochina.

Yet the French, even with the aid they were receiving from the United States, still could not defeat the Vietminh. Beginning in December 1946, General Giap launched a series of intense attacks against French positions in the principal towns in Tonkin. But his poorly armed troops were no match for the overwhelming French firepower, and they were quickly driven out of the urban areas. The Vietminh then turned to guerrilla warfare in the north just as they had done earlier in the south, fighting chiefly at night when it was hard for the French to bomb them from the air or batter them with heavy ground artillery. Their hit-and-run tactics frustrated the French who had difficulty separating the guerrilla forces from the general population. The Vietminh frequently infiltrated villages and fired at French troops, and often the French responded by destroying the villages and killing many innocent civilians. As a result, more and more enraged peasants either joined the guerrillas or at least gave them information about French movements. So although the French were able to exercise their authority in most of the cities and towns throughout Vietnam, the Vietminh controlled over half of the countryside and over half of the population.

But the French were determined to crush the Vietminh. In October 1947, they mounted a major offensive against the Vietminh base area in the mountains north of Hanoi. The French captured large stores of Vietminh food and ammunition, yet they could not destroy their elusive foe. The guerrillas easily disappeared into the jungle when they heard the distant roar of French tanks and trucks rumbling along the narrow roads. Not only were the gains minimal, but the costs were prohibitive. The Vietminh staged ambush after ambush as the overextended French soldiers retreated slowly down the roads winding through the jungle-covered mountains of northern Tonkin. The French suffered heavy casualties: over 1,000 killed and over 3,000 wounded. The Vietminh were encouraged by their success, and early in 1948 they increased their attacks on isolated French outposts and exposed French convoys.

Unable to win a decisive battlefield victory, the French soon began to search for a political solution for their troubles in Indochina. They ultimately decided to install a puppet government in Vietnam under former Emperor Bao Dai with the hope of uniting all noncommunist nationalists behind the new regime. Bao Dai had fled to Hong Kong after the establishment of the Democrat Republic of Vietnam, but the French succeeded in persuading him to return home and assume the appearance of power. In an agreement with Bao Dai in June 1948, the French declared their recognition of Vietnamese independence within the framework of the French Union. Yet the status of Cochinchina remained unsettled, and Vietnamese nationalists were skeptical about French intentions. In a second agreement with Bao Dai in March 1949, the French promised that Cochinchina would be reunited with Annam and Tonkin, but they stipulated that both the military affairs and foreign relations of Vietnam must remain in their hands. Because the French were not willing to grant Bao Dai real independence, most noncommunist nationalists refused to back his regime. And since many of these conservatives concluded that they had no alternative but to follow Ho Chi Minh, the Vietminh achieved complete control of the Vietnamese resistance movement.

Despite the fact that Bao Dai lacked popular support, however, the Truman administration decided to back him. Red China and Soviet Russia opened diplomatic relations with the Democratic Republic of Vietnam in late January 1950, and a week later the United States formally recognized the Bao Dai puppet government. Still not satisfied, the French asked the United States for more aid for their military operations in Indochina. Secretary of State Dean G. Acheson worried that every franc that the French spent in Vietnam was one less franc they could use for the defense of Europe. Besides their desire to provide financial relief for France, Acheson and his colleagues in the State Department hoped to use American aid as a lever to compel the French not only to agree to the rearmament of West Germany but also to grant independence to the Bao Dai regime. But the French responded to American pressure by warning that without more support from the United States they might have to withdraw from Vietnam. Although the French remained intransigent, President Truman approved a $15 million aid package on March 10 to underwrite the French war effort in Indochina. With that seemingly small step, taken just a few months before the outbreak of the Korean War, the United States significantly moved from affording indirect to direct support for French colonialism in Indochina.

The American decision to cross that bridge grew out of concerns over a profound dislocation in the international economic system following World War II. The United States had enormously expanded its industrial capacity during the war, and American leaders realized the need for an enlarged export trade to avoid falling back into the depths of a depression. They also understood that the industrial countries of Europe needed to import capital goods from the United States to get their devastated factories running once again. But the European nations, victors and vanquished alike, did not have enough dollars to pay for the vital products that they needed to buy from the United States. American leaders referred to this global economic disequilibrium as the "dollar gap" in world trade. The United States was exporting far more than it was importing, and as the American export surplus grew the dollar gap widened. In fact, the trade imbalance ballooned from $7.8 billion in 1946 to $11.6 billion a year later.

European countries responded to their shortage of dollars by resorting to a wide range of controls over their international economic transactions. They aimed to conserve their dollars by using them only for essential capital goods and not on less important products. European nations not only limited the amount of their currency that could be converted into dollars for the purchase of American merchandise, but they also erected high tariffs to protect their domestic industries from American competition. Besides impeding the flow of trade across the Atlantic with monetary restrictions and customs barriers, Europeans entered into bilateral barter arrangements that closed more doors against American commerce. Government officials and business leaders in the United States feared that if the dollar gap problem remained unsolved, these measures of economic nationalism would become permanent and the European countries would turn toward either state capitalism or socialism. In other words, they worried that the European governments would manage their economics and isolate their countries from world markets and thereby shatter the American dream of a liberal capitalist international community.

The Marshall Plan, formally called the European Recovery Program (ERP), was the major American response to the crisis in world capitalism. Between 1948 and 1952, the United States provided $17 billion for European economic recovery. This huge sum was a gift rather than a loan to the nations of Western Europe. The United States government decided against lending the money because when the time arrived for the European countries to service their debts they would have fewer dollars available to buy surplus American commodities. By giving the money without demanding repayment, the United States government aimed to reduce the European dollar deficit and thereby sustain a high level of American exports. The basic goal of the Marshall Plan was to reconstruct the industries of Western Europe and make them competitive in the markets of the world. If the European countries became strong enough to sell abroad, they could earn foreign exchange needed to buy goods from the United States. American leaders hoped to make European manufacturers lean and mean by insisting that they cut wages and pay less in taxes. They also demanded that European governments reduce social welfare spending and deflate their currencies in order to lower the price of their industrial products.

The State Department assumed the difficult task of convincing Congress of the need for the Marshall Plan. American diplomats did not think that Congress would appropriate funds to support the postwar reconstruction of Europe for humanitarian reasons. Nor did they believe that Congress understood the serious nature of the international economic crisis. But they knew that Congress was concerned about military security. In soliciting financial aid for the European Recovery Program, therefore, State Department officials emphasized strategic factors rather than humanitarian or economic considerations. They not only pointed to the communist coup in Czechoslovakia as an example of Russian expansion into Eastern Europe, but they also warned that countries in Western Europe might become communist if they remained impoverished. Besides exaggerating the Red menace in Europe, American diplomats assured Congress that the Marshall Plan was only a temporary measure required to meet an emergency situation. They likewise asserted that the program was a great success when the time came each year for Congress to appropriate money for European recovery.

But they knew that their claims were not completely true. While industrial production was increasing in the nations of Western Europe, these countries did not have adequate export markets where they could acquire foreign exchange needed to cover their trade deficit. Not only did the Soviet Union close the doors of Eastern Europe against the products of Western Europe, but the United States also maintained relatively high tariff rates on European goods. Although the State Department advocated a liberal commercial policy, Congress refused to lower customs duties and thereby incur the wrath of protectionist interests. Nor could Congress be convinced to extend the Marshall Plan, which was due to expire in 1952. After receiving repeated assurances about the success of the European Recovery Program, Congress was in no mood to appropriate another $17 billion for the next four years. Secretary of State Acheson explained the situation to President Truman in February 1950: "Put in its simplest terms the problem is that: as ERP is reduced, and after its termination in 1952, how can Europe and other areas of the world obtain the dollars necessary to pay for a high level of United States exports, which is essential both to their own basic needs and to the well-being of the United States economy? This is the problem of the 'dollar gap' in world trade."

Before the dollar gap had created a crisis in American diplomacy, many government officials and business leaders hoped that China would become a golden market for the United States. They were captivated by the vision of a New China, containing 400 million customers, emerging from the ashes of World War II as a modern nation under the conservative leadership of Chiang Kai-shek. El Dorado beckoned from across the Pacific. But to keep the potentially vast China market free from the danger of foreign domination, the United States needed to declaw the Japanese dragon. General Douglas MacArthur was therefore commissioned to occupy Japan as soon as the war came to a close. Between 1945 and 1947, the American occupational authorities disarmed Japan and purged the military caste to prevent the old warlords from ever again threatening the peace of the Far East. The American authorities also aimed during the first two years of the military occupation to destroy the zaibatsu system of family capitalism in Japan and thereby render the interlocking monopolies less capable of manufacturing the sinews of war.

But the United States quickly reversed the course of its occupational policy in Japan when it became evident that Mao Tse-tung and his communist followers would emerge triumphant in China. Beginning in 1947, American administrators in Japan shifted their emphasis away from political reform and toward economic recovery. Policymakers in Washington decided that the Japanese industrial structure should be rebuilt so that Japan could replace China as a large market for American products. They wanted Japan to be part of the trilateral core in a new liberal capitalist world system: the United States would be the major workshop in the Western Hemisphere; Western Europe would be a regional workshop centered around West Germany; and Japan would be the industrial workshop in the Far East. American policymakers also decided that the Japanese should be rearmed so that Japan could replace China as an important military ally of the United States. They wanted Japan to serve as the sheet anchor in an island chain of American military bases around the Asian rim. In short, Japan was to play a key role as a junior economic and strategic partner in the evolving Pax Americana.

The United States implemented the so-called Dodge Plan in 1949 in an effort to promote the postwar reconstruction of Japan. Like the Marshall Plan for Western Europe, the basic goal of the Dodge Plan was to revive industrial production in Japan and to make Japanese goods competitive in world markets. The United States did not, however, funnel billions of dollars into Japan for industrial renovation. Unlike the Europeans, therefore, the Japanese were forced to finance their own economic rehabilitation. The Dodge Plan required severe cuts in wages and social welfare services and the reinvestment of profits in plant modernization. In addition, it demanded a balanced budget as well as the suppression of labor strikes to keep inflation down and prices low. But the Dodge Plan failed for the very same reason that the Marshall Plan proved inadequate. Although their industrial output increased, the Japanese lacked export outlets where they could acquire foreign exchange needed to purchase American goods. Thus Japan, like the countries of Western Europe, continued to suffer from a large dollar deficit.

The State Department advocated a huge rearmament program as a short-run solution to the global dollar gap problem. American companies would be less dependent upon foreign markets for civilian commodities if they received large military orders from the armed forces of the United

States. Massive military spending would compensate both for the lack of foreign demand for American products and for the tariff wall that prevented foreign countries from obtaining a sufficient outlet for civilian goods in the United States. European countries and Japan could earn dollars if the armed forces of the United States purchased military hardware from overseas sources. In short, the offshore procurement of military equipment would replace foreign economic aid as a way of getting dollars to Europe and Japan. The State Department succeeded in persuading Congress to appropriate funds for a vast military buildup by playing upon fears of an international communist conspiracy to dominate the whole world. But the Mutual Security Program, conceived prior to the Korean War, was intended more as an interim solvent for the international economic crisis than as a check against Soviet expansion.

The State Department simultaneously called for the reintegration of colonial areas into a liberal international trading system as the long-run solution to the dollar gap problem. Before World War II, an important triangular trade pattern had evolved: the United States used dollars to buy raw materials from colonial areas; they in turn used these dollars to purchase industrial goods from European countries; and then they used the same dollars to pay for American products. For example, the United States purchased large quantities of rubber and tin from British Malaya with dollars, and British Malaya bought manufactured articles from Great Britain with these dollars, and finally the United Kingdom paid for American commodities with the same dollars. State Department officials hoped to reestablish this kind of triangular trade flow in order to restore international economic equilibrium, and they succeeded in getting federal funds earmarked for increasing the production of foodstuffs and raw materials in colonial areas. The precedent for this form of economic assistance was set in February 1950 when the Export-Import Bank received authorization to lend Indonesia $100 million to buy American equipment needed for the development of natural resources.

American policymakers believed that the expansion of primary commodity production in Southeast Asia was particularly important for the restoration of Japanese prosperity. They hoped that Japan would be able not only to obtain foodstuffs and raw materials in Southeast Asia without paying dollars for these essential imports but also to earn dollars by exporting manufactured goods to Southeast Asia. American leaders thought that in some parts of Southeast Asia the introduction of more irrigation would allow for the cultivation of two rice crops per year instead of the prevailing single crop. If these areas doubled their rice yield, they might also double their purchases of industrial products from Japan. Aiming to stimulate mineral and agricultural production throughout Southeast Asia, American economic experts estimated that by 1955 the region could absorb more than 50 percent of Japan's total exports. China had been Japan's most important market in the Far East before World War II, but after China fell to communism in 1949, American diplomats feared that Japan, if denied access to noncommunist markets in Southeast Asia, might become economically

dependent upon Red China and be lured into making a political accommodation with the communist bloc. Thus they hoped that Southeast Asia
would become Japan's major market in the Orient.

But Southeast Asia lacked political stability. Although the economic
task of increasing the production of primary commodities in that part of the
world would not require a large amount of American capital, the United
States faced a difficult political problem there. Communist rebels and conservative nationalists were challenging colonial rule in French Indochina,
British Malaya, and the Dutch East Indies. Regarding the military pacification of the region as a prerequisite for the economic revival of Japan,
American policymakers concluded that the United States would have to
help contain the rising tide of revolution in Southeast Asia. Before the
Japanese or anyone else could walk the commercial streets of Southeast
Asia, they repeatedly argued, those streets would have to be made safe from
communism. A joint report, made by the Departments of State and Defense
in January 1950, went to the heart of the matter: "Continuing, or even maintaining, Japan's economic recovery depends upon keeping Communism out
of Southeast Asia, promoting economic recovery there and in further developing those countries, together with Indonesia, the Philippines, Southern
Korea and India as the principal trading areas for Japan."

Concerned about Japan's need for noncommunist markets in Southeast
Asia, officials in both the State Department and the Pentagon regarded
French Indochina as vitally important to the political stability of the entire
region. They realized that Vietnam, Cambodia, and Laos could absorb only
a small amount of Japanese goods, but they perceived these French colonies
as the linchpin in the long crescent that stretched from Japan all the way to
India. French Indochina, while possessing little intrinsic commercial value
for Japan, occupied a key strategic position between Red China to the north
and the vast Malaya Archipelago to the south. Following the fall of China
to communism in 1949, American policymakers subscribed to what came to
be called the "domino theory," which held that if the Vietminh defeated the
French in Indochina the cancer of communism would spread throughout the
whole region. Guerrilla forces in other parts of Southeast Asia would not
only be encouraged by the success of their neighbors in overcoming
European colonialism, but they would also be able to obtain weapons from
nearby communist countries. American leaders therefore feared that if the
Vietnam domino fell to communism, it would tip over others until finally
the whole row would be knocked down.

Such dire prospects generated a debate in the State Department over the
wisdom of supplying direct American aid for the French military campaign
in Indochina. A few State Department officials were pessimistic about the
chances for a French victory because the Vietminh had widespread backing.
Noting that the French were fighting against a large portion of the
Vietnamese population, these skeptics concluded that the French would
ultimately lose even if they received a massive dose of American financial
and technical assistance. But Secretary of State Acheson and most of his
top aides argued that the United States should back the French and Bao Dai

even if the odds were heavily against them. While acknowledging that Bao Dai lacked popular support, they assumed that he was the only alternative to Ho Chi Minh. Acheson and his followers noted that Ho aimed to establish a communist government in Vietnam after he achieved his nationalist aspirations. They feared that if the French were driven out of Vietnam the rest of Southeast Asia would be in grave danger of succumbing to the forces of communism. They also worried that the French would object to American plans to include West Germany in a multilateral European military force if the United States refused to subsidize their war effort in Indochina.

Secretary Acheson and his colleagues in the State Department were determined to resist not only the expansion of Russian influence in Europe but also the spread of indigenous communism in Southeast Asia. They understood that communism was not monolithic and that all communist leaders did not take orders from Moscow. Marshal Tito, for example, had established an independent communist regime in Yugoslavia that remained free from Soviet domination. Acheson admitted in May 1949 that Vietnam might in fact develop as a "National Communist State on the pattern of Yugoslavia," but he thought that the United States should explore that possibility "only if every other avenue closed." While clearly preferring the puppet Bao Dai to a Titoist Ho Chi Minh, Acheson envisioned three different scenarios for the Indochina War: the Vietminh might defeat the French and become tools of the Kremlin; the Vietminh might win and establish an independent communist government in Vietnam that would remain free from Russian control; or the French might emerge victorious and stamp out the germ of communism before it infected the whole region. Given these choices, Acheson and his associates favored French colonialism rather than either international or indigenous communism.

The State Department believed that it was imperative for economic reasons to prevent any kind of communism from sweeping across Southeast Asia. American diplomats feared that even if Asian communists steered clear of Soviet political influence, they would follow the Russian model for economic growth. By emphasizing industrial development rather than the production of primary commodities, communist countries in Southeast Asia would become more self-sufficient and less dependent upon foreign commerce. Thus the spread of economic nationalism along with indigenous communism would restrict the opportunity for Japan and the capitalist countries of Western Europe to exchange manufactured goods for foodstuffs and raw materials produced in Southeast Asia. Prompted by such thoughts, the State Department decided in February 1950 to recommend direct American financial support for the French war effort in Indochina. Acheson and his colleagues urged that the United States should furnish money but not soldiers so that the war could be fought with American equipment and French troops. As already noted, President Truman gave his approval on March 10 to the proposal to provide the French with $15 million for their military operations in Indochina.

The Korean War, which began three months later, reinforced the

American determination to draw the line against the advance of communism in Southeast Asia. Although the conflict in Korea took American policymakers by surprise, it actually helped them accomplish their basic objectives in the Far East. The hostilities in Korea made it easier for the Truman administration to get Congress to appropriate larger and larger sums of money to fund the French struggle against the Vietminh. They also provided the United States with the opportunity to purchase more and more military equipment from Japan. But while the Japanese were temporarily able to earn dollars by selling military supplies to the American army fighting in Korea, President Truman and his advisers continued to regard Japanese economic integration with Southeast Asia as the permanent solution to the dollar gap problem in Japan. They likewise continued to worry that the Japanese would be pulled into the communist political and economic orbit if they were denied access to noncommunist markets in Southeast Asia. "Communist control of all Southeast Asia," a State Department memorandum warned in March 1952, "would remove the chief potential area for Japanese commercial development, and would so add to the already powerful mainland pulls upon Japan as to make it dubious that Japan could refrain from reaching an accommodation with the Communist bloc."

A Strategic Perspective on U.S. Involvement

ROBERT J. MCMAHON

Indochina became crucial to Truman administration planners by the late 1940s because of a perceived relationship between stability in Southeast Asia and economic recovery in Western Europe and Japan. U.S. intervention in Indochina formed part of a carefully conceived, if ultimately flawed, effort to preserve the economic resources of Southeast Asia for the West while denying them to the communist powers. It grew, in short, from America's overall Cold War strategy for containing Soviet power and influence, a strategy that led to a blurring of distinctions between core and periphery and elevated Southeast Asia into a national security concern of the first order. . . .

The future of French Indochina was but one of a bewildering galaxy of problems that required an early decision by the new president [Harry S Truman]. At first glance, this particular problem appeared a good deal less complex than most. During his last months in office, Franklin D. Roosevelt had assured French authorities, as he had their British and Dutch counterparts, that Washington would not oppose the reimposition of European control over colonial territories occupied by Japan during the war. Certain that he was simply following a well-established policy for the Japanese-

From Robert J. McMahon, "Harry S Truman and the Roots of U.S. Involvement in Indochina, 1945–1953," in David L. Anderson, ed., pp. 21–38 in *Shadow on the White House: Presidents and The Vietnam War, 1945–1975*, 1993 by the University Press of Kansas. Used by permission of the publisher.

occupied areas of Southeast Asia, Truman quickly conveyed the same message to French, British, and Dutch officials.

Truman's reassurances were entirely consistent with those given earlier by Roosevelt; they were meant to signal continuity, not change. Nonetheless, Truman's straightforward recognition of the colonial powers' claims to territorial sovereignty in Southeast Asia obscured the more complex reality surrounding the U.S. stance toward colonialism. Roosevelt's various wartime plans and pronouncements regarding European colonies in general, and French Indochina in particular, were sufficiently contradictory that Truman actually inherited a much more ambiguous legacy than he could possibly have realized. The emergence in September 1945 of an independent Vietnamese nationalist regime, demanding international recognition and framing its case in terms of American wartime statements and promises, drove home the complexities and contradictions of the Roosevelt legacy.

During the early years of World War II, Roosevelt and other top officials declared with some regularity that the United States supported the principle of self-determination for all peoples. The president, who took the lead on this issue, often prodded European officials about the need to commit themselves to a timetable for eventual colonial independence. Much to the discomfiture of America's European allies, Roosevelt and Secretary of State Cordell Hull proposed that a trusteeship system be established in the post-war period through which different developed nations, acting as trustees, would prepare local elites to assume the responsibilities of self-government. Trusteeship represented a compromise solution to Roosevelt; he believed that it would guarantee future independence while avoiding the danger of a premature transfer of power to inexperienced indigenous rulers.

Roosevelt's plans for the colonial world represented a nearly indistinguishable blend of American ideals and American interests. The president found the conditions under which so many subject peoples lived appallingly primitive. After passing through the British colony of Gambia in early 1942, for example, he railed against the poverty and disease he had witnessed everywhere, referring to the dependency as a "hellhole" and calling the experience "the most horrible thing I have ever seen in my life." Although Roosevelt never visited Indochina, the lack of personal contact did not prevent the president from berating the colony's French overlords in equally harsh terms. In fact, he considered the French the least enlightened of all the colonial powers and often singled out for particular censure their sorry record in Indochina. Despite "nearly one hundred years" of French rule in Indochina, he complained on one occasion, "the people are worse off than they were at the beginning."

Roosevelt's genuine humanitarian impulses coexisted with a more practical strain. The preservation of the colonial system stood as an impediment to the kind of world order most conducive to U.S. interests. Roosevelt was convinced that the imperial order, with its restrictive trading practices, economic exploitation, and political repression, would simply sow the seeds for future instability within the colonies and future conflicts among the great powers. The United States sought a more open world, one characterized by free trade and democratic principles. Only such a world, according to the president and his chief advisers, would ensure the peace, prosperity, stability, and security that the United States sought. Roosevelt's proselytizing on behalf of a more liberal approach to dependent areas thus bespoke an unsentimental calculation of national interests as much as it did a revulsion against imperialism's excesses.

Before his death, Roosevelt significantly modified his approach to colonial questions. Late in 1944 he jettisoned trusteeship planning for Indochina and other areas, offering instead a promise not to interfere with the reimposition of colonial rule in Southeast Asia. This policy shift reflected the president's essential pragmatism in the face of a series of complex, cross-cutting interests. From its inception, his trusteeship formula had generated heated rebukes from the colonial powers. British Prime Minister Winston Churchill, Roosevelt's most important ally, made clear on numerous occasions his unbending opposition to U.S. tampering with European colonies. Free French leader General Charles de Gaulle was no less adamant in opposing U.S. plans. The Roosevelt administration feared that an aggressive advocacy of trusteeship, in the face of such angry and unified opposition, might create intolerable strains within the wartime alliance and might jeopardize postwar cooperation in Western Europe, the most vital region of all to the United States. Defense needs also militated against persisting in an anticolonial campaign. Planners in the War and Navy Departments insisted that U.S. national security required exclusive control over the Japanese-mandated islands in the Pacific. With the president's concurrence, they intended to establish a permanent U.S. military presence throughout the Pacific in order to add depth and flexibility to the nation's air and naval capability. That high-priority goal, according to military experts, could not be compromised by trusteeship principles that could easily be applied to strategic U.S.-occupied territory as well as to European colonies. Broader political, strategic, and military concerns, in short, necessitated a tactical retreat from earlier anticolonial pronouncements and plans.

Ho Chi Minh's declaration of an independent Vietnamese state on September 2, 1945, brought to a head many of the contradictions embedded in the Roosevelt administration's colonial policy. Quoting liberally from the American Declaration of Independence in his own independence proclamation, the veteran nationalist leader was in effect offering the opening bid in what would prove to be a concerted, if ill-fated, campaign for U.S. backing. Later that day, a Vietnamese band joined the independence-day festivities in Hanoi with a rendition of the "Star-Spangled Banner." U.S. Army officers listened from the reviewing stand as a series of Vietnamese nationalists echoed Ho with their own glowing tributes to the United States' anticolonial heritage. The previous evening Ho had invited two members of the Office of Strategic Services (OSS) for dinner. After thanking them for the valuable material assistance rendered by the United States to his guerrilla movement during the war, he appealed for "fraternal collaboration" in the future.

A shrewd tactician with the instincts of a born politician, the man previously known as Nguyen Ai Quoc was a communist, a revolutionary, but above all a Vietnamese nationalist. He sensed that the momentous events set in motion by the Japanese occupation of Indochina and the Nazi conquest of France had created a historic opportunity for the realization of his lifelong dream: independence from French rule. From the outset Ho calculated that the United States, if it remained true to its wartime statements, could become his most useful ally. That view was not born of naiveté. It grew, instead, from the mutually beneficial collaboration between U.S. military and intelligence officers and Vietminh guerrillas that had taken place in the jungles of northern Tonkin during the struggle against Japan. It was nourished by the Vietnamese leader's belief that the United States' global interests would compel it to oppose the reestablishment of French colonialism.

Ho's assessment was not an unrealistic one. After all, Roosevelt had calculated that U.S. interests would best be served by the progressive evolution of colonial dependencies into self-governing states; the president's revulsion against French misrule in Indochina ran especially deep. Ho can hardly be faulted for failing to anticipate the shift in U.S. policy that occurred shortly before Roosevelt's death. Unaware that first Roosevelt and then Truman had reassured European allies that the United States would not block the reestablishment of the status quo antebellum, Ho appealed to Truman for recognition in a series of personal letters. "The carrying out of the Atlantic Charter and San Francisco Charter," he declared hopefully in one message, "implies the eradication of imperialism and all forms of colonial oppression."

Truman never responded to Ho's appeals. Neither he nor any of his top advisers ever seriously contemplated direct support for or diplomatic recognition of the Democratic Republic of Vietnam. To do so would have represented a sharp break with the policy Truman had inherited from Roosevelt in an area that ranked relatively low on the overall scale of U.S. priorities. Such a course must have seemed inconceivable to a president still overwhelmed by the myriad responsibilities of his new office. On August 29, during a White House meeting with de Gaulle, Truman signaled that there would be no such break. He reassured France's provisional president that the United States recognized the right of French authorities to reestablish sovereignty in Indochina. Ho's declaration of independence just three days later did not occasion a searching reexamination of that stance. Despite widespread respect for Ho's nationalist credentials and leadership abilities among U.S. intelligence and military personnel serving in Indochina, top U.S. policymakers were far more concerned with the needs and viewpoints of France. To alienate France, a country whose active support in Europe was crucial, would have undermined the overall foreign policy goals of the Truman administration. To do so on behalf of a national independence movement in remote Southeast Asia would have represented the height of diplomatic folly.

The United States instead pursued a policy of neutrality toward the colonial rebellion in Indochina, much as it did toward a contemporaneous colonial revolt in the Dutch East Indies. The Truman administration never questioned the legal right of the European sovereigns to reestablish control in Vietnam and Indonesia. At the same time, it realized that sheer pragmatism necessitated some concessions to indigenous nationalist movements. A harsh policy of political and military repression by the colonial powers would probably endanger not only the peace and order that the United States sought in Southeast Asia but the economic recovery and political stability that it sought in Western Europe.

Throughout 1945 and 1946, U.S. diplomats consequently urged their French counterparts to negotiate in good faith with Ho and his chief lieutenants in order to avert an outright conflict that would serve the interests of neither party. Washington applauded the conclusion of a preliminary Franco-Vietnamese accord on March 6, 1946, since it seemed to open the way for an amicable political compromise. Like Roosevelt administration planners before them, Truman administration analysts believed that only a more liberal approach to colonial issues, one pointing toward eventual self-government, could establish the essential preconditions for order, stability, and prosperity in the developing world.

Those broad principles served as a general guidepost for U.S. policymakers during the four years following Vietnam's proclamation of independence. Although the principles were certainly sound, they produced little more than frustration for the Truman administration in a period punctuated by false hopes, failed negotiations, and savage fighting. The promise of the March 6 accord soon gave way to stalemated negotiations at Dalat and Paris. Although he was willing to accept less than immediate independence for all of Vietnam, Ho could not condone the retention of French supremacy in the southern province of Cochinchina. To this ardent patriot, Tonkin, Annam, and Cochinchina formed one unified country; he would rather fight than accept division. And fight he did. Following abortive talks at Fontainebleau in the summer of 1946, the imperatives of diplomacy yielded inevitably to preparations for war. In November, hostilities erupted with shattering suddenness. Following a vicious French naval bombardment of Haiphong that claimed more than 6,000 Vietnamese lives, Ho Chi Minh and his supporters fled Hanoi. The French moved quickly to establish their administrative control in the north, and the Vietminh mobilized for another guerrilla struggle. Conflict soon engulfed much of Vietnam. No one at the time could have imagined how many years would pass before peace returned to that embittered land.

U.S. analysts privately expressed dismay with France's resort to the use of force. A colonial war of reconquest represented a regrettable return to the discredited methods of the past. Even worse, the French seemed to lack the military power necessary to accomplish their goals. John Carter Vincent, director of the State Department's Office of Far Eastern Affairs, offered a pessimistic appraisal of French prospects to Under Secretary of State Dean Acheson in a memorandum of December 23. "The French themselves admit that they lack the military strength to reconquer the country," he observed. Possessing "inadequate forces, with public opinion sharply at odds, [and] with a government rendered largely ineffective through internal division," the French were embarking on a most unpromising course. "Given the present elements in the situation," Vincent predicted, "guerilla warfare may continue indefinitely."

For all of its misgivings about French policy in Indochina, the State De-partment carefully avoided open criticism of its European partner. On December 23, Acheson told French Ambassador Henri Bonnet of Washington's deep concern about "the unhappy situation in which the French find themselves." Calling existing conditions in Indochina "highly inflammatory," the under secretary stressed the importance of reaching a settlement as soon as possible. Only the most sensitive of diplomats could have read even an implied criticism into Acheson's mild remarks. Indeed, he made it clear that even though the United States had no wish to offer its services as a mediator, it did want the French government "to know that we are ready and willing to do anything which it might consider helpful in the circumstances."

Nineteen forty-seven brought no respite to the fighting in Indochina— and no essential change in U.S. policy toward the conflict. The Truman administration continued to view French military exertions as a misguided effort to turn back the clock. In a February 3 cable to the U.S. Embassy in Paris, Secretary of State George C. Marshall expressed "increasing concern" with the stalemate in Indochina. He deplored both the "lack [of] French understanding [for] the other side" and their "dangerously outmoded colonial outlook and methods." At the same time, Washington displayed no inclination to intervene directly in yet another nettlesome regional conflict and even less interest in exerting unwanted pressure on an invaluable ally. "We have only [the] very friendliest feelings toward France," Marshall noted, "and we are anxious in every way we can to support France in her fight to regain her economic, political and military strength and to restore herself as in fact one of [the] major powers of [the] world." The enunciation in mid-1947 of the containment strategy and the Marshall Plan just underscored France's indispensability to the broader foreign policy aims of the Truman administration. Both initiatives were conceived as part of the administration's overall strategy for containing Soviet influence and power by fostering the economic recovery and political stability of Western Europe. In the intensifying Cold War struggle between the United States and the Soviet Union, no area was more vital than Western Europe and no country more crucial than France.

In view of its transcendent importance to the United States, France's persistence in a colonial conflict that most U.S. experts believed would leave it drained and weakened posed a fundamental dilemma to Truman and his senior advisers, one that they never adequately resolved. Precisely how could the United States help France recognize that its own self-interest required a nonmilitary solution in Indochina? And what specific course of action should the United States urge France to pursue? The dilemma was posed far more easily than it could be resolved. "Frankly we have no solution of [the] problem to suggest," Marshall conceded. "It is basically [a] matter for [the] two parties to work out [for] themselves."

The communist character of the Vietnamese independence movement and the absence of viable noncommunist alternatives further clouded an already murky picture. U.S. officials were keenly aware that the movement's outstanding figure had a long record as a loyal communist. Not only had Ho Chi Minh received political training in Moscow, but he had served for decades as a dedicated Comintern agent outside Indochina. Most U.S. diplomatic and defense officials worried that if Ho prevailed over the French, it would lead to "an independent Vietnam State which would be run by orders from Moscow." A handful of junior State Department officials dissented from that analysis, advancing the argument that Ho's ardent nationalism transcended any fraternal links to the Kremlin's rulers; they speculated that he might even emerge as an Asian Tito. Such unorthodox views never permeated the upper reaches of the Truman administration, however. Most senior policymakers calculated that, regardless of Ho's undeniably powerful credentials as a Vietnamese nationalist, the establishment of a Vietminh-dominated regime would benefit the Soviet Union. Moreover, other nations would almost certainly view the emergence of such a regime as a defeat for the West.

Yet, as the State Department acknowledged in September 1948, "we are all too well aware of the unpleasant fact that Communist Ho Chi Minh is the strongest and perhaps the ablest figure in Indochina and that any suggested solution which excludes him is an expedient of uncertain outcome." Much to Washington's consternation, the French search for an alternative figure with whom to negotiate produced only the weak and vacillating former emperor Bao Dai. Charles Reed, the U.S. consul in Saigon, reminded Washington that "the reputed playboy of Hong Kong" commanded little support. Bao Dai counted among his followers only "those whose pockets will be benefited if he should return." Notwithstanding U.S. reservations and objections, the French promoted the pliant Bao Dai as their answer to Ho Chi Minh. Most U.S. analysts viewed France's "Bao Dai solution" as a transparent effort to retain colonial control; they saw it as confirmation of the bankruptcy of French policy. The restoration of Bao Dai as titular head of an "impotent puppet Gov[ernmen]t" prompted concern within the State Department that the democracies might be forced to "resort [to] monarchy as [a] weapon against Communism."

In September 1948 the State Department offered an internal assessment of U.S. policy vis-à-vis the Indochina dispute, remarkable both for its candor and for its self-critical tone. "The objectives of US policy towards Indochina have not been realized," it admitted flatly. "Three years after the termination of war a friendly ally, France, is fighting a desperate and apparently losing struggle in Indochina. The economic drain of this warfare on French recovery, while difficult to estimate, is unquestionably large. The Communist control in the nationalist movement has been increased during this period. US influence in Indochina and Asia has suffered as a result." U.S. objectives could be attained only if France satisfied "the nationalist aspirations of the peoples of Indochina." Yet a series of fundamental impediments bedeviled all U.S. efforts to nudge the French in that direction: the communist coloration of the nationalist movement; the seeming dearth of popular noncommunist alternatives; the unwillingness of the Truman administration to offer unsolicited advice to an ally on such an emotional issue; Washington's "immediate interest in maintaining in power a friendly French government, to assist in the furtherance of our aims in Europe"; and, perhaps most basic of all, the administration's "inability to suggest any practicable solution of the Indochina problem."

Over the next year and a half, the Truman administration engaged in a wide-ranging reexamination of U.S. policy toward Southeast Asia. A series of unsettling global developments, which deepened the administration's appreciation for Southeast Asia's strategic and economic salience, lent urgency to the internal debate. As a result of its reassessment, the Truman administration abandoned its quasi-neutral approach to the Indochina dispute in favor of a policy of open support for the French. On February 7, 1950, Secretary of State Acheson formally announced U.S. recognition of the Bao Dai regime, the nominally independent entity established by France the previous year, and its sister regimes in Cambodia and Laos. Emphasizing U.S. concern that neither security, democracy, nor independence could exist "in any area dominated by Soviet imperialism," he promised economic aid and military equipment for France and the Associated States of Vietnam, Cambodia, and Laos.

The decision to lend U.S. money, equipment, and prestige to France's struggle against the Vietminh cannot be understood without reference to the wider forces shaping the foreign policy of the Truman administration in late 1949 and early 1950. Those forces led both to a searching reevaluation of the world situation and to a fundamental reassessment of U.S. tactics and strategy. In the six months preceding its commitment to the French, the Truman administration came face to face with probably the gravest global crisis of the entire postwar era. In the summer of 1949 the Soviet Union exploded its first atomic device, putting an end to the United States' brief atomic monopoly and posing a host of unprecedented challenges to U.S. national security. Truman and other leading officials feared that possession of the bomb might incline the Kremlin to take greater risks in an effort to extend its global reach and power. The collapse of the U.S.-backed Kuomintang regime in China and the establishment of a communist government in its stead provoked additional fears in U.S. policy circles. Events in China also gave rise to a round of nasty finger-pointing at home; a swelling chorus of Republican critics blamed the president personally for China's fate. Events outside the communist bloc appeared even more ominous to America's Cold Warriors. By the end of the year it was increasingly evident that the economic recoveries of Western Europe and Japan had stalled badly. U.S. decision makers feared that continued economic stagnation in those lands would generate social unrest and political instability, conditions that might prove a fertile breeding ground for communism.

Taken together, those developments portended a potentially catastrophic threat to U.S. national security. As the communist world gained strength and self-confidence, the United States and its allies seemed poised to lose theirs. To Truman and his senior strategists, the stakes in this global struggle for power were extraordinarily high, involving nothing less than the physical safety and economic health of the United States. "The loss of Western Europe or of important parts of Asia or the Middle East," wrote Acheson, "would be a transfer of potential from West to East, which, depending on the area, might have the gravest consequences in the long run." By early 1950, top U.S. diplomatic and defense officials concentrated much of their energy on defusing this hydra-headed crisis by resuscitating the economies of Western Europe and Japan and regaining the West's political and psychological momentum in the Cold War.

U.S. policymakers recognized that a multiplicity of links tied developments in Indochina to this daunting string of global crises. In Asia, the administration's overriding objective was to orient a politically stable and economically prosperous Japan toward the West. "Were Japan added to the Communist bloc," Acheson warned, "the Soviets would acquire skilled manpower and industrial potential capable of significantly altering the balance of world power." The secretary of state and other leading officials were convinced that Japan needed the markets and raw materials of Southeast Asia in order to spark its industrial recovery. The revitalization of Asia's powerhouse economy would create the conditions necessary for stability and prosperity within both Japan and Southeast Asia. U.S. geopolitical and economic interests in this regard formed a seamless web. Truman administration planners envisioned a revitalized Japan emerging once again as the dynamic hub of commercial activity throughout Asia. Achievement of this objective would give a much-needed boost to the regional and global economic systems, thwart communism's military threat and ideological appeal, and ensure Tokyo's loyalty to the West. According to the logic subscribed to by nearly all top U.S. strategists, Japan's economic health demanded that peace and stability prevail throughout Southeast Asia. Consequently, the Vietminh insurgency in Indochina, which posed the most serious threat to regional peace and stability, had to be vanquished with the greatest possible dispatch.

For a somewhat different set of reasons, U.S. strategic and economic interests in Europe pointed in the same direction. By the end of 1949, the optimism generated by the Marshall Plan on both sides of the Atlantic had long since dissolved. The unprecedented commitment of U.S. resources to the economic rehabilitation of Western Europe had not yet brought the dramatic transformation that the Truman administration so desperately sought. Instead, the United States' most important allies found themselves facing a frightening panoply of economic and political difficulties. The increasingly costly war in Indochina stretched France's resources to the breaking point, severely hampering its contribution to the European recovery program. Although West Germany's economic performance was not quite so dismal, U.S. officials continued to fret about the fragility of Bonn's commitment to the West. Certain that the ultimate success of the Marshall Plan required the reintegration of Germany into Europe, U.S. planners agonized about how to ease France's understandable fears about a resurgent Germany.

The enormous trade and currency imbalance between the United States and its European economic partners posed an even more immediate threat to U.S. interests. This so-called dollar gap continued to grow, reaching over $3.5 billion by the middle of 1949, and posed a particularly painful problem for Great Britain. "Unless firm action is taken," British Foreign Secretary Ernest Bevin implored Acheson in July 1949, "I fear much of our work on Western Union and the Atlantic pact will be undermined and our progress in the Cold War will be halted." Experts in Washington shared Bevin's fears. Former Assistant Secretary of State William Clayton spoke for many when he conjured up the image of "the patient little man in the Kremlin [who] sits rubbing his hands and waiting for the free world to collapse in a sea of economic chaos."

By early 1950, the Truman administration's senior planners were convinced that Western Europe's troubles, like Japan's, could be aided by the stabilization and pacification of Southeast Asia. France, Great Britain, and Holland had avoided a dollar gap problem during the prewar years through the establishment of triangular trading patterns in which their colonial dependencies in Southeast Asia earned dollars through the sale of raw materials to the United States. The health of the British sterling bloc had grown unusually dependent on American purchases of rubber and tin from Malaya. The disruption of traditional trading patterns as a result of raging colonial conflicts—an insurgency erupted in Malaya in 1948, joining those that already wracked Indochina and the East Indies—thus compounded the already desperate fiscal conditions plaguing Western Europe. The Truman administration's initial commitment to Southeast Asia, then, must also be placed within this context. U.S. officials believed that financial and material assistance to the French in Indochina would abet military pacification and political stabilization in Southeast Asia. At the same time, it would permit a more active French contribution to European recovery.

Political pressures reinforced Truman's inclination to link Southeast Asian developments to larger issues. The ferocity of the partisan assaults on Truman in the wake of Chiang Kai-shek's (Jaing Jieshi's) collapse increased the political pressure on the president to show greater resolution vis-à-vis the communist challenge in Asia. Aid to the French in Indochina enabled the beleaguered Truman to answer his critics' charges by demonstrating a determination to hold the line against further communist advances *somewhere*. It is of no small significance that the initial U.S. dollar commitment of February 1950 was drawn from funds earmarked by the president's congressional critics for the containment of communism within "the general area of China."

More diffuse psychological considerations also shaped the U.S. commitment to Southeast Asia. Administration analysts were convinced that the belief in many corners of the world was that historical momentum lay with communism and not with the West. U.S. strategists feared that such a perception, whether rooted in fact or fantasy, might take on a life of its own, producing a bandwagon effect that would have an extremely pernicious impact on U.S. global interests. In the words of NSC-68, an April 1950 administration document providing a comprehensive reappraisal of U.S. national security, the Soviet Union sought "to demonstrate that force and the will to use it are on the side of the Kremlin [and] that those who lack it are decadent and doomed." Because the fighting in Indochina was widely viewed as a contest between East and West, however erroneous that view might have been, the challenge it posed to Washington was almost as much psychological as it was geostrategic. State Department and Pentagon officials agreed that the U.S. commitment in Indochina helped meet that psychological challenge by demonstrating to adversaries and allies alike Washington's strength, resolution, and determination. The Truman administration's concern with such intangible matters as the United States' prestige, image, and reputation—in a word, its credibility—thus also entered into the complex policy calculus that made U.S. intervention in Southeast Asia seem as logical as it was unavoidable.

With the outbreak of the Korean War in June 1950, the strategic, economic, political, and psychological fears undergirding that initial commitment intensified. Convinced that Moscow and Beijing had become even more dangerously opportunistic foes, Truman and his senior advisers redoubled their efforts to contain the communist threat on every front. At the same time, they pursued with even greater vigor initiatives designed to strengthen the U.S. sphere of influence. Those vital global priorities demanded nothing less than an all-out effort to contain the communist threat to Southeast Asia, a threat manifested most immediately and most seriously by the Vietminh insurgency. Virtually all national security planners in the Truman administration agreed that Indochina was the key to Southeast Asia. If the Vietminh succeeded in routing the French, according to an analysis prepared by the Joint Strategic Survey Committee in November, "this would bring about almost immediately a dangerous condition with respect to the internal security of all of the other countries of Southeast Asia, as well as the Philippines and Indonesia, and would contribute to their probable eventual fall to communism." With uncommon unanimity, U.S. civilian and military policymakers agreed that a communist triumph in Indochina would represent a strategic nightmare for the United States. It would probably destabilize the entire region, disrupt important trading ties to Japan and Western Europe, deny to the West and make available to the communist powers important raw materials, endanger vital transportation and communication routes between the Pacific Ocean and the Middle East, and render vulnerable the United States' chain of off-shore military bases in the Pacific. "In addition, this loss would have widespread political and psychological repercussions upon other non-communist states throughout the world."

If the intersection of geostrategic, economic, political, and psychological imperatives helped crystallize U.S. policy objectives in Indochina, they did little to clarify the means necessary for the attainment of those objectives. By the autumn of 1950, the Vietminh had achieved a string of stunning military successes; the French, increasingly demoralized and immobilized, appeared on the verge of defeat. U.S. intelligence experts feared that open intervention by Chinese communist units, which were already providing material along with technical and training assistance to the Vietminh, might precipitate a complete French collapse. State Department consultant John Foster Dulles called attention in November 1950 to "what might be a hopeless military situation." A month later an interagency intelligence assessment, coordinated by the CIA, offered an equally grim prognosis. "If this [Chinese communist] aid continues and French strength and military resources are not substantially increased above those presently programmed," it forecast, "the Viet Minh probably can drive the French out of North Viet Nam (Tonkin) within six to nine months." The French position in the rest of Indochina would soon become untenable, leading eventually to "the transformation of Indochina into a Communist satellite."

Determined to help prevent such a calamitous occurrence, the Truman administration steadily accelerated its military and economic aid commitments to the French. By the end of 1950, Washington had committed over $133 million in aid to Indochina. By fiscal year 1951, the total value of U.S. military supplies earmarked for the Indochina war had swelled to approximately $316.5 million. Indochina ranked second by then, behind only Korea, as a recipient of U.S. military aid. That aid helped reinvigorate a faltering French military effort. Together with the appointment of the flamboyant and self-assured General Jean de Lattre de Tassigny as the commander of French forces in Indochina, it led to a substantial—albeit short-lived—improvement in French military fortunes throughout 1951. U.S. observers exulted, hoping that the most acute phase of the crisis might be behind them.

Still, realism tempered the Truman administration's appreciation of the de Lattre-inspired turnaround. Too much hinged on one man, an individual "not always concerned about how many eggs he breaks for his omelette." Furthermore, no matter how vigorous a military campaign the French waged, and no matter how much aid the United States pumped into Indochina, U.S. analysts understood that those factors could not by themselves resolve the Indochina crisis and secure Southeast Asia for the West. Reflecting a view widely shared within the Truman administration, the Joint Chiefs of Staff noted that "without popular support of the Indochinese people, the French will never achieve a favorable long-range military settlement of the security problem of Indochina."

U.S. officials in Washington, Saigon, and Paris were keenly aware that the political and military challenges of Indochina were inseparable. The more astute among them recognized as well that U.S. support for the French pacification effort might work at cross-purposes with U.S. encouragement of Vietnam's noncommunist elites. As early as May 1950, U.S. Ambassador to France David K. E. Bruce shrewdly put his finger on the core problem. The ultimate success of U.S. policy, he observed, "depends upon encouragement and support of both local nationalism and [the] French effort in Indochina. . . . Yet these two forces, brought together only by common danger of Communist imperialism, are inherently antagonistic and gains of one will be to some extent at expense of other." Much to the dismay of U.S. officials, the military dynamism of de Lattre found no political counterpart. The French, who remained extremely unpopular among the Indochinese, simply refused to transfer any genuine power to Bao Dai and his associates. The independence of the Associated States remained a sham; the peoples of Indochina accordingly viewed with disdain the coterie of local leaders serving as little more than French puppets. Lamented U.S. minister in Saigon Donald R. Heath, the "fact is that Ho Chi Minh is [the] only Viet[namese] who enjoys any measure of national prestige."

Notwithstanding its deep and well-founded misgivings about the direction of French policy, the United States carefully avoided open criticism of its European partner. Washington was footing a substantial portion of the bill for the Indochina war. Such a financial commitment would ordinarily bring a commensurate degree of leverage, but the Indochina conflict was anything but ordinary. The French military effort in Southeast Asia served U.S. interests at least as much as it served French interests, a point understood equally well in Paris and Washington. For all its dependence on the United States, France retained the ultimate leverage in the relationship. If U.S. advice became too meddlesome, or if the United States sought to tie strings to its aid, the French could simply withdraw from Indochina entirely. That threat, repeatedly made by French leaders, frightened U.S. decision makers, who worried that they might by default inherit direct responsibility for the Indochina morass.

From the outset of U.S. involvement in Indochina, the Joint Chiefs of Staff had insisted upon, and Truman had accepted, a critical limitation on available U.S. options: Namely, under no circumstances could U.S. troops be deployed in Southeast Asia. With U.S. resources already stretched to the breaking point by the nation's ever-expanding global commitments, the military establishment worried constantly about an increasingly dangerous over extension of U.S. power. Threats to U.S. interests may have been multiplying, but resources remained finite. John Ohly, deputy director of the Mutual Defense Assistance Program in the State Department, articulated the fundamental dilemma faced by U.S. planners. As he reminded Secretary of State Acheson: "We have reached a point where the United States, because of limitations in resources, can no longer simultaneously pursue all its objectives in all parts of the world and must realistically face the fact that certain objectives, even though they may be extremely valuable and important ones, may have to be abandoned if others of even greater value and importance are to be attained." Ohly's argument applied with especial force to Indochina, an area where U.S. interests had escalated far more rapidly than had the resources available to military planners. State Department and White House officials were convinced, as were their counterparts in the Pentagon, that the United States must contain the communist threat in Southeast Asia without using U.S. ground forces. That consensus also pointed to an unresolved—and perhaps unresolvable—contradiction at the root of U.S. policy toward Indochina. If Southeast Asia was so vital that its loss to communism would deal a severe blow to U.S. national security, how could the United States accept *any* limits on its actions?

Throughout 1952, in the course of an extended reexamination of U.S. policy toward Southeast Asia, the Truman administration struggled in vain to resolve that contradiction. Its efforts were carried out against the backdrop of a deteriorating French military position (made more ominous by the death of de Lattre in January of that year), renewed fears about the possibility of direct Chinese communist intervention, and growing concern that domestic political pressures might lead to a French withdrawal from Indochina. The numerous reappraisals prepared by the State Department, the Defense Department, and the National Security Council emphasized once again the critical importance of Southeast Asia to the United States. During a meeting of the National Security Council in March 1952, Secretary of Defense Robert A. Lovett referred to "the grave danger to U.S. security interests" that would occur "should Southeast Asia pass into the Communist orbit." Likewise, Acheson candidly informed British Foreign Secretary Anthony Eden several months later that "we are lost if we lose Southeast Asia without a fight," and thus "we must do what we can to save Southeast Asia."

According to NSC-124/2, a new statement of policy approved by Truman on June 25, 1952, "Communist domination, by whatever means, of all Southeast Asia would seriously endanger in the short term, and critically endanger in the longer term, United States security interests." The possibility of "overt or covert" aggression by Beijing posed the most immediate threat. If a single Southeast Asian nation succumbed as a result of Chinese intervention, it "would have critical psychological, political and economic consequences. In the absence of effective and timely counteraction, the loss of any single country would probably lead to relatively swift submission to or an alignment with communism by the remaining countries of the group." The long-term alignment of India and the nations of the Middle East with the communist bloc, the report noted, would almost certainly follow. "Such widespread alignment would endanger the stability of Europe." Further, a communist Southeast Asia would deprive the West of a range of strategic commodities, thus exerting even greater economic and political pressure on nations allied with the United States and probably impelling "Japan's eventual accommodation to communism."

It was a nightmarish—if familiar—scenario. The president and his top civilian and military advisers were agreed that a set of interdependent global interests made the preservation of a noncommunist Southeast Asia vital to U.S. security. Developing a consensus within the administration on the steps essential to secure that critical objective, however, proved more elusive. Certain that French resistance would crumble rapidly if Communist Chinese divisions entered the fray, military and civilian analysts agonized over how the United States might respond to such a move. Some Pentagon officials believed that only military action against China itself, or the threat of such action, could deter Beijing, raising the frightening question of whether preserving a noncommunist Indochina might necessitate another Sino-American conflict. The pragmatic Lovett suggested that the United States should be prepared instead to spend more money—"perhaps at the rate of a billion or a billion and a half dollars a year"—to support the French; "this would be very much cheaper," he argued, "than an all-out war against Communist China, which would certainly cost us fifty billion dollars."

Neither Truman, Acheson, Lovett, the service chiefs, nor any other senior administration official developed a satisfactory response to the multiple challenges posed by the Indochina conflict. In the end, the Truman administration had to content itself with an ever-deepening monetary commitment to the French. By the end of 1952, the United States was underwriting approximately 40 percent of the cost of the Indochina war. Obviously, as the formulators of U.S. policy themselves were quick to admit, it was an imperfect solution. "More and more dollars [are] being poured into an uninspired program of wait and see," acknowledged the service chiefs. At best, the United States' swelling financial commitment simply postponed the inevitable reckoning. Even if the much-discussed Chinese intervention never materialized, the United States could expect little more than a continuation of the present stalemate; and in the absence of meaningful French political concessions to noncommunist Vietnamese leaders, such a stalemate would simply play into the hands of the Vietminh. The blunt Army Chief of Staff General J. Lawton Collins doubtless spoke for many when he predicted in March 1952 that "that French will be driven out—it is just a question of time."

The Truman administration, which had done so much to elevate Southeast Asia to a diplomatic prize of the greatest importance, failed to develop the means necessary to secure that prize. It never reconciled strategy with tactics. Nor did the administration ever decide on an appropriate U.S. response should the French position suddenly collapse. Truman simply passed those daunting issues, along with an increasingly perilous U.S. commitment to Southeast Asia, on to his successor. It was a legacy fully as problematic and as wracked with contradictory currents as the one he had inherited from Roosevelt.

✗ *FURTHER READING*

Robert M. Blum, *Drawing the Line: The Origin of the American Containment Policy in East Asia* (1982)
Lucien Bodard, *The Quicksand War* (1967)
William Borden, *The Pacific Alliance* (1984)
Dorothy Borg and Waldo Heinrichs, *Uncertain Years: Chinese-American Relations, 1947–1950* (1980)
King C. Chen, *Vietnam and China* (1969)
Evelyn Colbert, *International Politics in Southeast Asia, 1941–1956* (1977)
Edward Drachman, *United States Policy Toward Vietnam, 1940–1945* (1970)
Peter M. Dunn, *The First Vietnam War* (1985)
Russell H. Fifield, *Americans in Southeast Asia: The Roots of Commitment* (1973)
John Lewis Gaddis, *Strategies of Containment* (1982)
Lloyd C. Gardner, *Approaching Vietnam* (1988)
George C. Herring, "The Truman Administration and the Restoration of French Sovereignty in Indochina," *Diplomatic History,* 1 (1977), 97–117

Gary R. Hess, "Franklin D. Roosevelt and Indochina," *Journal of American History,* 59 (1972), 353–368

———, *The United States' Emergence as a Southeast Asian Power* (1987)

———, "United States Policy and the Origins of the French-Vietminh War, 1945–1946," *Peace and Change,* 3 (1975), 21–33

Akira Iriye, *The Cold War in Asia* (1974)

Akira Iriye and Yonosuke Nagai, eds., *The Origins of the Cold War in Asia* (1977)

George McT. Kahin, *Intervention* (1986)

Melvyn P. Leffler, *A Preponderance of Power* (1992)

Robert J. McMahon, "The Cold War in Asia: Toward a New Synthesis?" *Diplomatic History,* 12 (1988), 307–27

———, "Toward a Post-Colonial Order: Truman Administration Policies in South and Southeast Asia," in Michael J. Lacey, ed., *The Truman Presidency* (1989)

Edgar O'Ballance, *The Indochina War, 1945–1954* (1964)

Ritchie Ovendale, "Britain, the United States, and the Cold War in Southeast Asia, 1949–1950," *International Affairs,* 63 (1982), 447–64

Archimedes L. Patti, *Why Vietnam?* (1981)

Lisle A. Rose, *Roots of Tragedy* (1976)

Andrew J. Rotter, *The Path to Vietnam* (1987)

Michael Schaller, *The American Occupation of Japan: The Origins of the Cold War in Asia* (1985)

Ronald H. Spector, *Advice and Support* (1983)

Marianne P. Sullivan, *France's Vietnam Policy* (1978)

Christopher Thorne, *Allies of a Kind* (1978)

Stein Tonnesson, *The Vietnamese Revolution of 1945* (1991)

CHAPTER

4

Dwight D. Eisenhower

and Vietnam:

Deepening the Commitment

When Dwight D. Eisenhower assumed the presidency in January 1953, no resolution of the Indochina conflict appeared in sight. Despite the considerable material investment in the French military effort that it had made, the Truman administration bequeathed to its successor a much more serious and complex problem. The American stake in the war had grown almost as quickly as the French position had deteriorated. The United States, which was then bearing nearly 40 percent of the cost of the conflict, watched with dismay as French territorial control was reduced to a series of small enclaves around Hanoi, Haiphong, and Saigon and a narrow strip along the Cambodian border, while the Vietminh, bolstered by Chinese aid, grew bolder and stronger. Faced with the unsettling prospect of a French collapse and a communist victory in Vietnam, Eisenhower made a number of momentous decisions that transformed the nature of the American commitment to Vietnam.

First, Eisenhower chose not to attempt a rescue of the trapped French garrison at Dienbienphu with direct U.S. military intervention. When the remnants of the French defending force at that remote outpost surrendered to their Vietminh attackers on May 7, 1954, the battle served as a potent symbol of France's imminent defeat. The president next opted to participate in the Geneva Conference on Indochina—and to acquiesce in its results. The Geneva Accords of July 21, 1954, provided for the cessation of hostilities in Indochina, established independent states in Laos and Cambodia, demarcated a temporary division of Vietnam at the seventeenth parallel, and stipulated procedures that would lead to the eventual unification of the country. Following the Geneva Conference, the Eisenhower administration constructed the Southeast Asia Treaty Organization (SEATO) in order to defend the region against possible communist aggression, and moved to assist in cre-

ating a viable, noncommunist regime in southern Vietnam under the leader-ship of Prime Minister Ngo Dinh Diem. The all-Vietnam elections called for in the Geneva Accords were never held; soon the temporary geographical division came to appear permanent. During the Eisenhower years, the United States made a vigorous commitment to the Diem regime, providing it with massive amounts of aid. Nevertheless, by 1960, the prime minister faced growing internal opposition from the reborn Vietminh (or "Vietcong.") guerrillas, a movement supported by the communist-dominated regime of Ho Chi Minh in the north.

In recent years, a vigorous scholarly debate about Eisenhower's foreign policy has emerged, and it has had a marked impact on historical assess-ments of the president's Vietnam policy. The following questions have proved especially controversial. Why did the president choose not to intervene at Dienbienphu? Did the United States violate the Geneva Accords? How should Eisenhower's ambitious nation-building program in South Vietnam be judged: as a partial success, or as an abject failure? Did Washington com-mit itself to too fragile a leader in Diem? Were there alternatives? What were the principal strengths and weaknesses of Diem's rule? How is the rebirth of a guerrilla movement in the south in the late 1950s best explained? And, in a broader sense, what were the domestic and interna-tional forces during the 1950s that catapulted Vietnam to such a position of prominence for the United States?

✗ D O C U M E N T S

In the first document, President Eisenhower appeals to British Prime Minister Winston S. Churchill for "united action" to help save the French garrison at Dienbienphu. The second selection is an excerpt from Eisenhower's press con-ference of April 7, 1954, in which he spells out what he means by the "domino theory" and its relationship to Indochina. Vo Nguyen Giap, the victorious Vietnamese commander at Dienbienphu, assesses the significance of that battle in the next document. The final declaration of the Geneva Conference, July 21, 1954, established a temporary division between northern and southern Vietnam and set forth procedures for eventual unification. It is reprinted here as the fourth document.

The remaining documents in this chapter focus on the regime of Ngo Dinh Diem in South Vietnam. On January 1, 1955, Central Intelligence Agency operative Edward G. Lansdale emphasized the importance of the South Vietnamese experiment in a memorandum to General J. Lawton Collins, the U.S. special representative in Vietnam. In an April 28, 1955, National Security Council discussion of the sect crisis that nearly toppled Diem from power, sharp differences among top U.S. officials on Diem's abilities come to light. The next document is a declaration by the government of Vietnam, issued on August 9, 1955, renouncing any negotiations with the communist regime in the north.

On January 1, 1957, U.S. Ambassador Elbridge Durbrow alerted Washing-ton to a series of difficulties that plagued Diem's regime. In the final docu-ment, a National Security Council discussion of May 9, 1960, Eisenhower and other leading officials ponder South Vietnam's deepening problems.

Dwight D. Eisenhower Appeals for British Help, 1954

Dear Winston:

I am sure that like me you are following with the deepest interest and anxiety the daily reports of the gallant fight being put up by the French at Dien Bien Phu. Today, the situation there does not seem hopeless.

But regardless of the outcome of this particular battle, I fear that the French cannot alone see the thing through, this despite the very substantial assistance in money and matériel that we are giving them. It is no solution simply to urge the French to intensify their efforts, and if they do not see it through, and Indochina passes into the hands of the Communists, the ultimate effect on our and your global strategic position with the consequent shift in the power ratio throughout Asia and the Pacific could be disastrous and, I know, unacceptable to you and me. It is difficult to see how Thailand, Burma and Indonesia could be kept out of Communist hands. This we cannot afford. The threat to Malaya, Australia and New Zealand would be direct. The offshore island chain would be broken. The economic pressures on Japan which would be deprived of non-Communist markets and sources of food and raw materials would be such, over a period of time, that it is difficult to see how Japan could be prevented from reaching an accommodation with the Communist world which would combine the manpower and natural resources of Asia with the industrial potential of Japan. This has led us to the hard conclusion that the situation in Southeast Asia requires us urgently to take serious and far-reaching decisions.

Geneva is less than four weeks away. There the possibility of the Communists driving a wedge between us will, given the state of mind in France, be infinitely greater than at Berlin. I can understand the very natural desire of the French to seek an end to this war which has been bleeding them for eight years. But our painstaking search for a way out of the impasse has reluctantly forced us to the conclusion that there is no negotiated solution of the Indochina problem which in its essence would not be either a face-saving device to cover a French surrender or a face-saving device to cover a Communist retirement. The first alternative is too serious in its broad strategic implications for us and for you to be acceptable. Apart from its effects in Southeast Asia itself, where you and the Commonwealth have direct and vital interests, it would have the most serious repercussions in North Africa, in Europe and elsewhere. Here at home it would cause a widespread loss of confidence in the cooperative system. I think it is not too much to say that the future of France as a great power would be fatally affected. Perhaps France will never again be the great power it was, but a sudden vacuum wherever French power is, would be difficult for us to cope with.

Somehow we must contrive to bring about the second alternative. The preliminary lines of our thinking were sketched out by Foster [Dulles] in his speech last Monday night when he said that under the conditions of today the imposition on Southeast Asia of the political system of Communist Russia and its Chinese Communist ally, by whatever means, would be a grave threat to the whole free community, and that in our view this possibility should now be met by united action and not passively accepted. He has also talked intimately with [British ambassador] Roger Makins.

I believe that the best way to put teeth in this concept and to bring greater moral and material resources to the support of the French effort is through the establishment of a new, *ad hoc* grouping or coalition composed of nations which have a vital concern in the checking of Communist expansion in the area. I have in mind in addition to our two countries, France, the Associated States, Australia, New Zealand, Thailand and the Philippines. The United States Government would expect to play its full part in such a coalition. The coalition we have in mind would not be directed against Communist China. But if, contrary to our belief, our efforts to save Indochina and the British Commonwealth position to the south should in any way increase the jeopardy to Hong Kong, we would expect to be with you there. I suppose that the United Nations should somewhere be recognized, but I am not confident that, given the Soviet veto, it could act with needed speed and vigor.

I would contemplate no role for Formosa or the Republic of Korea in the political construction of this coalition.

The important thing is that the coalition must be strong and it must be willing to join the fight if necessary. I do not envisage the need of any appreciable ground forces on your or our part. If the members of the alliance are sufficiently resolute it should be able to make clear to the Chinese Communists that the continuation of their material support to the Viet Minh will inevitably lead to the growing power of the forces arrayed against them.

My colleagues and I are deeply aware of the risks which this proposal may involve but in the situation which confronts us there is no course of action or inaction devoid of dangers and I know no man who has firmly grasped more nettles than you. If we grasp this one together I believe that we will enormously increase our chances of bringing the Chinese to believe that their interests lie in the direction of a discreet disengagement. In such a contingency we could approach the Geneva conference with the position of the free world not only unimpaired but strengthened.

Today we face the hard situation of contemplating a disaster brought on by French weakness and the necessity of dealing with it before it develops. This means frank talk with the French. In many ways the situation corresponds to that which you describe so brilliantly in the second chapter of "Their Finest Hour," when history made clear that the French strategy and dispositions before the 1940 breakthrough should have been challenged before the blow fell.

I regret adding to your problems. But in fact it is not I, but our enemies who add to them. I have faith that by another act of fellowship in the face of peril we shall find a spiritual vigor which will prevent our slipping into the quagmire of distrust.

If I may refer again to history, we failed to halt Hirohito, Mussolini and

Hitler by not acting in unity and in time. That marked the beginning of many years of stark tragedy and desperate peril. May it not be that our nations have learned something from that lesson?

So profoundly do I believe that the effectiveness of the coalition principle is at stake that I am prepared to send Foster or [Under Secretary of State Walter] Bedell [Smith] to visit you this week, at the earliest date convenient to you. Whoever comes would spend a day in Paris to avoid French pique, the cover would be preparation for Geneva.

Eisenhower Explains the Domino Theory, 1954

Q. Robert Richards, Copley Press: Mr. President, would you mind commenting on the strategic importance of Indochina to the free world? I think there has been, across the country, some lack of understanding on just what it means to us.

The President: You have, of course, both the specific and the general when you talk about such things.

First of all, you have the specific value of a locality in its production of materials that the world needs.

Then you have the possibility that many human beings pass under a dictatorship that is inimical to the free world.

Finally, you have broader considerations that might follow what you would call the "falling domino" principle. You have a row of dominoes set up, you knock over the first one, and what will happen to the last one is the certainty that it will go over very quickly. So you could have a beginning of a disintegration that would have the most profound influences.

Now, with respect to the first one, two of the items from this particular area that the world uses are tin and tungsten. They are very important. There are others, of course, the rubber plantations and so on.

Then with respect to more people passing under this domination, Asia, after all, has already lost some 450 million of its peoples to the Communist dictatorship, and we simply can't afford greater losses.

But when we come to the possible sequence of events, the loss of Indochina, of Burma, of Thailand, of the Peninsula, and Indonesia following, now you begin to talk about areas that not only multiply the disadvantages that you would suffer through loss of materials, sources of materials, but now you are talking about millions and millions and millions of people.

Finally, the geographical position achieved thereby does many things. It turns the so-called island defensive chain of Japan, Formosa, of the Philippines and to the southward; it moves in to threaten Australia and New Zealand.

It takes away, in its economic aspects, that region that Japan must have as a trading area or Japan, in turn, will have only one place in the world to go—that is, toward the Communist areas in order to live.

So, the possible consequences of the loss are just incalculable to the free world.

Vo Nguyen Giap on Dienbienphu (1954), 1964

Paramount Significance of the Great Dien Bien Phu Victory and of the Winter–Spring Victories

The historic Dien Bien Phu campaign and in general the Winter 1953-Spring 1954 campaign were the greatest victories ever won by our army and people up to the present time. These great victories marked a giant progress, *a momentous change in the evolution of the Resistance War for national salvation put up by our people against the aggressive French imperialists propped up by U.S. interventionists. . . .*

The great Dien Bien Phu victory and the Winter-Spring victories as a whole had a far-reaching influence in the world.

While the bellicose imperialists were confused and discouraged, the news of the victories won by our army and people on the battlefronts throughout the country especially the Dien Bien Phu victory, have greatly inspired the progressive people the world over.

The Dien Bien Phu victory was not only a great victory of our people but was regarded by the socialist countries as their own victory. It was regarded as a great victory of the weak and small nations now fighting against imperialism and old and new-colonialism for freedom and independence. Dien Bien Phu has become a pride of the oppressed peoples, a great contribution of our people to the high movement for national liberation which has been surging up powerfully since the end of World War II, and heralded the collapse of the colonial system of imperialism.

Dien Bien Phu was also a great victory of the forces of peace in the world. Without this victory, certainly the Geneva Conference would not be successful and peace could not be re-established in Indo-China. This substantiates all the more clearly that the victory won at Dien Bien Phu and in general the Resistance War put up by our people, and the victorious struggle for liberation waged by the oppressed people against imperialism and colonialism under all forms, played a role of paramount importance in weakening imperialism, thwarting the scheme of aggression and war of the enemy and contributing greatly to the defense of world peace. . . .

The aggressive war unleashed by the French imperialists in Indo-China dragged on for eight or nine years. Though they did their best to increase their force to nearly half a million men, sacrificed hundreds of thousands of soldiers, spent in this dirty war 2,688 billion French francs, squandered a great amount of resources, shed a great deal of blood of the French people, changed 20 cabinets in France, 7 high commissars and 8 commanders-in-chief in Indo-China, their aggressive war grew from bad to worse, met defeat after defeat, went from one strategic mistake to another, to end in the great Dien Bien Phu disaster. This is because the war made by the French colonialists was an unjust war. In this war the enemy met with the indomitable spirit of an entire people and therefore, no skillful general—be he Leclerc, De Tassigny, Navarre or any other general—could save the French Expeditionary Corps from defeat. Neither there would be a mighty weapon—cannon, tank or heavy bomber and even U.S. atomic bomb—

which could retrieve the situation. On the upshot, if in autumn 1953 and winter 1954, the enemy did not occupy Dien Bien Phu by paratroopers or if he occupied it and withdrew later without choosing it as the site of a do-or-die battle, sooner or later a Dien Bien Phu would come up, though the time and place might change; and in the end the French and U.S. imperialists would certainly meet with a bitter failure.

Final Declaration of the Geneva Conference on Indochina, 1954

1. The Conference takes note of the agreements ending hostilities in Cambodia, Laos, and Vietnam and organizing international control and the supervision of the execution of the provisions of these agreements.

2. The Conference expresses satisfaction at the end of hostilities in Cambodia, Laos, and Vietnam; the Conference expresses its conviction that the execution of the provisions set out in the present declaration and in the agreements of the cessation of hostilities will permit Cambodia, Laos, and Vietnam henceforth to play their part, in full independence and sovereignty, in the peaceful community of nations.

3. The Conference takes note of the declarations made by the Governments of Cambodia and Laos of their intention to adopt measures permitting all citizens to take their place in the national community, in particular by participating in the next general elections, which, in conformity with the constitution of each of these countries, shall take place in the course of the year 1955, by secret ballot and in conditions of respect for fundamental freedoms.

4. The Conference takes note of the clauses in the agreement on the cessation of hostilities in Vietnam prohibiting the introduction into Vietnam of foreign troops and military personnel as well as of all kinds of arms and munitions. The Conference also takes note of the declarations made by the Governments of Cambodia and Laos of their resolution not to request foreign aid, whether in war material, in personnel, or in instructors except for the purpose of the effective defense of their territory and, in the case of Laos, to the extent defined by the agreements of the cessation of hostilities in Laos.

5. The Conference takes note of the clauses in the agreement on the cessation of hostilities in Vietnam to the effect that no military base under the control of a foreign State may be established in the regrouping zones of the two parties, the latter having the obligation to see that the zones allotted to them shall not constitute part of any military alliance and shall not be utilized for the resumption of hostilities or in the service of an aggressive policy. The Conference also takes note of the declarations of the Governments of Cambodia and Laos to the effect that they will not join in any agreement with other States if this agreement includes the obligation to participate in a military alliance not in conformity with the principles of the Charter of the United Nations or, in the case of Laos, with the principles of the agreement on the cessation of hostilities in Laos or, so long as their

security is not threatened, the obligation to establish bases on Cambodian or Laotian territory for the military forces of foreign powers.

6. The Conference recognizes that the essential purpose of the agreement relating to Vietnam is to settle military questions with a view to ending hostilities and that the military demarcation line is provisional and should not in any way be interpreted as constituting a political or territorial boundary. The Conference expresses its conviction that the execution of the provisions set out in the present declaration and in the agreement on the cessation of hostilities creates the necessary basis for the achievement in the near future of a political settlement in Vietnam.

7. The Conference declares that, so far as Vietnam is concerned, the settlement of political problems, effected on the basis of respect for the principles of independence, unity, and territorial integrity, shall permit the Vietnamese people to enjoy the fundamental freedoms, guaranteed by democratic institutions established as a result of free general elections by secret ballot. In order to ensure that sufficient progress in the restoration of peace has been made, and that all the necessary conditions obtain for free expression of the national will, general elections shall be held in July 1956 under the supervision of an international commission composed of representatives of the Member States of the International Supervisory Commission, referred to in the agreement on the cessation of hostilities. Consultations will be held on this subject between the competent representative authorities of the two zones from July 20, 1955, onward.

8. The provisions of the agreements on the cessation of hostilities intended to ensure the protection of individuals and of property must be most strictly applied and must, in particular, allow everyone in Vietnam to decide freely in which zone he wishes to live.

9. The competent representative authorities of the North and South zones of Vietnam, as well as the authorities of Laos and Cambodia, must not permit any individual or collective reprisals against persons who had collaborated in any way with one of the parties during the war, or against members of such persons' families.

10. The Conference takes note of the declaration of the Government of the French Republic to the effect that it is ready to withdraw its troops from the territory of Cambodia, Laos, and Vietnam, at the request of the Governments concerned and within periods which shall be fixed by agreement between the parties except in the cases where, by agreement between the two parties, a certain number of French troops shall remain at specified points and for a specified time.

11. The Conference takes note of the declaration of the French Government to the effect that for the settlement of all the problems connected with the re-establishment and consolidation of peace in Cambodia, Laos, and Vietnam, the French Government will proceed from the principle of respect for the independence and sovereignty, unity and territorial integrity of Cambodia, Laos, and Vietnam.

12. In their relations with Cambodia, Laos, and Vietnam, each member of the Geneva Conference undertakes to respect the sovereignty, the

independence, the unity, and the territorial integrity of the above-mentioned States, and to refrain from any interference in their internal affairs.

13. The members of the Conference agree to consult one another on any question which may be referred to them by the International Supervisory Commission, in order to study such measures as may prove necessary to ensure that the agreements on the cessation of hostilities in Cambodia, Laos, and Vietnam are respected.

Edward G. Lansdale on the Importance of the South Vietnamese Experiment, 1955

1. Here is some New Year's thinking about the problem you and we face, and a request.

2. As a start, it is worth taking a look at the real value of the chips given to you by President Eisenhower for the game we are playing here. The chips are our direct aid to the Vietnamese. To most Americans, they mean money, material, and technical (advisory) manpower. In the eyes of the world, and especially Asia, they mean something more. In this view, the value of the chips becomes Asia itself and parts of the Middle East.

3. The Asian view is that "direct aid" means that Communism's strongest enemy, the United States, is now in close support of the Free Vietnamese against the Communists. Certainly each of the free nations which has a pact with the United States, in which we will give them close support against the Communists, sees a bit of itself in the situation of the Vietnamese. And, each of those nations, in varying degree, will be measuring what our support actually means. Thus, if we lose here or withdraw however gracefully, politically powerful people in those nations will read their own futures into our action. This means that the do-business-with-China folks of Japan, the anti-American-bases folks of the Philippines, and so on, will find their arguments strengthened locally to the critical strain point for the United States in places we now find difficult enough under neutralist and Communist political pressures. This is far beyond the usual observation of the loss of Vietnam opening Southeast Asia to the impact of Communist dynamism, which is dangerous enough in itself.

4. Thus, I feel that we have too much to lose to consider loosing [*sic*] or withdrawing. We have no other choice but to win here or face an increasingly grim future, a heritage which none of us wants to pass along to our offspring.

5. What will it take to win? It is going to take everything we are now doing and planning to do, plus more—and I believe that the "more" now exists here as a potential awaiting proper employment.

6. I have narrowed down the elements we need for winning the present struggle here to three, which is perhaps over-simplifying. I believe that if we can make these three elements a reality here, the initiative will pass to us and we will start winning. I feel, further, that we must have clear evidence by June 1955 that we can make the three elements a reality. They are:

a. Successful teamwork

b. Strengthen the free Vietnamese

c. Make the bulk of the population willing to risk all for freedom. . . .

7. *Strengthening Vietnamese.* I am concerned about whether all our aid and efforts here will strengthen the Vietnamese or merely make them more dependent upon us. Certainly none of us who must justify actions eventually at home would desire to place the U.S. in the position of continuing major help here for endless years, on the basis that if our aid were lessened then the enemy would win. Certainly the responsible Americans here would like to see the Vietnamese capably assuming an increasing share of their own burdens in all fields of national life.

8. Thus, I would like to see our efforts here geared as completely as possible to the operating philosophy of helping the Vietnamese to help themselves, not only Vietnamese government or army, but the people themselves. It will mean insisting on more extensive and effective use of our help by the Vietnamese—and our acceptance of workable Vietnamese standards rather than our own perhaps to a greater extent. This will increase proprietary interest in what is constructed (whether it be army division or individual farm), build the muscularity of national abilities, and start giving the Free Vietnamese the confidence in their own competence which the Vietminh have demonstrated so remarkably on their side. These are all factors of strength in a struggle with the Communists. It is also true that a man is more apt to defend what he has constructed for himself—and we will strengthen the Free Vietnamese as we increase the size or amount of what they want to defend from the Communists.

National Security Council Discussion of the Sect Crisis, 1955

General Collins, accompanied by Mr. Paul J. Sturm of the State Department, entered the Cabinet Room when Item 5 came up for discussion. Mr. Allen Dulles also asked permission for Mr. Kermit Roosevelt of the Central Intelligence Agency to be present while Mr. Dulles briefed the Council on the latest developments in Saigon.

Mr. Dulles explained that last night serious street fighting had broken out in the city of Saigon. A mortar shell had landed on the Presidential Palace, the residence of Prime Minister Diem, at 1:15 P.M. After two further shells had landed in the Palace grounds, Diem had telephoned General Ely and stated that he was ordering counterfire by the Vietnamese national forces. Eleven rounds of such counterfire had been counted by three o'clock in the afternoon. While there had since been rumors that a cease-fire had been arranged, Mr. Dulles doubted the validity of these reports, and said it seemed that Prime Minister Diem had ordered all-out action against the Binh Xuyen. In other words, Diem was proposing to force a showdown. It was not easy, continued Mr. Dulles, to say which side had actually been responsible for precipitating last night's events, but the real trouble had begun on April 26, when Prime Minister Diem had ordered the removal of the Chief of Police of Saigon, who was a member of the Binh Xuyen gangster group.

In a showdown fight, continued Mr. Dulles, and if the Vietnamese National Army remains loyal to the Prime Minister, there was little doubt that the Army could drive the Binh Xuyen forces out of Saigon. The difficulty was that such an attempt would almost certainly result in disturbances and civil war throughout South Vietnam. In addition, the street fighting might very well result in atrocities against French civilians living in Saigon. Finally, said Mr. Dulles, Diem has advised that he now intends to form a complete new Cabinet, and that he will announce its members tonight.

The President promptly inquired what General Ely was likely to do in the face of the situation which Mr. Dulles had described. General Collins replied that he believed that General Ely would do nothing unless a threat should develop to foreigners resident in Saigon. General Collins then produced a map of the city of Saigon and adjacent areas, and rapidly described the chief features of the city and the deployment of the Binh Xuyen and the National Army forces.

The President then asked General Collins whether the French were likely to interfere with American resupply of Prime Minister Diem's forces. General Collins thought that the French would not so interfere, and pointed out that the French have already offered an ammunition depot in Saigon to the Vietnamese forces.

At this point Mr. Dillon Anderson [special assistant to the president] reminded the Council of the decision with respect to U.S. policy toward South Vietnam which the Council had made in January of this year. While he was doing so, the Executive Secretary handed out a draft record of action prepared in the Department of State, which State suggested should be adopted in lieu of the earlier Council action of January. Secretary Dulles pointed out that the chief difference was that the earlier action had pinpointed Prime Minister Diem as the individual whose government the United States should support.

Secretary Dulles said that he would like to comment in general on the situation in which we found ourselves respecting South Vietnam. In his view, the present difficulties had two fundamental causes. First, the limitations of Prime Minister Diem as the head of a government. While Diem's good qualities were well known and need not be elaborated, it was a fact that he came from the northern part of the country and was not very trustful of other people, perhaps for good reason. Furthermore, he was not very good at delegating authority. Despite these shortcomings, Diem might have proved adequate to the situation if it had not been for the second fundamental limitation—namely, the lack of solid support from the French. While the top leaders of the French Government, such as Mendes-France, Faure and General Ely, have gone along with Diem reluctantly, French colonial officials on the scene in Vietnam have done their best to sabotage him. These two fundamental limitations in conjunction have brought about a situation that has finally induced General Collins to conclude that we must now look for a replacement for Diem.

As a matter of fact, continued Secretary Dulles, we have been telling the French for a considerable period that we would be prepared to consider an alternative to Diem if they could come up with one. They haven't as yet done so. Moreover, the mechanics of effecting a change at this time would be very difficult. A change of Premier would necessarily involve recourse to Bao Dai, and we have always felt that Bao Dai's influence would be invariably exerted in favor of the Binh Xuyen, which supplies his ample funds. We haven't therefore, been inclined to look with very much favor on a new South Vietnam government appointed by Bao Dai. On the contrary, we have felt that it was really essential that a showdown occur between Bao Dai and the rebellious sects. Such a showdown both Bao Dai and the French have consistently tried to avoid.

Late yesterday afternoon, however, we in the State Department dispatched a complicated series of cables to Saigon outlining ways and means of replacing Diem and his government. However, in view of the developments and the outbreak of last night, we have instructed our people in Saigon to hold up action on our plan for replacing Diem. The developments of last night could either lead to Diem's utter overthrow or to his emergence from the disorder as a major hero. Accordingly, we are pausing to await the results before trying to settle on [Pham Huy] Quat or Defense Minister [*sic*] Do as possible replacements. Secretary Dulles confessed that he was not much impressed with the Defense Minister. On the other hand, unless something occurs in the Saigon disorders out of which Diem will emerge as the hero, we will have to have a change. This is the view both of General Collins and General Ely, and Ely has played an honest game with us in this whole affair.

Secretary Dulles then pointed out that Bao Dai had actually threatened to take the matter in his own hands and establish a new government himself. Indeed, we are not absolutely sure that we can restrain him from so doing, since he so to speak represents the only existing source of legitimate governmental authority. Thus we find ourselves obliged to work with him and through him to some extent, until we are in a position to devise some alternative source of authority.

At the conclusion of his statement, Secretary Dulles asked General Collins to present his views. General Collins began by reminding the National Security Council of his earlier appearance before it prior to his departure for Saigon, and of the position he had taken at that time—namely, that there were five major factors on which the future of Free Vietnam would depend. He said that he would briefly run over these same five factors now.

1. The possibility of an overt attack on Free Vietnam by the Vietminh. Of this General Collins stated there was very little danger at the present time.

2. The loyalty of the Vietnamese National Army to Diem. General Collins emphasized that to date the Vietnamese National Army had been

loyal to Diem, but that loyalty would almost certainly not extend to supporting the Prime Minister in a civil war. The Army violently disliked the Binh Xuyen, but it also disliked the prospect of engaging in a civil war in South Vietnam which would also include the Hoa Hao and the Cao Dai sects, which were quite strong in the southern portions of Free Vietnam. The great danger of trying to drive the Binh Xuyen from their strongholds in Saigon, said General Collins, was precisely the danger that such an attempt would end in widespread civil war.

3. The problem of the sects. General Collins pointed out that we have feared all along that efforts to cut down the size of the private armies of the sects and to dry up their financial resources would cause trouble. This was probably inevitable, whether Diem or anyone else made the effort. On the other hand, General Collins insisted that Diem's handling of the problem of the sects had been anything but astute.

4. The attitude of the French. General Collins said that since this had been thoroughly covered by Secretary Dulles, he would add no more except to point out that there could be no doubt of the loyal role played with him by General Ely.

5. The personality of Diem. On this point General Collins said that as early as the end of his first week in Saigon he had come to entertain very serious doubts as to Diem's ability to govern. Diem betrayed no political knack whatsoever in his handling of men. His ineptitude in this respect was responsible for the series of resignations from his Cabinet. It was no mere matter of rats quitting a sinking ship. General Collins felt that it was a particular misfortune to lose Minh, the young Secretary of Defense, and Do, the older Secretary of Foreign Affairs, whom General Collins considered to be a man of very good judgment. If, said General Collins, Diem makes good on his statement that he would name a new Cabinet, this Cabinet would almost certainly consist of unknown individuals who had no public standing.

All this induced General Collins to conclude that Prime Minister Diem's number was up. Nor had he ever felt that Diem was the indispensable man. Accordingly, even without Diem the program adopted by the Council for South Vietnam could and should go forward without interruption, even though its estimated costs would be $40 million more this year than previously estimated. General Collins emphasized that he still felt that this U.S. policy and program was a gamble worth taking, although certainly a gamble. A long-term solution of the sect problem was vital to the success of the program. It was likewise vital to take control of the police away from the Binh Xuyen. Finally, it was essential to get genuine French support for the policy and program, no matter who was the Vietnamese Prime Minister.

The President commented that it was an absolute sine qua non of success that the Vietnamese National Army destroy the power of the Binh Xuyen. Otherwise any new government was bound to fail. To this General Collins replied that the attempt to destroy the Binh Xuyen by military action would almost certainly produce civil war in Vietnam. The Binh Xuyen, if removed from Saigon, would take to the Maquis and raise hell for years to come. Accordingly, General Collins said he personally preferred a political solution. He had wished Diem to form a genuine coalition government. He doubted very much whether Diem could be prevailed upon to try it, but such a political solution seemed most likely to bring success.

Secretary [of the Treasury George] Humphrey inquired how far the Communists were behind the disorders and outbreaks in Saigon. General Collins replied that there could be no doubt that they were stimulating and exploiting the disorders that existed.

At this point Mr. Anderson read the proposed record of action. The President inquired if there were any objections. There being none, the President observed that the proposed action sounded all right to him, and that he could not see what else we could do at this time.

At the close of the discussion, Mr. Allen Dulles commented that if it were any comfort to the Council, there was quite a good deal of evidence that the Vietminh were encountering considerable difficulty in their part of Vietnam.

South Vietnamese Statement on Reunification, 1955

In the last July 1955 broadcast, the Vietnamese national Government has made it clear its position towards the problem of territorial unity.

The Government does not consider itself bound in any respect by the Geneva Agreements which it did not sign.

Once more, the Government reasserts that in any circumstance, it places national interests above all, being resolved to achieve at all cost the obvious aim it is pursuing and eventually to achieve national unity, peace and freedom.

The Viet-Minh leaders have had a note dated July 19 transmitted to the Government, in which they asked for the convening of a consultative conference on general elections. This is just a propaganda move aimed at making the people believe that they are the champions of our territorial unity. Everyone still remembers that last year at Geneva, the Vietnamese Communists boisterously advocated the partition of our territory and asked for an economically self-sufficient area whereas the delegation of the State of Viet-nam proposed an armistice without any partition, not even provisional, with a view to safeguarding the sacred rights of the Vietnamese national and territorial unity, national independence and individual freedom. As the Vietnamese delegation states, the Vietnamese Government then stood for the fulfillment of national aspirations by the means which have been given back to Viet-nam by the French solemn recognition of the independence and sovereignty of Viet-nam, as a legal, independent state.

The policy of the Government remains unchanged. Confronted with the partition of the country, which is contrary to the will of the entire people, the Government will see to it that everybody throughout the country may live free from fear, and completely free from all totalitarian oppression. As a champion of justice, of genuine democracy, the Government always holds that the principle of free general election is a peaceful and democratic

means only if, first of all, the freedom to live and freedom of vote is sufficiently guaranteed.

In this connection, nothing constructive can be contemplated in the present situation in the North where, under the rule of the Vietnamese
Communists, the citizens do not enjoy democratic freedoms and fundamental human rights.

Elbridge Durbrow Assesses the Diem Regime, 1957

Certain problems now discernible have given us a warning which, if disre-
garded, might lead to a deteriorating situation in Viet Nam within a few
years.

Diem achieved notable successes in the first two years of his regime
and remains the only man of stature so far in evidence to guide this country. He has unified free Viet Nam, brought it relative security and stability,
and firmly maintains a pro-West, anti-communist position.

In the last year, however, Diem has avoided making decisions required
to build the economic and social foundations necessary to secure Viet
Nam's future independence and strength. He has made it clear that he
would give first priority to the build-up of his armed forces regardless of
the country's requirements for economic and social development. Events
abroad which increase the danger of communist infiltration and subversion,
and which threaten Viet Nam with possible isolation in this area have contributed to his concern and to his determination to strengthen his armed
forces.

Certain characteristics of Diem—his suspiciousness and authoritarianism—have also reduced the Government's limited administrative capabilities. He assumes responsibility for the smallest details of Government and
grants his Ministers little real authority.

At the same time, discontent is felt in different segments of the population for varied reasons. The base of the regime's popular support remains
narrow. The regime might overcome such discontent and finally win over
the loyalty of a majority of Vietnamese both in the North and South if it
could show its ability to give the country stronger protection and create
sound economic and social bases for progress. Progress, which is
demanded in Viet Nam as throughout Asia, is perhaps the touchstone of the
regime's enduring viability. Yet precisely because Diem is now procrasti-
nating in making decisions affecting fundamental problems of his country's
development, the lag between the people's expectations and the
Government's ability to show results will grow.

We consider it therefore of importance that we bring strong pressure on
the President to reach certain decisions basically in the economic and social
fields which have been before him for some months but on which he has not
acted. He has resented this and may resent it more, but in ours and his long
range interests we must do our utmost to cause him to move forward in
these fields.

The purpose of this evaluation of the present situation in Viet Nam is to examine the elements giving rise to some concern regarding certain developments in Viet Nam, to provide the Department [of State] and interested agencies salient background and to set forth conclusions and recommend certain broad courses of action. We feel that a frank discussion of the solution as we see it may be helpful to all concerned.

National Security Council Discussion of Diem's Growing Problems, 1960

Mr. [Robert] Amory [of the CIA] then reported that increasing troubles in South Vietnam were confronting Diem. For months Diem had been facing increased insurgent activity in the countryside similar to that which characterized the last days of the French regime. Moreover, Diem's own ranks had been crumbling. Critics of his one-man rule were becoming more vocal at all levels of government. This criticism asserted that Diem's administration had fostered corruption, condoned maladministration, and permitted dictatorial practices with the result that communism in South Vietnam was being promoted. Criticism of Diem was so far uncoordinated outside government circles but was becoming stronger, as indicated by a recent manifesto made public in Saigon by a group of former officials who called for extensive political reforms.

The President said he had received a stream of reports about South Vietnam. Heretofore we have been proud of Diem and had thought he was doing a good job. Apparently he was now becoming arbitrary and blind to the situation. Mr. Amory said one danger lay in the fact that Diem was not in direct touch with the people since he seldom went out into the countryside to see the people and talk with provincial leaders. He is inclined to leave this kind of activity, as well as the details of administration, to his brothers, who have all the evils and none of the assets needed to do a good job. The President wondered whether we were doing anything to try to persuade Diem to remain in closer touch with the people. Mr. Amory said our Ambassador to South Vietnam and General [Samuel T.] Williams [chief of the Military Assistance Advisory Group in Vietnam] were constantly advising Diem to keep in touch with the people.

Mr. [Livingston] Merchant [under secretary of state for political affairs] said Diem was more and more coming to be surrounded by a small group. He was leaving administration to his two brothers and was losing touch with the grass roots. However, Ambassador Durbrow was keeping in close touch with Diem. Mr. Merchant hoped that what happened to Syngman Rhee in Korea would give Diem pause.

The President said Diem seemed to be calm and quiet and to have an attractive personality unlike Rhee. The President then asked Mr. Merchant to consider whether the situation might be improved by a letter from him (the President) to Diem.

Mr. [Thomas S.] Gates [secretary of defense] remarked that South Vietnam internal security forces were not well equipped to handle insurgent forces in the swampy areas where most of the trouble occurred.

The President said the U.S. ought to do everything possible to prevent the deterioration of the situation in South Vietnam. We had rescued this country from a fate worse than death and it would be bad to lose it at this stage. Mr. Merchant believed that South Vietnam was getting as much economic assistance as it could effectively absorb. The President recalled that when Diem had first been attempting to acquire power in South Vietnam, a recommendation had been made to the Council that the U.S. should oppose him. The President said he hoped the Departments of State and Defense and CIA would consult together to see what could be done about the situation in South Vietnam.

X *E S S A Y S*

In the opening essay, Stephen E. Ambrose of the University of New Orleans, the author of an acclaimed two-volume biography of Dwight D. Eisenhower, praises the former general for staunchly resisting pressures for U.S. intervention in Indochina at the time of the Dienbienphu crisis of 1954. Ambrose suggests that Eisenhower deliberately imposed conditions on any prospective U.S. military action to help the French—requirements such as prior support from Congress and from U.S. allies in Europe—that he knew could not be met. Ambrose concludes that Eisenhower's decision was a wise and statesmanlike approach that kept the United States out of the Vietnamese morass.

In the next essay, David L. Anderson, a specialist in the history of American foreign relations who teaches at the University of Indianapolis, pays more attention to Eisenhower's post-Dienbienphu decisions. He contends that while Eisenhower may deserve high marks for choosing not to rescue the beleaguered French garrison at Dienbienphu, his administration's subsequent commitment to the Diem regime represented a massive intervention in Vietnamese affairs. Anderson says that the Eisenhower administration's generous economic, military, and political support for the Saigon government that it helped to establish never proved sufficient to create a viable nation. Instead, the United States became tied to a corrupt, inefficient, and unrepresentative regime in South Vietnam that never commanded popular support. In the process, it sowed the seeds for future troubles.

The Wisdom of U.S. Nonintervention

STEPHEN E. AMBROSE

The war raging in Vietnam [in early 1954] made the subject of massive retaliation more than academic. The French were holding their own, but barely. Paris was weary of war. The cost, in lives and money, had become unendurable. For the Americans, too, the situation was intolerable. A con-

From Stephen E. Ambrose, *Eisenhower,* vol. II, *The President,* pp. 173–85. Copyright © 1984 by Stephen E. Ambrose. Reprinted by permission of Simon & Schuster Inc.

tinued stalemate would drain French resources to such an extent that France would never be able to meet its NATO obligations, always a prime consideration with Eisenhower. Further, the French were demanding more American money, and even American planes and troops, and they were simultaneously using EDC [the European Defense Community], which Eisenhower very much wanted, to blackmail the United States. Without support in Indochina, the French were saying, they could not ratify EDC.

A French defeat in Vietnam would be worse than continued stalemate. There was first of all the global strategic balance to consider. As far back as December 1952, Dulles had told Eisenhower that "Korea is important, but the really important spot is Indochina, because we could lose Korea and probably insulate ourselves against the consequences of that loss; but if Indochina goes, and South Asia goes, it is extremely hard to insulate ourselves against the consequence of that." There was in addition the political position of the Republican Party to be considered. A major theme of Eisenhower's campaign had been a rejection of containment and an adoption of a policy of liberation. Now the Republicans had been in power for more than a year. They had failed to liberate any Communist slave anywhere. Indeed in Korea they had accepted an armistice that left North Korea in Communist hands. Eisenhower was keenly aware that by far his most popular act had been to achieve peace in Korea, but he was just as aware that Republican orators had been demanding to know, ever since 1949, "Who lost China?" Could he afford to allow Democrats to ask, "Who lost Vietnam?" He told his Cabinet he could not.

The obvious way out of the quandary was a French victory, but the problem was how to achieve it without introducing American planes and troops. Under no circumstances was Eisenhower going to send American troops back onto the Asian mainland less than a year after signing an armistice in Korea. Even had he wanted to do that, the New Look [Eisenhower's defense strategy] precluded such an effort—the troops simply were not available.

The only hope was through a judicious use of American resources to support allied forces, and not only the French. Eisenhower put Beetle Smith [Under Secretary of State Walter Bedell Smith] at the head of a committee to advise him. Smith recommended using Nationalist Chinese troops, adding that he had made a similar recommendation to Acheson in 1950 with regard to Korea. Smith admitted to Eisenhower that he and Acheson "had some very sharp words about this but I think I was right." Eisenhower thought he was wrong. Putting Chiang Kai-shek's troops into Vietnam would be a sure way to bring on a massive Red Chinese intervention. Besides, he told Smith, "We do not have an overall plan which provides for alternate lines of action in the event things go bad in Indochina regardless of our assistance."

What Eisenhower had in mind was a joint British-U.S. intervention, not with troops but with air support and military hardware. That would be in accord with his basic principle of collective security, it would relieve the Americans of the charge of colonialism, and it would save the French position. Convincing himself, however, was much easier than convincing the British, who wanted no part of an involvement in another war in Asia. Eisenhower wrote directly to Churchill, appealing to his sense of history. Eisenhower said that "I've been thinking a bit of the future. I am sure that when history looks back upon us of today it will not long remember any one of this era who was merely a distinguished war leader whether on the battlefield or in the council chamber." Rather, history would remember those who established ties among the free nations that would allow them to "throw back the Russian threat and allow civilization to continue its progress." In conclusion, Eisenhower declared, "Destiny has given priceless opportunity to some of this epoch. You are one of them. Perhaps I am also one of the company on whom this great responsibility has fallen."

Churchill was unimpressed by Eisenhower's dramatic presentation. Shortly after receiving it, Churchill met with Dulles. The Secretary of State reported to Eisenhower, "The Prime Minister followed his usual line. He said that only the English-speaking peoples counted; that together they could rule the world." Eisenhower deplored such thinking as hopelessly out of date, but he continued to work on Churchill.

Meanwhile, Eisenhower increased direct American military assistance to the French. How much of the war the Americans were paying for at this time is impossible to say because the figures were hidden in so many different ways, but the general estimate is around 75 percent. The French wanted more; specifically and immediately they wanted some B-26 bombers and the technicians to go with them. Eisenhower was terribly exasperated by the French—he blamed their refusal to grant full and free independence to the nations of Indochina for the continuation of the war—but the latest reports he was getting were quite positive about French chances. Eisenhower had not wanted to put American money and prestige into a losing cause, but his special study mission to Indochina, headed by General John O'Daniel, had just reported to him that the Dien Bien Phu fortress could "withstand any kind of attack the Vietminh are capable of launching." The French were on the offensive, or so they said, although Eisenhower found it difficult to see how putting their most famous units into a fortress that was surrounded by high ground that was held by the enemy constituted taking the offensive. But he needed the French vote for EDC; he wanted to keep the French fighting in Vietnam; he could not bear the thought of losing the place through neglect; perhaps this time, with the bombers, the French would stiffen their backs and really go after the enemy. Eisenhower decided to give them something less than half of what they asked for. The French had wanted twenty-five bombers and four hundred Air Force personnel to service them; Eisenhower gave them ten bombers and two hundred people.

On February 8, at a meeting of Republican leaders, Senator Leverett Saltonstall anxiously raised the question about American servicemen going to Indochina. Was yet another President, this one a Republican, going to take the country into yet another war by the back door? That was Saltonstall's implied question, and Eisenhower took it seriously. He carefully explained his reason for giving U.S. Air Force weapons to the French to be used against the Vietminh, and assured Saltonstall that none of the personnel would be in a combat zone. Eisenhower admitted that he was "frightened about getting ground forces tied up in Indochina," and promised that he would pull all two hundred men out of the area on June 15. "Don't think I like to send them there," he added, "but we can't get anywhere in Asia by just sitting here in Washington and doing nothing—my God, we must not lose Asia—we've got to look the thing right in the face." Then he allowed himself Beetle Smith's little fantasy: "I'd like to see Chiang's troops used in Indochina"—and immediately caught himself up— "but the political risk of Chinese Red moves would then be too great."

Still, for all Eisenhower's emphasis on reduced numbers and a definite date for withdrawal, he had sent the first American military personnel to Vietnam. Of course, as Eisenhower insisted, it was hardly an irrevocable step. But still, it had been taken. He was worried about what it might lead to. Earlier, in January, he had told the NSC (in the words of the stenographer), "For himself, said the President with great force, he simply could not imagine the United States putting ground forces anywhere in Southeast Asia, except possibly in Malaya, which we have to defend as a bulwark to our offshore island chain. But to do this anywhere else, said the President with vehemence, how bitterly opposed I am to such a course of action. This war in Indochina would absorb our troops by divisions!"

Long before the Gulf of Tonkin Resolution of 1964, Eisenhower was even more emphatic and prophetic about an American ground involvement in Vietnam. When writing his presidential memoirs, in 1963, he declared, "The jungles of Indochina . . . would have swallowed up division after division of United States troops, who, unaccustomed to this kind of warfare, would have sustained heavy casualties . . . Furthermore, the presence of ever more numbers of white men in uniform probably would have aggravated rather than assuaged Asiatic resentments." (When he published the memoirs, nearly a year later, he deleted that passage, because by then the country was getting involved in Vietnam and he did not want to be critical of the President.) Nevertheless, throughout the long period in 1954 of the French agony at Dien Bien Phu a grim specter dominated his thinking.

In mid-March, the upbeat reports from Vietnam suddenly reversed. Allen Dulles said the French now felt they had only a 50-50 chance at Dien Bien Phu. Furthermore, French Premier René Pleven told ambassador to France Douglas Dillon that "there was no longer the prospect of a satisfactory military solution." Eisenhower was distraught on learning of Pleven's defeatist attitude. "Why don't they withdraw request for military aid?" he wrote Smith. "Might be well to ask."

Eisenhower soon had a chance to ask himself. On March 23 French Army Chief of Staff Paul Ely came to Washington to discuss increasing the flow of American material. Eisenhower and Dulles had a series of meetings with Ely. He wanted additional American aircraft, while Eisenhower pressed him on the status of granting independence. Finally, Eisenhower agreed to furnish the French with some C-119 Flying Boxcars that could drop napalm, "which would burn out a considerable area and help to reveal enemy artillery positions." But Eisenhower would not commit the United States to any military policy of direct intervention until he "got a lot of answers" from Paris on outstanding issues, primarily EDC and Indochinese independence.

Then Eisenhower set about building the support he would need to withstand the strident demands for intervention that he knew would come when Dien Bien Phu fell. He did so by putting conditions on American involvement. They were deliberately created to be impossible of fulfillment, and there were a number of them. First, a full and clear grant of independence by the French. Second, British participation in any venture. Third, at least some of the nations of Southeast Asia had to be involved. Fourth, Congress had to give full and clear prior approval. Fifth, he would want the French to turn the war over to the Americans, but keep their troops in combat. Sixth, the French had to prove that they were not just asking the Americans to cover a fighting withdrawal.

Eisenhower's conditions, impossible as they were, seemed to him to be based on principles that could not be broken. As Dulles told Ely point-blank, the United States could "not afford to send its flag and its own military establishment and thus to engage the prestige of the United States," unless it expected to win. Eisenhower expressed for himself another basic principle, when in an unpublished portion of his memoirs he wrote that "the strongest reason of all for the United States [to stay out] is the fact that among all the powerful nations of the world the United States is the only one with a tradition of anti-colonialism. . . . The standing of the United States as the most powerful of the anti-colonial powers is an asset of incalculable value to the Free World. . . . The moral position of the United States was more to be guarded than the Tonkin Delta, indeed than all of Indochina."

So Eisenhower refused to go very far in meeting Ely's demands. The French general went to [Admiral Arthur W.] Radford, [chairman of the Joint Chiefs of Staff,] who was much more forthcoming. Together they approved joint U.S.-French plans, made in Saigon, for Operation Vulture, an air strike against the Vietminh around Dien Bien Phu. Ely's hope, and Radford's, was that as the end drew near at Dien Bien Phu, Eisenhower could not resist the pressure to intervene. Indeed, some of Eisenhower's aides thought that the French were deliberately losing at Dien Bien Phu in order to force an American intervention. Radford had reason to suppose the President might approve a strike too; just the day before he met with Ely, Eisenhower had told him that he would not "wholly exclude the possibility of a single strike, if it were almost certain this could prove decisive results." But as always, Eisenhower had put on a condition that was impossible to fulfill.

Eisenhower's most impossible conditions were the ones that required allied participation and congressional support. On March 29, Dulles in a speech put forward an idea that he had been given by Eisenhower, that the United States take the lead in forming a "United Action" in Vietnam.

Britain, France, Australia, New Zealand, Thailand, the Philippines, and the Associated States of Indochina would all intervene together. It was an absurd idea, except that it accomplished two objectives for Eisenhower—it allowed a national debate to take place on the wisdom of intervention (which debate, Eisenhower was sure, would convince most people that it was a mistake), and it began building the American fallback position. Eisenhower had reconciled himself to the loss of some of Vietnam, but not all, and certainly not all of Southeast Asia. Already he was committed, in other words, to a division of Vietnam, with the United States then coming in to support the non-Communist south. But he never said so in public, where he continued to insist that a negotiated settlement was out of the question. He still had some faint hopes that the French might pull themselves together, and that the British might at least put in a little material help.

For the record, and to protect himself against right-wing assaults, Eisenhower then tried to get both prior congressional approval and British participation. On April 2, with the situation at Dien Bien Phu growing worse every day, Eisenhower had Dulles and Radford meet with the leaders of both parties in Congress. Dulles said Eisenhower wanted a resolution from Congress that would give him the discretionary authority to use American air and sea power to prevent the "extension and expansion" of Communist aggression in Southeast Asia. The authority would expire on June 30, 1955, and would in no way "derogate from the authority of Congress to declare war." The congressmen, as Eisenhower expected would be the case, were aghast. They cried out "No more Koreas." The only way Eisenhower could get a resolution, they said (thus protecting themselves as carefully as Eisenhower was protecting himself), was if the British and other allies joined in, and if the French promised independence. Dulles decided not to submit the resolution to Congress.

On April 4, Eisenhower sent a telegram to Churchill. He expressed hope about Dien Bien Phu, but warned that "I fear that the French cannot alone see the thing through." Worse, defeat would mean "that the future of France as a great power would be fatally affected." He urged Churchill to join United Action, and between the lines implied to the Prime Minister that he had in mind putting the plan into effect after Vietnam was partitioned.

Then, Eisenhower drew the most telling historical parallel he could think of in appealing to Churchill: "We failed to halt Hirohito, Mussolini, and Hitler by not acting in unity and in time. That marked the beginning of many years of stark tragedy and desperate peril. May it not be that our nations have learned something from that lesson?" But for all the rhetoric, what Eisenhower was really doing was building a negotiating position for a conference in Geneva, scheduled for late April. The meeting had been called earlier to deal with Korea, but the Russians had insisted on putting Indochina on the agenda. Dulles was unhappy because he suspected, rightly, that the French wanted to use Geneva to negotiate themselves out of Vietnam. But he had failed to keep Indochina off the agenda, and partition was in the air, not least because of Dulles' United Action proposal. The Americans knew they had to prepare for the probability of a French withdrawal.

On the morning of April 5, Dulles called Eisenhower to inform him that the French had told Ambassador Dillon that their impression was that Operation Vulture had been agreed to, and hinted that they expected two or three atomic bombs to be used against the Vietminh. Eisenhower told Dulles to tell the French, through Dillon, that they must have misunderstood Radford. Eisenhower said that "such a move is impossible," that without congressional support an air strike would be "completely unconstitutional and indefensible." He told Dulles to "take a look to see if anything else can be done," then again warned, "We cannot engage in active war."

So Eisenhower had rejected intervention. But he had not decided to leave Southeast Asia to its own devices. He very definitely wanted to form a regional grouping for United Action that could draw a line and thus institute a policy of containment. As Truman had done in Europe in the late forties, Eisenhower would seal off the Communists in Southeast Asia. To achieve that goal, he first of all had to convince Congress, the American people, and the potential allies that Indochina was worth the effort. After all, if the Americans were not ready to fight beside the French, why should they, or anyone else, be prepared to fight for whatever was left of a non-Communist Indochina?

At his April 7 news conference, Eisenhower made his most important— and his most famous—declaration on Indochina. Robert Richards of Copley Press asked him to comment on the strategic importance of Indochina to the free world. Eisenhower replied that first of all, "You have the specific value of a locality in its production of materials that the world needs." Second, "You have the possibility that many human beings pass under a dictatorship that is inimical to the free world." Finally, "You have the broader considerations that might follow what you would call the 'falling domino' principle. You have a row of dominoes set up, you knock over the first one, and what will happen to the last one is the certainty that it will go over very quickly. So you could have a beginning of a disintegration that would have the most profound influences." He thought that the "sequence of events," if the United States abandoned Southeast Asia altogether, would be the loss of all of Indochina, then Burma, then Thailand, then Malaya, then Indochina. "Now you begin to talk about areas that not only multiply the disadvantages that you would suffer through loss of materials, sources of materials, but now you are talking really about millions and millions and millions of people." Even worse, the loss of Southeast Asia would be followed by the probable loss of Japan, Formosa, and the Philippines, which would then threaten Australia and New Zealand.

The President had painted a cataclysmic picture. If he was right about the probable consequences of the loss of Indochina, the need for United Action became clear and overwhelming. It was at this point, based on Eisenhower's reasoning, that the United States made its commitment to Vietnam. Not to the whole of Vietnam, but to whatever was left of non-

Communist Vietnam after the Geneva Conference finished partitioning the place. He was taking a halfway position, between those who were demanding an all-out effort to save the French at Dien Bien Phu and those who wanted America to get out and stay out of Southeast Asia.

As the situation at Dien Bien Phu deteriorated, demands for intervention from right-wing American politicians, military leaders, and from the French, increased. On April 16, the Vice-President spoke to the American Society of Newspaper Editors. Nixon was asked whether he thought the United States should send troops into Indochina if the French decided to withdraw. Nixon replied that if sending American boys was the only way to avoid further Communist expansion in Asia, "I believe that the Executive Branch of the government has to take the politically unpopular position of facing up to it and doing it, and I personally would support such a decision." Since Nixon mentioned neither Congress nor allied participation, his statement seemed to represent a major shift in policy. Eisenhower was in Augusta for the weekend, so [Press Secretary James] Hagerty had to face the reporters. He asked Nixon if there had indeed been a policy shift, but Nixon "played dumb" and said he was only answering hypothetical questions. Hagerty commented, "Think it was foolish for Dick to answer as he did but will make the best of it."

At a meeting of the Republican leaders the next week, [Representative] Charlie Halleck told Nixon that his statement "had really hurt" and that he hoped there would be no more talk of that kind. Eisenhower defended Nixon, saying that it was a good thing to keep the Communists guessing about American intentions.

By April 23, the situation at Dien Bien Phu had become desperate. Dulles, who was in Europe trying to get United Action under way, sent a series of alarming cables to Eisenhower. "France is almost visibly collapsing under our eyes," the Secretary declared. He deplored the worldwide publicity being given to Dien Bien Phu, because "it seems to me that Dien Bien Phu has become a symbol out of all proportion to its military importance." Dulles insisted that there was "no military or logical reason why loss of Dien Bien Phu should lead to collapse of French will, in relation both to Indochina and EDC." In another cable, Dulles said the French insisted there were only two alternatives; Operation Vulture or a request for a cease-fire. (There was great confusion about Vulture; Radford, Ely, and Nixon all believed it involved three atomic bombs, while Dulles thought it would be a "massive B-29 bombing" by U.S. planes using conventional bombs.)

Eisenhower phoned Beetle Smith. They agreed that there should be no intervention, no air strike, without allies. Eisenhower then cabled Dulles, saying that he could fully understand Dulles' frustration, but urging the Secretary to keep trying. Dulles replied that it was not at all certain in any case that an air strike would save Dien Bien Phu at this late date. "It is my opinion," the Secretary continued, "that armed intervention by executive action is not warranted. The security of the United States is not directly threatened."

On April 26, the opening day of the Geneva Conference, Eisenhower met with the Republican leaders. He told them that "the French are weary as hell," that Dien Bien Phu would fall within the week, although "the French go up and down every day—they are very voluble. They think they are a great power one day and they feel sorry for themselves the next day." When the congressmen asked the President why the British were so reluctant to get involved, he said that the Churchill government was "worried about Hong Kong and hope it will be left alone. They are fearful that if they move in Indochina the Chinese Reds will move against Hong Kong and could take it easily." Eisenhower said he tried to convince the British that "if we all went in together into Indochina at the same time, that would be fine but if they don't go in with us, they can't expect us to help them defend Hong Kong. We must have collective security or we'll fall." He then assured the leaders that "I don't see any reason for American ground troops to be committed in Indochina, don't think we need it," because "there are plenty of people in Asia, and we can train them to fight. It may be necessary for us eventually to use some of our planes or aircraft carriers off the coast and some of our fighting craft we have in that area for support."

[Senator Gene] Millikin said that if the British and French "deserted, we would have to go back to fortress America." Eisenhower turned on him angrily and ended the discussion by saying, "Listen, Gene, if we ever come back to fortress America, then the word 'fortress' would be entirely wrong in this day and age. Dien Bien Phu is a perfect example of a fortress. If we ever came back to the fortress idea for America, we would have one simple, dreadful alternative—we would have to explode an attack with everything we have. What a terrible decision that would be to make."

After the meeting, Eisenhower walked to the Oval Office with Hagerty. The President told his press secretary to prime a reporter to ask him at the next news conference about the Geneva Conference. Eisenhower would then try to emphasize "that all is not lost if Dien Bien Phu falls, which probably it will within a week."

Eisenhower then wrote a long, thoughtful letter to [General Alfred] Gruenther, [the Supreme Allied Commander, Europe] whom he depended upon as his most reliable link to the French leadership. After repeating once again that unilateral American intervention was out of the question ("it would lay us open to the charge of imperialism and colonialism or—at the very least—of objectionable paternalism"), Eisenhower complained that "ever since 1945 France has been unable to decide whether she most fears Russia or Germany. As a consequence, her policies in Europe have been nothing but confusion; starts and stops; advances and retreats!" Eisenhower said of Dien Bien Phu, "This spectacle has been saddening indeed. It seems incredible that a nation which had only the help of a tiny British Army when it turned back the German flood in 1914 and withstood the gigantic 1916 attacks at Verdun could now be reduced to the point that she cannot produce a few hundred technicians to keep planes flying properly in Indochina." Eisenhower thought the French problem was one of leadership and spirit. "The only hope is to produce a new and inspirational leader—and I do not mean one that is 6 feet 5 and who considers himself to be, by some miraculous biological and transmigrative process, the off-spring of Clemenceau and Jeanne d'Arc."

Then Eisenhower turned serious, ticking off points he wanted Gruenther to make to the French. The loss of Dien Bien Phu did not mean the loss of the war. The French should join United Action to stop "Communist advances in Southeast Asia": not to hurl back, but to stop such expansion; i.e., after partition. Eisenhower wanted the French Army to remain in Vietnam and promised that "additional ground forces should come from Asiatic and European troops already in the region" (that is, there would be no American troops but America would pay the bills). The French should grant independence. The ultimate goal, Eisenhower told the SACEUR to pass on the French, was to create a "concert of nations" in Southeast Asia on the NATO model.

This was Eisenhower's first direct mention of the idea of a Southeast Asia Treaty Organization (SEATO), and it was significant that he made it to the SACEUR. He thought first of NATO. His own vehement anti-Communism certainly played the major role in his Vietnam policy, tempered of course by his realism, but his anxieties about the French were also important considerations. He felt the French had to be dealt with like children, but he rejected the de Gaulle alternative. He had to support Pleven, now reportedly his only hope for getting EDC ratified by the French. And if EDC failed, German rearmament would be even more difficult to achieve. And without German rearmament, NATO would continue to be a hollow shell. In some part, then, SEATO came about because of the needs of NATO.

On the morning of April 29, at a news conference, Eisenhower referred obliquely to partition in response to a question from Joseph Harsch about Eisenhower's recent use of the phrase "*modus vivendi*" in Indochina. Eisenhower said he was "steering a course between two extremes, one of which, I would say, would be unattainable, and the other unacceptable." It would not be acceptable, he explained, "to see the whole anti-Communistic defense of that area crumble and disappear." But because the Vietminh were winning, there could be no hope of getting a "satisfactory answer" from them. "The most you can work out is a practical way of getting along." Eisenhower then mentioned divided Germany and Berlin as an example of "getting along one with the other, no more. Now, I think that for the moment, if you could get that, that would be the most you could ask."

Immediately after the news conference, Eisenhower went to a three-hour NSC meeting, most of it devoted to Vietnam. According to notes Nixon kept, "[Mutual Security Director Harold] Stassen said that he thought that decision should be to send ground troops if necessary to save Indochina, and to do it on a unilateral basis if that was the only way it could be done. The President himself said that he could not visualize a ground troop operation in Indochina that would be supported by the people of the United States and which would not in the long run put our defense too far out of balance. He also raised the point that we simply could not go in unilaterally because that was in violation of our whole principle of collective defense against communism in all places in the world."

Eisenhower told Stassen that there would be the most serious repercussions among the NATO allies, especially Britain, if the United States went in on its own. He then turned the discussion to a post-partition "Pacific coalition." Eisenhower said that future American efforts would be toward organizing a regional coalition, obtaining British support for it, and pressing France to grant independence. Eisenhower would not seek congressional approval for American participation in a collective intervention until a coalition could be put together.

The following morning, [National Security Adviser] Bobby Cutler brought him a draft of an NSC paper that was exploring the possibilities of using atomic bombs in Vietnam. Eisenhower told Cutler, "I certainly do not think that the atom bomb can be used by the United States unilaterally." Eisenhower turned on Cutler. "You boys must be crazy. We can't use those awful things against Asians for the second time in less than ten years. My God."

On May 7, Dien Bien Phu surrendered. Eisenhower tried to keep up the pretense that the French had lost only a battle, not the war. He told the NSC of his "firm belief that two, and only two, developments would really save the situation in French Indochina." First, Paris had to grant independence; second, the French needed to appoint a better general to take charge of the campaign. The French could still win, but time was running out. Cutler then joined Nixon and Stassen in again urging a unilateral American intervention. Eisenhower ignored them.

So Eisenhower's policy was set: to accept partition, although only after obstructing and delaying the process as long as possible, and then to create SEATO. He had managed to avoid involvement in the war, but he was determined to make as firm a commitment to the non-Communist remainder of Southeast Asia as America had made to the NATO countries.

Of all Eisenhower's reasons for staying out of Vietnam, the one that meant most to him was the potential effect of intervention on the American people. The Korean War had been divisive enough; Eisenhower shuddered to think of the consequences of getting into a war to fight for a French colony less than a year after the armistice in Korea. That was the reason for his stress on prior congressional approval; if he could get it, he would be leading a united nation. But he doubted that he could get it, precisely because the nation was badly divided.

Eisenhower's decision to stay out of Vietnam did not have the dramatic quality to it that his 1944 D-Day decision had, because it was made over a longer period of time. Nevertheless, it was as decisive, in its way, because in both cases what happened next depended solely upon his word. At any time in the last weeks of Dien Bien Phu he could have ordered an air strike, either atomic or conventional. Many of his senior advisers wanted him to do just that, including his chairman of the JCS, his Vice-President, his head of the NSC planning staff, his MSA adviser, and (sometimes) his Secretary of State. Eisenhower said no, decisively. He had looked at the military options, with his professional eye, and pronounced them unsatisfactory. On June 5, 1944, they had been satisfactory, and he said go; in April 1954, they were unsatisfactory, and he said don't go.

From that moment, Eisenhower supporters could claim, "He got us out of Korea and he kept us out of Vietnam."

The Tragedy of U.S. Intervention

DAVID L. ANDERSON

"The loss of South Vietnam would set in motion a crumbling process that could, as it progressed, have grave consequences for us and for freedom," President Dwight D. Eisenhower declared in an April 1959 speech. This statement reaffirmed the famous "falling domino" analogy that he had used five years earlier to explain the strategic importance of Indochina. If the states of Southeast Asia fell under "the Communist dictatorship," he asserted in April 1954, the result would be a "disintegration" with the "most profound influence" for "millions and millions and millions of people." Throughout his eight years as president, Eisenhower never wavered in his conviction that the survival of an independent, noncommunist government in southern Vietnam was a vital strategic imperative for the United States. This objective, which Eisenhower's successors in the White House would also support, was the cornerstone of his policies in Southeast Asia, but it left open the question of the means of achieving that goal.

Eisenhower and his foreign policy advisers went through two stages in attempting to devise a successful method of securing U.S. interests in Vietnam. The first approach, which lasted through 1954 and into 1955, was to continue the Truman tactic of working with and through the French and other Western allies to contain communism in Southeast Asia. During this early phase, Eisenhower showed remarkable restraint considering the administration's Cold War rhetoric about the global danger of communist expansionism. He managed to avoid involving the United States militarily in Indochina as France suffered a humiliating defeat at Dienbienphu at the hands of the communist-led Vietminh army. After the French surrender at Dienbienphu, an international conference at Geneva, Switzerland, arranged a Franco-Vietminh cease-fire in July 1954. In the following months, the Eisenhower administration tried to maintain an allied strategy in Indochina. It established the Southeast Asia Treaty Organization (SEATO) and sent a special mission to Vietnam headed by General J. Lawton Collins to attempt, among other things, to continue a joint U.S.-French program in the region.

By the spring of 1955, however, the administration had begun a second, essentially unilateral approach in which the United States sought to protect its strategic interests in Southeast Asia by building a new Vietnamese nation around a reclusive autocrat named Ngo Dinh Diem. For the

From David L. Anderson "Dwight D. Eisenhower and Wholehearted Support for Ngo Dinh Diem," in David L. Anderson, ed., pp. 43–59 in *Shadow on the White House: Presidents and the Vietnam War, 1945–1975*, 1993 by the University Press of Kansas. Used by permission of the publisher.

remainder of the Eisenhower presidency, the United States pegged its Vietnam policy on the questionable ability of Diem. In contrast to the cautious good judgment of the first phase that limited U.S. risks in Southeast Asia, the second phase exhibited a tragic irresponsibility by enmeshing the United States in the tangled web of Vietnamese politics and exposing Americans and American interests to considerable danger.

Eisenhower brought with him to the White House the conviction that the areas of the world "in which freedom flourishes" were under assault from a "Communist-regimented unity." In his first State of the Union address in February 1953, he described France's struggle against the Vietminh as holding "the line of freedom" against "Communist aggression throughout the world." As he prepared to leave office eight years later, his bipolar perception of the world divided between freedom and tyranny— with Southeast Asia at the center of that conflict—had not altered. Eisenhower's farewell address to the nation is remembered primarily for its warning against the dangerous influence of the military-industrial complex in America, but the speech opened with the stern reminder that the nation had faced and would continue to confront "a hostile ideology—global in scope, atheistic in character, ruthless in purpose, and insidious in method." The next day, on January 19, 1961, he warned president-elect John Kennedy that the civil war then raging in Laos threatened to spread communism throughout the entire region.

Besides his commitment to no compromise with world communism, the other hallmark of Eisenhower's policies in Indochina and elsewhere was cost reduction. In a strategy labeled the New Look, his administration sought the most economical ways to protect U.S. security. Commonly associated with the threat to use nuclear force for "massive retaliation," the New Look also called for a greater reliance on military alliances and covert operations.

The New Look was apparent during the initial phase of the administration's Indochina policies in the effort to work with France to defeat the Vietnamese communists. Although they shared the Truman administration's displeasure at the French intent to recolonize Indochina, the Republicans decided that the Cold War required them to stand with their North Atlantic Treaty Organization (NATO) ally. Secretary of State John Foster Dulles candidly admitted to the Senate Foreign Relations Committee that U.S. choices in this situation were distasteful, but in "the divided spirit" of the world today, the United States would have to tolerate the colonialists a bit longer to help block Soviet and Chinese infiltration of Southeast Asia. Dulles also felt compelled to cooperate with France in Indochina because he wanted French officials to accept a rearmed West Germany (a frightened prospect for many in France) as part of a U.S.-backed plan for NATO called the European Defense Community. To bolster French resolve in both Indochina and Europe, the Eisenhower administration increased U.S. aid to the point that it accounted for almost 80 percent of France's military expenditures in Southeast Asia by January 1954.

As the Eisenhower administration observed its first anniversary in office, however, Paris's perseverance was waning. The French public and politicians were tiring of the seven-year burden of the Indochina war. The resilient Vietminh, under the charismatic leadership of Ho Chi Minh, continued to exact a heavy price in blood and treasure from their would-be masters. To the regret of Washington, French leaders accepted a Soviet proposal for a multinational conference at Geneva, set to begin in April, that would attempt to structure a diplomatic settlement in Indochina. Then, in March, the Vietminh assaulted an entrenched French garrison at Dienbienphu with such overwhelming force that a French military disaster appeared possible on the eve of the truce talks. The French might decide at Geneva to capitulate to their communist foes.

The prospect of a socialist ally of the Soviet Union and the People's Republic of China (PRC) emerging triumphant over a member of NATO that had been openly aided by the United States deeply troubled U.S. leaders, who began serious consideration of the New Look's trump card—massive retaliation. Although this option implied the possibility of using nuclear weapons, few U.S. planners believed that the atomic bomb was necessary to balance the military scales at Dienbienphu. In this case, the proposal involved a staggering conventional bombardment of the attacking force using as many as 350 planes from U.S. aircraft carriers and from bases in Okinawa and the Philippines.

Throughout March and April, Eisenhower, Dulles, and other top administration officials weighed the air strike idea but never used it. In early May, the French garrison surrendered after sustaining heavy losses, and this outcome set the stage for the signing of a cease-fire agreement between France and the Vietminh at Geneva. This turn of events has long fascinated observers of Eisenhower's foreign policies. The president and his secretary of state encouraged the image that their hands were tied by congressional and allied reluctance to countenance a risky and perhaps unwarranted rescue of France's failed ambitions. Although this characterization made the White House appear passive, it paid excellent political dividends. It helped shield Eisenhower from personal attacks that he had "lost" something in Vietnam, as Truman had been excoriated for allegedly losing China.

While in office, Eisenhower was beloved by many Americans who admired his leadership of the Allied forces that defeated Nazi tyranny during World War II and who appreciated his humble demeanor and engaging grin. At the same time, however, he seemed to be a rather lackadaisical chief executive who presided over but did not propel his administration. The later declassification of confidential White House files reversed this picture dramatically. The record revealed Eisenhower to be directly and often decisively involved in key decisions such as those on Indochina in 1954. His management of the Dienbienphu crisis has become something of a centerpiece of the rehabilitation of his presidential image in recent years. He utilized the skills of talented subordinates such as Dulles and let them absorb some of the public pressure produced by controversial actions, but the president kept a firm, if hidden, hand on the administration's helm.

The origin of Eisenhower's leadership ability is clear. His rise to the pinnacle of the nation's military structure as a five-star general provided him with a wealth of experience that prepared him to be president. The military had been his leadership laboratory, and his advancement up the ranks in competition with other extremely able officers revealed that he was an adept student of management theory. His method of handling subordinates, for example, was carefully considered. During World War II, he delegated extensive responsibility to such forceful commanders as George Patton and Omar Bradley, but he retained the authority to call them to account when necessary. Similarly, his approach to public relations, contingency planning, and other areas of executive responsibility demonstrated active leadership and effective management style.

The details of the Dienbienphu decision have especially enhanced Eisenhower's reputation. Confronted with a military-diplomatic problem that corresponded to his personal experience, he confidently shaped the policy deliberations. Neither Dulles nor Vice-President Richard M. Nixon, both of whom often spoke out publicly and stridently on foreign policy, fashioned the administration's actions. The president made the decisions that kept U.S. ground and air forces out of combat. "It would be a great mistake for the United States to enter the fray in partnership only with France," Eisenhower believed; "united action by the free world was necessary, and in such action the U.S. role would not require use of its ground troops." The prudence of his course appears statesmanlike in contrast to the steps of later presidents who plunged U.S. forces into hostile action in Southeast Asia.

Yet praise for the decision can easily be overdrawn. Eisenhower's restraint had more to do with the immediate predicament of the French and the perception that Paris had lost the will to fight than with any careful reassessment of U.S. purposes in Vietnam. He was willing to accept a tactical setback in the Cold War at Dienbienphu but was not prepared to question the proclaimed importance of Indochina in the global balance of power. Also, it is a mistake to conclude that Eisenhower was an energetic leader just because the career soldier chose to involve himself personally in a national security issue. A few days after the French garrison surrendered, for example, the U.S. Supreme Court issued its momentous school desegregation decision, *Brown v. the Board of Education of Topeka*. On the matter of racial injustice, which burdened millions of American citizens every day, the president chose to stay uninvolved, declaring that he would express neither "approbation nor disapproval" of the Court's action.

When the Court ruled on the *Brown* case, U.S. delegates were sitting at the Geneva Conference deliberating the fate of Vietnam. The Vietminh victory at Dienbienphu made it likely that the French would accept a compromise with the communists. The Eisenhower administration took a largely passive role in the proceedings to avoid any responsibility for the outcome, but the United States maintained a presence there because the president and his advisers were not willing to embark on a separate, solitary course in the region. With Britain, the USSR, and the PRC mediating, the French and Vietminh reached a cease-fire agreement that temporarily partitioned the country at the 17th parallel. The communist-led Democratic Republic of Vietnam (DRV) would control the North, and France would regroup its military forces in the South. An all-Vietnam election was to be held in two years to determine the future political structure of the nation. The U.S. delegation publicly acknowledged these terms but did not sign or verbally endorse any of them.

Determined to salvage the southern part of Vietnam from communist domination and to do so by collective defense if possible, the Eisenhower administration championed the creation of SEATO in September 1954. Comprising the United States, France, Britain, Australia, New Zealand, the Philippines, Thailand, and Pakistan, this alliance was not a binding security pact like NATO, but it did provide a mechanism for possible joint action in future crises like Dienbienphu and especially in the event of overt aggression by the DRV or PRC. Under the terms of the Geneva Accords, Vietnam and neighboring Laos and Cambodia could not enter into military agreements, but the SEATO pact extended a vague commitment to their security in an attached protocol. Despite the treaty's weaknesses, Dulles hailed it as a "no trespassing" sign to warn away potential communist aggressors, and Eisenhower and his successors in the White House cited SEATO as the authority for U.S. intervention in the region's affairs.

Eisenhower's handling of Dienbienphu, Geneva, and SEATO, taken together, highlighted the strengths and weaknesses of his leadership style. He was managing the Vietnam issue politically but not solving it substantively. Using Dulles as his primary spokesman, Eisenhower had urged "united action" during the siege of Dienbienphu to counter the communist threat in Southeast Asia. With the formation of SEATO, such allied unity seemed possible. Opinion polls indicated that the American public favored this kind of multilateral approach over unilateral action. Similarly, Eisenhower's decision to maintain a discreet distance from the negotiations and final settlement at Geneva avoided a charge that he had accepted a compromise with communists—an allegation that critics had made against Franklin Roosevelt after the Yalta Conference of 1945. The American people wanted toughness in U.S. policy without the risk of war, and the administration's coolness toward the Geneva Accords and its creation of SEATO suited this public mood. In terms of policy, however, toughness alone was not a solution. The true alternatives were either to use force to break DRV power or to accept DRV success. The administration would do neither and hence only deepened the U.S. commitment in Southeast Asia with no realistic prospect for resolving the dilemma of how to protect U.S. interests without war.

Although France entered SEATO, U.S.-French cooperation in Southeast Asia after the Geneva Conference was strained almost to the breaking point. Eisenhower and many of his aides believed that Paris had essentially forfeited its influence on Western policies in Indochina with its weak performance against the Vietminh. The president complained that he was "weary" of the French and their "seemingly hysterical desire to be thought such a 'great power.'" Still, many of the French had strong economic and personal ties with Indochina and were loath to surrender what remained of their position.

In an effort to reestablish a working relationship with French officials in South Vietnam, Eisenhower sent General J. Lawton Collins, a trusted World War II colleague and former army chief of staff, to Saigon in November 1954 as his personal representative. "Lightning Joe" Collins was also to formulate "a crash program to sustain the Diem government and establish security in Free Vietnam." The president thought that French officials in Saigon would cooperate, but, if not, "we ought to lay down the law to the French," he told the National Security Council. "It is true that we have to cajole the French with regard to the European area," Eisenhower added, "but we certainly didn't have to in Indochina."

Collins had some success with military training programs and bureaucratic changes, but eventually his mission and U.S. policy in general reached an impasse with the French over the internal political structure of the South. At issue was the leadership of Ngo Dinh Diem. While the Geneva Conference was under way, Emperor Bao Dai had made Diem prime minister of the State of Vietnam, the vacuous regime that French officials had created as a Vietnamese nationalist alternative to the Vietminh and their alien Marxist ideology. It was this government, currently under the protection of the French in their regroupment zone south of the 17th parallel, that would face the DRV and its president Ho Chi Minh in the Geneva-mandated elections. Not all Vietnamese approved of the Vietminh, who had often ruthlessly silenced their political rivals, but the leaders of the DRV enjoyed the advantage of having forced the capitulation of the colonialists. Diem's regime would have to prove its ability and its patriotism if it was going to shake the appearance of dependence on the Westerners. Some Americans thought Diem might be able to meet this challenge, but only if the French allowed him the true independence to do so.

Diem himself was a complex individual. He was personally honest and courageous and had a well-established record of resistance to French domination of his homeland. These qualities were assets for a Vietnamese politician. He had genuine liabilities, though, that the French were quick to emphasize. He had no political base except his own large family, which had a well-earned reputation for clannish self-interest. His Catholic religion may have pleased the French but only served to isolate him from his predominantly Buddhist countrymen. His personality was aloof, even monkish—the opposite of the modern politician. In addition, he had lived briefly in the United States and knew some influential American politicians and church leaders, such as Senator Mike Mansfield (D-Mont.) and Francis Cardinal Spellman. In fact, it may have been Diem's ties to the United States that prompted Bao Dai to name him prime minister, in a move to court official U.S. support as French power waned in Vietnam.

How Bao Dai came to appoint Diem, a man whom he disliked immensely, is not known with certainty. Some accounts have speculated that the CIA or some other secret U.S. influence was behind the selection. There is no particular evidence available for this scenario, however, and

Bao Dai may well have had his own reasons. Clandestine American contact with Diem after he became prime minister has become well known. Covert initiatives were an explicit element of the New Look, and CIA Director Allen W. Dulles (the secretary of state's brother) sent a special agent to Saigon at the same time that Diem assumed office. Allen Dulles's choice was Air Force Colonel Edward G. Lansdale, an unconventional warfare officer who had aided the Philippine government's successful resistance of a communist rebellion. Lansdale quickly became Diem's confidant and an ardent advocate for firm U.S. support of the prime minister.

Despite endorsement of Diem from Lansdale and others, Eisenhower had given explicit instructions to Collins to evaluate Diem's leadership qualities. After five months of close observation, Collins reported that he judged Diem incapable of providing South Vietnam with the dynamic leadership it needed. Diem and his brothers were running a "practically one-man government," the general informed Washington, and they were stubbornly resistant to helpful advice. Collins recommended other Vietnamese officials whom he thought could better organize a broad-based coalition to compete with the communists. Collins's report shocked Secretary of State Dulles. Although initially dubious of Diem's prospects, the secretary had come to accept the argument of Diem's American friends that the prime minister was the best hope for a nationalist alternative to Ho and that all Diem needed was the confidence that he had the "*wholehearted backing*" of the United States.

Unlike the Dienbienphu discussions of the previous year, debate on the Diem issue in the spring of 1955 did not directly engage the president. Eisenhower chose to stand aside and let Secretary Dulles and General Collins reach a conclusion. The president was preoccupied with the Taiwan Straits crisis and the approach of his first summit conference with Soviet leaders. Meeting with Dulles and other State Department officials in Washington on April 25, Collins maintained his position that Diem was not indispensable, and the secretary reluctantly agreed. Literally at the moment these decisions were being made, street fighting erupted in Saigon. Probably instigated by Diem himself in a desperate demonstration to Washington, the violence enabled the prime minister to obtain enough backing from the fledgling South Vietnamese armed forces to quell the unrest. As Collins rushed back to Saigon to oversee U.S. interests in the unstable situation, Dulles's Asian advisers convinced him to reverse himself and to make wholehearted support of Diem the basis of U.S. policy. The aides argued that the violent outbreak proved that it was an inopportune time to tamper with Saigon's internal politics.

Once the Eisenhower administration had determined that it would stick with Diem, the task remained to convince the French to accept this course. In early May, exactly a year after the surrender of Dienbienphu, Dulles met several times with French premier Edgar Faure. The sessions were stormy, but Faure finally acquiesced to Dulles's insistence on Diem. It was clear that Paris no longer wished to contest Washington over the direction of Western policy in Vietnam. Through the rest of 1955, the French rapidly withdrew the remainder of their forces in South Vietnam and left the fate of the would-be nation to the Americans and their client Diem.

In the long-term history of U.S. involvement in Southeast Asia, Washington had turned an important corner. SEATO had provided a semblance of collective sanction to the U.S. intent to bolster South Vietnam, but the departure of the French demonstrated that the effort actually would be a unilateral U.S. program. The feasibility of the plan hinged on the questionable judgment that Diem could make it work. The administration entered a new and perilous policy phase.

With the basic decision having been made to build a nation around Diem, the implementation now fell to the foreign policy bureaucracy with little additional input from the president or Dulles. After Eisenhower suffered a heart attack in September 1955, many issues that his staff deemed routine, such as Vietnam, were kept from his schedule. The following year, Dulles developed abdominal cancer, and although he remained in office almost until his death in 1959, his personal agenda too became more restricted. Yet the course that Eisenhower and Dulles had set in Vietnam remained the administration's policy until the end of Eisenhower's presidency, and occasionally the two men would publicly reaffirm the concept of wholehearted support for Diem.

The task of nation building loomed large before the administration. The legitimacy of Diem's regime rested only on his appointment by the heir of Vietnam's last royal dynasty, and Sa Majesté Bao Dai had taken up permanent residence on the French Riviera. The State of Vietnam had a small army of 150,000 led by an inexperienced officer corps that, under the French, had never been allowed to have any command or staff authority. The civil bureaucracy consisted only of *fonctionnaires* trained to take orders, not to solve problems. Industry was virtually nonexistent in South Vietnam, and the agricultural base of rice and rubber, although potentially valuable, had been wrecked by exploitative landlords who had impoverished much of the peasantry. Diem himself had no political following that could compete with the regimented and motivated cadre in the DRV.

Diem's political weakness seemed especially important because of the national reunification elections that were supposed to occur in 1956. Although many observers of all ideological perspectives believed that Ho Chi Minh would win any truly free countrywide election, the chances of a referendum occurring were slim from the beginning. The Geneva conferees had drafted a vague proposal for elections because they could not fashion any workable political formula themselves. How the Vietnamese were to vote and on what was never specified. No official in North or South Vietnam had ever organized or conducted a free election, and there was no reason to expect that the Vietnamese would do so now under these strained circumstances. In the months following the Geneva Conference, it was clear that Diem and his American patrons had no enthusiasm for an election, but there was also no pressure for a vote from China, the Soviet Union, Britain, or France. None of these governments was inclined to assume any risk to itself to champion elections in Vietnam for the benefit of the DRV. The Eisenhower administration can be given little credit or blame for the failure of the election provisions of the Geneva agreements.

Even without the serious possibility of a reunification vote, Diem's specious political legitimacy posed grave difficulties for U.S. objectives. Kenneth T. Young, the State Department officer in charge of Southeast Asian affairs, saw the problem as a paradox. He believed that if South Vietnam did not become a republic the anachronistic State of Vietnam would be easy prey for the revolutionary line of the DRV. At the same time, though, he feared that voting for a representative assembly in the South might open the door to political anarchy. While Young and other Americans worried, Diem acted. He staged a lopsided referendum in October 1955 to depose Bao Dai and to make himself president of a newly created Republic of Vietnam (RVN). In March 1956, Diem organized an election of a constituent assembly, heavily stacked in his favor, to draft a constitution. The voting was not an exercise in democracy, but it was impressive evidence of the ability of the Ngo family, especially Diem's brothers Ngo Dinh Nhu and Ngo Dinh Can, to manipulate ballots. The RVN provided a facade of popular government for an ambitious family aspiring to centralized authority.

Evidence of the emerging Ngo family dictatorship mounted. Nhu and Can operated a secret organization, the Can Lao, that used bribery and intimidation to garner personal support for Diem from key members of the military and bureaucracy. Vietminh "suspects," that is, persons thought disloyal to the regime, were arrested and sent to "reeducation camps." An RVN ordinance abolished elected village councils and substituted government appointees to run local affairs. Some U.S. officials, including Secretary Dulles, excused this authoritarianism as typical of Asia and even saw it as prudent because it provided a measure of stability in a nation still developing its institutional structure. Among his criticisms of Diem, Collins had warned that the Ngos' penchant for self-protection would only isolate Diem from the people and weaken the regime. That caution had been rejected, however, in favor of wholehearted support for Diem. As Collins had predicted, the Ngos increasingly behaved as if they could take U.S. aid for granted regardless of how they acted.

The level of U.S. assistance to South Vietnam was high, almost $250 million annually through the end of the Eisenhower years. Some of these funds were designated for economic development. Very little aid went to the agricultural sector, but after U.S. urging, the Diem government announced some rent controls and land transfer plans, which went largely unimplemented. In the urban areas, a U.S.-designed Commercial Import Program made U.S. dollars available to subsidize imports. Rather than stimulate economic activity, however, the plan produced an influx of consumer goods, such as refrigerators and motorbikes, that created an appearance of prosperity but masked the lack of real economic growth.

The bulk of U.S. aid, about 80 percent of it, went directly to the South Vietnamese armed forces. During the Eisenhower presidency, the number of U.S. military personnel in the RVN never exceeded 700, but the large percentage of U.S. aid that went for military purposes revealed the high priority placed on the military security of the new nation. Eighty-five percent of the funds for paying, equipping, and training the RVN's 150,000-man force came from the U.S. Treasury.

Eisenhower and his advisers chose to declare Diem's leadership of South Vietnam a grand success, despite the repressive nature of the Saigon regime and its heavy dependency on aid. On May 8, 1957, the president himself stood on the hot parking apron at Washington National Airport to greet Diem as the RVN leader arrived for a highly publicized state visit. During the next four days, among lavish receptions and private meetings, Diem conferred with Eisenhower, Dulles, and other officials and addressed a joint session of Congress. This pageantry was part of a series of such events hosted by the administration for a number of Asian and African dignitaries. The purpose was to improve U.S. relations with the Third World, which, as Washington had learned during the Suez Canal crisis of 1956, could be vitally important. Diem was a beneficiary of this administration initiative in personal diplomacy.

Eisenhower and other American speakers hailed Diem as a "tough miracle man" and the "savior" of South Vietnam. The administration congratulated Diem and itself on his survival since 1954 and characterized the RVN as a stalwart ally in the struggle against world communism. Behind closed doors the rhetoric was friendly but somewhat more restrained. When Diem asked for an increase in U.S. aid, for example, Eisenhower rebuffed him with the explanation that U.S. global aid commitments prevented greater assistance. The Eisenhower-Diem summit reconfirmed the administration's earlier decisions to treat South Vietnam as strategically important and to give wholehearted endorsement to Diem's regime. It also showed that, even in a region of vital interest, the New Look principle of fiscal restraint still applied.

In the late 1950s, Congress too was determined both to contain foreign aid budgets and to continue assistance to the Diem regime. Only once during the decade did congressional committees hold hearings specifically on Indochina, and that occasion was an investigation of alleged corruption in the management of the aid program in Saigon. Although both Democratic and Republican members questioned the amounts and uses of some funds, the probe uncovered no serious misconduct. At no time during the Eisenhower presidency did Congress as a body challenge the goals of the administration's policies in Vietnam. During the Dienbienphu crisis, some congressional leaders, including Senator Lyndon B. Johnson (D-Tex.), urged the White House to avoid a unilateral U.S. intervention in the French war, but that position was already preferred by the president. Later, as the U.S. commitment to Diem grew, a bipartisan alignment of lawmakers— many of them in an interest group called the American Friends of Vietnam that included Senator John F. Kennedy (D-Mass.)—staunchly defended U.S. involvement in the region.

During Eisenhower's second term, two pressures largely shaped the conduct of U.S. policy in Southeast Asia: (1) the proclaimed value of South

Vietnam to U.S. security and (2) the need to manage economically the United States' global obligations. These twin concerns often exasperated the diplomats and military officers charged with devising and implementing appropriate actions. The problem was how to do more with less. With his attention on Sputnik, Cuba, and elsewhere, the president provided no additional direction to U.S. policymakers as conditions within Vietnam worsened.

By 1957 and 1958, terrorism and armed insurrection were on the rise in South Vietnam. This violence often represented retaliation and resistance to Diem's increasingly repressive regime. Most of these incidents occurred without the instigation of Hanoi. The DRV had not given up its objective of reuniting Vietnam under its rule, but its leaders had ordered their southern cadres to be patient. Hanoi preferred to try propaganda and other destabilizing techniques first rather than to plunge into an armed conflict that could prompt a U.S. military attack on the North. Southern resistance leaders, who faced being jailed and even executed, refused to wait, however, and began acting on their own with assassinations, firebombings, and small attacks on RVN military units and outposts.

Both Vietnamese and American officials in Saigon shared a mounting feeling of crisis, but the instructions from Washington remained clear that the nation-building program would have to make do with what it was already receiving, or likely even less, as the total foreign aid budget shrank. The result was a bitter and debilitating battle between American diplomats and the Ngo family and among the Americans themselves over how to utilize the available resources. The issue was whether to increase the already high percentage of U.S. funds that went to military use or to place more emphasis on economic development and political reform.

U.S. Ambassador in Saigon Elbridge Durbrow took the lead in arguing that the RVN government would remain under attack from within as a neo-colonialist dependent as long as it failed to take genuine steps toward improving the economic and social welfare of its citizens. He even went so far as to suggest to Washington that helicopters and other military items that Diem desired be withheld until the RVN president demonstrated progress on land reform, civil rights, and other abuses—urgent problems that were fueling the hostility toward his regime. Meanwhile, Diem and Nhu vehemently demanded more military aid of all types with which to increase the size and armament of their forces.

Lieutenant General Samuel T. Williams, the chief of the U.S. Military Assistance Advisory Group in Vietnam, took sharp exception to Durbrow's views and sided with the Ngos. He argued that economic and political reforms remained impossible until the partisan violence had been crushed militarily. He also considered it deplorable that Durbrow would propose threatening to deny matériel to Diem at a time when the RVN government was under attack by armed and ruthless opponents. The general complained privately that the ambassador was better suited to be a salesman in a ladies' shoe store than a diplomat in Asia. Williams got support from Lansdale, now a brigadier general in the Pentagon, who advised his Defense

Department superiors that Durbrow was "insulting, misinformed, and unfriendly" toward Diem.

Lansdale's and Williams's personal attacks on the ambassador demonstrated that there was more to the policy debate than just the merits of military versus economic aid. In question was the long-standing Eisenhower administration commitment to wholehearted support of Diem. The generals contended that rather than criticism and pressure, Diem needed Washington's acceptance and reassurance. With the backing of the State Department's Southeast Asia specialists, Durbrow maintained that no one, including Diem, was indispensable. In a pointed comment to his diplomatic colleagues, the ambassador recalled his Pentagon critic's past association with Diem: "We have to recognize that we are dealing with a somewhat more complicated situation in the case of the GVN [Government of Vietnam]," Durbrow declared, "and that we have left the 'Lansdale days' behind." The intensity with which both sides argued revealed how important these officials considered Vietnam to be to the United States. The debate also gave no indication that any of these policymakers thought of doing nothing and simply leaving the outcome in Vietnam up to the Vietnamese.

In January 1961, a few days before John Kennedy took the oath of office as Eisenhower's successor, Lansdale returned from an inspection visit to South Vietnam with a dire report. The RVN was in "critical condition," he declared, and the Vietcong (Washington's new term for Vietnamese communists) "have started to steal the country and expect to be done in 1961." His urgent tone may have derived in part from his ongoing debate over tactics with State Department officers, but it also revealed that the time had come for either reaffirmation or reassessment of the United States' wholehearted support of Diem and the RVN.

As Lansdale delivered his evaluation to the Pentagon, Eisenhower was briefing the president-elect on current world conditions. With a civil war under way in Laos in which the United States and the Soviet Union were supplying weapons to the contending sides, their discussion turned to Southeast Asia. The retiring chief executive claimed that the SEATO treaty obligated the United States to defend the region from communist encroachment. The United States should protect the area's security in cooperation with the SEATO allies if possible, but if not, Eisenhower advised, "then we must go it alone." The next day, January 20, Eisenhower's constitutional authority over the direction of U.S. foreign policy expired, but the course that he had charted in Vietnam would continue.

A review of the long-term significance of the two phases of Eisenhower's Vietnam policies reveals that the second or post-1955 stage with its unilateral and assertive commitment to South Vietnam prevailed over the original multilateral and cautious approach. The goal during both periods was the same: to deny Vietnam or as much of it as possible to the Vietnamese communists. Phase one was a setback to this objective because it ended with de facto acceptance of communist control of the northern half of the country. Eisenhower's negative decision—to avoid taking overt action to resist this outcome—appears as a wise, statesmanlike acceptance of the reality of the Vietminh's success in resisting French colonialism. It was a caution dictated by the immediate circumstances, however. The second phase was also based upon a negative decision—to avoid acceptance of an internal Vietnamese resolution of political authority in the country. This decision was far from statesmanlike. It failed to acknowledge Diem's neo-colonial dependence on U.S. support. It placed U.S. actions in conflict with the manifest Vietnamese desire for national independence. Yet Washington's wholehearted support of Diem continued. By the time Eisenhower left office in 1961, the goal of a noncommunist South Vietnam and the means of obtaining that objective—nation building premised on the survival of the Diem regime—were so deeply embedded in U.S. global strategy as to be virtually unassailable.

Eisenhower's personal strengths served him well during the first phase. His knowledge of military affairs and the politics of war enabled him to perceive clearly the military and political costs inherent in U.S. intervention in the French war. His talent for utilizing a good staff organization also enhanced his analysis of policy options and enabled him to present the outcome as a bureaucratic decision. This maneuvering mitigated potential criticism about being pusillanimous in Vietnam. During the second phase, these same strengths failed him. Once the Geneva cease-fire took effect, the issue in Vietnam was not one of military strategy but of the internal political and economic development of a new nation. Although his experience on General Douglas MacArthur's staff in the Philippines in the 1930s made Eisenhower sensitive to the aspirations of Asian nationalists and familiar with the frustrations of dealing with them, he had no personal acquaintance with any Vietnamese leaders and little grasp of the complex sociopolitical realities of the Asian communism that Diem faced. His one meeting with Diem was largely ceremonial. Similarly, his system of having his staff sift through options did not help alleviate this problem of comprehending complexity. Indeed, the key staff member upon whom he relied for foreign policy advice, Secretary Dulles, generally accepted the single-minded fixation on Diem. It could be argued that Eisenhower's 1955 heart attack made him excessively dependent on his staff, but even after his recovery and return to a rather heavy work load, he gave little personal attention to the details of Vietnam, which his staff presented to him as an issue that was being managed well. He accepted their optimistic assessments and, during Diem's 1957 visit, lent his voice to the chorus of praise for the RVN's achievements. Beneath the miracle facade, however, were serious problems: Diem's narrow political base, his regime's weak military structure, South Vietnam's weak economy, and the growing insurgency. When Eisenhower yielded the White House to Kennedy, the policy of wholehearted support of Diem remained in place not because it was achieving U.S. objectives but because to waver even slightly could risk collapse of the administration's eight-year effort to keep the dominoes from falling. Eisenhower's accomplishments in Vietnam were negative: no war, but no peace. It was a record of nonsolution and ever-narrowing options.

X *F U R T H E R   R E A D I N G*

David L. Anderson, *Trapped By Success: The Eisenhower Administration and Vietnam, 1953–1961* (1991)

James R. Arnold, *The First Domino* (1991)

Victor Bator, *Vietnam: A Diplomatic Tragedy* (1965)

Melanie Billings-Yun, *Decision Against War: Eisenhower and Dien Bien Phu, 1954* (1988)

John P. Burke and Fred I. Greenstein, *How Presidents Test Reality: Decisions on Vietnam 1954 and 1965* (1991)

James Cable, *The Geneva Conference of 1954 on Indochina* (1986)

Cecil B. Currey, *Edward Lansdale* (1988)

Philippe Devillers and Jean Lacouture, *End of a War: Indochina, 1954* (1969)

Robert A. Divine, *Eisenhower and the Cold War* (1981)

Bernard B. Fall, *Hell in a Very Small Place* (1966)

Russell H. Fifield, *Southeast Asia in United States Policy* (1963)

Lloyd C. Gardner, *Approaching Vietnam* (1988)

Melvin Gurtov, *The First Vietnam Crisis* (1967)

Ellen J. Hammer, *The Struggle for Indochina* (1966)

George C. Herring and Richard H. Immerman, "Eisenhower, Dulles, and Dienbienphu: 'The Day We Didn't Go to War' Revisited," *Journal of American History,* 71 (1984), 343–363

Richard H. Immerman, "The United States and the Geneva Conference of 1954: A New Look," *Diplomatic History,* 14 (1990), 43–66

Lawrence S. Kaplan, et al., eds., *Dien Bien Phu and the Crisis of Franco-American Relations, 1954–1955* (1990)

Yuen Foong Khong, *Analogies at War: Korea, Munich, Dien Bien Phu and the Vietnam Decisions of 1965* (1992)

Gabriel Kolko, *Anatomy of a War* (1985)

Edward Geary Lansdale, *In the Midst of Wars* (1972)

Peter Lyon, *Eisenhower* (1974)

Robert J. McMahon, "Eisenhower and Third World Nationalism: A Critique of the Revisionists," *Political Science Quarterly,* 101 (1986), 453–73

Frederick W. Marks III, "The Real Hawk at Dienbienphu: Dulles or Eisenhower?" *Pacific Historical Review,* 69 (1990), 297–322

Richard A. Melanson and David Mayers, eds., *Reevaluating Eisenhower* (1987)

Robert F. Randle, *Geneva 1954* (1969)

Chalmers M. Roberts, "The Day We Didn't Go to War," *Reporter,* 11 (September 14, 1954), 31–35

Jules Roy, *The Battle of Dienbienphu* (1965)

R. B. Smith, *Revolution Versus Containment* (1983)

Ronald H. Spector, *Advice and Support* (1983)

C H A P T E R

5

John F. Kennedy and Vietnam:

Incremental Escalation

✕

The administration of John F. Kennedy inherited an increasingly trouble-some commitment in Vietnam, a land that the young president had once described as the "cornerstone of the Free World in Southeast Asia." Fearful that the United States had lost the global initiative to the Soviet Union and China, Kennedy pursued a more activist foreign policy than his Republican predecessors. He especially sought to avoid additional Cold War defeats. In the spring of 1961, JFK supported—with some reluctance—a negotiated settlement in Laos that would lead to communist participation in a coalition government. Eager to avoid a similar compromise in Vietnam, where he believed that the stakes were much greater, Kennedy gradually increased the American presence there. In November 1961 he ordered the dispatch of several thousand U.S. military advisers to help to avert the collapse of the Diem government. Their number would swell to more than 16,000 by the end of Kennedy's presidency in 1963. When Diem's regime tottered in late 1963 in the face of challenges from both Vietcong guerrillas and Buddhist protesters, American officials backed a coup led by a group of South Vietnamese military officers. In the wake of the coup, Diem was murdered. Within weeks Kennedy himself would fall victim to an assassin's bullet.

JFK's role in the growing U.S. involvement in Vietnam has sparked intense scholarly scrutiny. Most historians agree that his decisions brought incremental, not dramatic, escalation and that he left his successors with deeper but still limited ties to South Vietnam. They differ on almost all other critical questions, including the underlying rationale for Kennedy's decisions, the significance of Vietnam to overall American foreign-policy objectives, the nature and strength of both Diem's regime and the Vietcong insurgency, the precise role of the United States in the coup against Diem, and the broader impact of Diem's ouster on the stability of South Vietnam and the U.S.–Vietnamese relationship. In view of Kennedy's sudden and untimely death, specialists have also speculated about what the president might have done with regard to the Vietnam problem had he lived—and had he been elected to a second term.

X *D O C U M E N T S*

The opening document is a cable of November 1, 1961, sent to President Kennedy by his military adviser, General Maxwell Taylor, recommending the introduction of a U.S. military force into South Vietnam. In a November 11 memorandum to the president, the second document, Secretary of State Dean Rusk and Secretary of Defense Robert S. McNamara also urge the commitment of U.S. troops. They call for the speedy dispatch of support and advisory troops and the development of plans for the possible later commitment of combat forces. In the third document, Jan Barry, a U.S. Army radio technician who served in South Vietnam from December 1962 to October 1963, reflects on his experiences there.

A memorandum from Senator Mike Mansfield to Kennedy is featured in the fourth document. Mansfield, an enthusiastic early supporter of Diem, questions the deepening American commitment in South Vietnam. On September 2, 1963, in a television interview with Walter Cronkite of CBS, Kennedy made a series of critical remarks about Diem's regime. One week later, he expressed similar dissatisfaction with Diem in another television interview while reiterating his belief in the domino theory. Kennedy's interviews are excerpted in the fifth and sixth documents.

The next reading is a cable of October 25, 1963, from Ambassador Henry Cabot Lodge in Saigon to national security adviser McGeorge Bundy, speculating on the prospects for a coup against Diem. The plotters included South Vietnamese General Tran Van Don and CIA agent Lucien Conein. In an October 30 cable to Lodge, the eighth document, Bundy expresses ambivalence about a U.S. role in any coup. The last selection, a transcript of Diem's final telephone conversation with Lodge, records the prime minister's fears for his safety after the outbreak of the rebellion in Saigon.

Maxwell Taylor Recommends the Dispatch of U.S. Forces, 1961

This message is for the purpose of presenting my reasons for recommending the introduction of a U.S. military force into SVN. I have reached the conclusion that this is an essential action if we are to reverse the present downward trend of events in spite of a full recognition of the following disadvantages:

a.   The strategic reserve of U.S. forces is presently so weak that we can ill afford any detachment of forces to a peripheral area of the Communist bloc where they will be pinned down for an uncertain duration.

b.   Although U.S. prestige is already engaged in SVN, it will become more so by the sending of troops.

c.   If the first contingent is not enough to accomplish the necessary results, it will be difficult to resist the pressure to reinforce. If the ultimate result sought is the closing of the frontiers and the clean-up of the insurgents within SVN, there is no limit to our possible commitment (unless we attack the source in Hanoi).

d.   The introduction of U.S. forces may increase tensions and risk escalation into a major war in Asia.

On the other side of the argument, there can be no action so convincing of U.S. seriousness of purpose and hence so reassuring to the people and Government of SVN and to our other friends and allies in SEA as the introduction of U.S. forces into SVN. The views of indigenous and U.S. officials consulted on our trip were unanimous on this point. I have just seen Saigon [cable] 575 to State and suggest that it be read in connection with this message.

The size of the U.S. force introduced need not be great to provide the military presence necessary to produce the desired effect on national morale in SVN and on international opinion. A bare token, however, will not suffice; it must have a significant value. The kinds of tasks which it might undertake which would have a significant value are suggested in Baguio [cable] 0005. They are:

a.   Provide a U.S. military presence capable of raising national morale and of showing to SEA the seriousness of the U.S. intent to resist a Communist takeover.

b.   Conduct logistical operations in support of military and flood relief operations.

c.   Conduct such combat operations as are necessary for self-defense and for the security of the area in which they are stationed.

d.   Provide an emergency reserve to back up the Armed Forces of the GVN [Government of (South) Vietnam] in the case of a heightened military crisis.

e.   Act as an advance party of such additional forces as may be introduced if CINCPAC [U.S. Commander in Chief, Pacific] or SEATO [Southeast Asia Treaty Organization] contingency plans are invoked.

It is noteworthy that this force is not proposed to clear the jungles and forests of VC guerrillas. That should be the primary task of the Armed Forces of Vietnam for which they should be specifically organized, trained and stiffened with ample U.S. advisors down to combat battalion levels. However, the U.S. troops may be called upon to engage in combat to protect themselves, their working parties, and the area in which they live. As a general reserve, they might be thrown into action (with U.S. agreement) against large, formed guerrilla bands which have abandoned the forests for attacks on major targets. But in general, our forces should not engage in small-scale guerrilla operations in the jungle.

As an area for the operations of U.S. troops, SVN is not an excessively difficult or unpleasant place to operate. While the border areas are rugged and heavily forested, the terrain is comparable to parts of Korea where U.S. troops learned to live and work without too much effort. However, these border areas, for reasons stated above, are not the places to engage our forces. In the High Plateau and in the coastal plain where U.S. troops would probably be stationed, these jungle-forest conditions do not exist to any great extent. The most unpleasant feature in the coastal areas would be the heat and, in the Delta, the mud left behind by the flood. The High Plateau offers no particular obstacle to the stationing of U.S. troops.

The extent to which the Task Force would engage in flood relief activities in the Delta will depend upon further study of the problem there. As reported in Saigon 537, I see considerable advantages in playing up this aspect of the TF mission. I am presently inclined to favor a dual mission, initially help to the flood area and subsequently use in any other area of SVN where its resources can be used effectively to give tangible support in the struggle against the VC. However, the possibility of emphasizing the humanitarian mission will wane if we wait long in moving in our forces or in linking our stated purpose with the emergency conditions created by the flood.

The risks of backing into a major Asian war by way of SVN are present but are not impressive. NVN is extremely vulnerable to conventional bombing, a weakness which should be exploited diplomatically in convincing Hanoi to lay off SVN. Both the D.R.V. and the Chicoms [Chinese communists] would face severe logistical difficulties in trying to maintain strong forces in the field in SEA, difficulties which we share but by no means to the same degree. There is no case for fearing a mass onslaught of Communist manpower into SVN and its neighboring states, particularly if our airpower is allowed a free hand against logistical targets. Finally, the starvation conditions in China should discourage Communist leaders there from being militarily venturesome for some time to come.

By the foregoing line of reasoning, I have reached the conclusion that the introduction of [word illegible] military Task Force without delay offers definitely more advantage than it creates risks and difficulties. In fact, I do not believe that our program to save SVN will succeed without it. If the concept is approved, the exact size and composition of the force should be determined by Sec Def in consultation with the JCS, the Chief MAAG [Military Assistance Advisory Group] and CINCPAC. My own feeling is that the initial size should not exceed about 8000, of which a preponderant number would be in logistical-type units. After acquiring experience in operating in SVN, this initial force will require reorganization and adjustment to the local scene.

As CINCPAC will point out, any forces committed to SVN will need to be replaced by additional forces to his area from the strategic reserve in the U.S. Also, any troops to SVN are in addition to those which may be required to execute SEATO Plan 5 in Laos. Both facts should be taken into account in current considerations of the FY [fiscal year] 1963 budget which bear upon the permanent increase which should be made in the U.S. military establishment to maintain our strategic position for the long pull.

Dean Rusk and Robert S. McNamara's Alternative Plan, 1961

1. United States National Interests in South Viet-Nam.

The deteriorating situation in South Viet-Nam requires attention to the nature and scope of United States national interests in that country. The loss of South Viet-Nam to Communism would involve the transfer of a nation of 20 million people from the free world to the Communist bloc. The loss of

South Viet-Nam would make pointless any further discussion about the importance of Southeast Asia to the free world; we would have to face the near certainty that the remainder of Southeast Asia and Indonesia would move to a complete accommodation with Communism, if not formal incorporation with the Communist bloc. The United States, as a member of SEATO, has commitments with respect to South Viet-Nam under the Protocol to the SEATO Treaty. Additionally, in a formal statement at the conclusion session of the 1954 Geneva Conference, the United States representative stated that the United States "would view any renewal of the aggression . . . with grave concern and seriously threatening international peace and security."

The loss of South Viet-Nam to Communism would not only destroy SEATO but would undermine the credibility of American commitments elsewhere. Further, loss of South Viet-Nam would stimulate bitter domestic controversies in the United States and would be seized upon by extreme elements to divide the country and harass the Administration. . . .

3. The United States' Objective in South Viet-Nam.

The United States should commit itself to the clear objective of preventing the fall of South Viet-Nam to Communist [sic]. The basic means for accomplishing this objective must be to put the Government of South Viet-Nam into a position to win its own war against the Guerillas. We must insist that that Government itself take the measures necessary for that purpose in exchange for large-scale United States assistance in the military, economic and political fields. At the same time we must recognize that it will probably not be possible for the GVN to win this war as long as the flow of men and supplies from North Viet-Nam continues unchecked and the guerillas enjoy a safe sanctuary in neighboring territory.

We should be prepared to introduce United States combat forces if that should become necessary for success. Dependent upon the circumstances, it may also be necessary for United States forces to strike at the source of the aggression in North Viet-Nam.

4. The Use of United States Forces in South Viet-Nam.

The commitment of United States forces to South Viet-Nam involves two different categories: (A) Units of modest size required for the direct support of South Viet-Namese military effort, such as communications, helicopter and other forms of airlift, reconnaissance aircraft, naval patrols, intelligence units, etc., and (B) larger organized units with actual or potential direct military mission. *Category (A) should be introduced as speedily as possible.* Category (B) units pose a more serious problem in that they are much more significant from the point of view of domestic and international political factors and greatly increase the probabilities of Communist bloc escalation. Further, the employment of United States combat forces (in the absence of Communist bloc escalation) involves a certain dilemma: if there is a strong South-Vietnamese effort, they may not be needed; if there is not such an effort, United States forces could not accomplish their mission in the midst of an apathetic or hostile population. Under present circumstances, therefore, the question of injecting United States and SEATO combat forces should in large part be considered as a contribution to the morale of the South Vietnamese in their own effort to do the principal job themselves.

5. Probable Extent of the Commitment of United States Forces.

If we commit Category (B) forces to South Viet-Nam, the ultimate possible extent of our military commitment in Southeast Asia must be faced. The struggle may be prolonged, and Hanoi and Peiping may overtly intervene. It is the view of the Secretary of Defense and the Joint Chiefs of Staff that, in the light of the logistic difficulties faced by the other side, we can assume that the maximum United States forces required on the ground in Southeast Asia would not exceed six divisions, or about 205,000 men (CINCPAC Plan 32/59 PHASE IV). This would be in addition to local forces and such SEATO forces as may be engaged. It is also the view of the Secretary of Defense and the Joint Chiefs of Staff that our military posture is, or, with the addition of more National Guard or regular Army divisions, can be made, adequate to furnish these forces and support them in action without serious interference with our present Berlin plans. . . .

In the light of the foregoing, the Secretary of State and the Secretary of Defense recommend that:

1. We now take the decision to commit ourselves to the objective of preventing the fall of South Viet-Nam to Communism and that, in doing so, we recognize that the introduction of United States and other SEATO forces may be necessary to achieve this objective. (However, if it is necessary to commit outside forces to achieve the foregoing objective our decision to introduce United States forces should not be contingent upon unanimous SEATO agreement thereto.)

2. The Department of Defense be prepared with plans for the use of United States forces in South Viet-Nam under one or more of the following purposes:

    a. Use of a significant number of United States forces to signify United States determination to defend Viet-Nam and to boost South Viet-Nam morale.

    b. Use of substantial United States forces to assist in suppressing Viet Cong insurgency short of engaging in detailed counter-guerrilla operations but including relevant operations in North Viet-Nam.

    c. Use of United States forces to deal with the situation if there is organized Communist military intervention.

3. We immediately undertake the following actions in support of the GVN:

    . . . c. Provide the GVN with small craft, including such United States uniformed advisers and operating personnel as may be necessary for quick and effective operations in effecting surveillance and control over coastal waters and inland waterways. . . .

e. Provide such personnel and equipment as may be necessary to improve the military-political intelligence system beginning at the provincial level and extending upward through the Government and the armed forces to the Central Intelligence Organization.
f. Provide such new terms of reference, reorganization and additional personnel for United States military forces as are required for increased United States participation in the direction and control of GVN military operations and to carry out the other increased responsibilities which accrue to MAAG under these recommendations. . . .
i. Provide individual administrators and advisers for insertion into the Governmental machinery of South Viet-Nam in types and numbers to be agreed upon by the two Governments. . . .

5. Very shortly before the arrival in South Viet-Nam of the first increments of United States military personnel and equipment proposed under 3., above, that would exceed the Geneva Accord ceilings, publish the "Jorden report" [a report by State Department official William J. Jorden that was critical of Diem] as a United States "white paper," transmitting it as simultaneously as possible to the Governments of all countries with which we have diplomatic relations, including the Communist states.

6. Simultaneous with the publication of the "Jorden report," release an exchange of letters between Diem and the President.

a. Diem's letter would include: reference to the DRV violations of Geneva Accords as set forth in the October 24 GVN letter to the ICC [International Control Commission] and other documents; pertinent references to GVN statements with respect to its intent to observe the Geneva Accords; reference to its need for flood relief and rehabilitation; reference to previous United States aid and the compliance hitherto by both countries with the Geneva Accords; reference to the USG statement at the time the Geneva Accords were signed; the necessity of now exceeding some provisions of the Accords in view of the DRV violations thereof; the lack of aggressive intent with respect to the DRV; GVN intent to return to strict compliance with the Geneva Accords as soon as the DRV violations ceased; and request for additional United States assistance in framework foregoing policy. The letter should also set forth in appropriate general terms steps Diem has taken and is taking to reform Governmental structure.
b. The President's reply would be responsive to Diem's request for additional assistance and acknowledge and agree to Diem's statements on the intent promptly to return to strict compliance with the Geneva Accords as soon as DRV violations have ceased. . . .

An Early U.S. Army Adviser Remembers His Experiences (1962-1963), 1981

I was nineteen and turned twenty when I was there. I joined the Army in May of 1962 and was in Vietnam in December, just as I finished radio school. That was my first assignment. I could've had orders, as everyone else in the class did, to Germany. Two of us had orders to Vietnam. Before I even joined the Army I ran into a guy who'd graduated from high school a year or two ahead of me. He had just gotten out of the Army from Alaska. He said, "Wow, the place to go is Vietnam. You get combat pay in addition to overseas pay. You can really clean up." In the Army there was an undercurrent that there was someplace in the world where you could get combat pay. But there was no real discussion in the newspapers, as I can recall.

Some people in the unit had no conception where they were in the world, they didn't care. It wasn't Tennessee. It wasn't the state they came from. So therefore they had no interest in learning anything. Other people were very interested and learned Vietnamese and became very close with a number of Vietnamese people. At some point you began to realize that the people around the military base were clearly cooperating with the guerrillas because they were able to infiltrate the inside of our bases and we hadn't the faintest idea where the guerrillas were.

When the Buddhist demonstrations began against the Diem government [1963], it became very clear to most Americans there who probably hadn't been paying attention that we were supporting a police state which, against its own people who were peaceably having demonstrations, would turn loose tanks and machine guns and barbed wire all over the country. From May of '63 all through the summer we'd get caught up in them, just trying to walk around in civilian clothes to go to bars. . . .

The entire contingent of Americans in Vietnam was so thinly spread out that there probably weren't more than five hundred in any one place. Tan Son Nhut had the highest concentration. And it was becoming apparent that the ARVN [Army of the Republic of Vietnam] might turn on us. That became a real worry in the summer of 1963. It became rather apparent from discussion going on that there was going to be a coup. I recall going to Saigon several times and hearing this undercurrent in bars where Vietnamese officers would be.

I left Vietnam in mid-October 1963 and the coup happened two weeks later. One of the people who was still there said that the night before the coup took place they were told to get packed up, be ready to leave the country, be ready to blow up their equipment. At that point one of the options was to completely leave Vietnam. . . .

Almost no one in the Washington area knew we had anything like what was going on in Vietnam. Those of us who had been there wore our military patches on our right shoulders, which denoted that we had been in the

From *Everything We Had* by Al Santoli, pp. 6–11. Copyright © 1981 by Albert Santoli and Vietnam Veterans of America. Reprinted by permission of Random House, Inc.

war. Colonels would stop me and say, "What war have you been in, son? Where is that? We have people fighting over there?"

Mike Mansfield Questions American Policy, 1962

Even assuming that aid over a prolonged period would be available, the question still remains as to the capacity of the present Saigon government to carry out the task of social engineering. Ngo Dinh Diem remains a dedicated, sincere, hardworking, incorruptible and patriotic leader. But he is older and the problems which confront him are more complex than those which he faced when he pitted his genuine nationalism against, first, the French and Bao Dai and then against the sects with such effectiveness. The energizing role which he played in the past appears to be passing to other members of his family, particularly Ngo Dinh Nhu. The latter is a person of great energy and intellect who is fascinated by the operations of political power and has consummate eagerness and ability in organizing and manipulating it. But it is Ngo Dinh Diem, not Ngo Dinh Nhu, who has such popular mandate to exercise power as there is in south Vietnam. In a situation of this kind there is a great danger of the corruption of unbridled power. This has implications far beyond the persistent reports and rumors of fiscal and similar irregularities which are, in any event, undocumented. More important is its effect on the organization of the machinery for carrying out the new concepts. The difficulties in Vietnam are not likely to be overcome by a handful of paid retainers and sycophants. The success of the new approach in Vietnam presupposes a great contribution of initiative and self-sacrifice from a substantial body of Vietnamese with capacities for leadership at all levels. Whether that contribution can be obtained remains to be seen. For in the last analysis it depends upon a diffusion of political power, essentially in a democratic pattern. The trends in the political life of Vietnam have not been until now in that direction despite lip service to the theory of developing democratic and popular institutions "from the bottom up" through the strategic hamlet program.

To summarize, our policies and activities are designed to meet an existing set of internal problems in south Vietnam. North Vietnam infiltrates some supplies and cadres into the south; together with the Vietnamese we are trying to shut off this flow. The Vietcong has had the offensive in guerrilla warfare in the countryside; we are attempting to aid the Vietnamese military in putting them on the defensive with the hope of eventually reducing them at least to ineffectiveness. Finally, the Vietnamese peasants have sustained the Vietcong guerrillas out of fear, indifference or blandishment and we are helping the Vietnamese in an effort to win the peasants away by offering them the security and other benefits which may be provided in the strategic hamlets.

That, in brief, is the present situation. As noted, there is optimism that success will be achieved quickly. My own view is that the problems can be made to yield to present remedies, *provided* the problems and their magnitude do not change significantly and *provided* that the remedies are pursued by both Vietnamese and Americans (and particularly the former) with great vigor and self-dedication.

Certainly, if these remedies do not work, it is difficult to conceive of alternatives, with the possible exception of a truly massive commitment of American military personnel and other resources—in short going to war fully ourselves against the guerrillas—and the establishment of some form of neocolonial rule in south Vietnam. That is an alternative which I most emphatically do not recommend. On the contrary, it seems to me most essential that we make crystal clear to the Vietnamese government and to our own people that while we will go to great lengths to help, the primary responsibility rests with the Vietnamese. Our role is and must remain secondary in present circumstances. It is their country, their future which is most at stake, not ours.

To ignore that reality will not only be immensely costly in terms of American lives and resources but it may also draw us inexorably into some variation of the unenviable position in Vietnam which was formerly occupied by the French. We are not, of course, at that point at this time. But the great increase in American military commitment this year has tended to point us in that general direction and we may well begin to slide rapidly toward it if any of the present remedies begin to falter in practice.

As indicated, our planning appears to be predicated on the assumption that existing internal problems in South Vietnam will remain about the same and can be overcome by greater effort and better techniques. But what if the problems do not remain the same? To all outward appearances, little if any thought has been given in Saigon at least, to the possibilities of a change in the nature of the problems themselves. Nevertheless, they are very real possibilities and the initiative for instituting change rests in enemy hands largely because of the weakness of the Saigon government. The range of possible change includes a step-up in the infiltration of cadres and supplies by land or sea. It includes the use of part or all of the regular armed forces of North Vietnam, reported to be about 300,000 strong, under Vo Nguyen Giap. It includes, in the last analysis, the possibility of a major increase in any of many possible forms of Chinese Communist support for the Vietcong.

None of these possibilities may materialize. It would be folly, however, not to recognize their existence and to have as much clarification in advance of what our response to them will be if they do.

This sort of anticipatory thinking cannot be undertaken with respect to the situation in Vietnam alone. The problem there can be grasped, it seems to me, only as we have clearly in mind our interests with respect to all of Southeast Asia. If it is essential in our own interests to maintain a quasi-permanent position of power on the Asian mainland as against the Chinese then we must be prepared to continue to pay the present cost in Vietnam indefinitely and to meet any escalation on the other side with at least a commensurate escalation of commitment of our own. This can go very far, indeed, in terms of lives and resources. Yet if it is essential to our interests then we would have no choice.

But if on the other hand it is, at best, only desirable rather than essential that a position of power be maintained on the mainland, then other courses are indicated. We would, then, properly view such improvement as may be obtained by the new approach in Vietnam primarily in terms of what it might contribute to strengthening our diplomatic hand in the Southeast Asian region. And we would use that hand as vigorously as possible and in every way possible not to deepen our costly involvement on the Asian mainland but to lighten it.

John F. Kennedy Criticizes the South Vietnamese Government, 1963

Mr. Cronkite: Mr. President, the only hot war we've got running at the moment is of course the one in Viet-Nam, and we have our difficulties there, quite obviously.

The President: I don't think that unless a greater effort is made by the Government to win popular support that the war can be won out there. In the final analysis, it is their war. They are the ones who have to win it or lose it. We can help them, we can give them equipment, we can send our men out there as advisers, but they have to win it, the people of Viet-Nam, against the Communists.

We are prepared to continue to assist them, but I don't think that the war can be won unless the people support the effort and, in my opinion, in the last 2 months, the government has gotten out of touch with the people.

The repressions against the Buddhists, we felt, were very unwise. Now all we can do is to make it very clear that we don't think this is the way to win. It is my hope that this will become increasingly obvious to the government, that they will take steps to try to bring back popular support for this very essential struggle.

Mr. Cronkite: Do you think this government still has time to regain the support of the people?

The President: I do. With changes in policy and perhaps with personnel I think it can. If it doesn't make those changes, I would think that the chances of winning it would not be very good.

Mr. Cronkite: Hasn't every indication from Saigon been that President Diem has no intention of changing his pattern?

The President: If he does not change it, of course, that is his decision. He has been there 10 years and, as I say, he has carried this burden when he has been counted out on a number of occasions.

Our best judgment is that he can't be successful on this basis. We hope that he comes to see that, but in the final analysis it is the people and the government itself who have to win or lose this struggle. All we can do is help, and we are making it very clear, but I don't agree with those who say we should withdraw. That would be a great mistake. I know people don't like Americans to be engaged in this kind of an effort. Forty-seven Americans have been killed in combat with the enemy, but this is a very important struggle even though it is far away.

We took all this—made this effort to defend Europe. Now Europe is quite secure. We also have to participate—we may not like it—in the defense of Asia.

Kennedy Reaffirms the Domino Theory, 1963

Mr. Huntley: Mr. President, in respect to our difficulties in South Viet-Nam, could it be that our Government tends occasionally to get locked into a policy or an attitude and then finds it difficult to alter or shift that policy?

The President: Yes, that is true. I think in the case of South Viet-Nam we have been dealing with a Government which is in control, has been in control for 10 years. In addition, we have felt for the last 2 years that the struggle against the Communists was going better. Since June, however— the difficulties with the Buddhists—we have been concerned about a deterioration, particularly in the Saigon area, which hasn't been felt greatly in the outlying areas but may spread. So we are faced with the problem of wanting to protect the area against the Communists. On the other hand, we have to deal with the Government there. That produces a kind of ambivalence in our efforts which exposes us to some criticism. We are using our influence to persuade the Government there to take those steps which will win back support. That takes some time, and we must be patient, we must persist.

Mr. Huntley: Are we likely to reduce our aid to South Viet-Nam now?

The President: I don't think we think that would be helpful at this time. If you reduce your aid, it is possible you could have some effect upon the government structure there. On the other hand, you might have a situation which could bring about a collapse. Strongly in our mind is what happened in the case of China at the end of World War II, where China was lost— a weak government became increasingly unable to control events. We don't want that.

Mr. Brinkley: Mr. President, have you had any reason to doubt this so-called "domino theory," that if South Viet-Nam falls, the rest of Southeast Asia will go behind it?

The President: No, I believe it. I believe it. I think that the struggle is close enough. China is so large, looms so high just beyond the frontiers, that if South Viet-Nam went, it would not only give them an improved geographic position for a guerrilla assault on Malaya but would also give the impression that the wave of the future in Southeast Asia was China and the Communists. So I believe it.

Mr. Brinkley: In the last 48 hours there have been a great many conflicting reports from there about what the CIA [Central Intelligence Agency] was up to. Can you give us any enlightenment on it?

The President: No.

Mr. Huntley: Does the CIA tend to make its own policy? That seems to be the debate here.

The President: No, that is the frequent charge, but that isn't so. Mr. [John A.] McCone, head of the CIA, sits in the National Security Council.

We have had a number of meetings in the past few days about events in South Viet-Nam. Mr. McCone participated in every one, and the CIA coordinates its efforts with the State Department and the Defense Department.

Mr. Brinkley: With so much of our prestige, money, so on, committed in South Viet-Nam, why can't we exercise a little more influence there, Mr. President?

The President: We have some influence. We have some influence and we are attempting to carry it out. I think we don't—we can't expect these countries to do everything the way we want to do them. They have their own interest, their own personalities, their own tradition. We can't make everyone in our image, and there are a good many people who don't want to go in our image. In addition, we have ancient struggles between countries. In the case of India and Pakistan, we would like to have them settle Kashmir. That is our view of the best way to defend the subcontinent against communism. But that struggle between India and Pakistan is more important to a good many people in that area than the struggle against the Communists. We would like to have Cambodia, Thailand, and South Viet-Nam all in harmony. but there are ancient differences there. We can't make the world over, but we can influence the world. The fact of the matter is that with the assistance of the United States and SEATO [Southeast Asia Treaty Organization], Southeast Asia and indeed all of Asia has been maintained independent against a powerful force, the Chinese Communists. What I am concerned about is that Americans will get impatient and say, because they don't like events in Southeast Asia or they don't like the Government in Saigon, that we should withdraw. That only makes it easy for the Communists. I think we should stay. We should use our influence in as effective a way as we can, but we should not withdraw.

Henry Cabot Lodge Discusses Coup Prospects, 1963

1. I appreciate the concern expressed by you [national security advisor McGeorge Bundy] in ref. a relative to the Gen. Don/Conein relationship, and also the present lack of firm intelligence on the details of the general's plot. I hope that ref. b will assist in clearing up some of the doubts relative to general's plans, and I am hopeful that the detailed plans promised for two days before the coup attempt will clear up any remaining doubts.

2. CAS [Classified American Source—reference to CIA] has been punctilious in carrying out my instructions. I have personally approved each meeting between Gen. Don and Conein who has carried out my orders in each instance explicitly. While I share your concern about the continued involvement of Conein in this matter, a suitable substitute for Conein as the principal contact is not presently available. Conein, as you know, is a friend of some eighteen years' standing with Gen. Don, and General Don has expressed extreme reluctance to deal with anyone else. I do not believe the involvement of another American in close contact with the generals would be productive. We are, however, considering the feasibility of a plan for the introduction of an additional officer as a cut-out between Conein and a

designee of Gen. Don for communication purposes only. This officer is completely unwitting of any details of past or present coup activities and will remain so.

3. With reference to Gen [Paul D.] Harkins' [chief of MAAG] comment to Gen. Don which Don reports to have referred to a presidential directive and the proposal for a meeting with me, this may have served the useful purpose of allaying the General's fears as to our interest. If this were a provocation, the GVN could have assumed and manufactured any variations of the same theme. As a precautionary measure, however, I of course refused to see Gen. Don. As to the lack of information as to General Don's real backing, and the lack of evidence that any real capabilities for action have been developed, ref. b provides only part of the answer. I feel sure that the reluctance of the generals to provide the U.S. with full details of their plans at this time, is a reflection of their own sense of security and a lack of confidence that in the large American community present in Saigon their plans will not be prematurely revealed.

4. The best evidence available to the Embassy, which I grant you is not as complete as we would like it, is that Gen. Don and the other generals involved with him are seriously attempting to effect a change in the government. I do not believe that this is a provocation by Ngo Dinh Nhu, although we shall continue to assess the planning as well as possible. In the event that the coup aborts, or in the event that Nhu has masterminded a provocation, I believe that our involvement to date through Conein is still within the realm of plausible denial. CAS is perfectly prepared to have me disavow Conein at any time it may serve the national interest.

5. I welcome your reaffirming instructions contained in CAS Washington [cable] 74228. It is vital that we neither thwart a *coup* nor that we are even in a position where we do not know what is going on.

6. We should not thwart a *coup* for two reasons. First, it seems at least an even bet that the next government would not bungle and stumble as much as the present one has. Secondly, it is extremely unwise in the long range for us to pour cold water on attempts at a coup, particularly when they are just in their beginning stages. We should remember that this is the only way in which the people in Vietnam can possibly get a change of government. Whenever we thwart attempts at a coup, as we have done in the past, we are incurring very long lasting resentments, we are assuming an undue responsibility for keeping the incumbents in office, and in general are setting ourselves in judgment over the affairs of Vietnam. Merely to keep in touch with this situation and a policy merely limited to "not thwarting" are courses both of which entail some risks but these are lesser risks than either thwarting all coups while they are stillborn or our not being informed of what is happening. All the above is totally distinct from not wanting U.S. military advisors to be distracted by matters which are not in their domain, with which I heartily agree. But obviously this does not conflict with a policy of not thwarting. In judging proposed coups, we must consider the effect on the war effort. Certainly a succession of fights for control of the Government of Vietnam would interfere with the war effort.

It must also be said that the war effort has been interfered with already by the incompetence of the present government and the uproar which this has caused.

7. Gen. Don's intention to have no religious discrimination in a future government is commendable and I applaud his desire not to be "a vassal" of the U.S. But I do not think his promise of a democratic election is realistic. This country simply is not ready for that procedure. I would add two other requirements. First, that there be no wholesale purges of personnel in the government. Individuals who were particularly reprehensible could be dealt with later by the regular legal process. Then I would be impractical, but I am thinking of a government which might include Tri Quang and which certainly should include men of the stature of Mr. Buu, the labor leader.

8. Copy to Gen. Harkins.

McGeorge Bundy Expresses Reservations, 1963

1. Your [cables] 2023, 2040, 2041 and 2043 examined with care at highest levels here. You should promptly discuss this reply and associated messages with Harkins whose responsibilities toward any coup are very heavy especially after you leave (see para. 7 below). They give much clearer picture group's alleged plans and also indicate chances of action with or without our approval now so significant that we should urgently consider our attitude and contingency plans. We note particularly Don's curiosity your departure and his insistence Conein be available from Wednesday night on, which suggests date might be as early as Thursday.

2. Believe our attitude to coup group can still have decisive effect on its decisions. We believe that what we say to coup group can produce delay of coup and that betrayal of coup plans to Diem is not repeat not our only way of stopping coup. We therefore need urgently your combined assessment with Harkins and CAS (including their separate comments if they desire). We concerned that our line-up of forces in Saigon (being cabled in next message) indicates approximately equal balance of forces, with substantial possibility serious and prolonged fighting or even defeat. Either of these could be serious or even disastrous for U.S. interests, so that we must have assurance balance of forces clearly favorable.

3. With your assessment in hand, we might feel that we should convey message to Don, whether or not he gives 4 or 48 hours notice that would (A) continue explicit hands-off policy, (B) positively encourage coup, or (C) discourage.

4. In any case, believe Conein should find earliest opportunity express to Don that we do not find presently revealed plans give clear prospect of quick results. This conversation should call attention important Saigon units still apparently loyal to Diem and raise serious issue as to what means coup group has to deal with them.

5. From operational standpoint, we also deeply concerned Don only spokesman for group and possibility cannot be discounted he may not be in

good faith. We badly need some corroborative evidence whether Minh and others directly and completely involved. In view Don's claim he doesn't handle "military planning" could not Conein tell Don that we need better military picture and that Big Minh could communicate this most naturally and easily to [General Richard] Stilwell [Harkins's Chief of Staff]? We recognize desirability involving MACV [U.S. Military Assistance Command, Vietnam] to minimum, but believe Stilwell far more desirable this purpose than using Conein both ways.

6. Complexity above actions raises question whether you should adhere to present Thursday schedule. Concur you and other U.S. elements should take no action that could indicate U.S. awareness coup possibility. However, DOD [Department of Defense] is sending berth-equipped military aircraft that will arrive Saigon Thursday and could take you out thereafter as late as Saturday afternoon in time to meet your presently proposed arrival Washington Sunday. You could explain this being done as convenience and that your Washington arrival is same. A further advantage such aircraft is that it would permit your prompt return from any point en route if necessary. To reduce time in transit, you should use this plane, but we recognize delaying your departure may involve greater risk that you personally would appear involved if any action took place. However, advantages your having extra two days in Saigon may outweigh this and we leave timing of flight to your judgment.

7. Whether you leave Thursday or later, believe it essential that prior your departure there be fullest consultation Harkins and CAS and that there be clear arrangements for handling (A) normal activity, (B) continued coup contacts, (C) action in event a coup starts. We assume you will wish Truehart as charge to be head of country team in normal situation, but highest authority desires it clearly understood that after your departure Harkins should participate in supervision of all coup contacts and that in event a coup begins, he become head of country team and direct representative of President, with [William] Truehart [Deputy Chief of Mission] in effect acting as POLAD [Political Adviser]. On coup contacts we will maintain continuous guidance and will expect equally continuous reporting with prompt account of any important divergences in assessments of Harkins and Smith.

8. If coup should start, question of protecting U.S. nationals at once arises. We can move Marine Battalion into Saigon by air from Okinawa within 24 hours—if available. We are sending instructions to CINCPAC to arrange orderly movement of seaborne Marine Battalion to waters adjacent to South Vietnam in position to close Saigon within approximately 24 hours.

9. We are now examining post-coup contingencies here and request your immediate recommendations on position to be adopted after coup begins, especially with respect to requests for assistance of different sorts from one side or the other also request you forward contingency recommendations for action if coup (A) succeeds, (B) fails, (C) is indecisive.

10. We reiterate burden of proof must be on coup group to show a substantial possibility of quick success; otherwise, we should discourage them

from proceeding since a miscalculation could result in jeopardizing U.S. position in Southeast Asia.

Diem's Final Appeal for U.S. Help, 1963

Diem: Some units have made a rebellion and I want to know what is the attitude of the U.S.?

Lodge: I do not feel well enough informed to be able to tell you. I have heard the shooting, but am not acquainted with all the facts. Also it is 4:30 a.m. in Washington and the U.S. Government cannot possibly have a view.

Diem: But you must have some general ideas. After all, I am a Chief of State. I have tried to do my duty. I want to do now what duty and good sense require. I believe in duty above all.

Lodge: You have certainly done your duty. As I told you only this morning, I admire your courage and your great contributions to your country. No one can take away from you the credit for all you have done. Now I am worried about your physical safety. I have a report that those in charge of the current activity offer you and your brother safe conduct out of the country if you resign. Had you heard this?

Diem: No. (And then after a pause) You have my telephone number.

Lodge: Yes. If I can do anything for your physical safety, please call me.

Diem: I am trying to re-establish order.

X *E S S A Y S*

Lawrence J. Bassett and Stephen E. Pelz of the University of Massachusetts, Amherst, offer a sharply critical assessment of Kennedy's Vietnam policy in the first essay. They assert that America's real enemies in South Vietnam were not the Soviet Union, China, and North Vietnam; rather, they were the southern Vietminh, who had suffered or gone into exile under Diem (organized as the National Liberation Front in 1960), and their peasant supporters. According to Bassett and Pelz, Kennedy profoundly misunderstood the conflict in Vietnam. His administration's thinking was shaped not by a sophisticated appreciation of Third World revolutions, as it liked to think, but by ingrained Cold War beliefs about the communist menace and the corresponding need to demonstrate U.S. credibility. Kennedy's commitments to the Diem regime also grew from political calculations, they suggest; the president feared that any sign of weakness in the face of the communist challenge in Southeast Asia might erode the political base of the Democratic party.

The second essay, by John M. Newman, explores the possibility that Kennedy, had he lived, might have withdrawn American troops from Vietnam. An active-duty army officer who has also taught Asian history at the army's Command and General Staff College, Newman argues that Kennedy intended to extricate U.S. forces from Vietnam regardless of the political fallout that such a decision might generate. The president, he says, recognized that political and military collapse were imminent for the Saigon regime, and he had consequently developed a careful plan for a phased American pullout. All the available evidence, Newman insists, points to the conclusion that Kennedy never would have committed American combat forces to Vietnam as Lyndon Johnson did just a year and a half later.

The Failed Search for Victory

LAWRENCE J. BASSETT AND STEPHEN E. PELZ

Two weeks before the United States's defeat at the Bay of Pigs, John Kenneth Galbraith, John F. Kennedy's new Ambassador to India, warned the President against "the surviving adventurism in the Administration. . . ." The always frank Galbraith recalled that the "futile campaign to the Yalu ruined the Democrats in 1950. . . . We Democrats with our reputation for belligerence and our basically hostile press have far less margin for mistakes than had the Republicans." During the following months, Galbraith also told Kennedy that South Vietnam was "a can of snakes," and speculated that Premier Ngo Dinh Diem's desperate efforts to cling to power might falter and draw the United States deeper into Indochina. Galbraith recommended that Kennedy send an emissary to explain the problem of Diem's pigheadedness to the State Department—"with pictures. . . . We are increasingly replacing the French as the colonial military force and we will increasingly arouse the resentment associated therewith." "Incidentally," he continued, "who is the man in your administration who decides what countries are strategic? I would like to have his name and address and ask him what is so important about this [Vietnamese] real estate in the space age." Galbraith concluded that "it is the political poison that is really at issue. The Korean war killed us in the early 50's; this involvement could kill us now."

John F. Kennedy himself decided that South Vietnam was strategically vital. He did so because he viewed the world and the methods for dealing with it differently from Galbraith, although he certainly agreed with the Ambassador about the domestic political dangers of ordering American infantry units to fight in South Vietnam. While Galbraith called for continuing a "conservative, thoughtful, nonbelligerent stance" toward the world, Kennedy wanted to lead his South Vietnamese allies to victory over the Vietnamese Communists without sending large numbers of American troops into battle. To this end the President stated repeatedly and publicly that the United States would help suppress the insurgency in South Vietnam; he warned the Soviets both publicly and privately against assisting the guerrillas; he increased economic aid to South Vietnam; he enlarged the South Vietnamese Army and police forces; he increased the number of American military advisers, logistic units, and pilots from approximately 700 to approximately 16,700; he allowed a number of the advisers to par-

Excerpted from *Kennedy's Quest for Victory: American Foreign Policy, 1961–1963,* edited by Thomas G. Paterson, pp. 223–225, 226–234, 237, 245, 252. Copyright © 1989 by Oxford University Press, Inc. Reprinted by permission.

ticipate in combat; he ordered assistance to the South Vietnamese for covert raids against North Vietnam; he helped launch the South Vietnamese strategic hamlet program; he encouraged the South Vietnamese military to assume political power; and he rejected suggestions that he try to neutralize South Vietnam—a solution which he had been willing to accept in Laos.

Early in his career Kennedy had formed an image of South Vietnam as a nation whose nationalist elite was caught between French colonialists and Communist insurgents. Since Kennedy believed Americans were not seen as colonialists, he expected that American advisers would be able to work with Vietnamese nationalists to establish and defend a pro-Western state in South Vietnam. Drawing the containment line at the South Vietnamese border was all the more important, because he had reluctantly accepted a neutralized Laos. In his determined search for victory in Vietnam, President Kennedy kept trying different tactics and personnel, but his efforts played into the hands of the National Liberation Front (NLF), a coalition of anti-Diem groups for which the Communists provided most of the leaders. By giving Diem money and men, Kennedy backed a system of landlord rule in the countryside, which was deeply unpopular with the peasants, and by aiding the South Vietnamese security forces in their attempts to impose Diem's will on the villages, he identified the Americans with a repressive *ancien regime.*

Peasants joined the NLF in increasing numbers, because the NLF cadres helped them achieve a rural revolution. Kennedy's program of industrialization, rural aid, resettlement, and helicopter assaults carried little appeal in the countryside. Kennedy nonetheless persisted in his quest for victory in Vietnam, even after repeated warnings that his methods were failing. He did so in part because he and his small senior staff did not spend much time searching for the realities behind the flow of daily cables from Saigon. Given the current state of documentation Kennedy's motives for this persistent quest for victory must remain something of a mystery. It appears, however, that he persevered in Vietnam not only to preserve his credibility as a successful practitioner of containment but also to maintain his reputation as an anti-Communist in the face of Republican attacks at home. . . .

In spite of considerable American economic and military aid, Diem was in trouble by 1959. In 1957-1958 he had restored landlord-gentry rule to many of the rural areas and put his northern and central Vietnamese Catholic Can Lao party members in control of much of the government, army, and police. In 1959 the southern Vietminh began reclaiming the countryside for the peasants, while decrying the harsh rule of "American Diem's" minions. In Long An province, not far from Saigon, for example, armed squads drove Diem's officials almost completely out of the villages with a campaign of terror which killed twenty-six people during the New Year's celebration of 1960. Vietminh cadres established peasant committees in the liberated areas and encouraged the newly empowered peasants to reduce land rents and redistribute the land of those Diemist officials who had fled. By 1961 the campaign had swayed about 80 percent of South Vietnam's villages toward their side, and Diem's government had to rely almost totally on American economic and military assistance to replace the taxes and recruits lost in the villages.

The Vietminh offensive in South Vietnam appeared to confirm Kennedy's picture of world politics in 1961. Although the United States was far superior to the Soviet Union in nuclear weaponry, Kennedy believed the United States faced a challenge to the global balance of power from both the Soviets and the Chinese Communists, who he claimed were merely vying with one another over the best way to bury the West. Because the Soviets possessed hydrogen bombs, Kennedy complained, Eisenhower's reliance on nuclear weapons represented a dangerous illusion; neither side could use such weapons for fighting conventional and brushfire wars. Kennedy therefore adopted a flexible response strategy to counter Communist-led insurgencies like the one in South Vietnam. The President and Secretary of State Dean Rusk also became particularly alarmed by the aggressive rhetoric of the People's Republic of China, which seemed to be gaining influence in Hanoi in 1962.

Kennedy had other reasons for taking the NLF challenge seriously. He had learned during the 1950s that he could win political rewards by advocating an anti-Communist counter-offensive. After all, he had grown up in the Massachusetts politics of anti-Communism, and Bay State voters had provided some of Joseph R. McCarthy's most loyal supporters. As a young congressman Kennedy had actually joined Republicans in criticizing the Democrats for losing East Germany, Poland, and China to the Soviets. He had also made headlines by pursuing alleged Communists in labor unions, and during his senatorial campaign of 1952, he charged that Henry Cabot Lodge, Jr., was soft on Communism. During his political campaigns he solicited support from a wide range of anti-Communist ethnic organizations—Italians, Poles, Germans, Hungarians, Czechs, Greeks, Lithuanians, and Russians.

The political arithmetic was simple—ethnic voters had supported Truman by a two-to-one margin in 1948, but they shifted in large numbers to Eisenhower in 1952. Due in part to his public McCarthyism, Kennedy was one of the few Democrats to buck the Republican tide in 1952. Although ethnic voters did not support McCarthyism in larger proportions than the general population, McCarthyism became the bridge over which formerly loyal Democratic voters in critical electoral college states left the decaying New Deal coalition. In 1956, 35 percent of Catholic *Democrats* voted against Stevenson. Kennedy knew good politics when he saw it. During his campaign, Kennedy portrayed himself as the man who could stand up to the Communists better than the Republicans, whom he accused of losing both Cuba and the Cold War. In the electoral college, Kennedy achieved a net gain of 22 votes due to the fortuitous concentration of ethnic blocs in key Northern and Midwestern states, and these votes were critical in the very close election of 1960.

The Republicans would hold Kennedy to his campaign promises of victories in the Cold War. In 1960, Richard M. Nixon had predicted that Kennedy was "the kind of man Mr. Khrushchev will make mincemeat of," and during his final briefing of the President-elect, Eisenhower told Kennedy he had to intervene militarily in Laos, with or without allies, if the Laotians invoked the Southeast Asia Collective Defense Treaty (SEATO). Kennedy had sought a second meeting with Eisenhower during the transition because he himself was leaning toward escalation in Laos, where leftist guerrillas were defeating American-backed rightists. For Eisenhower, an independent Laos was vital for holding the rest of Southeast Asia. According to one participant in this meeting, however, Eisenhower did leave an opening for a peaceful solution by saying that a coalition government which included the Communists might succeed in keeping Laos neutral indefinitely, but Kennedy concluded from this meeting that Eisenhower would prefer United States military intervention to any substantial Communist success in Laos. During this second meeting neither Eisenhower nor Kennedy thought Vietnam required emergency measures, for they did not mention the country.

At the start of his Administration, Kennedy believed Indochina demanded decisions. In spite of the best efforts of Central Intelligence Agency advisers, America's allies in Laos were in disarray, and the neutralist factions there were tilting toward cooperation with the Communists; the NLF was making steady gains in South Vietnam; Diem's regime was almost completely dependent upon the United States for funds; and the 675 American advisers in South Vietnam could not stir Diem's security forces to fight effectively. With Eisenhower's support, Kennedy might have declared the region a vital security zone and stationed regular American armed forces in South Vietnam, Laos, and Thailand, exposing those units to attrition by the guerrillas. Or he might have decided to increase military, economic, and political aid and advice to the Laotians and Vietnamese and rely on them to hold the line, exposing only American advisers to danger. Or, finally, he might have tried to negotiate a neutralization agreement with the Communist powers, leaving American allies in Laos and Vietnam to fight on with American dollar aid only, while drawing the military containment line at the Thai border. Kennedy chose the middle course— escalation short of sending United States combat troops—though he had to retreat from Laos and apply his strategy to South Vietnam.

Why did Kennedy intervene in Southeast Asia? Domestic politics played its part, but international factors were also important. Kennedy perceived the Laotian civil war as yet another Sino-Soviet challenge, and he became even more alarmed when Premier Nikita Khrushchev placated the Chinese by declaring Soviet support for wars of national liberation. Khrushchev added to Kennedy's uneasiness in 1961 by increasing Soviet airlifts to Congolese and Laotian insurgents and by augmenting aid to Castro's Cuba and to North Vietnam. Even more disturbing was Khrushchev's threat to resume the Berlin blockade. In October, just before the Berlin crisis eased, Kennedy told Arthur Krock of the *New York Times* that "it was a hell of a note . . . that he had to try to handle the Berlin situation with the Communists encouraging foreign aggressors all over the place . . . in Viet-Nam, Laos, etc."

In early 1961 Kennedy believed the United States lacked the strength to intervene with conventional forces in both Southeast Asia and Europe simultaneously, and, with the Berlin crisis looming, he certainly wanted enough troops available for service in Europe. Landlocked Laos presented difficult logistical problems, and the anticommunist Laotians showed little desire for combat. General Maxwell D. Taylor and Walt W. Rostow of the National Security Council (NSC) staff urged the President to commit the United States to direct military intervention if the Communists renewed their Laotian offensive. Kennedy demurred, replying that President Charles de Gaulle of France "had spoken with feeling of the difficulty of fighting in this part of the world." He also "emphasized the reluctance of the American people and of many distinguished military leaders to see any direct involvement of U.S. troops in that part of the world." Consequently, Kennedy chose to negotiate, and in April 1961 the Soviets and Chinese agreed to meet in Geneva to discuss Laos.

By careful maneuvering, Kennedy was able to limit Republican criticism of his plan for a Laotian coalition government. He neutralized Eisenhower by having British Prime Minister Harold Macmillan appeal directly to the ex-President, and on July 20 he arranged for General Douglas MacArthur to lecture congressional leaders on the inadvisability of deploying American troops in Southeast Asia. Kennedy hoped he could persuade the South Vietnamese and Thais to send their own forces into Southern Laos, if the need arose. Rostow concluded that Kennedy wanted "indigenous forces used to the maximum," and "should we have to fight, we should use air and seapower to the maximum and engage minimum U.S. forces on the Southeast Asian mainland." The Geneva Conference on Laos began in May 1961 and lasted until June 1962, when the conferees agreed to set up a neutral government. Although they promised to respect Laotian neutrality and avoid establishing foreign military bases in Laos, by late 1962 both sides were covertly violating the agreement. The shaky arrangement held together, decreasing the need for overt American intervention after June 1962.

Kennedy's concessions in Laos raised the stakes for him in South Vietnam. During the Laos negotiations, Dean Rusk told Andrei Gromyko that "there must be a cessation of the increasingly open attacks against South Viet Nam by the DRV [North Vietnam]. . . . Both the Soviets and the DRV should understand that we are deeply committed to South Vietnam and cannot and will not accept its destruction." In spite of Rusk's claim, the Eisenhower Administration had not formally committed Kennedy to defend South Vietnam. The SEATO treaty required only that member nations consult with one another and meet common dangers according to their own "constitutional processes." Eisenhower had conditioned the large United States aid program on proper performance by Diem—a performance which Elbridge Durbrow, the United States Ambassador in Saigon, 1960–1961, found lacking. Eisenhower's policy toward South Vietnam left Kennedy with options other than to support a Diemist regime, but Kennedy was determined to help the South Vietnamese defeat the Communists.

Even before deciding to negotiate a Laotian settlement, Kennedy had gradually increased American military and economic aid to South Vietnam. At the outset of his Administration Kennedy had expressed doubt that Eisenhower had been doing enough in South Vietnam, and he asked his NSC staff, "How do we change morale; how do we get [South Vietnamese] operations in the north [North Vietnam]; how do we get moving?" In order to shift "from the defense to the offense," Kennedy authorized a 50,000–man increase in ARVN, sent in more American training staff, deployed 400 Green Berets to lead 9,000 border tribesmen against North Vietnam's infiltration routes, ordered the Central Intelligence Agency to organize commando raids against North Vietnam, armed the South Vietnamese provincial Civil Guard forces with heavy weapons, and added $42 million to an aid program which was already spending $220 million per year. In May 1961 Diem assured Vice President Lyndon B. Johnson that this impressive military and economic buildup would enable the ARVN to go on the offensive. Kennedy also prompted SEATO to declare publicly that it would refuse to "acquiesce in [a] takeover of [South Vietnam by] . . . an armed minority . . . supported from outside. . . ." In spite of these emergency actions, 58 percent of South Vietnam was under some degree of Communist control in May 1961, according to the Department of Defense.

When Kennedy personally tried to warn off the Russians, however, he hit a roadblock. At the Vienna summit in June, Kennedy brought up Khrushchev's speech in support of national liberation wars, and he told the Soviet leader that the "problem was how to avoid direct contact between [the] two countries as we support respective groups; [he] referred to Vietnam guerrilla activity and said we do not believe they represent [the] popular will. . . ." Khrushchev said the Soviets found it necessary to support such wars, because they were the only way oppressed peoples could throw off their oppressors. He also warned that American meddling in such wars might bring the "terrible prospect of mutual destruction." While Kennedy found Khrushchev to be threatening in this encounter, the young President may well have misperceived the degree of Soviet aggressiveness. During the Vienna summit, Kennedy gave as good as he got, and Khrushchev's moves in Germany, Laos, and the Congo might well have been defensive. In Berlin, the East Germans were losing growing numbers of refugees to the West; in Laos, the Communists were counterattacking against an American-backed rightist offensive; and in the Congo, Eisenhower had winked at the Belgian-sponsored Katanga secession and had driven Patrice Lumumba, a nationalist leader, to seek Soviet military aid. Even Khrushchev's much quoted speech called for disarmament negotiations and increased East-West trade, not just national liberation wars. The Soviet Union was not a principal opponent in South Vietnam.

Who was the enemy in South Vietnam? The People's Republic of China was hardly a consistent or enthusiastic ally of the Vietnamese Communists, for Beijing had joined Moscow in forcing Ho Chi Minh to accept the division of Vietnam during the 1954 Geneva Conference, and the Chinese Communists continued to compete with the North Vietnamese for influence over the Pathet Lao in Laos. Until 1960 the Chinese had not been enthusiastic about reviving the insurgency in South Vietnam. Given this record, the majority of the North Vietnamese preferred to lean to the side of the more distant Russians rather than to the side of the nearby Chinese. And just before Kennedy decided to escalate American efforts drastically in South Vietnam, Zhou Enlai walked dramatically out of the Twenty-second Congress of the Communist Party of the Soviet Union on October 23, 1961. As the Sino-Soviet dispute widened in 1961–1963, the North Vietnamese were able to play off both Communist powers to secure somewhat increased aid, but even the Chinese stressed that the independent strength of internal revolutionaries, not outside aid, was the prerequisite for victory in national liberation wars. Although the 1950s' line of peaceful coexistence did disappear from Communist rhetoric, neither the Chinese nor the Russians wanted to press national liberation wars to a direct superpower confrontation, and both recognized the centrality of indigenous sources to revolutionary success.

The North Vietnamese were not even the primary enemy in South Vietnam, for they hoped to avoid a full-scale conventional war with the American-advised Army of the Republic of Vietnam. They planned to mobilize the peasantry by a socio-political campaign and convert urban dwellers and disgruntled ARNV officers to their cause by nationalistic appeals, and then set up a coalition government after a general uprising and coup. In order to appeal to nationalists, the North Vietnamese urged the Southern Vietminh to organize the NLF. After the coup, the North Vietnamese probably planned to ease the Americans out of the country and then move the noncommunist elements out of the coalition. This program would let Hanoi finish its new five-year economic plan for the north by 1966. The North Vietnamese, then, did not constitute the *primary* enemy in South Vietnam during the Kennedy Administration, though they certainly provided leadership, some supplies, and encouragement to southern NLF fighters.

The two main enemies of the United States in South Vietnam were the peasants, who supported the NLF for reasons which Kennedy did not understand, and the southern Vietminh (later NLF) leaders who had suffered or gone into exile under Diem. Under Ho Chi Minh's direction from 1945 to 1954 the southern Vietminh had established the legitimacy of their movement by helping to defeat the Japanese, by driving the French colonialists from the country, and by extending the Vietminh revolution to at least 60 percent of the South, only to see Diem re-impose landlord control in the rural areas and arrest those suspected of Communist connections or opposition sympathies. By 1961 the NLF-inspired peasants were steadily liberating themselves from Diemist rule, while supplying their village militias with arms purchased or captured from the ARVN or brought home by numerous ARVN deserters. Although they received trained leaders from among the southerners who had fled North and returned, and although they received some arms from China, the NLF-led peasants could sustain a guerrilla campaign and control the countryside without major infiltration or arms shipments from North Vietnam or China.

The NLF had so many advantages that the insurgency spread rapidly. Its land program carried great appeal in the Delta region, where tenant farmers comprised the great majority, as well as in central Vietnam where landholdings were very small. Tenants customarily paid around 50 to 60 percent of their crop to the landlord, in addition to taxes and bribes, leaving them far poorer than Kennedy and Gullion supposed; the Diemists also represented an old, Westernizing, landlord regime, symbolized by Catholicism, which distinguished it from the majority of its Confucian, Buddhist, and Animist countrymen. By the fall of 1961, the peasant revolutionaries had won control of the villages in many regions of South Vietnam, although some experts have maintained that the Delta region was still hotly contested as late as 1963. Walt Rostow and Roger Hilsman, Kennedy's principal counter-insurgency war theorists, did not understand the attraction of the people's war strategy for the peasantry. They believed the Communists were primarily terrorists and guerrilla fighters, whose challenge was as much military as socio-economic, though Rostow stressed the military side of the struggle more than Hilsman. If Kennedy had felt politically free to do so, and if he had understood the strength of the people's war strategy, he might well have accepted coalition governments in both Laos and South Vietnam and drawn the counter-insurgency line instead in Thailand, a country which had not suffered the social divisions of colonialism and which did not suffer from a major insurgency.

By fall 1961 Diem's regime was in far deeper trouble than Kennedy had realized. In September, NLF armed forces tripled their attacks and consolidated their hold on much more of the countryside. Diem requested a bilateral security treaty with the United States and, with less enthusiasm, the dispatch of regular American combat forces. Kennedy then sent General Taylor, his personal military counselor, and Rostow of the NSC staff, two hawkish advisers, to South Vietnam to explore the seriousness of the setback and the need to meet Diem's requests. After their return the President began to consider his options. Through early November, the debate among Kennedy's principal advisers centered on a variety of escalatory alternatives. There were five main policies suggested, each of which reflected the organizational origins of its sponsor. . . .

Kennedy ruled out neutralization, but he also vetoed the Pentagon's plan to send regular combat troops to South Vietnam. Although the proposal for troops had gained wide support within the Administration, Taylor reported that Kennedy was "instinctively" against it. The CIA supported the President by predicting that the North Vietnamese would match American deployments with increased infiltration. On November 11, Kennedy vetoed sending regular combat troops. Instead, he decided to increase economic aid as well as send more advisers to ARVN and to South Vietnamese intelligence and government agencies. The United States also promised air reconnaissance, air transport, and helicopter units to improve ARVN reactions to NLF movements. Kennedy ordered that American advisers be assigned to ARVN field battalions, rather than division headquarters (thereby allowing them to help plan and direct operations). The President also followed Lansdale's advice by seeking the insertion of American advisers into the South Vietnamese government to provide operational guidance at all levels. The advisory effort, he said, "should be substantial otherwise we will give the wrong impression. . . . Are we prepared to send in hundreds and hundreds of men and dozens and dozens of ships? If we would just show up with 4 or 5 ships this will not do much good. . . . As I said on Saturday concerning Laos—we took actions which made no difference at all." In return for all of this United States assistance Diem would have to mobilize his nation fully, broaden his government, and give his generals the power to move troops without prior clearance from Saigon. Kennedy directed Ambassador Nolting to tell Diem that the "missions being undertaken by our own forces . . . are more suitable for white foreign troops than garrison duty or seeking out of Viet Cong personnel submerged in the Viet-Nam population." Nevertheless, Kennedy had committed Americans to fly helicopters and planes and accompany ARVN troops when they engaged the NLF.

In mid-November, Kennedy tried to dissuade Bundy, Taylor, Rostow, McNamara, and the Joint Chiefs from their campaign to send regular troops by telling them foreign troops were only "a last resort." The President added that he did not want a war with China. He did agree to allow the Pentagon to plan for the introduction of SEATO troops, but that was as far as he would go. Vietnam, he explained, was unlike Korea, because it was not a clear-cut victim of aggression, and, consequently, neither the Democrats in Congress nor the British nor the French would support SEATO intervention there. And the United States did not have enough troops to go around. Nor was it clear why American soldiers should be sent into South Vietnam, but not into Cuba: "The President said that he could even make a rather strong case against intervening in an area 10,000 miles away against 16,000 guerrillas with a native army of 200,000, where millions have been spent for years with no success." The Joint Chiefs remained unconvinced, replying that they favored invading Cuba as well. The Chiefs doubted that the Lansdale counterinsurgency approach would work, for Vietnam was not like the Philippines or Malaya. They told General Taylor in October that the Malay counter-insurgency campaign was not comparable to Vietnam, because the Thais and British were able to control Malaya's borders; because colonial police were able to isolate ethnic Chinese insurgents from the majority of the population; because food was scarce, enabling strategic hamlet programs to work; and because the British, not the Malays, were in command. In January 1962 the Joint Chiefs reiterated their request for the dispatch of regular American troops, but by then the alternative program was well under way.

Diem expressed disappointment and anger. He had requested a bilateral alliance and massive aid, not an Americanization of his government. He told Nolting, "Viet Nam did not want to be a protectorate." After tense negotiations, he agreed only to *consult* American advisers whom he helped select, and he avoided significant changes in his military command structure, because he remained fearful of a coup. Kennedy was trapped by the contradictions in his own policy toward Diem. He could not force a sup-posedly independent nationalist leader to accept American tutelage without appearing to undermine him, and Diem was already publicizing Kennedy's demands. Kennedy gave way. On December 15, the two governments announced their joint partnership—but on Diem's terms. A solid political foundation was essential to successful prosecution of the war, but the State Department had lost another round in its fight to make Diem more efficient, democratic, and popular. And on February 18, 1962, Robert F. Kennedy confirmed the State Department defeat by declaring unconditionally during a visit to Saigon, "We are going to win in Viet-Nam. We will remain here until we do win."

Diem regained some favor with Washington by accepting another part of the Kennedy plan for South Vietnam—strategic hamlets. Roger Hilsman, director of the State Department's Bureau of Intelligence and Research, correctly concluded that the villages of South Vietnam willingly provided supplies and the great majority of recruits to the NLF. He argued that the South Vietnamese government had to provide villagers with civic action programs and physical security by creating fortified hamlets linked by radio. The strategic hamlets would receive developmental aid and close police scrutiny. In addition, the hamlets' own militias would defend them and call in roving Civil Guard units if the NLF attacked. Because they lacked food and replacements, the NLF bands would have to attack in strength, rather than starve, and the Civil Guard and newly mobile ARVN could then crush them by ambush or conventional engagement.

While Hilsman had a somewhat more accurate perception of the insur-gency than the Pentagon, his proposed solution proved unrealistic. His pro-posed village militias consisted of the fathers, uncles, and brothers of the NLF village guerrillas, and his expectation that one relative would starve or even shoot another in return for a medical clinic, a school, and a new well was strange at best. Diem, and his brother Ngo Dinh Nhu, who was in charge of the secret police and internal security, pushed the hamlet program rapidly as a means of reclaiming the villages. Land reform was notably absent and other benefits slow in coming, while the peasants often had to purchase the building materials and barbed wire which they used to fence themselves in.

At first, the military side of Kennedy's counter-insurgency campaign appeared to show progress. Aided by helicopters and growing numbers of American advisers, the ARVN bedeviled the NLF in the first half of 1962. With ARVN's fortunes appearing to prosper, the Kennedy Administration flirted briefly with negotiations. In July 1962, Harriman, who was just wrapping up the Laos settlement, offered the North Vietnamese a neutrality agreement similar to the one he had just concluded for Laos. Ho Chi Minh replied that the NLF had already suggested such a plan: the United States would withdraw its advisers; a cease-fire would go into effect; the great powers would guarantee the neutralization and independence of Vietnam; the Vietnamese would establish a coalition government, which would include both Diem and the NLF; and the coalition government would end the strategic hamlet program, hold free elections, and begin talks to reunify the country. In late 1962 the NLF also offered a cease-fire which did not first require the withdrawal of the Americans. Given the strength of the NLF in the countryside, free elections would almost certainly have resulted in a government dominated by the NLF. Although the NLF proposal opened the prospect of a decent interval between the time of American withdrawal and the time of a prospective defeat of Diem, Kennedy rejected the NLF offer. The President preferred to seek victory, rather than accept defeat, however much disguised or delayed.

By the end of 1962 Kennedy had sent 11,000 American military personnel to South Vietnam, along with 300 military aircraft, 120 helicopters, and additional heavy weapons. American pilots helped to fly combat missions, and the Americans supplied napalm bombs to the South Vietnamese air force. At Binh Hoa in January 1962 an air strike killed five civilians, including a two-year-old boy, a five-year-old girl, and a seven-year-old boy. If their parents had not been active supporters of the NLF before the raid, they most probably joined after this tragedy. Kennedy put General Paul D. Harkins, a former tank officer, in charge of the military assistance program in Saigon, and Harkins adopted a strategy based on the United States Army's tradition of achieving victory via attrition and destruction of the enemy's army. Harkins left the problem of village militias largely to the Vietnamese Civil Guards and Self Defense Corps, while he tried to break the enemy's will by using ARVN regulars to smash the enemy's main guerrilla forces. Taylor and Harkins wanted to put continuous pressure on the NLF regulars by exploiting American air mobility—a strategy which they believed had worked against guerrillas in both Greece and Korea. When ARVN succeeded in surrounding the NLF regulars with overwhelming numbers, they were supposed to use artillery and air strikes to flush them into combat with superior blocking forces.

For a variety of reasons ARVN could not implement this strategy. Its divisions were trained and armed to deter a conventional invasion from the north, and they were unsuited to chase lightly armed guerrillas who disappeared into the countryside. Nor did many of the units in the field want to fight. A number of senior officers were mercenaries who had served in the colonial French Army, and Diem compounded the problem by putting his favorite officers in charge of the best units and keeping them in garrison, while sending poorly trained units into combat. American advisers could not energize ARVN because they did not speak Vietnamese, control promotions, make aid allocations (which came through Diem), or command troops (as they had done in Korea). Intelligence operations also faltered. American and South Vietnamese intelligence officers sought order-of-battle information on regular NLF units, rather than try to identify members of the local village militias and political committees, who were the mainstays of the insurgency. In 1962 air mobility allowed ARVN to achieve some early surprise victories, but the NLF soon adapted to the helicopters by making quicker hit-and-run attacks and placing heavy machine guns in village tree lines. Even if ARVN had been able to destroy the main force units which they were vainly chasing, they would still have faced the much more numerous village militias. The only solution to the village militias was to occupy the villages, reduce land rents, and recognize the NLF's land redistributions. But American military advisers believed in the Clausewitzian goal of destroying their enemy's army, not clearing and holding peasant villages, and Diem believed in control by his bureaucrats and the landlords, not reform for peasant hamlets.

Given the advanced state of the NLF revolt, Kennedy's counterinsurgency strategy was proving unworkable. As 1962 gave way to 1963, the strategic hamlet program also developed trouble. Diem, Nhu, and Harkins had pushed the program far out into enemy territory, resettling some hamlets in which as many as one-third of the men were missing—they had probably joined the NLF. The sullen strategic hamlet militias often did not defend their villages against the insurgents, and the Self-Defense Corps and Provincial Civil Guard units were unable or unwilling to take on company-sized NLF attacks. By the spring of 1963 only 1500 of 8500 strategic hamlets remained viable. By contrast, in June 1963 the NLF was levying taxes in 42 of South Vietnam's 44 provinces.

Organizational problems also undermined Kennedy's strategy. General Lyman Lemnitzer, the Chairman of the Joint Chiefs of Staff, and General Earle G. Wheeler, Army Chief of Staff, proved unsympathetic to counterinsurgency ideas. Kennedy failed to appoint anyone of stature to ride herd in South Vietnam on Harkins, Diem, and Nhu, while in Washington the successive Vietnam task force directors also lacked the rank to force independent government departments to coordinate their activities. Consequently the military campaigns and strategic hamlet programs did not mesh well. Kennedy kept most of the decisions in his own hands, and he lacked the time or energy to be an effective Vietnam desk officer. Nor could he play the role of an Under Secretary of State or Defense in seeking intelligence or reviewing policy, except in crises such as occurred during the fall of 1961. His small NSC staff were primarily European-oriented generalists who lacked Asian expertise or the time to develop a sophisticated set of questions which would have revealed the nature of the NLF revolution. The NSC staff members maintained the illusion of being in touch by having mountains of cables routed through the White House, but they lacked the time and background to put them in their proper perspective. Sorensen is correct in saying that Vietnam "never received the attention it should have . . . at the highest levels." Kennedy remained convinced that the methods of counterinsurgency would gradually bring victory in the countryside. In his State of the Union message of 1963, he confidently declared, "The spearpoint of aggression has been blunted in Viet-Nam."

In early 1963 Kennedy's optimism waned briefly after Senator Mansfield reported on his recent trip to Southeast Asia. Mansfield warned that the United States might ultimately be forced to accept a dominant combat role if Kennedy did not withdraw the American advisers. Mansfield's prediction reportedly angered the President, who was even less pleased when he heard of the very poor ARVN showing in combat at Ap Bac in the

Delta. With the American press present, a large ARVN force, aided by American-donated helicopters and armored personnel carriers, allowed a much smaller NLF force to escape. In the process, the NLF inflicted heavy casualties on ARVN and shot down five helicopters. Three American advisers died. Kennedy was puzzled by "the Vietnam troops and their lack of courage," and he asked his aides to reassess the rice paddy war. Hilsman and Michael V. Forrestal, the NSC staffer assigned to expedite Vietnam policy, saw no need to "make any sudden and dramatic change," though they questioned Harkins's penchant for large-scale operations. The generals themselves remained optimistic. Wheeler reported that "[we] are winning slowly on the present thrust," and Harkins trumpeted that "improvement is a daily fact . . . and we are confident of the outcome."

Besides ARVN and strategic hamlet failures, Kennedy had to contend with charges that the United States was using "dirty-war" tactics in Vietnam. Kennedy had indeed ordered a limited, experimental program of trail clearing and crop destruction using defoliants and herbicides such as Agent Orange. In doing so, he not only set an unfortunate precedent for much larger applications of chemicals during the Johnson Administration but he also provided the NLF and North Vietnam with an opportunity to launch a propaganda campaign and appeal to the International Control Commission. It was a high political price to pay for a program which proved militarily worthless.

Much worse problems arose when South Vietnamese troops fired into a crowd of Buddhists in Hué on May 8, 1963. The Buddhist marchers were flying religious banners during a celebration of Buddha's birthday, in spite of a ban on such symbols issued by Diem's brother, Ngo Dinh Thuc, the Archbishop of Hué. The ARVN killed nine marchers and wounded many others, triggering Buddhist demonstrations and self-immolations. In the major South Vietnamese cities students took to the streets to support Buddhist charges of religious discrimination and authoritarianism against the Ngos. Diem and Nhu countered with raids on pagodas, mass arrests, and martial law, each of which provoked more marches and self-immolations, creating a cycle which would persist through the fall of the Ngos in November. Madame Ngo Dinh Nhu, the security chief's wife and Diem's sister-in-law, callously dismissed the immolations as "barbecues" and offered to supply matches and gasoline in the future. The Kennedy Administration attempted repeatedly to induce Diem to compromise with the Buddhists. Diem said he would seek reconciliation, but he never kept his promise.

During his first two years in office Kennedy had tried to minimize the seriousness of the Vietnam problem, and he had largely succeeded. In spite of [presidential assistant Theodore C.] Sorensen's advice, Kennedy chose not to make a major speech at the end of 1961 explaining his decision to escalate, and thus he delayed public debate. As American advisers went into combat, congressmen yielded to Kennedy's appeals for support and Congress routinely approved increases in American aid programs to South Vietnam. In the summer of 1963, however, the Buddhist crisis brought increasingly critical newspaper reports from Homer Bigart and David Halberstam of the *New York Times* and Neil Sheehan of United Press International. At first Kennedy believed that having the American mission in Saigon bring reporters "into our confidence" would generate an "accurate story [of] our Viet-Nam program," but the journalists' well-founded distrust of the Diem regime and the American mission doomed the effort. In late October Kennedy even tried to persuade *New York Times* publisher Arthur H. Sulzberger to remove Halberstam from South Vietnam, but to no avail. Vietnam became a big story in August and September 1963, and increasingly the criticism included both Kennedy and Diem. Kennedy finally had to conclude, "The way to confound the press is to win the war."

As the election campaigns for 1964 began, bipartisan support for Kennedy's foreign policy broke down. During the summer and fall of 1963, conservatives attacked the foreign aid bill, the American wheat sale to the Soviet Union, and the nuclear test ban treaty. Nelson Rockefeller, Nixon, and Goldwater were waiting for Kennedy to make serious mistakes in South Vietnam and then exploit such errors in the presidential campaign. Senator Richard Russell of Georgia, a member of the President's own party, presaged the debate by chiding the Administration for "trying to fight this [Vietnam] problem as if it were a tournament of roses." He called for the "dirty-tricks department" to offer rewards for NLF guerrillas—dead or alive. To Kennedy, experienced as he was in the politics of anti-Communism, these criticisms foreshadowed another debate about "who lost China?"

While Kennedy watched the Buddhist crisis in South Vietnam with growing dismay, he faced a similar crisis closer to home: the civil rights conflict in the American South. The civil rights issue worried Kennedy's pollsters and political advisers, who warned that he might lose critical Southern and Midwestern votes in the next election. By August 1963, half of those polled said he was pushing integration too fast. Louis Harris's analysis of the 1960 results indicated the Republicans might make real inroads in the region in 1964, and a Lubell survey of former Kennedy voters in Birmingham, Alabama, turned up only one white who would again vote for Kennedy.

The probable political loss of the South made the retention and expansion of the Democratic vote in the North vital, but Kennedy's advisers warned him he was in trouble there as well. . . .

Thus, in addition to Kennedy's personal and ideological commitment to containment in South Vietnam, there also existed a political imperative to quiet the Buddhist crisis, stabilize the South Vietnamese regime, and convince the South Vietnamese to fight effectively. But Kennedy had little luck with Diem. In fact, Kennedy's efforts to persuade Diem to mollify the Buddhists aggravated the underlying conflict between Saigon and Washington. Diem resented the rapid American advisery buildup and the American advisers' penchant for meddling in Vietnamese decisions. The South Vietnamese dictator also feared—quite correctly—the Americans might encourage his enemies among the South Vietnamese generals to depose him. The CIA reported that Diem might request a reduction in the number of American advisers. When asked about Diem's complaints at a news conference, Kennedy responded that withdrawal of the advisers would be premature, with "still a long, hard struggle to go" and no "brightening in the skies that would permit us to withdraw troops or begin to by the end of this year." Actually, back in 1962 when the war seemed to be going well, the Pentagon had prepared plans for an orderly withdrawal. If Kennedy had wanted to, he might have used these plans to implement a withdrawal of aid and advisers in stages as a means of forcing the generals and Diem to reform.

During June and July intelligence officials warned Kennedy that Diem had alienated the nationalist elites which Kennedy had identified in the 1950s as vital to building a stable Third World. Thomas Hughes of the State Department reported that discontent was widespread in the civil bureaucracy, in the military establishment, among students, and even within the Catholic hierarchy. Hughes, Hilsman, and the CIA warned that a coup against Diem was a distinct possibility, and Hughes and the CIA assured Kennedy that "a reasonably large pool of . . . experienced and trained manpower" existed which "could provide reasonably effective leadership for the government [of South Vietnam] and [for] the war effort."

On June 27 the Administration announced the nomination of Henry Cabot Lodge, former senator from Massachusetts and Republican candidate for Vice President in 1960, as Ambassador to Saigon. According to the CIA, a "considerably disturbed" Diem correctly interpreted the appointment to mean "that the United States [now] planned to wield a 'big stick.' . . ." Lodge's appointment also gave the Administration political sea room to act against Diem; one magazine predicted Lodge's appointment would "make the Republicans think twice before attacking Administration policy in troublesome South Viet Nam." Lodge arrived in Saigon on August 22, the day after Nhu's American-trained Special Forces raided Buddhist pagodas in Saigon, Hué, and elsewhere and made mass arrests. Diem had presented Lodge with a fait accompli: he had curbed the Buddhists before Lodge could press him to accommodate them. Rumors even circulated that Diem and Nhu were considering serious negotiations with North Vietnam. Kennedy had instructed Lodge to persuade Diem to treat his non-Communist opponents better, and if Diem resisted, work for Diem's removal. In fact, since July a group of ARVN generals led by Duong Van Minh, Tran Van Don, and Tran Thien Khiem had been exploring the possibility of an American-supported coup with American CIA agents.

In Washington, many senior officials were on vacation at the time of the August raids on the pagodas, and the anti-Diem faction in the White House and State Department urged swift action. Forrestal urged the President to "move before the situation in Saigon freezes." With the aid of George Ball, the Under Secretary of State, who was filling in for Rusk, Harriman, Hilsman, and Forrestal persuaded Kennedy over the telephone to instruct Lodge on August 24 to compel Diem to drop Nhu from his administration and accept American advice on how to run his government and army. If

Diem did not comply, then the United States was to give "direct support" to the ARVN generals in the event of Diem's ouster. Kennedy assured Lodge, "We will back you to the hilt on actions you take to achieve our objectives." Perhaps with the Bay of Pigs fiasco in mind, Kennedy did want time to review plans for the coup to assure that the American-backed generals would succeed. He warned Lodge on August 29, "I know from experience that failure is more destructive than the appearance of indecision. . . . When we go, we must go to win. . . ." Consequently, Kennedy reserved the right to "change course and reverse previous instructions." But he continued to allow the Ambassador wide discretion in the execution of his Vietnam policy, authorizing Lodge to suspend aid to Diem "at a time and under conditions of your choice." Although Lodge was eager to act immediately, the ARVN generals were unable to line up enough military support in the Saigon area to risk a coup.

Kennedy continued to apply pressure to Diem. On television on September 2 he remarked that the war could not be won without popular support from the South Vietnamese, and, he added, "in my opinion, in the last 2 months, the government has gotten out of touch with the people." Kennedy predicted that Diem could only regain such support "with changes in policy and perhaps with [changes in] personnel." Otherwise, the choices for victory "would not be very good." But Kennedy disagreed "with those who say we should withdraw. That would be a great mistake. . . . Forty-seven Americans have been killed in combat with the enemy, but this is a very important struggle even though it is far away." Between October 2 and October 5, Kennedy signaled his displeasure with Diem by applying a variety of "selective pressures": Kennedy canceled some future economic aid shipments; threatened to cut off American support for Nhu's Special Forces, unless they were placed under the command of the ARVN General Staff and moved from Saigon into the field; recalled the CIA station chief in Saigon, who was too closely identified with Nhu; and announced publicly that 1,000 American advisers would be withdrawn from South Vietnam by the end of 1963 and all American advisers would be out by the end of 1965, provided that the war in the countryside continued to go well.

By cutting aid to Diem, Kennedy helped revive—apparently unwittingly—the ARVN generals' interest in a coup. On October 3, Duong Van Minh, Chief of the General Staff, asked for reassurance that the Americans would not oppose a coup, and he suggested the possibility that the plan might include the assassination of two Ngo brothers, Nhu and Can. Lucien Conein, Minh's CIA contact, assured him that Washington would provide economic and military assistance to a new regime which promised to cooperate with the United States, regain popular support, and try to win the war. CIA Director John McCone neither encouraged nor deplored the recommendation for the assassination of Diem's brothers, although he did warn Saigon that Diem himself should not be killed. On October 25, Lodge alerted Kennedy that a coup would occur sometime before November. In the days just before the coup, Kennedy and McGeorge Bundy worriedly questioned Lodge about prospects for success and the possibility of achieving plausible deniability of the American role in the coup. Once the attempted overthrow began, however, they told Lodge it was "in the interests of the U.S. Government that it should succeed."

On the morning of November 1, Lodge met for the last time with Diem. A few hours later the coup finally began, with CIA agent Conein at coup headquarters to report to the embassy, advise the coup leaders, and distribute cash, if needed. At 4:30 p.m. that same day a frantic Diem telephoned the United States Ambassador. Lodge relayed an offer of safe conduct out of the country from the coup leaders, but he claimed disingenuously that the United States government had no policy toward the coup. While Diem and Nhu escaped to the Cholon section of Saigon, both to die the following day at the hands of General Minh's lieutenants, Lodge went to bed. On November 8, Washington officially recognized the new military regime in Saigon. A week later, in response to a *New York Times* editorial which suggested a negotiated settlement of the war, Rusk instructed Lodge to tell the generals that the United States government "cannot envisage any points that would be negotiable." The Secretary of State reassured the South Vietnamese government that North Vietnam would have to end its "subversive aggression" and allow the new South Vietnamese regime to "extend its authority throughout South Vietnam before the United States would withdraw."

The events of 1963 shattered one expectation—that Diem would listen to American advice, reform his government, and win the war—and created another—that the generals would do the same. Before the coup Kennedy and his Washington advisers simply assumed that the ARVN generals would be an improvement over Diem, but they were wrong. Many of the members of the South Vietnamese Military Revolutionary Council had been collaborators with the French colonialists, and Robert Thompson, the British counter-insurgency expert, thought they "lacked the experience or ability to command much more than a regiment, let alone a country." Within three months, another military faction overthrew Minh and the Revolutionary Council, starting a topsy-turvy pattern of coup and counter-coup which continued for some time. Even the Buddhist protest marches and self-immolations continued to occur.

Before Minh fell, however, Kennedy himself died. His remarks prepared for delivery on November 22 in Dallas, Texas, a destination he never reached, included the words: "We in this country in this generation—by destiny rather than choice—the watchmen on the walls of world freedom. . . . Our assistance to . . . nations can be painful, risky and costly, as is true in Southeast Asia today. But we dare not weary of the task." And in another speech he intended to deliver that night can be seen the outline of his anticipated 1964 campaign. The New Frontier had gotten the country moving again—America's economy was growing, its space effort thriving, its military power expanding, and its containment policy working from Berlin to Latin America to Southeast Asia. On the day he died he still hoped for victory in South Vietnam and vindication of the doctrine of counter-insurgency.

Why did Kennedy persist in Vietnam under such unpromising conditions? After all, many leaders, ranging from Charles de Gaulle and Douglas MacArthur to Mike Mansfield and John Kenneth Galbraith, had warned Kennedy against a deepening Vietnam adventure. He chose to ignore their warnings. His defenders claimed that the Eisenhower Administration left him no choice but to pursue the war in Vietnam. But he might well have drawn the containment line in Thailand, while letting Diem fight his own battles with generous grants of money and arms. Instead, he sent in 16,000 advisers, 100 of whom had died by the end of 1963; he sponsored the strategic hamlet program; he unleashed a war of attrition against the NLF; and he allowed the military to use napalm, defoliation, and helicopter envelopment tactics, rather than a clear and hold strategy. Why did he do it? Both Khrushchev and Mao Zedung may have helped to draw him in, for they had exaggerated their support for national liberation wars, thereby lending substance to Kennedy's fears. In fact, however, the fragmentation of the Communist world was accelerating in these years, as Kennedy could read in his own intelligence reports. If Kennedy had negotiated a deal on South Vietnam, he might have encouraged détente with the Soviet Union and hastened a Sino-Vietnamese split.

Kennedy's self-confident definition of the South Vietnamese problem was an important reason for his persistence. The President believed that Diem and the generals constituted a third force of nationalists who could lead peasants and workers in a fight against Communism. Because Americans were nation-builders, not colonialists, they could persuade the South Vietnamese to apply American technology, tactics, and organizational techniques to the problems of the Vietnamese countryside, with its problems of underdevelopment, terrorism, and guerrilla warfare. The struggle would be long and hard, but success would come eventually—if only the right combination of Vietnamese nationalist leaders could be found. The misapplied analogs of Greece and Malaya reinforced his belief in nation-building and counter-insurgency. Kennedy's image of Vietnam proved false. In the minds of the peasants, Diem and the generals represented the old regime. The people of the countryside craved land, power, and the promise of economic justice and national liberation, not wells, clinics, films, strategic hamlets, or infantry sweeps through their villages. The NLF program also contained more political and economic change and less coercion and violence than Kennedy comprehended. Kennedy's expectations for the future were unrealistic as well. American advisers could not transform the ARVN into an effective force, nor persuade Diem and Nhu to appeal to the peasantry.

Kennedy's decision-making system failed to correct the President's false image of Vietnam's prospects. His small staff lacked an understanding of the socio-economic appeal of the Chinese and Vietnamese revolutions to the peasantry. The NSC did not produce an accurate picture which would shatter the President's strongly held image of a nationalist elite waiting for outside inspiration to mobilize a neutral peasantry against Communist terrorists. Although Kennedy's collegial style of decision-making has received considerable praise, it also did not work well in the case of Vietnam. Until the Buddhist crisis of 1963 Kennedy usually treated Vietnam as a fairly routine foreign policy problem, which he assumed he could handle with limited resources. His staff, with the exception of the hyperactive Walt Rostow, tended to coast along the lines of established policy, recommending more of the same. Not until November 1961 did a major review of the options emerge. Even then, however, the list of options which were staffed out and fully considered was incomplete, for none of the key debaters, with the brief exception of Harriman, was a serious advocate of neutralization and a retreat to Thailand. Kennedy never gave negotiations a chance. Nor were there many advocates for withholding advisers while giving Diem enough money and arms to sink or swim on his own. Instead of a sophisticated image of the problem of rural revolution in Southeast Asia, ingrained Cold War thinking about the credibility of containment shaped Administration deliberations. Consequently, the debate always centered on escalation, with Kennedy curbing the hawks in the Pentagon and choosing counter-insurgency.

The politics of anti-Communism also played a large role in shaping Kennedy's decisions. He had survived and prospered in the McCarthyite atmosphere of the fifties, and he feared the loss of swing anti-Communist votes to the Republicans and the Dixiecrats in the increasingly turbulent politics of the sixties. The lesson of the so-called loss of China remained with him, and the Republicans repeatedly peppered him with charges of appeasement on a host of issues. During the 1960 campaign he had promised to turn the tide of the Cold War, and he was preparing to claim considerable progress in 1964. With Laos neutralized, Cuba hostile, and East Berlin sealed off, Vietnam became a testing ground by his own definition. Though some of his defenders have claimed he would have withdrawn the United States from Vietnam after being re-elected in 1964, they underestimate the degree to which Kennedy had committed himself and the country to supporting a non-Communist Vietnam. Kennedy would have had to admit the failure of his major counter-insurgency effort, which was designed to discourage national liberation wars everywhere. More likely than withdrawal was a continued search for the right combination of means and men to win the war in South Vietnam. Kennedy would probably have ruled out sending in United States Army infantry divisions, but short of that limit, he would probably have continued to make a major effort to succeed.

In any case, by late 1963 Kennedy had radically expanded the American commitment to Vietnam. By putting American advisers in harm's way and allowing the press to chronicle their tribulations and casualties, he helped to engage American patriotism in a war against Vietnamese people. By arguing that Vietnam was a test of the West's ability to defeat the people's war strategy and a test of American credibility in the Cold War, he raised the costs of withdrawal for his successor. By launching a strategic hamlet program, he further disrupted peasant society. By allowing Harkins and the ARVN to bomb, shell, search, and destroy, he made so many recruits for the NLF that he encouraged North Vietnam and the NLF to move the war into its final military phase. By participating in Diem's removal, he brought warlord politics to Saigon. By downplaying publicly the American role in Vietnam, he discouraged a constitutional debate about the commitment of American advisers to battle. By publicly and privately committing the United States to the survival of an anti-Communist state in South Vietnam, he made it much more difficult for his successors to blame the South Vietnamese government for its own failures and to withdraw. And by insisting that military victory was the only acceptable outcome, he ignored the possibility that negotiations might lead to an acceptable process of retreat. Kennedy bequeathed to Lyndon B. Johnson a failing counterinsurgency program and a deepened commitment to the war in South Vietnam.

Kennedy's Plan for American Withdrawal

JOHN M. NEWMAN

It was November 12, [1963], just ten days before the assassination, when Senator Wayne Morse had a riveting talk with President Kennedy. "I went down to the White House," Morse recalls, "and handed him his education bills, which I was handling on the Senate floor." Morse remembers making "two to five speeches a week against Kennedy on Vietnam." The Senator says his colleagues used to kid him, saying, "Wayne, haven't you covered that subject?" He would respond: "Apparently not. We teachers know the value of repetition in the learning process." Morse described what happened with Kennedy that day:

> I'd gone into President Kennedy's office to discuss education bills, but he said, "Wayne, I want you to know you're absolutely right in your criticism of my Vietnam policy. Keep this in mind. I'm in the midst of an intensive study which substantiates your position on Vietnam. When I'm finished I want you to give me half a day and come over and analyze it point by point."

Surprised, Morse asked if Kennedy understood his objections. Kennedy replied, "If I don't understand your objections by now, I never will."

What was this "intensive study" on Vietnam that Kennedy was in the midst of? Since early in the year his plan had been to wait until after the 1964 election to pull out. He had agreed with Mansfield that announcing the withdrawal would lead to "a wild conservative outcry against returning him to the Presidency for a second term. Morse is not the only person who knew Kennedy was reconsidering his Vietnam policy: so did [NSC staff member Michael] Forrestal, who found out about it nine days later. Forrestal, of course, knew something Wayne Morse did not: that Kennedy had already given the order to withdraw 1,000 Americans from Vietnam by the end of the year. Kennedy's rethinking appears to have been prompted

From John M. Newman, *JFK and Vietnam: Deception, Intrigue, and the Struggle for Power,* Warner Books, 1992.

by the sudden shift in reporting on the battlefield situation in early November and his nervousness about what this might mean for the upcoming election campaign.

The shift in Kennedy's thinking led him to modify his public position on the withdrawal and to make a far clearer commitment to carrying it out. A brief review demonstrates how this came about. By waiting until after the election to fully withdraw he could steer clear of a conservative backlash; and, by beginning to bring a few men home, supposedly because of the success on the battlefield, he could fend off the liberals, like [Senator J. William] Fulbright, who argued that Kennedy was bogging the U.S. down in a hopeless quagmire. The crux of his public position was to stay in the middle while letting his military advisors emphasize that they were winning the war. Consequently, he had distanced himself from the optimistic withdrawal timetable announced publicly by McNamara on October 2. In keeping with this plan, Kennedy included a requirement for secrecy when he actually implemented the 1,000-man withdrawal with NSAM-263, putting this secrecy requirement right in the directive itself.

In this way Kennedy moved forward as planned, well insulated from attacks on either side as the upcoming election approached. The potential problem, of course, was what to do if the battlefield situation made staying on the fence untenable politically. The President's remarks at the October 2 NSC meeting clearly indicate his fear that the situation could change at any time, and his statements at an October 9 press conference demonstrate his concern that this uncertain situation could be a problem in the election campaign. He said:

> I cannot tell what our relations will be in Southeast Asia a year from now. I know what results our policy is attempting to bring. But I think the result ought to be judged in the summer of '64 and the fall of '64. . . . I would not want to make those judgments now, because I think we still have a long way to go before next summer. . . . I would say we are going to have a hard, close [election campaign] fight in 1964.

As the moment drew nearer for the 1,000-man withdrawal, Kennedy still maintained secrecy about his decision to implement it. On October 31 Kennedy was asked point-blank whether he intended to speed up the withdrawal from Vietnam. He responded:

> Well as you know, when Secretary McNamara and General Taylor came back, they announced that we would expect to withdraw a thousand men from South Vietnam before the end of the year and there has been some reference to that by General Harkins. *If* we were able to do that, that would be our schedule. I think the first unit or first contingent would be 250 men who are not involved in what might be called front-line operations. It would be our hope to lessen the number of Americans there by 1,000, as the training intensifies and is carried on in South Vietnam. [emphasis added]

These remarks show that the President, three weeks after the fact, was still not prepared to acknowledge that he *had* agreed to this timetable. His public position remained that the 1,000-man withdrawal was still an "if" at this point.

Then came the sudden turnaround of reporting in early November, as the CIA joined the State Department in decrying the state of the battlefield. The manner in which this reversal occurred—citing MACV's own statistics—thoroughly impugned Harkins' reporting, and any possibility of maintaining the fiction of battlefield success was dashed. It had become crystal clear to Kennedy, by this time, that the battlefield would not hold until the following summer. It was surely this unwelcome fact that forced him to reconsider his public stance on the war. This new situation was the context of the President's conversation on November 12 with Wayne Morse. In a press conference two days later someone asked Kennedy for his appraisal of Vietnam and what the purpose was for the Honolulu conference. In reply he said this:

> Because we do have a *new* situation there, and a new government, we hope, an increased effort in the war. The purpose of the meeting at Honolulu—Ambassador Lodge will be there, General Harkins will be there, Secretary McNamara and others, and then, as you know, later Ambassador Lodge will come here—is to attempt to assess the situation: what American policy should be, and what our aid policy should be, how we can intensify the struggle, how we can bring Americans out of there. [emphasis added]

This was strange: gone from his list of American objectives was winning the war—it had been replaced by the phrase "intensify the struggle."

Earlier, at his September 12 press conference, Kennedy had said his policy was "simple" and listed three objectives: win the war, contain the communists, and bring the Americans home. That was *before* the change in reporting on the battlefield in early November. At the November 12 press conference he restated the American objectives this way:

> Now, that is our object, *to bring Americans home,* permit the South Vietnamese to maintain themselves as a free and independent country, and permit democratic forces within the country to operate—which they can of course, much more freely when the assault from the inside, and which is manipulated from the north, is ended. So the purpose of the meeting in Honolulu is how to pursue these objectives. [emphasis added]

This was a stronger emphasis on withdrawing Americans than the President had ever made publicly before: he now placed it at the head of America's objectives in Vietnam. In this statement too there was no provision for winning the war. He merely refers to permitting "democratic forces within the country to operate," a formulation that was only a step away from a political solution along the lines he had pursued in Laos.

Kennedy followed up this declaration with another substantive change: he lifted the secrecy requirement from the 1,000-man withdrawal. Two days after this press conference, the MAAG Chief in Vietnam, Major General Charles Timmes, made it official: 1,000 American soldiers would be coming

home by the end of December. Kennedy himself did not issue a press statement; he was at Palm Beach, Florida, at the time, where a White House
spokesman would neither confirm nor deny the number of troops to be
withdrawn. The spokesman did say, however, that the number "was being
determined by the Department of Defense." Any high-level announcement
in Washington would await the results of the Honolulu meeting.

Kennedy asked Forrestal to go along and then to proceed to Cambodia,
which had been making charges of U.S. interference in its affairs. Before
leaving, Forrestal met with Kennedy on November 21. Forrestal reports
what Kennedy said in that encounter:

> He asked me to stay a bit; and he said: "When you come back, I want you
> to come and see me, because we have to start to plan for what we are going
> to do now, in South Vietnam." He said: "I want to start a complete and very
> profound review of how we got into this country; what we thought we
> were doing; and what we now think we can do." He said: "I even want to
> think about whether or not we should be there."

Kennedy told Forrestal that because this "was in the context of an election
campaign," he could not consider a quick, "drastic change" of policy but
instead how "some kind of a gradual shift in our presence in South Vietnam
could occur."

Kennedy's dilemma was how to engineer this gradual shift while the
battlefield situation was rapidly declining, and would perhaps do so even
faster as the U.S. pulled out. His last remark about Vietnam, made in Fort
Worth the morning he died, could not have stated this dilemma more
clearly: "Without the United States, South Vietnam would collapse
overnight." . . .

At 12:30 P.M., on November 22, the shots rang out in Dealy Plaza that
took the President's life. His Vietnam policy died with him. On the surface,
the shift in the war effort seemed gradual: it was fifteen months before the
first American Marines waded ashore at Da Nang, South Vietnam. Some
aspects of the reversal, however, were more sudden—almost instantaneous.
The underlying reason why the larger change took as long as it did was that
Johnson faced the same problem Kennedy had: the 1964 presidential election. The key to understanding how this campaign problem differed for
these two men is this: Kennedy had to disguise a withdrawal; Johnson had
to disguise intervention. . . .

The first phase of the Vietnam War during the Kennedy administration
lasted from the inauguration until the first days of May 1961.
Overshadowed by the debacle in Cuba and the failure in Laos, Vietnam policy languished as the bureaucracy in Washington charged with developing
it paid more attention to turf battles than those waged by the Viet Cong. The
program produced—the Counterinsurgency Plan (CIP)—made the desperately needed new American aid dependent on reforms by Diem, a man
whose record demonstrated that he would not implement them. The attempt
to force him to do so turned into an ugly parody of intrigue in Saigon, wast-

ing three precious months in the process. By the time the linkage between aid and reform was dropped and the Vice President sent out to patch things up, the Viet Cong had expanded their operations in Vietnam and captured most of the key terrain in Laos that would later become known as the Ho Chi Minh Trail.

The options, which the administration ended up facing in the summer of 1963, were already apparent by this stage: get out of Vietnam; instigate a coup against Diem; or say three Hail Marys and hope for the best with him. These choices were not clearly posed to the President, but he did not provide clear leadership either. The policy that emerged by default was the Hail Mary option. It was a sloppy, sluggish American slide into deeper commitment, more aid, and acquiescence to Diem.

What was painfully lacking in Washington was a concerted effort to define the nature of Vietnamese society; the insurgency raging there; and the nature of Diem's policies to cope with it. What would such an effort have revealed? At the minimum: a rural society whose political engine was driven by the simple aims of freedom from foreign bondage and government interference; a ferocious runaway insurgency that had long since ruthlessly harnessed this engine to its goal of a unified communist country; and a repressive and authoritarian regime in Saigon that stood in the path not only of the communist insurgency in the countryside, but also of the educated, noncommunist urban element of the population seeking a more democratic alternative for the country. By this time the autocratic nature of Diem's regime was simply one more unsavory aspect of his naked struggle for political power.

Even if such a systematic examination had been undertaken, it is doubtful that these sobering conclusions would have been accepted at the decision-making level in Washington. For the United States was already too deeply entrenched in Vietnam. The situation was well out of hand by the time Kennedy was elected, and the hope, enthusiasm, and vigor he symbolized only helped to forestall serious consideration of the true nature of the problem and the long odds America faced in Vietnam. The President began to understand, in those first three months, that the intrigues that had preoccupied both Saigon and Washington had not served U.S. policy well. Above all else he learned this: that his advisors—including the Vice President—wanted to intervene in Southeast Asia and that he did not.

The second phase of the war during the Kennedy years begins with NSAM-52 in early May 1961, and runs through the initial implementation of NSAM-111 at the end of the year. During the period between these two directives, three elements were on the rise: the success of the communist insurgency, the American commitment, and the resultant discord in Washington over what to do. NSAM-52 committed U.S. policy to preventing communist domination in Vietnam and dispatched 400 U.S. Special Forces advisors, while NSAM-80 in October dispatched the first Air Force Jungle Jim unit to participate in the war. In both instances the President, in making these decisions, had resisted a recommendation to send in combat troops, pushed mainly by the military in May, but largely supported by civilian advisors as well in October. The pressure for combat troops continued to build, especially when Taylor too, after his trip in late October, joined the chorus.

Kennedy's final decision—NSAM-111, issued on November 22, 1961—against intervention, was arrived at after all the arguments for it that could be made had been mustered: when the intelligence unequivocally showed the battlefield situation was desperate, when all his top advisors agreed that the fate of Vietnam hung in the balance, and when most of them believed that vital U.S. interests in the region and the world were at stake. Clearly, then, it was the major Vietnam decision of his presidency, drawing, as it did, a line that he never crossed. One of the principal theses of this work, derived from that decision, is that Kennedy would never have placed American combat troops in Vietnam. He did, nevertheless, make a commitment short of that, giving in to the urgency of the situation and to the pressure from his advisors, for NSAM-111 unleashed a flood of advisors, helicopters, and other equipment into Vietnam in the hope that American technology and know-how might somehow work a miracle.

Yet, here, again, this momentous decision was made without the benefit of answers to the most basic questions: Why were the Viet Cong winning? Why wouldn't Diem mend his ways? At what point and under what conditions would the U.S. have to withdraw? The Hail Mary solution prevailed: a long shot with time running out. More advisors, more airplanes, and more helicopters were sent but the Viet Cong kept on growing. Kennedy had not faced the music; he had only taken the "bucket of slop," as [Richard] Bissell [former deputy director of the CIA] called paramilitary operations, from the CIA and handed it to the military. The irony was that by the time Kennedy ruled out American combat troops, once and for all, the size of the Viet Cong had grown to the point where there was little hope that the South Vietnamese Army could contain it.

Kennedy had cleaned house in Washington and firmly taken charge, and the policy that emerged was his alone. Although he would not accept the recommendations of his advisors for combat troops—an act of great moral courage—neither would he accept defeat. Here was where the President became more personally entangled in the agony that his decision helped to prolong, and where his purpose became blurred by his own need to retain political power.

The third phase of the war during the Kennedy presidency, which lasted for the first half of 1962, was marked by the continued and dramatic growth of the Viet Cong and a sudden reversal toward optimism in the U.S. military's reporting on the war. Since this change occurred well before the new Kennedy program had any chance to influence the situation, it was suspicious—all the more so considering the military's long record of dire reports on the state of the battlefield. One of the theses of this work is that this reversal in reporting went well beyond the deception of official optimism and the denial of the true extent of U.S. involvement that the administration was engaging in. Rather, it was conducted at the top secret level and went so far as to eliminate from the order of battle more than half of the hard-core Viet Cong forces.

Because the President was cognizant of—and encouraged—the first level of this deception, and was, at the same time, the target of the second, the phrases "deception within a deception" or "inside deception" have been used to characterize the deepening web of intrigue that followed Kennedy's refusal to put combat troops into Vietnam. That refusal was the baseline from which all planning had to proceed. The Viet Cong's explosion, in the spring of 1962, beyond the ability of the South Vietnamese Army's ability to cope with them meant that the advisory effort was not working. The reason this was hidden from the President probably was because, of the two military choices available, withdrawal or intervention, his bar against combat troops would have meant withdrawal.

Prompted in April by [U.S. ambassador to India John Kenneth] Galbraith, Kennedy appeared to entertain the thought of a neutralist solution in Vietnam but was dissuaded by a consensus of his military and civilian advisors. Here the deception of progress looms large in building the case for a lengthier American presence and in encouraging hope for victory. Although Kennedy decided to pursue that course, McNamara made clear—probably at the President's urging—that there was still a limit to how long U.S. participation could last because the public would not accept American casualties indefinitely.

The fourth phase of the war in the Kennedy years extends from the summer of 1962 to the spring of 1963. This phase began while the false story of success continued to build the hopes of Kennedy and McNamara in ultimate victory. At this point, consumed by the Cuban Missile Crisis, they let Vietnam policy run its course. Too little attention was paid to the fact that the illusion of success somehow always seemed to require more men, more planes, more helicopters and other equipment to sustain it. Eventually, Kennedy and McNamara found themselves trapped in a deepening vortex of military escalation in which victory seemed ever more elusive. By the spring of 1963 the involvement had become so deep that the failure unfolding on the battlefield began to have foreboding implications for Kennedy's chances at a second term as President.

It was not that the American military had not done its job in Vietnam. It had. The advisors had counseled the South Vietnamese Army, and the intelligence specialists had been accurate and honest in reporting on the enemy. In retrospect, these men are the real heroes of the early stages of the war; but they were up against impossible odds. The South Vietnamese Army was too small and Diem was reluctant to let them fight anyway. The organization and training of South Vietnamese forces in general was wholly inappropriate to counterinsurgency operations, and MACV failed to pass on to Washington the observations of American advisors about the resulting problems. The harsh judgment of history on the American military performance in Vietnam during the Kennedy years should not fall on the privates, sergeants, lieutenants, and captains; it should fall on the command level and the senior leadership in Washington.

The final phase of Kennedy's developing dilemma in Vietnam, then, began in the spring of 1963. The Buddhist crisis and subsequent political collapse of the Saigon regime in the summer transformed his predicament into a nightmare. The President reconciled himself to pulling the U.S. out of the war and to the unpopularity he was sure this decision would bring. Perhaps a sense of guilt over his own role clouded his vision and helped move him to conclude that *only* his reelection could extricate America from the mess in Vietnam. The elements of his plan to accomplish this became increasingly desperate as the situation continued to deteriorate into the fall and Diem met his grim fate.

Kennedy's plan to pull out contained four components, three of which were present by the time the design was firmly put into place in the spring. First and foremost was his belief that the bulk of the withdrawal could not take place before the election without sparking another Joe McCarthy-style red scare that might dash the chance for extrication. Unfortunately, this part of the plan required that Kennedy project an image to the conservatives that did not reflect his true views on the war. The second element of the plan was to trickle out some of the Americans *during* the campaign in order to neutralize the growing criticism from liberals who felt the U.S. was becoming bogged down in the war. To begin such a limited withdrawal without provoking the conservative backlash he feared was difficult to do. The key to accomplishing it was the third ingredient of the plan: linking the 1,000-man withdrawal to the MACV success story emanating from Saigon.

If, by this time, Kennedy had not given up entirely on the notion of winning, he at least had deep suspicions about MACV's reporting. In hindsight, his willingness to tie the 1,000-man pullout to the story of success is indicative of the desperation that began creeping into his actions, and it raises the more fundamental issues of candor and presidential prerogative. At the time, however, this tie-in to success was so vital to his plan that the veracity of the success story probably seemed minor compared to the goal he sought: resolution of the seemingly intractable American problem in Vietnam.

The fourth and final component to his plan resulted from the political collapse in Saigon. That both the military and political sides of the struggle there were collapsing threatened the tie-in to success. Kennedy would be vulnerable to attacks from *both* sides of the aisle if he publicly justified the 1,000-man withdrawal by a presumption of battlefield success and that "success" then turned into a failure (especially if this occurred during an election campaign). Therefore, the last girder he put into place in the fall was the arrangement for his top military advisors to publicly make the case for this linkage (1,000-man withdrawal linked to success on the battlefield) while he remained at a safe political distance from any potentially damaging implications.

There seems little doubt that Kennedy was headed for a total withdrawal—come what may—from Vietnam when he left for Texas. Whether the comments he made to Senator Morse and Mike Forrestal indicate he was thinking of accelerating his plan is an intriguing idea but one that remains unproven. Any such modification, as well as the plan itself, were snuffed out on November 22, 1963. The vague sentence in NSAM-273 on withdrawal—however much we contrast its nuances with the clear-cut words of NSAM-263—became a fig leaf of continuity in the hands of the new President. The tragedy in Texas, in the end, brought about the outcome that Kennedy had opposed throughout his presidency: full-scale American intervention in Vietnam.

Many unanswered questions remain about Kennedy and Vietnam. For example, just what was the new study he was in the midst of when he died? Would he have been willing to face the consequences of accelerating the pullout and seeking a neutral South Vietnam during an election year? Why did his last press conferences no longer include winning the war as an American objective? These questions may not be answered with authority, but one question can be: would Kennedy have sent in the combat troops as Johnson did? The answer to that is no. That perennial question has been the focus of debate for nearly thirty years, but its politicization has obscured the more fundamental questions raised by the way he dealt with this issue. These questions strike at the very heart of the American presidency and processes of government and have great relevance for the study of the subsequent administrations.

Kennedy's public duplicity on the issue of American intervention has made it all too easy for Johnson apologists to seize on Kennedy's statements as proof that he too would have sent in the troops. The speech he would have delivered at the Trade Mart in Dallas, had he lived, was the last example of this questionable pretense. The speech contained this passage:

> Our assistance to these nations can be painful, risky and costly, as is true in Southeast Asia today. But we dare not weary of the task. For our assistance makes possible the stationing of 3.5 million allied troops along the Communist frontier at one-tenth the cost of maintaining a comparable number of American soldiers. A successful Communist breakthrough in these areas [like Southeast Asia], *necessitating direct United States intervention,* would cost us several times as much as our entire foreign aid program, and might cost us heavily in American lives as well. [emphasis added]

The Kennedy apologists who ignore such statements are no more helpful than his critics who rely on them exclusively. Disregarding them only subverts the truth. The fact is that he made them, and did so continuously, up to the day he died. However high or noble his larger purpose may have been, in so doing he besmirched his own reputation and that of the office he held.

There is no need to restate here the evidence that Kennedy would not have sent in combat troops; it is sufficient to say that the top secret NSC meetings of 1961 more than resolve the question. There is also no need to revisit the sad litany of his misleading public statements. Both of these subjects have been dealt with in detail and at length in this work. The real questions posed by the Janus-like nature of his public and private postures go to the core of the American political system: What is the legitimate national interest? Who shall decide this? When is it permissible for the President to mislead the public about his intentions with respect to war? With respect to anything? Is there a higher end that justifies these means? If one President may deceive to stay out of a war, cannot another do likewise to go into one?

Kennedy concluded that a retreat from Vietnam could not happen unless he was reelected. Although subsequent events appear to have justified such a conclusion, the fact is that he had the option to withdraw when he realized that failure was inevitable and to fight honestly for his beliefs in the campaign, relying on strong leadership and example. To do so meant rising above the personal goal of political power, and attempting to inspire and unify friends and foes alike as he did in his inaugural address. This course would have been risky, but so was the one he was pursuing. By taking his case directly to the people the onus would have been placed upon those arguing for intervention.

The Dallas Trade Mart speech contains another passage that merits attention:

> We in this country, in this generation, are—by destiny rather than choice—the watchmen on the walls of freedom. We ask, therefore, that we may be worthy of our strength with wisdom and restraint, and that we may achieve in our time and for all time the ancient vision of "peace on earth, good will toward men." That must always be our goal, and the righteousness of our cause must always underlie our strength. For as was written long ago: *except the Lord keep the city, the watchman waketh in vain.*
> [emphasis in original]

Perhaps lying veiled in this old parable is Kennedy's recognition and his acceptance of the fact that his efforts at one place along that long wall had met defeat: Vietnam. Still, speaking about policy in parables, however eloquent, was no way to take his case to the people.

In raising these questions, the intent is not to demean Kennedy and his many accomplishments; but failing to raise them would demean both. We can no longer afford to look at just one side of Camelot, to do so trivializes Kennedy's life and the price the nation paid for his death. We can still admire him for the great courage he showed in ruling out the use of American combat troops in Vietnam, and point out that he had been deceived, for a time, about the state of the war effort, understanding that that deception was instrumental in the choices he made. Had he lived, he still would have had time to take his case truthfully to the American people in 1964, and he might have done so. That he never had the chance was his misfortune and the nation's as well. Finally, it must be pointed out that Kennedy was not the President who sent in the troops. As a highly decorated U.S. Army General said in 1968: "Let us not lay on the dead the blame for our own failures."

Clearly the most tragic consequence of Kennedy's death was the subsequent escalation of the war. One may argue about which aspect of war policy was altered, changed, or reversed, and how suddenly or gradually it happened, but the fact is that it did happen. Scholars with august reputations steer clear of looking seriously at this question in part because it is so politically charged and, like Kennedy's war policies, it raises basic and alarming questions about American democratic institutions.

The American people have never been satisfied with the official explanation of the Kennedy assassination, nor has the Congress for that matter. Nevertheless, it is psychologically less troubling to believe that Johnson carried on Kennedy's Vietnam policy than to acknowledge the reverse. If that premise, and the Warren Commission's conclusion that Lee Harvey Oswald acted alone, are dispelled, where, then, does honest inquiry lead? Until now, such inquiry has been off-limits for serious political scientists and historians because of the conspiratorial presumptions that appear inherent in the material. The implication seems to be that any study that dares examine the possibility of a recent conspiracy is somehow un-American. Yet, in fact, it is *that* idea that is un-American. That we the people have not only the right but the duty to examine such questions is a basic assumption of our most treasured political institutions.

Hopefully the passage of time has begun to erode fears of looking critically at the role of the assassination in the subsequent escalation of the war. Unfortunately, appropriate educational background and rigorous analytical methodology is virtually absent among those few who have tackled the subject. The one exception that comes to mind is Professor Peter Dale Scott, a serious early researcher who was stigmatized for his effort; in 1972 he persuasively argued that the assassination played a major role in the escalation of the war. The problem that Scott faced in the six years he had spent researching the subject was a lack of adequate documentation, not the least of which is the gaping documentary hole in *The Pentagon Papers* between the end of October 1963 and the assassination. Scott's chapter in volume 5 of the Senator Gravel edition of *The Pentagon Papers* was a monumental effort to unlock the mysteries of NSAM-273—without actually having seen the document—an effort that even Sherlock Holmes would have admired.

The final version of NSAM-273 was declassified a few years later but it was not until 1991, when an early draft of it and many of the secret documents from the last half of 1963 were declassified, that a more robust foundation for analyzing and interpreting that period was established. Perhaps the present work will encourage further examination of this subject as well as the broader political issues involved. How the war progressed after Kennedy's death, and the assassination itself, are subjects beyond the scope of this work. One lesson the author learned in the process of researching and writing this book is that preconceived and simplistic ideas most often do not hold up under careful scrutiny. For that reason no effort will be made here to offer quick answers to these profound questions. It is hoped, however, that this work will help to establish the respectability of this subject matter as a legitimate field of inquiry.

Finally, the sometimes startling nature of the events detailed and the preliminary interpretations in this work should be considered no more than a first attempt to reopen this lost chapter of American history and to draw the lessons we must from its mistakes. The issues at stake go beyond the Kennedy administration and the Vietnam War: they touch upon the entire spectrum of our political institutions and Western moral and ethical traditions.

✗ FURTHER READING

David Burner, *John F. Kennedy and a New Generation* (1988)
Noam Chomsky, *Rethinking Camelot: JFK, the Vietnam War, and U.S. Political Culture* (1993)
James N. Giglio, *The Presidency of John F. Kennedy* (1991)
David Halberstam, *The Making of a Quagmire* (1965)
Ellen J. Hammer, *A Death in November : America in Vietnam, 1963* (1987)
Jim F. Heath, *Decade of Disillusionment* (1975)
Roger Hilsman, *To Move a Nation* (1967)
Douglas Kinnard, *The Certain Trumpet* (1991) (on Maxwell Taylor)
Henry Cabot Lodge, *The Storm Has Many Eyes* (1973)
John Mecklin, *Mission in Torment* (1965)
Herbert S. Parmet, *JFK* (1983)
Thomas G. Paterson, "Bearing the Burden: A Critical Look at JFK's Foreign Policy," *Virginia Quarterly Review,* 54 (1978), 193–212
———, ed., *Kennedy's Quest for Victory* (1989)
Stephen E. Pelz, "John F. Kennedy's 1961 Vietnam War Decisions," *Journal of Strategic Studies,* 4 (1981), 356–385
Walt W. Rostow, *The Diffusion of Power* (1972)
Dean Rusk, *As I Saw It* (1990)
William J. Rust, *Kennedy in Vietnam* (1985)
Arthur M. Schlesinger, Jr., *Robert Kennedy and His Times* (1978)
———, *A Thousand Days* (1965)
Thomas J. Schoenbaum, *Waging Peace and War* (1988) (on Dean Rusk)
Neil Sheehan, *A Bright Shining Lie* (1988) (on John Paul Vann)
R. B. Smith, *The Kennedy Strategy* (1985)
Richard J. Snyder, ed., *John F. Kennedy* (1988)
Theodore C. Sorensen, *Kennedy* (1965)
Maxwell D. Taylor, *Swords and Ploughshares* (1972)
Richard Tregaskis, *Vietnam Diary* (1963)
Richard J. Walton, *Cold War and Counter-Revolution: The Foreign Policy of John F. Kennedy* (1972)
Geoffrey Warner, "The United States and the Fall of Diem," Part I: "The Coup that Never Was," *Australian Outlook,* 29 (1974), 245–58
———, "The United States and the Fall of Diem," Part II: "The Death of Diem," *Australian Outlook,* 29 (1975), 3–17

Lyndon B. Johnson's Decisions for War

✕

In the months following the Diem and Kennedy assassinations, political chaos gripped South Vietnam. Combined with spreading guerrilla insurgency in the South, this turmoil made American officials worry that the survival of the Saigon government hung in the balance. In December 1963 Defense Secretary Robert S. McNamara warned President Lyndon B. Johnson that without a reversal of current trends within the next two or three months, the most likely result would be a communist-controlled state. Many of Johnson's advisers urged military escalation, recommending bombing reprisals against the North and the dispatch of U.S. combat forces to the South.

In August 1964, in response to alleged attacks against U.S. naval vessels by North Vietnamese warboats in the Gulf of Tonkin, Congress passed a resolution that granted the president sweeping powers. It authorized him to take "all necessary measures to repel any armed attacks against the forces of the United States and to prevent further aggression." Nevertheless, Johnson moved cautiously. In July 1965, fearing the imminence of Saigon's collapse, he acted. After a lengthy deliberative process, LBJ ordered a sustained bombing campaign against North Vietnam and authorized the introduction of combat forces to stem the insurgency in the South. Those decisions committed the United States to a major land war in Asia.

Because Johnson's escalation of U.S. involvement in Vietnam had such profound consequences, his decisions have understandably generated much heated public and scholarly debate. How were the decisions reached? Did Johnson dominate the deliberative process? Or did he simply follow the recommendations of his principal advisers? Why did LBJ and senior policymakers dismiss the doubts raised by Under Secretary of State George Ball? What specific goals did Johnson expect to achieve through the use of combat troops and the air offensive? Did he expect to defeat the communists? Or only to prevent the fall of the South Vietnamese regime? How did he view the stakes involved in Vietnam? Did his concern with the likely domestic political fallout from the loss of South Vietnam to the communists affect his

thinking? Did he seek merely to buy time for his Great Society reform pro-
gram? What did he believe would be the international ramifications for the
United States if its South Vietnamese ally perished?

X D O C U M E N T S

The first document features excerpts from National Security Action Memorandum 288 of March 17, 1964, which set forth U.S. objectives in South
Vietnam. The Tonkin Gulf Resolution (the second document), which passed
the Senate on August 10, 1964, with only two dissenting votes, authorized the
president to use whatever force he deemed necessary in Vietnam. In the third
selection, a speech of April 7, 1965, at Johns Hopkins University, President
Johnson explains why the United States is fighting in Vietnam.

   The fourth document, a memorandum to the president from Secretary of
Defense McNamara, recommends a substantial expansion of U.S. military
pressure against the Vietcong in the South and the North Vietnamese in the
North. Under Secretary of State Ball offers contrary advice to the president in
a memorandum of July 1, the fifth document. An excerpt from Johnson's
memoir *The Vantage Point,* in which he reflects on his decision to accept
McNamara's advice, is the next document. The final selection gives a soldier's
perspective on the war. Reprinted from Philip Caputo's best-selling memoir *A*
Rumor of War, it captures the innocence and idealism that some American
fighting men brought with them to Vietnam.

Reassessment of U.S. Objectives in South Vietnam, 1964

[The United States' policy is] to prepare immediately to be in a position on
72 hours' notice to initiate the full range of Laotian and Cambodian
"Border Control actions" . . . and the "Retaliatory Actions" against North
Vietnam, and to be in a position on 30 days' notice to initiate the program
of "Graduated Overt Military Pressure" against North Vietnam. . . .

   We seek an independent non-Communist South Vietnam. We do not
require that it serve as a Western base or as a member of a Western Alliance.
South Vietnam must be free, however, to accept outside assistance as
required to maintain its security. This assistance should be able to take the
form not only of economic and social measures but also police and military
help to root out and control insurgent elements.

   Unless we can achieve this objective in South Vietnam, almost all of
Southeast Asia will probably fall under Communist dominance (all of
Vietnam, Laos, and Cambodia), accommodate to Communism so as to
remove effective U.S. and anti-Communist influence (Burma), or fall under
the domination of forces not now explicitly Communist but likely then to
become so (Indonesia taking over Malaysia). Thailand might hold for a
period without help, but would be under grave pressure. Even the
Philippines would become shaky, and the threat to India on the West,
Australia and New Zealand to the South, and Taiwan, Korea, and Japan to
the North and East would be greatly increased.

All of these consequences would probably have been true even if the U.S. had not since 1954, and especially since 1961, become so heavily engaged in South Vietnam. However, that fact accentuates the impact of a Communist South Vietnam not only in Asia but in the rest of the world, where the South Vietnam conflict is regarded as a test case of U.S. capacity to help a nation to meet the Communist "war of liberation."

Thus, purely in terms of foreign policy, the stakes are high. . . .

We are now trying to help South Vietnam defeat the Viet Cong, supported from the North, by means short of the unqualified use of U.S. combat forces. We are not acting against North Vietnam except by a modest "covert" program operated by South Vietnamese (and a few Chinese Nationalists)—a program so limited that it is unlikely to have any significant effect. . . .

There were and are some sound reasons for the limits imposed by the present policy—the South Vietnamese must win their own fight; U.S. intervention on a larger scale, and/or GVN actions against the North, would disturb key allies and other nations; etc. In any case, it is vital that we continue to take every reasonable measure to assure success in South Vietnam. The policy choice is not an "either/or" between this course of action and possible pressure against the North; the former is essential and without regard to our decision with respect to the latter. The latter can, at best, only reinforce the former. . . .

Many of the actions described in the succeeding paragraphs fit right into the framework of the [pacification] plan as announced by Khanh. Wherever possible, we should tie our urgings of such actions to Khanh's own formulation of them, so that he will be carrying out a Vietnamese plan and not one imposed by the United States.

The Tonkin Gulf Resolution, 1964

To promote the maintenance of international peace and security in southeast Asia.

Whereas naval units of the Communist regime in Vietnam, in violation of the principles of the Charter of the United Nations and of international law, have deliberately and repeatedly attacked United States naval vessels lawfully present in international waters, and have thereby created a serious threat to international peace; and

Whereas these attacks are part of a deliberate and systematic campaign of aggression that the Communist regime in North Vietnam has been waging against its neighbors and the nations joined with them in the collective defense of their freedom; and

Whereas the United States is assisting the peoples of southeast Asia to protect their freedom and has no territorial, military or political ambitions in that area, but desires only that these peoples should be left in peace to work out their own destinies in their own way: Now, therefore, be it *Resolved by the Senate and House of Representatives of the United States of America in Congress assembled,* That the Congress approves and supports the determination of the President, as Commander in Chief, to take all necessary measures to repel any armed attack against the forces of the United States and to prevent further aggression.

SEC. 2. The United States regards as vital to its national interest and to world peace the maintenance of international peace and security in southeast Asia. Consonant with the Constitution of the United States and the Charter of the United Nations and in accordance with its obligations under the Southeast Asia Collective Defense Treaty, the United States is, therefore, prepared, as the President determines, to take all necessary steps, including the use of armed force, to assist any member or protocol state of the Southeast Asia Collective Defense Treaty requesting assistance in defense of its freedom.

SEC. 3. This resolution shall expire when the President shall determine that the peace and security of the area is reasonably assured by international conditions created by action of the United Nations or otherwise, except that it may be terminated earlier by concurrent resolution of the Congress.

Lyndon B. Johnson Explains Why Americans Fight in Vietnam, 1965

Why must this nation hazard its ease, its interest, and its power for the sake of a people so far away?

We fight because we must fight if we are to live in a world where every country can shape its own destiny, and only in such a world will our own freedom be finally secure.

This kind of world will never be built by bombs or bullets. Yet the infirmities of man are such that force must often precede reason and the waste of war, the works of peace.

We wish that this were not so. But we must deal with the world as it is, if it is ever to be as we wish.

The world as it is in Asia is not a serene or peaceful place.

The first reality is that North Viet-Nam has attacked the independent nation of South Viet-Nam. Its object is total conquest.

Of course, some of the people of South Viet-Nam are participating in attack on their own government. But trained men and supplies, orders and arms, flow in a constant stream from North to South.

This support is the heartbeat of the war.

And it is a war of unparalleled brutality. Simple farmers are the targets of assassination and kidnapping. Women and children are strangled in the night because their men are loyal to their government. And helpless villages are ravaged by sneak attacks. Large-scale raids are conducted on towns, and terror strikes in the heart of cities.

The confused nature of this conflict cannot mask the fact that it is the new face of an old enemy.

Over this war—and all Asia—is another reality: the deepening shadow of Communist China. The rulers in Hanoi are urged on by Peking. This is a regime which has destroyed freedom in Tibet, which has attacked India and has been condemned by the United Nations for aggression in Korea. It is a nation which is helping the forces of violence in almost every continent. The contest in Viet-Nam is part of a wider pattern of aggressive purposes.

Why are these realities our concern? Why are we in South Viet-Nam?

We are there because we have a promise to keep. Since 1954 every American President has offered support to the people of South Viet-Nam. We have helped to build, and we have helped to defend. Thus, over many years, we have made a national pledge to help South Viet-Nam defend its independence.

And I intend to keep that promise.

To dishonor that pledge, to abandon this small and brave nation to its enemies, and to the terror that must follow, would be an unforgivable wrong.

We are also there to strengthen world order. Around the globe from Berlin to Thailand are people whose well being rests in part on the belief that they can count on us if they are attacked. To leave Viet-Nam to its fate would shake the confidence of all these people in the value of an American commitment and in the value of America's word. The result would be increased unrest and instability, and even wider war.

We are also there because there are great stakes in the balance. Let no one think for a moment that retreat from Viet-Nam would bring an end to conflict. The battle would be renewed in one country and then another. The central lesson of our time is that the appetite of aggression is never satisfied. To withdraw from one battlefield means only to prepare for the next. We must say in Southeast Asia—as we did in Europe—in the words of the Bible: "Hitherto shalt thou come, but no further."

There are those who say that all our effort there will be futile—that China's power is such that it is bound to dominate all Southeast Asia. But there is no end to that argument until all of the nations of Asia are swallowed up.

There are those who wonder why we have a responsibility there. Well, we have it there for the same reason that we have a responsibility for the defense of Europe. World War II was fought in both Europe and Asia and when it ended we found ourselves with continued responsibility for the defense of freedom.

Our objective is the independence of South Viet-Nam and its freedom from attack. We want nothing for ourselves—only that the people of South Viet-Nam be allowed to guide their own country in their own way.

We will do everything necessary to reach that objective and we will do only what is absolutely necessary.

In recent months attacks on South Viet-Nam were stepped up. Thus, it became necessary for us to increase our response and to make attacks by air. This is not a change of purpose. It is a change in what we believe that purpose requires.

We do this in order to slow down aggression.

We do this to increase the confidence of the brave people of South

Viet-Nam who have bravely borne this brutal battle for so many years with so many casualties.

And we do this to convince the leaders of North Viet-Nam—and all who seek to share their conquest—of a simple fact:

We will not be defeated.

We will not grow tired.

We will not withdraw, either openly or under the cloak of a meaningless agreement.

We know that air attacks alone will not accomplish all of these purposes. But it is our best and prayerful judgment that they are a necessary part of the surest road to peace.

We hope that peace will come swiftly. But that is in the hands of others besides ourselves. And we must be prepared for a long continued conflict. It will require patience as well as bravery—the will to endure as well as the will to resist.

I wish it were possible to convince others with words of what we now find it necessary to say with guns and planes: armed hostility is futile—our resources are equal to any challenge—because we fight for values and we fight for principle, rather than territory or colonies, our patience and our determination are unending.

Once this is clear, then it should also be clear that the only path for reasonable men is the path of peaceful settlement. . . .

These countries of Southeast Asia are homes for millions of impoverished people. Each day these people rise at dawn and struggle through until the night to wrestle existence from the soil. They are often wracked by diseases, plagued by hunger, and death comes at the early age of forty.

Stability and peace do not come easily in such a land. Neither independence nor human dignity will ever be won though by arms alone. It also requires the works of peace. The American people have helped generously in times past in these works, and now there must be a much more massive effort to improve the life of man in that conflict-torn corner of our world.

The first step is for the countries of Southeast Asia to associate themselves in a greatly expanded co-operative effort for development. We would hope that North Viet-Nam would take its place in the common effort just as soon as peaceful co-operation is possible.

The United Nations is already actively engaged in development in this area, and as far back as 1961 I conferred with our authorities in Viet-Nam in connection with their work there. And I would hope tonight that the Secretary General of the United Nations could use the prestige of his great office and his deep knowledge of Asia to initiate, as soon as possible, with the countries of that area, a plan for co-operation in increased development.

For our part I will ask the Congress to join in a billion dollar American investment in this effort as soon as it is underway.

And I would hope that all other industrialized countries, including the Soviet Union, will join in this effort to replace despair with hope and terror with progress.

The task is nothing less than to enrich the hopes and existence of more than a hundred million people. And there is much to be done.

The vast Mekong River can provide food and water and power on a scale to dwarf even our own T.V.A.

The wonders of modern medicine can be spread through villages where thousands die every year from lack of care.

Schools can be established to train people in the skills needed to manage the process of development.

And these objectives, and more, are within the reach of a cooperative and determined effort.

I also intend to expand and speed up a program to make available our farm surpluses to assist in feeding and clothing the needy in Asia. We should not allow people to go hungry and wear rags while our own warehouses overflow with an abundance of wheat and corn and rice and cotton.

So I will very shortly name a special team of outstanding, patriotic, and distinguished Americans to inaugurate our participation in these programs. This team will be headed by Mr. Eugene Black, the very able former president of the World Bank.

This will be a disorderly planet for a long time. In Asia, and elsewhere, the forces of the modern world are shaking old ways and uprooting ancient civilizations. There will be turbulence and struggle and even violence. Great social change—as we see in our own country—does not always come without conflict.

We must also expect that nations will on occasion be in dispute with us. It may be because we are rich, or powerful, or because we have made some mistakes, or because they honestly fear our intentions. However, no nation need ever fear that we desire their land, or to impose our will, or to dictate their institutions.

But we will always oppose the effort of one nation to conquer another nation.

We will do this because our own security is at stake.

But there is more to it than that. For our generation has a dream. It is a very old dream. But we have the power, and now we have the opportunity to make that dream come true.

For centuries nations have struggled among each other. But we dream of a world where disputes are settled by law and reason. And we will try to make it so.

For most of history men have hated and killed one another in battle. But we dream of an end to war. And we will try to make it so.

For all existence most men have lived in poverty, threatened by hunger. But we dream of a world where all are fed and charged with hope. And we will help to make it so.

Robert S. McNamara Recommends Escalation, 1965

Introduction

Our objective is to create conditions for a favorable settlement by demonstrating to the VC/DRV that the odds are against their winning. Under present conditions, however, the chances of achieving this objective are small—and the VC are winning now—largely because the ratio of guerrilla to anti-guerrilla forces is unfavorable to the government. With this in mind, we must choose among three courses of action with respect to South Vietnam: (1) Cut our losses and withdraw under the best conditions that can be arranged; (2) continue at about the present level, with US forces limited to, say, 75,000, holding on and playing for the breaks while recognizing that our position will probably grow weaker; or (3) expand substantially the US military pressure against the Viet Cong in the South and the North Vietnamese in the North and at the same time launch a vigorous effort on the political side to get negotiations started. An outline of the third of these approaches follows.

I. Expanded Military Moves

The following military moves should be taken together with the political initiatives in Part II below.

A. Inside South Vietnam.   Increase US/SVN military strength in SVN enough to prove to the VC that they cannot win and thus to turn the tide of the war. . . .

B. Against North Vietnam.   While avoiding striking population and industrial targets not closely related to the DRV's supply of war material to the VC, we should announce to Hanoi and carry out actions to destroy such supplies and to interdict their flow into and out of North Vietnam. . . .

II. Expanded Political Moves

Together with the above military moves, we should take the following political initiatives in order (a) to open a dialogue with Hanoi, Peking, and the VC looking toward a settlement in Vietnam, (b) to keep the Soviet Union from deepening its military involvement and support of North Vietnam until the time when settlement can be achieved, and (c) to cement the support for US policy by the US public, allies and friends, and to keep international opposition at a manageable level. While our approaches may be rebuffed until the tide begins to turn, they nevertheless should be made. . . .

III. Evaluation of the Above Program

A. Domestic US Reaction.   Even though casualties will increase and the war will continue for some time, the United States public will support this course of action because it is a combined military-political program designed and likely to bring about a favorable solution to the Vietnam problem.

B. Communist Reaction to the Expanded Programs.

1. *Soviet.* The Soviets can be expected to continue to contribute materiel and advisors to the North Vietnamese. Increased US bombing of Vietnam, including targets in Hanoi and Haiphong, SAM [surface-to-air missile] sites and airfields, and mining of North Vietnamese harbors, might oblige the Soviet Union to enter the contest more actively with volunteers and aircraft. This might result in minor encounters between US and Soviet personnel.

2. *China.* So long as no US or GVN troops invade North Vietnam and so long as no US or GVN aircraft attack Chinese territory, the Chinese probably will not send regular ground forces or aircraft into the war. However, the possibility of a more active Soviet involvement in North Vietnam might precipitate a Chinese introduction of land forces, probably dubbed volunteers, to preclude the Soviets' taking a pre-eminent position in North Vietnam.

3. *North Vietnam.* North Vietnam will not move towards the negotiating table until the tide begins to turn in the south. When that happens, they may seek to counter it by sending large numbers of men into South Vietnam.

4. *Viet Cong.* The VC, especially if they continue to take high losses, can be expected to depend increasingly upon the PAVN [People's Army of Vietnam, regular forces of North Vietnam] forces as the war moves into a more conventional phase; but they may find ways of continuing almost indefinitely their present intensive military, guerrilla and terror activities, particularly if reinforced with some regular PAVN units. A key question on the military side is whether POL [petroleum-oil-lubricants], ammunition, and cadres can be cut off and if they are cut off whether this really renders the Viet Cong impotent. A key question on the political side is whether any arrangement acceptable to us would be acceptable to the VC.

C. Estimate of Success.

1. *Militarily.* The success of the above program from a military point of view turns on whether the increased effort stems the tide in the South; that in turn depends on two things—on whether the South Vietnamese hold their own in terms of numbers and fighting spirit, and on whether the US forces can be effective in a quick-reaction reserve role, a role in which they have not been tested. The number of US troops is too small to make a significant difference in the traditional 10-1 government-guerrilla formula, but it is not too small to make a significant difference in the kind of war which seems to be evolving in Vietnam—a "Third Stage" or conventional war in which it is easier to identify, locate and attack the enemy. (South Vietnam has 141 battalions as compared with an estimated equivalent number of VC battalions. The 44 US/3d country battalions mentioned above are the equivalent of 100 South Vietnamese battalions.)

2. *Politically.* It is frequently alleged that such a large expansion of US military personnel, their expanded military role (which would put them in

close contact and offer some degree of control over South Vietnamese citizens), and the inevitable expansion of US voice in the operation of the GVN economy and facilities, command and government services will be unpopular; it is said that they could lead to the rejection of the government which supported this American presence, to an irresistible pressure for expulsion of the Americans, and to the greatly increased saleability of Communist propaganda. Whether these allegations are true, we do not know.

The political initiatives are likely to be successful in the early stages only to demonstrate US good faith; they will pay off toward an actual settlement only after the tide begins to turn (unless we lower our sights substantially). The tide almost certainly cannot begin to turn in less than a few months, and may not for a year or more; the war is one of attrition and will be a long one. Since troops once committed as a practical matter cannot be removed, since US casualties will rise, since we should take call-up actions to support the additional forces in Vietnam, the test of endurance may be as much in the United States as in Vietnam.

3. *Generally (CIA estimate).* Over the longer term we doubt if the Communists are likely to change their basic strategy in Vietnam (i.e., aggressive and steadily mounting insurgency) unless and until two conditions prevail: (1) they are forced to accept a situation in the war in the South which offers them no prospect of an early victory and no grounds for hope that they can simply outlast the US and (2) North Vietnam itself is under continuing and increasingly damaging punitive attack. So long as the Communists think they scent the possibility of an early victory (which is probably now the case), we believe that they will persevere and accept extremely severe damage to the North. Conversely, if North Vietnam itself is not hurting, Hanoi's doctrinaire leaders will probably be ready to carry on the Southern struggle almost indefinitely. If, however, both of the conditions outlined above should be brought to pass, we believe Hanoi probably would, at least for a period of time, alter its basic strategy and course of action in South Vietnam.

Hanoi might do so in several ways. Going for a conference as a political way of gaining a respite from attack would be one. Alternatively it might reduce the level of insurgent activity in the hopes that this would force the US to stop its punishment of the North but not prevent the US and GVN from remaining subject to wearying harassment in the South. Or, Hanoi might order the VC to suspend operations in the hopes that in a period of temporary tranquillity, domestic and international opinion would force the US to disengage without destroying the VC apparatus or the roots of VC strength. Finally, Hanoi might decide that the US/GVN will to fight could still be broken and the tide of war turned back again in favor of the VC by launching a massive PAVN assault on the South. This is a less likely option in the circumstances we have posited, but still a contingency for which the US must be prepared.

George Ball Dissents, 1965

1. *A Losing War:* The South Vietnamese are losing the war to the Viet Cong. No one can assure you that we can beat the Viet Cong or even force them to the conference table on our terms, no matter how many hundred thousand *white, foreign* (U.S.) troops we deploy.

No one has demonstrated that a white ground force of whatever size can win a guerrilla war—which is at the same time a civil war between Asians—in jungle terrain in the midst of a population that refuses cooperation to the white forces (and the South Vietnamese) and thus provides a great intelligence advantage to the other side. Three recent incidents vividly illustrate this point: (a) the sneak attack on the Da Nang Air Base which involved penetration of a defense perimeter guarded by 9,000 Marines. This raid was possible only because of the cooperation of the local inhabitants; (b) the B-52 raid that failed to hit the Viet Cong who had obviously been tipped off; (c) the search and destroy mission of the 173rd Air Borne Brigade which spent three days looking for the Viet Cong, suffered 23 casualties, and never made contact with the enemy who had obviously gotten advance word of their assignment.

2. *The Question to Decide:* Should we limit our liabilities in South Vietnam and try to find a way out with minimal long-term costs? The alternative—no matter what we may wish it to be—is almost certainly a protracted war involving an open-ended commitment of U.S. forces, mounting U.S. casualties, no assurance of a satisfactory solution, and a serious danger of escalation at the end of the road.

3. *Need for a Decision Now:* So long as our forces are restricted to advising and assisting the South Vietnamese, the struggle will remain a civil war between Asian peoples. Once we deploy substantial numbers of troops in combat it will become a war between the U.S. and a large part of the population of South Vietnam, organized and directed from North Vietnam and backed by the resources of both Moscow and Peiping.

The decision you face now, therefore, is crucial. Once large numbers of U.S. troops are committed to direct combat, they will begin to take heavy casualties in a war they are ill-equipped to fight in a non-cooperative if not downright hostile countryside.

Once we suffer large casualties, we will have started a well-nigh irreversible process. Our involvement will be so great that we cannot—without national humiliation—stop short of achieving our complete objectives. *Of the two possibilities I think humiliation would be more likely than the achievement of our objectives—even after we have paid terrible costs.*

4. *Compromise Solution:* Should we commit U.S. manpower and prestige to a terrain so unfavorable as to give a very large advantage to the enemy—or should we seek a compromise settlement which achieves less than our stated objectives and thus cut our losses while we still have the freedom of maneuver to do so.

5. *Costs of a Compromise Solution:* The answer involves a judgment as to the cost to the U.S. of such a compromise settlement in terms of our

relations with the countries in the area of South Vietnam, the credibility of our commitments, and our prestige around the world. In my judgment, if we act before we commit substantial U.S. troops to combat in South Vietnam we can, by accepting some short-term costs, avoid what may well be a long-term catastrophe. I believe we tended grossly to exaggerate the costs involved in a compromise settlement. An appreciation of probable costs is contained in the attached memorandum.

6. With these considerations in mind, I strongly urge the following program:

a. Military Program

1. Complete all deployment already announced—15 battalions—but decide not to go beyond a total of 72,000 men represented by this figure.
2. Restrict the combat role of the American forces to the June 19 announcement, making it clear to General Westmoreland that this announcement is to be strictly construed.
3. Continue bombing in the North but avoid the Hanoi-Haiphong area and any targets nearer to the Chinese border than those already struck.

b. Political Program

1. In any political approaches so far, we have been the prisoners of whatever South Vietnamese government that was momentarily in power. If we are ever to move toward a settlement, it will probably be because the South Vietnamese government pulls the rug out from under us and makes its own deal *or* because we go forward quietly without advance prearrangement with Saigon.
2. So far we have not given the other side a reason to believe there is *any* flexibility in our negotiating approach. And the other side has been unwilling to accept what *in their terms* is complete capitulation.
3. Now is the time to start some serious diplomatic feelers looking towards a solution based on some application of a self-determination principle.
4. I would recommend approaching Hanoi rather than any of the other probable parties, the NLF, ——— or Peiping. Hanoi is the only one that has given any signs of interest in discussion. Peiping has been rigidly opposed. Moscow has recommended that we negotiate with Hanoi. The NLF has been silent.
5. There are several channels to the North Vietnamese, but I think the best one is through their representative in Paris, Mai van Bo. Initial feelers of Bo should be directed toward a discussion both of the four points we have put forward and the four points put forward by Hanoi as a basis for negotiation. We can accept all but one of Hanoi's four points, and hopefully we should be able to agree on some ground rules for serious negotiations—including no preconditions.

6. If the initial feelers lead to further secret, exploratory talks, we can inject the concept of self-determination that would permit the Viet Cong some hope of achieving some of their political objectives through local elections or some other device.

7. The contact on our side should be handled through a non-governmental cutout (possibly a reliable newspaper man who can be repudiated).

8. If progress can be made at this level a basis can be laid for a multinational conference. At some point, obviously, the government of South Vietnam will have to be brought on board, but I would postpone this step until after a substantial feeling out of Hanoi.

9. Before moving to any formal conference we should be prepared to agree once the conference is started:
    a. The U.S. will stand down its bombing of the North
    b. The South Vietnamese will initiate no offensive operations in the South, and
    c. The DRV will stop terrorism and other aggressive action against the South.

10. The negotiations at the conference should aim at incorporating our understanding with Hanoi in the form of a multinational agreement guaranteed by the U.S., the Soviet Union and possibly other parties, and providing for an international mechanism to supervise its execution.

Johnson Recalls His Decision to Commit Troops (1965), 1971

We discussed Ball's approach for a long time and in great detail. I think all of us felt the same concerns and anxieties that Ball had expressed, but most of these men in the Cabinet Room were more worried about the results, in our country and throughout the world, of our pulling out and coming home. I felt the Under Secretary had not produced a sufficiently convincing case or a viable alternative.

Dean Rusk expressed one worry that was much on my mind. It lay at the heart of our Vietnam policy. "If the Communist world finds out that we will not pursue our commitments to the end," he said, "I don't know where they will stay their hand."

I felt sure they would *not* stay their hand. If we ran out on Southeast Asia, I could see trouble ahead in every part of the globe—not just in Asia but in the Middle East and in Europe, in Africa and in Latin America. I was convinced that our retreat from this challenge would open the path to World War III.

Our consultations had only begun. I met the next day with the Joint

From *The Vantage Point: Perspectives of the Presidency, 1963–1969* by Lyndon Baines Johnson, pp. 147–152. Copyright © 1971 by HEC Public Affairs Foundation. Reprinted by permission of Henry Holt and Company, Inc.

Chiefs of Staff and the Secretaries of the military services. In the afternoon I met again for nearly an hour and a half with Rusk, McNamara, Ball, General Wheeler, Bundy, and several civilian advisers, including Clark Clifford, John McCloy, and Arthur Dean. Later that day I went up to Camp David to reflect. I invited several advisers to join me there for further long discussions on Sunday, July 25.

Secretary McNamara, Ambassador to the United Nations Arthur Goldberg, and Clark Clifford, then Chairman of the President's Foreign Intelligence Advisory Board, joined me in the Aspen Lodge at Camp David in the afternoon. One of the things we wanted to discuss was whether we should take any action in the United Nations in connection with Vietnam. The weight of opinion was against a major effort to persuade the United Nations to act at that time. Most of my advisers felt that the leaders in Hanoi would turn down any UN proposal, because they had consistently declared that Vietnam was not a proper matter for UN involvement. Moreover, it was virtually certain that the Soviet Union would veto any proposal Hanoi might have trouble accepting.

At this session my old friend Clark Clifford was in a reflective and pessimistic mood. "I don't believe we can win in South Vietnam," he said. "If we send in 100,000 more men, the North Vietnamese will meet us. If North Vietnam runs out of men, the Chinese will send in volunteers. Russia and China don't intend for us to win the war."

He urged that in the coming months we quietly probe possibilities with other countries for some way to get out honorably. "I can't see anything but catastrophe for my country," he said.

I told Clifford that he was expressing worries that many Americans, including the President, were experiencing. No one was more concerned than I was, but we could not simply walk out. Nor was I prepared to accept just any settlement as a cover-up for surrender. What we needed was a way to start real negotiations and I intended to keep pressing our offer to talk peace.

We continued our review of the military situation and the requirement for additional forces. Our military commanders had refined their estimates and indicated they could meet the immediate demand with 50,000 men. I called a meeting of the National Security Council two days later, on July 27. I asked McNamara at that time to summarize again the current need as he saw it.

McNamara noted that the Viet Cong had increased in size through local recruitment and replacements from the North. Regular North Vietnamese army units had increased in number and strength. Communist control of the countryside was growing. A dozen provincial capitals were virtually isolated from surrounding rural areas. The South Vietnamese army was growing, but not nearly fast enough to keep pace with the expanding enemy forces. Without additional armed strength, South Vietnam would inevitably fall to Hanoi. I told the NSC there were five possible choices available to us.

"We can bring the enemy to his knees by using our Strategic Air

Command," I said, describing our first option. "Another group thinks we ought to pack up and go home."

"Third, we could stay there as we are—and suffer the consequences, continue to lose territory and take casualties. You wouldn't want your own boy to be out there crying for help and not get it."

"Then, we could go to Congress and ask for great sums of money; we could call up the reserves and increase the draft; go on a war footing; declare a state of emergency. There is a good deal of feeling that ought to be done. We have considered this. But if we go into that kind of land war, then North Vietnam would go to its friends, China and Russia, and ask them to give help. They would be forced into increasing aid. For that reason I don't want to be overly dramatic and cause tensions. I think we can get our people to support us without having to be too provocative and warlike.

"Finally, we can give our commanders in the field the men and supplies they say they need."

I had concluded that the last course was the right one. I had listened to and weighed all the arguments and counterarguments for each of the possible lines of action. I believed that we should do what was necessary to resist aggression but that we should not be provoked into a major war. We would get the required appropriation in the new budget, and we would not boast about what we were doing. We would not make threatening noises to the Chinese or the Russians by calling up reserves in large numbers. At the same time, we would press hard on the diplomatic front to try to find some path to a peaceful settlement.

I asked if anyone objected to the course of action I had spelled out. I questioned each man in turn. Did he agree? Each nodded his approval or said "yes." . . .

There was more to it than listening to the arguments and dissents, the explanations and justifications of my wisest advisers in and out of government. When a President faces a decision involving war or peace, he draws back and thinks of the past and of the future in the widest possible terms. On his sworn oath, a President pledges he will protect the nation. The security of the whole country is the foremost responsibility of the Chief Executive. The most important question I had to face was: How will the decisions we make in Vietnam or elsewhere affect the security and the future of our nation?

A President searches his mind and his heart for the answers, so that when he decides on a course of action it is in the long-range best interests of the country, its people, and its security.

That is what I did—when I was alone and sleepless at night in the Executive Mansion, away from official cables and advisers; when I sat alone in the Aspen Lodge at Camp David; when I walked along the banks of the Pedernales River or looked out over the Texas hill country. In those lonely vigils I tried to think through what would happen to our nation and to the world if we did not act with courage and stamina—if we let South Vietnam fall to Hanoi.

This is what I could foresee: First, from all the evidence available to me it seemed likely that all of Southeast Asia would pass under Communist control, slowly or quickly, but inevitably, at least down to Singapore but almost certainly to Djakarta. I realize that some Americans believe they have, through talking with one another, repealed the domino theory. In 1965 there was no indication in Asia, or from Asians, that this was so. On both sides of the line between Communist and non-Communist Asia the struggle for Vietnam and Laos was regarded as a struggle for the fate of Southeast Asia. The evidence before me as President confirmed the previous assessments of President Eisenhower and of President Kennedy.

Second, I knew our people well enough to realize that if we walked away from Vietnam and let Southeast Asia fall, there would follow a divisive and destructive debate in our country. This had happened when the Communists took power in China. But that was very different from the Vietnam conflict. We had a solemn treaty commitment to Southeast Asia. We had an international agreement on Laos made as late as 1962 that was being violated flagrantly. We had the word of three Presidents that the United States would not permit this aggression to succeed. A divisive debate about "who lost Vietnam" would be, in my judgment, even more destructive to our national life than the argument over China had been. It would inevitably increase isolationist pressures from the right and the left and cause a pulling back from our commitments in Europe and the Middle East as well as in Asia.

Third, our allies not just in Asia but throughout the world would conclude that our word was worth little or nothing. Those who had counted so long for their security on American commitments would be deeply shaken and vulnerable.

Fourth, knowing what I did of the policies and actions of Moscow and Peking, I was as sure as a man could be that if we did not live up to our commitment in Southeast Asia and elsewhere, they would move to exploit the disarray in the United States and in the alliances of the Free World. They might move independently or they might move together. But move they would—whether through nuclear blackmail, through subversion, with regular armed forces, or in some other manner. As nearly as one can be certain of anything, I knew they could not resist the opportunity to expand their control into the vacuum of power we would leave behind us.

Finally, as we faced the implications of what we had done as a nation, I was sure the United States would not then passively submit to the consequences. With Moscow and Peking and perhaps others moving forward, we would return to a world role to prevent their full takeover of Europe, Asia, and the Middle East—*after* they had committed themselves.

Philip Caputo Remembers His Idealism (1965), 1977

On March 8, 1965, as a young infantry officer, I landed at Danang with a battalion of the 9th Marine Expeditionary Brigade, the first U.S. combat unit sent to Indochina.

For Americans who did not come of age in the early sixties, it may be hard to grasp what those years were like—the pride and overpowering self-assurance that prevailed. Most of the thirty-five hundred men in our brigade, born during or immediately after World War II, were shaped by that era, the age of Kennedy's Camelot. We went overseas full of illusions, for which the intoxicating atmosphere of those years was as much to blame as our youth.

War is always attractive to young men who know nothing about it, but we had also been seduced into uniform by Kennedy's challenge to "ask what you can do for your country" and by the missionary idealism he had awakened in us. America seemed omnipotent then: the country could still claim it had never lost a war, and we believed we were ordained to play cop to the Communists' robber and spread our own political faith around the world. Like the French soldiers of the late eighteenth century, we saw ourselves as the champions of "a cause that was destined to triumph." So, when we marched into the rice paddies on that damp March afternoon, we carried, along with our packs and rifles, the implicit convictions that the Viet Cong would be quickly beaten and that we were doing something altogether noble and good. We kept the packs and rifles; the convictions, we lost.

The discovery that the men we had scorned as peasant guerrillas were, in fact, a lethal, determined enemy and the casualty lists that lengthened each week with nothing to show for the blood being spilled broke our early confidence. By autumn, what had begun as an adventurous expedition had turned into an exhausting, indecisive war of attrition in which we fought for no cause other than our own survival.

✗ *E S S A Y S*

The opening selection is taken from journalist David Halberstam's best-selling book *The Best and the Brightest*. A former *New York Times* reporter whose dispatches from Vietnam earned him a Pulitzer Prize in the early 1960s, Halberstam ascribes President Johnson's decisions for escalation to a combination of personal and political factors. The president, he argues, proved supremely confident of America's ability to prevail against its adversaries. In the second essay, Brian VanDeMark, a recent recipient of a doctoral degree in history from the University of California, Los Angeles, maintains that Johnson believed he had no choice but to follow the global containment strategy devel-

From *A Rumor of War* by Philip Caputo, pp. xii–xx. Copyright © 1977 by Philip Caputo. Reprinted by permission of Henry Holt and Company, Inc.

oped by his predecessors in the White House. The imperatives of that strategy, in VanDeMark's view, demanded that communist advances be halted in Southeast Asia. Political considerations also influenced Johnson, he contends. Another reason that LBJ sent combat troops to Vietnam stemmed from his desire to buy time for his ambitious Great Society reforms. Johnson, Van-DeMark emphasizes, feared that the "loss" of South Vietnam to the communists might trigger a right-wing reaction that would prove as crippling to his legislative agenda as it would be to his public support and political future.

To Achieve a Victory

DAVID HALBERSTAM

Lyndon Johnson had to decide. The pressures were enormous both ways, there was going to be no easy way out. A few friends like [Senator] Dick Russell were warning him not to go ahead, that it would never work; Russell had an intuitive sense that it was all going to be more difficult and complicated than the experts were saying, but his doubts were written off as essentially conservative and isolationist, and it was easily rationalized that Russell, like [Senator J. William] Fulbright, did not care about colored people. Besides, Johnson had bettered Russell in the Senate and now here was Johnson surrounded by truly brilliant men (years later when there were free fire zones in the South—areas where virtually uncontrolled air and artillery could be used—which led to vast refugee resettlement, Russell would pass on his doubts about the wisdom of this as policy to the White House, saying, "I don't know those Asian people, but they tell me they worship their ancestors and so I wouldn't play with their land if I were you. You know whenever the Corps of Engineers has some dam to dedicate in Georgia I make a point of being out of state, because those people don't seem to like the economic improvements as much as they dislike being moved off their ancestral land"). But even Russell was telling the President that he had to make a decision, that he had better move, get off the dime, and Russell would support the flag.

Men who knew Johnson well thought of him as a man on a toboggan course in that period. Starting the previous November [1964] and then month by month as the trap tightened, he had become increasingly restless, irritable, frustrated, more and more frenetic, more and more difficult to work with. He was trapped and he knew it, and more than anyone else around him he knew that he was risking his great domestic dreams; it was primarily his risk, not theirs. The foreign policy advisers were not that privy to or that interested in his domestic dreams, and his domestic advisers were not that privy to the dangers ahead in the foreign policy. As a politician Johnson was not a great symbolic figure who initiated deep moral stirrings in the American soul, a man to go forth and lead a country by image, but quite the reverse, and he knew this better than most. His image

From *The Best and the Brightest* by David Halberstam, pp. 641–646, 694–697, 716–718. Copyright © 1972 by David Halberstam. Reprinted by permission of Random House, Inc.

and his reputation and his posture were against him; at his ablest he was a shrewd infighter. Despite the bombast he was a surprisingly cautious man (in guiding the Senate against [Senator Joseph] McCarthy he had been the epitome of caution, so cautious as to not receive any credit for it, which was probably what he wanted, it was not an issue to be out in front on). He was very good at measuring his resources, shrewdly assessing what was needed for a particular goal: was it there, was it available, was the price of accomplishing it too high? He had advised against going into Dienbienphu in 1954, not because he thought there was anything particularly wrong with intervention, but because he felt that immediately after the Korean War the country simply could not absorb and support another Asian land war; indeed, it was the very psychology of exhaustion with the Korean War which had put Eisenhower into office.

Now he was facing fateful decisions on Vietnam just as he was getting ready to start the Great Society. With his careful assessment of the country, he was sure the resources were there, that the country was finally ready to do something about its long-ignored social problems. The time was right for an assault on them, and he, Lyndon Johnson, would lead that assault, cure them, go down in history as a Roosevelt-like figure. He was keenly aware of these resources, and in late 1964 and early 1965 he began to use the phrase "sixty months of prosperity" as a litany, not just as party propaganda to get credit for the Democrats, but as a way of reminding the country that it had been having it good, very good, that it was secure and affluent, that it now had to turn its attention to the needs of others. Yet he knew he would not have the resources for both the domestic programs and a real war, and as a need for the latter became more and more apparent, he became restless and irritable, even by Johnsonian standards irascible, turning violently on the men around him. Those who knew him well and had worked long for him knew the symptoms only too well; it was, they knew, part of the insecurity of the man, and they talked of it often and gradually among themselves, since they all were subject to the same abuse. Unable to bear the truth about himself if it was unpleasant, he would transfer his feelings and his anger at himself to others, lashing out at Lady Bird [the President's wife], or George Reedy, or Bill Moyers, or particularly poor Jack Valenti [presidential advisers], but really lashing out at himself. And so in early 1965 this great elemental man, seeing his great hopes ahead and sensing also that they might be outside his reach, was almost in a frenzy to push his legislation through, a restless, obsessed man, driving himself and those around him harder and harder, fighting a civil war within himself.

He knew it would not be easy, that the bombing was a tricky business, not as tricky as ground troops, there was, after all, an element of control in bombing ("If they [the Air Force] hit people I'll bust their asses," he said at the start) but tricky nonetheless. And yet, and yet. "If I don't go in now and they show later I should have gone, then they'll be all over me in Congress. They won't be talking about my civil rights bill, or education, or beautification. No sir, they'll push Vietnam up my ass every time. Vietnam. Vietnam. Vietnam. Right up my ass." Cornered, and having what he would consider the Kennedy precedent to stand in Vietnam, a precedent which Kennedy set, but probably never entirely believed, and with all the Kennedy luminaries telling him to go ahead, even Rusk's uneasiness having been resolved ("He would look around him," said Tom Wicker later, "and see in Bob McNamara that it was technologically feasible, in McGeorge Bundy that it was intellectually respectable, and in Dean Rusk that it was histori- cally necessary"), he went forward. Of course he would; after all, it could be done. He was a can-do man surrounded by other can-do men. If we set our minds to something, we did not fail. If Europeans were wary of this war, if the French had failed, and thus were warning the Americans off, it was not because they had lived more history and seen more of the folly of war, it was because they had become cynical, they had lost the capacity to believe in themselves, they were decadent. We were the first team.

So it all came down to Lyndon Johnson, reluctant, uneasy, but not a man to be backed down. Lyndon would not cut and run, if it came to that; no one was going to push Lyndon Johnson around. Lyndon Johnson knew something about people like this, like the Mexicans back home, they were all right, the Mexicans, but "if you didn't watch they'll come right into your yard and take it over if you let them. And the next day they'll be right there on your porch, barefoot and weighing one hundred and thirty pounds, and they'll take that too. But if you say to 'em right at the start, 'Hold on, just wait a minute,' they'll know they're dealing with someone who'll stand up. And after that you can get along fine." Well, no one would push Lyndon Johnson of Texas around. This was Lyndon Johnson representing the United States of America, pledged to follow in the tradition of Great Britain and Winston Churchill—Lyndon Johnson, who, unlike Jack Kennedy, was a believer, not a cynic about the big things. Honor. Force. Commitments. Who believed in the omnipotence of American power, the concept of the frontier and using force to make sure you were clearly understood, believ- ing that white men, and in particular Americans, were just a bit superior, believing in effect all those John Wayne movies, a cliché in which real life had styled itself on image (paint the portrait of Johnson as a tall tough Texan in the saddle, he had told Pierre Salinger, although he was not a good rider). And in the Dominican crisis he sent word through McGeorge Bundy for Colonel Francisco Caamano Deno, the rebel leader: "Tell that son of a bitch that unlike the young man who came before me I am not afraid to use what's on my hip."

For *machismo* was no small part of it. He had always been haunted by the idea that he would be judged as being insufficiently manly for the job, that he would lack courage at a crucial moment. More than a little insecure himself, he very much wanted to be seen as a man; it was a conscious thing. He was very much aware of *machismo* in himself and those around him, and at a moment like this he wanted the respect of men who were tough, real men, and they would turn out to be the hawks. He had always uncon- sciously divided the people around him between men and boys. Men were activists, doers, who conquered business empires, who acted instead of talked, who made it in the world of other men and had the respect of other men. Boys were the talkers and the writers and the intellectuals, who sat around thinking and criticizing and doubting instead of doing. There were good boys, like Horace Busby and for a time Dick Goodwin, who used their talent for him, and there were snot noses, and kids who were to be found at the State Department or in the editorial rooms of the Washington *Post* or the *New York Times* using their talents against him. Bill Moyers was a boy who was halfway to becoming a man, a writer who was moving into operational activities. Hubert Humphrey, Vice-President or no, was still a boy, better than most liberals, but too prone to talk instead of act, not a person that other *men* would respect in a room when it got down to the hard cutting; real men just wouldn't turn to Hubert, he didn't have the weight, and so when Humphrey voiced his doubts on Vietnam he was simply excluded from the action until he muffled his dissent.

Now, as Johnson weighed the advice he was getting on Vietnam, it was the boys who were most skeptical, and the men who were most sure and confident and hawkish and who had Johnson's respect. Hearing that one member of his Administration was becoming a dove on Vietnam, Johnson said, "Hell, he has to squat to piss." The *men* had, after all, done things in their lifetimes, and they had the respect of other men. Doubt itself, he thought, was an almost feminine quality, doubts were for women; once, on another issue, when Lady Bird raised her doubts, Johnson had said of course she was doubtful, it was like a woman to be uncertain. Thus as Vietnam came to the edge of decision, the sides were unfair, given Johnson's make-up. The doubters were not the people he respected; the men who were activists were hawks, and he took sustenance and reassurance that the real men were for going ahead. Of the doves, only George Ball really had his respect. Ball might be a dove, but there was nothing soft about him. He had made it in a tough and savage world of the big law firms, and his approach was tough and skeptical. He did not talk about doing good or put Johnson off by discussing the moral thing to do, rather he too was interested in the exercise of power and a real world that Johnson could understand. He was a doer, an activist, and Johnson would tell him again and again, even as Ball dissented, "You're one of these can-do fellows too, George."

Thus the dice were loaded; the advocates of force were by the very nature of Johnson's personality taken more seriously, the doubters were seen by their very doubts as being lesser men. So he would go ahead, despite his own inner instincts, that the rosy predictions were in fact not likely to be so rosy, that it was likely to be tougher and darker, that George Ball's doubts had a real basis. The thrust to go forward was just too great. Everyone else seemed so convinced of America's invincibility. Even Ball, arguing at the time that it was the right moment to cut our losses, sensed this feeling of American invincibility and will, and would write that by negotiating out, the United States could become a "wiser and more mature nation." But those lessons would have to come the hard way; there were too few restraints. All the training of two decades had been quite the reverse. They had come to the end of one path. They were cornered by bad policies on Asia which they had not so much authored as refused to challenge, both in the fifties when out of power, and in the sixties when in power. And so now they bombed. They did this in place of combat troops, and they believed that it would not last long, perhaps a few months. . . .

The forces pushing against Lyndon Johnson as he came closer and closer to a decision seemed terribly imbalanced. On the one side were the Chiefs and the Saigon generals, wanting troops, sure of themselves, speaking for the Cold War, for patriotism, and joined with them were his principal national security advisers, all believers in the use of force. Those committed to peace were not as well organized, not as impressive, and seemingly not as potent politically; if anything, in making their case to him, they seemed to unveil their weaknesses more than their strengths. One incident revealed how frail the peace people seemed to Johnson. On the first weekend in April the Americans for Democratic Action were holding their annual convention, and a group of the leadership asked to see the President, specifically to protest the bombing. The meeting was granted and about a dozen ADA officials went over to see the President. Some of the ADA people were quite impassioned; the bombing of the North, they said, simply had to stop. It was wrong, it was against everything America stood for. Johnson himself tried as best he could to deflect the criticism. He was under great pressure from the military to use more force, he said; he had tried to negotiate, but Hanoi continued to be the aggressor. He read at great length from a speech that he intended to give on the Mekong River development project; he was, he said, trying to do there what he was doing here at home. But he was not able to assuage their feeling. It was a sharp and tough exchange. The ADA people were particularly worried about McNamara's role, and several of them criticized the growing power of the Secretary of Defense, whom they visualized as being a major hawk. Johnson moved to set them at ease. "Why are you people always complaining about McNamara?" he asked. "Why, Mac Bundy here"—pointing to Bundy—"is a much bigger hawk than McNamara." But even the ADA people did not seem to be particularly unified; there were divisions within the group, and John Roche, a Brandeis professor who was the outgoing chairman, seemed quite sympathetic to the Johnson position. As the group was leaving, it passed through the White House press room, and Joe Rauh, one of the ADA officials, told the waiting reporters that the exchanges had been sharp ones, that the ADA had expressed its opposition to the bombing in very strong terms. At that point Roche tried to soften Rauh's statement, and the two clashed over the wording, Roche wanting a more subdued description.

The whole incident immediately convinced Johnson that he could handle the liberals, that they had no real muscle, that they were divided among themselves. Even as he said good-bye to the ADA representatives, he showed in the Joint Chiefs, plus McNamara and Rusk, for one of the pressing meetings on the use of ground troops. Because he liked to begin each meeting by referring to the one which preceded it, the President now reached into the wastebasket and scooped up the notes which the ADA people had brought to the meeting and written to each other during it. Then, mimicking his previous guests to perfection, he began to read the notes to the assembled Chiefs, pausing, showing great relish in ridiculing each, adjusting his voice as necessary, taking particular pleasure in one that Rauh had written: "Why doesn't he take the issue of Vietnam to the United Nations?" That one in particular broke them up. Then the liberals dispensed with, they got down to more serious things, such as the forthcoming decisions on ground troops.

Nor was Johnson's instinct to use force tempered in April by the experience in the Dominican Republic. When the frail political legitimacy of the Dominican government began to fall apart, and when leftist rebels began to make a challenge, Johnson moved quickly to stop another Cuba. Presidents in the past had been soft on Cuba and had paid for it. No one would accuse Lyndon Johnson of that. So despite the fact that the reports from the Dominican were remarkably unclear, with the American ambassador filing wildly exaggerated estimates on the amount of violence taking place, and totally unconfirmed reports on the extent of Communist subversion, Johnson moved swiftly. He would use force. No one at a high level in the Administration dissented, or suggested that the United States had no legal justification for moving in with force, or indeed that it did not even know what was happening. Force it was, overkill, not just the Marines, but the Airborne as well, 22,000 troops, and they went in, and whatever the uprising was—the Administration seemed unclear about that—it was put down. American muscle had determined the outcome. Oh, there had been protests from the left, and from people nervous about things like this, but Johnson had paid no attention and it had worked out—or seemed to work out. So if the same liberals were making the same soft sounds on Vietnam, why pay attention? People forgot about these things if they worked out, and there was no doubt what would happen when real men walked into one of these fourth-rate countries and set things right. So there was, out of the Dominican, an impression confirmed that if you just stood tall, why, things would come your way, though of course the difference between the depth and root of the insurgency in Vietnam and the sheer political frustration and chaos of the Dominican was very, very great. But the Dominican, whatever else, did not discourage Lyndon Johnson from the use of force. Nor, of course, the men around him.

The President was increasingly concerned about the situation in Vietnam, but he was less wary of the French experience than Taylor or Ball; he was more confident of what *Americans* could do. In addition, and this was to be important later as the question of enclave strategy versus search-and-destroy strategy arose, he was not a man to sponsor a defensive strategy, to send American boys overseas, to see American boys killed, and then yet be involved in a long, unrewarding war. He was not a man for that kind of war, a man to be charged with a no-win policy. The political trap of the Korean War was real to him: he knew what it was like to be attacked for failing to win a war, for getting in with a no-win policy. If Americans were going to be there, they had better be aggressive. Clean it all up and get home. Show Ho what Americans could do, and get him to the table. . . .

So Johnson made his decision; it was, he thought, a personal challenge from Ho. If Ho wanted a challenge, a test of will, then he had come to the right man. Lyndon Johnson of Texas would not be pushed around, he would not try to negotiate with Ho and those others, as he said, walking in the streets of Saigon. He was a man to stand tall when the pressure was there. To be counted. He would show Ho his mettle, show the toughness of this country, and then they could talk. Rusk agreed; this was one democracy that was not going to show itself weak, it had the right leader (later during the Glassboro meetings with the Soviet leadership, Karl Mundt, as conservative a senator as could be found, was appalled to find that the Soviet Union's Kosygin did not have the kind of power to go to war that Johnson seemed to have). Johnson would not shirk from this test of wills. Besides, it was above all a political decision and a domestic one at that; it was a question of how he read the country, and when he found doubters on his own staff, some of the younger people, he would tell them, You boys don't understand, you don't know the relationship between the Congress and Asia. It was an emotional thing; they had never seen it because during their political lifetime it had been bottled up, but it was still there. He would lose his presidential possibilities, he said, if Ho was running through the streets of Saigon. Listen, he added, Truman and Acheson had never been effective from the time of the fall of China. Lyndon Johnson had a mandate for the moment. But this way if he failed on Vietnam it would be gone quickly. McNamara and Bundy seemed to be saying it could be done quickly, perhaps in six months, perhaps a little more. And the test cases were also quick. The Cuban missile crisis had gone quickly and that was a dry run for it, and the Dominican Republic, hell, he had sent a few troops in there and he had put out the fire in a few days. Hardly a shot fired. Look what had happened in the Dominican, when American boys had gone ashore. So this one would be quick too. Just give him six months. Of course, six months later he would be unmovable, too deeply involved in something that was going badly to talk rationally. It was one more sad aspect of Lyndon Johnson that there was the quality of the bully, and the reverse quality as well; he was, at his best, most open, most candid, most easy to reach, most accessible when things were going well, but when things went poorly, as they were bound to on Vietnam, he became impossible to reach and talk to. His greatest flexibility and rationality on the subject came before he had dispatched the first bombers and the first troops; from then on it would all be downhill. Doubters would no longer be friendly doubters, they would be critics and soon enemies; and worse, soon after that, traitors. There was no way to reach him, to enter his chamber, to gain his ear, other than to pledge total loyalty. Only one man would be able to change him, to dissent and retain his respect—and even that was a tenuous balancing act which virtually destroyed one of his oldest friendships, and that was Clark Clifford in 1968.

So, cornered, he would go ahead. He was not just reading their country, which was small, Asian, fourth-rate, bereft of bombers and helicopters; he was above all a political animal and he was reading his *own* country and in that he may have misread it; he read the politics of the past rather than the *potential* politics of the country, which his very victory of 1964 illuminated. (He had won as a peace candidate, and it is likely that had a new China policy been openly debated, with Johnson in favor of it and Goldwater opposing, it might have enlarged his margin; at the least it would have had little negative effect, probably would not have cut into his margin in any appreciable sense, and would have liberated him from one of the dominating myths of the past. But as the issue had been dormant by both liberal and conservative consent for a decade—the liberals giving consent, the conservatives owning the policy—there was no desire to change it.) The Democrats, who had been hurt by the issue in the past, were quite content to keep it bottled up. As was Johnson, a good and traditional liberal who was also a man of the fifties and of Texas in the fifties, where McCarthyism had been particularly virulent, an era of potentially monolithic Communism, where the fewer questions about how monolithic it was, the better.

To Avoid a Defeat

BRIAN VANDEMARK

Vietnam divided America more deeply and painfully than any event since the Civil War. It split political leaders and ordinary people alike in profound and lasting ways. Whatever the conflicting judgments about this controversial war—and there are many—Vietnam undeniably stands as the greatest tragedy of twentieth-century U.S. foreign relations.

America's involvement in Vietnam has, as a result, attracted much critical scrutiny, frequently addressed to the question, "Who was guilty?"—Who led the United States into this tragedy?" A more enlightening question, it seems, is "How and why did this tragedy occur?" The study of Vietnam should be a search for explanation and understanding, rather than for scapegoats.

Focusing on one important period in this long and complicated story—the brief but critical months from November 1964 to July 1965, when America crossed the threshold from limited to large-scale war in Vietnam—helps to answer that question. For the crucial decisions of this period resulted from the interplay of longstanding ideological attitudes, diplomatic assumptions, and political pressures with decisive contemporaneous events in America and Vietnam.

Victory in World War II produced a sea change in America's perception of its role in world affairs. Political leaders of both parties embraced a sweepingly new vision of the United States as the defender against the perceived threat of monolithic communist expansion everywhere in the world. This vision of American power and purpose, shaped at the start of the Cold

Excerpted from *Into the Quagmire: Lyndon Johnson and the Escalation of the Vietnam War* by Brian VanDeMark, pp. xiv–xvi, 212–221. Copyright © 1991 by Brian VanDeMark. Reprinted by permission of the author and Oxford University Press, Inc.

War, grew increasingly rigid over the years. By 1964–1965, it had become an ironbound and unshakable dogma, a received faith which policymakers unquestioningly accepted—even though the circumstances which had fostered its creation had changed dramatically amid diffused authority and power among communist states and nationalist upheaval in the colonial world.

Policymakers' blind devotion to this static Cold War vision led America into misfortune in Vietnam. Lacking the critical perspective and sensibility to reappraise basic tenets of U.S. foreign policy in the light of changed events and local circumstances, policymakers failed to perceive Vietnamese realities accurately and thus to gauge American interests in the area prudently. Policymakers, as a consequence, misread an indigenous, communist-led nationalist movement as part of a larger, centrally directed challenge to world order and stability; tied American fortunes to a noncommunist regime of slim popular legitimacy and effectiveness; and intervened militarily in the region far out of proportion to U.S. security requirements.

An arrogant and stubborn faith in America's power to shape the course of foreign events compounded the dangers sown by ideological rigidity. Policymakers in 1964–1965 shared a common postwar conviction that the United States not only should, but could, control political conditions in South Vietnam, as elsewhere throughout much of the world. This conviction had led Washington to intervene progressively deeper in South Vietnamese affairs over the years. And when—despite Washington's increasing exertions—Saigon's political situation declined precipitously during 1964–1965, this conviction prompted policymakers to escalate the war against Hanoi, in the belief that America could stimulate political order in South Vietnam through the application of military force against North Vietnam.

Domestic political pressures exerted an equally powerful, if less obvious, influence over the course of U.S. involvement in Vietnam. The fall of China in 1949 and the ugly McCarthyism it aroused embittered American foreign policy for a generation. By crippling President Truman's political fortunes, it taught his Democratic successors, John Kennedy and Lyndon Johnson, a strong and sobering lesson: that another "loss" to communism in East Asia risked renewed and devastating attacks from the right. This fear of reawakened McCarthyism remained a paramount concern as policymakers pondered what course to follow as conditions in South Vietnam deteriorated rapidly in 1964–1965.

Enduring traditions of ideological rigidity, diplomatic arrogance, and political vulnerability heavily influenced the way policymakers approached decisions on Vietnam in 1964–1965. Understanding the decisions of this period fully, however, also requires close attention to contemporary developments in America and South Vietnam. These years marked a tumultuous time in both countries, which affected the course of events in subtle but significant ways.

Policymakers of 1964–1965 lived in a period of extraordinary domestic political upheaval sparked by the civil rights movement. It is difficult to overstate the impact of this upheaval on American politics in the mid-1960s. During 1964–1965, the United States—particularly the American South—experienced profound and long overdue change in the economic, political, and social rights of blacks. This change, consciously embraced by the liberal administration of Lyndon Johnson, engendered sharp political hostility among conservative southern whites and their deputies in Congress—hostility which the politically astute Johnson sensed could spill over into the realm of foreign affairs, where angry civil rights opponents could exact their revenge should LBJ stumble and "lose" a crumbling South Vietnam. This danger, reinforced by the memory of McCarthyism, stirred deep political fears in Johnson, together with an abiding aversion to failure in Vietnam.

LBJ feared defeat in South Vietnam, but he craved success and glory at home. A forceful, driving President of boundless ambition, Johnson sought to harness the political momentum created by the civil rights movement to enact a far-reaching domestic reform agenda under the rubric of the Great Society. LBJ would achieve the greatness he sought by leading America toward justice and opportunity for all its citizens, through his historic legislative program.

Johnson's domestic aspirations fundamentally conflicted with his uneasy involvement in Vietnam. An experienced and perceptive politician, LBJ knew his domestic reforms required the sustained focus and cooperation of Congress. He also knew a larger war in Vietnam jeopardized these reforms by drawing away political attention and economic resources. America's increasing military intervention in 1964–1965 cast this tension between Vietnam and the Great Society into sharp relief.

Johnson saw his predicament clearly. But he failed to resolve it for fear that acknowledging the growing extent and cost of the war would thwart his domestic reforms, while pursuing a course of withdrawal risked political ruin. LBJ, instead, chose to obscure the magnitude of his dilemma by obscuring America's deepening involvement as South Vietnam began to fail. That grave compromise of candor opened the way to Johnson's eventual downfall.

Events in South Vietnam during 1964–1965 proved equally fateful. A historically weak and divided land, South Vietnam's deeply rooted ethnic, political, and religious turmoil intensified sharply in the winter of 1964–1965. This mounting turmoil, combined with increased communist military attacks, pushed Saigon to the brink of political collapse.

South Vietnam's accelerating crisis alarmed American policymakers, driving them to deepen U.S. involvement considerably in an effort to arrest Saigon's political failure. Abandoning the concept of stability in the South *before* escalation against the North, policymakers now embraced the concept of stability *through* escalation, in the desperate hope that military action against Hanoi would prompt a stubbornly elusive political order in Saigon.

This shift triggered swift and ominous consequences scarcely anticipated by its architects. Policymakers soon confronted intense military, political, and bureaucratic pressures to widen the war. Unsettled by these largely unforeseen pressures, policymakers reacted confusedly and defensively. Rational men, they struggled to control increasingly irrational forces. But their reaction only clouded their attention to basic assumptions and ultimate costs as the war rapidly spun out of control in the spring and summer of 1965. In their desperation to make Vietnam policy work amid this rising tide of war pressures, they thus failed ever to question whether it could work—or at what ultimate price. Their failure recalls the warning of a prescient political scientist, who years before had cautioned against those policymakers with "an infinite capacity for making ends of [their] means."

The decisions of 1964–1965 bespeak a larger and deeper failure as well. Throughout this period—as, indeed, throughout the course of America's Vietnam involvement—U.S. policymakers strove principally to create a viable non-communist regime in South Vietnam. For many years and at great effort and cost, Washington had endeavored to achieve political stability and competence in Saigon. Despite these efforts, South Vietnam's political disarray persisted and deepened, until, in 1965, America intervened with massive military force to avert its total collapse.

Few policymakers in 1964—1965 paused to mull this telling fact, to ponder its implications about Saigon's viability as a political entity. The failure to re-examine this and other fundamental premises of U.S. policy— chief among them Vietnam's importance to American national interests and Washington's ability to forge political order through military power— proved a costly and tragic lapse of statesmanship. . . .

President Johnson's July 1965 decisions climaxed a series of steps, reaching back to the summer of 1964, which locked the United States on a path toward massive military intervention in Vietnam. That path eventually destroyed LBJ's presidency and polarized American society.

How had LBJ reached this critical juncture in America's Vietnam odyssey? The road to 1964–1965 had been charted years before, at the dawn of the Cold War, when U.S. leaders fixed a course of global containment that, over the decades, assumed the status of political writ—unassailable, unchangeable, unquestionable.

The compass of global containment, in turn, had eventually pointed to South Vietnam. It proved a fateful destination for the United States. Riven by chronic political factionalism, profound social antagonisms, and a nationalist movement tragically usurped by the communists, South Vietnam remained a quicksand of instability—treacherous ground on which to build a growing American effort.

That fact escaped few U.S. leaders, who felt Washington's strategic interests mortgaged to a succession of corrupt, inept, and repressive Saigon regimes well aware, as one early 1965 Buddhist leaflet put it, that "[w]e can insult the Americans as much as we please and they must still do our bidding and grant us aid." Dean Rusk, in a moment of private despair, dubbed this "the tyranny of the weak." William Bundy called it the "black cloud hanging over everything" America did. But Lyndon Johnson, characteristically, put it best: "I didn't like the smell of it. I didn't like anything about it," he later said, "but I think the situation in South Vietnam bothered me most. They never seemed able to get themselves together down there. Always fighting with one another. Bad. Bad."

And as South Vietnam's deterioration quickened in 1964–1965, the pressures to escalate intensified sharply. All through this critical period, President Johnson navigated reluctantly and furtively, continually pushed forward by events in Vietnam and growing bureaucratic momentum, while struggling to limit and conceal the war's domestic repercussions.

It was a difficult and ambiguous course befitting LBJ's difficult and ambiguous problem. Complex, intractable, and full of danger, the war aroused Johnson's bitterness, resentment, and anger. He confronted Vietnam as an unsure and troubled leader grappling with an unwanted and ominous burden. For a domestic reformer who, in the words of one acquaintance, "would chop off the rest of the world if he could," the war represented a loathsome threat to his dreams.

LBJ perceived his dilemma acutely. On the one hand, he recognized the dangers a larger war posed to the Great Society. On the other hand, he judged a lost war ruinous to his political standing and legislative effectiveness. Johnson later described his predicament vividly: "If I left the woman I really loved—the Great Society—in order to get involved with that bitch of a war on the other side of the world, then I would lose everything at home. All my programs. All my hopes to feed the hungry and shelter the homeless. All my dreams to provide education and medical care to the browns and the blacks and the lame and the poor. But if I left that war and let the Communists take over South Vietnam, . . . there would follow in this country an endless national debate—a mean and destructive debate—that would shatter my Presidency, kill my administration, and damage our democracy." LBJ felt trapped, in [journalist] Walter Lippmann's apt phrase, "between the devil of unlimited war and the deep blue sea of defeat."

As a result, Johnson moved cautiously and warily, constantly shifting and hesitating in the face of momentous decisions like the beginning of bombing in February and the deployment of major combat forces in July. At each turning point, LBJ acted with marked reluctance, saying nothing more than absolutely necessary, and oftentimes considerably less. That is why Johnson appeared, to many of those around him, "always reacting, always responding" to successive Vietnam crises.

But the ultimate crisis, in LBJ's mind, involved the "loss" of South Vietnam, which he feared would trigger a right-wing reaction devastating to his presidency and the Great Society. This prospect terrified Johnson. He resolved to prevent it by preserving South Vietnam at increasing military and political risk. LBJ dreaded these increasing risks, but he dreaded defeat even more. Johnson summed up his feelings with a bittersweet parable. "That reminds me of two Indians," he said at one point during the July deliberations. "The first invited the second home to dinner. 'What are you having?' asked the second. 'Crow,' said the first. 'Crow—that's not fit to eat, is it?' complained the second. 'Better'n owl,' replied the first."

Haunted by his plight, LBJ tried to hide it from the country. To him, Vietnam seemed an ugly and insoluble problem best kept from public scrutiny. "If you have a mother-in-law with only one eye and she has it in the center of her forehead," he grimly joked during this period, "you don't keep her in the living room."

Instead, Johnson kept Vietnam in the back closet. To some, like McGeorge Bundy, LBJ's action seemed "an extreme case of guarding one's hand." To others, like journalist Hugh Sidey, it seemed indicative of Johnson's compulsive secretiveness—his lifelong habit of thinking "the shortest distance between two points was through a tunnel." But the most fateful legacy of LBJ's furtiveness, as William Bundy observed, was that it "sowed dragon's teeth in terms of [the] credibility gap charge."

Johnson sowed those dragon's teeth when he realized Vietnam's escalating costs themselves jeopardized the Great Society. This stinging realization compelled LBJ to mask the scope and price of a war he shuddered to lose. But Johnson's behavior, in time, alienated the American public profoundly. The resulting decline in LBJ's credibility, together with Vietnam's spiraling costs, ultimately undid both his Presidency and the Great Society. In his struggle to avert the disastrous "loss" of Vietnam, Johnson slid into a major war which proved equally disastrous. Here lay the most tragic irony of LBJ's Vietnam ordeal.

The legacy of Vietnam, like the war itself, remains a difficult and painful subject for Americans. As passions subside and time bestows greater perspective, Americans still struggle to understand Vietnam's meaning and lessons for the country. They still wonder how the United States found itself ensnared in an ambiguous, costly, and divisive war, and how it can avoid repeating such an ordeal in the future.

The experience of Lyndon Johnson and his advisers during the decisive years 1964–1965 offers much insight into those questions. For their decisions, which fundamentally transformed U.S. participation in the war, both reflected and defined much of the larger history of America's Vietnam involvement.

Their decisions may also, one hopes, yield kernels of wisdom for the future; the past, after all, can teach us lessons. But history's lessons, as Vietnam showed, are themselves dependent on each generation's knowledge and understanding of the past. So it proved for 1960s policymakers, whose ignorance and misperception of Southeast Asian history, culture, and politics pulled America progressively deeper into the war. LBJ, Rusk, McNamara, Bundy, Taylor—most of their generation, in fact—mistakenly viewed Vietnam through the simplistic ideological prism of the Cold War. They perceived a deeply complex and ambiguous regional struggle as a grave challenge to world order and stability, fomented by communist China acting through its local surrogate, North Vietnam.

This perception, given their mixture of memories—the West's capitulation to Hitler at Munich, Stalin's postwar truculence, Mao's belligerent rhetoric—appears altogether understandable in retrospect. But it also proved deeply flawed and oblivious to abiding historical realities. Constrained by their memories and ideology, American policymakers neglected the subtle but enduring force of nationalism in Southeast Asia. Powerful and decisive currents—the deep and historic tension between Vietnam and China; regional friction among the Indochinese states of Vietnam, Laos, and Cambodia; and, above all, Hanoi's fanatical will to unification—went unnoticed or unweighed because they failed to fit Washington's worldview. Although it is true, as Secretary of State Rusk once said, that "one cannot escape one's experience," Rusk and his fellow policymakers seriously erred by falling uncritical prisoners of their experience.

Another shared experience plagued 1960s policymakers like a ghost: the ominous specter of McCarthyism. This frightful political memory haunted LBJ and his Democratic colleagues like a barely suppressed demon in the national psyche. Barely ten years removed from the traumatic "loss" of China and its devastating domestic repercussions, Johnson and his advisers remembered its consequences vividly and shuddered at a similar fate in Vietnam. They talked about this only privately, but then with genuine and palpable fear. Defense Secretary McNamara, in a guarded moment, confided to a newsman in the spring of 1965 that U.S. disengagement from South Vietnam threatened "a disastrous political fight that could . . . freeze American political debate and even affect political freedom."

Such fears resonated deeply in policymakers' minds. Nothing, it seemed, could be worse than the "loss" of Vietnam—not even an intensifying stalemate secured at increasing military and political risk. For a President determined to fulfill liberalism's postwar agenda, Truman's ordeal in China seemed a powerfully forbidding lesson. It hung over LBJ in Vietnam like a dark shadow he could not shake, an agony he would not repeat.

McCarthyism's long shadow into the mid-1960s underscores a persistent and troubling phenomenon of postwar American politics; the peculiar vulnerability besetting liberal Presidents thrust into the maelstrom of world politics. In America's postwar political climate—dominated by the culture of anti-communism—Democratic leaders from Truman to Kennedy to Johnson remained acutely sensitive to the domestic repercussions of foreign policy failure. This fear of right-wing reaction sharply inhibited liberals like LBJ, narrowing what they considered their range of politically acceptable options, while diminishing their willingness to disengage from untenable foreign commitments. Thus, when Johnson did confront the bitter choice between defeat in Vietnam and fighting a major, inconclusive war, he reluctantly chose the second because he could not tolerate the domestic consequences of the first. Committed to fulfilling the Great Society, fearful of resurgent McCarthyism, and afraid that disengagement meant sacrificing the former to the latter, LBJ perceived least political danger in holding on.

But if Johnson resigned never to "lose" South Vietnam, he also resigned never to sacrifice his cherished Great Society in the process. LBJ's determination, however understandable, nonetheless led him deliberately and seriously to obscure the nature and cost of America's deepening involvement in the war during 1964–1965. This decision bought Johnson the short-term political maneuverability he wanted, but at a costly long-term political price. As LBJ's credibility on the war subsequently eroded, public confidence in his leadership slowly but irretrievably evaporated. And this, more than any other factor, is what finally drove Johnson from the White House.

It also tarnished the presidency and damaged popular faith in American government for more than a decade. Trapped between deeply conflicting pressures, LBJ never shared his dilemma with the public. Johnson would not, or felt he dare not, trust his problems with the American people. LBJ's decision, however human, tragically undermined the reciprocal faith between President and public indispensable to effective governance in a democracy. Just as tragically, it fostered a pattern of presidential behavior which led his successor, Richard Nixon, to eventual ruin amid even greater popular political alienation.

Time slowly healed most of these wounds to the American political process, while reconfirming the fundamental importance of presidential credibility in a democracy. Johnson's Vietnam travail underscored the necessity of public trust and support to presidential success. Without them, as LBJ painfully discovered, Presidents are doomed to disaster.

Johnson, in retrospect, might have handled his domestic dilemma more forthrightly. An equally serious dilemma, however, remained always beyond his—or Washington's—power to mend: the root problem of political disarray in South Vietnam. The perennial absence of stable and responsive government in Saigon troubled Washington policymakers profoundly; they understood, only too well, its pivotal importance to the war effort and to the social and economic reforms essential to the country's survival. Over and over again, American officials stressed the necessity of political cooperation to their embattled South Vietnamese allies. But to no avail. As one top American in Saigon later lamented, "[Y]ou could tell them all, 'you've got to get together [and stop] this haggling and fighting among yourselves,' but how do you make them do it?" he said. "How do you make them do it?"

Washington, alas, could not. As Ambassador Taylor conceded early in the war, "[You] cannot order good government. You can't get it by fiat." This stubborn but telling truth eventually came to haunt Taylor and others. South Vietnam never marshaled the political will necessary to create an effective and enduring government; it never produced leaders addressing the aspirations and thus attracting the allegiance of the South Vietnamese people. Increasing levels of U.S. troops and firepower, moreover, never offset this fundamental debility. America, as a consequence, built its massive military effort on a foundation of political quicksand.

The causes of this elemental flaw lay deeply imbedded in the social and political history of the region. Neither before nor after 1954 was South

Vietnam ever really a nation in spirit. Divided by profound ethnic and religious cleavages dating back centuries and perpetuated under French colonial rule, the people of South Vietnam never developed a common political identity. Instead, political factionalism and rivalry always held sway. The result: a chronic and fatal political disorder.

Saigon's fundamental weakness bore anguished witness to the limits of U.S. power. South Vietnam's shortcomings taught a proud and mighty nation that it could not save a people in spite of themselves—that American power, in the last analysis, offered no viable substitute for indigenous political resolve. Without this basic ingredient, as Saigon's turbulent history demonstrated, Washington's most dedicated and strenuous efforts will prove extremely vulnerable, if not futile.

This is not a happy or popular lesson. But it is a wise and prudent one, attuned to the imperfect realities of an imperfect world. One of America's sagest diplomats, George Kennan, understood and articulated this lesson well when he observed: "When it comes to helping people to resist Communist pressures, . . . no assistance . . . can be effective unless the people themselves have a very high degree of determination and a willingness to help themselves. The moment they begin to place the bulk of the burden on us," Kennan warned, "the whole situation is lost." This, tragically, is precisely what befell America in South Vietnam during 1964–1965. Hereafter, as perhaps always before—*external* U.S. economic, military, and political support provided the vital elements of stability and strength in South Vietnam. Without that *external* support, as events following America's long-delayed withdrawal in 1973 showed, South Vietnam's government quickly failed.

Washington's effort to forge political order through military power spawned another tragedy as well. It ignited unexpected pressures which quickly overwhelmed U.S. policymakers, and pulled them ever deeper into the war. LBJ and his advisers began bombing North Vietnam in early 1965 in a desperate attempt to spur political resolve in South Vietnam. But their effort boomeranged wildly. Rather than stabilizing the situation, it instead unleashed forces that soon put Johnson at the mercy of circumstances, a hostage to the war's accelerating momentum. LBJ, as a result, began steering with an ever looser hand. By the summer of 1965, President Johnson found himself not the controller of events but largely controlled by them. He had lost the political leader's "continual struggle," in the words of Henry Kissinger, "to rescue an element of choice from the pressure of circumstance."

LBJ's experience speaks powerfully across the years. With each Vietnam decision, Johnson's vulnerability to military pressure and bureaucratic momentum intensified sharply. Each step generated demands for another, even bigger step—which LBJ found increasingly difficult to resist. His predicament confirmed George Ball's admonition that war is a fiercely unpredictable force, often generating its own inexorable momentum.

Johnson sensed this danger almost intuitively. He quickly grasped the dilemma and difficulties confronting him in Vietnam. But LBJ lacked the inner strength—the security and self-confidence to overrule the counsel of his inherited advisers.

Most of those advisers, on the other hand—especially McGeorge Bundy and Robert McNamara—failed to anticipate such perils. Imbued with an overweening faith in their ability to "manage" crises and "control" escalation, Bundy and McNamara, along with Maxwell Taylor, first pushed military action against the North as a lever to force political improvement in the South. But bombing did not rectify Saigon's political problems; it only exacerbated them, while igniting turbulent military pressures that rapidly overwhelmed these advisers' confident calculations.

These advisers' preoccupation with technique, with the application of power, characterized much of America's approach to the Vietnam War. Bundy and McNamara epitomized a postwar generation confident in the exercise and efficacy of U.S. power. Despite the dark and troubled history of European intervention in Indochina, these men stubbornly refused to equate America's situation in the mid-1960s to France's earlier ordeal. To them, the United States possessed limitless ability, wisdom, and virtue; it would therefore prevail where other western powers had failed.

This arrogance born of power led policymakers to ignore manifest dangers, to persist in the face of ever darkening circumstances. Like figures in Greek tragedy, pride compelled these supremely confident men further into disaster. They succumbed to the affliction common to great powers throughout the ages—the dangerous "self-esteem engendered by power," as the political philosopher Hans Morgenthau once wrote, "which equates power and virtue, [and] in the process loses all sense of moral and political proportion."

Tradition, as well as personality, nurtured such thinking. For in many ways, America's military intervention in Vietnam represented the logical fulfillment of a policy and outlook axiomatically accepted by U.S. policymakers for nearly two decades—the doctrine of global containment. Fashioned at the outset of the Cold War, global containment extended American interests and obligations across vast new areas of the world in defense against perceived monolithic communist expansion. It remained the lodestar of American foreign policy, moreover, even as the constellation of international forces shifted dramatically amid diffused authority and power among communist states and nationalist upheaval in the postcolonial world.

Vietnam exposed the limitations and contradictions of this static doctrine in a world of flux. It also revealed the dangers and flaws of an undiscriminating, universalist policy which perceptive critics of global containment, such as the eminent journalist Walter Lippmann, had anticipated from the beginning. As Lippmann warned about global containment in 1947:

> Satellite states and puppet governments are not good material out of which to construct unassailable barriers [for American defense]. A diplomatic war conducted as this policy demands, that is to say conducted indirectly, means that we must stake our own security and the peace of the world

upon satellites, puppets, clients, agents about whom we can know very little. Frequently they will act for their own reasons, and on their own judgments, presenting us with accomplished facts that we did not intend, and with crises for which we are unready. The "unassailable barriers" will present us with an unending series of insoluble dilemmas. We shall have either to disown our puppets, which would be tantamount to appeasement and defeat and loss of face, or must support them at an incalculable cost. . . .

Here lay the heart of America's Vietnam troubles. Driven by unquestioning allegiance to an ossified and extravagant doctrine, Washington officials plunged deeply into a struggle which itself dramatized the changed realities and complexities of the postwar world. Their action teaches both the importance of re-examining premises as circumstances change and the costly consequences of failing to recognize and adapt to them.

Vietnam represented a failure not just of American foreign policy but also of American statesmanship. For once drawn into the war, LBJ and his advisers quickly sensed Vietnam's immense difficulties and dangers—Saigon's congenital political problems, the war's spiraling military costs, the remote likelihood of victory—and plunged in deeper nonetheless. In their determination to preserve America's international credibility and protect their domestic political standing, they continued down an ever costlier path.

That path proved a distressing, multifaceted paradox. Fearing injury to the perception of American power, diminished faith in U.S. resolve, and a conservative political firestorm, policymakers rigidly pursued a course which ultimately injured the substance of American power by consuming exorbitant lives and resources, shook allied confidence in U.S. strategic judgment, and shattered liberalism's political unity and vigor by polarizing and paralyzing American society.

Herein lies Vietnam's most painful but pressing lesson. Statesmanship requires judgment, sensibility, and, above all, wisdom in foreign affairs—the wisdom to calculate national interests prudently and to balance commitments with effective power. It requires that most difficult task of political leaders: "to distinguish between what is desirable and what is possible, . . . between what is desirable and what is essential."

This is important in peace; it is indispensable in war. As the great tutor of statesmen, Carl von Clausewitz, wrote, "Since war is not an act of senseless passion but is controlled by its political object, the value of this object must determine the sacrifices to be made for it in *magnitude* and also in *duration.* Once the expenditure of effort exceeds the value of the political object," Clausewitz admonished, "the object must be renounced. . . ." His maxim, in hindsight, seems painfully relevant to a war which, as even America's military commander in Vietnam, General William Westmoreland, concluded, "the vital security of the United States was not and possibly could not be clearly demonstrated and understood. . . ."

LBJ and his advisers failed to heed this fundamental principle of statesmanship. They failed to weigh American costs in Vietnam against

Vietnam's relative importance to American national interests and its effect on overall American power. Compelled by events in Vietnam and, especially, coercive political pressures at home, they deepened an unsound, peripheral commitment and pursued manifestly unpromising and immensely costly objectives. Their failure of statesmanship, then, proved a failure of judgment and, above all, of proportion.

F U R T H E R   R E A D I N G

Anthony Austin, *The President's War* (1971)

George W. Ball, *The Past Has Another Pattern* (1982)

David M. Barrett, *Uncertain Warriors: Lyndon Johnson and His Vietnam Advisers* (1993)

Larry Berman, *Planning a Tragedy* (1982)

Vaughan Bornet, *The Presidency of Lyndon B. Johnson* (1983)

John P. Burke and Fred I. Greenstein, *How Presidents Test Reality* (1991)

Clark Clifford, *Counsel to the President* (1991)

Warren I. Cohen, *Dean Rusk* (1980)

————, and Nancy B. Tucker, *Lyndon B. Johnson Confronts the World* (1994)

Chester L. Cooper, *The Lost Crusade* (1972)

David L. DiLeo, *George Ball, Vietnam, and the Rethinking of Containment* (1991)

J. William Fulbright, *The Price of Empire* (1989)

John Galloway, *The Gulf of Tonkin Resolution* (1970)

Leslie H. Gelb and Richard K. Betts, *The Irony of Vietnam* (1979)

Philip Geyelin, *Lyndon B. Johnson and the World* (1966)

Joseph C. Goulden, *Truth Is the First Casualty: The Gulf of Tonkin Affair* (1969)

David Halberstam, *The Best and the Brightest* (1972)

Doris Kearns, *Lyndon Johnson and the American Dream* (1976)

Yuen Foong Khong, *Analogies at War* (1992)

Gregory Palmer, *The McNamara Strategy and the Vietnam War* (1978)

Dean Rusk, *As I Saw It* (1990)

Deborah Shapley, *Promise and Power* (1993) (on Robert McNamara)

Anthony Short, *The Origins of the Vietnam War* (1989)

Eugene C. Windchy, *Tonkin Gulf* (1971)

CHAPTER

7

U.S. Military Strategy

X

From the introduction of U.S. ground forces in 1965, President Johnson, General William C. Westmoreland, and other top civilian and military officials sought to define a strategy appropriate to U.S. objectives in Vietnam. How could American superiority in firepower and technology be brought to bear on an elusive enemy in an inhospitable climate? Were America's goals primarily military or political? What role, if any, should the United States play in the political stabilization of its South Vietnamese ally? Those essential questions defied easy solutions for LBJ and his successors.

American military strategy in Vietnam provoked an intense debate among scholars, military officers, and politicians. That debate, which began with the escalation of the American commitment in the mid-1960s, has raged unabated since then; it remains nearly as lively today as at the height of the war. Certain issues have proved especially troublesome. Was the attrition strategy wise? Might alternative military tactics have been more effective? Why did the United States adopt the tactics and strategy that it did? To what extent did the United States understand its foe—and its ally? How clear were the objectives for which it was fighting? Did Hanoi and the National Liberation Front evolve tactics and strategy superior to those of Washington? And, perhaps the most controversial question of all, could the United States have won the war? If so, how?

X *DOCUMENTS*

In the first document, a November 30, 1965, memorandum to President Johnson, Defense Secretary Robert McNamara recommended additional American troop deployments while admitting that even those deployments could not guarantee victory. George F. Kennan, former U.S. ambassador to the Soviet Union and author of the containment strategy that guided much of post–World War II American foreign policy, criticized the U.S. military commitment to

243

Vietnam in a publicized appearance before the Senate Foreign Relations Committee. Excerpts from Kennan's statement are reprinted as the second document. The next document, a Central Intelligence Agency memorandum of May 12, 1967, offers a candid assessment of the American bombing campaign against North Vietnam, acknowledging its shortcomings. A public statement by McNamara on the improved military outlook for the United States in Vietnam follows. Ironically, at the same time he was issuing this optimistic public prognostication, his private doubts about the war effort were growing.

In the next document, General William C. Westmoreland offers a retrospective justification of the attrition strategy. The last selection presents a soldier's perspective on the experience of combat in Vietnam.

Robert S. McNamara Urges Additional Troop Deployments, 1965

The [Nguyen Cao] Ky [Prime Minister of South Vietnam, 1965–67] "government of generals" is surviving, but not acquiring wide support or generating actions; pacification is thoroughly stalled, with no guarantee that security anywhere is permanent and no indications that able and willing leadership will emerge in the absence of that permanent security. (Prime Minister Ky estimates that his government controls only 25% of the population today and reports that his pacification chief hopes to increase that to 50% two years from now.)

The dramatic recent changes in the situation are on the military side. They are the increased infiltration from the North and the increased willingness of the Communist forces to stand and fight, even in large-scale engagements. The Ia Drang River Campaign of early November is an example. The Communists appear to have decided to increase their forces in SVN both by heavy recruitment in the South (especially in the Delta) and by infiltration of regular NVN forces from the North. . . . The enemy can be expected to enlarge his present strength of 110 battalion equivalents to more than 150 battalion equivalents by the end of calendar 1966, when hopefully his losses can be made to equal his input.

As for the Communist ability to supply this force, it is estimated that, even taking account of interdiction of routes by air and sea, more than 200 tons of supplies a day can be infiltrated—more than enough, allowing for the extent to which the enemy lives off the land, to support the likely PAVN/VC force at the likely level of operations.

To meet this possible—and in my view likely—Communist buildup, the presently contemplated Phase I forces will not be enough (approx. 220,000 Americans, almost all in place by end of 1965). Bearing in mind the nature of the war, the expected weighted combat force ratio of less than 2-to-1 will not be good enough. Nor will the originally contemplated Phase II addition of 28 more U.S. battalions (112,000 men) be enough; the combat force ratio, even with 32 new SVNse battalions, would still be little better than

2-to-1 at the end of 1966. The initiative which we have held since August would pass to the enemy; we would fall far short of what we expected to achieve in terms of population control and disruption of enemy bases and lines of communications. Indeed, it is estimated that with the contemplated Phase II addition of 28 U.S. battalions, we would be able only to hold our present geographical positions. . . .

3. We have but two options, it seems to me. One is to go now for a compromise solution (something substantially less than the "favorable out once" I described in my memo of Nov. 3) and hold further deployments to a minimum. The other is to stick with our stated objectives and with the war, and provide what it takes in men and materiel. If it is decided not to move now toward a compromise, I recommend that the U.S. both send a substantial number of additional troops and very gradually intensify the bombing of NVN. Amb. Lodge, Wheeler, Sharp and Westmoreland concur in this prolonged course of action, although Wheeler and Sharp would intensify the bombing of the North more quickly.

(Recommend up to 74 battalions by end-66: total to approx 400,000 by end-66). And it should be understood that further deployments (perhaps exceeding 200,000) may be needed in 1967. Bombing of NVN. . . . over a period of the next six months we gradually enlarge the target system in the northeast (Hanoi-Haiphong) quadrant until, at the end of the period, it includes "controlled" reconnaissance of lines of comm throughout the area, bombing of petroleum storage facilities and power plants, and mining of the harbors. (Left unstruck would be population targets, industrial plants, locks and dams.)

4. Pause in bombing NVN. It is my belief that there should be a three- or four-week pause in the program of bombing the North before we either greatly increase our troop deployments to VN or intensify our strikes against the North. (My recommendation for a "pause" is not concurred in by Lodge, Wheeler or Sharp.) The reasons for this belief are, first, that we must lay a foundation in the minds of the American public and in world opinion for such an enlarged phase of the war and second, we should give NVN a face-saving chance to stop the aggression. I am not seriously concerned about the risk of alienating the SVNese, misleading Hanoi, or being "trapped" in a pause; if we take reasonable precautions, we can avoid these pitfalls. I am seriously concerned about embarking on a markedly higher level of war in VN without having tried, through a pause, to end the war or at least having made it clear to our people that we did our best to end it.

5. Evaluation. We should be aware that deployments of the kind I have recommended will not guarantee success. U.S. killed-in-action can be expected to reach 1000 a month, and the odds are even that we will be faced in early 1967 with a "no-decision" at an even higher level. My over-all evaluation, nevertheless, is that the best chance of achieving our stated objectives lies in a pause followed, if it fails, by the deployments mentioned above.

George F. Kennan Criticizes the American Military Commitment, 1966

I have not been anxious to press my views on the public but I gladly give them to you for whatever they are worth, claiming no particular merit for them except perhaps that they flow from experience with Communist affairs that runs back now for some thirty-eight years, and also from the deepest and most troubled sort of concern that we should find the proper course, the right course, at this truly crucial moment.

The first point I would like to make is that if we were not already involved as we are today in Vietnam, I would know of no reason why we should wish to become so involved, and I could think of several reasons why we should wish not to. Vietnam is not a region of major military, industrial importance. It is difficult to believe that any decisive developments of the world situation would be determined in normal circumstances by what happens on that territory. If it were not for the considerations of prestige that arise precisely out of our present involvement, even a situation in which South Vietnam was controlled exclusively by the Viet Cong, while regrettable, and no doubt morally unwarranted, would not, in my opinion, present dangers great enough to justify our direct military intervention.

Given the situation that exists today in the relations among the leading Communist powers, and by that I have, of course, in mind primarily the Soviet-Chinese conflict, there is every likelihood that a Communist regime in South Vietnam would follow a fairly independent course. There is no reason to suspect that such a regime would find it either necessary or desirable in present circumstances to function simply as a passive puppet and instrument of Chinese power. And as for the danger that its establishment there would unleash similar tendencies in neighboring countries, this, I think, would depend largely on the manner in which it came into power.

In the light of what has recently happened in Indonesia, and on the Indian subcontinent, the danger of the so-called domino effect, that is the effect that would be produced by a limited Communist success in South Vietnam, seems to me to be considerably less than it was when the main decisions were taken that have led to our present involvement. Let me stress, I do not say that that danger does not exist. I say that it is less than it was a year or two ago when we got into this involvement. From the long-term standpoint, therefore, and on principle, I think our military involvement in Vietnam has to be recognized as unfortunate, as something we would not choose deliberately, if the choice were ours to make all over again today, and by the same token, I think it should be our government's aim to liquidate this involvement just as soon as this can be done without inordinate damage to our own prestige or to the stability of conditions in that area.

It is obvious, on the other hand, that this involvement is today a fact. It creates a new situation. It raises new questions ulterior to the long-term problems which have to be taken into account; a precipitate and disorderly withdrawal could represent in present circumstances a disservice to our own interests and even to world peace greater than any that might have been involved by our failure to engage ourselves there in the first place. This is a reality which, if there is to be any peaceful resolution of this conflict, is going to have to be recognized both by the more critical of our friends and by our adversaries.

But at the same time, I have great misgivings about any deliberate expansion of hostilities on our part directed to the achievement of something called "victory," if by the use of that term we envisage the complete disappearance of the recalcitrance with which we are now faced, the formal submission by the adversary to our will, and the complete realization of our present stated political aims. I doubt that these things can be achieved even by the most formidable military successes.

There seems to be an impression that if we bring sufficient military pressure to bear, there will occur at some point something in the nature of a political capitulation on the other side. I think this is a most dangerous assumption. I don't say that it is absolutely impossible, but it is a dangerous assumption in the light of the experience we have had with Communist elements in the past. The North Vietnamese and the Viet Cong have, between them, a great deal of space and manpower to give up if they have to, and the Chinese can give them more if they need it. Fidelity to the Communist tradition would dictate that if really pressed to extremity on the military level, these people should disappear entirely from the open scene and fall back exclusively on an underground political and military existence rather than to accept terms that would be openly humiliating and would represent in their eyes the betrayal of the future political prospects of the cause to which they are dedicated.

Any total rooting-out of the Viet Cong from the territory of South Vietnam could be achieved, if it could be achieved at all, only at the cost of a degree of damage to civilian life and of civilian suffering, generally, for which I would not like to see this country responsible. And to attempt to crush North Vietnamese strength to a point where Hanoi could no longer give any support for Viet Cong political activity in the South would almost certainly, it seems to me, have the effect of bringing in Chinese forces at some point, whether formally or in the guise of volunteers, thus involving us in a military conflict with Communist China on one of the most unfavorable theaters of hostility that we could possibly choose.

This is not the only reason why I think we should do everything possible to avoid the escalation of this conflict. There is another one which is no less weighty, and this is the effect the conflict is already having on our policies and interests further afield. This involvement seems to me to represent a grievous misplacement of emphasis on our foreign policies as a whole. Not only are great and potentially more important questions of world affairs not receiving, as a consequence of our involvement in Vietnam, the attention they should be receiving, but in some instances assets we already enjoy and hopefully possibilities we should be developing, are being sacrificed to this unpromising involvement in a remote and secondary theater. Our relations with the Soviet Union have suffered grievously, as was to be expected, and this at a time when far more important things were involved in those relations than what is ultimately involved in Vietnam and when we had special reason, I think, to cultivate those relations. And more unfortunate still, in my opinion, is the damage being done to the feelings entertained for us by the Japanese people; the confidence and the good disposition of the Japanese is the greatest asset we have had and the greatest asset we could have in East Asia. As the greatest industrial complex in the entire Far East, and the only place where the sinews of modern war can be produced on a formidable scale there, Japan is of vital importance to us and indeed to the prospects generally of peace and stability in East Asia.

There is no success we could have in Vietnam that would conceivably warrant, in my opinion, the sacrifice by us of the confidence and good will of the Japanese people.

The Central Intelligence Agency's Assessment of the Bombing Campaign, 1967

Through the end of April 1967 the US air campaign against North Vietnam—Rolling Thunder—had significantly eroded the capacities of North Vietnam's limited industrial and military base. These losses, however, have not meaningfully degraded North Vietnam's material ability to continue the war in South Vietnam.

Total damage through April 1967 was over $233 million, of which 70 percent was accounted for by damage to economic targets. The greatest amount of damage was inflicted on the so-called logistics target system—transport equipment and lines of communication.

By the end of April 1967 the US air campaign had attacked 173 fixed targets, over 70 percent of the targets on the JCS list. This campaign included extensive attacks on almost every major target system in the country. The physical results have varied widely.

All of the 13 targeted petroleum storage facilities have been attacked, with an estimated loss of 85 percent of storage capacity. Attacks on 13 of the 20 targeted electric power facilities have neutralized 70 percent of North Vietnam's power-generating capacity. The major losses in the military establishment include the neutralization of 18 ammunition depots, with a loss capacity of 70 percent. Over three fourths of the 65 JCS-targeted barracks have been attacked, with a loss of about one fourth of national capacity. Attacks on 22 of the 29 targeted supply depots reduced capacity by 17 percent. Through the end of April 1967, five of North Vietnam's airfields had been attacked, with a loss of about 20 percent of national capacity.

North Vietnam's ability to recuperate from the air attacks has been of a high order. The major exception has been the electric power industry. One small plant—Co Dinh—is beyond repair. Most of the other plants would require 3–4 months to be restored to partial operations, although two plants—Haiphong East and Uong Bi—would require one year. For complete restoration, all of the plants would require at least a year. Restoration of these plants would require foreign technical assistance and equipment.

The recuperability problem is not significant for the other target systems. The destroyed petroleum storage system has been replaced by an effective system of dispersed storage and distribution. The damaged military target systems—particularly barracks and storage depots—have simply been abandoned, and supplies and troops dispersed throughout the country. The inventories of transport and military equipment have been replaced by large infusions of military and economic aid from the USSR and Communist China. Damage to bridges and lines of communications is frequently repaired within a matter of days, if not hours, or the effects are countered by an elaborate system of multiple bypasses or pre-positioned spans.

McNamara on the Improved Military Outlook, 1967

On the military field, let me say to start with, the military commanders I met with—and I met with all of the senior military commanders in the field, all of the senior Vietnamese commanders, many of the Allied commanders, Korean, and New Zealanders, for example, and many of the middle-ranking and junior U.S. officers—all of the military commanders stated that the reports that they read in the press of military stalemate were, to use their words, the "most ridiculous statements that they had ever heard."

In their view military progress had occurred and was continuing. How did they measure this? They measured it in particular by the success of what they called the large-unit actions. These are battalion-sized and larger actions.

They felt that these actions that General [William C.] Westmoreland had organized and carried on over the past several months, particularly in II and III Corps, had a spoiling effect on the Viet Cong and North Vietnamese. Before they could concentrate their troops to launch an offensive, Westmoreland, through his intelligence sources, had obtained information about the intended enemy plans and had struck the troop concentrations as they were developing, spoiling the potential of the enemy for carrying out these offensive actions.

Moreover, as you know, it has been General Westmoreland's strategy over the past several months to attack the base areas, particularly those in the II and III Corps, using B-52 strikes in some cases but in particular using a coordinated ground and air attack against these base areas to destroy the facilities, the stocks—the recuperation areas that the Viet Cong and the North Vietnamese had used.

The military commanders felt, as a result of this combination of spoiling attacks and attacks on the base areas, the pressure had been so great on the North Viet Cong that they had tended to shift their area of activity. Whereas up until very recently, the activity had been concentrated primarily in the II and III Corps, the offensive activities more recently—they had moved their area of action to the I Corps.

This is understandable because in the II and III Corps—with the loss of their base areas—they were at the end of a very long line of communication over which their men and supplies moved from the supply centers in North Viet-Nam. This line of communications moved down the panhandle of North Viet-Nam across into Laos, down Laos to the Cambodian border, and across into South Viet-Nam—a very, very long line of communication that was under very intense air attack, as a matter of fact.

And because this was a handicap to them—particularly so in connection with the strategy that Westmoreland was carrying out against them—they shifted their area of activity to I Corps.

This accounts for their military actions there in the past several weeks. Now they have the advantage of short lines of communication extending down to the southern border of Viet-Nam, very close to the point where the troops are now very active.

Perhaps the most dramatic change that I saw that reflects the military situation was the opening of the roads.

Highway No. 1, which is the coastal route that runs from the 17th parallel—the line of demarcation between North Viet-Nam and South Viet-Nam—clear south to Saigon, has been broken for many, many months in literally hundreds of places, and traffic on the route has been minimal.

But within the past several months, as a result of these military actions—planned and carried out by the free-world forces—that route has gradually been reopened in large segments.

As a matter of fact, day before yesterday, the route from the southern border of the II Corps up to Dong Hai, which is very close to the DMZ—just a few miles south of the DMZ—was opened for traffic.

There will continue to be ambushes, I presume, and Viet Cong strikes against it, but as I flew over the road after this long stretch was opened, literally hundreds of bicycles and scores of cars and trucks—civilian cars and trucks—were using it.

The same thing is true of many of the feeder roads in III and IV Corps—roads that are of importance to move vegetables or rice to market or otherwise serving as an underpinning of the day-to-day life of the society.

I don't want to exaggerate this or imply all roads are open—far from it. I don't even want to suggest that many of the roads being used can be used freely night and day. They can't. But there has been a very, very noticeable—when I say "noticeable," I mean one flying over the area can notice a very substantial increase in the miles of roads that are open to traffic and the volume of traffic on the roads.

Perhaps a word about the air operations is in order.

We have suffered materially in air operations because of night vision—the difficulty of acquiring targets at night.

There have been some very significant changes in technology. I don't want to go into the details of them other than to say they have greatly increased the capability of our forces to carry on all-weather attacks on the lines of communication, both in South Viet-Nam and in North Viet-Nam.

These, in conjunction with new weapons, new types of ordnance, that have been designed and developed in recent years and brought into production in recent months in combination have increased the effectiveness of the airstrikes. As a matter of fact, they have reduced the losses of both planes and pilots. The losses of planes, for example, are rather significantly lower than we had previously estimated.

Now a word on the pacification program. You are all aware that within the past few weeks there has been a reorganization of the American effort in pacification, an integration of the civilian and military staffs.

The responsibility for pacification has been assigned to General Westmoreland, whose deputy, Mr. Robert Komer, has been placed in direct charge of it. I was very pleased with what I saw.

The frictions that I had read about in the paper perhaps existed at one time but certainly have been dampened down, if not completely eliminated. Both civilian and military officers that I visited at the sector level, the provinces, and the subsector levels of the villages and hamlets, were working effectively together and appeared to have benefited from this integration and reorganization of the pacification efforts.

However, having said that, I should state to you that to be candid I must report the progress in pacification has been very slow. I think that the momentum will increase as the new organization gains in experience, but what we are really trying to do here is engage in nation-building. It is an extraordinarily complex process. I would anticipate progress in what is really a very significant field would continue to be slow.

I am sure that the first question you would ask me, if I didn't anticipate it, would be about additional military personnel; so I will address myself to that. I think some more U.S. military personnel will be required. I am not sure how many. I am certain of one thing: that we must use more effectively the personnel that are presently there.

When I say that, I am speaking of all free-world personnel. As you know, the Vietnamese, the Koreans, the Australians, the New Zealanders, the Filipinos, as well as we, have all contributed forces to the support of the operations in Viet-Nam.

There has been a very rapid buildup of those forces. We now have in uniform of the free-world forces over 1,300,000 men. As you might expect in any organization that has expanded as fast as this one has, there are bound to be areas of waste and inefficiency that can be corrected and eliminated—that must be corrected when we are considering additional troop requirements.

William C. Westmoreland Reflects on a War of Attrition, 1977

In response to changes in national policy, there were basically six strategies adopted between 1954 and 1969. The first involved bolstering the South

"The Military Attrition," by William C. Westmoreland, from *The Lessons of Vietnam*, pp. 57–60, 71. W. Scott Thompson and Donaldson D. Frizzell, eds. 1977, Taylor & Francis/Crane Russak & Co. Reproduced with permission. All rights reserved.

Vietnamese by sending advisers and logistical and economic support in the hope that this could stop and reverse the subversive efforts of the Communists within South Vietnam. The second was an overall strategy of gradually escalating pressure against North Vietnam in the hope of convincing the North to halt its support of the insurgency in the South. This was essentially a strategy based on bombing. The third was a base-security strategy, which was an adjunct of the decision to bomb North Vietnam but which can be called a strategy in that it represented the first commitment of American ground troops to the fighting, albeit in a defensive role. The fourth was an enclave strategy, which assumed protection by American troops of five important areas of South Vietnam but still left most of the fighting to the South Vietnamese. The fifth involved a gradual buildup of forces in the South for purposes of putting maximum pressure on the Communist structure and forces in the South, emphasizing pacification and nation building, expanding control by the South Vietnamese Government over the population, and, at the same time, escalating pressure on the North with air and naval power. The political objective was to bring the enemy to the conference table. The final strategy comprised maximum expansion of the Vietnamese armed forces, increased efforts to pacify all of South Vietnam and to build a viable nation, coupled with gradual withdrawal with or without negotiations.

The decision to launch an air campaign of rising intensity against the North was made against a background of anguished concern over the threat of South Vietnam's imminent collapse. Although the basic objective was to try to convince the North to end its support of the insurgency, another objective was to bolster the morale and strengthen the resolve of the South Vietnamese, who had long been absorbing punishment while the supporters of the insurgency enjoyed impunity.

Two basic considerations lay behind the gradual escalation of the campaign. First, a modest bombing effort might be enough to convince the North of American resolve and, if negotiations developed, might compensate for some of the leverage the Viet Cong victories gave the other side. Secondly, the fear of Chinese Communist intervention was always of immense concern to American officials. Since the Chinese had responded to earlier bombings in muted tones, policy makers in Washington deduced that a gradually increasing campaign might ruffle the Chinese less than would a sudden massive onslaught. The Administration was faced with a dilemma—mobilizing too much support for the war might produce "war fever" and cause the American people to look upon the war as a "great crusade." Nevertheless, I believe a better job could have been done in explaining the nature of our objectives to the American people and the historical background of our involvement.

The strategy of gradually escalating pressure was a new concept; the Joint Chiefs of Staff disagreed with it. It was not, to them, an early "win" policy. Most military men are accustomed to thinking in terms of terminating a war in the shortest practical time and at least cost, following a decision to fight. It is perhaps unnecessary to make the point that there is a relationship between the length of a war and its cost.

By early April 1965, it had become apparent that the new strategy, even with its adjunct of base security, was having no visible effect on the will of the North Vietnamese to continue to support the insurgency. As someone has put it, the United States was signaling Hanoi with a new alphabet that Hanoi could not or would not read. The realization that the air war alone was not doing the job—or at least would take a long time to do it—led to a belief that some new step had to be taken directly against the insurgency in the South. So long as the Viet Cong—reinforced at that point by North Vietnamese troops—continued to win, the leaders in the North, in expectation of ultimate victory, probably would endure the punishment the limited bombing campaign was inflicting.

Taking a new step against the Viet Cong clearly meant actively involving American troops, yet President Johnson and most of his advisers still shied from such a fateful step. Once committed, planes and ships could be readily withdrawn; not so with ground troops. Furthermore, how well would American troops with their sophisticated equipment perform in an Asian insurgency environment? Better to devise some kind of strategy that stopped short of unrestricted commitment, one that would further signal American resolve yet at the same time provide escape valves.

That was the thinking behind the enclave strategy whereby American troops were to take full responsibility for defense of five coastal enclaves and to be prepared to go to the rescue of South Vietnamese forces within fifty miles of the enclaves. Yet, as I pointed out at the time, it put American troops in the unfortunate position of defending static defensive positions with their backs to the sea—in effect, holding five embattled beachheads. It also left the decision of ultimate success or failure in the hands of South Vietnamese troops whose demonstrated inability to defeat the Viet Cong was the reason for committing American troops.

In the face of continuing crisis, my view, and that of the Joint Chiefs of Staff, prevailed. President Johnson's decision of July 1965 carried the United States across the threshold in Vietnam. Before 1965 ended, the United States was to have 184,000 military personnel in Vietnam, including an Army air-mobile division and a Marine division.

Based on my personal experience with the problems on the ground in South Vietnam—political and military—and considering my perception of the aims of the enemy, I anticipated in 1965 that this nation was becoming involved in a protracted war of attrition in which our national will would be sorely tried. As a student of the history of war, and remembering the relatively recent Korean War experience, I was aware of the likelihood that a limited war, fought with limited means for limited objectives, would put special strain on the body politic of a system of government such as ours.

It was in such a context that I recommended continuation of the one year tour that had been set for advisers. It was my belief that lengthy involuntary tours would more likely bring about a hue and cry to "bring the boys home" than a tour in which the "boys would come home" after one year unless they volunteered to stay longer. Also, in anticipation of a long war, it seemed to me that the burden of service should be shared by a cross section of American youth. I did not anticipate that numbers of our young men would be allowed by national policy to defer service by going to a college campus.

I hoped, perhaps with folly, that an emerging sense of South Vietnamese nationalism and a revitalized national will in South Vietnam—manifested in a viable government and a proficient fighting force—would in the long run compensate for the inevitable waning of public support in the United States for a difficult war. . . .

From a military standpoint, it clearly would have been better to have moved much earlier against the enemy's sanctuaries in Laos and Cambodia and possibly even in the southern reaches of North Vietnam. Yet that is speaking without consideration for the political consequences. Further, if the military could have employed air and naval power in accordance with its best judgment, our strategy could have been accelerated. However, the same caution may not have been exercised and the dangers of provoking China to get more deeply involved could have been enhanced.

The Vietnam conflict was an undeclared and limited war, with a limited objective, fought with limited means against an unorthodox enemy, and with limited public support. The longest war in our history, it was the most reported and the most visible to the public—but the least understood. It was more than a military confrontation; ideological, economic, psychological, political, and nation-building problems were involved. Our national involvement in Southeast Asia became an emotional public controversy and hence a political issue. This new and traumatic experience by our nation should provide lessons for our people, our leadership, the news media, and our soldiers.

A Soldier's Perspective on Combat in Vietnam, 1977

Writing about this kind of warfare is not a simple task. Repeatedly, I have found myself wishing that I had been the veteran of a conventional war, with dramatic campaigns and historic battles for subject matter instead of a monotonous succession of ambushes and fire-fights. But there were no Normandies or Gettysburgs for us, no epic clashes that decided the fates of armies or nations. The war was mostly a matter of enduring weeks of expectant waiting and, at random intervals, of conducting vicious manhunts through jungles and swamps where snipers harassed us constantly and booby traps cut us down one by one.

The tedium was occasionally relieved by a large-scale search-and-destroy operation, but the exhilaration of riding the lead helicopter into a landing zone was usually followed by more of the same hot walking, with the mud sucking at our boots and the sun thudding against our helmets while an invisible enemy shot at us from distant tree lines. The rare

From *A Rumor of War* by Philip Caputo, pp. xii–xx. Copyright © 1977 by Philip Caputo. Reprinted by permission of Henry Holt and Company, Inc.

instances when the VC chose to fight a set-piece battle provided the only excitement; not ordinary excitement, but the manic ecstasy of contact. Weeks of bottled-up tensions would be released in a few minutes of orgiastic violence, men screaming and shouting obscenities above the explosions of grenades and the rapid, rippling bursts of automatic rifles.

Beyond adding a few more corpses to the weekly body count, none of these encounters achieved anything; none will ever appear in military histories or be studied by cadets at West Point. Still, they changed us and taught us, the men who fought in them; in those obscure skirmishes we learned the old lessons about fear, cowardice, courage, suffering, cruelty, and comradeship. Most of all, we learned about death at an age when it is common to think of oneself as immortal. Everyone loses that illusion eventually, but in civilian life it is lost in installments over the years. We lost it all at once and, in the span of months, passed from boyhood through manhood to a premature middle age. The knowledge of death, of the implacable limits placed on a man's existence, severed us from our youth as irrevocably as a surgeon's scissors had once severed us from the womb. And yet, few of us were past twenty-five. We left Vietnam peculiar creatures, with young shoulders that bore rather old heads. . . .

There is also the aspect of the Vietnam War that distinguished it from other American conflicts—its absolute savagery. I mean the savagery that prompted so many American fighting men—the good, solid kids from Iowa farms—to kill civilians and prisoners. . . . War by its nature, can arouse a psychopathic violence in men of seemingly normal impulses.

There has been a good deal of exaggeration about U.S. atrocities in Vietnam, exaggeration not about their extent but about their causes. The two most popularly held explanations for outrages like My Lai have been the racist theory, which proposes that the American soldier found it easy to slaughter Asians because he did not regard them as human beings, and the frontier-heritage theory, which claims he was inherently violent and needed only the excuse of war to vent his homicidal instincts.

Like all generalizations, each contains an element of truth; yet both ignore the barbarous treatment the Viet Cong and ARVN often inflicted on their own people, and neither confront the crimes committed by the Korean division, probably the most bloody-minded in Vietnam, and by the French during the first Indochina war.

The evil was inherent not in the men—except in the sense that a devil dwells in us all—but in the circumstances under which they had to live and fight. The conflict in Vietnam combined the two most bitter forms of warfare, civil war and revolution, to which was added the ferocity of jungle war. Twenty years of terrorism and fratricide had obliterated most reference points from the country's moral map long before we arrived. Communists and government forces alike considered ruthlessness a necessity if not a virtue. Whether committed in the name of principles or out of vengeance, atrocities were as common to the Vietnamese battlefields as shell craters and barbed wire. The marines in our brigade were not innately cruel, but on landing in Danang they learned rather quickly that Vietnam was not a place where a man could expect much mercy if, say, he was taken prisoner. And men who do not expect to receive mercy eventually lose their inclination to grant it.

At times, the comradeship that was the war's only redeeming quality caused some of its worst crimes—acts of retribution for friends who had been killed. Some men could not withstand the stress of guerrilla-fighting: the hair-trigger alertness constantly demanded of them, the feeling that the enemy was everywhere, the inability to distinguish civilians from combatants created emotional pressures which built to such a point that a trivial provocation could make these men explode with the blind destructiveness of a mortar shell.

Others were made pitiless by an overpowering greed for survival. Self-preservation, that most basic and tyrannical of all instincts, can turn a man into a coward or, as was more often the case in Vietnam, into a creature who destroys without hesitation or remorse whatever poses even a potential threat to his life. A sergeant in my platoon, ordinarily a pleasant young man, told me once, "Lieutenant, I've got a wife and two kids at home and I'm going to see 'em again and don't care who I've got to kill or how many of 'em to do it."

General Westmoreland's strategy of attrition also had an important effect on our behavior. Our mission was not to win terrain or seize positions, but simply to kill: to kill Communists and to kill as many of them as possible. Stack 'em like cordwood. Victory was a high body count, defeat a low kill-ratio, war a matter of arithmetic. The pressure on unit commanders to produce enemy corpses was intense, and they in turn communicated it to their troops. This led to such practices as counting civilians as Viet Cong. "If it's dead and Vietnamese, it's VC," was a rule of thumb in the bush. It is not surprising, therefore, that some men acquired a contempt for human life and a predilection for taking it.

Finally, there were the conditions imposed by the climate and country. For weeks we had to live like primitive men on remote outposts rimmed by alien seas of rice paddies and rain forests. Malaria, blackwater fever, and dysentery, though not the killers they had been in past wars, took their toll. The sun scorched us in the dry season, and in the monsoon season we were pounded numb by ceaseless rain. Our days were spent hacking through mountainous jungles whose immensity reduced us to an antlike pettiness. At night we squatted in muddy holes, picked off the leeches that sucked on our veins, and waited for an attack to come rushing at us from the blackness beyond the perimeter wire.

The air-conditioned headquarters of Saigon and Danang seemed thousands of miles away. As for the United States, we did not call it "the World" for nothing; it might as well have been on another planet. There was nothing familiar out where we were, no churches, no police, no laws, no newspapers, or any of the restraining influences without which the earth's population of virtuous people would be reduced by ninety-five percent. It was the dawn of creation in the Indochina bush, an ethical as well as a geographical wilderness. Out there, lacking restraints, sanctioned to kill, confronted by a hostile country and a relentless enemy, we sank into a brutish state. The descent could be checked only by the net of a man's inner moral values, the attribute that is called character. There were a few—and I suspect Lieutenant [William] Calley [implicated in the My Lai atrocity] was one—who had no net and plunged all the way down, discovering in their bottommost depths a capacity for malice they probably never suspected was there.

Most American soldiers in Vietnam—at least the ones I knew—could not be divided into good men and bad. Each possessed roughly equal measures of both qualities. I saw men who behaved with great compassion toward the Vietnamese one day and then burned down a village the next. They were, as Kipling wrote of his Tommy Atkins, neither saints "nor blackguards too/But single men in barricks most remarkable like you." That may be why Americans reacted with such horror to the disclosures of U.S. atrocities while ignoring those of the other side: the American soldier was a reflection of themselves.

✗ E S S A Y S

Harry G. Summers, Jr., a U.S. army colonel who served as a battalion and corps operations officer in Vietnam, criticizes both military strategy and civilian leadership during the Vietnam War. He believes that a different strategy could have brought victory to the United States. A selection from his influential book *On Strategy* is the first essay. Next, Gary R. Hess of Bowling Green State University summarizes and critiques the alternative strategies suggested by Summers and another military officer, General Bruce Palmer. Finally, Loren Baritz, a historian and administrator at the University of Massachusetts, Amherst, argues that the Vietnam War was a product of American culture. He contends that that culture, with its faith in technological superiority and managerial sophistication, spawned a self-defeating military strategy.

A Critical Appraisal of American Strategy

HARRY G. SUMMERS, JR.

One of the continuing arguments about the Vietnam war is whether or not a formal declaration of war would have made any difference. On the one hand there are those who see a declaration of war as a kind of magic talisman that would have eliminated all our difficulties. On the other hand there are those who see a declaration of war as a worthless anachronism. The truth is somewhere in between. A declaration of war is a clear statement of *initial* public support which focuses the nation's attention on the enemy. (Continuation of this initial public support is, of course, contingent on the

Reprinted with permission from the book *On Strategy* by Harry G. Summers Jr., pp. 21–23, 120–124, 1982, as published by Presidio Press, 31 Pameron Way, Novato, CA 94949.

successful prosecution of war aims.) As we will see, it was the lack of such focus on the enemy and on the political objectives to be obtained by the use of military force that was the crux of our strategic failure.

Further, a declaration of war makes the prosecution of the war a shared responsibility of both the government and the American people. . . . Without a declaration of war the Army was caught on the horns of a dilemma. It was ordered into battle by the Commander in Chief, the duly elected President of the United States. It was sustained in battle by appropriations by the Congress, the elected representatives of the American people. The legality of its commitment was not challenged by the Supreme Court of the United States. Yet, because there was no formal declaration of war, many vocal and influential members of the American public questioned (and continue to question) the legality and propriety of its actions.

This dilemma needs to be understood. It transcends the legal niceties over the utility of a declaration of war. It even transcends the strategic military value of such a declaration. It should not be dismissed as a kind of sophisticated "stab in the back" argument. As will be seen, the requirement for a declaration of war was rooted in the principle of civilian control of the military, and the failure to declare war in Vietnam drove a wedge between the Army and large segments of the American public.

It is not as if we did not know better. We knew perfectly well the importance of maintaining the bond between the American people and their soldiers in the field, and that this bond was the source of our moral strength. As early as the Revolutionary War this moral strength was a primary factor in our defeat of the British, then a major world power. As a result of this experience we wrote the rules for invoking the national will into our Constitution. Article 1, Section 8 states them clearly:

> The Congress shall have Power . . . To declare War . . . To raise and support Armies . . . To make Rules for the Government and Regulation of the land and naval forces . . .

Implicit in this rule was the rejection of an 18th century-type army answerable only to the Executive. The American Army would be a people's Army to be committed only by the will of the people. As Alexander Hamilton explained:

> The whole power of raising armies [is] lodged in the *Legislature,* not in the *Executive;* This Legislature [is] to be a popular body, consisting of the representatives of the people, periodically elected . . . a great and real security against the keeping of troops without evident necessity.
>
> . . . The power of the President would be inferior to that of the Monarch
>
> . . . That of the British King extends to the *Declaring* of war and to the Raising and Regulating of fleets and armies; All which by the Constitution . . . would appertain to the Legislature.

Hamilton's remarks highlight a critical distinction. In other nations a declaration of war by the chief executive alone (emperor, king, premier, party chairman) may or may not represent the *substance* of the will of his people. By requiring that a declaration of war be made by the representatives of the people (the Congress), rather than by the President alone, the Founding Fathers sought to guarantee this substance and insure that our armed forces would not be committed to battle without the support of the American people. Ironically, President Johnson seemed to know that. In a peculiar passage in light of what was to follow, he said:

> I believed that President Truman's one mistake in courageously going to the defense of South Korea in 1950 had been his failure to ask Congress for an expression of its backing. He could have had it easily, and it would have strengthened his hand. I made up my mind not to repeat that error. . . .

Like President Truman in 1950, President Johnson could probably have had a declaration of war in August 1964 after the Gulf of Tonkin incidents when two American destroyers were attacked by North Vietnamese patrol boats. Instead of asking for a declaration of war, however, President Johnson asked Congress for a resolution empowering him to "take all necessary measures to repel an armed attack against the forces of the United States and to prevent further aggression.". . .

Because they made the cardinal military error of underestimating the enemy, our military leaders failed in their role as "the principal military advisors to the President." There are some who have yielded to the temptation to blame everything on the Commander in Chief, President Johnson. But even his severest critics would have to admit that he certainly did not set out to put the nation in turmoil, ruin his political career, and lose the Vietnam war. It was the duty and responsibility of his military advisors to warn him of the likely consequences of his actions, to recommend alternatives, and, as Napoleon put it, to tender their resignations rather than be the instrument of their army's downfall. In failing to press their military advice they allowed the United States to pursue a strategic policy that was faulty from the start. Instead of deliberately adopting the *strategic defensive,* and tailoring our strategies and tactics to that posture, we slipped into it almost unaware and confused it with the *strategic offensive.* In so doing we lost sight of our strategic purpose and found the truth in the Clausewitzian observation: "Defense without an active purpose is self-contradictory both in strategy and in tactics." By their own failure to understand what we were about, our military leaders were not able to warn our civilian decision-makers that the strategy we were pursuing could never lead to conclusive results.

Although from 1965 until 1975 (with the exception of Tet-68 and the ill-fated Eastertide Offensive of 1972) the North Vietnamese were also in a defensive posture, there was a critical difference. The North Vietnamese were on the tactical defensive as part of a strategic offensive to conquer South Vietnam. Our adoption of the strategic defensive was an end in itself and we had substituted the negative aim of counterinsurgency for the positive aim of isolation of the battlefield. This was a fatal flaw. As Clausewitz said, "A major victory can only be obtained by positive measures aimed at a *decision,* never by simply waiting on events. In short, even in the defense, a major stake alone can bring a major gain. The North Vietnamese had a major stake—the conquest of Indochina. It was the United States that was "simply waiting on events."

. . . Clausewitz defined critical analysis as "not just an evaluation of the means actually employed, but of *all possible means.* . . . One can, after all, not condemn a method without being able to suggest a better alternative." From a "purely military" standpoint it might appear that the better alternative would have been a strategic offensive against North Vietnamese armed forces and their will to fight. But, as Clausewitz warned, there is no such thing as a "purely military" strategy. Military strategy exists to serve political ends, and, . . . for a variety of very practical political reasons an invasion of North Vietnam was politically unacceptable.

We were faced with essentially the same dilemma we had faced in the Korean war. Our political policy was to contain the expansion of communist power, but we did not wish to risk a world war by using military means to destroy the source of that power. We solved that dilemma in Korea by limiting our political objectives to containing North Korean expansion and successfully applied our military means to achieve that end. In Vietnam we began with just such limited objectives. Our mistake was in failing to concentrate our military means on that task. It would appear that we sensed this deficiency, since the Korean war model was essentially the alternative that General Vien, General Westmoreland and the JCS recommended. It was not identified as such because it did not fit the frame of reference we had established for ourselves. For one thing, establishment of a Korean war-type objective in the mid-1960s would have branded Army leadership as hopelessly anachronistic. . . . From the perspective of our total victory in World War II, Korea still looked like a defeat and it is only from the perspective of our actual defeat in Vietnam that we can see that Korea was actually a victory. Further, there was the tyranny of fashion. Counterinsurgency, not conventional tactics, appeared to be the wave of the future. Finally, their plans hinged on the mobilization of the Reserves, a political price President Johnson was not prepared to pay.

Time and bitter experience has removed these distortions from our frame of reference. In 1977, General Bruce Palmer, Jr. (USA, Retired), former commander of U.S. Army Vietnam and former Vice Chief of Staff, U.S. Army, saw clearly what should have been done. In a seminar at the U.S. Army War College, he said that, together with an expanded Naval blockade, the Army should have taken the tactical offensive along the DMZ across Laos to the Thai border in order to isolate the battlefield and then *deliberately* assume the strategic and tactical defensive. While this strategy might have entailed some of the same long-term costs of our Korean strategy, it would (like that strategy) have furthered our political objective of containing communist expansion. He said that in his opinion this could have been accomplished *without reserve mobilization,* without invading North Vietnam and running the risk of Chinese intervention, and with substantially fewer combat forces than were actually deployed to Vietnam.

In brief, General Palmer's strategic concept called for a five-division force (two U.S., two ROK [Republic of Korea] and one ARVN along the DMZ with three more U.S. divisions deployed to extend the defensive line to the Lao-Thai border). An additional U.S. division would have been used to stabilize the situation in the central highlands and in the Saigon area. The Marine divisions would have been held in strategic reserve, to be available to reinforce the DMZ and to pose an amphibious threat, thereby tying down North Vietnamese forces in coastal defense.

General Palmer believed that the advantages of such a strategy would have been enormous. It would have required four fewer divisions than the ten and two-thirds divisions we actually deployed. "Moreover," he said, "the bulk of these forces would have fought on ground of their choosing which the enemy would be forced to attack if he wanted to invade South Vietnam. [This would have provided U.S. forces with a clear and under-standable objective—a peace-keeping operation to separate the belliger-ents.] In defending well-prepared positions, U.S. casualties would have been much fewer. . . . The magnitude and likelihood and intensity of the so-called 'Big War,' involving heavy fire power, would have been lessened [one of the main causes of U.S. public disenchantment with the war]." He went on to say that a much smaller U.S. logistics effort would have been required and we would have avoided much of the base development that was of no real value to the South Vietnamese. "Cut off from substantial out-of-country support, the Viet Cong was bound to wither on the vine and gradually become easier for the South Vietnamese to defeat," he concluded. This conclusion was recently reinforced by statements of former South Vietnamese leaders who believed that by providing a military shield behind which South Vietnam could work out its own political, economic, and social problems, the United States could have provided a reasonable chance for South Vietnamese freedom and independence.

Writing after the U.S. withdrawal from Vietnam, Brigadier Shelford Bidwell, editor of *RUSI*, the distinguished British military journal of the Royal United Services Institute, commented on the view that the war in Vietnam was unwinnable. "This is rubbish," he said, blaming our failure on our election of a strategy which "not only conferred on the North Vietnamese the privilege of operating on safe exterior lines from secure bases but threw away the advantages of a tactical and strategic initiative." He went on to note that by "using firepower of crushing intensity" we suc-ceeded in defeating both the insurgency and the 1972 North Vietnamese offensive but at the strategic price of "American society in turmoil. . . . All this . . . would have been avoided," he said, "by adopting the classical prin-ciples of war by cutting off the trouble at the root. . . . If this was not polit-ically realistic, then the war should not have been fought at all."

Just as the North Koreans and their Chinese allies were the "root of the trouble" in the Korean war, so the root in the Vietnam war was North Vietnam (*not* the Viet Cong). In Vietnam as in Korea our political objec-tives dictated a strategic defensive posture. While this prevented us from destroying the "root" at the source through the strategic offensive, Korea proved that it was possible to achieve a favorable decision with the strategic defensive. It restored the status quo ante, prevented the enemy from achieving his goals with military means, and provided the foundation for a negotiated settlement. All of this was within our means in Vietnam.

Were There Viable Alternative Strategies?

GARY R. HESS

The tenth anniversary of the fall of Saigon occasioned an outpouring of reflections on the American experience in Vietnam. When contrasted with the national sentiments of a decade earlier, the recent press and television analyses of the Vietnam War underline the extent to which scholarly and popular attitudes have changed. With the collapse of South Vietnamese military resistance in the spring of 1975, American soul-searching followed what had become conventional thinking about U.S. involvement in Southeast Asia. The commitment to South Vietnam, it was generally assumed, had been a mistake, a tragic gamble to save a weak and unpopular regime. An immoral and seemingly endless war, forced upon the country by deceitful leaders, was over at last, and with ominous implications for America's global position. The titles of the essays in a special issue of the *New Republic* reflected the national mood. The lead editorial was entitled "On the Disaster," followed by essays with these suggestive titles: "Our SOBs . . . The End is the Beginning . . . Grand Illusion . . . Pushing Sand . . . The Secret War . . . Myths and Interests . . . Hubris: National and Personal . . . The Elite Protects Itself . . . Lies and Whispers."

In those essays and others by prominent foreign policy analysts, the meaning of Vietnam typically found expression in references to the illusions of anti-communism, ignorance of Vietnamese culture and history, and the arrogance of power. Within a decade, however, the terms of thinking about Vietnam have shifted dramatically. Writing from various perspectives, revisionists have defended U.S. intervention, exculpated American warfare of any wrongdoing, and judged the military effort a success. Illusions, and ignorance, and arrogance have given way to hints of a "stab in the back" by the media, Congress, or critics of the war. In its 29 April 1985 issue, marking the tenth anniversary of the fall of Saigon, the *New Republic* embodied, as it had in 1975, the predominant intellectual trend. The editors found the "right lesson" in what they titled "The Myths of Revolution." Other essays, contributed mostly by writers little known in 1975, included a former war critic reflecting on "My Change of Heart" and a Vietnamese dissident coauthoring "Vietnam's Opposition Today." Reflecting the reassessment of the military effort, the issue included "How We Lost." Finally, "Reconsideration of *Fire in the Lake*" criticized the

Gary R. Hess, "The Military Perspective on Strategy in Vietnam: Harry G. Summers's *On Strategy* and Bruce Palmer's *The 25-Year War*," *Diplomatic History*, 10 (Winter 1986), pp. 91–106. Reprinted by permission.

romantic idealization of Vietnamese communism in Frances FitzGerald's prize-winning 1972 book. (FitzGerald had been a contributor to the journal's 1975 Vietnam issue.)

Revisionism and political developments in Indochina and the United States have been mutually reinforcing. Hanoi's imposition of rigid control over the south and its invasion of Cambodia have made the Vietnamese government increasingly repugnant to Americans, even those who had criticized U.S. intervention. The "silent majority" of Americans demanded—and eventually achieved in the leadership of President Ronald Reagan—a reaffirmation of pride, patriotism, and militant anti-communism. As part of this conservative resurgence, the Vietnam War has been elevated, in the president's words, to a "noble cause."

An important force in the reinterpretation of the American experience in Vietnam has been the extensive writings from the military perspective. This literature is comprised of two types: the accounts of fighting men and the reflections of higher commanders. In the popular consciousness, the former have been especially influential. Never before have the horrors of a particular war become so widely known in such a short time. Ignored a decade ago, the soldiers have since told their stories to a receptive audience. Vietnam veterans typically portray themselves as the victims of betrayal by the American government and society. In a spate of individual and collective memoirs and novels, several of which have been dramatized on television, Americans have been reminded of how hundreds of thousands of patriotic youth went to Vietnam only to become quickly disillusioned in a mindless war that measured success by the "body count" and taught contempt for "gooks." Survival became an obsession, but those who did survive returned to an America that was, at best, indifferent and, at worst, hostile to those who had fought in an unpopular war. The image of the betrayed Vietnam soldier has been widely cultivated by television and motion pictures, especially in the popular and controversial films *Apocalypse Now, Coming Home,* and *The Deer Hunter.*

The views of military commanders have reinforced the bitter recollections of the troops. Frustrated by the confusing directives from the Pentagon and by the restraints imposed upon American power, high-ranking officers generally have placed responsibility for failure on ineffective civilian leadership. General William C. Westmoreland's memoir, *A Soldier Reports,* criticizes especially the Johnson administration's refusal to provide the support necessary to achieve objectives in Vietnam and the ineffectiveness of U.S. negotiations with North Vietnam. In a more comprehensive history of the war, *Summons of the Trumpet,* Major General Dave Richard Palmer, who was an adviser to the South Vietnamese Army (ARVN), likewise traced American frustrations principally to ineffective political leadership in Washington. In *The War Managers,* Brigadier General Douglas Kinnard, who served in Vietnam from 1966 to 1967 and again from 1969 to 1970, documented the extent of the military leadership's disillusionment. In their responses to an extended questionnaire, over one hundred generals, who had commanded in Vietnam, saw their mission hampered by confusing objectives (only 29 percent considered them to be "clear and understandable"), slowness in building up ARVN (73 percent believed that Vietnamization should have been emphasized much earlier), and by hostile reporting of the war (52 percent characterized television coverage as "not a good thing . . . sensational . . . counterproductive"). These findings related closely to the generals' responses as to what should be changed "if we had to do it again": fully 91 percent identified, as overriding priorities, "defining the objectives" and "improving the ARVN."

Besides revealing sympathy with many of Westmoreland's reflections on the war, the generals in *The War Managers* also implicitly criticized his leadership. They divided sharply over the concept and execution of the search-and-destroy strategy, criticized the kill ratio as a measure of success (55 percent judged it a "misleading device"), and decried an inadequate understanding of the enemy (56 percent observed that its "will and determination . . . [were] not sufficiently considered").

Reservations about U.S. strategy are central to the extended critiques provided by Colonel Harry G. Summers, Jr., and General Bruce Palmer, Jr. Like many analysts of the Vietnam War, Summers and Palmer essentially ask what went wrong. Unlike others who agree that the war was winnable, they do not focus blame on Congress, the media, or the antiwar movement. Neither do they see the war as "won" in 1967–68 or 1972–73 and "lost" because of irresolute leadership. There is no hint of a congressional "stab in the back" after "victory" in the Paris peace negotiations, as Richard Nixon self-servingly argues in *No More Vietnams.* Instead, Summers and Palmer place the responsibility for failure on both the nation's civilian and military leadership. What clearly emerges are the efforts of two thoughtful officers to come to grips with the most wrenching experience in the history of the institution to which they dedicated their lives.

The Summers and Palmer arguments are similar, each having influenced the other. In his book, Palmer refers approvingly to *On Strategy,* while Summers praises Palmer's basic views on Vietnam as set forth in a 1977 lecture. Recently, Summers described *The 25-Year War* as "especially valuable" for its stress on "the need for intellectual honesty and moral quality" on the part of army officers.

In analyzing the army's failure to measure up to national expectations, Summers and Palmer follow different approaches. *On Strategy* resulted from Summers's research at the Strategic Studies Institute at the U.S. Army War College, Carlisle Barracks, Pennsylvania, where he later held the General Douglas MacArthur Chair of Military Research. Beginning in 1981 as a War College project to examine the "application of military science to the national defense," *On Strategy* has become an influential book, and Summers has become something of a celebrity. Originally published by the Army War College, then by Presidio Press in 1981, *On Strategy* has since been issued in a Dell paperback edition. Summers's views have received much attention in major journals and on television; he was omnipresent during the tenth anniversary media reflections, and he was the author of the aforementioned *New Republic* article on "How We Lost." Recently he became a columnist for *U.S. News and World Report.* Summers's combat experience lends authority to his arguments. An infantry squad leader during the Korean War, he served as a battalion and company operations officer in Vietnam. What makes his argument most compelling, however, is his application of the principles of warfare set forth by Carl von Clausewitz to U.S. tactics and strategy in Vietnam. As Summers relentlessly demonstrates in case after case, the Americans failed especially to follow the principles of the objective, offensive, mass, economy of force, and maneuver. While observing that the enemy almost consistently adhered to those principles, Summers views the "lesson" of Vietnam as self-evident.

Palmer builds principally upon his considerable experience in Washington and Vietnam between 1963 and 1974. Few officers enjoyed a comparable opportunity to observe both the conflict itself and the decision-making process. As a staff officer of Lieutenant General Harold K. Johnson, deputy chief of Staff for Army Operations from September 1963 to April 1965, Palmer was in a position to follow the concerns and the influence of the Joint Chiefs of Staff (JCS) during the critical first steps of direct U.S. involvement. In early 1965, President Lyndon B. Johnson sent him on a tour of Vietnam, Laos, Cambodia, and Thailand. Like other observers at that time, Palmer was distressed by South Vietnam's vulnerability. After one year as commander of U.S. forces in the Dominican Republic, which brought him into contact with Ambassador Ellsworth Bunker, and then one year at Fort Bragg, Palmer was given command of II Field Force in Vietnam in March of 1967. (He is included among the generals in the Kinnard survey.) Subsequently he was made Westmoreland's deputy at the headquarters of the U.S. Army in Vietnam. After experiencing the tumultuous events of 1967–68, Palmer returned to Washington with Westmoreland in July 1968, becoming the army's vice-chief of Staff. From that position he followed the American withdrawal and the Vietnamization policy before retiring in 1974. Although throughout his memoir Palmer leaves little doubt of his judgment of the men whom he observed—high regard for Dean Rusk, Westmoreland, and Bunker; disdain for the arrogance of Lyndon Johnson, Henry Kissinger, and (mixed with some respect) Alexander Haig—he generally sticks to the larger question of understanding the Vietnam failure. His views already have attracted considerable attention, and *The 25-Year War,* first published by the University Press of Kentucky, is now also available in a Simon and Schuster paperback edition.

Since the arguments of Summers and Palmer move along similar lines and tend to be mutually reinforcing, piecing them together should provide an overview of what has become a widely held perspective on the Vietnam War. Summers and Palmer stress several related themes: the deficiency of preintervention military planning and advice, the failure to issue a declaration of war, the ineffectiveness of Westmoreland's strategy, and the potential success of strategic alternatives. Their analyses seek to explain what Summers labels the American record of "tactical victory, strategic defeat" and to show how the army, operating under the constraints imposed by Washington, could have attained the nation's basic objectives.

Much of the U.S. frustration in Vietnam can be traced to the failure of the nation's military leadership to fulfill basic responsibilities. Strategic planning was not prepared for the Vietnam contingency. Accordingly, when the Joint Chiefs should have expressed doubts about intervention, they muted their serious reservations and endorsed air and ground operations of dubious effectiveness.

Ill-conceived strategic planning, Summers argues, was at the base of U.S. frustration. The army learned the wrong lesson from the Korean War. In that conflict the Chinese intervention forced a fundamental change in strategic operations; no longer could war be carried to the homeland of the enemy. The army had adjusted and brought political and military objectives into balance by waging a war against the Chinese that resulted in the restoration of the prewar status quo. Still bound by World War II concepts of "victory," however, the army drew the incorrect conclusion that Korea "taught" the necessity to avoid a land war with China. A second factor guiding strategy was the overriding fear of nuclear destruction, which placed limits on American options and meant the loss of "escalation dominance." Summers sees pre-Vietnam strategy directed by the "counsel of our fears":

> Instead of seeing that it was possible to fight and win a limited war in Asia regardless of Chinese intervention, we again (as we had done with nuclear war) took counsel of our fears and accepted as an article of faith the proposition that we should never again become involved in a land war in Asia.

Then, as the Johnson administration was moving in 1964–65 to take the United States to war, Palmer contends that the military leaders failed in their obligations to civilian authority. During the deliberations of the JCS, General Earle G. Wheeler, as chairman, insisted upon an "agreed-position" system of recommendations, pressuring those who disagreed with the majority, or with the direction of administration policy, to forego their objections. Therefore, a consensual "no harm in trying . . . it's worth the effort" mentality contributed to the JCS recommendation for air warfare, thus ignoring the reservations of army and navy leaders. Subsequent questions about the functions of ground troops also were not considered adequately. At no point did the service chiefs warn the president and secretary of defense of the likelihood of failure. No one wanted to appear "disloyal," and a "can-do" attitude overwhelmed objections. The civilian leadership needed to know the points of disagreement, but the JCS ignored its responsibilities.

Palmer's criticism of the JCS raises the intriguing question of whether or not reservations about intervention would have restrained President Johnson. He would have had good reason to reflect because the JCS had been assigning increased strategic importance to Indochina. At the time of the 1954 crisis the JCS had urged restraint, holding that "Indochina is devoid of decisive military objectives and the allocation of more than token U.S. armed forces in Indochina would be a serious diversion of limited U.S.

capabilities." By 1961, in the words of Leslie Gelb and Richard Betts, the JCS had "[done] an apparent somersault." Embracing the "domino theory," they recommended in 1962 that the United States "take expeditiously all actions necessary to defeat communist aggression in South Vietnam." In justifying their stand, they argued:

> The immediate strategic importance of Southeast Asia lies in the political value that can accrue to the Free World through a successful stand in that area. Of equal importance is the psychological impact that a firm position by the United States will have on the countries of the world—both free and communist. On the negative side, a United States political and/or military withdrawal . . . would have an adverse psychological effect of even greater proportion, and one from which recovery would be both difficult and costly.

While the JCS record of support for increased U.S. commitments to Indochina should have given added credence to any reservations, had they been expressed in 1965, it is questionable whether any words of caution would have altered the momentum toward intervention. Indeed, Palmer's insights add to an understanding of a policymaking process that President Johnson dominated and which discouraged debate over Vietnam initiatives. Concerns about the costs of attaining American objectives and doubts about the chances for success were common within the Department of State, Department of Defense, National Security Council, and elsewhere, but the system did not allow for debate. Recent studies have emphasized the extent to which Johnson took the initiative in Vietnam decision making in 1964–65, forcing consideration of issues in ways that led seemingly inescapably to U.S. intervention. Characteristically manipulating the civilian and military advisers, Johnson evidently had become convinced that the Vietnam problem could be solved quickly through sufficient American power to force North Vietnam to end its war in the south. In the charged atmosphere prevailing in Washington at the time of the Gulf of Tonkin and Pleiku incidents, Johnson would have likely dismissed any JCS reservations against intervention just as he did those of Vice-President Hubert Humphrey and Undersecretary of State George Ball. The president's humiliation of Humphrey was not lost on those who sought influence in the Johnson White House.

When the United States made its crucial decisions of 1965, Summers argues at length, and Palmer concurs, Johnson drastically miscalculated by failing to seek a declaration of war. Only through a declaration could the national attention be focused on the enemy, the war effort become a shared responsibility of government and people, mobilization have resulted appropriately, and sanctions have been imposed against those who aided the enemy. "All of America's previous wars," Summers writes, "were fought in the heat of passion. Vietnam was fought in cold blood, and that was intolerable to the American people." Palmer agrees:

> It seems rather obvious that a nation cannot fight a war in cold blood, sending its men and women to distant fields of battle without arousing the

emotions of the people. I know of no way to accomplish this short of a declaration of war by the Congress and national mobilization.

Johnson's decision not to inflame national passions—a result partly of his assumptions about the duration of the war and his determination to focus attention on domestic reform—undermined the war effort from the beginning. Summers and Palmer both cite the president's failure to seek a war declaration as one of their principal indictments of civilian leadership. Their charges raise a number of questions.

First, were all of America's earlier conflicts fought in the "heat of passion," and is that essential? Korea, which Summers refers to as the strategic model for Vietnam, also lacked a declaration of war and was waged without any sustained heat of passion. The dismissed MacArthur's call for victory stirred deep passions during his triumphant American return in 1951. The Korean conflict clearly illustrated the immense difficulties of gaining support for a limited war, and the erosion of Truman's popularity foreshadowed Johnson's fate fifteen years later. Korea also demonstrated, however, that, even in the absence of the level of national commitment implicit in a war declaration, it was possible to attain objectives in a limited war.

Second, would Congress have declared war? According to Summers, Johnson "could probably have had a declaration of war in August 1964 after the Gulf of Tonkin incidents." He cites Arthur M. Schlesinger, Jr., to the effect that Johnson "could certainly have obtained Congressional authorization beyond the Tonkin resolution for a limited war in 1965." But would a declaration of war have been justified in 1964 or 1965 on the basis of national security? Not according to Palmer, who writes: "National security was a legitimate interest . . . but South Vietnam was not vital to the United States." The sketchy "encounters" in the Gulf of Tonkin incident did not touch off a national demand for military retaliation. The passage of the Tonkin resolution should not be interpreted as indicative of congressional willingness to declare war. To members of Congress, as well as the public generally, a declaration of war constitutes a serious commitment; congressional resolutions allowing presidents wide latitude in foreign crises were seen, at least in 1964, as relatively innocuous. In the previous decade, Congress, without serious consequences, had given President Dwight D. Eisenhower such resolutions regarding the Middle East and the Formosa Strait. In the summer of 1964, Johnson's popularity and respect among the American public were overwhelming, and few questioned the sincerity of his campaign promise to avoid war in Vietnam.

Third, would a declaration of war have made a substantial difference in popular support? Would national passions—assuming that they could have been generated in 1964 or 1965—have been sustained? Popular disenchantment with the war developed slowly, reflecting war weariness, disappointment, and distrust. The public still would have witnessed the horrors of war on television, and those images would have been just as compelling had war been declared. The erosion of popular support that became pronounced in late 1967 and early 1968 seems to have been principally the result of mounting frustrations and uncertainties, which a declaration would have reduced only marginally. A declaration of war in 1917 had not precluded substantial opposition to, and criticism of, President Woodrow Wilson's leadership, and a declaration of war in 1941 did not prevent mounting weariness as casualties increased and victory seemed far away, even in the most popular of wars.

Finally, is it not more difficult to keep a declared war safely limited? Arousing the national passions has ominous implications in the nuclear age. The United States, in Vietnam as in Korea and other lesser commitments of its forces in the last forty years, has faced serious dilemmas in using and restricting its power. A declaration of war, even for essentially defensive objectives, increases risks of a wider conflict.

If the strategic planning lacked cohesion and the JCS ignored realities, the American military mission, not surprisingly, had to be improvised. "Insufficient timely discussion" in Washington preceded the dispatch of American forces. General Maxwell Taylor, then ambassador in Saigon, favored a defensive strategy much like the "enclave" approach advocated publicly by Lieutenant General James M. Gavin, which would have restricted American offensive operations to the vicinity of base areas, usually near the coast. Westmoreland, however, advocated taking the war to the enemy, thereby defeating the Vietcong and North Vietnamese units in the south. A war of attrition resulted. To apply General Omar Bradley's famed dictum on MacArthur's Korean strategy to the Summers-Palmer assessment of the Vietnam situation, it amounted to "the wrong war, at the wrong place, at the wrong time, and with the wrong enemy." The attrition strategy, Summers emphasizes, violated basic principles of warfare. By failing to take the offensive, Westmoreland's plan "committed the United States Army . . . to the strategic defensive in pursuit of the negative aim of wearing the enemy down." As it committed itself to counterinsurgency throughout South Vietnam, the army's operations became inefficient and futile; this strategy ignored Clausewitz's principles of mass, economy of force, maneuver, and simplicity.

A central question for both Summers and Palmer concerns the ability of the United States to bring its superior weaponry, especially its massive firepower, to bear against an elusive enemy. They agree that the search-and-destroy strategy was seriously flawed. In Palmer's analysis, search and destroy frequently resulted in heavy American casualties without fully engaging the enemy. While Summers believes that such operations were usually successful tactically, they cost a "fatal strategic price" because much of the domestic opposition to the war focused on the brutality of search-and-destroy tactics. The tragedies at Ben Suc and My Lai resulted from such operations. An alternative approach—gradual extension of control over a large area, such as the methods employed in Operation Junction City—likewise resulted, in Palmer's estimate, in substantial casualties without appreciable long-term gains.

The central flaw of Westmoreland's strategy was its assumption about North Vietnamese determination and capability. The military, Summers argues, made the "cardinal error of underestimating the enemy." Palmer believes that the evidence was there from the beginning to see that attrition would not work. Central Intelligence Agency estimates, which he credits with being consistently more reliable than military intelligence, projected that North Vietnam could indefinitely replace losses inflicted by the Americans.

Committed to this ill-conceived strategy of attrition, the growing U.S. military presence lacked direction and coherence. The "most pernicious policy" was the base camp, an "albatross" draining men and resources. During his tours, Palmer was appalled by the "nine-to-five" routine of officers who were helicoptered twice daily between headquarters at Long Binh and villas at the nearby city of Bien Hoa. The one-year rotation policy resulted in frequent turnover of experienced personnel and in inadequately trained recruits, a situation that could have been avoided had the United States been mobilized and the reserves called for Vietnam duty.

Air operations were as ill-conceived as the war on the ground. The all-out bombing campaign advocated by the JCS was compromised by President Johnson's decision to serve as "target officer." His piecemeal application of the aerial firepower, together with the numerous bombing halts to encourage negotiations, condemned the air arm to discard the Clausewitzian principles of mass, surprise, and consistency. Moreover, civilian leaders, not for the first time, overestimated the effectiveness of bombing campaigns.

A poor command structure, while not the cause of defeat, consistently undermined effective operations. While the North Vietnamese followed Clausewitz's precept of unity of command, Summers contends, the United States lacked a coherent command structure, which was symptomatic of the even greater failure to focus on the military objective. The command problems irritated Palmer during his tours of duty in Vietnam, as well as in Washington, and he details the cumbersome structure. In charge of American operations was the Commander, U.S. Military Assistance Command, Vietnam (COMUSMACV), but that office suffered from poor coordination with ARVN and other allied units in Vietnam. Its chain of command ran from Washington through the Commander in Chief, Pacific (CINPAC) at Hawaii through to Vietnam. COMUSMACV also lacked responsibility for air operations against North Vietnam, these being directed by CINPAC through the Pacific air and naval commanders. Moreover, COMUSMACV was both an army and a joint command; a separate army command was needed. In retrospect, few would question Palmer's assessment that "undivided responsibility and unified direction were conspicuously absent."

These problems in southeast Asia were compounded by other complications in Washington. The JCS lacked sufficient responsibility to direct the war, a situation that Palmer attributes partly to the creation of the Department of Defense which placed the secretary of defense between each of the service chiefs and the president. In this arrangement the JCS functioned as an indirect advisory group which he describes as a "recipe for destruction in wartime." Based on his observations during the Vietnam War, Palmer argues that, "in time of crises, emergency, or war, the operational chain of command should run from the president/commander-in-chief directly to the JCS and thence to unified commanders."

Management of the army's mission in Vietnam, Palmer readily acknowledges, was consistently undermined by Johnson's disregard of advice. Representing Westmoreland at cabinet meetings in 1968, Palmer observed firsthand the Johnson techniques. At one session the presidential photographer was present throughout, "taking an endless series of snapshots of the president from every conceivable angle." Johnson was "in constant motion, receiving or making phone calls, pressing the buzzer under the top of his desk to give orders . . . and frequently interrupting anyone trying to articulate his views." In an "atmosphere hardly conducive to meaningful discussion," Johnson paid "scant attention" to what was said, for the meeting was evidently a "pro forma gathering designed to support the claim of undivided support." The civilians' disregard for the JCS continued into the Nixon administration, and Kissinger especially dominated decisionmaking.

Still, the American failure flowed ultimately from its flawed strategy. By leaving the initiative to the enemy, the United States invited the Tet Offensive, in which North Vietnamese and Vietcong units achieved their one instance of strategic surprise and won a major strategic victory despite a tactical defeat. The domestic frustrations from the lack of progress in a war of attrition contributed both to the imperative of American withdrawal and to the South Vietnamese believing that their country was being abandoned.

Both Summers and Palmer maintain that the United States should have followed a strategy of carrying the war to strong points in North Vietnam. Counterinsurgency dealt only with the periphery: Hanoi's "screen" in the south. The basic American objective should have been to prevent North Vietnamese infiltration. "If the infiltration could not be brought under control," Summers states, "South Vietnam could never solve its internal problems." In essence, Vietnam was a conventional conflict—a war of North Vietnamese aggression—but the counterinsurgency emphasis of the early 1960s, and the misread "lessons of Korea," blinded the United States to realities. Palmer specifically suggests a strategy of denying North Vietnam access to the Demilitarized Zone (DMZ), which was one of its points of strength throughout the conflict. The United States should have defended the strongest points in the area just to the south of the DMZ and extending across Laos, holding it by developing bases and ports with a substantial international force. If denied authority to send forces into Laos, the United States still could have secured the area through raids into that country. An effective American and South Vietnamese defense of the DMZ would have threatened to trap North Vietnamese units in the south and to cut their lines of supply. Denied support, the Vietcong would have "wither[ed] on the vine." While shielding South Vietnam at the DMZ, the United States could have concentrated on the "primary mission" of building up the ARVN to give it responsibility for countering Vietcong insurgency.

Palmer and Summers also agree that the United States should have kept up continual pressure directly against North Vietnam. Strategic bombing was unnecessary, but air interdiction in sparsely populated areas of North Vietnam and Laos, and along the DMZ, was essential. U.S. air and naval power, moreover, should have blockaded northern ports, and a large amphibious presence should have been maintained in the Gulf of Tonkin to keep the North Vietnamese guessing about American intentions. The "major mistake" of the war, according to Palmer, was signaling North Vietnam that the United States did not intend to invade its territory. That gave the enemy the assurance—one it should not have enjoyed—of realizing that national survival was never at stake. Summers attributes this shortcoming to the publicly expressed fear of nuclear warfare; this cost the United States "a major strategic advantage—*escalation dominance*—the ability to pose a threat to the enemy to raise the level of warfare beyond his ability (or willingness) to respond."

When the Nixon administration finally moved aggressively against the North Vietnamese lines of supply, these analysts found the results generally disappointing because of the earlier strategic shortcomings. The Cambodian incursion of 1970 came too late; its military effect was limited, while its domestic repercussions in the United States were disastrous. Sending ill-prepared ARVN units into Laos in 1971 only revealed the belatedness of Vietnamization; Palmer describes it as "very much [like] sending a boy to do a man's job in an extremely hostile environment." On the other hand, Summers and Palmer both praise Nixon's Christmas 1972 bombing—one of the few times that the United States achieved strategic surprise—because it forced Hanoi into the January 1973 settlement.

The Summers-Palmer alternative seems to offer a means of attaining American objectives at a reasonable cost. It also suggests a mission more compatible with Washington's determination to limit the commitment of U.S. forces. The attrition strategy constantly required additional troops. The cycle of escalation, with each step justified by promises of meeting future needs when, in fact, much intelligence indicated otherwise, led not only to popular disillusionment but also to deep debate within the Johnson administration, culminating in the denial of additional forces in 1968. Furthermore, the alternative approach of restricting the American presence would have been less offensive to the people and leaders of South Vietnam than the virtual Americanization of its government, society, and economy. The prospects for meeting the challenge of nation-building would therefore have been enhanced. Finally, the Summers-Palmer plan seems strategically sound: the enemy is clearly identified; the objective is unequivocal; the logistics are relatively simple; economy of force is practiced; American power is concentrated against enemy strength; and escalation is an option. Moreover, when related to the Summers-Palmer position on a declaration of war, this military mission would have been undertaken with a strong national commitment.

Such reflections on Vietnam hold much relevance as U.S. policymakers confront today's issues. In a 28 November 1984 speech, Secretary of

Defense Caspar Weinberger outlined "six major tests" to be applied when considering the use of American combat forces overseas: the importance of the area to national security; a "clear intention of winning"; well-defined interests; willingness to reassess "size, composition, and disposition" of those forces; recognition that the use of American units was a "last resort"; and, finally, that "[be]fore the U.S. commits combat forces . . . [it has a] reasonable assurance [of] . . . the support of the American people and their elected representatives in Congress." Drawing specifically upon the "lessons" of Vietnam, Weinberger added that "we cannot fight a battle with the Congress at home while asking our troops to win a war overseas, or, as in the case of Vietnam, in effect asking our troops not to win but just to be there." While one may challenge the utility of Weinberger's six major tests, as Secretary of State George Shultz did with respect to the "guaranteed public support in advance" test, such efforts to redefine the terms of military engagement clearly reflect the impact of the Vietnam experience.

The Summers-Palmer alternative, however, also raises a number of military and political questions. From a military viewpoint, was this option feasible, given the situation in Vietnam in 1965? Considering the chronic instability of the Saigon government and the evidence of the Vietcong-North Vietnamese strength in the south, the prospects for a defensive strategy looked bleak at that time. Carrying the war to the enemy seemed imperative.

Could the south have been sealed effectively? Summers draws upon an earlier example: "The United States could (as it had done in Korea) bring the infiltration under control." This is a somewhat facile comparison. The analogy between the North Koreans and North Vietnamese infiltration is open to question. Preventing movement of forces in the terrain of the Korean peninsula was a vastly different mission from deterring small units in jungles in an area with few natural barriers. Stopping North Vietnamese movement into the south likely would have necessitated extending forces over a wider area than the DMZ position. Palmer notes that the DMZ was one of the North Vietnamese points of strength, albeit the most easily defensible. In view of the versatility and determination of the North Vietnamese, the Americans actually might have had to face the situation described by Westmoreland: "Some have considered it practicable to seal the land frontiers against North Vietnamese infiltration. . . . Yet small though [South Vietnam] is, its land frontiers extend for more than 900 miles." To have defended that entire frontier on a scale similar to Korea would have required "many millions of troops." Like others, Westmoreland was skeptical of projects aimed at sealing the DMZ, such as the proposed "McNamara line" of mines, sensors, fortifications, and barbed wire. He argued, however, for the presence of an international force along the DMZ, which could have called immediate attention to North Vietnamese violations of the border. Such a presence might have had an intimidating effect on Hanoi.

Finally, would the alternative strategy have significantly altered political developments? A positive assessment assumes that, given time and support, a lasting national structure could have been established in the south. Throughout its twenty-five year history, the Republic of Vietnam confronted the immense challenge of trying to build national consciousness in an environment lacking essential characteristics for nation-building. The Saigon government owed its existence to the United States. Opposition to that government and its problems of dependence might have been lessened, but not eliminated, by the concentration of U.S. forces near the DMZ and the buildup of the ARVN. After all, opposition to the Saigon government was not a creation of North Vietnam, and the eventual manipulation and exploitation of the Vietcong by Hanoi should not obscure the southern origins of the insurgency. What were needed were leaders who could have inspired sacrifice, ended the widespread corruption, and brought reforms into rural areas.

Summers and Palmer, like those under whom they served, approach the war with the same assumptions as American policymakers who considered the division of Vietnam to be permanent and expected to dissuade Hanoi from its objective of national unification. Those convictions ran counter to the facts. The government at Hanoi could lay claim to a Nationalist legitimacy that the American client in the south lacked. The determination and resourcefulness of the enemy in Vietnam impressed many Americans who served there, including Palmer and Summers. As they note, the war was "everything" to North Vietnam—the completion of the Communist-Nationalist revolution begun in 1945. Fighting in South Vietnam could never mean as much to the United States, especially since American security was not at stake, as Palmer bluntly acknowledges. This is not intended to romanticize Ho Chi Minh and his followers, for their totalitarian tactics understandably offend U.S. ideals. "What was wrong in backing a weak, corrupt, inefficient regime against a brutally powerful, fanatically puritanical, ruthlessly efficient adversary," David Fromkin and James Chace write, "was that our side was likely to lose." The American effort was consistently undermined by the history of French colonialism and the French-Viet Minh War. "To an incredible degree," David Halberstam once reflected, "we were haunted and indeed imprisoned by the past." Because the South Vietnamese government eventually collapsed does not mean that its political history might not have been changed. The odds against the U.S. effort were substantial, however, and the Vietnam problem most likely defied American solution.

These works are of importance to diplomatic historians. The arguments of Summers and Palmer, by essentially reinforcing the complaints of fighting men about the conduct of the war, will likely help shape popular consciousness concerning the Vietnam conflict. Also, *On Strategy* and *The 25-Year War* are bound to influence military strategists and may come to represent a widely held interpretation on the mistakes of Vietnam.

Summers and Palmer, together with the generals in the Kinnard study, represent the views of one generation of military leaders on America's lost war. Their advice to the next generation of officers is bound to exert influence upon strategic thinking for years to come. Finally, these authors consider the Vietnam War under the conditions that the United States actually faced, and that alone is a singularly useful service. Regardless of whether or not one agrees with their strategic assessments and prescriptions, Summers and Palmer force serious reflection on the objectives and potential of American warfare in Vietnam.

The Limits of Technological Warfare

LOREN BARITZ

War is a product of culture. It is an expression of the way a culture thinks of itself and the world. Different cultures go to war for different reasons and fight in different ways. There is an American way of war. Our Vietnam War was started and fought in ways our culture required.

All the critics of General Westmoreland's "strategy" of a conventional big-unit war of attrition argued that he failed to understand that the guerrillas were more important than the conventional forces of North Vietnam. Most of the "pacification" devotees made the same point. None of them understood the relationship between American culture and the American way of war.

Lieutenant Colonel Zeb B. Bradford was a better cultural critic than the civilian and academic experts. He explained that Americans could not have fought successfully as guerrillas or antiguerrillas. It was thus necessary for Americans to have concentrated on our own way of war:

> The great strength of US fighting forces historically has been precisely that they have exploited their peculiarly American qualities and attributes. Highly mechanized and technical warfare reinforces our tendencies and talents and serves as a vehicle for evolutionary advance—counterinsurgency goes against the grain. We are a rich, industrial, urban country. Highly technical forces are compatible with our characteristics and resources.

Zeb Bradford wrote what is indisputable: Mostly white, English-speaking soldiers could not fight as guerrillas in Asia. We would make superb guerrillas if we were fighting in the United States.

The counterinsurgency fad was a direct consequence of President Kennedy's uninformed enthusiasm, and it confused the American effort for many years after his death. When the army Chief, General George Decker, told President Kennedy that "any good soldier can handle guerrillas," the President first lectured him and six months later fired him. The military brass got the message. On the surface, counterinsurgency was in. JFK's support of the stylish Green Berets was consistent with his athletic patriotism, and was based on the assumption that military training could some-

From *Backfire: A History of How American Culture Led Us into Vietnam and Made Us Fight the Way We Did* by Loren Baritz. Copyright © 1985 by Loren Baritz. Reprinted by permission of William Morrow and Co., Inc.

how overcome culture and race. Peer De Silva, the CIA's chief of station of Saigon, remembered that Robert and John Kennedy believed that "if a Vietcong *can* lie for hours under water in a rice paddy, breathing air through a straw, so *can* we." It was harder to train them to climb out of the water, mix with the villagers, and remain undetectable. The American way of life and war meant that we could not succeed as counterinsurgents.

American political culture—the self-righteousness of our nationalism—merged with the impulses of our technological culture—tell us what to do and we'll do it, no questions asked. President Kennedy's enthusiasm for counterinsurgency led the nation to assume that we could successfully intervene in Vietnamese politics in ways that were foreign to America's genius. Our managerial sophistication and technological superiority resulted in our trained incompetence in guerrilla warfare.

The conclusion is obvious: If this nation cannot use its managerial and technological strengths in international conflict, it would be wise to avoid engagement. If our expensive weapon systems will not contribute to victory, it would be wise not to pretend that we have other resources.

The only circumstance where this conclusion does not apply is when the imbalance between us and our enemy is ludicrous, as in the adventure on the island of Grenada. This conclusion, however, did apply to our peacekeeping force in Lebanon, where our massed technology could not protect the marines from one terrorist's truck. Our Vietnam experience had revealed that we could not stop what we did not stop in Lebanon. That is because military intelligence, not missiles or an armada of warships, is necessary to stop terrorism. If the intelligence is available, one bullet may be all the technology necessary. If it is unavailable, our soldiers will surely die.

The entire ecology of America's military bureaucracy depends on weapons—increasingly complex, difficult to maintain, and expensive. Thus, General Westmoreland's strategy of conventional war was consistent with the realities of American culture, obviously including its bureaucratic and corporate values. There was nothing else he could do. In a gigantic confusion of means and ends, the Pentagon, both then and now, appears to conceive of its weapons as national strategy and its budget as foreign policy. This is a revealing symptom of the technicians' mentality: Quantity shall overcome. The Israelis and the North Vietnamese might have taught us otherwise. This dependence on quantity has some meaning in conventional warfare, but certainly not in guerrilla war, and, within limits, probably not in the calculus of nuclear deterrence.

The technician's mind is organized around the question *how*. He is motivated by a desire, sometime a need, to solve problems. He is rational, practical, hardheaded, and believes that if an idea can be transformed into a solution that actually works, the idea was true. Most of the war's planners exhibited these traits. Three other attributes of the technological mentality had an even more direct impact on the war. The technician's language is amoral, dispassionate, and optimistic. For example, Secretary McNamara's perception of Vietnam as a limited war reveals all these habits of mind:

"The greatest contribution Vietnam is making—right or wrong is beside the point—is that it is developing an ability in the United States to fight a limited war, to go to war without the necessity of arousing the public ire."

A technician's war would be muddied by the public's passion. Thus, the Vietnam War was cold-blooded. Secretary Rusk said that "we tried to do in cold blood perhaps what can only be done in hot blood, when sacrifices of this order are involved." None of the Presidents attempted to stir passion about this war. General Westmoreland mistakenly said that the reason was that the political leaders "were more afraid of stirring up the hawks than the doves, a very ironical development. . . . Therefore, a policy decision was made to keep the war low key." The war was fought for reasons of state, not out of anger. If the American public was whipped into anger, the political engineers might not have been able to attempt to fine-tune Vietnam to just the right level of death. They might not have been able so precisely to control a more passionate war. The very idea of limited war was at stake.

According to Colonel Harry Summers, an operations officer in Vietnam, the cold-bloodedness was a result of the academic sources of the theories about limited war. "As we . . . read the writings of the political scientists and systems analysts on limited war, they are noteworthy for their lack of passion. The horror, the bloodshed and the destruction of the battlefield are remarkably absent." He quoted Karl von Clausewitz, the classic theorist of war, who wrote about 150 years ago: "It would be an obvious fallacy to imagine war between civilized peoples as resulting merely from a rational act on the part of the government. . . ." Crackpot rationalism, to paraphrase C. Wright Mills, was understood a very long time ago. Colonel Summers mistakenly believed that the academics could be forgiven for their bloodless rationalism, "but we in the military knew better." The military was guilty of not talking, of cooperating with the deceptions, and of not forcing the issue when the Presidents decided to avoid exciting the middle class.

The belief that the public should coolly and unemotionally support a war was a result of the desire to make the war conform to the technological mind. We were to fight the war for calculated reasons. This was not war as the American people fondly remembered their good wars, especially The Big One. When the people finally became angry, their anger was more often aimed at the Presidents than at the enemy. Americans, as others, need to perceive the enemy's threat, and the threat needs to be real enough to frighten them, and the fright needs to be metabolized into anger. Then they will support war.

A war over ideology is not enough for the people, however exercised over the abstractions the leaders and other "responsible" elites became. These groups believed in abstractions: dominoes, national credibility, and the significance of counterinsurgency. They were merely convinced, not passionate. That is never enough for the people. It is right to insist on becoming fighting mad. Anger could not be factored into the technician's equations.

North Vietnam finally won its war because it was willing to accept more death than we considered rational. That is why the bombing campaigns failed. It is not that our technology failed. Our cultural perceptions failed when so many intelligent men in high positions simply assumed that our enemy's culture was sufficiently like ours that he would quit at a point where we believed we would quit.

We lost the war because we were never clear about the guerrillas, their popular support, the North Vietnamese, or ourselves. Our marvelously clever technology did not help us to understand the war and, in fact, confused us even more because it created our unquestioning faith in our own power. Finally, the North's decision to continue fighting, and our decision to stop, were each consistent with the cultural imperatives of each nation. Because the army of South Vietnam was trained by us to fight in the American style, it was forever dependent on a supply of hardware and fuel. That army was incongruent with the culture it was trying to defend.

This is why the military's continuing claim that we could have won the war if it had been allowed to fight differently is pointless. We could not have fought it differently. The constraints on the tactics of the war, and the absence of a political goal to shape those tactics, were products of American culture at the time. It is meaningless to argue that "next time we'll do it differently and win." The only reasonable prediction about the cultural pressures surrounding a "next time" is that they will at least resemble those that existed in the 1960s and exist now.

Americans continue to believe that managerial expertise and war technology will contribute to the security of the nation and the peace of the world. Such a belief is consistent with who we are, but inconsistent with our experience in Vietnam. We did not know when, where, or how to make use of our tools. It is important to have the right tools. We have them. But it is also important to know when and how to use them. This is why the debate about whether anything useful can be learned from Vietnam is not very enlightening. What we must learn from Vietnam is not tactics or strategy, not technique, but who we are, what our culture requires.

One of the slogans used to tranquilize the people in George Orwell's *Nineteen Eighty-Four* is "Ignorance is Strength." In America since Hiroshima, that slogan turned out to be backward. For postwar America, strength was ignorance. We were so strong, we thought we did not need to know about others. We mistakenly thought we knew ourselves and that was all that mattered. Our power was thought somehow to immunize us against failure, at least against colossal failure.

Because culture creates war, it also creates peace. Some people now argue that the peculiar set of circumstances we encountered in Vietnam will never occur again. There are many ways to remain ignorant about Vietnam. The best way is to remain ignorant about America. Another is to insist that the war was unique, so different from other wars that it holds no important lessons. Every historical event is unique, after all. James Thomson, who resigned from the NSC in 1966, expressed this idea much too cleverly: "The only lesson we should learn from Vietnam is never again to fight a nationalist movement dominated by Communists in a former French colony." This emphasis on Vietnam's uniqueness has three implications: it ignores American culture; it dismisses Vietnam as an aberration; and, it does not prevent future intervention on what is now thought to be the inappropriate model of Vietnam.

For all the criticism that the Vietnam War was unnecessarily militarized, a parallel fact was that America's managerial fetish "civilized" the military. General Westmoreland was the chief bureaucratic supervisor who reported to the bureaucratic Joint Chiefs who reported to Secretary McNamara who wrote the book on bureaucracy in the Defense Department. The symptoms of an increasingly managerial military establishment were evident in the military's conception of itself as just "doing a job," of its men as managers and workers, and its careerism, bureaucratic sensitivities, and fixation on accounting controls and statistical indexes. These are the lasting legacies of Secretary McNamara's indisputably brilliant tenure. The military's overwhelming investment in engineering was (and is) severely criticized. But this emphasis was (and is) consistent with our national values. It produced the weapons. The Pentagon could not do otherwise.

Colonel Summers acknowledged that the job of the political leaders of the war was to provide the political strategy of the war, its reasons and purpose. The job of the systems analysts was to provide the means to accomplish the purpose. What was missing was a military strategy for the use of the available means to accomplish the stated purpose. He thought we had the *why* and the *what,* but not the *how.* Yet, true to his trade, Colonel Summers swept politics under the rug. We could no more answer why we were in Vietnam than we could explain how to use our cascade of weapons. The single great American accomplishment of the war was in supplying the weapons, and that was not enough.

Having weapons without a purpose or a strategy led to the policy of attrition. If we exploded enough bombs and fired enough rounds, we assumed the enemy would quit. At some point, he would have. General Westmoreland always knew where that point was. The alternative to attrition, he said, was "a war of annihilation." The military struggle could have succeeded only if all of Vietnam had been utterly devastated, with the people dead and buried, or at least dead. Someone once said that the military wanted to carry Vietnam away in the ashtrays of its cars. . . .

. . . The military, despite the agony of Vietnam, felt then and feels now that they did not lose the war. They think that victory was denied them by political decisionmakers who liked to play with soldiers.

The argument that civilian interference prevented the military from winning has been widely accepted, with almost half of the American public (and 82 percent of combat vets) agreeing. This easy assignment of blame obviously permits all of us to growl at the politicians and be done with it. But the ticket-punching careerist officers were not invented by civilians. The utter failure to develop military tactics effectively to utilize the technology was not the fault of civilians. The strategy of attrition and the dizzying rotation of officers were not made in Washington. The cover-ups and deceptive optimism were the military's own. The interservice rivalries were not required by politicians. The bureaucratization of William Westmoreland's mind was the military's own. The unwillingness to stop the blizzard of heroin was the military's own. The subversion of the Special Forces, the insistence on using B-52s, and spreading the use of Agent Orange were all military decisions.

It is, however, true that the military could not have "won" the war. Neither it nor the politicians knew what *winning* meant. By sheer force of firepower the military won its battles, but it could never have made these victories add up to victory. What was the military's responsibility for the failure of the Presidents and their aides to formulate a strategy? It was not the fault of the politicians that the leading generals and admirals bit their tongues when their candor was indispensable. Unless, of course, they had nothing to say. Colonel Summers, for one, rejected the military's argument that politicians' meddling prevented a victory: "Our problem was not so much political interference as it was the lack of a coherent military strategy—a lack for which our military leaders share a large burden of responsibility." In any case, the military's traditional emphasis on its own experience and judgment was unavailable to the nation's leaders as the Chiefs routinely snapped off a salute with the standard "Can do, sir!" Wind-up bureaucratic dolls should not complain that others did not let them win.

✗ *F U R T H E R   R E A D I N G*

Mark Baker, *Nam* (1981)
Larry Berman, *Lyndon Johnson's War* (1989)
Douglas S. Blaufarb, *The Counterinsurgency Era* (1977)
Larry E. Cable, *Conflict of Myths* (1986) (on counterinsurgency)
Larry E. Cable, *Unholy Grail: The US and the War in Vietnam, 1965–1968* (1991)
Cincinnatus, *Self-Destruction: The Disintegration and Decay of the United States Army During the Vietnam Era* (1978)
Mark Clodfelter, *The Limits of Air Power: The American Bombing of North Vietnam* (1989)
William E. Colby, *Lost Victory* (1989)
Phillip B. Davidson, *Secrets of the Vietnam War* (1990)
Frederick Downs, *The Killing Zone* (1978)
Robert L. Gallucci, *Neither Peace nor Honor* (1975)
James William Gibson, *The Perfect War* (1986)
Lawrence E. Grinter, "South Vietnam: Pacification Denied," *Southeast Asia Spectrum,* 3 (1975), 49–78
George C. Herring, "American Strategy in Vietnam: The Postwar Debate," *Military Affairs,* 46 (1982), 57–63
Walter L. Hixson, "Containment on the Perimeter: George F. Kennan and Vietnam," *Diplomatic History,* 12 (1988), 149–163
Edwin Hooper et al., *The United States Navy and the Vietnam Conflict* (1976)
Richard A. Hunt and Richard H. Shultz, Jr., *Lessons from an Unconventional War* (1981)
Douglas Kinnard, *The War Managers* (1977)
Andrew F. Krepinevich, Jr., *The Army and Vietnam* (1986)
Guenther Lewy, *America in Vietnam* (1978)
Raphael Littauer and Normal Uphoff, eds., *The Air War in Indochina* (1972)
Robert Mason, *Chickenhawk* (1983)

Drew Middleton, *Air War—Vietnam* (1978)

Harold G. Moore and Joseph L. Galloway, *We Were Soldiers Once . . . And Young* (1992)

Donald J. Mrozek, *Air Power and the Ground War in Vietnam* (1989)

John Mueller, "The Search for the Breaking Point in Vietnam," *Strategic Studies,* 24 (1980), 497–519

Robert E. Osgood, *Limited War Revisited* (1979)

Bruce Palmer, Jr., *The 25-Year War* (1984)

Dave Richard Palmer, *Summons of the Trumpet* (1978)

Gregory Palmer, *The McNamara Strategy and the Vietnam War* (1978)

Bernard W. Roger, *Cedar Falls–Junction City: A Turning Point* (1974)

John Schlight, *The United States Air Force in Southeast Asia* (1988)

Deborah Shapley, *Promise and Power* (1993) (on Robert McNamara)

U. S. Grant Sharp, *Strategy for Defeat* (1978)

Lewis Sorley, *Thunderbolt: General Creighton Abrams and the Army of His Times* (1993)

Shelby L. Stanton, *The Rise and Fall of an American Army* (1985)

James C. Thompson, *Rolling Thunder* (1980)

Earl H. Tilford, Jr., *Crosswinds: The Air Force's Setup in Vietnam* (1993)

Henry L. Trewhitt, *McNamara* (1971)

Francis J. West, *The Village* (1972)

William C. Westmoreland, *A Soldier Reports* (1976)

Robert H. Whitlow, *U.S. Marines in Vietnam* (1976)

CHAPTER

8

The Enemy: North Vietnam and the "Vietcong"

Following the Geneva Conference of 1954, Ho Chi Minh and most of the former Vietminh leadership devoted their energies to the establishment of a socialist state in the territory north of the seventeenth parallel: the Democratic Republic of Vietnam. In the area south of the parallel, Ngo Dinh Diem, with strong American backing, attempted to consolidate his hold on power in the Republic of Vietnam. By 1956, any lingering hope that the all-Vietnam elections promised at Geneva would be held had been dashed, and the two "regroupment areas" increasingly resembled independent countries.

The northern leaders had not abandoned the goal of national unification. Opposition to Diem spread throughout the countryside during the late 1950s; a revolutionary guerrilla movement reemerged in the south at that time, composed in part of former Vietminh cadres. At least by 1960, Hanoi was giving active support to that movement, and in November of that year the National Liberation Front (NLF) was founded as a broad populist coalition that sought to appeal to all groups opposed to Diem's regime.

The nature and extent of Hanoi's involvement in the southern revolution stands as one of the most controversial aspects of the Vietnam War. The issue divided scholars, activists, and policymakers at the height of American involvement, and it continues to spark lively debate. The following questions rank among the most significant: Did North Vietnam orchestrate the revolution in the south from its inception? Were the "Vietcong" guerrillas and the NLF merely puppets of Hanoi? or did the southern revolution have important internal roots? How and why did the Vietcong gain such a strong foothold in the countryside so quickly? Did the communist program appeal to the peasants, and, if so, how? What role, if any, did the Soviet Union and China play in the deepening conflict in Vietnam? Finally, from the perspective of the United States, who were America's principal enemies in Vietnam?

✗ D O C U M E N T S

After the conclusion of the Geneva Agreements, Ho Chi Minh urged all Vietnamese to comply with their provisions. His appeal of July 22, 1954, appears as the first document. In the second reading, Troung Nhu Tang, an opponent of the Diem regime, recalls the events that led to the formation of the National Liberation Front. The NLF's manifesto of December 1960, the third selection, reflected the organization's interest in attracting the broadest possible coalition in opposition to the Diem government.

The next two documents present personal testimony from peasants who were recruited by Vietcong cadres in the early 1960s. Nguyen Tan Thanh, who eventually rose to become a senior captain and deputy commander in the main forces of the Vietcong, explains how the land question prompted his decision to join the insurgency. Le Ly Hayslip, in an excerpt from her remarkable memoir *When Heaven and Earth Changed Places,* recounts how an innocent young girl metamorphosed into a dedicated Vietcong supporter.

In the sixth document, dating from 1961, Vo Nguyen Giap spells out the essential strategy of what he called a "people's war," insisting that even an insufficiently equipped people's army, by devising right tactics and strategy, could defeat a modern army. Nguyen Chi Thanh, a South Vietnamese communist who would later command all communist forces in the south, offered a similarly optimistic perspective in an article published in July 1963, reproduced here as the seventh document. He stressed that a powerful North Vietnam and an effective revolutionary movement in the south were mutually complementary and required careful coordination. In the final document, a speech delivered over Radio Hanoi on July 17, 1966, Ho displays characteristic determination in the face of growing American military pressure.

Ho Chi Minh's Appeal After the Geneva Agreements, 1954

The Geneva Conference has come to an end. It is a great victory for our diplomacy.

On behalf of the Government, I cordially make the following appeal:

1. For the sake of peace, unity, independence, and democracy of the Fatherland, our people, armymen, cadres, and Government have, during these eight years or so, joined in a monolithic bloc, endured hardship, and resolutely overcome all difficulties to carry out the Resistance; we have won many brilliant victories. On this occasion, on behalf of the Government, I cordially congratulate you, from North to South. I respectfully bow to the memory of the armymen and people who have sacrificed their lives for the Fatherland, and send my homages of comfort to the wounded and sick armymen.

This great victory is also due to the support given us in our just struggle by the peoples of our brother countries, by the French people, and by the peace-loving people of the world.

Thanks to these victories and the efforts made by the delegation of the Soviet Union at the Berlin Conference, negotiations were opened between our country and France at the Geneva Conference. At this conference, the struggle of our delegation and the assistance given by the delegations of the Soviet Union and China have ended in a great victory for us: The French Government has recognized the independence, sovereignty, unity, and territorial integrity of our country; it has agreed to withdraw French troops from our country, etc.

From now on, we must make every effort to consolidate peace and achieve reunification, independence, and democracy throughout our country.

2. In order to re-establish peace, the first step to take is that the armed forces of both parties should cease fire.

The regroupment in two regions is a temporary measure; it is a transitional step for the implementation of the armistice and restoration of peace, and paves the way for national reunification through general elections. Regroupment in regions is in no way a partition of our country, neither is it an administrative division.

During the armistice, our army is regrouped in the North; the French troops are regrouped in the South, that is to say, there is a change of regions. A number of regions which were formerly occupied by the French now become our free zones. Vice versa, a number of regions formerly liberated by us will now be temporarily occupied by the French troops before they leave for France.

This is a necessity; North, Central, and South Viet-Nam are territories of ours. Our country will certainly be unified, our entire people will surely be liberated.

Our compatriots in the South were the first to wage the war of Resistance. They possess a high political consciousness. I am confident that they will place national interests above local interests, permanent interests above temporary interests, and join their efforts with the entire people in strengthening peace, achieving unity, independence, and democracy all over the country. The Party, Government, and I always follow the efforts of our people and we are sure that our compatriots will be victorious.

3. The struggle to consolidate peace and achieve reunification, independence, and democracy is also a long and hard struggle. In order to carry the day, our people, armymen, and cadres from North to South must unite closely. They must be at one in thought and deed.

We are resolved to abide by the agreements entered into with the French Government. At the same time, we demand that the French Government correctly implement the agreements they have signed with us.

We must do our utmost to strengthen peace and be vigilant to check the maneuvers of peace wreckers.

We must endeavor to struggle for the holding of free general elections throughout the country to reunify our territory.

We must exert all our efforts to restore, build, strengthen, and develop our forces in every field so as to attain complete independence.

We must do our utmost to carry out social reforms in order to improve our people's livelihood and realize genuine democracy.

We further tighten our fraternal relations with Cambodia and Laos.

We strengthen the great friendship between us and the Soviet Union, China, and other brother countries. To maintain peace, we enhance our solidarity with the French people, the Asian people, and people all over the world.

4. I call on all our compatriots, armymen, and cadres to follow strictly the lines and policies laid down by the Party and Government, to struggle for the consolidation of peace and the achievement of national reunification, independence, and democracy throughout the country.

I eagerly appeal to all genuine patriots, irrespective of their social class, creed, political stand, and former affiliation, to cooperate sincerely with us and fight for the sake of our country and our people so as to bring about peace and achieve reunification, independence, and democracy for our beloved Viet-Nam.

If our people are as one, if thousands of men are like one, victory will certainly be ours.

Long live a peaceful, unified, independent, and democratic Viet-Nam.

Truong Nhu Tang on the Origins of the National Liberation Front (1957–1959), 1985

By the time 1957 merged into 1958, Ngo Dinh Diem had exhausted the patient hopefulness that had initially greeted his presidency. From the first he had moved ruthlessly to consolidate his personal power, crushing the private army of the Binh Xuyen,* then subduing the armed religious sects. From there he attacked those suspected of communist sympathies in what was called the To Cong ("Denounce the Communists") campaign, jailing and executing thousands who had fought against the French. Each of these moves was carried out with surprising energy, and in their own terms they succeeded. As he surveyed the political landscape three years after assuming power, Diem could see no well-organized centers of opposition to his rule. The National Assembly was wholly dominated by his brother's National Revolutionary Movement, the troublesome private armies had been severely handled, and the Communist-dominated resistance veterans were cowed and in disarray.

But Diem's successes had all been of a negative sort. Though he had asserted his authority and gained time, he had done nothing about establishing positive programs to meet the nation's economic and social needs. He had not used the time he had gained. After three years it was apparent that the new president was a powermonger, not a builder. For those who could see, the fatal narrowness of his political understanding was already evident.

---

* A tightly run organized crime syndicate that controlled underworld activities in Saigon and Cholon and was not adverse to injecting itself into politics.

Excerpt from *A Vietcong Memoir,* Copyright © 1985 by Truong Nhu Tang, David Chanoff, and Doan Van Toai, reprinted by permission of Harcout Brace & Co.

In the first place, Diem's armed enemies had for the most part only been mauled, not destroyed. Elements of the defeated sect armies went underground, licking their wounds and looking for allies. Gradually they began to link up with groups of former Vietminh fighters fleeing from the To Cong suppression. The core of a guerrilla army was already in the making.

Even as old enemies regrouped, Diem was busy adding new ones. In the countryside he destroyed at a blow the dignity and livelihood of several hundred thousand peasants by canceling the land-redistribution arrangements instituted by the Vietminh in areas they had controlled prior to 1954. He might have attempted to use American aid to compensate owners and capitalize on peasant goodwill; instead he courted the large landholders. Farmers who had been working land they considered theirs, often for years, now faced demands for back rent and exorbitant new rates. It was an economic disaster for them.

In 1957 Diem promulgated his own version of land reform, ostensibly making acreage available, though only to peasants who could pay for it. But even this reform was carried out primarily on paper. In the provinces it was sabotaged everywhere by landowners acting with official connivance. The result of all this was a frustrated and indignant peasantry, fertile ground for anti-Diem agitation.

Meanwhile, the city poor were tasting their own ration of misery. In Saigon the government pursued "urban development" with a vengeance, dispossessing whole neighborhoods in favor of modern commercial buildings and expensive apartments, which could only be utilized by Americans and the native upper classes. Not a few times, poorer quarters were completely razed by uncontrollable fires (Khanh Hoi and Phu Nuan were particularly calamitous examples). Few thought these fires were accidental; they were too closely followed by massive new construction. The displaced moved onto sampans on the river or to poorer, even more distant districts. In the slums and shanty villages resentment against the Americans mixed with a simmering anger toward the regime.

In the highland regions of the Montagnards too, Diem's policies were cold-blooded and destructive. Attempting to make the tribespeople more accessible to government control, troops and cadres forced village populations down out of the mountains and into the valleys—separating them from their ancestral lands and graves. In Ban Me Thuot and other areas, the ingrained routines of social life were profoundly disrupted by these forced relocations, which seemed to the tribespeople nothing more than inexplicable cruelty.

By the end of 1958, Diem had succeeded brilliantly in routing his enemies and arrogating power. But he had also alienated large segments of the South Vietnamese population, creating a swell of animosity throughout the country. Almost unknown at first, in a few short years he had made himself widely detested, a dictator who could look for support only to the Northern Catholic refugees and to those who made money from his schemes. Most damning of all, he had murdered many patriots who had fought in the struggle against France and had tied his existence to the patronage of the United States, France's successor. To many nationalist-minded Vietnamese, whose emotions were those of people just emerging from a hundred years of subjection to foreigners, Diem had forfeited all claims to loyalty.

In light of Diem's conduct of the presidency, two facts were clear: First, the country had settled into an all too familiar pattern of oligarchic rule and utter disregard for the welfare of the people. Second, subservience to foreigners was still the order of the day. We had a ruler whose overriding interest was power and who would use the Americans to prop himself up—even while the Americans were using him for their own strategic purposes.

As far as I was concerned, this situation was intolerable. Replacing the French despots with a Vietnamese one was not a significant advance. It would never lead to either the broad economic progress or the national dignity which I (along with many others) had been brooding about for years. Among my circle of friends there was anger and profound disappointment over this turn of events. We were living, we felt, in historic times. A shameful, century-long era had just been violently closed out, and a new nation was taking shape before our eyes. Many of us agreed that we could not acquiesce in the shape it was taking. If we were not to be allowed a say about it from within the government, we would have to speak from without.

By the end of 1958, those of us who felt this way decided to form an extralegal political organization, complete with a program and plan of action. We had not moved toward this decision quickly; it was an undertaking of immense magnitude, which would require years of effort before giving us the strength to challenge Diem's monopoly on power. To some, that prospect seemed quixotic at best. But most of us felt we had little choice.

From casual discussions, we began to meet in slightly more formal groups, sometimes only a few of us, sometimes eight or ten together. Two doctors, Duong Quynh Hoa and Phung Van Cung, took active roles, as did Nguyen Huu Khuong, a factory owner, Trinh Dinh Thao, a lawyer, and the architect Huynh Tan Phat. We were joined by Nguyen Van Hieu and Ung Ngoc Ky, who were lycee teachers, and other friends such as Nguyen Long and Tran Buu Kiem. Our first order of business was to identify and make contact with potential allies for what we knew would be a long and bitter struggle.

To do this we formed what we called the mobilization committee, whose members were myself, Hieu, Kiem, Ky, Long, Cung, and architect Phat. Through friends, relatives, business and political contacts we began to establish a network of people who felt as we did about Diem and his policies. Phat and a few of the others were old resisters and had kept their ties with fellow veterans of the French war, many of whom were hiding with friends and family from the To Cong hunters. They too were beginning to organize, and they had colleagues and sympathizers in every social stratum throughout the country. They were natural allies.

Among us we also had people with close ties to the sects, the legal political parties, the Buddhists. In each group we made overtures, and everywhere we discovered sympathy and backing. Sometimes individuals would indicate their desire to participate actively. More often we would receive assurances of quiet solidarity. At the same time, we sent Nguyen Van Hieu to Hanoi to begin working out a channel of support from our Northern compatriots.

At each stage we discussed carefully the ongoing search for allies, wary about how to gather support and still retain our own direction and freedom of action. It was a delicate and crucial problem, of the utmost complexity. The overwhelming strength of our enemy urged us to acquire whatever assistance we could, from whatever source. In addition, the anticolonial war had not simply ended in 1954; a residual Vietminh infrastructure was still in place and was beginning to come alive again. For better or worse, our endeavor was meshed into an ongoing historical movement for independence that had already developed its own philosophy and means of action. Of this movement, Ho Chi Minh was the spiritual father, in the South as well as the North, and we looked naturally to him and to his government for guidance and aid. . . . And yet, this struggle was also our own. Had Ngo Dinh Diem proved a man of breadth and vision, the core of people who filled the NLF and its sister organizations would have rallied to him. As it was, the South Vietnamese nationalists were driven to action by his contempt for the principles of independence and social progress in which they believed. In this sense, the Southern revolution was generated of itself, out of the emotions, conscience, and aspirations of the Southern people.

The complexity of the struggle was mirrored in the makeup of our group. Most were not Lao Dong ("Workers' Party"—the official name of the Vietnamese Communist Party) members; many scarcely thought of themselves as political, at least in any ideological way. Our allies among the resistance veterans were also largely nationalist rather than political (though they had certainly been led and monitored by the Party). But we also had Party activists among us, some open, some surreptitious. Tran Buu Kiem, the architect Phat, and the teachers Hieu and Ky I knew as politically-minded individuals, who had been leaders of the New Democratic Party during their student years at Hanoi University in the early forties. This militant student union had been absorbed by the Lao Dong in 1951, some of its members enrolling in the Party, some defecting altogether, some simply accepting the change in leadership without themselves becoming Communists. What I didn't know was that Phat had been a secret Party member since 1940 while Hieu, Ky, and Kiem had rallied to the Party in 1951.

But I was not overly concerned at that point about potential conflicts between the Southern nationalists and the ideologues. We were allies in this fight, or so I believed. We needed each other, and the closest ties of background, family, and patriotism united us in respect for each other's purposes. This was my reading of the situation in 1959 as the yet-to-be-named National Liberation Front gathered momentum. I was not alone in drawing this conclusion. And I was not the only one whom time would disabuse.

Manifesto of the National Liberation Front, 1960

Compatriots in the country and abroad!

Over the past hundred years the Vietnamese people repeatedly rose up to fight against foreign aggression for the independence and freedom of their fatherland. In 1945, the people throughout the country surged up in an armed uprising, overthrew the Japanese and French domination and seized power. When the French colonialists invaded our country for the second time, our compatriots, determined not to be enslaved again, shed much blood and laid down many lives to defend their national sovereignty and independence. Their solidarity and heroic struggle during nine years led the resistance war to victory. The 1954 Geneva Agreements restored peace in our country and recognized "the sovereignty, independence, unity and territorial integrity of Viet Nam."

Our compatriots in South Viet Nam would have been able to live in peace, to earn their livelihood in security and to build a decent and happy life.

However, the American imperialists, who had in the past helped the French colonialists to massacre our people, have now replaced the French in enslaving the southern part of our country through a disguised colonial regime. They have been using their stooge—the Ngo Dinh Diem administration—in their downright repression and exploitation of our compatriots, in their maneuvres to permanently divide our country and to turn its southern part into a military base in preparation for war in Southeast Asia.

The aggressors and traitors, working hand in glove with each other, have set up an extremely cruel dictatorial rule. They persecute and massacre democratic and patriotic people, and abolish all human liberties. They ruthlessly exploit the workers, peasants and other labouring people, strangle the local industry and trade, poison the minds of our people with a depraved foreign culture, thus degrading our national culture, traditions and ethics. They feverishly increase their military forces, build military bases, use the army as an instrument for repressing the people and serving the US imperialists' scheme to prepare an aggressive war.

Never, over the past six years, have gun shots massacring our compatriots ceased to resound throughout South Viet Nam. Tens of thousands of patriots here have been murdered and hundreds of thousands thrown into jail. All sections of the people have been living in a stifling atmosphere under the iron heel of the US-Diem clique. Countless families have been torn away and scenes of mourning are seen everywhere as a result of unemployment, poverty, exacting taxes, terror, massacre, drafting of manpower and pressganging, usurpation of land, forcible house removal, and herding of the people into "prosperity zones," "resettlement centres" and other forms of concentration camps.

High anger with the present tyrannical regime is boiling among all strata of the people. Undaunted in the face of barbarous persecution, our compatriots are determined to unite and struggle unflaggingly against the US imperialists' policy of aggression and the dictatorial and nepotic regime of the Ngo Dinh Diem clique. Among workers, peasants and other toiling people, among intellectuals, students and pupils, industrialists and traders, religious sects and national minorities, patriotic activities are gaining in scope and strength, seriously shaking the US-Diem dictatorial regime.

The attempted coup d'etat of November 11, 1960 in Saigon in some respects reflected the seething anger among the people and armymen, and the rottenness and decline of the US-Diem regime. However, there were among the leaders of this coup political speculators who, misusing the patriotism of the armymen, preferred negotiation and compromise rather than to overthrow Ngo Dinh Diem. Like Ngo Dinh Diem, they persisted in following the pro-American and traitorous path, and also used the anti-communist signboard to oppose the people. That is why the coup was not supported by the people and large numbers of armymen and, consequently, ended in failure.

At present, our people are urgently demanding an end to the cruel dictatorial rule; they are demanding independence and democracy, enough food and clothing, and peaceful reunification of the country.

To meet the aspirations of our compatriots, the *South Viet Nam National Front for Liberation* came into being, pledging itself to shoulder the historic task of liberating our people from the present yoke of slavery.

The *South Viet Nam National Front for Liberation* undertakes to unite all sections of the people, all social classes, nationalities, political parties, organizations, religious communities and patriotic personalities, without distinction of their political tendencies in order to struggle for the overthrow of the rule of the US imperialists and their stooges—the Ngo Dinh Diem clique—and for the realization of independence, democracy, peace and neutrality pending the peaceful reunification of the fatherland.

The *South Viet Nam National Front for Liberation* calls on the entire people to unite and heroically rise up as one man to fight along the line of a program of action summarized as follows:

1. To overthrow the disguised colonial regime of the US imperialists and the dictatorial Ngo Dinh Diem administration—lackey of the United States—, and to form a national democratic coalition administration.

2. To bring into being a broad and progressive democracy, promulgate freedom of expression, of the press, of belief, of assembly, of association, of movement and other democratic freedoms. To grant general amnesty to all political detainees, dissolve all concentration camps dubbed "prosperity zones" and "resettlement centres," abolish the fascist 10–59 law and other anti-democratic laws.

3. To abolish the economic monopoly of the United States and its henchmen, to protect home-made products, encourage home industry and trade, expand agriculture and build an independent and sovereign economy. To provide jobs for the unemployed, increase wages for workers, armymen and office employees. To abolish arbitrary fines and apply an equitable and rational tax system. To help those who have gone South to return to their native places if they so desire, and to provide jobs for those among them who want to remain in the South.

4. To carry out land rent reduction, guarantee the peasants' right to till present plots of land, redistribute communal land and advance toward land reform.

5. To do away with enslaving and depraved US-style culture, build a national and progressive culture and education. To wipe out illiteracy, open more schools, carry out reforms in the educational and examination system.

6. To abolish the system of American military advisers, eliminate foreign military bases in Viet Nam and build a national army for the defence of the fatherland and the people.

7. To guarantee equality between men and women and among different nationalities, and the right to autonomy of the national minorities; to protect the legitimate interests of foreign residents in Viet Nam; to protect and take care of the interests of Vietnamese living abroad.

8. To carry out a foreign policy of peace and neutrality, to establish diplomatic relations with all countries which respect the independence and sovereignty of Viet Nam.

9. To re-establish normal relations between the two zones, pending the peaceful reunification of the fatherland.

10. To oppose aggressive war; to actively defend world peace.

Compatriots!

Ours are a heroic people with a tradition of unity and indomitable struggle. We cannot let our country be plunged into darkness and mourning. We are determined to shatter the fetters of slavery, and wrest back independence and freedom.

Let us all rise up and unite!

Let us close our ranks and fight under the banner of the *South Viet Nam National Front for Liberation* to overthrow the rule of the US imperialists and Ngo Dinh Diem—their henchmen.

Workers, peasants and other toiling people! The oppression and misery which are now heavily weighing on you must be ended. You have the strength of tens of millions of people. Stand up enthusiastically to save your families and our fatherland.

Intellectuals! The dictatorial rulers have stripped us of the most elementary human rights. You are living in humiliation and misery. For our great cause, stand up resolutely!

Industrialists and traders! A country under the sway of foreign sharks cannot have an independent and sovereign economy. You should join in the people's struggle.

Compatriots of all national minorities! Compatriots of all religious communities! Unity is life, disunity is death. Smash all US-Diem schemes of division. Side with the entire people in the struggle for independence, freedom and equality among all nationalities.

Notables! The interests of the nation are above all else. Support actively the struggle for the overthrow of the cruel aggressors and traitors.

Patriotic officers and soldiers! You have arms in your hands. Listen to the sacred call of the fatherland. Be definitely on the side of the people. Your compatriots have faith in your patriotism.

Young men and women! You are the future of the nation. You should devote your youthful ardour to serving the fatherland.

Compatriots living abroad! Turn your thoughts toward the beloved fatherland, contribute actively to the sacred struggle for national liberation.

At present the movement for peace, democracy and national independence is surging up throughout the world. Colonialism is irretrievably disintegrating. The time when the imperialists could plunder and subjugate the people at will is over. This situation is extremely favourable for the struggle to free South Viet Nam from the yoke of the US imperialists and their stooges. Peace-loving and progressive people in the world are supporting us. Justice is on our side, and we have the prodigious strength of the unity of our entire people. We will certainly win! The US imperialist aggressors and the Ngo Dinh Diem traitorous clique will certainly be defeated. The cause of liberation of South Viet Nam will certainly triumph.

Compatriots around the country!

Let us write and march forward confidently and valiantly to score brilliant victories for our people and our fatherland!

A Vietcong Recruit Explains Why He Joined the Revolution (1961), 1986

I joined the VC [Vietcong] when I was thirty-five years old. I was married and had four children. I was leasing farmland—one hectare [about 2.5 acres]—that was very poor in quality, almost sterile. That was why the owner rented it out to us. Despite working hard all year round, we got only about 100 *gia* of rice out of it. Of this amount, 40 *gia* went to the landlord. We borrowed money to buy ducks and geese. We lived a very hard life. But I cultivated the land carefully, and in time it became fertile. When it did, the owner took it back; my livelihood was gone. I had to go back to my parents, to raise ducks for my father.

I was poor. I had lost my land and I didn't have enough money to take care of my children. In 1961 propaganda cadres of the Front [National Liberation Front] contacted me. These guys had joined the resistance against the French, and after Geneva they had stayed underground in the South. They came to all the poor farmers and made an analysis of the poor and rich classes. They said that the rich people had always served the French and had used the authority of the French to oppress the poor. The majority of the people were poor, not because they wasted their money but because they had been exploited by the landlords who had worked with the French. In the past, the ancestors of the poor had broken ground for tillage. Then powerful people had seized their land. Without any other means to live, the poor had become slaves of the landlords. The cadres told us that if the poor people don't stand up the rich people, we would be dominated by

Nguyen Tan Thanh interview, from *Portrait of the Enemy* by David Chanoff and Doan Van Toai, pp. 42–43. Copyright © 1986 by David Chanoff and Doan Van Toai. Reprinted by permission of Random House Inc.

them forever. The only way to ensure freedom and a sufficient life was to overthrow them.

When I heard the cadres, I thought that what they said was correct. In my village there were about forty-three hundred people. Of these, maybe ten were landlords. The richest owned five hundred hectares [1,236 acres], and the others had at least twenty hectares [49 acres] apiece. The rest of the people were tenants or honest poor farmers. I knew that the rich oppressed the poor. The poor had nothing to eat, and they also had no freedom. We had to get rid of the regime that allowed a few people to use their money and authority to oppress the others.

So I joined the Liberation Front. I followed the VC to fight for freedom and prosperity for the country. I felt that this was right.

A South Vietnamese Peasant Girl Becomes a Vietcong Supporter (c. 1961), 1989

Before I was twelve and knew better, I played war games with the children in my village. These games were popular because we had been taught since birth that the legendary king, Dinh Bo Linh, had won his crown by excelling at such things. So, like children everywhere, we copied what we admired. Some of us pretended to be Republican soldiers (who were just like surly policemen), while others would be Viet Cong, whom we supposed were only gangsters. When one force was too badly outnumbered, some of us switched sides, although others refused to play the game at all unless a certain person was "the enemy" or was "on my side"—whichever side that happened to be on that day. The old war between the Viet Minh and the French seemed a lifetime away (it had been many years since Ky La had seen fighting and the village, in fact, had been renamed "Binh Ky" by the new Republic as part of its total break with the past), and armies of this new war, the Viet Cong and the Republic, were both filled with Vietnamese. "How bad can this be?" we asked ourselves during rests between mock battles. "A family feud? A spat between brothers?" We had seen plenty of those in our own families. We could not imagine such a war to be real.

Still, I never enjoyed the game. When I played a Republican, I always imagined that the laughing face at the end of my stick-rifle was my brother Bon Nghe, who had gone to Hanoi and who might one day come back to fight around Ky La. When I played a Viet Cong, I could think only of my sister Ba in Danang, who, being married to a policeman, locked her door every night out of fear of "those terrorists" who blew up power stations and cars and took potshots at the officials for whom her husband worked. I could not accept the idea that either my brother or sister must somehow become my enemy.

From *When Heaven and Earth Changed Places* by Le Ly Hayslip, pp. 35–37, 41–42. Copyright © 1989 by Le Ly Hayslip and Charles Jay Wurts. Used by permission of Doubleday, a division of Bantam Doubleday Dell Publishing Group, Inc.

In school, the pressure to make sides was enormous. Our teacher, a villager named Manh, who was paid by the government, asked us, "What will you do if you see a Viet Cong, or hear about someone who's helping them?" We answered in chorus, "Turn him in to the soldier!" Manh praised us for our answer and told us that the Republicans would pay our families big rewards for every Viet Cong we helped them capture. Still, when we played among ourselves, there was no shortage of Viet Cong fighters, and the children who pretended to be Republicans usually did so halfheartedly. . . .

The first time I saw a Viet Cong fighter close up it was just about dark and I was cleaning up our kitchen. I happened to gaze out the window to the house next door, which (although it was owned by Manh, who had been my teacher) was often used by villagers for gambling. Without a sound, a half-dozen strangers scampered into Manh's house and then shouted "Nobody move!" The oil lamp in Manh's window went out and people began running from the house. At first I thought it was Republican soldiers raiding the gamblers, as they had done several times before, but it soon became obvious that this was not that kind of raid.

Manh was the last one out, led at gunpoint with his hands atop his head. I could hear this familiar voice arguing with the strangers: "But—I don't know what you're talking about!" and "Why? Who told you that?" I leaned into the window to get a better view when I saw one of the strangers standing just outside. He wore black garments, like everyone else, and had on a conical sun hat, even though it was already dark. His sandals were made from old tires and his weapon had a queer, curved ammunition clip that jutted down from the stock like a banana. He seemed to be keeping an eye on the dusty road that ran by Manh's house and he was so close to me that I was afraid to run away or even duck down for fear that he would hear me.

Suddenly one of the strangers barked an order in an odd, clipped accent (I found out later this was how everyone talked in the North) and two of his *comrades* prodded Manh to the edge of the road. I could still hear Manh begging for his life when two rifle shots cut him short. The strangers then ran a Viet Cong flag up the pole that stood outside our schoolhouse and left as quickly as they had come. The leader shouted over his shoulder: "Anyone who touches that flag will get the same thing as that traitor!"

The guard who was standing by my window glanced over and gave me a wink, showing he knew I had been there all the time and had learned the lesson he had come to teach; he then followed his troop into the night. The handsome, cocky face beneath the sun hat reminded me of my brother Bon Nghe, but it stimulated me the way my thoughts of brother Bon never did.

By now all the villagers were out of their houses, staring curiously into the darkness and chattering wildly among themselves. Manh's wife ran with her relatives to the road and retrieved his body while his six children— two of whom had been my playmates—looked after them, too stunned to leave their house or even to cry. Finally, the youngest called out her father's name and ran off, just as my own father's hand fell upon my shoulder.

"Bay Ly," he said quietly—with none of the alarm I heard in the other voices. "Do you know what you've just seen?"

"My teacher—" I said, suddenly aware of the catch in my throat, "they killed him! The Viet Cong shot him! But he was nice to us! He never hurt anyone!"

"He was Catholic," my father said, sounding like a teacher himself. "And a follower of President Diem. He talked too much about how Buddhists were ruining the country."

"But we're Buddhists, Father! He never said bad things about us!"

"No." My father cradled my head against his chest. "But what he said endangered others—and some of those people lost their lives. I am sorry for Manh and his wife and children. But Manh's own careless words got him into trouble. We'll give him a decent burial, but you remember what you've seen—especially when you think about talking again to the soldiers."

On the very next day, the Republicans came back to Ky La—more than we'd ever seen—with trucks full of steel girders and cement and barbed wire. They chopped down the Viet Cong flag and told the farmers to build defenses around the village. The ditches left over from the French occupation, now overgrown with weeds, were made deeper and bamboo trees were cut down to make spikes and watchtowers. During the weeks of construction, the soldiers told us to stay indoors and keep our houses dark at night. As soon as the sun went down, the Republicans set up ambushes around the village and waited for the dogs to bark—a sure sign that intruders were lurking outside.

But nothing happened. After a while, the Republican troops pulled out and left us in the hands of the "Popular Force"—the *Dan De*—local villagers who had been given small arms and a little training in how to use them. Because the war seemed to leave with the soldiers, the PF officials declared peace and Ky La, despite its new necklace of stakes and barbed wire, tried very hard to believe them.

Unfortunately, the peace didn't last very long. A few days later, my father awakened me in the middle of the night and took us to the place where the Republicans had left their biggest cache of materials, including some long metal poles. Within a few minutes, we were joined by most of our neighbors. One PF officer said, "Here—take these poles and hide them so that the Republicans won't find them. Our fighters need them for protection against enemy tanks."

Without further discussion, we took as many poles as we could carry and hurried off to bury them outside our house. "Oh yes," the PF officer added. "If you have a watchdog, give him to a relative out of town or boil him up for supper. We can't have any dogs barking the next time our freedom fighters come to the village!"

Although I wanted badly to ask my father what was happening, I obediently helped him carry some twenty poles to our house. By the time we finished burying them, a huge bonfire had been started in a clearing behind our house, with most of the villagers—including the children—collected around it. In the light of the dancing flames, I recognized the handsome Viet Cong soldier who had winked at me on the night my teacher Manh was killed. He just strolled along, cradling his weapon, wearing the amused smile I'd seen many young men wear when they eyed pretty girls at the market. The Viet Cong cadre, and many of the villagers, piled onto the fire everything the Republicans had given them to defend the village—bamboo stakes, fence posts, and thatching from the watchtowers. The only thing that was spared was the material from our half-completed schoolhouse.

"Save the school!" the cadre leader told us in his funny Northern accent. "Your children need their education but we will teach them what they should know. The first thing they must learn is that on this night, Ky La was saved." He gestured to the black-uniformed troops around the fire, "We are the soldiers of liberation! That is how you will call us. We are here to fight for our land, and our country! Help us stop the foreign aggression and you will have peace. Help us win and you will keep your property and everything else you love. Ky La is *our* village now—and yours. We have given it back to you."

As he spoke, another soldier ran yet another Viet Cong flag up the pole beside the schoolhouse.

"Know where your bunkers are, comrades, and be ready to fill them soon! The battle is on its way!"

The Viet Cong soldiers who had up to this time been everywhere in the village—ripping down the Republican construction and prodding the villagers out to the meetings—now fell into ranks behind their leader. As they moved into the jungle, the leader turned and told us, "Down the road you will find two traitors. I trust they are the last we will see in Ky La. We must leave now, but you will see us again.". . .

When the Viet Cong could not be found (they spent most of their time, after all, hiding in caverns underground with entrances hidden by cookstoves, bushes, false floors, or even underwater by flowing rivers themselves), the Republican soldiers took out their frustration on us: arresting nearby farmers and beating or shooting them on the spot, or carting anyone who looked suspicious off to jail. As these actions drove even more villagers to the Viet Cong cause, more and more of our houses were modified for Viet Cong use. The cadremen told us that each family must have a place in which liberation troops could hide, so my father dug an underground tunnel beneath our heavy cookpot which could house half a dozen fighters. While my father and other villages worked on their tunnels, we children were taken to a clearing beyond the village graveyard, on the threshold of the swamp, where we were taught revolutionary songs. One of the first we learned was in praise of Uncle Ho—Ho Chi Minh—who, we were told, awaited news of our heroism like a kindly grandfather:

> The full moon shines on our land,
> So that we can sing and dance
> And make wishes for Uncle Ho.
> Uncle Ho—we wish you a long life!
> We wish you a long beard that we can stroke
> While you hold us in your arms
> And tell us how much you love us and our country!

We were also taught what we were expected to do for our village, our families, and the revolution. If we were killed, we were told we would live on in history. We learned that, like the French, men of another race called *Americans* wanted to enslave us. "Their allies are the traitorous Republicans of Ngo Dinh Diem!" the Viet Cong shouted. "Just as our fathers fought against the French and their colonial administrators, so must we now fight against these new invaders and their running dogs!" We learned that cheating, stealing from, and lying to Republican soldiers and their allies were not crimes, and that failing to do these things, if the situation demanded it, was treason of the highest sort. Girls were shown the pattern of the Viet Cong flag—half blue (for the North—the direction of peace), half red (for the bloody South), with a yellow star (for the union of yellow-skinned people) in between—and told to sew as many as they could for use in demonstrations or whenever one was asked for by a fighter. Even when the hated Republicans were in our village and our flag could not be displayed, we were to fly it proudly in our hearts. We then sang songs to celebrate those brothers and fathers that went north to Hanoi in 1954. I sang loudly and thought of Bon Nghe and knew he would be proud.

Although it was nearly dawn when I got home from the first meeting, my parents were still awake. They asked what I'd been doing and I told them proudly that I was now part of the "political cadre"—although I had no idea what that meant. I told them we were to keep an eye on our neighbors and make sure the liberation leaders knew if anyone spoke to the hated Republicans. I told my mother to rejoice, that when her son—my beloved brother Bon—came back from Hanoi, he would be a leader in the South, just as the leaders of our own cadre had been trained in Hanoi and now were helping our village gain victory over the invaders.

Although my mother was not sure that my involvement with the cadre was a good idea, she seemed happy that through them, somehow, Bon's return might be hastened. My father, however, looked at me with an expression I had never seen before and said nothing. Although Ky La's first big battle had yet to be fought, it was as if he had seen, in my shining, excited, determined little face, the first casualty of our new war.

Vo Nguyen Giap on People's War, 1961

The Vietnamese people's war of liberation was a just war, aiming to win back the independence and unity of the country, to bring land to our peasants and guarantee them the right to it, and to defend the achievements of the August Revolution. That is why it was first and foremost a people's war. To educate, mobilise, organise and arm the whole people in order that they might take part in the Resistance was a crucial question.

The enemy of the Vietnamese nation was aggressive imperialism, which had to be overthrown. But the latter having long since joined up with the feudal landlords, the anti-imperialist struggle could definitely not be separated from anti-feudal action. On the other hand, in a backward colonial country such as ours where the peasants make up the majority of the population, a people's war is essentially a peasant's war under the leadership of the working class. Owing to this fact, a general mobilisation of the whole people is neither more nor less than the mobilisation of the rural masses. The problem of land is of decisive importance. From an exhaustive analysis, the Vietnamese people's war of liberation was essentially a people's national democratic revolution carried out under armed form and had a twofold fundamental task: the overthrowing of imperialism and the defeat of the feudal landlord class, the anti-imperialist struggle being the primary task.

A backward colonial country which had only just risen up to proclaim its independence and install people's power, Viet Nam only recently possessed armed forces, equipped with still very mediocre arms and having no combat experience. Her enemy, on the other hand, was an imperialist power [France] which has retained a fairly considerable economic and military potentiality despite the recent German occupation [during World War II] and benefited, furthermore, from the active support of the United States. The balance of forces decidedly showed up our weaknesses against the enemy's power. The Vietnamese people's war of liberation had, therefore, to be a hard and long-lasting war in order to succeed in creating conditions for victory. All the conceptions born of impatience and aimed at obtaining speedy victory could only be gross errors. It was necessary to firmly grasp the strategy of a long-term resistance, and to exalt the will to be self-supporting in order to maintain and gradually augment our forces, while nibbling at and progressively destroying those of the enemy; it was necessary to accumulate thousands of small victories to turn them into a great success, thus gradually altering the balance of forces, in transforming our weakness into power and carrying off final victory.

At an early stage, our Party was able to discern the characteristics of this war: a people's war and a long-lasting war, and it was by proceeding from these premises that, during the whole of hostilities and in particularly difficult conditions, the Party solved all the problems of the Resistance. This judicious leadership by the Party led us to victory.

From the point of view of directing operations, our *strategy and tactics had to be those of a people's war and of a long-term resistance.*

Our strategy was, as we have stressed, to wage a long-lasting battle. A war of this nature in general entails several phases; in principle, starting from a stage of contention, it goes through a period of equilibrium before arriving at a general counter-offensive. In effect, the way in which it is carried on can be more subtle and more complex, depending on the particular conditions obtaining on both sides during the course of operations. Only a long-term war could enable us to utilise to the maximum our political trump cards, to overcome our material handicap and to transform our weakness into strength. To maintain and increase our forces, was the principle to which we adhered, contenting ourselves with attacking when success was certain, refusing to give battle likely to incur losses to us or to engage in hazardous actions. We had to apply the slogan: to build up our strength during the actual course of fighting.

The forms of fighting had to be completely adapted that is, to raise the fighting spirit to the maximum and rely on heroism of our troops to overcome the enemy's material superiority. In the main, especially at the outset of the war, we had recourse to guerrilla fighting. In the Vietnamese theatre of operations, this method carried off great victories: it could be used in the mountains as well as in the delta, it could be waged with good or mediocre material and even without arms, and was to enable us eventually to equip ourselves at the cost of the enemy. Wherever the Expeditionary Corps came, the entire population took part in the fighting; every commune had its fortified village, every district had its regional troops fighting under the command of the local branches of the Party and the people's administration, in liaison with the regular forces in order to wear down and annihilate the enemy forces.

Thereafter, with the development of our forces, guerilla warfare changed into a mobile warfare—a form of mobile warfare still strongly marked by guerilla warfare—which would afterwards become the essential form of operations on the main front, the northern front. In this process of development of guerilla warfare and of accentuation of the mobile warfare, our people's army constantly grew and passed from the stage of combats involving a section or company, to fairly large-scale campaigns bringing into action several divisions. Gradually, its equipment improved, mainly by the seizure of arms from the enemy—the material of the French and American imperialists.

From the military point of view, *the Vietnamese people's war of liberation proved that an insufficiently equipped people's army, but an army fighting for a just cause, can, with appropriate strategy and tactics, combine the conditions needed to conquer a modern army of aggressive imperialism.*

Nguyen Chi Thanh on Communist Strategy, 1963

In 1954, the U.S. imperialists, taking advantage of the French colonialists' defeat at Dien Bien Phu, drove the French out of south Viet Nam and set up a puppet regime headed by Ngo Dinh Diem. In essence, this meant that U.S. neocolonialism replaced French old colonialism and became dominant in south Viet Nam.

The United States thought that, with its numerous arms, dollars, rich political and military experience and a faithful lackey Ngo Dinh Diem, it could solve all the problems in south Viet Nam in a very short time. Events, however, have proved this to be sheer wishful thinking. . . .

U.S. capital is world-renowned for its cleverness in clicking the abacus for cold-blooded exploitation. However, it can hardly be found in the annals of U.S. imperialism where its political and military leaders committed such serious blunders and long-standing errors as they did in appraising the situation in south Viet Nam. This is understandable since what is involved here is not a business calculation but brain-racking "political arithmetic."

Their formula is perhaps something like this:

Step 1. Set up a puppet regime (headed by Ngo Dinh Diem or any other lackey).

Step 2. Consolidate this puppet regime and take measures to stabilize the situation in south Viet Nam: direct their main efforts on suppressing the revolutionary forces and the former Resistance forces, and gradually eliminate the French influences so as to clear the way for further U.S. economic, political, military and cultural penetrations.

Step 3. Strengthen the puppet regime, turn south Viet Nam into a stable colony of a new type and a complete military base under absolute U.S. control.

The above formula appears at first sight to be well thought out. Its greatest fallacy, however, lies in the fact that it only suits the United States and disregards all others. The United States does not see the other factors in this situation.

It is true that U.S. neo-colonialism has scored certain successes in some parts of the world. In south Viet Nam, however, it is "born at the wrong time," or to borrow from business language, it will not "pay off." This is because the United States has overlooked a fundamental factor, that is, when U.S. neo-colonialism made its way to south Viet Nam, it ran into certain unexpected circumstances, which may be listed as follows:

• Great, sharp social contradictions exist between U.S. imperialism and north Viet Nam which is advancing towards socialism.

• With the restoring of peace, social contradictions in south Viet Nam, instead of being eased, have further sharpened and matured. These are contradictions between the south Vietnamese people on the one hand and the U.S. imperialists, the feudal landlord class and comprador capital represented by Ngo Dinh Diem on the other.

• The south Vietnamese people have learned much from their struggle and have been able to utilize correct methods to resolve the social contradictions in south Viet Nam. These methods have been crystallized in the clear-sighted programmes of the South Viet Nam National Liberation Front and of the People's Revolutionary Party of South Viet Nam.

• Generally speaking, the world situation is not favourable to U.S. imperialism. The socialist camp is mightier than the imperialist camp; the movements for democracy and national independence are gaining momentum. These are great and ever-sharpening contradictions, driving the U.S. imperialists into a situation in which they can no longer do as they please.

It appears that south Viet Nam is the focus of many contradictions. The United States should have used algebra in gauging the situation there; instead it used simple arithmetic. Consequently it has run into a blind alley. The United States tries to find a way out by sending a batch of generals and over ten thousand troops to south Viet Nam. This will not help, now or ever. It now appears that the United States may "change the horse in the middle of the stream," but the substitution of one traitor for another will come to nothing. Such a change will not save the U.S.-Diem rule from ruin.

When the U.S. imperialists dispatched ten thousand troops to south Viet Nam, they believed that the rebellious forces could be put down within eighteen months. Later they said it would probably take ten years. Now, some people in the United States are not at all sure if they could succeed in eighteen years.

U.S. imperialism is certainly not ready to reconcile itself to its defeat in south Viet Nam. But it is an indisputable fact that it is being confronted with a crisis in its political line, which has, in turn, given rise to crises in military strategy and tactics.

The causes of these crises lie in the following:

• The fundamental cause is that the U.S. imperialists are doing an unjust thing—invading another country—and therefore they meet with the firm resistance of the south Vietnamese people, are disapproved of by the American people, condemned by other peoples, and even disliked by some of their henchmen in the Ngo Dinh Diem administration.

• Pursuing its aggressive aims, the United States egged Ngo Dinh Diem on to adopt a number of stupid policies, which aggravated the contradictions within the Ngo Dinh Diem regime.

• The U.S.-Diem clique faces an opponent who, although lacking American dollars, arms and other material, is full of anti-imperialist spirit, full of patriotism and revolutionary courage, and experienced in political and military struggles.

Although ultimate conclusions cannot yet be reached insofar as the struggle is still going on in south Viet Nam, we may however put forth the following views:

1. The U.S. imperialists are not invincible. Compared with imperialists of other countries, they are mightier, but compared with the revolutionary forces and the forces of the people of the world, they are not at all strong. If the proletarian revolution and people of the world resolutely struggle against U.S. imperialism, they can surely repel it step by step and narrow down its domain.

We do not have any illusions about the United States. We do not underestimate our opponent—the strong and cunning U.S. imperialism. But we are not afraid of the United States. The strategic concept thoroughly pervades the revolutionary line of south Viet Nam and is the fundamental factor determining the success of the revolution. If, on the contrary, one is afraid of the United States and thinks that to offend it would court failure, and that firm opposition to U.S. imperialism would touch off a nuclear war, then the only course left would be to compromise with and surrender to U.S. imperialism.

2. A powerful north Viet Nam will be a decisive factor in the social development of our entire country. But this does not mean that simply because the north is strong, the revolutionary movement in the south will automatically succeed. The powerful north Viet Nam and the revolutionary movement of the south Vietnamese people are mutually complementary and

must be closely coordinated; the building of the north itself cannot replace the resolution of the inherent social contradictions of south Viet Nam. Adhering to this correct view, we have avoided opportunistic mistakes. If, on the contrary, we had feared the United States and had no faith in the success of our struggles against it, we would have called on the people in south Viet Nam to "wait" and "coexist peacefully" with the U.S.-Diem clique, and committed an irreparable error. We have correctly handled the relations between north and south Viet Nam. This is a Marxist-Leninist strategic concept which is in conformity with the latest experience in the world developments and those in our own country.

Ho Vows to "Fight Until Complete Victory," 1966

Compatriots and fighters throughout the country!

The barbarous U.S. imperialists have unleashed a war of aggression in an attempt to conquer our country, but they are sustaining big defeats.

They have rushed an expeditionary corps of about 300,000 men into the southern part of our country. They have used a puppet administration and a mercenary army fostered by them as instruments of their aggressive policy. They have resorted to extremely savage means of warfare—toxic chemicals, napalm bombs, and so forth. With such crimes they hope to subdue our southern compatriots.

But under the firm and wise leadership of the NFLSV [National Front for the Liberation of South Vietnam, or NLF], the South Viet-Nam army and people, closely united and fighting heroically, have scored very glorious victories and are determined to struggle until complete victory with a view to liberating the South, defending the North, and subsequently achieving national reunification.

The U.S. aggressors have brazenly launched air attacks on North Viet-Nam in an attempt to get out of the quagmire in the South and to impose negotiations on us on their terms.

But North Viet-Nam will not falter. Our army and people have shown redoubled eagerness in the emulation to produce and fight heroically. So far we have blasted out of the skies more than 1,200 aircraft. We are determined to defeat the enemy's war of destruction and at the same time to extend all-out support to our dear compatriots in the South.

Of late the U.S. aggressors hysterically took a very serious step further in the escalation of the war: They launched air attacks on the suburbs of Hanoi and Haiphong. That was an act of desperation comparable to the agony convulsions of a grievously wounded wild beast.

Johnson and his clique should realize this: They may bring in 500,000 troops, 1 million, or even more to step up the war of aggression in South Viet-Nam. They may use thousands of aircraft for intensified attacks against North Viet-Nam. But never will they be able to break the iron will of the heroic Vietnamese people to fight against U.S. aggression, for national salvation. The more truculent they are, the further they will aggravate their crime. The war may still last ten, twenty years, or longer. Hanoi,

Haiphong, and other cities and enterprises may be destroyed, but the Vietnamese people will not be intimidated! Nothing is more precious than independence and freedom. When victory day comes, our people will rebuild our country and endow it with bigger and more beautiful construction.

It is common knowledge that each time they are about to step up their criminal war, the U.S. aggressors always resort to their peace talks swindle in an attempt to fool world opinion and blame Viet-Nam for unwillingness to enter into peace talks!

President Johnson! Reply publicly to the American people and the peoples of the world: Who has sabotaged the Geneva Agreements which guarantee the sovereignty, independence, unity, and territorial integrity of Viet-Nam? Have Vietnamese troops invaded the United States and massacred Americans: Is it not the U.S. Government which has sent U.S. troops to invade Viet-Nam and massacre the Vietnamese?

Let the United States end its war of aggression in Viet-Nam, withdraw from this country all U.S. and satellite troops, and peace will return here at once. . . .

The Vietnamese people cherish peace, genuine peace, peace in independence and freedom, not sham peace, American peace.

For the defense of the independence of the fatherland and for the fulfillment of our obligation to the peoples struggling against U.S. imperialism, our people and army, united as one man, will resolutely fight until complete victory, whatever the sacrifices and hardships may be. In the past we defeated the Japanese fascists and the French colonialists in much more difficult junctures. Today the conditions at home and abroad are more favorable; our people's struggle against U.S. aggression for national salvation is sure to win a total victory.

E S S A Y S

In the first essay, written at the height of the war, Douglas Pike examines the appeal of Vietnamese communism. Currently a member of the Institute of East Asian Affairs at the University of California, Berkeley, he ascribes the National Liberation Front's success to a combination of organizational expertise and revolutionary mystique. Yet Pike also argues that Marxism-Leninism was un-Vietnamese in nature because it stood at variance from the most deeply ingrained Vietnamese views of the universe. In the second essay, Eric M. Bergerud of Lincoln University probes Vietcong success at the local level by focusing on developments in Hau Nghia province. Strategically situated between Saigon and the Cambodian border, that Mekong River valley province lay at the very heart of the Vietcong insurgency. Bergerud analyzes the complex mix of factors that enabled the insurgency to gain control over Hau Nghia by the early 1960s.

Revolutionary Mystique

DOUGLAS PIKE

To those outside Vietnam there was a general perception, one shared neither by Vietnamese nor by foreigners within the country, that South
Vietnam was a place of terror and sudden death, of coups d'etat and bombings, of alarms and excursions by night. These things did exist. Yet somehow they remained in perspective and did not dominate the lives of either
Americans or Vietnamese, in or out of Saigon. Tolstoy, although writing of
another time and place, described exactly how it was:

> The tales and descriptions of that time without exception speak only of the
> self-sacrifice, patriotic devotion, despair, grief, and the heroism. . . . But
> it was not really so. It appears so to us because we see only the general
> historic interest of that time and do not see all the personal human inter-
> ests that people had. Yet in reality those personal interests of the moment
> so much transcend the general interests that they always prevent the pub-
> lic interest from being felt or even noticed. Most of the people at that time
> paid no attention to the general progress of events but were guided only by
> their private interests. . . .

Thousands of Vietnamese villagers lived through the entire 1960–1965
period without being involved in, and hardly ever being inconvenienced by,
either the NLF's armed struggle or the GVN's military operations.
Although subjected to great NLF organizational and political attention, the
average rural Vietnamese was seldom if ever a direct victim of its violence
program. The mental picture held by most Americans of rural Vietnam as a
vast, boiling battlefield, of innumerable military engagements by day, of
villages again and again torn apart by ARVN-guerrilla clashes, of a people
in the midst of constant fighting and bloodshed, with no place to hide, living in a sort of no man's land between two contending armies—that picture
simply does not hold up under scrutiny.

A villager of course would be monumentally affected if his village
found itself under guerrilla attack, was the scene of a battle between ARVN
troops and the guerrillas, or, if in a liberated area, was bombed or
napalmed. But the odds of this happening in the 1960–1964 period were not
much greater than the odds of being hit by lightning. If, on a statistical
basis, a single rural villager was selected at random and studied in terms of
how much the war impinged on his life, how often he witnessed combat or
even saw combatants, it is most likely that he never would have been
directly affected to any degree. The author talked to innumerable villagers
in all parts of Vietnam, and most of them spoke of the effects of the war on
others but admitted that it had never fallen on them.

The average rural Vietnamese could plant his rice, watch it grow, harvest it, and begin the cycle again, placidly unconcerned, unaffected by the

From Douglas Pike, *Viet Cong: The Organization and Techniques of the National Liberation Front of South Vietnam*, pp. 372–382. Copyright © 1966. Reprinted by permission of MIT Press.

swirl around him. The result was that he did not perceive the situation in Vietnam as a "war" in the same way that Americans regard the Vietnam "war." Thus the frequently stated observation that the Vietnamese peasant "has known nothing but war for twenty years," although technically accurate, is also misleading. An American reading this formed a mental picture of the peasant in "war" under circumstances quite different from reality.

The basic characteristics of the NLF and its activities were the use of a united-front organization to establish a mass base of support; organization of the rural people, employing both rational appeals to self-interest and coercion, and then using the specially created social movements in antigovernmental activity; heavy use of various techniques for the communication of ideas to foment social strife; use of specialized military actions, selective in nature and psychological in intent; use of the Communist party *apparat,* and Communist doctrine among the leaders and full-time cadres, to establish orthodoxy and maintain discipline. The goal was control of the population and, through this control, organization of the people as a weapon against the government. But it was more than this. It was more than simply the inculcation of new beliefs or differing attitudes. The NLF's ultimate objective taken together with other activities was to create a new socialization pattern.

The NLF was concerned with the deepest social values. It sought to create a new system of formal and informal groupings by which the socialization was to be accomplished and behavior regulated. It manipulated economic activities, the base for all human activities, in such a way as to increase the degree of communalism or collectivization and thus to some degree alter the village means of production; it introduced a new political structure to keep internal order and to regulate contact within South Vietnam, particularly with respect to villagers hostile to the NLF; it manipulated educational and other intellectual activities within the village. It apparently attempted to substitute a disguised brand of Marxism for traditional religious beliefs, although in an oblique manner; and it introduced new language terminology, social mythology, and folklore. In short, it attempted to work within the totality of village life and provide a new cultural focus.

Understanding sociopolitical developments in Vietnam involves cataloging the various social and political groups, organizations, cliques, and clans—some of them covert and almost all of them parochial or regional in nature—and then mapping the interrelationships among these various forces. Political infighting consists not so much of open confrontation with one's opponent (or even directly and forcibly destroying him) as it does of drowning, absorbing, splintering, fragmenting, discrediting, turning him aside, or, if necessary, joining him and working at his side to eliminate him. The immediate goal is usually status or prestige more than pure political power. The NLF was superior in this type of political struggle—especially in the rural areas—chiefly because success in this effort depends on good organizational ability and skilled management of social movements. Therefore the secret of NLF success in the early years—and they were many—was organization. Probably the NLF expended more time, money, and manpower on organizational activity than on all other activities combined. Further, this effort was concentrated in what was an organizational vacuum.

In those areas of the country where it had firm and continuous social control the NLF was in effect a society within a society, with its own social structure, values, and coercive instruments. The NLF cadres made a conscious and massive effort to extend political participation, even if it was manipulated, on the local level so as to involve the people in a self-contained, self-supporting revolution. The functional liberation associations at the village level attempted to serve each individual member in terms of his own personal interests while at the same time developing a deep revolutionary consciousness. Ironically, as the result of increased coercion on the part of the NLF, as its popular support dwindled, its actual authority increased. What had been essentially a persuasive mechanism became basically a coercive one, not so much because of the failure of the original NLF social organization pattern as because of the arrival of Northern cadres who were unwilling to trust the original form because they felt in the long run that it would not serve the interests of the Party and indeed might become a threat to it. Once again, the not unfamiliar story of the revolution betrayed. But the organization at all times, whether persuasive or coercive, remained the central NLF activity in the village.

That the leaders of this enterprise were professionals must be evident from the structure they created. It is difficult, however, to estimate the number of NLF leaders and cadres who were professional revolutionaries. Most of them were vastly experienced, some by choice, some by circumstance. The initial NLF leadership corps was made up of the ex-Viet Minh. Many of these, probably the majority, were professionals such as doctors, lawyers, and teachers. They were competent and enjoyed high status among their followers. Most of them had been in the movement, either Viet Minh or NLF, for most of their lives, although generally the guerrilla leaders had served longer than the civilians. Within the NLF these early leaders came to hold the main-line administrative posts or became the commanders of the Main Force units. They were inclined to be more nationalistic and less doctrinal than those who came after them, and they were far less pro-DRV. Those who rose in prominence after the launching of the NLF, that is, in the early 1960's, were more politically oriented, less apt to have a professional background, and therefore of somewhat lower status in the eyes of the rank and file. They were more doctrinal, more anti-GVN, pro-DRV, and pro-Communist. With the regularization came both cadres and top leaders from the North; their great social trauma had been the Viet Minh war. Most had been young cadres during the Viet Minh war and had climbed the status ladder in the North according to DRV standards, which meant they excelled in Communist virtues, technical competence, zeal, discipline, and unwavering faith in the cause. They had a vested interest in victory through following orders from Hanoi, for it was there that their homes were located, their families lived, and their careers were rooted. Their motivation was quite different; it was North Vietnamese whether or not they had originally come from the South. Above all, these Northern-trained leaders, and they were found chiefly in the NLF military apparatus, were professionals, less marked by the self-righteous puritanism that characterized the earliest NLF leadership group or the individual initiative and revolutionary consciousness that marked those who rose in the ranks during the early stages of the insurgency. They were less moved by the deep sense of frustration that drove the earlier leaders, and their devotion to the cause stemmed more from career building than from ideology or hatred.

One of the most persistent questions asked about the NLF follower was "Why did he join?" The implication in the question is that for one or more rational or emotional reasons the individual Vietnamese decided to enlist in the cause, did so, and thus entered as a believer. . . . Almost the reverse was the case. The Vietnamese youth was first surrounded by a social organization that he had no hand in creating but to which he somehow belonged. Through a process of insinuation the youth came to realize that he was part of the NLF, never quite sure of how this happened and never with any overt choice presented to him. The process of glacially slow recruitment came first, the mystique was developed later. Or, as it has been aptly put, conversion followed subversion. Therefore not motives but circumstances must be considered in understanding the recruitment pattern and its contribution to the NLF mystique.

The most common answer given by a *quy chanh* [defector from the NLF] to questions concerning the circumstances under which he became part of the NLF indicated that he was initially drawn into the organization and later recruited. He might first be asked to act as a messenger, or to take part in a struggle movement, or to deliver leaflets to an agent in the provincial capital. Then he would be urged to join his friends in a study group that might also be a literacy class. Then he would be asked to commit some act of violence; at this point, whether he knew it or not, he was in the net. When handled skillfully, subtly, and gradually, a teen-aged youth did not realize that he was involved until he was already enmeshed. This technique succeeded, for the most part, not in areas where the GVN was exerting itself but in the remote villages where the NLF and the Viet Minh before it were the only visible "government" the youth had ever known. And so the *quy chanh* would say, "Everyone seemed to think it was the correct thing to do," often adding plaintively, "There didn't seem to be any danger. The Saigon government was so far away I didn't think they would ever know about me." Of course a small minority actually sought out and joined the NLF. These included draft dodgers, military deserters, those who hated the government for some personal reason, opportunists, the ambitious who were seeking status, the rejected, the adventurers, and all the others in [philosopher] Eric Hoffer's categories of the True Believer.

For the most part, however, the supporters were recruited under circumstances where there was no alternative. Most recruitment was from among social groups such as the religious sects, with grievances against the government, and less effort was placed on the recruitment of individuals at random. At the same time the NLF sought to create situations that would give rise to grievances among such groups so as to facilitate recruitment. Once the youth was recruited, the training and indoctrination work supplied the rationale for belonging.

Americans and others often assumed that the NLF army members were fanatics. Because they performed well in combat, it was argued, they were highly motivated, which meant dedication to an ideological cause. Thus the search was for the essence of this belief. It proved elusive, largely because it did not exist. The best of the military units—the Main Force units—were highly effective because they were composed of professionals. These were not green young Vietnamese farmers, only recently introduced to the rifle, but experienced guerrillas who had been fighting most of their adult lives. What impelled them was not ideology so much as professional competence, much like the United States Marine or the French Foreign Legionnaire. The men in the best of these units were very good; their discipline was superb; they knew how to use camouflage well, a requirement for survival; they were well skilled in small-unit tactics, especially the ambush in its many variations; they trained hard, rehearsed, and practiced attacks until letter perfect, and then they fought hard. Their mystique should be attributed chiefly to a unit *esprit de corps* that stemmed from the consensus that each man in the unit was a superior and vastly experienced professional.

The strength of the NLF was the result of careful organization building, not the product of some unique spirit or élan. The mystique, to the degree that it existed and bound together the separate building blocks of the movement, resulted from indoctrinational efforts, shared social myths, and leader-led relations. The mystique's functions were, first, identity, stemming from the doctrinal course of the Revolution, the ideology of communism, and the recruitment pattern; and, second, unity, resulting from the nature of the leadership, the indoctrination itself, and individual self-motivating standards of behavior.

The various pseudoscientific laws that the leadership regarded as governing the Revolution were at no time themselves challenged by the NLF followers, nor was the principle that such definitive laws existed, as asserted in these terms in an early NLF document:

> A revolution develops according to objective laws, which exist independently of man's wish. The revolutionary should not rely on his subjective wish but should rely on objective reality, on the objective law of social development, to act and promote the development of history. To lead the Revolution correctly is to act in such a manner that under concrete historical conditions one can mobilize and organize all forces that can be mobilized in order to bring the Revolution to victory. . . .

The leadership considered its chief doctrinal task to be the translation of abstract theory into the setting of a traditional society. It did this by placing prime value on loyalty, as perhaps all such groups must. The Revolution assumed a pragmatic, not greatly intellectual, cast, and it was characterized by an absence of agonizing. It lacked the depth of thought marked by, say, the Russian Revolution and far more resembled the Chinese revolution. To both the NLF and the PRP [People's Revolutionary Party, the Communist Party of South Vietnam], determinants of success were twofold: revolutionary capability, including the proclivity for revolution by the Vietnamese people themselves, and PRP leadership, which is to say Communist leadership. The people's revolutionary capability was more asserted than proven, and the Party's monopolistic leadership imposed rather than prescribed. Both developed into articles of faith, a mystic belief in the power and loyalty of the people and a sense of trust in the omniscience of the Party. What was then required was to put the formula to work: The people would support the Revolution if only the cadres would show them that their interests were identical to the cause, would constantly agitate them so as to prevent loss of ardor, and would develop them into creatures of initiative who would act and not merely react.

No evidence was ever uncovered to indicate that schisms existed in the early years on the proper course of the Revolution. The quarrel that did develop . . . lay in writing the final act of the revolutionary drama—whether it should consist of the General Uprising, the Mao-Giap third stage, or negotiated settlement. The dispute was resolved in favor of the Mao-Giap thesis, not through discussion or by successfully decimating the two other alternatives but because the new supraleadership in Hanoi concluded that it represented the correct course to pursue and used its Northern-trained and Northern-loyal cadres to force acceptance of its decision.

However, even in the days when it was the dominant doctrine, the leadership consistently overestimated its progress and several times erroneously believed that the moment of the General Uprising had arrived. Internal documents from a Lao Dong Youth League conference in June 1961, for example, stated that speakers at that time asserted flatly that the General Uprising would take place in the first three months of 1962 and that all cadres must plan accordingly. After the overthrow of the Diem government and again in the spring of 1965 the leadership apparently believed the moment had come, only to have their hopes again dashed. These failures undoubtedly contributed to the decision to "militarize" the struggle and pursue victory by means of the Mao-Giap third stage. But this triggered a new level of American response, which meant that from a doctrinal standpoint it had failed as much as had the General Uprising thesis.

In sum, from a standpoint of mystique the General Uprising served the NLF well through the golden days of the Revolution. It was not mere window dressing but the justification and rationalization for the insurgency, the cement that held the effort together, and a powerful tool for agit-prop team use in working with villagers. In the end it failed because it was not sufficiently rooted in reality, because it could work only if the Communists' assessment of the social milieu in the South was correct, which it was not.

The NLF and the people it influenced lived in a muzzy, myth-filled world of blacks and whites, good and evil, a simplistic world quite out of character with the one to which the Vietnamese was accustomed. But it created a powerful external image for the Vietnamese immersed in the cause, restructuring his reality, providing him with a new identity and a boundless sense of unity. The elements of this mystique were fourfold.

First, it was characterized by great moralism and was far more moral than ideological. Virtue was the golden word. The cause consisted of moral duties based on moral absolutes, guided by moral imperatives; duty itself, under a virtuous leadership, was the highest value. Preoccupation with law and legality was not simply an effort to establish legitimacy but a justification of the moral correctness of the cause. Because he was virtuous, the NLF supporter was morally superior to the enemy and hence politically and militarily superior. The moralism manifested itself in a spirit of sincerity; the NLF surrounded its words and actions with an aura of sincerity.

Second, it was characterized by extreme romanticism. The NLF leaders, like Mao Tse-tung and Ho Chi Minh before them, were romantic rebels who saw themselves as idealists. Idealistic appeals abounded: the promise of the good life in utopian terms; the opportunity to revolt against all the evil, injustice, and inequity of this world; the chance to be part of a great crusade. But behind these was the romantic lure of the struggle itself; the means not the ends counted. There was more glory along the road than at its end. The clandestine organization made up of multitudes of inner groups, cults, and secret arrangements played on the Vietnamese individual's romantic love of the devious. . . . Yet in general the NLF mystique was less a positive cause than a negation. But this too had lure to the romantic—the lure of anarchy, beyond which, if it failed, lay the lure of martyrdom. The NLF in creating its mystique was acutely sensitive to the age-old Asian attitude of fatalism.

Third, its mystique was imitative and therefore militantly defensive, which probably should be counted as a weakness. The NLF leader was driven by a compulsive search for answers from elsewhere, anywhere. Examples were taken from other places and they were forced, and from other times and they were distorted. If the NLF was not slavishly copying Mao Tse-tung on the Long March, it was employing the Viet Minh's analysis of French Maginot Line thinking as it applied to the Americans, or calling on all cadres to repeat in a literal manner some victory scored a few months earlier in another part of Vietnam. The constant scanning of the horizon was part of a preoccupation with contemplation and self-analysis. Cadres, in a curious form of intellectualism, would explain the Revolution over and over to their most disinterested students—the rural Vietnamese. Copied though it was, it provided the supporter with a worldview that might not be understood but was satisfactory. Through indoctrination and even socialization he received needed psychological support and release from cultural tensions. (The same psychiatrist said the NLF was a father image led by Ho Chi Minh.)

And finally there was a will to believe, perhaps a characteristic of any mystique. It grew from the sense of universality of a movement representing Vietnam, the world, excluding not even a full social class (the enemies in Saigon and Washington). It was based on an assessment of the world environment that the NLF believed made Revolution in Vietnam irresistible and doomed GVN and U.S. prowess to steady deterioration. It was based on faith in the Vietnamese people's revolutionary capability, faith in the doctrinal approach, faith in revolutionary guerrilla warfare consisting of the combined armed and political struggle, and the infallible wisdom of the Party's leaders, who from long experience could divine the laws of history.

Marxism-Leninism as filtered through first Chinese and then Vietnamese thought contributed much to the NLF mystique. After the regularization efforts not only Communist thought but the communist-society goal was proclaimed openly, as previously it had been asserted internally. For example, the PRP asserted in a Radio Liberation broadcast, December 9, 1964, that its ultimate objective was a communist state, and the only question was whether this would come early or late:

> The [enemy] slanders us saying that our Party monopolizes the Front and that our Party's solidarity policy is nothing more than a trick for the present. . . . It says the Party's strategic objectives are against those of the Front, such as national independence, democracy, peace, and neutrality, and they say that our Party cannot pursue a sincere and lasting policy of solidarity with the Front. This argument proves that the enemies of our people do not understand anything about our Party of Marxism-Leninism. . . . The general Marxist-Leninist principles of the working class are aimed at rallying the majority of the forces into a united national front, a worker-peasant alliance led by the working class. . . . Our Party does not conceal its ultimate objective, which is to achieve socialism and communism. But our Party has never ceased pointing out that the path leading to that objective is long, and that the objective cannot be achieved in a few years, but several score years. . . .

A Communist condition had prevailed within the NLF from the start and was assumed as a matter of course by Vietnamese of all political shadings. With respect to the mystique the matter of communism's paramountcy became somewhat more complex. Partly it was a matter of definition.

If a Communist is one who believes that man's future is shaped by his tools of production, that history is dominated by a class struggle for control of those means of production, that capitalism must grow increasingly evil, and that a brotherhood of workers and farmers swearing allegiance to an international ideal must unite to seize power and build its own society led by the vanguard, the proletariat, and in turn by the vanguard of the vanguard, the Communist party—if this is a Communist, then there were few Communists among the NLF. If, however, a Communist is one who swears blind allegiance to the world movement whose loci of power are Moscow and Peking, from which in this instance via Hanoi he draws through a political umbilical cord sustenance and strength that he cannot, and does not want to, supply himself, then most of the NLF's leaders, cadres, and true believers were Communists.

It was the difference between philosophic communism and alliance communism. For, in the first instance, to be a Communist meant mastering Marxism-Leninism, which NLF Vietnamese found notoriously difficult to understand since it is distinctly un-Vietnamese in nature and at variance with their most deeply ingrained views of the universe. (For example, it must have been indeed a Herculean task for a cadre to convince a Vietnamese that matter and not God or Spirit is the ultimate reality, or that nothing is inherently unknowable.) The second instance meant simply establishing identity and achieving unity in which an NLF supporter had only to approve of the powerful foreign forces that stood behind him and his cause. Only among the higher-echelon cadres, and even here not with total acceptance, was communism regarded as a new body of wisdom to be learned, understood, and put to use.

Thus the NLF was Communist not because it incorporated Communist doctrine but because it linked itself to foreign states that did. This distinction, or weakness, meant that the strengths that hold Communists and Communist movements together during dark days elsewhere were largely absent in Vietnam.

The Success of Communist Strategy at the Village Level

ERIC M. BERGERUD

It would scarcely be possible to understand the course of events in Hau Nghia after 1963 without a general look backward at the years following the Geneva Conference of 1954. In this period, the NLF gained both the political initiative over the Diem government and an increasingly favorable balance of political and military forces. Also during this period, Saigon attempted to combat the growing threat to its existence with methods that clearly foreshadowed later American efforts.

When the Geneva Conference adjourned in July of 1954, South Vietnam was in a state of near chaos. Economic uncertainty, the inherent difficulties of establishing a new government apparatus, streams of refugees, the bizarre activities of the religious sects and bandit groups, and malicious intrigues between French and American agents made impossible an orderly transition from colonial domination to independence. Even worse was the provisional nature of the Geneva Accords. The Final Declaration of the conference, calling for national elections in two years, was crippled from the start because it was left unsigned, only accepted orally, denounced by Saigon, and accepted only with reservations by the United States. Clearly, war or rebellion might return in the near future. Therefore, it is not correct to view the Vietnam conflict during the 1955–1959 period as a steady erosion of the Saigon government's power at the hands of Communist-led insurgents. Rather, a power vacuum existed throughout South Vietnam, which Diem rushed to fill.

Initially, Diem had several advantages. First, there was an undeniable war weariness and desire for some sort of stability on the part of the vast majority of the population, both rural and urban. Second, despite plots by

Reprinted from Eric M. Bergerud, *The Dynamics of Defeat: The Vietnam War in Hau Nghia Province*, 1991, pp. 12–23, 54–68, 82–84, by permission of Westview Press, Boulder, Colorado.

the departing French, Diem had managed to secure the support of the United States. Backed by U.S. aid, which continued unabated after the Geneva Accords, Diem's promises of reform and prosperity were plausible. Diem had been anti-French, in contrast to top South Vietnamese military leaders and the completely discredited Emperor Bao Dai. Therefore, many non-Communist elements within the Viet Minh could be expected if not to support the new government, then at least to await developments and see if Diem could establish a genuine government. Most important, although perhaps not fully appreciated by Diem, was the attitude of the Communist leadership, both north and south.

Apparently, there were few illusions within the higher echelons of the Party concerning the likelihood of the nationwide elections and reunification talks agreed to at Geneva. Nevertheless, the Party had claimed that Geneva was a great victory; immediate action against Diem would contradict this line. It also dismissed the possibility of a truly popular Saigon government being established in the rural areas because of class conflict and structural contradictions. Furthermore, establishing a strong socialist government in Hanoi and rebuilding war-ravaged areas throughout the North was the top priority of the Party. Therefore, Party leadership adopted a two-pronged strategy; regroupment of essential cadres to North Vietnam and reorganization of a secret Party apparatus in the South. An underground cadre from Cholon later described the situation:

> The main guideline for the people who were to stay was there was to be no public violation of the Agreement. We were supposed to maintain our legal identities as ordinary citizens. Organizations were to be maintained at the most minimal levels; no written communications or papers were to be utilized in any way. The object was complete, total secrecy. . . . We were told that Diem might honor the Agreement or he might not. But in either case we had to continue the movement, keep people warmed up and keep the organizations going. If there really were elections, then we would be able to capitalize on the situation more quickly if the networks were in place. And if there weren't we would be better prepared to resume the struggle. In any event, the Party could never sleep on its victories.

Consistent with this strategy, most of the trained military cadres along with any technical specialists, moved north. Because the Geneva Accords theoretically offered protection to former resistance fighters, a sizable number of Party members in the rural areas registered with Saigon authorities and began a legal existence. However, the most dedicated Party members, who had managed to maintain a secret existence during hostilities, remained underground and totally reorganized the Party on the basis of a secret cell system. The main task of the illegal segment of the Party was to prepare political action in case of elections or to lay the groundwork for future political resistance if, as was believed likely, no elections were held. With memories still fresh of the 1945 Hanoi general uprising, which led to the establishment of the Democratic Republic of Vietnam under Ho Chi Minh, the Party directed much effort toward strengthening its position in

Saigon. According to the Geneva Accords, no Communist military units were to be left in the South, but the new Party apparatus carefully established the nucleus for a new military strike force. Old weapons were taken to the North, and new ones were hidden. In areas where terrain allowed secret activity, small main force units remained in existence. Nevertheless, the primary attention of the Party was centered on the North, and the Party in the South was relatively disarmed.

With his most dangerous enemy occupied elsewhere and for the moment honoring the Geneva Accords, Diem amazed his many American detractors by moving quickly and skillfully to establish some sort of government in the South. First, in April 1955, he succeeded in crushing the Binh Xuyen, a well-entrenched criminal organization centered in Saigon. More bloodshed followed when the Cao Dai and Hoa Hao, two religious sects with private armies and originally allied with the Binh Xuyen, were also dispersed or forced to submit to Diem's authority. Strengthened by this show of force, Diem next conducted a referendum that ended the Vietnamese monarchy and proclaimed himself president of a new Republic of Vietnam. All the while, Nhu, Diem's eccentric but powerful brother, developed the Can Lao political party and propagated a strange proto-Fascist "personalist" ideology.

Diem and Nhu knew perfectly well that the remnants of the Viet Minh would ultimately be their principal enemy. Indeed, Party-inspired mass demonstrations extolling the "victory at Geneva" were commonplace events. Therefore, while preparing action against the Binh Xuyen, Diem and Nhu initiated the Anti-Communist Denunciation Campaign, which rapidly developed into a manhunt directed against the Party. The hunt increased in scope and energy with each Diem victory. Predictably, the Cong An, Diem's police, were hardly discriminating. It proved easy to accuse any potential enemy of having Communist affiliations. Jails filled, and an uncommonly large number of prisoners were shot while attempting escape. According to a later study prepared for the U.S. Defense Department, "There can be no doubt, on the basis of reports of the few impartial observers, that innumerable crimes and absolutely senseless acts of suppression against both real and suspected Communists and sympathizing villagers were committed. Efficiency took the form of brutality and a total disregard for the difference between determined foes and potential friends."

It may be that Diem created as many enemies as he neutralized with his indiscriminate approach. Nevertheless, his campaign left the Party reeling. In fact, the Party was quite unprepared for what had transpired. Although a strong clandestine tradition existed, the Party had organized quite openly in the rural areas while fighting the French; much of rural Vietnam had been, after all, totally under Party control. Furthermore, many underground Viet Minh followers had surfaced, and others had moved north. As previously mentioned, Party leaders had discounted the possibility of creating a strong central government. On the contrary, they were confident that chaos would continue and had hopes of a coup or general uprising in the near future.

Diem's campaign, therefore, had the advantage of surprise. Party leaders were rounded up in the cities and, where possible, in the rural villages. Every time a cell, the Party's basic three-person organizational building block, was compromised, it had to be rebuilt. Often, a cell had to be reorganized many times over.

With the situation in the South deteriorating and the Geneva Accords appearing more and more a dead letter, bitter debate began within the Party leadership on how best to proceed. Le Duan and others proposed a rapid switch to armed struggle. Truong Chinh, Gen. Nguyen Vo Giap, and other "northerners" urged patience. In December 1956, a compromise was agreed to at the Central Committee's Eleventh Plenum, calling for both continuing political agitation in the near term and long-range preparations for armed struggle. Southern cadres were not fully privy to these deliberations. Furthermore, they had to face the Cong An on a daily basis and were both fearful and impatient. Morale within the Party dropped, and many apparently felt betrayed by Ho Chi Minh and the Soviet Union. Because the Party had claimed publicly that the Accords would be carried out while actually expecting a quick end to the Diem regime, confidence in the judgment of the leadership fell and defections rose. Diem had seized the initiative, and prospects for the Party seemed bleak. However, Diem could not yet claim victory. Saigon's authority had not yet been extended to cover the countryside, where some 80 percent of the population lived. By 1956, attempts by the Saigon government to achieve this control were under way.

Diem's efforts were both administrative and military. He began by abolishing the elective village councils that Bao Dai had established. In June 1956, Diem decreed, without benefit of statute as legally required, that, henceforth, elective councils would be replaced by three- to five-man committees appointed by the province chief. Furthermore, four months later, Saigon proclaimed that the province chiefs would be appointed directly by the president and would be responsible for all administration within the province. In early 1957, the power of the province chief was further enhanced by making him commander of all military forces controlled by the province. From this time on, most province chiefs were ARVN (Army of the Republic of Vietnam) field-grade officers. These measures were all intended to centralize power within South Vietnam. However, because loyalty to Diem was obviously the first requisite for appointment, all too often the new province chiefs and lesser officials proved to be corrupt cronies of Nhu or one of his allies.

While Diem was centralizing administrative power in his own hands, the South Vietnamese army was kept busy with sweeps through rural areas. After a village or hamlet was apparently cleared of enemy forces, a six-man Civic Action cadre team moved in, when available. The cadre teams, a personal creation of Diem and Nhu, were a transparent copy of the Viet Minh cadres who had played the central role in the struggle against France. They were necessary for Diem because he had virtually no political constituency in rural Vietnam outside Catholic areas. (Diem, the quintessential Vietnamese urban aristocrat, knew almost nothing about agrarian life. His few journeys to the countryside while president were carefully stage-managed affairs.) Team leaders reported directly to a presidential office and, in theory, operated independently of village and province officials. A primary role for a cadre, on paper, was to serve as a sort of people's ombudsman, capable of passing complaints against bad officials directly to Saigon. The cadre teams were to gain the confidence of the villagers by living with them and by establishing self-help projects, made possible with U.S. aid. Once the proper rapport had been established, the cadres were to propagandize against the Communists and praise Diem and the Can Lao Party. Villagers, no doubt wisely, would go through the motions in more or less good humor. Gerald Hickey, the prominent American anthropologist, witnessed some propaganda meetings:

> Every Saturday evening there is a hamlet Communist denunciation meeting, and the hamlet chief and five-family leaders are responsible for seeing that all male residents over 18 years are in attendance. On the fifteenth day of each lunar month there is a general Communist denunciation meeting held at the dinh [communal temple]. . . . Villagers dutifully assist at these meetings, but most do not appear particularly attentive. Some squat outside the dinh chatting in low tones while a few read newspapers. After one denunciation meeting, a young farmer regaled his friends in one of the nearby shops by imitating the speaker of the evening.

According to the recollections of a cadre leader of this period, many villagers simply disbelieved the message: "We were supposed to explain why the communists were bad and why the people must follow the government. But during the Resistance the communists had been the only ones in the village to fight against the French, so when we tried to explain that the communists were evil people, the villagers just didn't listen to us."

The Civic Action cadre teams were a parody of political development. Aid programs, when properly and honestly administered, were welcomed by the peasants. Corruption, however, was the rule. Team members were well paid; consequently, like the military and civilian administrators, they were usually appointed because of political or family ties rather than merit. Invariably, they came from outside the area and rarely were from rural backgrounds. Diem's cadres differed from the Party's in yet another respect: Regardless of their independence, the Civic Action cadres were yet another projection of state power coming from the outside. There was no internal recruitment or organic link with the community, two fundamental characteristics of the Viet Minh and, later, the Front cadres. The Civic Action cadres were *in* rural Vietnam, not of it. Furthermore, beyond some strange and foreign ideology and a few material trinkets, they had nothing to offer. Their task was futile, and their role was minor. They are worth mentioning only because they foreshadow the large and theoretically crucial Revolutionary Development Cadre program launched by Americans ten years later.

As Saigon attempted to extend its control throughout the countryside, it was forced to face the explosive issue of landownership. In the years before World War II, landholding patterns in Cochin (which is what the French called the southern third of Vietnam) had degenerated, in the words of an American economist, into a static "mechanism for widespread economic exploitation and social abuse." Large French and Vietnamese absentee landholders dominated the Mekong Delta especially. The upper 2.5 percent of landowners held approximately 45 percent of the land. With the population expanding and new land progressively more expensive to develop, the result was a steady increase in rent demanded of tenants, until it reached 40 to 60 percent of the annual rice harvest. At the same time, caloric consumption declined after 1930. Many of the landless lived on the edge of survival. Naturally, the Viet Minh were quick to capitalize on this situation. When war against France began, French-held land and large Vietnamese-owned estates were confiscated, and remaining large landowners were driven into the cities. This land, in turn, was distributed to the landless. Small landowners were left in peace, reflecting the Viet Minh's united-front strategy. Where land was still rented, limits were placed on rents and tenants assured of long-term rentals. As might be imagined, this policy was extremely popular and earned for the Viet Minh the loyalty and gratitude of hundreds of thousands of poor peasants.

The Geneva Accords in 1954 brought an uncertain situation concerning landholding. As the landowners constituted an important bloc supporting Diem and the Saigon government, Diem did not have the option of accepting the land redistribution that had taken place during the fighting as permanent. Rather, as Saigon extended its forces into the countryside, the landlords and their agents also returned. To prevent the worst type of exploitation seen during French rule, Diem, under American pressure, issued a series of regulations limiting rents to between 15 and 25 percent of the annual harvest, providing secure tenure rights, and limiting individuals to 100 hectares of cropland. Land over this limit was to be purchased by the government and resold to the peasants.

However, such measures, which would have been progressive thirty years earlier, had little appeal to peasants who had received land expropriated by the Viet Minh. Furthermore, in execution, Diem's program was a dreadful failure. To begin with, regulations concerning rents were frequently ignored. A 1967 U.S. study showed that rents in government-controlled areas were in the 25 to 40 percent range. Naturally, landlords held on to the best land if they were actually forced to sell a portion of their holdings. The decree did not cover land devoted to cash crops, and implementation of the program was laborious and required a great amount of paperwork. Loopholes existed in all phases of the program and were often exploited by the landowners to slow or stop implementation. Another counterproductive aspect of the program was the 100-hectare limit. Because only a few very rich landowners had title to more than 100 hectares, middle-level landowners were not touched at all. Worse yet, influential politicians and members of Diem's families used the program to gain ownership of much of the land expropriated by the government. Indeed, the GVN itself became the largest landlord in the country by far. Rents on government land went into the provincial coffers and were a prime source of graft. Frequently, local officials doubled as land agents for private owners or for government holdings. Lastly, Diem's measures did not truly come to grips with the problem of the landless peasant. In the Mekong Delta, where most of the peasants lived, figures from 1960–1961 show that 62 percent of all land was rented and only 22 percent of the peasantry owned all of the land they farmed. Locally, distribution might be even worse. In Long An province (part of which was soon to be transferred to Hau Nghia), for example, only 10 percent of the 75,000 hectares of rented rice land was subject to expropriation. Due to delays and corruption, only some 3 percent of the estimated 35,000 families renting land in Long An ever gained title under the program.

Diem's land policy soon proved a bonus for the Party. Not only was redistribution largely illusory but the peasants were also forced to sign contracts with the landowners, reaffirming the latter's rights of title. Naturally, the Party propagandized against Diem's program. . . .

The land issue was only one among many that the Party exploited. Other economic ills, such as inflation, were attacked, along with the ubiquitous corruption of GVN officials. Diem's connections with the United States were condemned, as was his abrogation of the Geneva Accords. The charismatic Ho Chi Minh was contrasted in personal terms with Diem and Nhu. Therefore, the period 1957–1959 was a time of general recovery for the Party. Many of the most vulnerable cadres already had been imprisoned or killed in 1956; survivors were in safe areas or in deep cover. As the situation stabilized, much effort was concentrated on forming worker-peasant alliances and on proselytizing the peasant conscripts of Diem's armed forces. However, Party members were ready to concede that Diem's policies, particularly the land issue that so antagonized the peasantry, were more important than the Party's political work in aiding the recovery.

Throughout 1957–1959 the Party adhered to the policy of political rather than violent resistance. However, because its apparatus had proven too vulnerable to the Cong An, Diem's secret police, the Party decided to answer in kind. Although the small main force armed units that survived Diem's 1956 offensive sought to avoid contact with government forces, another type of armed activity was initiated. Called tru gian by the Party ("extermination of traitors"), this revived policy, which had been employed heavily against the French, called for the assassination of government officials and agents considered dangerous to the Party.

The "extermination" policy was conducted in absolute secrecy. The Party denied responsibility for acts of terror and attempted to blame Saigon. The "traitors" picked for death fell into several categories. First and foremost were Cong An agents and other government officials who proved successful in tracking down members of the secret Party apparatus. Other victims included locally influential anti-Communist teachers, Civic Action Cadres who took their task too seriously, and local government officials. In the latter category, the Party was careful to target officials who proved honest and effective; the corrupt and inefficient were left in peace. Although some of the executions might have been the result of local vendettas, tru gian was unquestionably a premediated policy with a long pedigree in the Party's history. (During and after World War II, the Party waged a ruthless campaign of assassination and intimidation against anti-Communist nationalist groups competing for leadership of the anti-French crusade.) It was a dangerous tactic. Just as many Vietnamese followed the Party because of their hatred for the GVN security services, relatives and friends of tru gian victims might well become enemies of the revolution out of hatred. Indeed, many of the most dedicated and skilled of the Party's opponents were driven by a desire for personal revenge. Nevertheless, the Party persevered in their role in the cycle of terror in Vietnam and, as shall be seen, later increased it greatly. There were very good reasons to do so. The "extermination" campaign protected Party cadres, sowed fear among GVN officials, and encouraged corruption and inefficiency on the part of government officials. In the words of a former Party leader in Dinh Tuong province, "In principle, the Party tried to kill any (government) official who enjoyed the people's sympathy and left the bad officials unharmed in order to wage propaganda and sow hatred against the government."

It should be stressed, however, that, until 1960, even the extermination program was a small-scale and secret effort. The Party did not consider it as a move toward the armed struggle phrase, during which the GVN would be challenged openly and assaulted with all possible vigor. The Party also kept secret its major role in sporadic fighting between GVN forces and remnants of the religious sects. In general, despite pleas for armed resistance coming from many southern cadres, the Party leadership in Hanoi continued its political—as opposed to armed—strategy.

In Saigon, Diem appeared to be riding high. Government armed forces were lightly opposed and, thanks to U.S. aid, growing in size. Administration was expanded and tightened down to the village level. The government was increasingly able to collect taxes. A village militia (Dan Ve) and a Civil Guard (Bao An) were organized to protect village and district officials and installations, respectively. Cong An agents were active everywhere, identifying potential enemies of the regime. Diem convinced the Americans in Saigon (and he may have believed this himself) that continued insurgent activity was, in fact, a futile "last gasp" of a movement that had been defeated politically. In 1959, Diem launched his most intensive campaign against the Party. Military and Cong An operations increased steadily, and, in May, Diem promulgated Law 10/59, which provided for harsh punishment for virtually any antigovernment activity. . . .

Perhaps the Party waited too long before striking back. Events, however, vindicated the leadership. Though doctrinal disputes in the politburo and pressure to adhere to Moscow's peaceful coexistence policy of the late 1950s played a role in the decision to delay armed struggle, much more important was the Party's view of the essential nature of Diem's regime. The Saigon government was considered by its very nature to be corrupt, repressive, and inefficient. The urban, and often Catholic, moneyed elite that supported Diem was viewed by the Party as predatory in relation to the rural masses. Although the Party no doubt underestimated Diem in the short run, strategists in Hanoi believed that his military and administrative advances ultimately would count for nothing and actually would aid the Party. The leadership expected that Saigon's performance would prove to the peasants the truth of the Party's propaganda line. The Party was certain that, as Diem's administrative control of the rural areas extended, it would bring with it corruption, hated landlords, an unpopular draft and militia requirements, travel restrictions, bad administration, and an American presence that the masses would find humiliating. Thus, any apparent success for Saigon would be superficial and temporary. As Diem's regime revealed its true face to the masses, the Party was confident that an ever more favorable political situation would evolve. When the time was ripe, the Party would begin armed struggle, and the entire Diem apparatus, however imposing on paper, would collapse in short order. Events would show that the Party was entirely correct in its assessment. However difficult the local situation might become, the Party was determined to be patient and to allow Diem's oppression to create the political preconditions for armed struggle. The following quote from a high-level defector outlines Party policy at this time:

> The general situation, as I know from my own areas, and as cadres from other areas told me, was that the cadres and the people were terribly anxious to cross to the armed phase, but that the Central Committee sought every means to prolong the political phase according to its concept of the "ripe situation." What is a "ripe situation"? It is one in which the masses have been brought to a point where, if not a majority, then at least a certain number must follow the path laid out by the Party: They must see no other escape from their predicament. How does one create a "ripe situation"? That is the purpose of political struggle. During that period Diem's terrorist policy was becoming more blatant day by day, and the alienation of the people from the government was becoming greater and greater. Thus the Party pushed the struggle movement, which increased the terrorism. But the more the people were terrorized, the more they reacted in opposition, yet the more they reacted, the more violently they were terrorized. Continue this until the situation is truly ripe, and it will explode, according to a saying of Mao Tse-tung: "A firefly can set a whole field ablaze." Yet for a firefly to set a whole field ablaze the field must be extremely dry. "To make the field dry" in this situation meant that we had to make the people suffer until they could no longer endure it. Only then would they carry out the Party's armed policy. That is why the Party waited until it did.

In any event, the Party's patience provided ample rewards. In May 1959 (the exact date is uncertain), the Party Central Committee in Hanoi decided to begin armed struggle in closest coordination with continuing political struggle. This change in direction, eagerly sought by the southern cadres, quickly brought about a dramatic change in the overall balance of forces between Diem and his opponents. Throughout Vietnam, main force provincial battalions were reformed, and traditional base areas were rebuilt. Everywhere, preparations were under way to engage Diem's forces in selective combat.

The switch to armed struggle was best evidenced by a sharp increase in terrorism. The "extermination of traitors" campaign was quickened in the last half of 1959. In early 1960, the Party launched a ferocious assault on Diem's rural political apparatus, highlighted by coordinated assassinations during the 1960 Tet celebrations of January 18–25. South Vietnamese figures supplied to the U.S. Embassy listed 233 assassinations in 1959, 143 of them taking place in the last two quarters. In the first five months of 1960, this figure surged to 780.

It is difficult to overrate the importance of the terror campaign. Previously, Saigon officials had virtual freedom of movement in the countryside. Many appointed officials lived in the villages to which they were assigned. But Party members had to move in extreme secrecy and were in continued peril. The great upswing in the "extermination of traitors" campaign changed the situation virtually overnight. Local officials were forced back into fortified compounds located in district or province capitals. Movement became hazardous. More hazardous still, on the part of an official, was a display of competence or genuine anti-Communist zeal. Most important, by forcing the government of officials back into the towns, the Party was able to reestablish its political presence in the countryside. Political agitation, political and military recruitment, administration reorganization, and taxation could be undertaken with a degree of safety unknown to the Party for years, particularly at night.

Ultimately, the Party's success in isolating the Saigon government from the rural population in most of South Vietnam would prove fatal to Diem. However, in terms of immediate impact in 1959, both domestically and internationally, the initiation of main force combat was nearly as important, and it more clearly represented the mortal threat coming from the Party toward the Diem regime. From the beginning, the Party's military efforts were characterized by careful planning, which, when combined with strict secrecy, ensured that insurgent forces would attack with local superiority. Regular combat began on 26 September 1959 when 2d Liberation Battalion ambushed two companies of the ARVN 23d Division, inflicted 26 casualties, and captured most of their weapons. A more spectacular assault occurred on 25 January 1960 when the same insurgent battalion, reinforced with local guerrillas, penetrated the compound of the 32d Regiment, 21st ARVN Division at Tay Ninh. The insurgents succeeded in killing 23 government soldiers and capturing a large number of arms. This assault was a very grim portent. According to Lt. Gen. Samuel Williams, head of the U.S. military advisory group, the defeat at Tay Ninh was a "severe blow to the prestige of the Vietnamese Army and an indication of the VC ability to stage large-size well-planned attacks."

Taken individually, small military actions reduced Diem's power not a bit. Party-led forces were still far too small to threaten ARVN with defeat in the field. However, victories over Diem's army were excellent propaganda and served to raise the morale of those attempting to destroy the government. Developments were truly ominous from Diem's point of view. Not only were the insurgents quickly succeeding in destroying Saigon's control over the countryside and replacing it with a functioning administration, they were also establishing a military apparatus that could protect the insurgency and allow it to expand. In retrospect, it is clear that the Party seized the initiative from Saigon in late 1959–1960. It was not to be relinquished until well after American intervention. The speed of the collapse of Diem's rural political apparatus in many parts of South Vietnam is the best testimony concerning the Saigon government's lack of legitimacy in the countryside. . . .

Diem had been murdered by his generals, but he was destroyed by the Front. By late 1963, the Party had succeeded in fashioning a revolutionary movement that the GVN could not handle. Soon, American and North Vietnamese intervention would change the nature of the conflict in fundamental ways. Consequently, at this point, it is appropriate to analyze in greater detail how the Front operated in Hau Nghia province. By doing so, we can examine the indigenous "people's war" in South Vietnam at high tide, before the intervention of outside forces. Hopefully, it will also be possible to better appreciate the depth of the catastrophe that faced Americans in Vietnam when they stepped in after Diem's demise to prevent a Front victory.

Although other scholars have described the organizational structure of the Front and Party in great detail, a summary is required here. Because the general direction of the insurgency was firmly in the hands of the Party, the highest organizational echelon was the Central Committee in Hanoi. No major policy was developed without its consent. Operationally, however, the second echelon—the Party's bureau of southern affairs, called COSVN by the Americans—was more important. In practice, the distinction between COSVN and the Central Committee was not rigid; some members of COSVN were also members of the Central Committee, thus allowing the bureau to set policy on all but the most vital matters. Although overall policy was determined at COSVN or the Central Committee, descending organizational echelons were responsible for implementing directives in a manner appropriate to local conditions. . . .

Although the village committee was the lowest echelon on the organizational chart, it was considered by the Party to be the most important for the purpose of waging revolutionary war. The Party worked tirelessly at strengthening the village apparatus. The village chapter, made up of small cells of Party members, was directly responsible for the implementation of Party policy at the village and hamlet level. This included everything from propagandizing the masses to collecting taxes to finding recruits for the local military units. Everywhere, Front organizations, such as the Farmers' Liberation Association or the Women's Liberation Association, were organized to more fully mobilize the peasantry. The emphasis placed by the Party on the village yielded crucial dividends. Because the insurgents, whether Party members or not, were locally recruited, they were able to identify directly with the rural population and exploit bonds of family and friendship. The revolutionaries were personally intimate with the population and therefore could identify, pressure, intimidate, or, if necessary, eliminate individuals opposed to their movement. Unless someone was picked for promotion or assigned service in main force divisions, followers of the revolution rarely had to leave their home provinces and normally operated in or near their home hamlets. This situation not only was good for morale but also made possible the superb intelligence apparatus that was characteristic of the insurgency. The Party's village emphasis also facilitated timely and relentless propaganda. As Jeffrey Race has pointed out, the Party was careful to subordinate every political effort to the struggle with the GVN and to keep the village apparatus from developing into a mere administrative unit.

In general, the Party and Front were skillfully organized, combining the ability to centralize policy formulation and implementation, on one hand, with the ability to react to local conditions and events, on the other. The Party leadership combined organizational brilliance with an uncanny ability to exploit genuine grievances, put their opponents in the worst possible light, mobilize political-military action, generate fear among their enemies, and, most importantly, convince supporters that victory was inevitable. Political, psychological, physical, and military factors continually interacted in the Party's calculation. The weave of revolutionary warfare was so complex that it is difficult to know where to begin to unravel it for the purposes of analysis. The land issue, however, is an obvious place to start.

In a traditional agrarian society, even one like Vietnam where much was changing quickly, the individual's relationship to the land is central to economic and social existence. Just as land was fundamental in determining wealth and status, it was fundamental in defining political position. Indeed, more than anything else, it was the land issue that ultimately brought Diem to ruin. . . . Diem attempted to restore the position of Vietnamese landlords who had been dispossessed by the Viet Minh. Although he tried to placate the peasantry with a feeble and corrupt land reform plan, his land policy, as recounted by a founder of the NLF, was a disaster:

> In the countryside he destroyed at a blow the dignity and livelihood of several hundred thousand peasants by canceling the land-redistribution arrangements instituted by the Viet Minh in the areas they had controlled prior to 1954. He might have attempted to use American aid to compensate owners and capitalize on peasant goodwill; instead he courted the large landholders. Farmers who had been working land they considered their own, often for years, now faced demands for back rent and exorbitant new rates. It was an economic disaster for them. . . . The result of all this was a frustrated and indignant peasantry, fertile ground for anti-Diem agitation.

With the land issue, Diem provided the Party leaders with a perfect tool to begin the process of integrated political and military struggle that the Party called dau tranh. At any given phase of the war, debate took place within the Party over which strategy was appropriate to the balance of forces as they existed at the moment. Nevertheless, the leadership was always in agreement on one point: Political struggle and military struggle must be linked continually. The hammer and anvil was a common metaphor. Political struggle, naturally, had to dominate in the initial stage of a protracted conflict. Measures had to be calculated to simultaneously increase the power of the revolution and decrease the power of the "puppet" regime. Eventually, persuasive and coercive measures were directed toward every sector of Vietnamese society and all organs of the GVN's political-military apparatus. First of all, however, the Party had to nurture its revolutionary core, the foundation upon which the entire effort was based. In Hau Nghia, as in much of rural Vietnam, this core was the landless peasantry.

Hau Nghia province was not destitute, but it was poor. Land in Hau Nghia, unlike that in the Mekong Delta proper to the south, did not allow double rice harvests. The population density, however, was high. Consequently, many peasant families lived an existence that was uncomfortably close to dire need. Although precise figures from Hau Nghia are not available, the number of landless peasants must have been very high. As previously mentioned, large plantations were a prominent fixture during the French period. According to GVN figures from 1964, in the southern region of South Vietnam, which included Hau Nghia, 44.4 percent of the peasants were landless in 1961. Another 28.5 percent rented some land, and only 22 percent of the peasants farmed their own land exclusively. In land area, this meant that 62.5 percent of land was rented and 35.2 percent privately owned. Large landowners, in Vietnamese terms, dominated. According to an exhaustive American study done in 1968, the upper 9.5 percent of landowners owned 54.7 percent of the land in the same southern region in 1966. On the other end of the scale, the bottom 26.6 percent of the landowners owned less than one hectare and accounted for only 2.5 percent of the land owned. In neighboring Long An province, the percentages were even more unbalanced: In 1968, 79 percent of the peasantry were landless.

Students of the Vietnam War have long realized the critical nature of the land issue for the Party. Douglas Pike wrote:

> "He should own the land who rubs it between his hands each season," runs an ancient Vietnamese proverb, expressing the great hunger that only the landless who work the land can ever fully understand. In a primarily agrarian society such as Vietnam, concern for land and land tenure problems is second only to concern for weather, and the NLF in those areas where land was a major issue, the Mekong Delta and the coastal lowlands, made full use of it. . . . Cadres were instructed to turn every issue into land terms.

Gabriel Kolko maintains that the struggle for land was "the single most important issue not only of the war in the south after 1960 but in the entire history of the Revolution."

Despite the importance of the issue, it is a very tricky one to analyze because of its multiple manifestations. Obviously, it touched on material conditions. Landless peasants, for instance, had to do stoop labor. Unless a landless peasant had the good fortune of having sustained access to fertile land, housing would be of the crudest variety and diet monotonous, even if adequate. A poor landless peasant would probably own almost no consumer goods. Psychological stress stemming from uncertainty over the future added a bleakness to life. Land, along with the family, was security. Bad weather, political disturbance, or blight could turn a marginal existence into a nightmare very quickly. Likewise, social status was largely determined by landholding. Village affairs were traditionally dominated, although not exclusively so, by landowners. Weddings, funerals, and Tet celebrations, so important in village life, were usually very meager affairs for a poor peasant. Even gravesites, so central to Ong Ba, were far more humble for the landless. Having only labor to sell, few landless peasants could afford to properly educate their children. Obviously, these inequities provided boundless opportunities for Front cadres with an equalitarian message preaching class conflict.

There was considerable debate within the Party over what constituted a "class enemy" and a "landlord." The requirements of revolutionary warfare posed a dilemma for the Party that had no obvious solution. On one hand, by their very nature, "Front tactics" required reaching out to a large part of the social spectrum. Indeed, it was central to dau tranh to have political struggle across the entire social spectrum at all times. On the other hand, the "base element" of the revolution, the poor peasantry and urban workers, had to be convinced that the social struggle was uniquely theirs. Only if this were done could the Party ask for the sacrifices inherent in the struggle. This presented no problem in the area of propaganda and indoctrination: As will be seen directly, the Party was skilled at developing propaganda themes to suit every group. However, in terms of social action in realms controlled by the Party, principally "liberated areas" and within the Front apparatus itself, the problem was direct and pressing. The debate was entirely tactical because, as shown in dramatic fashion by the bloody "land reform" carried out in North Vietnam during the late 1950s, collectivization was considered the ideal answer to the land question. This fact, of course, was not advertised to the peasants who had "reactionary" views on the matter.

In general, the Party accepted a rather lenient definition of "landowner." The Party line on the subject was described by a middle-ranking civilian cadre of the Central Nam Bo (an area including Hau Nghia) Propaganda Culture Indoctrination Section. The man was from Duc Hoa and was assigned to work in a liberated zone in Duc Hue district. Although he was considered to be from a "good element" of society because of his Front sympathies, he was not asked to join the Party because he was well educated and his father-in-law was a large landowner. As he later described it, his section was employed in "propaganda, mass culture, indoctrination and training work. The word 'mass' here refers only to workers and agricultural laborers. The Section is supposed to follow the thinking of the mass in order to put it right and to strengthen it." The man gave a succinct definition of "landowner":

Those who live on their agricultural revenues and don't work at all with their hands. They hire laborers or collect land rent. The amount of their property differs according to the region. Landowners who have sold their land are still considered landowners and may be denounced as are others in their class.

The man also gave a more comprehensive description of the Party's view of the class structure in the countryside:

The VC classified the country people as follows:
A. Exploiter country people:
    1. Entirely [hoan toan] exploiters and our enemies, that is the landowners.
    2. Exploiters to a certain degree and our allies for the time being, that is the rich farmers who don't work much.
B. Middle farmers classified as:
    1. Middle farmers, near the rich farmers, somewhat exploiters.
    2. Middle farmers.
    3. Middle farmers, just up-graded from poor farmers. The middle farmers are further classified as old and new middle-farmers. The latter are those who have been up-graded since 1945 and are considered worthier than old middle farmers.
C. Poor farmers who have only little and whose work is the main source of revenue.
D. Landless farmers.

It should be pointed out that the "poor" and "landless" farmers listed above would have constituted at least 70 percent of the population of Hau Nghia province.

Any researcher using the interrogation reports of Front and Party defectors must be struck by the extremely high proportion of poor peasants among them. A very typical example was given in 1966 by a former squad leader in a Front main force battalion operating in Hau Nghia province, who recalled his decision to join the Front:

I became active in the Front in January 1964. I was working as a laborer in a ricefield about a kilometer from my village when a VC cadre came and persuaded me to join the Front. . . . He said I would be working for the people and the nation, and thus for the liberation of the peasants from feudalism and landlordism and the nation from American domination. Besides I would be given 2 hectares of land which I would then be able to farm as my own. . . . The aim that appealed to me most was the overthrow of landlordism, as I believed land would be distributed to the peasants, particularly to those who worked for the Revolution. . . . I was dissatisfied with my life, because my family was very poor. I only thought of having land to help my parents lead a better life.

In practice, the Front moved carefully in the matter of land redistribution. The details were left to the village cadres and, as might be imagined, had to be worked out with great care to minimize painful and divisive disputes among tenants. For the most part, they were careful not to antagonize middle-level peasants. Large holdings owned by absentee landlords or the GVN were confiscated and distributed to the tenants, with most peasants receiving between one-half and one hectare of land. Rents, where still paid, were frequently less than 10 percent—a much lower total than was the case in GVN areas. The Front also introduced a policy of progressive taxation that both lowered most peasants' tax bills considerably and discouraged the ownership of surplus land. Land was distributed conditionally. Peasants were expected to support the Front with taxes, with membership in mass organizations, or, if necessary, militarily. If a peasant refused to do so, his land could be lost. Obviously, all the advantages gained by Front reforms would be lost if the GVN prevailed. Thus, the land reform program was more than a strategy to gain popularity. Above all, it was aimed at gaining peasant commitment to the Front.

As the Front began to prevail in Hau Nghia, the land distribution process was started. In Loc Giang village, for instance, the Front had controlled most of the hamlets since 1961. Land distribution, however, did not begin until at least one year later. A Front rallier from Loc Giang, quoted earlier, recalled that land was allocated on the basis of need and family size: A family of four might get half a hectare, a family of eight, an entire hectare. This man believed that yields increased only somewhat, if at all, but he did not see increased production as the major reward: "The only good thing in land distribution was that the poor didn't have to work as hired laborers any more, because they had their own land to work on."

Difficulties were inevitable. Although the details are not clear, apparently the Front was initially too aggressive at redistribution in some locales and antagonized middle-level peasants. The education officer of Tay Ninh province (which included Trang Bang district until October 1963) had served first the Viet Minh and then the Front for over twenty years; he recalled that, in 1961, a furious debate took place over the pace of redistribution. In some areas, he recalled, land had been distributed to middle-level peasants. Later, the Party reversed course and wanted to "inflict punitive measures" against class enemies. This included redistributing the land given to some well-off peasants in favor of the very poor. Militants carried the day in Tay Ninh, but, as time went on, the Front increasingly sought "solidarity with middle farmers."

The Party used the land issue to begin the momentum of revolutionary struggle. It touched many people, it was immediately understandable, and it led to direct commitment on the part of many toward the Front. If the Party's position on land struck a chord with the peasants, an issue that they knew intimately, then it was natural for them to believe the Party on issues that were more distant and unfamiliar. Yet, the struggle in rural Vietnam was far more complex and dynamic than a simple matter of grievance and response. In many respects, commitment was more important than any particular issue. Certainly, the method of transmitting the message was as important as the message itself.

Various Front mass political organizations had a crucial role in the indoctrination of the peasantry. The Farmers' Liberation Association was the largest and most important. Among others were the Women's Liberation Association and Youth Liberation Association. Within these, various cadres worked at "educating" and developing the "class consciousness" of the peasantry. Mass gatherings, study sessions, and Chinese-inspired self-criticism meetings were continual. In the words of one captured education cadre from Hau Nghia, the Front "assigned a great many people to the education mission in order to continuously develop the culture of the people." The rallier from Loc Giang recalled, "There were all kinds of cadres for all categories of the villagers. Young men had young man cadres, young women had young woman cadres, old men had old man cadres and old women had old woman cadres, etc."

The theme stressed most often was class hatred. If the class enemy could be linked with foreign imperialism, all the better. The following propaganda motif came from Duc Hue:

> This village-chief's family has its members educated in town. They are pilots and officers for the Americans and the puppet government. His sons and grandsons strafe and bomb our village and hamlets. By that you can see that landowners always go hand in hand with the imperialists to fight against us peasants and workers.

The national appeal was also used with the peasantry to great effect but was secondary until American intervention. The following is a line developed for Front schools in the Hau Nghia area:

> There is only one Vietnam Nation. There is only one Vietnamese People. North and South are under the same roof. Therefore when the Americans come to Vietnam, it is the duty of the Vietnamese people to throw them out of the country. They come here as aggressors. They come to invade Vietnam, therefore the Vietnamese people are determined to chase them out of the country, to liberate the South and to unify the nation.

Naturally, the GVN was constantly mocked and criticized. Inflation, high prices, corruption by officials, and "decadent" Western culture were all recurring themes.

The Front also exploited resistance to conscription. Although many young men drafted by the GVN were able to serve near home, the Front offered the opportunity to avoid uniformed service altogether. Before American intervention, the Front usually refrained from forcing young men to join revolutionary military forces. Membership in one of the various organizations was sufficient commitment initially. Naturally, Front cadres hoped a young man would volunteer for more arduous and risky tasks as indoctrination and peer pressure did their work. As the military defector from Loc Giang remembered:

> Most of the fighters were draft dodgers. At first, the cadres said they could come to their area to dodge the GVN draft without having to work for the Front. The cadres let them go free for a few months before they started forming study sessions for these draft dodgers and sending female cadres to proselyte them.

Even when a young man chose to "hold the Front's gun," service had its attractions. A hamlet guerrilla lived a largely civilian existence at home and played a military role only when necessary.

Convincing someone to join main force military units that required full-time service away from home was much harder. The indoctrination cadre asserted that even Party members were often reluctant to leave their home villages for risky service with main force units. He also recalled that young men were hiding from both the Front and the GVN outside many villages, being fed secretly by their families. Front cadres would do their best to convince these families to have their sons come home. More testimony on the subject comes from the interrogation of current affairs chief of the Youth Group Committee from Trang Bang district. This man had fought the French, gone north in 1954, returned to Trang Bang in 1963, and surrendered in 1966. He claimed that most young men were war weary:

> I've dealt with youths of three areas—contested areas, weak areas and deep areas. Most of the youths in the deep areas have relatives working for the VC, so they support the revolution. Moreover, they are poor. They either join the Front troops or stay home to do farming, but they hide themselves when the GVN or Americans make operations to the area. The youths in contested areas are pacifistic, they avoid both sides. We call them uncommitted youths. They don't work for the GVN and don't work for the Front full-time, they only dig trenches, build combat fences, etc. These kinds of youths follow whichever side makes better propaganda. The youths in weak areas, like cities and strategic hamlets, don't approve of communism and VC, but they don't want to be drafted by the GVN because they think they will be killed by the VC in battles. Therefore, they try all means to avoid the draft. These kinds of youths have low morale in serving the revolution, so we select the good ones among them to educate and propagandize.

As this quote illustrates, it was one thing to create a climate of sympathy for the aims of the Front but quite another to actually mobilize individuals to face the risks and harsh life required to carry the revolution to victory. Grievances alone, no matter how genuine, do not make revolutions. The direction, inspiration, and energy for struggle had to be supplied by the Front cadres.

It is impossible here to do justice to the role played by the cadres from top to bottom. The Party, of course, was an archetype Leninist organization. Consequently, the top cadres made policy and expected it to be implemented faithfully down each rung of the organizational ladder. Local initiative, however, was expected and encouraged. Local cadres also had the key role of reporting on the local situation, which was crucial for Party strategists in determining the balance of forces and creating appropriate policy.

Equally important, local cadres served as examples of revolutionary virtue. They were expected to be honest, sincere, and brave. After the war, COSVN commander Gen. Tran Van Tra defined revolutionary virtue and explained its importance:

Virtue is manifested in behavior between people, between the general and the specific, in the family and in society. Everyone must love and respect each other, and be faithful, sincere and loyal. . . . It must be Vietnamese morality and communist morality, which combine to form the virtue of Ho Chi Minh. . . . If words are not accompanied by action they have no value, theory not demonstrated by reality is only empty theory. Every individual must be exemplary in study, work, combat, production, and one's way of life, and life in an exemplary, close-knit family and an orderly, harmonious society. If we are not exemplary no one will listen to us, and if families are not harmonious and exemplary there is no way to create an orderly, just society.

General Tra was describing an ideal. It was an ideal, however, that Front and particularly Party cadres took very seriously. Compared to their GVN counterparts, Front cadres had many advantages. GVN officials were usually members of the urban elite. In contrast, because most Front cadres came from rural Vietnam and frequently were from the area in which they operated, they dressed like, lived like, and thought like the local peasantry. Whereas GVN officials, whether honest or corrupt, received status and material benefit from their position, Front cadres worked for a pittance. Standard pay was 3$ (about 3 cents) per day and 20 to 25 kilos of rice per month. The military rallier from Loc Giang, quoted earlier, described the propaganda advantages of this point:

The cadres always cultivated hatred toward the GVN in the people during study sessions. Why could they do that? Because they said they didn't get paid to work as cadres for the Front; they worked because the Front has the just cause to work for.

Mistreatment of villagers on the part of GVN officials or soldiers was a continual grievance. The Hiep Hoa finance cadre, also quoted earlier, recounted the Party's policy on personal behavior:

I should point out that all VC cadres are subject to a very strict set of rules of behavior laid down by the Party. For example, a cadre may drink, but may not get drunk. Drunkenness is punishable by dismissal, although I have known of cases where individuals have been given several warnings for this offense. No cadre may steal anything, especially from the people. A stolen chicken from a farmer will result in dismissal from the Party.

The same man described the Party's policy toward the issue of civilian casualties, an area where the GVN was frequently indifferent:

Mistreating the people is a very serious offense, although sometimes a regrettable incident occurs when innocent civilians are killed or wounded by one of our mines or booby-traps. In Hiep Hoa, whenever this happened, we would always attempt to visit the family to offer apologies, and explain that the incident was an accident of war. It was bad for our cause when this happened, and we always tried to smooth over the damage when possible.

A different rejoinder might be used if the war damage was material only. A production cell leader in a tiny arms factory in Cu Chi described how the

Front handled complaints from villagers concerning battle damage to their hamlet:

> Peasants would complain to neighbors that VC hiding in houses were to blame for damage (which was slight); VC would answer, "We would not complain if we lost our lives to defend the people, so why do the people complain loudly when they suffer a little damage to their property? You have no constructive spirit."

The cell leader also described the deep impact made on villagers by the cadres' willingness to sacrifice:

> People knew life with ARVN was much easier: They got paid monthly and suffered no hardship. The VC life is very hard. The VC used the earth as their beds, and the open sky as their mosquito nets. This was what the people said, but in the meeting organized by the VC they said that their life was full of glory and their death full of greatness. They asked the people to join the Revolutionary movement. Besides, their attitude toward the people was very courteous; therefore, the people were very glad to join the VC.

Finally, the same man recalled the excellent behavior of Front military forces when in the area, in sharp contrast to ARVN's reputation for haughty conduct:

> Front solders came frequently to help build combat villages and fight ARVN. The population liked them very much because they were always ready to help them with their pit digging or their gardening. The people listened to them very eagerly whenever they told the stories of their lives. All the young men in my hamlet who were to be drafted by ARVN joined the Front.

Front cadres tirelessly dispensed indoctrination and propaganda to villagers. The primary recipients of the Front's message, however, were the cadres themselves. Even the lowest-level cadre was required to attend training courses. The ideological component of these courses for village cadres did not contain elaborate Marxist analysis: their Leninism was decidedly secondhand. A longtime province-level education cadre noted that most village or hamlet cadres had only a vague idea about communism and, in the recent past, were "merely oppressed people" that had risen, thanks to the Front, to become "some sort of VIP in the village." They were content with their lot and followed the ideological lead of their superiors without question. Higher up the ladder, however, cadres received more and more extensive training in ideological matters. Whereas hamlet and village cadres followed the Front primarily because of rural issues, such as land, higher cadres tended to stress the international struggle against "American Imperialism." Whatever the precise motives of the individuals involved, the Front was very successful in instilling in their political cadres a faith in their cause and a powerful faith in ultimate victory. As we shall see, enough of them kept this faith, despite extraordinary military pressure, to frustrate the American war effort in the Vietnamese countryside.

Regardless of a cadre's level, self-criticism sessions were frequent. These sessions were normally a type of group therapy with members of the group criticizing and praising themselves and others. Cadres were urged to always remember that they were there to serve the people and should never forget the lot of the poor peasant. Another aim of self-criticism was the prevention of complacency and self-delusion. The Cu Chi district youth secretary was asked during interrogation to explain the Party's reasons for self-criticism:

> Because they want the people to tell the truth. Because they think that if we are doing wrong, the only way we can be corrected is to do it ourselves, not to wait until the other person does it. You don't have to wait until the other person corrects you. Do it yourself, purge yourself. Secondly, it's a method of self-help and we also need the help of the other people.

If a cadre were suspected of losing this zeal or, worse, becoming corrupt, self-criticism was more akin to a trial than therapy. Under such circumstances, the individual was well advised to confess promptly if guilty. If he did not, and was later found to be culpable, punishment, in one cadre's words, could be "stiff, very stiff."

Various internal difficulties impeded Front efforts. After 1960, a large number of "regroupee" cadres came to the South after having lived and trained in the DRV since the Geneva Accords were signed in 1954. This was not a north/south problem per se because most of these individuals were southern born. Their experiences and perspectives were different, however. The regroupees were frequently given senior positions and expected the respect and deference they believed their due because of their long experience and sacrifice. Military regroupees had more experience in handling larger groups of men than did their younger counterparts. The more recent cadres believed that the regroupees frequently had lost touch with southern conditions. In the military area, younger fighters had experienced combat against modern weapons (such as helicopters and armored personnel carriers) employed by ARVN since 1962, which had not been used during the Viet Minh period. There was also the apparently well-founded suspicion that a few of the regroupees had grown weary of struggle and came to the South because of homesickness or hatred of life in the North.

Illicit love affairs also were a frequent cause of morale problems. Sexual morality in rural Vietnam was traditionally quite conservative. The Front pointed to prostitution, drug use, and other forms of moral debauchery as manifestations of a malignant capitalist culture being imposed on Vietnam by the United States. In general, the Front tried to pose as the defender of traditional Vietnamese family values. On the other hand, the Front took a very progressive stance, in Vietnamese terms, on women's equality. Women were widely employed at all levels of the revolution, except main force combat. Consequently, a great many young men and women found themselves together outside traditional settings. As recalled by the finance cadre from Hiep Hoa, the Front tried to encourage a puritanical code of conduct:

> Second wives and mistresses are forbidden. If the woman is single, the punishment is dismissal. If she is married, the punishment may be confinement as well as dismissal. It does not matter if the woman is the wife of a fellow-VC cadre or of a GVN soldier or official. The first is frowned upon because it can only create dangerous dissension in the ranks. The latter is regarded as dangerous because of the security risk of consorting with the wife of an enemy.

Nevertheless, pregnancy, jealousy, and other domestic strife was very common. One cadre recounted a most uncomfortable incident in Duc Hoa:

> I lived in a security cadre's house near the GVN post. One day a drunkard in the neighborhood shouted: "You false revolutionaries, you have availed yourself of the revolution to make a woman pregnant, then have abandoned her." I asked my host to go out and make him hold his tongue. He reluctantly went out but didn't succeed. Later I was told that he himself was the culprit. Such cases were very common in the country since young men and girls are working together.

The youth secretary from Trung Lap showed resignation when commenting on a similar incident: "The whole country's in heat. Especially when the people are mixed up, all thrown in together there, it's bound to happen.". . .

Despite all difficulties, Front cadres built on a foundation left by the Viet Minh and succeeded in creating a sympathetic political climate in Hau Nghia province. An American researcher studying Hau Nghia in 1968 was startled to find some families that had supported the Viet Minh-NLF for three generations. The researcher remarked on how deeply the Party's view of events had penetrated:

> The everyday speech patterns of the people of the district reflect the characteristic expressions of the Viet Cong. Peasants referred to the central government as "Diem-My" (Diem-American) usually followed in VC terminology by "clique" or "gang."

In 1962, Gerald Hickey made a strikingly similar observation on the attitudes of the people of Cu Chi:

> The people here have learned from early childhood to view reality through the prism of Viet Cong ideas, beliefs and prejudices. Success in turning these people toward actual allegiance to a nationalist government would thus require extraordinary measures applied over a long period of time.

Yet, the Front's success in rural areas like Hau Nghia was not entirely due to its great ability to exploit real or imagined grievances and present an alternative view of the future. The cynical manipulation of fear in all of its manifestations was a central component in the Party's theory and practice of struggle. Most notorious was the brutal use of terror against enemies of the revolution. The Party was careful to direct its violence at the very worst or very best of GVN officials. "Punishing" (the Party's euphemism for murder) a despicable official gained the Party popularity; killing good officials sowed fear. By making efficiency and anti-Communist zeal very dangerous, the Party encouraged bad and dishonest administration in GVN areas. This, in turn, reinforced negative feelings toward Saigon on the part of the villagers. A low-level civilian cadre later described this process in a hamlet in Cu Chi:

> People said that all the good officials were either killed or chased away by the VC and they were replaced by bad officials. The VC started in 1960, killing first the Village council member in charge of police and then the hamlet chiefs. . . . All the other government officials were afraid and resigned their positions under threats from the VC; the village chief, the finance members, the Secretary of the council, all resigned. The council member in charge of police was replaced by a Civil Guard from the outpost. He was very haughty and arrogant. The new village chief was a stranger in the village. He was disliked by the population because he often tried to squeeze money.

Despite later Party efforts to pass off much of the terror campaign as the unauthorized work of "overzealous" cadres, there can be no doubt that virtually all assassinations were premeditated and came by order of high Party officials. The veteran political and education cadre quoted earlier discussed precisely this point during his interrogation:

> I can say that for every act of terrorism that happened in that province, then that is the work of the Party secretary, because he is the only one who is responsible for this kind of action. He directs all security agents to commit such acts of terror. . . . As far as killing or slaughtering is concerned, I can say that sort of thing is done entirely by the decision of the higher authority. Of course in every country or in every region there are some bad guys who act upon their own will. In the Front such a person would be subjected to punitive measures.

Probably more important than genuine acts of terror was the climate of fear and disorientation that such deeds created for those people who were undecided or indifferent toward the struggle. After all, if the GVN could not protect its own functionaries, what could a simple villager do? Questioning any Front policy would bring accusations of "reactionary thinking." A doubter would certainly be wise to watch his or her tongue, as a loose word might well be relayed to supporters of the revolution and become the topic in a self-criticism session. Furthermore, Front propaganda relentlessly propagated a stream of disinformation about the GVN and Americans. When the Front took over a hamlet, it was common to force the villagers to destroy their identity cards, thus putting them in danger of arrest if they ventured into GVN areas. Low level supporters of the Front were told that the GVN would torture them if they attempted to switch sides. U.S. aid projects were pictured as sinister tricks. The cumulative effect was to greatly encourage supporters of the revolution and intimidate both opponents and those sitting on the fence. . . .

By the end of 1965, the NLF had won the war in Hau Nghia province. PROVN [the Program for the Pacification and Long-Term Development of South Vietnam, a U.S. government study of March 1966] estimated that the insurgents controlled 53 percent of the population and "influenced" 42 percent more. Government control was put at less than 5 percent. The authors further estimated that 4,291 insurgents were active in Hau Nghia, broken down into the following categories: a 60-man "provincial hard-core" company, 1,085 cadres, 987 irregular guerrillas, 979 secret self-defense corps, and 1,180 people's self-defense corps. Enemy forces were credited with the ability to disrupt the economy, control lines of communication, and recruit, tax, and "terrorize" the population. Enemy control, according to the American officers, was due to efforts to identify the insurgency with the problems of the villagers, the exploitation of kinship ties and the use of "a 'sweet' approach, supplemented by terroristic murders, kidnappings, and torture." Furthermore, the CIA representative in Hau Nghia concluded that 98 percent of the insurgents in the province were local and that they neither got nor needed substantial aid from Hanoi—in particular, they were capable of producing their own grenades and other weapons locally.

In the face of enemy energy and strength, government forces, as described in PROVN, were capable of only feeble efforts. . . .

To the extent that the PROVN researchers were able to determine the sentiments of the population, government weakness was again revealed. A behavioral scientist, assigned to PROVN, interviewed villagers and concluded that the local inhabitants judged the GVN and the Front above all on their respective ability to provide security. Obviously, the government was considered the inferior of the two in this regard. Interviews also indicated that, where the government's presence was felt (which was only near the district towns and Bao Trai), the inhabitants did not believe that the government had any genuine interest in their welfare. Officials were aloof and shunned contact with individual villagers. In contrast, the PROVN researchers noted, the NLF made every effort to identify the movement with the problems of the villagers.

The situation in Hau Nghia by the end of 1965 was perhaps not entirely typical of the country as a whole. Certainly, the insurgency was stronger there than in some provinces, but the situation was not at all unique. Several other provinces (some of which, like Long An or Binh Dinh, were larger and more important than Hau Nghia) had likewise fallen under the nearly complete control of the NLF. Unfortunately for Saigon, these provinces had important characteristics in common—they were ethnically Vietnamese, heavily populated, and agricultural. Given that a majority of South Vietnam's people were ethnically Vietnamese, non-Catholic, and rural, it is readily apparent that, by 1965, Saigon had lost the allegiance of the largest and most important segment of the population. Consequently, the government was in a very nearly hopeless position. Only the badly flawed ARVN stood in the way of victory for the NLF. And, during 1965, ARVN was being destroyed piecemeal. It is impossible to determine how much time may have passed before the Front would have forced a favorable political or military outcome to the war. It *is* possible, however, to conclude that only the introduction of American ground forces temporarily prevented the fall of the anti-Communist government in Saigon.

✗ *F U R T H E R   R E A D I N G*

William Andrews, *The Village War* (1973)
King C. Chen, "Hanoi's Three Decisions and the Escalation of the Vietnam War," *Political Science Quarterly,* 90 (1975), 239–259
Hoang Van Chi, *From Colonialism to Communism* (1964)
Nguyen Thi Dinh, *No Other Road to Take* (1976)
William J. Duiker, *The Communist Road to Power in Vietnam* (1981)
Frances FitzGerald, *Fire in the Lake: The Vietnamese and the Americans in Vietnam* (1972)
V. C. Funnell, "Vietnam and the Sino-Soviet Conflict," *Studies in Comparative Communism,* 11 (1978), 142–199
Vo Nguyen Giap, *Big Victory, Big Task* (1967)
_____, *Unforgettable Days* (1978)
William Darryl Henderson, *Why the Vietcong Fought* (1979)
P. J. Honey, *Communism in North Vietnam* (1963)
Neil L. Jamieson, *Understanding Vietnam* (1993)
Jean Lacouture, *Ho Chi Minh: A Political Biography* (1968)
Michael Lee Lanning and Dan Cragg, *Inside the VC and the NVA* (1992)
Greg Lockhart, *Nation in Arms: The Origins of the People's Army of Vietnam* (1991)
Peter Macdonald, *Giap: The Victor in Vietnam* (1993)
Edwin E. Moise, *Land Reform in China and North Vietnam* (1983)
Daniel S. Papp, *Vietnam: The View from Moscow, Peking, Washington* (1978)
Douglas Pike, *History of Vietnamese Communism* (1978)
_____, *PAVN: People's Army of Vietnam* (1986)
_____, *Vietnam and the Soviet Union* (1987)
Samuel L. Popkin, *The Rational Peasant* (1979)
Ken Post, *Revolution, Socialism and Nationalism in Viet Nam* (vols. 1–3) (1989)
Jeffrey Race, *War Comes to Long An* (1972)
Robert L. Sansom, *The Economics of Insurgency in the Mekong Delta of Vietnam* (1970)
W. R. Smyser, *The Independent Vietnamese: Vietnamese Communism Between Russia and China, 1956–1969* (1980)
Russell Stettler, ed., *The Military Art of People's War* (1970)
James Trullinger, *Village at War* (1980)
Robert F. Turner, *Vietnamese Communism: Its Origins and Development* (1975)
Alexander B. Woodside, *Community and Revolution in Vietnam* (1976)
Donald S. Zagoria, *Vietnam Triangle* (1967)

CHAPTER
9

The Tet Offensive

✕

The Tet lunar holidays of 1968 broke across South Vietnam like a thunder-clap as the North Vietnamese and Vietcong launched a series of well-coordi-nated attacks throughout the country. The offensive heralded a new, much bolder phase in communist military and political strategy. Although Ameri-can and South Vietnamese forces ultimately repelled the attacks, inflicting heavy casualties on their adversary, the Tet offensive raised fundamental questions about the efficacy of American policy that reverberated throughout the United States. Most important, it forced a wrenching reexamination of Washington policy that culminated in President Lyndon B. Johnson's deci-sions in March 1968 to call for negotiations and to set a ceiling on U.S. troop levels.

Most analysts now agree that the communists suffered heavily for their boldness. They point especially to the devastating losses of Vietcong cadres in the fighting. Following Tet, North Vietnamese troops were compelled to play an increasingly heavy role in the struggle. Specialists agree as well that the offensive dealt the United States a powerful psychological blow, generating strong opposition to the war among elite groups and the general public. They differ, however, in their evaluation of Tet's precise military and politi-cal effects. Two questions predominate in recent studies: why was Tet such a turning point for the United States, and should it have been?

✕ D O C U M E N T S

The first three documents reflect the immediate response to Tet. First is an excerpt from Lyndon Johnson's news conference on February 2, 1968, in which the president offers his initial appraisal of the Tet offensive. Two days later, Robert McNamara and Dean Rusk presented their assessment during a joint television interview. Then on February 8, Senator Robert F. Kennedy called for a reevaluation of America's Vietnam policy, denouncing the illusions

337

that had been guiding the U.S. war effort. The next document contains extracts from a report of February 27 by General Earle G. Wheeler, chairman of the Joint Chiefs of Staff. Wheeler evaluated the military situation in the wake of the Tet attacks and repeated General William Westmoreland's request for more than 200,000 additional troops. In the fourth document, written in March 1968, the southern branch of the Vietnamese communist party gives an early evaluation of the offensive's contributions and shortcomings.

The next three readings are personal reminiscences. First, Eunice Splawn, a U.S. Air Force nurse, recalls the fears and pressures brought on by the Tet attacks. Next, Robert Komer, head of the pacification program in South Vietnam, recollects Tet's impact on U.S. officials in Saigon and Washington. Finally, Clark Clifford, who replaced McNamara as defense secretary on March 1, 1968, remembers the critical questions that he posed to top administration figures at that time.

The last selection is Johnson's public address of March 31, in which he called for a bombing halt and the beginning of negotiations with North Vietnam—and then stunned his audience with the announcement of his withdrawal from the 1968 presidential race.

Lyndon B. Johnson on the Failed Communist Offensive, 1968

Q. Do you see anything in the developments this week in these attacks in Viet-Nam that causes you to think, to reevaluate, some of the assumptions on which our policies and strategy there has been based? I am thinking in terms of the security ratings, amount of population that is considered under government control? Do you think the basic assumption is still valid?

The President: We do that every week. I would see nothing that would indicate that that should not be done. We must, all the time, try to keep up and to be sure we have not made any mistakes. If you are saying, Have we felt that what happened could not happen? the answer is "No." As a matter of fact, . . . if you have seen any of the intelligence reports, the information has been very clear that two things would happen:

One is that there would be a general uprising, as I stated.

Two, there would be a general invasion and attempt to secure military victory and that the objective would be to get a military victory and a psychological victory. That is one of the great problems the President has to deal with. He is sitting there reading these information reports while his own people, a good many of the best intentioned, are supplying him with military strategy, and the two do not fit in.

So you have to be tolerant and understand their best intentions while you are looking at the other fellow's hole card. That is what General Westmoreland has been doing while all of these Monday morning quarterbacks are pointing out to him that this is the way he should move or this is the way you should not move.

This is part of what happens when you look at history. It may be that General Westmoreland makes some serious mistakes or that I make some. We don't know. We are just acting in light of the information we have. We believe we have information about what they are trying to do there. We have taken every precaution we know of. But we don't want to give you assurance that all will be satisfactory. We see nothing that would require any change of great consequence.

We will have to move men from this place to that one. We will have to replace helicopters. Probably we had 100-odd helicopters and planes seriously damaged, and we will have to replace them. Secretary McNamara told me he could have that done very shortly.

We will have to replace the 38 planes lost, but we have approximately 5,900 planes there. We anticipate that we will lose 25 or 30 every month just from normal crashes and so forth. . . .

I am not a great strategist and tactician. I know that you are not. Let us assume that the best figures we can have are from our responsible military commanders. They say 10,000 died and we lost 249 and the South Vietnamese lost 500. That does not look like a Communist victory. I can count. It looks like somebody has paid a very dear price for the temporary encouragement that some of our enemies had.

We have approximately 5,900 planes and have lost 38 completely destroyed. We lost 100-odd that were damaged and have to be repaired. Maybe Secretary McNamara will fly in 150 shortly. Is that a great enemy victory?

In Peking today they say that we are in panic. You have to judge that for yourself. In other Communist capitals today they say that we have definitely exhibited a lack of power and that we do not have any military strength. You will have to judge that for yourself.

But General Westmoreland evaluating this for us and the Joint Chiefs of Staff reviewing it for him tell me that in their judgment their action has not been a military success.

I am measuring my words. I don't want to overstate anything. We do not believe that we should help them in making it a psychological success either.

Robert McNamara and Dean Rusk Assess the Tet Offensive, 1968

Mr. Able: Secretary McNamara, it is 3 years this week since we started bombing North Viet-Nam. It was also in '65 that we started the big buildup on the ground. What happened this week? How do you relate the ability of the Viet Cong to stage as major an offensive as this one was to the efforts we have been making these past 3 years?

Secretary McNamara: Three years ago, or more exactly, 2 1/2 years ago, in July of 1965, President Johnson made the decision—announced to our people the decision to move significant numbers of combat troops into South Viet-Nam. At that time the North Vietnamese and their associates, the Viet Cong, were on the verge of cutting the country in half and of destroying the South Vietnamese Army. We said so at the time, and I think hindsight has proven that a correct appraisal. What has happened since that time, of course, is that they have suffered severe losses, they have failed in their objective to destroy the Government of South Viet-Nam, they have failed in their objective to take control of the country. They have continued to fight.

Just 4 days ago I remember reading in our press that I had presented a gloomy, pessimistic picture of activities in South Viet-Nam. I don't think it was gloomy or pessimistic; it was realistic. It said that while they had suffered severe penalties, they continued to have strength to carry out the attacks which we have seen in the last 2 or 3 days.

Mr. Able: Mr. Secretary, are you telling us the fact that the Viet Cong, after all these years, were able to, temporarily at least, grab control of some 20-odd Provincial capitals and the city of Saigon—are you telling us this has no military meaning at all?

Secretary McNamara: No; certainly not. I think South Viet-Nam is such a complex situation—one must always look at the pluses and the minuses, and I don't mean to say there haven't been any minuses for the South Vietnamese in the last several days. I think there have been, but there have been many, many pluses. The North Vietnamese and the Viet Cong have not accomplished either one of their major objectives: either to ignite a general uprising or to force a diversion of the troops which the South Vietnamese and the United States have moved into the northern areas of South Viet-Nam, anticipating a major Viet Cong and North Vietnamese offensive in that area.

And beyond that, the North Vietnamese and the Viet Cong have suffered very heavy penalties in terms of losses of weapons and losses of men in the past several days. They have, of course, dealt a very heavy blow to many of the cities of South Viet-Nam.

Mr. Frankel: Secretary Rusk, the administration has naturally been stressing the things that they think the Viet Cong did not achieve in this week of attacks—didn't cause an uprising, which you say may have been one of their goals, didn't seize cities for any permanent period. But yet we have also been given to understand that the real name of this game out there is "Who can provide safety for whom?" And haven't they in a very serious way humiliated our ability in major cities all up and down this country to provide the South Vietnamese population that is listed as clearly in our control with a degree of assurance and safety that South Vietnamese forces and American forces together could give them?

Secretary Rusk: There is almost no way to prevent the other side from making a try. There is a way to prevent them from having a success.

I said earlier that I thought there would be a number of South Vietnamese who would take a very grumpy view over the inability of the Government to protect them against some of the things that have happened in the last 3 or 4 days. But the net effect of the transaction is to make it clear that the Viet Cong are not able to come into these Provincial capitals and seize Provincial capitals and hold them; that they are not able to announce the formation of a new committee, or a coalition or a federation, and have it pick up any support in the country; that they are not able to undermine the solidarity of those who are supporting the Government.

No; I think there is a psychological factor here that we won't be able to assess until a week or two after the event, and I might say also that we know there is going to be some hard fighting ahead. We are not over this period at all. As a matter of fact, the major fighting up in the northern part of South Viet-Nam has not yet occurred, so there are some hard battles ahead. . . .

Mr. Frankel: Secretary McNamara, let me take advantage of your valedictory mood. Looking back over this long conflict and especially in this rather agonized week in Viet-Nam, if we had to do it all over again, would you make any major changes in our—

Secretary McNamara: This is not an appropriate time for me to be talking of changes, with hindsight. There is no question but what 5 or 10 or 20 years from now the historians will find actions that might have been done differently. I am sure they will. . . . I am learning more and more about Viet-Nam every day. There is no question I see better today than I did 3 years ago or 5 years ago what might have been done there.

On balance, I feel much the way the Asian leaders do. I think the action that this Government has followed, policies it has followed, the objectives it has had in Viet-Nam, are wise. I do not by any means suggest that we have not made mistakes over the many, many years that we have been pursuing those objectives.

Mr. Frankel: You seem to suggest that we really didn't—that none of us appreciated what we were really getting into.

Secretary McNamara: I don't think any of us predicted 7 years ago or 15 years ago the deployment of 500,000 men to Viet-Nam. I know I didn't.

Robert F. Kennedy Calls Vietnam an Unwinnable War, 1968

Our enemy, savagely striking at will across all of South Vietnam, has finally shattered the mask of official illusion with which we have concealed our true circumstances, even from ourselves. But a short time ago we were serene in our reports and predictions of progress.

The Vietcong will probably withdraw from the cities, as they were forced to withdraw from the American Embassy. Thousands of them will be dead.

But they will, nevertheless, have demonstrated that no part or person of South Vietnam is secure from their attacks: neither district capitals nor American bases, neither the peasant in his rice paddy nor the commanding general of our own great forces.

No one can predict the exact shape or outcome of the battles now in progress, in Saigon or at Khesanh. Let us pray that we will succeed at the lowest possible cost to our young men.

But whatever their outcome, the events of the last two weeks have taught us something. For the sake of those young Americans who are fighting today, if for no other reason, the time has come to take a new look at the war in Vietnam; not by cursing the past but by using it to illuminate the future.

And the first and necessary step is to face the facts. It is to seek out the austere and painful reality of Vietnam, freed from wishful thinking, false hopes and sentimental dreams. It is to rid ourselves of the "good company," of those illusions which have lured us into the deepening swamp of Vietnam.

We must, first of all, rid ourselves of the illusion that the events of the past two weeks represent some sort of victory. That is not so.

It is said the Vietcong will not be able to hold the cities. This is probably true. But they have demonstrated despite all our reports of progress, of government strength and enemy weakness, that half a million American soldiers with 700,000 Vietnamese allies, with total command of the air, total command of the sea, backed by huge resources and the most modern weapons, are unable to secure even a single city from the attacks of an enemy whose total strength is about 250,000. . . .

For years we have been told that the measure of our success and progress in Vietnam was increasing security and control for the population. Now we have seen that none of the population is secure and no area is under sure control.

Four years ago when we only had about 30,000 troops in Vietnam, the Vietcong were unable to mount the assaults on cities they have now conducted against our enormous forces. At one time a suggestion that we protect enclaves was derided. Now there are no protected enclaves.

This has not happened because our men are not brave or effective, because they are. It is because we have misconceived the nature of the war: It is because we have sought to resolve by military might a conflict whose issue depends upon the will and conviction of the South Vietnamese people. It is like sending a lion to halt an epidemic of jungle rot.

This misconception rests on a second illusion—the illusion that we can win a war which the South Vietnamese cannot win for themselves.

You cannot expect people to risk their lives and endure hardship unless they have a stake in their own society. They must have a clear sense of identification with their own government, a belief they are participating in a cause worth fighting for.

People will not fight to line the pockets of generals or swell the bank accounts of the wealthy. They are far more likely to close their eyes and shut their doors in the face of their government—even as they did last week.

More than any election, more than any proud boast, that single fact reveals the truth. We have an ally in name only. We support a government without supporters. Without the efforts of American arms that government would not last a day.

The third illusion is that the unswerving pursuit of military victory, whatever its cost, is in the interest of either ourselves or the people of Vietnam.

For the people of Vietnam, the last three years have meant little but horror. Their tiny land has been devastated by a weight of bombs and shells greater than Nazi Germany knew in the Second World War.

We have dropped 12 tons of bombs for every square mile in North and South Vietnam. Whole provinces have been substantially destroyed. More than two million South Vietnamese are now homeless refugees.

Imagine the impact in our own country if an equivalent number—over 25 million Americans—were wandering homeless or interned in refugee camps, and millions more refugees were being created as New York and Chicago, Washington and Boston, were being destroyed by a war raging in their streets.

Whatever the outcome of these battles, it is the people we seek to defend who are the greatest losers.

Nor does it serve the interests of America to fight this war as if moral standards could be subordinated to immediate necessities. Last week, a Vietcong suspect was turned over to the chief of the Vietnamese Security Services, who executed him on the spot—a flat violation of the Geneva Convention on the Rules of War.

The photograph of the execution was on front pages all around the world—leading our best and oldest friends to ask, more in sorrow than in anger, what has happened to America?

The fourth illusion is that the American national interest is identical with—or should be subordinated to—the selfish interest of an incompetent military regime.

We are told, of course, that the battle for South Vietnam is in reality a struggle for 250 million Asians—the beginning of a Great Society for all of Asia. But this is pretension.

We can and should offer reasonable assistance to Asia; but we cannot build a Great Society there if we cannot build one in our own country. We cannot speak extravagantly of a struggle for 250 million Asians, when a struggle for 15 million in one Asian country so strains our forces, that another Asian country, a fourth-rate power which we have already once defeated in battle, dares to seize an American ship and hold and humiliate her crew.

The fifth illusion is that this war can be settled in our own way and in our own time on our own terms. Such a settlement is the privilege of the triumphant: of those who crush their enemies in battle or wear away their will to fight.

We have not done this, nor is there any prospect we will achieve such a victory.

Unable to defeat our enemy or break his will—at least without a huge, long and ever more costly effort—we must actively seek a peaceful settlement. We can no longer harden our terms every time Hanoi indicates it may be prepared to negotiate; and we must be willing to foresee a settlement which will give the Vietcong a chance to participate in the political life of the country.

These are some of the illusions which may be discarded if the events of last week are to prove not simply a tragedy, but a lesson: a lesson which carries with it some basic truths.

First, that a total military victory is not within sight or around the corner; that, in fact, it is probably beyond our grasp; and that the effort to win such a victory will only result in the further slaughter of thousands of innocent and helpless people—a slaughter which will forever rest on our national conscience.

Second, that the pursuit of such a victory is not necessary to our national interest, and is even damaging that interest.

Third, that the progress we have claimed toward increasing our control over the country and the security of the population is largely illusory.

Fourth, that the central battle in this war cannot be measured by body counts or bomb damage, but by the extent to which the people of South Vietnam act on a sense of common purpose and hope with those that govern them.

Fifth, that the current regime in Saigon is unwilling or incapable of being an effective ally in the war against the Communists.

Sixth, that a political compromise is not just the best path to peace, but the only path, and we must show as much willingness to risk some of our prestige for peace as to risk the lives of young men in war.

Seventh, that the escalation policy in Vietnam, far from strengthening and consolidating international resistance to aggression, is injuring our country through the world, reducing the faith of other peoples in our wisdom and purpose and weakening the world's resolve to stand together for freedom and peace.

Eighth, that the best way to save our most precious stake in Vietnam— the lives of our soldiers—is to stop the enlargement of the war, and that the best way to end casualties is to end the war.

Ninth, that our nation must be told the truth about this war, in all its terrible reality, both because it is right—and because only in this way can any Administration rally the public confidence and unity for the shadowed days which lie ahead.

No war has ever demanded more bravery from our people and our Government—not just bravery under fire or the bravery to make sacrifices—but the bravery to discard the comfort of illusion—to do away with false hopes and alluring promises.

Reality is grim and painful. But it is only a remote echo of the anguish toward which a policy founded on illusion is surely taking us.

This is a great nation and a strong people. Any who seek to comfort rather than speak plainly, reassure rather than instruct, promise satisfaction rather than reveal frustration—they deny that greatness and drain that strength. For today as it was in the beginning, it is the truth that makes us free.

Earle G. Wheeler's Report on Military Prospects After Tet, 1968

1. The Chairman, JCS and party visited SVN on 23, 24 and 25 February. This report summarizes the impressions and facts developed through conversations and briefings at MACV and with senior commanders throughout the country.

2. *Summary*

• The current situation in Vietnam is still developing and fraught with opportunities as well as dangers.

• There is no question in the mind of MACV that the enemy went all out for a general offensive and general uprising and apparently believed that he would succeed in bringing the war to an early successful conclusion.

• The enemy failed to achieve this initial objective but is continuing his effort. Although many of his units were badly hurt, the judgment is that he has the will and the capability to continue.

• Enemy losses have been heavy; he has failed to achieve his prime objectives of mass uprisings and capture of a large number of the capital cities and towns. Morale in enemy units which were badly mauled or where the men were oversold the idea of a decisive victory at TET probably has suffered severely. However, with replacements, his indoctrination system would seem capable of maintaining morale at a general adequate level. His determination appears to be unshaken.

• The enemy is operating with relative freedom in the countryside, probably recruiting heavily and no doubt infiltrating NVA units and personnel. His recovery is likely to be rapid; his supplies are adequate; and he is trying to maintain the momentum of his winter-spring offensive.

• The structure of the GVN held up but its effectiveness has suffered.

• The RVNAF held up against the initial assault with gratifying, and in a way, surprising strength and fortitude. However, ARVN is now in a defensive posture around towns and cities and there is concern about how well they will bear up under sustained pressure.

• The initial attack nearly succeeded in a dozen places, and defeat in those places was only averted by the timely reaction of US forces. In short, it was a very near thing.

• There is no doubt that the RD [rural development, or pacification] Program has suffered a severe set back.

• RVNAF was not badly hurt physically—they should recover strength and equipment rather quickly (equipment in 2–3 months—strength in 3–6 months). Their problems are more psychological than physical.

• US forces have lost none of their pre-TET capability.

• MACV has three principal problems. First, logistic support north of Danang is marginal owing to weather, enemy interdiction and harassment and the massive deployment of US forces into the DMZ/Hue area. Opening Route 1 will alleviate this problem but takes a substantial troop commitment. Second, the defensive posture of ARVN is permitting the VC to make rapid inroads in the formerly pacified countryside. ARVN, in its own words, is in a dilemma as it cannot afford another enemy thrust into the cities and towns and yet if it remains in a defensive posture against this contingency, the countryside goes by default. MACV is forced to devote much of its troop strength to this problem. Third, MACV has been forced to deploy 50% of all US maneuver battalions into I Corps, to meet the threat there, while stripping the rest of the country of adequate reserves. If the enemy synchronizes an attack against Khe Sanh/Hue-Quang Tri with an offensive in the Highlands and around Saigon while keeping the pressure on throughout the remainder of the country, MACV will be hard pressed to meet adequately all threats. Under these circumstances, we must be prepared to accept some reverses.

• For these reasons, General Westmoreland has asked for a 3 division-15 tactical fighter squadron force. This force would provide him with a theater reserve and an offensive capability which he does not now have.

    3. The situation as it stands today:
        a. Enemy capabilities
            (1) The enemy has been hurt badly in the populated lowlands, but is practically intact elsewhere. He committed over 67,000 combat maneuver forces plus perhaps 25% or 17,000 more impressed men and boys, for a total of about 84,000. He lost 40,000 killed, at least 3,000 captured, and perhaps 5,000 disabled or died of wounds. He had peaked his force total to about 240,000 just before TET, by hard recruiting, infiltration, civilian impressment, and draw-downs on service and guerrilla personnel. So he has lost about one-fifth of his total strength. About two-thirds of his trained, organized unit strength can continue offensive action. He is probably infiltrating and recruiting heavily in the countryside while allied forces are securing the urban areas. . . .

    4. What does the future hold?
        a. Probable enemy strategy. . . . We see the enemy pursuing a reinforced offensive to enlarge his control throughout the country and keep pressures on the government and allies. We expect him to maintain strong threats in the DMZ area, at Khe Sanh, in the highlands, and at Saigon, and to attack in force when conditions seem favorable. He is likely to try to gain control of the country's northern provinces. He will continue efforts to encircle cities and province capitals to isolate and disrupt normal activities, and infiltrate them to create chaos. He will seek maximum attrition of RVNAF elements. Against US forces, he will emphasize attacks by fire on airfields and installations, using assaults and ambushes selectively. His central objective continues to be the destruction of the Government of SVN and its armed forces. As a minimum he hopes to seize sufficient territory and gain control of enough people to support establishment of the groups and committees he proposes for participation in an NLF dominated government.
        b. MACV Strategy:
            (1) MACV believes that the central thrust of our strategy now must be to defeat the enemy offensive and that if this is done well, the situation overall will be greatly improved over the pre-TET condition.
            (2) MACV accepts the fact that its first priority must be the security of Government of Vietnam in Saigon and provincial capitals. MACV describes its objectives as:
    • First, to counter the enemy offensive and to destroy or eject the NVA invasion force in the north.
    • Second, to restore security in the cities and towns.

- Third, to restore security in the heavily populated areas of the countryside.
- Fourth, to regain the initiative through offensive operations.
    c. Tasks:
        (1) *Security of Cities and Government.* MACV recognizes that US forces will be required to reinforce and support RVNAF in the security of cities, towns and government structure. At this time, 10 US battalions are operating in the environs of Saigon. It is clear that this task will absorb a substantial portion of US forces.
        (2) *Security in the Countryside.* To a large extent the VC now control the countryside. Most of the 54 battalions formerly providing security for pacification are now defending district or province towns. MACV estimates that US forces will be required in a number of places to assist and encourage the Vietnamese Army to leave the cities and towns and reenter the country. This is especially true in the Delta.
        (3) *Defense of the borders, the DMZ and the northern provinces.* MACV considers that it must meet the enemy threat in I Corps Tactical Zone and has already deployed there slightly over 50% of all US maneuver battalions. US forces have been thinned out in the highlands, notwithstanding an expected enemy offensive in the early future.
        (4) *Offensive Operations.* Coupling the increased requirement for the cities and subsequent reentry into the rural areas, and the heavy requirement for defense of the I Corps Zone, MACV does not have adequate forces at this time to resume the offensive in the remainder of the country, nor does it have adequate reserves against the contingency of simultaneous large-scale enemy offensive action throughout the country.
    5. Force Requirements:
        a. Forces currently assigned to MACV, plus the residual Program Five forces yet to be delivered, are inadequate in numbers and balance to carry out the strategy and to accomplish the tasks described above in the proper priority. To contend with, and defeat, the new enemy threat, MACV has stated requirements for forces over the 525,000 ceiling imposed by Program Five.

A Communist Party Evaluation, 1968

I. *Great and unprecedented successes recorded in all fields during the first-month phase of the General Offensive and General Uprising.*

Since the beginning of Spring this year, the "Anti-U.S. National Salvation" resistance war of our people in the South has entered a new phase:

In this phase of General Offensive and General Uprising, after a month of continuous offensives and simultaneous uprisings conducted on all battlefields in the South, we have recorded great and unprecedented victories in all fields, inflicting on the enemy heavier losses than those he had suffered in any previous period.

1. We wore down, annihilated and disintegrated almost one-third of the puppet troops' strength, wore down and annihilated about one-fifth of U.S.

combat forces, one-third of the total number of aircraft, one-third of the total number of mechanized vehicles, and an important part of U.S. and puppet material installations; destroyed and forced to surrender or withdraw one-third of the enemy military posts, driving the enemy into an unprecedentedly awkward situation: from the position of the aggressor striving to gain the initiative through a two-prong tactic [military action and rural pacification], the enemy has withdrawn into a purely passive and defensive position, with his forces dispersed on all battlefields in the South for the purpose of defending the towns, cities and the main lines of communications. The struggle potential and morale of U.S. and puppet troops have seriously weakened because our army and people have dealt thundering blows at them everywhere, even at their principal lairs, and because they are facing great difficulties in replenishing troops and replacing war facilities destroyed during the past month.

2. We attacked all U.S.-puppet nerve centers, occupied and exerted our control for a definite period and at varying degrees over almost all towns, cities and municipalities in the South, and destroyed and disintegrated an important part of puppet installations at all levels, seriously damaging the puppet administrative machinery.

3. We liberated additional wide areas in the countryside containing a population of 1.5 million inhabitants; consolidated and widened our rear areas, shifted immense resources of manpower and material, which had been previously robbed by the enemy in these areas, to the support of the front-line and of victory; encircled and isolated the enemy, and reduced the enemy's reserves of human and material resources, driving him into a very difficult economic and financial situation.

4. We have quantitatively and qualitatively improved our armed forces and political forces which have become outstandingly mature during the struggle in the past month. Our armed forces have progressed in many aspects, political organizations are being consolidated and have stepped forward, much progress has been realized in leadership activities and methods and we have gained richer experiences.

The above-mentioned great and unprecedented successes in all fields have strongly encouraged and motivated compatriots in towns and cities and areas under temporary enemy control to arise to seize the state power, have created a lively and enthusiastic atmosphere and inspired a strong confidence in final victory among compatriots in both the North and the South. These successes have moreover won the sympathy and support of the socialist countries and the world's progressive people (including the U.S. progressive people) for our people's revolutionary cause, seriously isolated the U.S. imperialists and their lackeys, deepened their internal contradictions and thereby weakened the U.S. will of aggression.

The above-mentioned great successes in all fields have been recorded thanks to the clear-sighted and correct policy, line and strategic determination of the Party, the wise and resolute leadership of the Party Central Committee, the correct implementation of the Party's policy and line by Nam Truong and Party committee echelons, the sacrifice and devotion of all Party cadres and members who have in an exemplary manner carried out the Party's strategic determination, the eagerness for independence and freedom of the people in the South who are ready to shed their blood in exchange for independence and freedom, the absolute loyalty to the Party's and masses' revolution of the People's armed forces who have fought with infinite courage, the great assistance from the northern rear area and brotherly socialist countries, and the sympathy and support from the world people.

· We have won great successes but still have many deficiencies and weak points:

1. In the military field—From the beginning, we have not been able to annihilate much of the enemy's live force and much of the reactionary clique. Our armed forces have not fulfilled their role as "lever" and have not created favorable conditions for motivating the masses to arise in towns and cities.

2. In the political field—Organized popular forces were not broad and strong enough. We have not had specific plans for motivating the masses to the extent that they would indulge in violent armed uprisings in coordination with and supporting the military offensives.

3. The puppet troop proselyting failed to create a military revolt movement in which the troops would arise and return to the people's side. The enemy troop proselyting task to be carried out in coordination with the armed struggle and political struggle has not been performed, and inadequate attention had been paid to this in particular.

4. There has not been enough consciousness about specific plans for the widening and development of liberated rural areas and the appropriate mobilization of manpower, material resources and the great capabilities of the masses to support the front line.

5. The building of real strength and particularly the replenishment of troops and development of political forces of the infrastructure has been slow and has not met the requirements of continuous offensives and uprisings of the new phase.

6. In providing leadership and guidance to various echelons, we failed to give them a profound and thorough understanding of the Party's policy, line and strategic determination so that they have a correct and full realization of this phase of General Offensive and General Uprising. The implementation of our policies has not been sharply and closely conducted. We lacked concreteness, our plans were simple, our coordination poor, control and prodding were absent, reporting and requests for instructions were much delayed.

The above-mentioned deficiencies and weak points have limited our successes and are, at the same time, difficulties which we must resolutely overcome.

II. *The present form of the war between the enemy and us and prospects of future developments.*

1. Our present "Anti-U.S. National Salvation" resistance war has a very new form and is more favorable to us than ever.

a.   We are in a completely active and offensive position; we have brought the war into towns and cities, the enemy's rear areas and important and densely populated areas close to towns and cities; our rear areas have increasingly expanded to form a strong, linked-up position which gradually and tightly encircles the enemy's last strong points. Throughout the three areas, the masses have continuously risen up and strengthened their position of mastery with a higher and higher revolutionary spirit. In towns and cities particularly, in the face of the enemy's recent murderous and savage actions against the people, including puppet troops' and civil servants' dependents, the masses, boiling with anger, have been supporting our troops and awaiting favorable occasions to arise, eradicating wicked [enemy] individuals, sweeping the enemy's state power, and building the people's revolutionary state power. All intermediary classes of people are leaning toward the revolution's side.

b.   The enemy is in a passive position, being encircled, divided and dispersed on all battlefields. He is facing difficulties in all aspects such as: a stalemate in strategy; passiveness in tactics; difficulties in replenishing troops and replacing war facilities which had been destroyed; difficulties in the economic field because of the restriction of their reserve of manpower and material resources. Because of their serious isolation in the political field and the state of confusion of the puppet army, the puppet regime is gradually losing authority and running toward total failure.

2.   Although the enemy is suffering heavy defeat and is in a passive and confused situation, he still has strength and is very stubborn. In his death throes he will resort to more murderous and savage actions. He will massacre the people, thrust out to break the encirclement and create many new difficulties for us. The struggle between the enemy and us will become fiercer, particularly in areas adjoining the towns and cities. Therefore, we must be extremely vigilant, urgently and actively exploit our past successes, overcome all difficulties and hardships with determination to secure final victory and be ready to fight vigorously should the war be prolonged and widened.

However, it must be clearly realized that this will be but the enemy's convulsions before death, his reaction from a weak, not a strong position. The situation will continue to develop in a way favorable to us and detrimental to the enemy with the possibility of sudden developments which we must be ready to take advantage of in order to secure final victory.

A U.S. Air Force Nurse Remembers
the Tet Offensive (1968), 1987

It was around that time that I Corps, up the road from us a small distance, was almost overrun. One of the guys from the ambulance group said to me,

From *In the Combat Zone* by Kathryn Marshall, pp. 95–96. Copyright © 1987 by Kathryn Marshall. By permission of Little, Brown and Company.

"Come on!" so I went. I remember going up to a place close to I Corps headquarters where they had a big cement landing strip. It was lined up, row after row, with Viet Cong people that had been killed the first night of Tet. How many I saw, I don't know. But I remember a Marine gunny [gunship] sergeant came in to see me and was extremely upset—he had realized that some of those bodies laying out there were women, and he was afraid he had possibly killed a woman. I explained to him that when someone has a gun and is shooting at you, you don't look to see if it's a man or a woman. This was very difficult for him to accept.

The first two days of the Tet offensive, we worked something like thirty hours without sleep.

I remember going down to the hospital. It was night, and the area was not secure at all—there were fires everywhere, and rockets and mortars were dropping all along the runway. Some of the girls were running on ahead of me. When they passed the wing commander's trailer, a guy said, "Halt! Who goes there?" One of the girls said, "We're nurses. We're on our way to the hospital—" I distinctly heard her say that, but apparently he didn't. Well, I had just gotten past the guy when I heard the loudest sound of my life—even with all the rockets and sirens, I heard him move the safety catch of his M-16. I stopped dead still, right in my tracks. Very slowly I turned to him and said, "We are nurses. We are on our way to the hospital." And this little voice said, "OK, ma'am." I realized then how scared he was—how close we'd come to getting mowed down by one of our own guys.

That night at the hospital, the chaplain and I crawled around underneath beds with patients who were not able to go to the bunkers—you took as many as you could to the bunkers, and the ones who could not go to the bunkers, you put them on stretchers and got them underneath the bed. Some of them were mental patients, guys who had just broken under all the strain. Myself, I'm sure I felt some anxiety, but there was so much to be done I didn't have time to feel it. For one thing, I was in charge of the ward and had to set up the triage area. So you had to triage—you had to decide which ones were critical, which ones had to be treated first, which ones would make it and which ones wouldn't. And you had to get their medicines attended to, and get their dressings changed. You had to get them bedded down if they were going to spend the night or get them set up to go on the ambuses if they were going out on air evac—during Tet, we'd get three or four flights out before midnight, because somewhere near midnight was usually when Charlie would start hitting us.

So you constantly had something or other going—you didn't have time to stand around and worry about the next rocket attack. You just kept working as long as you could. At one point during those first thirty hours we were told to get a few moments' sleep, and some little guy said, "Here, ma'am, take part of my mattress." For ten or fifteen minutes I shared a mattress with someone, I don't know who he was. But there was no way I could get any sleep.

Robert Komer Recalls Tet's Impact (1968), 1987

What really surprised us about Tet—and boy it was a surprise, lemme tell you, I was there at Westy's [General Westmoreland] elbow—was that they abandoned the time-tested Mao rural strategy where the guerrillas slowly strangle the city, and only at the end do they attack the seat of imperial power directly. At Tet they infiltrated right through our porous lines and attacked some forty cities. They abandoned the countryside where they were doing very well, and boy did they get creamed in the cities. For once, the enemy, who we could not find out there in the triple canopy jungle, who could control his losses by deciding to cut and run every time we got after him, for once we could find him. He was right there shooting at us in our own headquarters, and the cost to him was enormous militarily.

I always felt that the Tet offensive was a desperate gamble on the part of Hanoi. They saw the American presence going up and up and up, they saw us beginning to get a pacification program going, and they decided they better go for broke. And they did dislocate us. It cost them enormously. They had snuffed out the best of the southern cadre by sending them into the cities. We had a startling success in pacification after the Tet offensive because the enemy had sacrificed the core of his guerrilla movement. After Tet it really became an NVA war.

But he had also fatally weakened us at the center of our political structure. I mean Washington panicked. LBJ panicked. Bus Wheeler, Chairman of the Joint Chiefs, panicked. *We* [American officials in South Vietnam] didn't panic, mainly because we were too goddamn busy. But after the first day we knew we were back on top. The one place where after three days we were still out of control was Hue. Now that was two North Vietnamese divisions. And that was a big problem. They really had to be dug out, and we didn't finish it until February twenty-sixth [nearly a month after the offensive began].

It was the Tet shock to the American psyche that made me first think we might lose. And the shock in Washington was materially increased by the fact that the top command—Bunker and Westmoreland in particular—had come back in late November and reported confidently to the President that "Boss, finally all this stuff you have given us is beginning to pay off, and we look forward to 1968 as a big year of success for us." Westy has great plans for pushing back the NVA. Finally we have an elected government even though it's Thieu and not Ky, and so on.

We were not engaging in deception. We genuinely believed at the end of 1967 that we were getting on top. Hell, I was there in the top three or four Americans in Saigon. Westmoreland believed, Abrams believed, Bunker believed, and I believed that finally, with five hundred thousand goddamn troops and all that air, and pacification finally getting underway, with the Vietnamese having set up a constitution and elections, we really

Kim Willenson, et al., *The Bad War: An Oral History of the Vietnam War,* pp. 95–97. Copyright © 1987, Newsweek, Inc. Reprinted with permission.

were winning. We couldn't quite see clearly how soon, but this wasn't public relations, this wasn't Lyndon Johnson telling us to put a face on it. We genuinely thought we were making it.

And then boom, forty towns get attacked, and they didn't believe us anymore. Bus Wheeler with his three dwarfs, [Phil] Habib, [George] Carver, and [Gen. William] DePuy, comes out about the twelfth of February. The Chiefs have decided, because they too panicked, that we're losing. Besides which, there's the *Pueblo* incident [the seizure by North Korea of an American naval vessel] in Korea, and maybe there's another Berlin crisis brewing. We have no strategic reserve; it's all either out in Vietnam or on the way. The Chiefs want to go to the President and say "We've got to call up the reserves, because if we get a second front in Korea there's not a goddamn thing we could do about it."

Wheeler comes out and asks Westmoreland "What do you need if we call up the reserves and the wraps are off." Westmoreland says "Look, if you call up the reserves and we've got five hundred thousand more men to play with, I would like two hundred thousand more." He pulls out of the drawer a request he had made in the spring of 1967, which was turned down, and has his guys burn a little midnight oil to update it. He gives it to Wheeler and he says "Look, this is to speed up the pace of victory. We think we have creamed them at Tet. They are on the run now. By God, if you'll give me the resources I'll chase them back into Cambodia, Laos and North Vietnam." He also has some plans that he tells Wheeler about: A hook around the DMZ at Cua Viet and go up there north of Dong Ha. Go into Laos. Go into Cambodia. He wants to hit the enemy in his sanctuaries. He says "We've got them on the run. They're going to retreat to the sanctuaries, and by God let's follow them in there and we'll win this war." Nothing big like taking Haiphong or anything like that. It's a conditional request. Westy is saying "If you're going to call up reserves and the other theater commanders are bidding, I too am going to put in a bid: two hundred thousand more men in two tranches, a hundred thousand in '68 and a hundred thousand in '69. I'll win your war for you in three or four years."

And then they decide not to do anything about the *Pueblo,* and the Berlin crisis proves evanescent. By the time Wheeler gets back, the whole case for calling up the reserves, which the JCS have argued for since the day we entered Vietnam, has disappeared—except the Vietnam case. But the fact that Westmoreland's conditional requisition, which is based on A. calling up the reserves and B. letting him use these troops to go into the sanctuaries, none of that is ever mentioned by Wheeler to either the President or to McNamara. By God they would have thrown him out on his ear. Can you imagine? So the perception in Washington is that we have just suffered a massive defeat and here's the commander saying "Boy, I've just won a massive victory. Give me some more guys and I'll clean this thing up fairly quickly."

So the three gnomes, Habib, Carver, and DePuy, go and talk to the President with Wheeler's patronage, and they say "Those guys in Saigon are smoking opium. We think the situation is much worse than they do. We have just been out there and we disagree with Komer's optimism, with Westmoreland's optimism, with Bunker's optimism and Thieu's optimism. Those guys just got surprised. Who wants to listen to them? We are in deep trouble, and that's why we need more men—not to insure victory but to stave off defeat." And of course this is leaked by some civilian who knows nothing of the conditionality of the request. The Chiefs never tell anybody anything. The goddamn Chiefs of Staff. Wheeler's the evil genius of the Vietnam war in my judgment.

Clark M. Clifford Remembers
His Post-Tet Questions (1968), 1969

I took office on March 1, 1968. The enemy's Tet offensive of late January and early February had been beaten back at great cost. The confidence of the American people had been badly shaken. The ability of the South Vietnamese Government to restore order and morale in the populace, and discipline and esprit in the armed forces, was being questioned. At the President's direction, General Earle G. Wheeler, Chairman of the Joint Chiefs of Staff, had flown to Viet Nam in late February for an on-the-spot conference with General Westmoreland. He had just returned and presented the military's request that over 200,000 troops be prepared for deployment to Viet Nam. These troops would be in addition to the 525,000 previously authorized. I was directed, as my first assignment, to chair a task force named by the President to determine how this new requirement could be met. We were not instructed to assess the need for substantial increases in men and matériel; we were to devise the means by which they could be provided.

My work was cut out. The task force included Secretary Rusk, Secretary Henry Fowler, Under Secretary of State Nicholas Katzenbach, Deputy Secretary of Defense Paul Nitze, General Wheeler, CIA Director Richard Helms, the President's Special Assistant, Walt Rostow, General Maxwell Taylor and other skilled and highly capable officials. All of them had had long and direct experience with Vietnamese problems. I had not. I had attended various meetings in the past several years and I had been to Viet Nam three times, but it was quickly apparent to me how little one knows if he has been on the periphery of a problem and not truly in it. Until the day-long sessions of early March, I had never had the opportunity of intensive analysis and fact-finding. Now I was thrust into a vigorous, ruthlessly frank assessment of our situation by the men who knew the most about it. Try though we would to stay with the assignment of devising means to meet the military's requests, fundamental questions began to recur over and over.

Clark M. Clifford, "A Vietnam Reappraisal: The Personal History of One Man's View and How It Evolved," *Foreign Affairs* (July 1969), pp. 609–612, 613. Reprinted by permission of *Foreign Affairs*, July 1969. Copyright © 1969 by the Council on Foreign Relations, Inc.

It is, of course, not possible to recall all the questions that were asked nor all of the answers that were given. Had a transcript of our discussions been made—one was not—it would have run to hundreds of closely printed pages. The documents brought to the table by participants would have totaled, if collected in one place—which they were not—many hundreds more. All that is pertinent to this essay are the impressions I formed, and the conclusions I ultimately reached in those days of exhausting scrutiny. In the colloquial style of those meetings, here are some of the principal issues raised and some of the answers as I understood them:

"Will 200,000 more men do the job?" I found no assurance that they would.

"If not, how many more might be needed—and when?" There was no way of knowing.

"What would be involved in committing 200,000 more men to Viet Nam?" A reserve call-up of approximately 280,000, an increased draft call and an extension of tours of duty of most men then in service.

"Can the enemy respond with a build-up of his own?" He could and he probably would.

"What are the estimated costs of the latest requests?" First calculations were on the order of $2 billion for the remaining four months of that fiscal year, and an increase of $10 to $12 billion for the year beginning July 1, 1968.

"What will be the impact on the economy?" So great that we would face the possibility of credit restrictions, a tax increase and even wage and price controls. The balance of payments would be worsened by at least half a billion dollars a year.

"Can bombing stop the war?" Never by itself. It was inflicting heavy personnel and matériel losses, but bombing by itself would not stop the war.

"Will stepping up the bombing decrease American casualties?" Very little, if at all. Our casualties were due to the intensity of the ground fighting in the South. We had already dropped a heavier tonnage of bombs than in all the theaters of World War II. During 1967, an estimated 90,000 North Vietnamese had infiltrated into South Viet Nam. In the opening weeks of 1968, infiltrators were coming in at three to four times the rate of a year earlier, despite the ferocity and intensity of our campaign of aerial interdiction.

"How long must we keep on sending our men and carrying the main burden of combat?" The South Vietnamese were doing better, but they were not ready yet to replace our troops and we did not know when they would be.

When I asked for a presentation of the military plan for attaining victory in Viet Nam, I was told that there was no plan for victory in the historic American sense. Why not? Because our forces were operating under three major political restrictions: The President had forbidden the invasion of North Viet Nam because this could trigger the mutual assistance pact between North Viet Nam and China; the President had forbidden the mining of the harbor at Haiphong, the principal port through which the North received military supplies, because a Soviet vessel might be sunk; the President had forbidden our forces to pursue the enemy into Laos and Cambodia, for to do so would spread the war, politically and geographically, with no discernible advantage. These and other restrictions which precluded an all-out, no-holds-barred military effort were wisely designed to prevent our being drawn into a larger war. We had no inclination to recommend to the President their cancellation.

"Given these circumstances, how can we win?" We would, I was told, continue to evidence our superiority over the enemy; we would continue to attack in the belief that he would reach the stage where he would find it inadvisable to go on with the war. He could not afford the attrition we were inflicting on him. And we were improving our posture all the time.

I then asked, "What is the best estimate as to how long this course of action will take? Six months? One year? Two years?" There was no agreement on an answer. Not only was there no agreement, I could find no one willing to express any confidence in his guesses. Certainly, none of us was willing to assert that he could see "light at the end of the tunnel" or that American troops would be coming home by the end of the year.

After days of this type of analysis, my concern had greatly deepened. I could not find out when the war was going to end; I could not find out the manner in which it was going to end; I could not find out whether the new requests for men and equipment were going to be enough, or whether it would take more and, if more, when and how much; I could not find out how soon the South Vietnamese forces would be ready to take over. All I had was the statement, given with too little self-assurance to be comforting, that if we persisted for an indeterminate length of time, the enemy would choose not to go on.

And so I asked, "Does anyone see any diminution in the will of the enemy after four years of our having been there, after enormous casualties and after massive destruction from our bombing?"

The answer was that there appeared to be no diminution in the will of the enemy. . . .

And so, after these exhausting days, I was convinced that the military course we were pursuing was not only endless, but hopeless. A further substantial increase in American forces could only increase the devastation and the Americanization of the war, and thus leave us even further from our goal of a peace that would permit the people of South Viet Nam to fashion their own political and economic institutions. Henceforth, I was also convinced, our primary goal should be to level off our involvement, and to work toward gradual disengagement.

Johnson Calls for Negotiations, 1968

Good evening, my fellow Americans. Tonight I want to speak to you of peace in Viet-Nam and Southeast Asia.

No other question so preoccupies our people. No other dream so absorbs the 250 million human beings who live in that part of the world. No other goal motivates American policy in Southeast Asia.

For years, representatives of our Government and others have traveled the world seeking to find a basis for peace talks.

Since last September, they have carried the offer that I made public at San Antonio.

That offer was this: that the United States would stop its bombardment of North Viet-Nam when that would lead promptly to productive discussions—and that we would assume that North Viet-Nam would not take military advantage of our restraint.

Hanoi denounced this offer, both privately and publicly. Even while the search for peace was going on, North Viet-Nam rushed their preparations for a savage assault on the people, the Government, and the allies of South Viet-Nam.

Their attack—during the Tet holidays—failed to achieve its principal objectives.

It did not collapse the elected government of South Viet-Nam or shatter its army, as the Communists had hoped.

It did not produce a "general uprising" among the people of the cities, as they had predicted.

The Communists were unable to maintain control of any of the more than 30 cities that they attacked. And they took very heavy casualties.

But they did compel the South Vietnamese and their allies to move certain forces from the countryside into the cities. They caused widespread disruption and suffering. Their attacks, and the battles that followed, made refugees of half a million human beings.

The Communists may renew their attack any day. They are, it appears, trying to make 1968 the year of decision in South Viet-Nam—the year that brings, if not final victory or defeat, at least a turning point in the struggle.

This much is clear: If they do mount another round of heavy attacks, they will not succeed in destroying the fighting power of South Viet-Nam and its allies.

But tragically, this is also clear: Many men—on both sides of the struggle—will be lost. A nation that has already suffered 20 years of warfare will suffer once again. Armies on both sides will take new casualties. And the war will go on.

There is no need for this to be so.

There is no need to delay the talks that could bring an end to this long and this bloody war.

Tonight I renew the offer I made last August—to stop the bombardment of North Viet-Nam. We ask that talks begin promptly, that they be serious talks on the substance of peace. We assume that during those talks Hanoi will not take advantage of our restraint.

We are prepared to move immediately toward peace through negotiations. So tonight, in the hope that this action will lead to early talks, I am taking the first step to deescalate the conflict. We are reducing—substantially reducing—the present level of hostilities. And we are doing so unilaterally and at once.

Tonight I have ordered our aircraft and our naval vessels to make no attacks on North Viet-Nam, except in the area north of the demilitarized zone where the continuing enemy buildup directly threatens Allied forward positions and where the movements of their troops and supplies are clearly related to that threat.

The area in which we are stopping our attacks includes almost 90 percent of North Viet-Nam's population and most of its territory. Thus there will be no attacks around the principal populated areas or in the food-producing areas of North Viet-Nam.

Even this very limited bombing of the North could come to an early end if our restraint is matched by restraint in Hanoi. But I cannot in good conscience stop all bombing so long as to do so would immediately and directly endanger the lives of our men and our allies. Whether a complete bombing halt becomes possible in the future will be determined by events.

Our purpose in this action is to bring about a reduction in the level of violence that now exists.

It is to save the lives of brave men and to save the lives of innocent women and children. It is to permit the contending forces to move closer to a political settlement.

And tonight I call upon the United Kingdom and I call upon the Soviet Union, as cochairmen of the Geneva conferences and as permanent members of the United Nations Security Council, to do all they can to move from the unilateral act of deescalation that I have just announced toward genuine peace in Southeast Asia.

Now, as in the past, the United States is ready to send its representatives to any forum, at any time, to discuss the means of bringing this ugly war to an end.

I am designating one of our most distinguished Americans, Ambassador Averell Harriman, as my personal representative for such talks. In addition, I have asked Ambassador Llewellyn Thompson, who returned from Moscow for consultation, to be available to join Ambassador Harriman at Geneva or any other suitable place just as soon as Hanoi agrees to a conference.

I call upon President Ho Chi Minh to respond positively and favorably to this new step toward peace.

But if peace does not come now through negotiations, it will come when Hanoi understands that our common resolve is unshakable and our common strength is invincible.

Tonight, we and the other allied nations are contributing 600,000 fighting men to assist 700,000 South Vietnamese troops in defending their little country.

Our presence there has always rested on this basic belief: The main burden of preserving their freedom must be carried out by them—by the South Vietnamese themselves.

We and our allies can only help to provide a shield behind which the people of South Viet-Nam can survive and can grow and develop. On their efforts—on their determinations and resourcefulness—the outcome will ultimately depend. . . .

The actions that we have taken since the beginning of the year to reequip the South Vietnamese forces; to meet our responsibilities in Korea, as well as our responsibilities in Viet-Nam; to meet price increases and the cost of activating and deploying Reserve forces; to replace helicopters and provide the other military supplies we need—all of these actions are going to require additional expenditures.

The tentative estimate of those additional expenditures is $2.5 billion in this fiscal year and $2.6 billion in the next fiscal year.

These projected increases in expenditures for our national security will bring into sharper focus the Nation's need for immediate action, action to protect the prosperity of the American people and to protect the strength and the stability of our American dollar.

On many occasions I have pointed out that without a tax bill or decreased expenditures next year's deficit would again be around $20 billion. I have emphasized the need to set strict priorities in our spending. I have stressed that failure to act—and to act promptly and decisively—would raise very strong doubts throughout the world about America's willingness to keep its financial house in order.

Yet Congress has not acted. And tonight we face the sharpest financial threat in the post-war era—a threat to the dollar's role as the keystone of international trade and finance in the world. . . .

One day, my fellow citizens. there will be peace in Southeast Asia.

It will come because the people of Southeast Asia want it—those whose armies are at war tonight and those who, though threatened, have thus far been spared.

Peace will come because Asians were willing to work for it—and to sacrifice for it—and to die by the thousands for it.

But let it never be forgotten: Peace will come also because America sent her sons to help secure it.

It has not been easy—far from it. During the past 4-1/2 years, it has been my fate and my responsibility to be Commander in Chief. I lived daily and nightly with the cost of this war. I know the pain that it has inflicted. I know perhaps better than anyone the misgivings that it has aroused.

Throughout this entire long period, I have been sustained by a single principle: that what we are doing now in Viet-Nam is vital not only to the security of Southeast Asia, but it is vital to the security of every American.

Surely we have treaties which we must respect. Surely we have commitments that we are going to keep. Resolutions of the Congress testify to the need to resist aggression in the world and in Southeast Asia.

But the heart of our involvement in South Viet-Nam—under three different Presidents, three separate administrations—has always been America's own security.

And the larger purpose of our involvement has always been to help the nations of Southeast Asia become independent and stand alone, self-sustaining as members of a great world community—at peace with themselves and at peace with all others.

With such an Asia, our country—and the world—will be far more secure than it is tonight.

I believe that a peaceful Asia is far nearer to reality because of what America has done in Viet-Nam. I believe that the men who endure the dangers of battle—fighting there for us tonight—are helping the entire world avoid far greater conflicts, far wider wars, far more destruction, than this one.

The peace that will bring them home some day will come. Tonight I have offered the first in what I hope will be a series of mutual moves toward peace.

I pray that it will not be rejected by the leaders of North Viet-Nam. I pray that they will accept it as a means by which the sacrifices of their own people may be ended. And I ask your help and your support, my fellow citizens, for this effort to reach across the battlefield toward an early peace. . . .

Throughout my entire public career I have followed the personal philosophy that I am a free man, an American, a public servant, and a member of my party, in that order always and only.

For 37 years in the service of our nation, first as a Congressman, as a Senator and as Vice President and now as your President, I have put the unity of the people first. I have put it ahead of any divisive partisanship.

And in these times as in times before, it is true that a house divided against itself by the spirit of faction, of party, of region, of religion, of race, is a house that cannot stand.

There is division in the American house now. There is divisiveness among us all tonight. And holding the trust that is mine, as President of all the people, I cannot disregard the peril to the progress of the American people and the hope and the prospect of peace for all peoples.

So I would ask all Americans, whatever their personal interests or concern, to guard against divisiveness and all its ugly consequences.

Fifty-two months and 10 days ago, in a moment of tragedy and trauma, the duties of this Office fell upon me. I asked then for your help and God's, that we might continue America on its course, binding up our wounds, healing our history, moving forward in new unity, to clear the American agenda and to keep the American commitment for all of our people.

United we have kept that commitment. United we have enlarged that commitment.

Through all time to come, I think America will be a stronger nation, a more just society, and a land of greater opportunity and fulfillment because of what we have all done together in these years of unparalleled achievement.

Our reward will come in the life of freedom, peace, and hope that our children will enjoy through ages ahead.

What we won when all of our people united just must not now be lost in suspicion, distrust, selfishness, and politics among any of our people.

Believing this as I do, I have concluded that I should not permit the Presidency to become involved in the partisan divisions that are developing in this political year.

With America's sons in the fields far away, with America's future under challenge right here at home, with our hopes and the world's hopes for peace in the balance every day, I do not believe that I should devote an hour or a day of my time to any personal partisan causes or to any duties other than the awesome duties of this Office—the Presidency of your country.

Accordingly, I shall not seek, and I will not accept, the nomination of my party for another term as your President.

But let men everywhere know, however, that a strong, a confident, and a vigilant America stands ready tonight to seek an honorable peace—and stands ready tonight to defend an honored cause—whatever the price, whatever the burden, whatever the sacrifices that duty may require.

Thank you for listening.

Good night and God bless all of you.

✗ ESSAYS

William S. Turley, a specialist in Vietnamese history who teaches at Southern Illinois University, analyzes the origins and results of the Tet offensive in the first essay. Focusing especially on North Vietnam and the National Liberation Front, he concludes that Hanoi accomplished its minimum objective of sparking a psychological crisis in Washington that hastened American deescalation, but it paid a heavy price of crippling losses. Gabriel Kolko of York University (Toronto) explores Tet's impact on Washington decision-makers in the next essay. He argues that the offensive proved the decisive turning point for U.S. involvement in Vietnam. Kolko contends that the American business and financial communities exerted powerful pressures on the Johnson administration to limit the U.S. commitment because of their concern with the budget deficits and gold and dollar crises spawned by the war. U.S. leaders feared that another escalation in Vietnam would severely damage America's economic position at home and abroad while further eroding its military strength.

Tactical Defeat, Strategic Victory for Hanoi

WILLIAM S. TURLEY

At midnight on January 31, 1968, a million tiny explosions roared across the city. The bright flashes of firecrackers glowed and flickered against the buildings and rising smoke. It was Tet in Saigon, the beginning of the New Year, a sacred time of reunion and renewal. Two and one-half hours later, an old Renault taxi and a small truck crept through the now silent streets and stopped in front of the U.S. Embassy. Nineteen sappers piled out, blew a hole in the compound wall, and rushed in. Meanwhile, some 84,000 communist troops moved toward their targets in five municipalities, thirty-six province capitals, and sixty-four district seats. The Tet Offensive was under way.

William S. Turley, *The Second Indochina War: A Short Political and Military History, 1954–1975,* pp. 99–117. Copyright © 1986, Westview Press. Reprinted by permission.

For weeks the Communists had meticulously stocked weapons, ammunition, and food in the homes and businesses of urban sympathizers. Vegetable carts bound for market had carried rifles. A ship from Hong Kong had unloaded crates of ammunition marked "firecrackers" onto a dock in Saigon. Combatants and agitators had trickled into the cities one by one or in small groups aboard buses, bicycles, or on foot. Others had gathered at secret locations on the outskirts of the cities. Political cadres had made discreet contact with urban dissidents.

Not every movement went undetected, and by late January, it was apparent that something was about to happen. But the rumors had been heard before, and the evidence hinted at something too audacious to be believed. The attacks achieved almost complete surprise. Despite three years of massive U.S. involvement, the communist offensive was bigger and more complicated than ever before. It struck the very centers of previously inviolable cities. The bulk of the assault forces were indigenous Southern irregulars, and the preparations for the offensive required at least the passive collusion of many of its supposed victims. No matter how the fighting ended, U.S. claims of military victory would not be able to erase the impression that all the blood and expense had been, and always would be, for naught.

The Tet strategy was hardly a new idea for the Vietnamese Communists. Its germ was the August Revolution, in which the Communists had provided a nucleus of armed force for the popular uprisings that had brought the party to power in 1945. Party doctrine subsequently held that surrounding the cities with rural revolution, as Maoists advocated, was insufficient in Vietnam. For if cut off from the countryside, the cities could still hold out with support from the "imperialist" hinterland. Moreover, given Vietnam's cramped geography, enemies that controlled the cities could launch powerful attacks into liberated areas if not distracted by turbulence in their own rear. The strategic solution, called "general offensive and general uprising," was to mount simultaneous armed attacks and popular uprisings at all geographical points. Even if this plan did not sweep the revolution to power, the Communists theorized, it would destroy the enemy's illusion of success.

The idea exercised a powerful hold on revolutionaries who saw themselves as ordained to lead a small, impoverished nation in resistance against more powerful foes. It was especially popular among party members whose revolutionary careers had begun amidst the patriotic fervor that had seized the cities in August 1945. Many believed that the proper stimulus could make the cities explode again. Party leaders had never neglected to consider the cities in their plans and had considered attack in the enemy's most secure areas, in coordination with region-wide popular uprisings, as their ultimate weapon. The Central Committee's resolution 9 in 1963 had foreseen the need for a "general offensive and general uprising," and in 1964, COSVN had drawn up tentative plans, selected targets, and subdivided Saigon into five "lines of attack." Fairly detailed planning was under way by mid-1966.

The Communists realized they could not simply replay the August Revolution, however. The United States and the "puppet" Saigon regime presented a much more formidable obstacle than the shaky Japanese-installed administration a few mobs had overwhelmed in 1945. Much more military power would have to be projected now into the cities to have great effect. But unlike the situation in 1945, power was now available and securely based in the North. The party also had a large organization in the South with which leaders believed they controlled nearly 4 million people. If they bypassed U.S. positions, revolutionary forces stood a chance of destroying the "puppet."

In June 1967, Nguyen Chi Thanh traveled to Hanoi to present a draft plan for attacking the cities to the Political Bureau. Several considerations weighed in the Political Bureau's deliberations. U.S. bombing had taken such a toll that communist leaders were impatient for it to end, if only so they could strengthen the North's capacity to support the war in the South. Yet U.S. leaders still appeared to believe in the possibility of military victory, and rural struggle alone seemed unlikely in the near future to make them believe differently. New difficulties would arise if the United States prolonged its involvement or invaded the North. It was imperative to ward off such moves and tilt the United States toward negotiation, which the Communists believed could be done by destroying U.S. confidence. If that effort succeeded, it would be necessary also for the Communists to break up pacification and recover control in the countryside so that "fighting-while-negotiating" could be conducted from a position of strength. After heated discussion, the Political Bureau reached agreement that the time had come for the big blow.

Thanh's plan for an all-out effort apparently encountered resistance, however. General Giap, for one, doubted that Southern irregulars could do the job unaided but was loathe to place precious main forces at risk. Differences over strategy stemmed partly from disagreement over the realism of seeking the immediate termination of U.S. involvement as opposed to preempting further U.S. escalation. Thanh's death on July 6, 1967, may have cleared the way for agreement on a scaled-down version of his plan. In an article serialized in *Nhan dan* (The People) during September, Giap gave his grudging approval but warned against expecting quick victory. Orders went out to Southern command organs the same month. PLAF units and Southern irregulars, those orders made clear, were to bear the main burden of attacking the cities while the PAVN created diversions and stood in reserve.

What, then, did the Communists hope to achieve? Party leaders differed in expectations but agreed it should be possible to jolt the war into a new phase leading toward, if not immediately causing, U.S. withdrawal. The most optimistic hope was that the offensive would paralyze the Thieu regime's military and administrative apparatus, generate popular demand for Thieu to step aside, and end in coalition government. Thus deprived of the "puppet" on whom the United States depended to justify intervention, the United States would have no choice but to fix a date for its withdrawal.

Somewhat less sanguine was the hope that the offensive would convince U.S. leaders of the futility of their "limited war" strategy. If, as the Communists surmised, the United States would be unable to escalate further, it would have to give up hope of military victory and seek a way out through negotiations.

The cities up to this time had experienced a few terrorist incidents, but never had the fighting in the countryside pushed into their confines. A person born in Saigon, Hue, Danang, or Can Tho easily could have reached maturity without feeling any direct effect of the war. For many urbanites, U.S. intervention brought jobs and larger pay packets, not pain and suffering. The only sound of combat audible in Saigon was the low rumble of B-52 strikes thirty kilometers away. City youth also were more likely than rural youth to qualify for student draft deferment or to have families with the financial or political means to arrange avoidance of military service altogether. Urbanites were largely oblivious to the terror endured by peasants in "contested" areas and could, if they wished, regard the war as someone else's misfortune.

However, the combined effects of rural insecurity, the destructiveness of U.S. tactics, and economic distortions also had stimulated a cityward migration. The proportion of total population living in the countryside had dropped from 80 to about 70 percent, a trend that would continue and be largely irreversible. This movement threatened to shrink the Communists' base of support in rural areas where they had their main strength. But it also gave them reason to hope that in the bidonvilles spreading in the outskirts and back streets of Saigon and in Danang, Qui Nhon, Cam Ranh, and a dozen lesser provincial capitals, they might find an enlarged pool of urban supporters.

Noteworthy, too, was the changing political scene in Saigon. The era of revolving-door juntas had ended, and Nguyen Van Thieu was safely ensconced in Independence Palace. On the surface it seemed that a new elite—younger, more career-oriented, and more susceptible to U.S. influence by comparison with the mandarin Francophiles it displaced—had consolidated a firm hold on power. Thieu certainly typified the new group. Born a Buddhist in 1923, Thieu was from a modest, provincial background. Emerging from the first war a major in the French Army, he had transferred to the ARVN and in 1957 had gone for training in the United States. The next year, at the height of the Diem era, he had married into a wealthy Catholic family and converted. With his wife's connections, the right patrons, and a knack for clever maneuver, Thieu was admirably equipped to rise in the armed forces but not to provide inspiring leadership.

The consolidation of the Thieu regime had begun with elections for a Constituent Assembly in 1966 when Thieu as chief of state still shared power with Premier Nguyen Cao Ky. Elections for village councils and hamlet chiefs had followed in spring 1967, a genuine if fragile accomplishment that laid a basis for the rehabilitation of Saigon-sponsored local government. At the top, however, Thieu and Ky had parted over which of them should run for the presidency provided in the new constitution. Leaders of opposing cliques, they threatened to split the military once again. Only when it became clear that the majority of senior officers as well as the United States supported Thieu had Ky agreed in June to run for vice president on Thieu's ticket.

Attention then shifted to culling the civilian candidacies, partly to reduce their exorbitant number but also to remove some genuine electoral threats. Maneuvers in the Constituent Assembly disqualified General Duong Van "Big" Minh, who had announced his intention of returning from exile on the tennis courts of Bangkok. The popular, former minister of economics, Au Truong Thanh, who revealed he once had withheld a gold sales distributorship from the chief of police, also was eliminated. Further manipulations pared down the number of slates to eleven. Of these, the best known of the civilian tickets was headed by Phan Khac Suu and Dr. Phan Quang Dan, both of whom had gained repute by spending time in Diem's jails. Another, headed by Tran Van Huong and Mai Tho Truyen, could count on the aging Huong's prominence as a lay leader of the Southern Buddhist Association to win support among Buddhists in the deep south. A third slate consisting of Truong Dinh Dzu and Tran Van Chieu lacked personal distinction but captured attention by calling for negotiations to end the war. The Dzu-Chieu slate was promptly dubbed the peace ticket.

The campaign was to have begun with a tour of the provinces by all eleven slates of candidates. But Thieu and Ky refused to join, and the air force C-47 that was to carry the other candidates to their first destination delivered them to the wrong airport. Huong claimed that "the government purposely arranged the trip to humiliate us and make clowns out of us." The tour fell apart, and though a second was arranged, the civilians held the military responsible for irregularities that continued down to the end of the campaign. Thieu and his associates, however, were constrained from blatantly rigging the election by the realization that this would create insurmountable problems in Washington and that the election would take place under the scrutiny of a huge foreign press corps and other observers. On September 3, according to the published results, 83.8 percent of the South's registered voters cast ballots. The Thieu-Ky ticket won, but with only 34.8 percent of the votes. The pattern of local results suggested that Thieu and Ky did best where the military felt most free to help; they lost in Hue, Danang, and Saigon. If the results were at all accurate, it was clear that not one of the slates was the first choice of any significant segment of the electorate.

U.S. officials naturally pointed to the turnout as evidence that most South Vietnamese preferred a noncommunist government. But the election did little to confirm the stature of Thieu as the man to head it. Moreover, it had taken U.S. pressure to assure that elections were held and to unify the military. It was also obvious that civilian elites, once united in opposition to Diem, were now antagonistic to the military government, and the elections had helped to sharpen that antagonism. These elites were also deeply divided among themselves. The threat of collective defeat by the revolution was no more sufficient in 1967 than in 1964 to restrain personal ambition or vanity. Although the city scene was changing, none of this change suggested any worsening of prospects for the Communists.

Communist strategy called for luring U.S. forces away from population centers, and so the Tet Offensive began neither at Tet nor in the cities. It began at Khe Sanh, the remote outpost of a U.S. Marine rifle company near the western end of Route 9. Located on an open plateau, the marine camp and nearby Khe Sanh village faced peaks over 850 meters high, behind which forested hills rolled into Laos and the demilitarized zone. There the marines found the PAVN 325c division digging into the peaks during spring 1967.

The small marine camp was highly vulnerable. Though supported by artillery at the Rock Pile and Camp Carroll, it was just fourteen kilometers from the terminus of an improved road over which the PAVN could move heavy equipment. The marines therefore sent in two battalions of reinforcements. After a few sharp engagements the PAVN division shifted eastward to join other units in feints and jabs along Route 9. Infantry assaults on strong points, then artillery barrages, made northern Quang Tri province once again a major focus of U.S. attention.

The 325c was accompanied by the 304th division when it returned to the Khe Sanh area in December 1967. More marine reinforcements plus an ARVN battalion brought the number of base defenders up to 6,000. Finally, on January 21, the two PAVN divisions broke the suspense with attacks on hilltop outposts and a massive artillery barrage that destroyed the base's largest ammunition dump, crated the runway, and damaged a dozen helicopters. The "siege" of Khe Sanh had begun.

Reports of PAVN divisions maneuvering in the hills around Khe Sanh conjured up the spectre of Dien Bien Phu. The U.S. command pulled 15,000 elite troops from all over the South's five northern provinces to reinforce the Route 9 combat bases, and soon a total of 50,000 U.S. troops were tied down at Khe Sanh or in its support. By the end of January, as communist assault forces assembled on city outskirts, attention in Saigon and Washington was riveted on the mountains. For days after the Tet attacks in the cities, Westmoreland and Thieu believed Khe Sanh was the "real" target and the city attacks the diversion, such a hold did Dien Bien Phu have on their thoughts.

PAVN commanders surely would have been happy to overrun Khe Sanh if given the opportunity. But the victors of Dien Bien Phu could not have been less aware than Westmoreland of the differences between the two battlefields. In the first place, Khe Sanh was not really remote, as Dien Bien Phu had been. It was barely 50 kilometers from the sea and half an hour by air from the huge airbase at Danang. The French, by contrast, had bottled themselves up in rugged mountains over 300 kilometers from their support in Hanoi. Compared to the 325 assorted aircraft available to the French Union force, the United States could draw from 2,000 aircraft including big C-123 and KC-130 transports to supply Khe Sanh with almost constant aerial cover and supplies in excess of need. Second, Khe Sanh was not a valley ringed by mountains but a plateau facing hills on one side only, and the marines held several of the peaks. The possibility of encircling the base from high ground did not exist as it had at Dien Bien Phu. Finally, although the PAVN used more firepower at Khe Sanh (122-mm artillery, 122-mm rockets, 120-mm mortars, Soviet-built PT-76 light amphibious tanks) than in any single engagement up to that time, it faced, aside from the base's own ample artillery, the 175-mm guns of Camp Carroll and massive, all-weather aerial bombardment. By the time the siege eased in mid-April, U.S. aircraft had dropped more than 100,000 tons of bombs (including 60,000 tons of napalm) on a battlefield of a dozen square kilometers.

The 20,000 PAVN troops deployed at Khe Sanh were less than one-half the number used at Dien Bien Phu (a deployment indicative of PAVN strategists' true objectives), though the PAVN had tripled in size since 1954. U.S. estimates of PAVN casualties were less than one-half the 23,000 suffered in the earlier battle. The PAVN attempted to dig siege trenches, but it was a belated effort. The PAVN never tunneled beneath marine positions as required for an all-out assault. The level of effort was sufficient to sustain a credible diversion, but not to mount a realistic attempt to overrun the base so long as the United States was determined to hold it.

The deputy editor of *Quan doi nhan dan* (People's Army) newspaper, interviewed in Hanoi in 1984, affirmed that Khe Sanh was never intended to be another Dien Bien Phu. The earlier battle took place after seven years of war had worn down the French, whereas the United States in 1968 was at the peak of its military power. Another Dien Bien Phu at Khe Sanh, this officer said, would have been "impossible." Rather, he went on, the Khe Sanh battle, aside from providing a strategic diversion, was a test of the U.S. reaction to the PAVN's use of the demilitarized zone (DMZ). The PAVN command wanted to determine how the United States would respond if the PAVN staged attacks from the zone, specifically whether the United States would send troops into the North.

Hanoi derided the Western preoccupation with the Dien Bien Phu analogy as it applied to Khe Sanh. Communist commentators pointed instead to Lang Vei, a Special Forces/Civil Indigenous Defense Group (CIDG) camp eight kilometers east of the besieged marines. Led by eleven PT-76s, PAVN forces on February 7 completely overran the camp, killing 250 montagnard and 24 U.S. defenders.

As the PAVN hit Khe Sanh and several other highland targets, assault forces slipped around lowland outposts to penetrate the cities. Some struck prematurely at Qui Nhon, Kontum, Pleiku, Darlac, and Nha Trang on January 29, but U.S. and ARVN intelligence missed the attacks' significance. More than one-half the ARVN was on leave for Tet. If a skittish commander had not pulled several U.S. battalions closer to Saigon in early January, the city would have been almost completely devoid of reaction forces. General Westmoreland's intelligence officer later admitted that communist plans seemed so "preposterous" that no one would have believed what was about to happen had anyone known them in detail. The

U.S. and ARVN commands so poorly understood the strategy of their enemy that they could not take seriously the evidence of its intentions. So in the wee hours of Tet the cities lay open.

The estimated 67,000 maneuver forces and 17,000 hastily recruited guerrillas that attacked the cities had been led to believe final victory was at hand. Instructions to local party cadres spoke of annihilating Saigon's administrative apparatus and organizing the masses to help consolidate revolutionary power. At higher levels, however, it was understood that these were maximum objectives. During an interview with the author in 1973, a former PLAF colonel who helped plan the attack on Saigon-Cholon remarked that "the party did not say certain places had to be held for so long, but that what could be occupied should be held as long as possible, the longer the better. Any occupation for some length of time was in some measure a success, a victory."

The wave of attacks that broke on January 31 was the first of three violent surges planned for 1968. The assault on the U.S. Embassy was but the tiny if symbolically devastating kickoff. An estimated 4,000 troops joined in the attacks on Saigon, hitting Tan Son Nhut airfield, the ARVN general staff compound, government ministries, and Independence Palace. Battalion-sized forces invested several neighborhoods in Cholon. Tanks and helicopter gunships, sent to evict them, reduced entire city blocks to rubble. Forces that seized large portions of several delta towns were destroyed along with the buildings they occupied. In the large majority of cases, the attacks were beaten back in a few days.

Only in Hue did attacking forces hold out longer. The estimated 7,500-man assault force, one of the few consisting largely of uniformed PAVN regulars, entrenched itself behind the walls of the old city and fought until February 24. Roughly two-thirds of the attackers and nearly 500 ARVN and U.S. troops died in bitter door-to-door fighting, artillery shelling, and aerial bombardment that left 100,000 civilian refugees. In the aftermath, 2,800 bodies were found in mass graves, and another 2,000 people were missing, leaving behind them questions that are hotly disputed to this day (that is, who or what killed them and why).

The first wave of attacks spluttered to an end with mortar and rocket barrages against several cities. Though U.S. and ARVN forces held the streets, half of all U.S. maneuver battalions were tied down in I Corps, and the ARVN had pulled back into defensive positions, leaving the countryside undefended. On April 20, a handful of dissident intellectuals presented themselves as the Vietnam Alliance of National Democratic and Peace Forces and declared adherence to the NLF in a move to broaden the revolution's appeal. A second wave of attacks in early May attempted to build on the momentum of the first, but, lacking surprise, the attacks were quickly beaten back. A third still weaker wave brought the offensive to a close in August.

Despite initial panic, neither the ARVN nor the Saigon government had collapsed. Students and sympathizers had helped to form a "revolutionary administration" in Hue and Tra Vinh, but the population mostly had taken to shelter when banner-waving activists appeared in the streets. Cadres who had freely entered rural communities as ARVN and U.S. forces withdrew to defend the cities found themselves exposed when those forces pushed back out into the countryside to resume pacification. The U.S. estimate of 40,000 communist troops killed in the first wave of attacks was inflated, but the losses were cripplingly high. Communist battalion-sized attacks tapered off, and Washington and Saigon claimed a military victory.

But the military balance hardly mattered. As the fighting subsided in Hue, General Westmoreland claimed the Communists had used up all of their "military chips" in one last "throw of the dice." Now weakened and overextended, he said, they were vulnerable as never before, and their vulnerability presented a "great opportunity" to go for the kill. With the agreement of the Joint Chiefs, Westmoreland proposed an "amphibious hook" around the demilitarized zone to destroy bases and staging areas, attacks on sanctuaries in Laos and Cambodia, and intensified bombing of the North. Westmoreland's proposal required 206,000 more troops, an increase that would require mobilization of the reserves.

Westmoreland's request was submitted in a report by General Earle G. Wheeler, chairman of the Joint Chiefs, which presented a bleak prospect if the request were not granted. Though crafted to win approval, the report, dated February 27, 1968, was more realistic than many that had preceded it. Reproduced in *The Pentagon Papers,* it made the following points:

• The current situation in Vietnam is still developing and fraught with opportunities as well as dangers.

• There is no question in the mind of MACV that the enemy went all out for a general offensive and general uprising and apparently believed that he would succeed in bringing the war to an early successful conclusion.

• The enemy failed to achieve this initial objective but is continuing his effort. Although many of his units were badly hurt, the judgment is that he has the will and the capability to continue.

• Enemy losses have been heavy; he has failed to achieve his prime objectives of mass uprisings and capture of a large number of the capital cities and towns. However, with replacements, his indoctrination system would seem capable of maintaining morale at a generally adequate level. His determination appears to be unshaken.

• The enemy is operating with relative freedom in the countryside, probably recruiting heavily. . . . His recovery is likely to be rapid; his supplies are adequate; and he is trying to maintain the momentum of his winter-spring offensive.

• The structure of the GVN [Government of Vietnam, i.e., Saigon] has held up but its effectiveness has suffered.

• The [ARVN] held up against the initial assault. . . . However, ARVN is now in a defensive posture around towns and cities and there is concern about how well they will bear up under sustained pressure.

• The initial attack nearly succeeded in a dozen places, and defeat in those places was only averted by the timely reaction of U.S. forces. In short, it was a very near thing.

The report then came to its sober conclusion:

• MACV has three principal problems. First, logistic support north of Danang is marginal owing to weather, enemy interdiction and harassment and the massive deployment of U.S. forces into the DMZ/Hué area. Opening Route 1 will alleviate this problem but takes a substantial troop commitment. Second, the defensive posture of ARVN is permitting the VC to make rapid inroads in the formerly pacified countryside. ARVN, in its own words, is in a dilemma as it cannot afford another enemy thrust into the cities and towns and yet if it remains in a defensive posture against this contingency, the countryside goes by default. MACV is forced to devote much of its troop strength to this problem. Third, MACV has been forced to deploy 50 percent of all U.S. maneuver battalions into I Corps, to meet the threat there, while stripping the rest of the country of adequate reserves. If the enemy synchronizes an attack against Khe Sanh/Hue-Quang Tri with an offensive in the Highlands and around Saigon while keeping the pressure on throughout the remainder of the country, MACV will be hard pressed to meet adequately all threats. Under these circumstances, we must be prepared to accept some reverses.

The report was partly a political ploy to alarm the president into expanding the war. But coming less than three months after Westmoreland had said the end of the war was in sight, it only confirmed the pessimism of the new secretary of defense, Clark Clifford, and caused the president to turn to dovish civilians for advice. Disclosure of the troop request on March 10 in the *New York Times* provoked a public uproar. The official optimism of years past suddenly seemed proof of incompetence or deception. Moreover, no one could be certain that even with 206,000 additional troops the United States could impose a military solution or intimidate Hanoi into submission. Something messier seemed just as likely.

The Senate Foreign Relations Committee meanwhile had held hearings on the Tonkin Gulf Incident that cast doubt on Johnson's version of that pivotal event. Hitherto solid congressional support for the war began to ebb away. In mid-March, Senator Eugene McCarthy, the "peace candidate" for the Democratic party's presidential nomination, took 45 percent of the vote in the New Hampshire primary, inspiring Senator Robert Kennedy to join the race on an anti-war platform. Though Johnson won the primary, he sensed impending defeat. If he stood for reelection, the campaign would divide the nation; if he won, his presidency would be ineffectual. So on March 31, Johnson announced he would not seek nomination for another term, declared a bombing halt over the North except for a narrow strip above the demilitarized zone, and called on Hanoi to agree to peace talks. Hanoi accepted on condition that the talks begin by discussing a halt to the bombing altogether, and formal talks opened in Paris in May.

The Tet Offensive demolished the credibility of officials who had claimed progress, improvement, and "light at the end of the tunnel." Dovish opinion gained respectability within the administration itself. But in large measure, it was Lyndon Johnson who had defeated both himself and his policies by refusing to make hard choices. A consensus-seeking, centrist politician, he had sought to hoard the capital of his 1964 landslide victory by antagonizing no one. Fearful of the right, he had refused to "sell out" Saigon and withdraw. Reluctant to antagonize the left, he had given the Joint Chiefs less than what they asked. Needing support for domestic reforms, he had abhorred becoming the first U.S. president to lose a war. At each moment that called for decision, Johnson had chosen only to stave off defeat. But absence of defeat was a recipe for stalemate, and endless war was acceptable to no one.

Public support in the United States for the Vietnam War was about what it had been for the Korean War, though less than for World War II and a good deal more than for World War I. Support fell in response mainly to the rise in casualties and apparent inconclusiveness of the fighting. . . . Vocal opposition was largely confined to the intellectual, nonunion left. As for the anti-war protest movement, it is credited by a student of U.S. wartime opinion with electing Richard Nixon twice: once in 1968 by withholding votes that would have given victory to Hubert Humphrey, and once in 1972 by capturing control of the Democratic party and nominating George McGovern, "the worst presidential candidate any party has put forward in modern times."

How did the Communists view Tet and its aftermath? The first COSVN assessment on January 31 claimed success in "paralyzing" the Saigon administration, confusing the U.S. command, and inflicting heavy damage. But efforts to seize "primary objectives" and to "motivate the people to stage uprisings and break the enemy's oppressive control" were disappointing. The Communists realized from the start that they were unlikely to achieve their maximum aims.

In March, a fuller COSVN assessment directed attention to the successful disruption of the enemy's "two-prong tactic" of military action and rural pacification. U.S. and ARVN forces, the assessment observed, had been forced to disperse in order to defend the towns, cities, and lines of communication. In consequence, "additional wide areas in the countryside containing a population of 1.5 million inhabitants" had been liberated. The revolution had gained access to "immense resources of manpower and material." But the offensive had failed to eliminate much of the enemy armed force, the urban attacks had "not created favorable conditions for motivating the masses to arise," and recruitment was insufficient to sustain "continuous offensives and uprisings." Only in a fleeting reference to "internal contradictions" that "weakened the U.S. will of aggression" did the assessment include the Tet Offensive's U.S. domestic scene. Some kind of victory was still sought in altering the actual balance of military and political forces inside South Vietnam.

The Communists barely acknowledged the opening of the Paris talks as they proceeded in May with their second wave of planned attacks. "The Americans," *Quan doi nhan dan* editorialized, "have not given up, so our people will have to suffer more before we can win final victory." In fact, Southern cadres had begun to question whether they should do all of the suffering to obtain relief for the North alone; others wondered why, if negotiations had begun, they had to go on fighting. General Van Tien Dung, the PAVN chief of staff, felt constrained to point out that a bombing halt was essential if the North were to strengthen its role as the "great rear area" for the Southern revolution, and a COSVN directive dated January 10 castigated cadres who had thought the campaign would be a "one-blow affair."

The U.S. agreement to an unconditional bombing halt and to NLF participation in four-party talks allowed the Communist party to claim a satisfactory outcome. The United States, cadres were told, had been forced to deescalate, cease bombing of the North, and join Hanoi at the conference table. Final victory was conceded to lie in an indeterminate future, but the "limited war" strategy had been discredited. U.S. plans to escalate had been preempted, and the war had entered the penultimate phase of "fighting-while-negotiating."

The party's official history describes the Tet Offensive as a great victory, and in the only sense that mattered—the strategic outcome—it was. But many cadres had hoped to turn the tide of battle *inside South Vietnam* and regretted the cost they had had to pay just for psychological impact inside the United States. Former PLAF leader Madame Nguyen Thi Dinh described the post-Tet period to the author as an "especially difficult time" for the Southern revolution. Just why it was difficult has been explained in bitter detail by one of the offensive's chief planners, General Tran Van Tra:

> In Tet 1968, we did not correctly assess the concrete balance of forces between ourselves and the enemy. Nor did we fully realize that the enemy still had considerable capabilities while ours were limited. Consequently, we set requirements that exceeded our actual strength. That is, we based our action not on scientific calculations or careful weighing of all factors but, in part, on an illusion which arose from subjective desire. Although the decision was wise, ingenious and timely . . . and created a significant strategic turning point in Vietnam and Indochina, we suffered heavy losses of manpower and material, especially of cadres at various echelons, which caused a distinct decline in our strength. Subsequently, we not only were unable to preserve all the gains we had made but also had to endure myriad difficulties in 1969–70 so that the revolution could stand firm in the storm. While it is obvious that the road to revolution is never a primrose path, . . . in Tet, 1968, had we considered things more carefully and set forth correct requirements in conformity with the balance of forces between the two sides, our victory would have been even greater, our cadres, troops and people would have spilled less blood, and the subsequent development of the revolution would have been much different.

Whether Tra blamed himself or others is not clear. But Southern cadres tended to believe that things would have been different if Nguyen Chi Thanh had lived. He, many believed, would have kept the more cautious high command in Hanoi from scaling down his plan, and his genius for mass organization would have guaranteed a better popular response in the cities. The first wave of attacks would have been more powerful, touching off uprisings that would have made the second wave more powerful still. Each successive surge of violence would have been stronger than the last. As it was, complained one former regroupee captain, the campaign had "an elephant's trunk and a snake's tail": It started small and ended smaller. Behind such views lay the firm conviction, held even by defectors, that what had prevented the masses from rising to support the revolution was fear of reprisal. If the enemy's "oppressive apparatus" had been broken, the people would have flocked to the revolution's banner. A short leap of faith sustained Southern cadres' confidence that more force and better organization would inspire greater uprisings next time. As General Tra wrote, "Tet 1968 was an extremely valuable practical experience."

A Decisive Turning Point

GABRIEL KOLKO

The Tet offensive revealed the structural constraints on policy and decision making in contemporary America and compelled the Johnson administration and Congress to acknowledge, to an extent none of their predecessors ever had, the limits that economic, military, and political realities inexorably imposed on them. The sense of crisis that emerged was justified primarily because America's leaders, not only in Washington but in all the major sectors of social power and influence, had to confront candidly the meaning of Vietnam, its symbolism to the region and the world, and its role as a test of national strategy and might. Until 1968 the costs of illusions and errors were not so apparent, and support for a large war existed among the country's leaders.

Only during crises does the real locus of power and interest expose the decisive constraints on political decision makers. To the extent that a society then defines its core needs and goals, the state's alleged autonomy and discretion in the balance of forces and power within a society tend to disappear. The presidency itself is brought to heel before what may roughly be designated as the larger interests of the American system and of those who have the capacity to define it. To the degree that those interests can be clearly and factually articulated, either by those at home or by those foreign nations linked into the U.S.-led world economic, political, and military order, the executive's options are circumscribed. Men whose ideas had earlier led the nation in different directions, as was true of the President's key advisers from 1963 until early 1968, now cease to prove influential. Their myopia, ambitions, or individual styles of work no longer have anything more than incidental interest. Should the institutional order at this point make basic errors of policy, it would be due to broader social illusions and an unrealistic consensus rather than to the caprice of this or that faction or person. In brief, bureaucratic forces are no longer decisive in a framework where choices are visibly not discretionary and the irrationality of conventional wisdom is not yet blind to the dangers of self-destruction. Decisions at this late stage reflect the interests and imperatives of a system. The Tet

From *Anatomy of a War* by Gabriel Kolko, pp. 312–326, 334–337. Copyright © 1985 by Gabriel Kolko. Reprinted by permission of Pantheon Books, a Division of Random House, Inc.

offensive's most decisive effect was to articulate clearly the fact that the United States was now confronting a potentially grave crisis. The first three months of 1968 were therefore the most important in the history of the entire American aggression in Vietnam.

Just as one must see America's intervention in Vietnam as contextually motivated—with its desire for credibility, regional domination, the propping up of dominoes, and the devising of a successful local-war strategy all evoking greater involvement—so one must comprehend the global events which compelled the infinitely slow process of American disengagement and defeat in the Vietnam War. Even before Tet, increasing institutional and political constraints began casting their shadows on American efforts in Vietnam. The war itself dramatically exacerbated older economic difficulties, but there were yet other dilemmas confronting the administration. These ranged from such intractable problems as the mounting racial tension in American cities and the war's debilitating impact on U.S. military power to the decline of its strategic manpower reserves for other world or even domestic crises. The significance of this erosion was dramatically illustrated in early 1968 when North Korea seized the USS *Pueblo* and its eighty-three crew members on January 23, an act which humiliated the administration and made it appear helpless. Tensions along the thirty-eighth parallel also led the South Koreans at the end of January to consider an immediate withdrawal of their 49,000 men from South Vietnam, and Washington was confronted with the possibility of having to replace them at the very moment of the Tet offensive. The danger of war along Korea's thirty-eighth parallel momentarily appeared real.

Yet it was the gold and dollar crisis that created the most sustained and irresistible pressures on Washington. Although the administration's promises to lower its deficits had managed to keep the gold pool with Europe alive after December, steady gold purchases showed that Europe's bankers remained extremely nervous. They were especially concerned because Congress refused to act on the President's tax surcharge proposal to reduce the deficits. It was in this context that the President's advisers considered their responses to a possible imminent defeat, and McNamara's parting advice to the President was not to allow another troop escalation in Vietnam to ruin the dollar abroad and the economy at home.

The gold and dollar crisis colored all of Washington's thoughts on responses to the precarious military situation in South Vietnam. At the end of February Senator Jacob Javits of New York called for an end to the gold pool, triggering a panic, and $118 million was withdrawn from the pool in only two days. For two weeks, as the United States reached an impasse in the war in Vietnam, the highly complex and technical dollar-gold problem traumatized Washington and the Western capitals, consuming vast amounts of the time of the President and his advisers. "The specter of 1929 haunted him daily," Doris Kearns reports of her intimate later interviews with him; "he worried that if the economy collapsed, history would subject Lyndon Johnson to endless abuse."

On March 4, Treasury Secretary [Henry] Fowler warned the President that the gold rush and the flight from the dollar were serious and could worsen rapidly, with a gold embargo leading to "exchange rate wars and trading blocs with harmful political as well as economic effects." At the same time other key advisers were carefully and pessimistically assessing the consequences of any additional troop buildup to European bankers' confidence in the dollar. While Europe's gold-pool members had agreed in early March to sustain the dollar, on March 11 banks rushed the pool, which lost nearly a billion dollars in gold before it suspended operations four days later. "We can't go on as is," [National Security Adviser Walt W.] Rostow warned the President on March 14, and on the same day several European nations began to redeem dollars for U.S. Treasury gold to recoup the bullion they had lost in support of the dollar. That afternoon, having lost $372 million that day, and fearing a loss of a billion dollars the following day, the Treasury arranged immediately to close the gold market. With memos and meetings constantly before him and with his chief economic adviser's late January warning of a possible world depression still fresh in his mind, Johnson on March 15 wrote to the European prime ministers that "these financial disorders—if not promptly and firmly overcome—can profoundly damage the political relations between Europe and America and set in motion forces like those which disintegrated the Western world between 1929 and 1933."

At first the White House wanted its allies to accept unlimited amounts of dollars without gold backing, but Fowler and [Federal Reserve Board Chairman William McChesney] Martin opposed this as both unrealistic and a license to continue fiscal irresponsibility. Instead, European central bankers were called to Washington for an emergency meeting on March 16. As antiwar pickets paraded outside their secret sessions, reminding them that the war was the origin of the dollar crisis, the key decisions over the future of the dollar were being made by Europeans. Abolishing the pool altogether, Europe's bankers refused to use their gold to save the dollar. They categorically rejected an American request that they forgo their right to claim gold for dollars from the U.S. Treasury. They offered restraint only if the administration acted more responsibly in managing its economy. In effect, if it refused to place the defense of the dollar above all other considerations, then they reserved the power to demand a reckoning that could profoundly upset America's position in the world economy, with all that this implied for its political leadership.

After Tet the administration finally acknowledged that any increase of troops to Vietnam threatened not just the country's economy but all of its domestic and international priorities. Those in Washington who had for some time opposed the war's overshadowing of other military and regional commitments now became more outspoken. Although they were especially strong among civilians in the Pentagon, there was a near consensus in the government that the war should not cause the nation to sacrifice its other responsibilities, especially to NATO. With America stretched thin globally and with a crisis brewing in Korea, the Joint Chiefs of Staff immediately revived its earlier request for a call-up of reserves—a politically unpopular move for the President—and its chairman, General Wheeler, spent the rest of February conniving to get more men for the military services. In a virtuoso performance he flew to Saigon and after four days was back in Washington on February 27 with an extremely pessimistic report and a demand, allegedly from Westmoreland himself, for 206,000 men. Vietnam had greatly weakened the strategic manpower reserves for crises elsewhere in the world, and Wheeler gambled that he could rebuild them by claiming that the 206,000 were essential to reverse the tide of the war. To deny him the full request, Wheeler argued, was to jeopardize the position of the commander in Vietnam, if not to imperil his forces. One hundred thousand of the new men, however, he planned to send elsewhere than to Vietnam.

The guileless Westmoreland later sharply rebuked Wheeler for pretending that he was the author of the famous 206,000 request, but Wheeler was in fact dissembling largely out of concern for the mounting pressure in Washington over the weakening of the U.S. military elsewhere. Indeed, the President himself was worried that there would be insufficient regular forces to cope with the anticipated summer turmoil in American cities—an anxiety that was justified when huge riots broke out in Washington and in over fifty cities after the Reverend Martin Luther King was assassinated the following April 4. The most immediate result of the request for 206,000 more men, however, was that the President on February 28 asked Clark Clifford, his new Secretary of Defense, to create a committee to study it—and it was this committee's effort to turn its attention to a full-scale review of the war that became the main focus of opposition to further escalation among key Washington decision makers.

When men who have heretofore perceived no limits to their power confront reality, there will always be drama and tension. There were, of course, very dramatic moments during February and March 1968; remorse and doubt led to a debilitating loss of self-confidence unknown among American leaders for decades. But from the inception of Tet to Johnson's epoch-making speech of March 31, there was an inexorability to Washington's command decisions.

The American military's first response was a paralyzing incredulity at their gross underestimation of their enemy's resources and their failure after nearly three years of massive efforts to blunt the Revolution's growing offensive capabilities. Even while Wheeler was actively cajoling Westmoreland to call for reinforcements, the JCS itself on February 12 recommended deferring a decision to send them. By the time Wheeler had mobilized the Joint Chiefs behind him, he confronted other opposition from all sides. While the civilians in the Pentagon were the most aggressive, they had the backing of most of the CIA and the State Department for their immediate contention that sending more troops to South Vietnam would be futile. Not only would more troops encourage the already inefficient ARVN to fight even less well, the opponents of Wheeler's request pointed out, but the critical battles then taking place would be decided long before new soldiers could reach Vietnam. It was also in response to these conflicting views that the President had created the Clifford committee to help him reach his decision.

The Clifford committee began by gathering the basic facts. Initially, it did not intend to question the efficacy of the war. The departing McNamara had warned the President that 400,000 men and $10 billion would be required if he approved the commitment of a large new offensive force. The JCS contended that the 108,000 men definitely intended for South Vietnam out of the 206,000 requested, would tip the scale in the otherwise stalemated war. But even Rostow, who had earlier endorsed the new escalation, now had to admit that the DRV would meet any American buildup. Also crucial in the committee's discussion was the argument that the war was causing the United States to sacrifice its many interests elsewhere in the world, impairing its overall international objectives. Piece by piece, the case for continuing the war by escalating was destroyed. The CIA, especially, argued that the war was stalemated and that the Communists retained the strategic initiative. By the time the Clifford committee's intense discussions and analyses were completed on March 3, Clifford had changed his position and no one favored the 206,000 plan save Wheeler and the JCS. "1968 will be the pivotal year" of the war, Wheeler had correctly argued.

The result was a nominal stalemate among the President's key advisers, which meant a continuation of the status quo, though in fact opinions were changing subtly with the burden of reality. While the possibility of committing 206,000 men was left open on a "week by week" basis, only 22,000 men already authorized were to go immediately as "all we can give at the moment," as the President put it. Johnson later asserted he had rejected the 206,000-man request by early March, but in fact he remained quite ambivalent and unwilling to accept the growing constraints on his freedom of action. Even after the *New York Times* on March 10 revealed the secret debates, he hesitated, although the publicity hurt the advocates of escalation. What the Clifford committee proposed was that the administration do nothing decisive until it could complete a basic reassessment of "political and strategic guidance" of the war. But for two weeks, apart from a desultory consensus that much more had to be done to get the ARVN to assume a far greater role in the war, nothing new was decided on Vietnam, and the President was under the greatest pressure of his life as every conceivable problem weighed on him.

"I felt," he later confided, "that I was being chased on all sides by a giant stampede coming at me from all directions." There was Vietnam, but also the economy. Blacks were rioting, students protesting, and hysterical reporters pressing. "And then the final straw. The thing I feared from the first day of my Presidency was actually coming true. Robert Kennedy had openly announced his intention to reclaim the throne. . . ." The strain on Johnson made his behavior erratic; rumors of his overwrought emotional state and exotic religious experiences abounded—and later enough of them were confirmed to reveal that the President had indeed lost touch. Antiwar Senator Eugene McCarthy's 42 percent vote in the New Hampshire primary on March 12 reinforced the President's desperation.

Politics and economics now merged to affect the future of the war. Clifford, perhaps the shrewdest adviser to Presidents in the post-1945 era, was a critical link in this synthesis. As he was to recount later that month to Rusk and Rostow, "I make it a practice to keep in touch with friends in business and the law across the land. I ask them their views about various matters. Until a few months ago, they were generally supportive of the war. They were a little disturbed about the overheating of the economy and the flight of gold, but they assumed that these things would be brought under control; and in any event, they thought it was important to stop the Communists in Vietnam. Now all that has changed. . . . these men now feel we are in a hopeless bog. The idea of going deeper into the bog strikes them as mad. . . . It would be very difficult—I believe it would be impossible—for the President to maintain public support for the war without the support of these men." In fact, two days after the McCarthy victory, Kennedy approached Clifford and proposed not to run for the presidency if Johnson would create a commission to study and change Vietnam policy. Clifford presented the offer to Johnson, who rejected it brusquely, only to see Kennedy announce his candidacy.

Clifford, meanwhile, was not happy with the President's paralysis and incapacity to reverse the disastrous course toward escalation. The opinions of his corporate friends reinforced his own real but habitually cautious desires to redefine the nation's Vietnam strategy. "I was more conscious each day of domestic unrest in our own country," he wrote the following year. "Just as disturbing to me were the economic implications of a struggle to be indefinitely continued at ever-increasing cost." On March 19 he proposed to Johnson that he call another session of the Senior Advisory Group of the State Department—the so-called Wise Men who the preceding fall had strongly supported the President's war policy. Dean Acheson. its chairman, had since late February, at the President's request, been informally reviewing the war and its conflict with American interests elsewhere in the world, and he had become highly critical of the unlimited commitment. On March 15 he had informed Johnson that the JCS was giving him very poor advice and that it was time to disengage from the unpopular war. Clifford knew he had a powerful friend in the former secretary of state, whose prestige with Johnson was enormous, and he also sensed what his group would advise. Johnson consented to the project probably aware of its likely position, and the Wise Men picked up the debate the Clifford committee had left hanging.

The role of the Wise Men was illustrative of the parameters of power and ideas in the United States in moments of crisis. The basic military, economic, and political facts which so profoundly influenced the Wise Men had already reached most of the President's key advisers and the President himself. Even arch-hawks like Rostow admitted that though putting the country on a war footing in February had been possible, "the changing political environment at home and the international financial crisis of March reduced that possibility." Nothing could change those realities, and in a certain sense the ideas of the Wise Men were anticlimactic, reflecting the tide of events rather than shaping them.

The world of big industry and finance, so amorphous to those outside it but so real to those in it, had been for the war because its members believed in the objectives of American foreign policy which had led to the intervention. Yet key individuals were often called on, both formally and informally, to comment on economic affairs that the war strongly affected, such as budget deficits and inflation. While they had never assumed a critical position on the war before 1968, they consistently favored efforts to eliminate these economic challenges. Such expediency meant that should the nation's financial difficulties become sufficiently serious, they would oppose escalation and might even favor a reduction of the war to economically manageable proportions. Such a stance was strictly pragmatic and graphically revealed the contradictions which led to American involvement in the first place, for its ideal would have been for the United States to have won the war both quickly and cheaply. The Wise Men—who included men with close links to the world of finance, corporate law, and big business like George Ball, Douglas Dillon, Cyrus Vance, John J. McCloy, McGeorge Bundy, Arthur Dean, Robert Murphy, and Henry Cabot Lodge—understood such nuances. It was virtually certain that impersonal calculations of this kind would influence their recommendations. As men used to confronting facts and their implications, they were better able to internalize the larger material balance of forces in the war than most, particularly because it was not their personal reputations that were at stake but their class interests.

Also important during this decisive month was the state of public opinion and that of politicians who instinctively thrive on relating to it, quite unconcerned with their own past inconsistencies on the war. The entry of McCarthy and Kennedy in the race for the Democratic nomination would not have been such a formidable challenge to the President had the polls on March 16 not shown him to be at the lowest point of popularity since he came to office. The public's feelings about the war had become consistently more critical since 1966; by the end of 1967 they were evenly divided. The Tet offensive caused opposition to rise sharply. By the summer of 1968 those Americans who thought the sending of troops to Vietnam was a mistake far outnumbered those in favor of it. This trend profoundly affected many officials, who felt that growing public impatience was imposing a real limit on how long politicians could continue to sustain the war. And the emergence of a larger and more militant antiwar movement on campuses, especially among the children of the elite, struck key defenders of the war personally. By the end of March 1968, it was quite clear that even ignoring the military and economic constraints, the administration was confronting an unprecedented postwar situation in the virtually total collapse of the crucial foreign policy consensus between the executive, the traditional establishment, and the public.

However belligerent or aggressive the President appeared to his advisers or the press at this time, it was clear that he was now implementing the Clifford committee's cautious policy of no further escalation. However, the committee failed to alter the President's basic commitment to an ongoing war. On March 22 the final allotment of new men to South Vietnam was reconfirmed at 24,000 more, nearly half of whom were already there, and the request for 206,000 men was shelved permanently. As with all his fateful March decisions, Johnson later offered the explanation that his freezing the commitment to the war at existing levels after six years of steady escalation was due to a variety of factors, foremost of which was the expectation that there would be no additional NLF offensives and the belief that the ARVN was now fighting harder. But, in fact, both premises proved incorrect, and Johnson still did not escalate when the second Tet wave came, because his other concerns were quite decisive. These included "especially our financial problems," with the gold crisis and budget deficit still hanging over the economy, as well as public opinion. And for a consummate parliamentarian like Johnson, the conviction during March that Congress would no longer support escalation undoubtedly also weighed heavily in his calculations. Whatever his bluster and style, the facts had sunk into the President's consciousness. U.S. policy would get neither worse—nor better.

The famous, often detailed meetings of the Wise Men on March 25–26 only confirmed this reality. Acheson was firmly in command of its proceedings and so preconceived in his judgments that he brooked little opposition from a minority which preferred not to offend the President's martial instincts. The war was stalemated, and the nation could not afford to commit more resources without sacrificing its economy and other global interests in an effort to win it. The public, too, both in South Vietnam and in the United States, was now deeply opposed to the effort. Most of the Senior Advisory Group favored the ending of escalation and the taking of steps toward disengagement—ranging from less bombing of the DRV to a reduction of American forces and the transfer of greater responsibility for the war to RVN.

For the President, emotionally overwrought during these weeks and merging the greatest personal crisis of his lifetime with the most important failure of American military and foreign policy in this century, the last days of March were excruciating. The shrewdest politician Texas ever produced was for the first time wholly isolated and compelled to assume the burden not simply of his own political errors in Vietnam but also of the failure of an entire class in pursuing the war and the hegemonic goals of American foreign policy, a class that was now abandoning escalation and the President's commitment to it. Carrying the weight of failure, Johnson hesitated and considered persisting with the war without any inhibitions. After terrible days of intense emotional strain, he also decided to withdraw from the race for the 1968 presidential nomination and to retreat to the tranquillity of his Texas ranch.

The President's March 31 speech touched on everything from a bombing halt to negotiations, but the most important and tangible part of it was the announcement of his decision to retire from politics. His erstwhile concessions of a bombing halt in all but vague areas north of the seventeenth parallel in return for reciprocal DRV actions was within only a day to embarrass the administration when planes attacked sites nearly five hundred kilometers north of that line. Rather than extricating himself from the war in a forthright manner, Johnson quickly raised basic doubts about his intentions and further alienated domestic and world opinion. By April and May, bombing attacks against the DRV were far greater than in February or March. From this time until October 31, when Johnson called a total bombing halt over the DRV in a last-ditch effort to win votes for Hubert Humphrey's faltering campaign for the presidency, it was obvious that bombing would both become a tool of public relations and politics for himself and set a precedent for his successor. For while the March 31 speech was an explicit pledge not to escalate the war, the President remained very much committed to sustaining the struggle until he left office, and Rusk and Rostow reinforced his devotion to bombing. Clifford and those who wanted to redefine national policy and scale down the war knew that the President would never agree with them, whatever they said, and all they could do for the remainder of 1968 was try to keep Johnson tied to what they regarded as a schizoid policy and prevent it from becoming something even worse. It was not, in their opinion, to get better.

Johnson's open offer for negotiations was soon mired when the United States retracted its proposal to meet the Communists anywhere, embarrassing the administration even before the long, futile Paris talks were to begin the following May. Conceding that he would not raise troop levels by more than 24,000 or escalate the war, the President asked for Congress's help in solving the budget deficit, the gold and dollar crisis, and the other economic problems that his past escalations had unleashed. The most prominent new proposal in the President's message, which became the basis of Nixon's subsequent Vietnamization policy, was an expanding of the RVN's military forces to take a progressively larger share of combat and, implicitly, lay the basis for a reduced dependency on American troops. It was only here that the advice of the Wise Men may actually have moved the President.

The American presence in Vietnam was directly related to the RVN's chronic military and political weaknesses, and interpreting its performance during the weeks after Tet was central to Washington's definitions of its own role and alternatives. The first, careful reports were highly pessimistic, and the persistent internecine political struggles between Thieu and Ky in the midst of a life-and-death struggle particularly discouraged officials. The CIA believed that the political dimension was critical, but it also confessed that if there was no chance of reform, a U.S. role, regardless of its size, would prove hopeless. The State Department called the RVN's collapse "a strong present possibility over the next few months." By the end of March, however, General Creighton Abrams, who had already been designated quietly to replace Westmoreland, was arguing that the ARVN suddenly had far better morale than earlier. With the bulk of military opinion on the RVN highly skeptical, and the legacy of experience even more negative, the Wise Men focused on the linkage of reconstituting the ARVN and American disengagement, fully aware that it was unlikely to succeed. Yet the notion of a decent interval to conceal the failure of American forces was clearly articulated. Publicly committed to the myth of the RVN's growing successes and strength, the administration saw the claim as the pretense which would justify eventual troop reductions. Even if there was no clear timetable, the unspoken assumption in Washington's plans was that victory was unobtainable and that "Vietnamizing" the war would buy time for whatever diplomatic or political alternatives might arise—or at least postpone the need to confront the very real defeat until after the election.

Given the absence in Johnson's speech of any references to credibility, dominoes, and the like, the implicit shift of emphasis in his statement was crucial. American war aims were neither victory nor some other abstraction but providing the RVN a "shield" behind which it could grow. On the efforts of the RVN's people "the outcome will ultimately depend." This redefinition of basic national objectives conformed both to military, political, and economic necessity and to the overwhelming opinion of leading advisers and decision makers. It was this new American readiness to limit its commitments and later partially to disengage, however amorphously stated and defined at this time, that was the major outcome of the Tet offensive.

Vietnam became America's first foreign war since 1812 to produce a profound domestic social crisis and political polarization. During the First and Second World Wars, political leadership in Washington made key decisions gradually and deliberately as changes occurred in the global balance of forces. Not so with Vietnam. Unlike all earlier wars, it aggravated many of the problems of American capitalism rather than relieving them. Amid a protracted trauma in race relations, the war increasingly became the focus of protest and dissent for millions of people who knew what the President was privately being told: so long as the war absorbed so much money, it was impossible to deal with internal social needs.

The vast bulk of Americans who opposed the war had no basis for analyzing it coherently, and the efforts of the Left within the antiwar movement to explain it failed. While they were incapable of truly perceiving its horror for the average Vietnamese, the gore of television coverage notwithstanding, a sense of this terrible experience nonetheless penetrated their consciousness. The issue of war crimes entered the debates over the war, and the enormity of the damage the United States was inflicting profoundly disquieted the consciences of a small minority. However inchoate opinion and attitudes were, there was a growing appreciation of the vast, ever-larger gap between conventional wisdom and reality, filling some Americans with a deepening sense of outrage and many more with a growing skepticism and sense of alienation. If, in the end, analytic conceptions never caught up with the sheer magnitude of the events, they nonetheless broke the apathy and consensus which had given the successive administrations the freedom from political pressure to test their strategies in Southeast Asia. This growth of skepticism and radicalization accelerated after 1967 to become a serious variable in the politics of the war. Even if protest waned with events and no one group could unify it, the accumulated opposition to the war now became a permanent reality which would emerge periodically to challenge the government in multiple and often exotic and complex ways, ranging from extremely polite middle-class constituents entreating their congressmen to forms of direct action. While no single effort made a difference, collectively all such activity indicated that for the first time in modern American history the national consensus or apathy on foreign policy was irretrievably broken, thereby creating the mass basis for opposition. The politics of opposition evolved not deductively or ideologically but as a part of a cumulative set of choices the state presented to people whose responses were based on an enormous variety of motives. Time and events were shaping consciousness, and thereby action, especially among those who had the most to lose from the war. Vast numbers were being politicized, and Tet was a powerful catalyst in this process. A new reality was being created in the American political universe.

Confronting unprecedented opposition from traditional elites as well as from the public, the White House chose a way out of the impasse that was extremely tortuous but whose direction was clear. It was on the defensive even though no one in government dared to admit total defeat. Only days after Johnson made his March 31 speech, black rioting erupted and for weeks took up much of the administration's attention. In part because the May 1968 riots in France subdued the French ardor for making gold central to the world exchange system, the United States was able to breathe more freely on that question for the remainder of the year, though the precariousness of the dollar remained an inhibition to any costly new adventures. Yet although its military, economic, and political options had been drastically reduced, the administration made the fateful decision to struggle in a losing context to save its "credibility" by relying on two major, interrelated efforts to gain time during 1968 for alternatives it could only vaguely envision—a policy which was guaranteed to lose the election for virtually any Democrat who chose to run.

The first was merely to continue the war at the same high level of combat and firepower which American forces permitted, with a full awareness of their inability to alter the military equation and shorten the war. This desperate dependence on firepower was symbolic, concealing failure with brutal revenge, as well as a means of obtaining time for the second approach—namely, to begin to transfer the war to the various RVN armies. For Johnson this meant essentially continuing the war within those constraints he abhorred and turning it over to his successor with the strongest military position possible.

American leaders knew that more firepower would not change the position of the Revolution militarily or reduce its ability to mobilize recruits. Still, when the President promised a pause in the bombing of the DRV to encourage negotiated solutions to the war and reciprocity, the Air Force immediately increased its fighter-bomber sorties over the DRV, setting a wartime record during July. The DRV's skepticism toward American initiatives naturally rose with them. The tonnage of bombs dropped on the DRV during 1968 nearly equaled that of 1967, but bombing greatly increased in the south, where a growing part of "the countryside," one American general reported in 1969, "looked like the Verdun battlefields." This emphasis on firepower meant, of course, that the administration would fight what it increasingly knew to be a futile war in ways which could only further wreck South Vietnam's human, social, and economic fabric. As the American generals continued the habitual search-and-destroy tactics throughout 1968, some reported their "coldly realistic, if not pessimistic" conclusions back to Washington that the strategy was still ineffectual.

The successive waves of combat which began on Tet created nearly one million refugees, and over $200 million in capital goods were destroyed during Tet alone. Agricultural output and private-sector output dropped sharply in 1968, as did the revenues of the RVN, which was now more dependent on aid than ever and less able to take over the military responsibilities the Americans proposed to transfer to it. Linked to this mounting economic burden was the accelerating transformation and urbanization of the society. The Americans were impressed that the urban population had shown a distinct apathy toward the RVN's ordeal, even, in some places, engaging in low-level cooperation with the NLF. "The ineffective GVN political response may still further improve the VC cause in the cities, as well as in the countryside," the Clifford committee had presciently warned. In effect, the war created structural forces, such as urbanization, that might define the context of the RVN's politics, so that even if an articulate portion of the urban population did not rally openly to the NLF, the RVN, with its sordid struggles between Thieu and Ky, might nonetheless further alienate them.

The administration's decision to concentrate on strengthening the RVN's various armed forces was crucial both politically and structurally. To the extent that the administration planned to transform the nature of the war from a conflict between Americans and the Revolution to one between the RVN and the Revolution, it was making a fateful choice, since scarcely anyone knowledgeable believed that the RVN had the ability to win such a conflict. The Party had calculated this very question before Tet, and forcing such clarity on the United States was a prime objective of the effort. The new strategy was an excuse for leaving some Americans in South Vietnam at a time when pressure at home was mounting for their removal. While this was a consideration for the White House, many in Washington really saw Vietnamization as a face-saving formula for acknowledging their own failures.

Ironically, the creation of a larger RVN military machine was to become another vehicle for guaranteeing the defeat of its cause. For the RVNAF's growing role goaded the peasantry and urban masses, including many elements indifferent or even hostile to the NLF, to oppose the RVN's war policies. In the spring of 1968 the RVN declared a general mobilization of eighteen- and nineteen-year-olds. All men between eighteen and thirty-eight were now subject to induction and required to stay in a branch of the fulltime military until forty-five, while sixteen- and seventeen-year-olds and thirty-nine- to fifty-year-olds were subject to incorporation into the largely unarmed, part-time People's Self-Defense Forces. By 1969, 150,000 new men had been added to the ARVN and 250,000 to the RF/PF [Regional Forces/Provincial Forces]. The mass levee at a time of growing

RVN economic difficulties further profoundly distorted the wholly artificial nature of the RVN social system, imposing a vast new tax on it.

The forced recruitment of the nation's sons alienated the people in multiple ways. The most obvious was their personal and economic losses, so that such families more and more perceived the RVN as the main burden on their lives. For the rest of the nation, the ARVN was a growing tax as looting, which had reached new levels during Tet, increased with the mounting economic problems confronting soldiers. "Looting and other misconduct by Republic of Vietnam Armed troops toward the civilian populace have undermined the confidence of the people in RVNAF," the NSC's early 1969 assessment concluded, and they saw no way of reversing it. The ARVN became less cohesive, despite its new arms. The rate of desertions rose substantially, especially among new recruits, and the so-called ghost soldiers became even more common. Their officers were equally unprepared for their tasks, which contributed to growing demoralization. "All agencies agree that the RVNAF could not," the NSC stated early in 1969, "either now or even when fully modernized, handle both the VC and a sizable level of NVA forces without U.S. combat support in the form of air, helicopters, artillery, logistics and some ground forces." Increasing the size of the RVN's army only weakened it as a fighting organization, further undermining the entire social order and leaving its economy more dependent and vulnerable. Unwilling and unable to confront these dilemmas, the Johnson administration preferred to bequeath them all to its successor. . . .

The [Vietnamese Communist] Party has ever since 1968 regarded the Tet offensive as the turning point in war and as a decisive triumph, the consequences of which would eventually mature in final victory. By 1968 the Vietnam War had become much more difficult to analyze, for the very process of protracted conflict had made it not only a military struggle but one in which the political, economic, and ideological and human domains became increasingly crucial. Of all the factors, none alone was decisive, but their growing interactions were the raw materials that would shape the final outcome of the war.

For the United States, Tet was a long-postponed confrontation with reality; it had been hypnotized until then by its own illusions, desires, and needs. The belated realization that it had military tactics and technology but no viable military strategy consistent with its domestic and international priorities made Tet the turning point in the administration's calculations. Those who had earlier favored the war finally made a much more objective assessment of the balance of forces. To attribute Washington's new perceptions to falsehood on the Communists' part or to naiveté by the American media, as Johnson and various generals were later to do, is to beg the central question of the impact of the military events which imposed a sense of reality on the administration's leading advisers and authorities. For despite the shift in public opinion as a consequence of Tet, it was still not yet so great as to make the difference to those called on to evaluate policy. It was true, of course, that Tet caused the media to become more skeptical of official reports on the war, but they were never to become critical of the imperialist politics that had led to the intervention in the first place. Another reason for their new disbelief, apart from the Revolution's attaining successes the Pentagon had alleged were impossible, was that those U.S. spokesmen who dealt with the media were frequently ignorant of the nature of the war themselves. Having also been treated with condescension and a great deal of intentional distortion, the media's readiness to break with official illusions was quite predictable, not least because many in the administration themselves no longer shared these misconceptions.

Decision making on Vietnam had until 1968 been subject to optional policies because the consequences of those choices had not yet reached insupportable levels, and the magnitude of the costs of errors to the overall stability and interests of the system was still obscure, while the advantages of victory to the assertion of American power geopolitically and militarily were quite clear. The weight of opinion was therefore for war to the extent needed to attain quite rational objectives: the hegemony of American power over social trends in the Third World. By 1968 the costs of the war to the system were measurable, and, whatever their earlier impulses, the small circle of critical advisers reached a basic consensus on the interests of the system. Most of the bureaucrats gave in to the weight of opinion in 1968 for the same reason they had gone along with the dominant conventional wisdom earlier—their own futures depended on operating within a consensus. The dissenters who wanted more war were now just as rare as those who favored less war had been two years earlier.

After Tet it was not the ever-present differences between various groups and personalities which shaped Washington's command decisions but rather the political order's relationship and interaction with all of the powerful economic, political, and social institutions and people which exist in an informal but real fashion to constitute power in the American social system. The chemistry of human and institutional interaction, from ambition to weakness, will always be extremely diverse within predictable parameters. Tet revealed that it was time to focus on the limits of the system. To have pursued the scale of escalation to an even higher level would have wreaked an untold amount of damage on America's economic position at home and abroad, on its military power elsewhere, and on its political life—a price scarcely any serious person proposed to pay.

The offensive brought these processes to a head, and from this viewpoint the Revolution had attained a decisive advantage in its overall struggle. More crucial yet, however, since the wheels of the U.S. political process grind pragmatically and slowly, was its impact on Washington's comprehension of the centrality of the RVN in the war effort. Without exception, all senior officials involved in guiding future policy would have agreed with the CIA when it noted, "The will and capability of the GVN and its armed forces remain the keys to the eventual outcome." The infusion of this understanding more deeply into the American consciousness was perhaps the most important Party goal, and in this regard it succeeded entirely. Even those U.S. generals who later severely criticized the administration's decisions, knew they could not win the war without the RVN's assuming a far greater burden militarily and being far less irresponsible politically. "Vietnamizing" the Vietnam War, ironically, at this late date became the last pillar of American strategy, leaving its position wholly dependent on its own dependents. It was the reluctant acceptance of this unhappy greater reliance on others that guaranteed the Party's eventual victory, for nearly all who were closely connected with the war greatly doubted in private that the RVN could grasp the military victory that had eluded over half a million GIs.

In this sense the Revolution attained the main strategic objectives of the Tet offensive, compelling the United States to leave the realm of desire and confront that of necessity. But the very framework of the epic struggle, for the Revolution as well as for its enemies, was altering. The very process of conflict was disorganizing the entire social order, affecting values and desires. The transformation of the nation, the brutal urbanization, the Americanization of the mores of the youth, and all the scourges of occupation and war were changing the goals of many Vietnamese.

The emergence of new social strata in the burgeoning cities meant that in certain regards both the RVN and the NLF were growing weaker. Yet, while the urban difficulties the Party faced were tactical, and sufficient to undermine its efforts during Tet, for the RVN they were matters of basic survival. As a ruling administrative structure, the RVN needed support and some measure of enthusiasm from those not on its payroll. The passivity and apathy shown to it by the urban population during Tet was extremely ominous. The RVN's potentially fatal dilemma was that it lacked an ideological, economic, and organizational basis for transforming itself into a real political force, able to function and exist independently of the Americans. The very process of egoism and depoliticization which was so troublesome to the Communists was now the RVN's main nemesis, for without a political consensus there could only be cohesion based on repression and avarice. And, given the costliness [of] the economic adhesive of massive corruption which maintained the Thieu regime in power, it was by 1968 quite impossible that the RVN could transcend this fatal contradiction. Indeed, the very nature of the RVN's economic system would eventually produce new issues and grievances around which a new opposition might form. For it had the burden of regulating the social system to minimize the war's dislocations and to meet human needs. In fact it was greatly adding to them.

South Vietnam's rural structure was changing as well, and each mass exodus accelerated this pattern. By the end of 1968 rural Vietnam bore significantly less resemblance to the environment in which the NLF was born. People increasingly desired security from the war's ravages, and this more and more shaped their politics. The collapse or destruction of the NLF infrastructure in many places did not make the RVN any more palatable to the peasants, since what they wanted most—peace—the RVN could not give them. Worse yet, its mounting demands on the peasantry broadened the bases of its grievances even as the land system's traditional economic role altered to make it less onerous. To some extent, and depending on the region, the classic confrontation between the Revolution and its enemies was paralleled by developments in the intricate play of changing peasant values, needs, and politics to which neither the NLF nor the RVN responded wholly. While the NLF's power declined visibly, the RVN could not fill the vacuum. The process of mutual erosion began during Tet, when the Revolution drove the RVN out of a large part of the country yet could not permanently remain there.

Tet was the threshold in the war's development, a major turning point guaranteeing that the Revolution would not be defeated. All the rapidly evolving social, economic, human, and organizational dimensions were increasingly significant for the final outcome, and however nebulous and ambiguous they appeared then, it was clear by the end of 1968 that they would prove decisive.

X *FURTHER READING*

Larry Berman, *Lyndon Johnson's War* (1989)
Peter Braestrup, *Big Story* (1977)
Bernard Brodie, "The Tet Offensive," in Noble Frankland and Christopher
    Dowling, eds., *Decisive Battles of the Twentieth Century* (1976), 321–34
Clark Clifford, *Counsel to the President* (1991)
Orrin DeForest and David Chanoff, S*low Burn: The Rise and Fall of American
    Intelligence in Vietnam* (1990)
William J. Duiker, *The Communist Road to Power in Vietnam* (1981)
Leslie H. Gelb and Richard K. Betts, *The Irony of Vietnam* (1979)
Townsend Hoopes, *The Limits of Intervention* (1970)
Lyndon B. Johnson, *The Vantage Point* (1971)
Guenther Lewy, *America in Vietnam* (1978)
Don Oberdorfer, *Tet* (1971)
Bruce Palmer, Jr., *The 25-Year War* (1984)
Robert Pisor, *The End of the Line: The Siege of Khe Sanh* (1982)
John Prados and Ray Stubble, *Valley of Decision: The Siege of Khe Sanh* (1991)
Herbert Y. Schandler, *The Unmaking of a President* (1977)
Ronald H. Spector, *After Tet* (1993)
Harry G. Summers, Jr., *On Strategy: A Critical Analysis of the Vietnam War* (1982)
William C. Westmoreland, *A Soldier Reports* (1976)
John L. Wiltz, *The Tet Offensive: Intelligence Failure in War* (1991)

The Ally: South Vietnam

✗

A consistent aim of American policy from the late 1940s was the creation of an alternative to communist rule in Vietnam. After the defeat of the French, that objective centered on the establishment of an independent regime in the south that would prove capable of resisting both internal and external military threats. It also encompassed the development of effective political, economic, and social institutions, a process often referred to by American officials as nation building. As the American military presence in Vietnam ballooned during the 1960s, America's fate increasingly became tied to the fortunes of its Saigon ally. Washington's military objective in Vietnam—the defeat of the communists—could not easily be dissociated from its political goal—the establishment of a viable state in South Vietnam.

Although the nature of the South Vietnamese regime inspired a flood of polemical tracts in the United States during the 1960s and early 1970s, relatively few scholars have probed deeply into the underlying structure of the government in Saigon. The most basic questions can be posed simply: Did South Vietnam have the potential to emerge as a viable, independent state? or were its inherent weaknesses so great that it can only be characterized as a doomed dependency?

✗ *D O C U M E N T S*

In the first document, a conversation between Presidents Diem and Eisenhower, the South Vietnamese ruler discusses his country's pressing defense needs and requests additional aid from the United States. The discussion took place at the White House on March 9, 1957. Tran Van Don, one of the leaders in the coup against Diem, reflects in the second document on South Vietnam's need for political and economic reforms following Diem's ouster. The third document, excerpted from the memoirs of former South Vietnamese president Nguyen Cao Ky, reiterates a complaint that South Vietnamese leaders often made of their American allies: that they were insensitive, patronizing, and arrogant. On April 7, 1969, Ky's successor, Nguyen Van Thieu, announced his position on a negotiated settlement to the National Assembly; it appears here as the fourth document. The speech, issued on the eve of the Paris peace talks, left little room for compromise with the communists. In the final document, American serviceman Bobby Muller bitterly recalls his experience with South Vietnamese troops. His blunt disparagement of their fighting ability and commitment to the struggle reflects a viewpoint that many other U.S. soldiers shared.

Ngo Dinh Diem Requests Additional U.S. Aid, 1957

After introductory remarks by the President praising President Diem for the excellent achievements he has brought about in the last three years in stabilizing the situation in Viet-Nam, President Eisenhower asked President Diem to outline the principal problems he is facing today.

President Diem replied that his country has gone through a very grave and serious crisis and has been able to hold on despite strong pressures from all sides. The principal problem of establishing internal security and building up their defense posture has been achieved to a considerable extent. The principal reason Viet-Nam has been able to hold out against these pressures has been because of the sympathy and encouragement given by the United States despite the fact that for a time even some people in the United States did not think that the Diem government could maintain itself.

At the present time Viet-Nam is faced with the possibility of a strong Communist offensive from the Vietminh who have 400 thousand men under arms. Fortunately, however, the Vietminh are faced with serious problems such as high taxes needed to maintain this large force and must have other controls which have caused discontent among the population in the North. Diem feels that Red China is faced with the same problems. They are maintaining a large army which requires heavy taxes and controls over the people, which Diem hopes in the long run will force the Chinese Government to demobilize a considerable portion of their forces and treat the people in a more liberal manner. There is, nevertheless, the possibility that the Vietminh with their large army might try to attack now while they have a superiority in numbers. The Vietminh during the first year after the Geneva Conference did not think it would be necessary to use armed force to take over the South; they thought the government in the South would crumble and they could take over without difficulty. With internal stability in Free Viet-Nam and the build-up of their own armed forces, they have now the possibility of holding out for a few years more during which time Diem reiterated the strain and drain on the economy of the Vietminh may cause them to demobilize some of their forces and adopt a more liberal attitude toward the population. . . .

Diem [stated] that Viet-Nam has attained stability due primarily to the volume of American aid. He pointed out that the magnitude of American aid permitted the US Government to have a large number of advisers and consultants in Viet-Nam who not only can assist Viet-Nam with its problems but also follow closely developments and the use to which aid is placed. In contrast, the small amounts of aid given to other countries, such as 20/30 million dollars, does not permit the US Government to maintain such close control over developments in other countries as is the case in Viet-Nam. Diem pleaded for the maintenance of the present aid level of 250 million dollars a year of which 170 million dollars is allocated for defense purposes. This aid has permitted Viet-Nam to build up its armed strength and thus play an important role in Southeast Asia. If this aid should be cut both the military and economic progress would have to be reduced. This would cause serious repercussions not only in Viet-Nam but among neighboring countries in Southeast Asia who look on Viet-Nam as an example of the good US aid can bring. Any cut would also bring serious political repercussions in Viet-Nam.

Tran Van Don on the Need for Reforms After the Coup Against Diem (1963), 1978

Immediately after the success of the coup d'etat [against Diem], a provisional constitutional charter was proclaimed. It provided for General Big Minh to be the chairman of the MRC [Military Revolutionary Council], which was composed of twelve generals, and for a civilian cabinet of fifteen ministers to be headed by a prime minister who would be responsible to the MRC and to Minh as head of state. This was appropriate because Minh was our leader and known by all as the hero of the coup. Mr. Nguyen Ngoc Tho, former vice president of the republic under the Diem regime was appointed prime minister. He was chosen because of his long administrative experience which would help to smooth this transition phase. In addition, he was a long-time friend of Big Minh and we felt we could trust him.

Having promoted the coup, we were well aware of the difficulties that always follow a sudden change of regime. We understood that this provisional government structure should be replaced as soon as a definitive constitution could be promulgated. Another closely related problem involved our decision to purge the administration and the army of elements we knew to be inept, despotic, or corrupt. We expected a certain breakdown in the functioning of the administration because of this, but thought that the good psychological effect on the people and the purifying influence of new officials would more than overcome any disruptions.

Students, priests, and those politically opposed to the previous government were immediately released from prison and instructions were issued prohibiting arbitrary arrest and confinement. Freedom of the press and of religious belief were solemnly proclaimed and welcomed with enthusiasm. Hard labor in the rural areas was abolished in connection with the strategic hamlet program, and we attempted to obtain support for our new government from the religious sects Hoa Hao and Cao Dai.

Reprinted with permission from the book *Our Endless War* by Tran Van Don, pp. 115, 116–118. © by Presidio Press, 31 Pamaron Way, Novato, CA 94949.

The economic and financial situation was disturbing, however, because American aid had been temporarily suspended during the months preceding the coup. Further, the Tho cabinet was having difficulty since its members could not agree with each other. Part of the problem was that Tho, the former vice president under Diem, was inflexible and narrow in his policies. . . .

Toward the end of January, after a series of contacts with many political, religious, and military leaders, I had been able to plan out the main orientation of our revolutionary program. On January 27, I gave my reform program to Big Minh and [General] Khiem for further submission to the government. It suggested many radical changes, political, economic, social, and cultural, and handed power over to a new revolutionary cabinet under a different prime minister. Especially important were the roles to be entrusted to the youth of the nation for the realization of our revolutionary goals.

I knew that if the war were to be won against the Communists military measures alone would not suffice. Our struggle against the NLF had to be waged with political, economic, cultural, and social considerations as well. The NLF strategy had been to occupy and control the countryside and turn it into a springboard for advancing to the cities. We, therefore, had to make our presence felt in the same rural areas, winning the people's support, seducing them away from Communist influences, and enlisting their participation in a full-scale struggle. My concept was that the war in Vietnam was between two factions of Vietnamese, so it should have been settled between ourselves by all means available. Aid obtained from our Free World friends should have been confined to moral, technical, and material support. Our national policy should have been geared toward solving simultaneously the two overall goals of winning the support of the population and then annihilating the enemy's armed forces.

We also wanted to show the people that we meant what we said, that we truly intended to do away with graft and corruption and special privileges for the governors. I proposed to my colleagues that we lead austere lives, turn in the official limousines so prized by the Diem administration, and sell off the luxurious homes maintained at the expense of the common people. We had to get ourselves used to the idea that we had to get closer to the people, living our lives more like them.

In our military mission we needed to destroy the enemy's secret bases, prevent infiltration of men, weapons, equipment, and supplies, and neutralize his units. Local organizations such as the civil guard and the police were to be responsible for law and order within the local areas. Their purpose was to protect the villages and the people living in them from the political and military cadres of the NLF. In areas that were so rugged that our troops would have unusual difficulty conducting normal military operations, we might have had to request air support such as helicopter transport from our allies.

In winning the support of the populace, we had to remove the insidious influence of the NLF from the villages. This had to be the principal object of the war, with all necessary resources utilized for this purpose. We had to help the people develop their individual capabilities and get them to understand their political rights and enjoy them. To achieve this they needed a great number of well-trained and sympathetic local officials capable of replacing the Communist cadres who had been working with them. Once the people in the countryside, who were 80 percent of our overall population, were won over to the national cause, the NLF could no longer be sustained because it would have lost its main source of support.

I still believe that these objectives were obtainable because the NLF had not yet achieved such power in the countryside as to deny us access to the populace. It is good to remember that no large-scale infiltration of North Vietnamese regular units had yet occurred so that we were faced only by the irregular cadres. The principle we wanted to follow in pacifying the countryside was that of an "oil spot" spreading out from a safe area, making it larger and larger as we gradually made whole provinces secure. Eventually these spots would meet and after a certain time full sections of the country would be thoroughly under government control. Then we would go on to destroy enemy secret bases that had been set up and interrupt the infiltration routes, such as the Ho Chi Minh trail. After all this had been accomplished, we might feel secure enough to contemplate active operations against the North in order to try to unify the national territory.

These plans would, I believe, have permitted our government to secure the countryside and make South Vietnam a safer and better place to live. We had our chance. We had seized power and had the overwhelming mass of the people with us. We were inexperienced, but this probably was in itself something of an advantage. We certainly did not want to continue the sins of the past.

But, our hopes and aspirations were not to be realized.

Nguyen Cao Ky on the Battle for Hearts and Minds, 1976

Alongside the military war, fought with bombs and bullets, we had to fight another war—one to convince our own people that South Vietnam offered a way of life superior to that of the Communists. It was a war for the hearts and minds of the people.

It was not, as some thought, a matter of simple materialism, a philosophy that started with filling bellies. Ambassador Ellsworth Bunker was hopelessly wrong when he told me on one occasion, "People are drifting toward Communism because they are poor. If you give the people everything they want—television sets, automobiles, and so on—none of them will go over to Communism."

Poor Bunker! He was trying to impose American standards of life on people he did not understand, people who basically had no desire for the so-called good things of the American way of life.

From Nguyen Cao Ky, *Twenty Years and Twenty Days,* pp. 135–138, 154, 1976. Published by BookCrafters.

Like so many well-meaning Americans, Bunker, when he came to Vietnam, was unable to grasp the fact that he had made an excursion into a culture as different from America's as an African Negro's is different from that of an Eskimo. No man could hope to span the differences in American and Vietnamese culture and heritage in the short time of his appointment in our land. How could I explain to Bunker's Western mind, for example, that while an American would be lost without a future to conquer, a Vietnamese is lost without the refuge of the past.

"Material goods are not the answer," I replied. "It's much more important to win the hearts and minds of the people than to give them TV sets."

Bunker shook his head disbelievingly, and I felt, watching him, that he was wondering how this young upstart dared to utter such nonsense. But then Bunker no doubt believed in Napoleon's dictum that an army marches on its stomach, and saw no reason why civilians should be any different. But they were.

Among my first priorities when I became prime minister was to introduce some form of social revolution, a term I later amended to "social justice." My aims, my hopes, were very simple: I wanted my people to get a proper reward for their efforts. I wanted a man working eight hours a day to receive twice as much as a man working four hours a day. It takes very little to make the Vietnamese happy. Our needs are simple because we are Asians; we are influenced by the sayings of Confucius. We are not interested in material gain like Westerners; commercial success does not attract us as it does Americans, so we can be happy with little. On the other hand, we do not like to feel exploited, and there lay the root of our problem.

For above all else, the Communist cadres, infiltrating from the North, exploited our corruption and black marketeering as they tried to win over puzzled (yet at heart loyal) peasants to the cause of Ho Chi Minh. They were diabolically clever, for they made no spectacular promises; they held out no bribes. Like Churchill, they offered nothing but blood, sweat, toil, and tears, but they were able to build up the image of a simple, Spartan leader as great in his way as Churchill, and contrast it with our squabbling, corrupt politicians, as squalid in their way as the French politicians in 1940 who bickered among themselves while the Germans streamed across their land.

Yet we had one ace in our hand, if only we could play the hand properly, an ace that did not even exist in the Communist deck of cards. It was freedom, the world's most precious—yet most elusive—treasure. The freedoms that Roosevelt had preached, not only the freedom from fear and want, but the freedom for us to choose our leaders, and the freedom to boot them out if they proved unworthy of the trust reposed in them.

I felt we had to start at the top—and at the bottom. We needed to establish free elections at all levels—in the village tribunal as well as the presidential palace. We needed to introduce fair systems of compensation, provisions for social welfare—all things that are taken for granted in the West.

We achieved more than we were given credit for, though all our efforts were made against a backdrop of a bitter fight for survival. The draft continued in Vietnam until virtually the end, and at the height of the fighting every family in the country had one member, if not two or three, in uniform.

But if we held an ace, we also held a deuce. For while I was preaching the need for freedom, I was not always free myself. True, we were not puppets, yet we never achieved the standing or appearance of an independent, self-governing country. The Americans criticized us for not having a highly developed system of government, but how could we have that when every Vietnamese in Saigon referred to the American ambassador as "the Governor General"?

The Americans did not seek this; they were not colonists, but South Vietnam had been a colony until the defeat of the French, and in many ways it remained virtually a colony, though without the restrictions imposed by the French. We still lacked our own identity.

We never produced a leader to unite the country with its many religious and political factions. The North had one in Ho Chi Minh; rightly or wrongly, the Communists believed in him and fought and died for him. He had a charisma that won many supporters even in the West and not all of them were Communists. Neither Diem, nor Thieu—both backed by the Americans—won the hearts of even the South Vietnamese.

The Americans controlled the fighting of the war. American aid financed the country; without it we could not survive. Americans selected or influenced the selection of our politicians and leaders, even at village level, and had a natural tendency to pick the most compliant rather than the most gifted. American culture—its films, television, and advertising—swamped our own.

Conscious of their dollar-bought superiority, the Americans patronized us at all levels. GIs thoughtlessly but hurtfully referred to Vietnamese as Dinks and Gooks, Slants and Slopes. (Charlie, Chuck, and Claude were reserved for the Viet Cong.)

Their contemptuous attitude was typified by an announcer on the American Forces Radio in 1970: "For those of you staying on in 'Nam, here's a little advice regarding our Vietnamese friends. As you know, they're kind of jumpy now, so please remember the golden rule. Never pat a Vietnamese on the head. Stand on low ground when you talk to them. They kind of resent looking up to you. Okay?"

Certainly the Vietnamese resented being patted on the head. The battle for the hearts and minds of the people was more fundamental to success even than air power or fire power. Yet someone, presumably a GI, painted in white letters on an old warehouse by the river in Saigon the legend: "Just grab the Gooks by the balls and their hearts and minds will follow.". . .

Once more I reiterate that we needed America; we could never have fought the Communists alone. But how much better it would have been if the Americans had never appeared in the picture and we had combined patience with American economic aid and expertise to improve the lot of the average Vietnamese family and the skill of our fighting men. I am convinced that slowly but surely we could have won the war, simply because all the people would have been behind us once the social revolution had been won.

Nguyen Van Thieu's Address to the National Assembly, 1969

Today, in this forum, I wish to solemnly confirm once more to the world, to our allies, to our fellow countrymen, and to our enemy that in our constant search for a constructive solution to the conflict, we consider that the following six points constitute a reasonable and solid basis for the restoration of peace in Viet-Nam:

1. Communist aggression should stop.

Communist North Viet-Nam should give up its attempts to conquer the RVN by force. It should stop violating the DMZ and the frontiers of the RVN, and stop its wanton attacks against the innocent population of the RVN.

2. Communist North Vietnamese and auxiliary troops and cadres should be completely withdrawn from the Republic of Viet-Nam.

As the military and subversive forces of Communist North Viet-Nam are withdrawn, infiltration ceases, and the level of violence thus subsides, the RVN will ask its allies to remove their forces, in accordance with the Manila joint-communique of seven nations in October, 1966.

3. The territories of the neighboring countries of the RVN should not be violated and used by Communist North Viet-Nam as bases and staging areas for aggression against the RVN.

Communist North Vietnamese troops and cadres illegally introduced and stationed in Laos and Cambodia should be withdrawn from these countries. Communist North Viet-Nam military installations in these countries should be dismantled.

4. The RVN adopts the policy of National Reconciliation.

Those now fighting against us, who renounce violence, respect the laws, and faithfully abide by the democratic processes, will be welcomed as full members of the National Community. As such, they will enjoy full political rights and assume the same obligations as other lawful citizens under the National Constitution.

5. The reunification of the two Viet-Nams is to be decided by the free choice of the entire population of Viet-Nam through democratic processes.

To establish the atmosphere conducive to national reunification, after peace has been reestablished, modalities of economic and cultural exchanges between the two Viet-Nams and other countries of this area, can be actively explored, together with other intermediary measures of peaceful coexistence so that, pending reunification, the two Viet-Nams can participate more fully and more constructively in the various undertakings of the international community.

6. There must be an effective system of international control and reliable international guarantees against the resumption of Communist aggression.

The control mechanisms should be freed from the paralyzing effects of the Veto system. It should have sufficient personnel and adequate means to detect any violation of peace agreement. When violations are committed, and aggression is renewed, there should be prompt and effective response from a reliable system of international guarantees, otherwise any peace agreement will be only a sham device used by the Communists to weaken our system of defense, and not a basis for long lasting peace and stability for this part of the world.

An American Serviceman's View of the South Vietnamese Army, 1987

Probably the first two months I was there, I spent out in the bush. Out there the war was easy in a way because there was no ambiguity. Anybody you met out there was hard core NVA regular. No "good guy, bad guy" problem. Later, when we came back to work the coastal area where there were villages and refugees, that's when things started to go "wait a second." Cam Lo, which is one I remember very well, was a refugee village where people had been taken from another place called Gio Linh, ten or fifteen miles away. I didn't understand it then, but for Vietnamese, villagers, their rice paddy and their little ancestral burial ground defines their universe. You take them away as we did and you've totally disrupted what they relate to. And in Cam Lo what I experienced was just hatred in the eyes of people.

The Vietnamese did not like us and I remember I was shocked. I still naively thought of myself as a hero, as a liberator. And to see the Vietnamese look upon us with fear or hatred visible in their eyes was a shock. The only thing we were good for is to sell us something. And frankly every time we operated around Cam Lo we got fucked with. Any patrol, any operation, any convoy passing by would get a smack. So the people that I thought would regard us as heroes were the very people that we were fighting, and all of a sudden my black-and-white image of the world became real gray and confused.

Then I came into contact with the ARVN and that was all the more absurd. First there were some joint operations and then I went with MACV as an advisor and worked with three different ARVN battalions and that's when everything just went screwy in my head. Every night I slept with the battalion commander. We had personal bodyguards and the reason was that a good percentage of the guys in the ranks were VC or even North Vietnamese. The bodyguards were to protect us against getting blown away by the guys we were fighting with. We went out into the A Shau valley for what was supposed to be a ten-day operation and it wound up being ten weeks, and we lost a good number of guys not because of firefights but because they took as much rice as they could carry and they split. The A

From *Everything We Had* by Al Santoli, pp. 111–112. Copyright © 1981 by Albert Santoli and Vietnam Veterans of America. Reprinted by permission of Random House, Inc.

Shau was badlands. It was not a friendly place. And when you leave your unit out in the A Shau you ain't leaving to go bring in the crops back at the farm. You're leaving because you're joining the other side.

It was a joke. The enemy was a tough, hard, dedicated fucking guy, and the ARVN didn't want to hear about fighting. It was LaLa Land. Every, every, every, *every* firefight that we got into, the ARVN broke, the ARVN fucking ran. I was with three different battalions and the story never changed. I almost fell over laughing once. I had an Australian I was working with, and this NVA unit had just ambushed us. We had two companies of ARVN, and finally they got on line to counterattack, and the company commanders give the order to move and nobody moves. And they have to run up and down line with little sticks, beating these guys and kicking them in the fucking rear end to get them up out of their holes. And the Aussie and I look at each other, and we know then and there that this ain't going to work.

✗ E S S A Y S

Gabriel Kolko of York University (Toronto) investigates the inherent structural limitations of the South Vietnamese regime in the opening essay. He sees a government hopelessly dependent on American aid and reliant on a pervasive system of corruption for its survival. Such a regime, Kolko argues, had little prospect for widening its narrow political base or blunting the communist appeal to the peasantry.

In the second essay, Bui Diem, former South Vietnamese ambassador to the United States, acknowledges many of the government's shortcomings while insisting that South Vietnam could have evolved into a viable state. Under the most difficult circumstances, real accomplishments were made; others were possible, including the development of a more democratic political system. The United States, he contends, must bear considerable responsibility for failing to use its leverage as a catalyst for reform and for the arrogant manner with which it treated its ally. Bui Diem now serves as a member of George Mason University's Indochina Institute.

A Doomed Dependency

GABRIEL KOLKO

The war's economic and social impact on South Vietnam between 1965 and 1970 was decisive to its eventual military conclusion. The accumulated effects of war produce their own internal dilemmas and contradictions as well as unintended consequences which may prove far more consequential to a war's outcome than anyone's conscious desires, thereby fixing the boundaries of historical possibilities. The U.S. intervention in Vietnam pro-

From *Anatomy of a War* by Gabriel Kolko, excerpts from pp. 199–224. Copyright © 1985 by Gabriel Kolko. Reprinted by permission of Pantheon Books, a Division of Random House, Inc.

duced such ironies from the inception, but by the late 1960s their impact was decisive and irreversible.

These economic and social trends appeared less than critical to American leaders, and measured in the form of numbers—the only index available to men whose values preclude empathy—they were quite elusive. Even today, information on South Vietnam's demography, the class structure, or the economy is poor and masks unconscionably the enormous human drama and suffering of fully one-half of a nation. It offends the sense of real human experiences to attempt to reduce such events to aggregate, measurable proportions, but to fathom their meaning and importance is to understand, as fully as frail human capacities allow, controlling factors in war and history, the forces which decide the outcome of the more easily described, much more closely studied world of battles or of decision making.

The nature of South Vietnamese society was not incidental to the U.S. effort, but a critical factor, by itself sufficient to determine whether Washington's fate would be victory or defeat. It explains not only the sources of the Revolution's initial efforts in the south but also the subsequent directions imposed upon it, the nature of its triumph, and the peace that followed. The strength, fragility, and evolution of the U.S. dependent determined the very viability of its undertaking and the extent of the obligation the Americans assumed in their naive optimism.

Firepower shaped the demography of South Vietnam after 1964, reducing the issue for a substantial portion of the peasantry to one of physical survival. At the core of the vast panorama of events emerging from this protracted conflict were men and women whose commitments and lives were ceaselessly affected by innumerable challenges and travails. Their responses ranged across the whole spectrum of possible individual reactions, from heroism and conscious efforts to resolve their problem through collective action against foreign invaders to an elemental decision to survive physically as a person by whatever means necessary. To comprehend that process of constant choice for most of the adults is quite impossible, because the destruction, grief, and physical anguish around them, the extremes of human bravery and human degradation, defy description.

The United States in Vietnam unleashed the greatest flood of firepower against a nation known to history. The human suffering was monumental. The figures on all aspects of this enormous trauma are inadequate, and between 1968 and 1970 the refugee reporting system alone underwent three major revisions. The Pentagon's final estimate of killed and wounded civilians in South Vietnam between 1965 and 1972 ran from 700,000 to 1,225,000, while Senate numbers for the same period were 1,350,000. Deaths in these two assessments ranged from 195,000 to 415,000; "enemy" killed were 850,000 minimum, and a substantial part of these were civilians. The Revolution's figures are much higher. In a nation of about 18 million people in 1970, the war exacted an immensely high toll in killed and wounded.

Munitions was the primary cause of casualties, and the vast bulk of it was employed by the United States and the ARVN which accounted for nearly all the artillery and 100 percent of that delivered by air. In 1969, internal U.S. discussions admitted, "the information available . . . on the overall scale and incidence of damage to civilians by air and artillery . . . is less than adequate." They did know, however, that in the single month of January 1969 over four million people, nearly a quarter of the population, had one or more air strikes within three kilometers of their hamlet. The U.S. and RVN pacification programs sought to empty the NLF-dominated regions of their population, not merely by firepower but also by defoliation, forced removals into strategic hamlets, and other means of separating the peasants from their land. While the reasons for this vast population displacement were both political and military, American officials also considered it "desirable" in making available the huge labor pool they required for their own bases and logistics. And once displaced, the peasants had to be kept, the Americans believed, from returning home. For all these reasons, [Robert] Komer said in April 1967, the United States should "[s]tep up refugee programs deliberately aimed at depriving the VC of a recruiting base."

In essence, a substantial part of the peasantry was consciously forced off the land against its will, permanently transforming the nature of South Vietnamese society. The most conservative estimates are that at least half of the peasants were pushed into refugee camps or urban settings one or more times, many repeatedly. The statistics are, again, far from precise, not least because the United States was hardly inclined to expend the effort to document accurately the brutal consequences of its policies. Senate figures for 1964–72 give only 5.8 million persons as refugees, but additional data show that provinces under the NLF, primarily north of Saigon, and in the Mekong as well, generated the largest proportion of refugees. The correlation between firepower and population displacement is very close. RVN numbers on refugees or war victims during 1965–72 are substantially higher than U.S. figures, about 7 million people, or about one-third of the population or well over half the peasantry. Once in refugee camps, the peasants saw their standard of living drop by about two-thirds, and their psychic loss was incalculable. The result was the urbanization of a rural society in a manner unique in this century, for it was far more brutal and disorienting to the population than any that a large Third World nation has ever experienced.

Urban Vietnam before 1960 had been remarkably comfortable, its cities scarcely more than colonial enclaves. The French had controlled them until 1954, of course, but the Chinese also were always vital economically and physically. Even in 1966 one-fifth of South Vietnam's urban population, comprising about a million persons, was Chinese. The virtual Chinese monopoly over important economic activities left little space for newcomers, whose commerce was really marginal subsistence. A portion of them made up the most dynamic, entrepreneurial sector, and were in the best position to amass the benefits of the new foreign presence. Into this turbulent world came millions of peasants after 1964.

In 1960, 20 percent of South Vietnam's population lived in urban areas. The proportion had reached 26 percent by 1964, 36 percent by 1968, and 43 percent by 1971—a growth rate of five times that of all less developed nations during the same decade. Saigon's expansion, though great in the surrounding suburbs, was astonishingly small in the metropolitan area, and far less than that of such provincial towns as Can Tho, Danang, Bien Hoa, Hue, and cities closer to actual combat. Danang and Nha Trang grew fourfold between 1960 and 1971, mainly after 1964, while Can Tho's population tripled. . . .

Forced urbanization not only produced a wholly untenable RVN economy but also created a profoundly disturbed human order, fraught with immense political implications. Looked at objectively, the United States in less than a decade did more damage to an entire society than other colonial nations or the urbanization process elsewhere accomplished over generations. No one, the Revolution included, at first fully perceived the magnitude of this cultural assault, which touched the basic question of the nature of politics and individual commitments in a social context of personal and family crisis. By necessity, this experience can affect people in various ways, one of which is egoism, personalism, and *attentisme* or apathy toward politics. The adult peasantry forced into cities became profoundly alienated from a culture and society succumbing to Americans who devoured their sons and daughters, patronized successive juntas, and wreaked havoc on Vietnamese lands and traditions. One split in urban society which emerged was between those who had absorbed the officially sanctioned urban mores and those who remained rural and traditional in either their economic lives or their values. More dangerous, the newly arrived city dwellers were alienated from their children. . . .

A critical problem for the NLF was whether the former peasantry's involuntary rupture with its rural origins and the Revolution was irreversible, but the decisive question for the United States and the RVN was whether it would ever leave its cocoon of private concerns to sustain the RVN in some effective fashion. For while the Revolution had other means of struggling, without a measure of support from the urban population the RVN would remain politically unstable and the cities only a fatal economic burden.

The social order that urbanization created was ultimately the functional outcome of many policies, and though the new society was largely incremental and ad hoc in nature, aspects of it were certainly planned. Urbanization was the unavoidable logic of the high-firepower war, and its cultural form was strongly influenced by the over two million GIs who passed through the country. Many in America and Saigon regarded population reconcentration as both an opportunity and a hidden blessing. That Washington did not understand the critical economic and political implications of the war's demography until it was too late was one of its great miscalculations in the war.

Thousands of Americans were involved in "nation building" projects, including social scientists eager to test their wares in practice. These ranged from the surrounding of air bases with civilians they attempted to make happy with subsidies of every kind so that they would not aid the NLF (a policy that failed dismally) to an effort to write a Vietnamese equivalent of the song "God Bless America" to win over the masses. The radio propaganda that incessantly swept the nation had very little impact, even in the opinion of the RVN's experts, and the most powerful tool that both the United States and the RVN had to consolidate their influence among the masses was the dollar—a weapon which worked best among the youth on the streets but proved also to be finite both in quantity and in effectiveness.

The dollar's assault on the culture, whether traditional or Revolutionary, profoundly alienated a significant element of the older urban dwellers, particularly the students and intelligentsia who had the leisure to observe and think about it. Secondary school and university enrollment increased over ten times between 1954 and 1970, when the RVN claimed there were about 680,000 in the two categories. The children of the petite bourgeoisie, merchants, and even civil servants and RVN functionaries, many transcended their class position and related to their own peer culture in much the same way the children of uprooted peasants did.

The intellectuals, too, were as fragile in South Vietnam as they are anywhere, full of moods, variations, and typical equivocations, but many became increasingly sympathetic to the NLF as they observed what the United States was doing to the nation and its culture, though a significant portion always did what those in power demanded. Many among them, particularly teachers, were poorly paid. The students, especially, reacted to the nightmare of human degradation around them, and some preserved their capacity for action, even as many retreated into their privileged private worlds. Among people in these social categories, the NLF certainly increased its influence as a by-product of the American cultural offensive, and a significant portion of this crucial social stratum was always alienated from the RVN and the United States.

The final test was less the alienated urban intelligentsia's relationship to the Revolution than its willingness to make those commitments and sacrifices necessary to maintain the existing order in power, and the effects of urbanization prevented this from occurring. As a physical solution to the problem of cooperation between the Revolution and peasantry, the urbanization of the south appeared sensible to the United States. Despite its immediate advantages, however, it was by the late 1960s increasingly alienating the expanding urban population, leaving a growing political, economic, and psychological void. France's struggle against the Communists had not altered the rural society's structure, character, and values in any basic way. Even during its entire colonial reign, only a small minority of the people had been affected ideologically. But the American style of war was far more damaging to the population's identity and existence. The reconciliation of the economic and political contradictions in its policies was almost immediately beyond Washington's abilities. Ultimately, the cumulative effects of urbanization on the RVN's economic, political, and military system immeasurably aided its total collapse.

The Communist Party's virtual monopoly on the opposition to French and American imperialism reflected the impact of colonialism on the Vietnamese class structure and its evolution. All of its potential challengers were too divided, too sectarian, or too ambitious to fill the void in the political system, and religious differences, especially in the south, gravely weakened the non-Marxist opposition. Chinese domination of the economy meant that the stratum with the most to gain from the status quo was unable directly to relate politically to the rest of the system and was mobile, should need arise, and no other potential class-based leadership existed. This vacuum in power and politics was institutionalized for most of the RVN's brief life in the hands of two men, producing hybrid ruling elites without an autonomous class constituency and dependent ultimately on foreign support. Diem's nearly decade-long rulership at the inception of the RVN's twenty-two-year existence, with his systematic attacks on the fragile French bureaucratic legacy and class-based elites, the Chinese particularly, further narrowed the social basis of rulership, reducing it essentially to his clique and the military—the only large institutional force he could not abolish or decrease in functional power. Put simply, the military was the only non-Communist stratum able to succeed Diem and to aspire to power.

The RVN was very much in the same position as many non-Asian Third World states dependent on foreign aid or created in a vacuum to perform a comprador role for a foreign imperialism, and the military in this context traditionally serves as the political arena and instrument of political succession, even though the sponsoring state—the United States in this case—hopes also to utilize it primarily as a way of transferring the techniques of violence and administration necessary to maintain foreign influence. Should the army's political function become its dominant preoccupation, then its tools of violence will ultimately be crucial only within the military establishment's political process, for arms will become the only real or potential means of political change—making its concern for external threats to the state quite secondary. And where the militarized political structure defines the nature and boundaries of economic development and accumulation to a critical extent, corruption drastically erodes its fighting capacities. In brief, politics neutralizes military capabilities decisively by making all purely military considerations subordinate to the control of political and economic power. The state, the economy, and military and political power all become integrated. The overcoming of this contradiction is the United States' main dilemma every time it creates a dependency on which it in turn becomes dependent to attain its own national objectives.

Such a context makes the social nature and function of the officers a fundamental issue, their class origins and linkages being facts of potentially great significance to their definition of their social and economic role as well as their personal aspirations. This is especially true when the military in underdeveloped nations with a vacuum in institutional power is the dominant mechanism within which rulership is determined. The marginality or stability of a class society at its various levels is critical where a cohesive opposition exists, and it becomes a crucial factor in determining how wars are concluded.

The officers in the RVN's armed forces, some 25,000 by 1967, as well as the tiny elite of senior officers at the rank of major or higher, were homogenous to an astonishing degree. The junior officers, composing 95 percent of the total number of officers, were very young. Since they had to have at least a high school diploma, they were overwhelmingly urbanized and born into families that could afford to educate their children. Soldiers could not rise through the ranks to become officers. A quarter were born in the north, and the percentage of Catholics was double South Vietnam's average, which meant that the military was an important avenue of social mobility for displaced refugees coming from the DRV after 1954. Economically, though, the profession was poorly paid, second lieutenants earning but $55 monthly in 1967 and enjoying few legal perquisites. For the majority who were married and had families, this fact became critical to their real functions. At least one major distinction between officers was their training academy and their year of graduation. Without a definable class or ideological differentiation among the officers, the "school tie" became inordinately important. The National Military Academy at Dalat produced 13 percent of the officers in the military in 1967, but 30 percent of the general-ranking officers graduated from it, while Thu Duc academy graduated two-thirds of the officers and a mere 5 percent of the generals and 30 percent of the field-grade officers. Catholics accounted for a third of the generals.

Of a sample of sixty generals in 1972, one-third were the sons of landowners, another quarter of government officials, and over a quarter of officers and urban professionals and middle- and upper-class elements. They were upwardly mobile; their families were not yet important but at a point where they might aspire to be, and this profoundly affected their use of power. Thieu, for example, was the son of a small landlord, and he graduated from Dalat. A scant majority were graduates of Dalat academy, 14 percent of Thu Duc. Nearly all had begun their careers under the French. The military, given the role of war in the French and the RVN's priorities, was the chief channel of social and economic mobility for an important sector of the marginalized middle classes ready to work for the dominant colonial power.

The motive of the senior officers after Diem's death was simple: power in the form of careers and money. This was just as true of the congeries of civilian miniparties, factions, or religious sects who were always moving in and out of various coalitions or plotting on the sidelines. Where neither coherent class interest nor ideology exists, there is no basis of collective action and responsibility, and personal welfare becomes the motive of politics, resulting in individual corruption as an institutionalized dimension of society.

The Americans always watched this charade with the utmost cynicism. Perhaps the most dangerous aspect of this period was the effort of civilians to link up with military factions and encourage them, which was a guarantee of continuous turmoil and, by mid-1966, of various degrees of warlordism in the four military regions into which the RVN was divided, particularly MR I in the north. Indeed, as the successive military juntas passed through Saigon, mutual suspicions justifiably became axiomatic among those in the perpetual imbroglio the United States was sustaining. As they conspired and as membership in the ruling juntas changed, the system was made ripe for a superior political fixer, and in Nguyen Van Thieu the senior officers met their master.

Thieu was surely the ablest politician to emerge in the RVN's history, and his conversion from Buddhism to Catholicism to advance his career proved he was supremely flexible. He was a member in the June 1965 junta representing the "Young Turks" with no close past ties to the French and Diem. From there he moved unobtrusively to find ways of maneuvering around potential opponents and, above all, to try to find the price or weakness of any who might resist him. Unlike Diem, he had no serious ideological pretensions, and the initial key to his success was his readiness co-optively to share the spoils. Thieu was much more interested in obtaining stable control over power rather than a monopoly of it, and not until 1973 was he to seek total authority in his own hands.

In the wake of Diem's death, one of the most important factors in his rise to power was the aid he obtained from the Chinese business elite. Thieu's sister-in-law married Ly Luong Than, who was already one of the richest Chinese in Saigon, held a U.S. passport in his traditionally abundant collection, and was a key figure in the Fukienese *bang* [Chinese merchant organizations]. Than brought Thieu together with Francis Koo, first secretary of the Taiwanese embassy in Saigon and a senior figure in SEATO intelligence circles. Koo decided Thieu would serve the embattled Chinese community well and provided him funds and contacts to advance his career. When Nguyen Cao Ky, his main rival, in early 1966 excoriated speculators and had one Chinese publicly executed as a warning to the others, the still nervous Chinese elite gave Thieu massive financial backing and intervened on his behalf with U.S. officials. Thieu was a shrewd operator in his own right, but his access to funds also smoothed his way. He had far more tact and cash to employ than Ky did. The United States' obsessive desire to see military unity was the single most important element in bringing Thieu to power, but his Chinese connection undoubtedly shaped the regime's distribution of economic benefits.

Thieu in 1967 was the sole general with sufficient talent to survive the chaos of Saigon politics and create a powerful political machine. In June 1967 he had the junta nominate him for the new presidency, after he promised to abide by the will of a collective leadership. Even when he was most powerful, Thieu neutralized, co-opted, and pressured many of his military and civilian elite rivals far more gently than Diem did, trying to divide the rewards of office widely to gain time to enjoy the prerogatives of power and, above all, to prevent any threats to his increasingly durable machine from the other senior military commanders. As for the Chinese, one of his first acts in 1967 was to allow them to reestablish their *bangs* and to return their associations' confiscated property.

The moment he came to office, in September 1967, Thieu embarked on building a largely private power machine which integrated the military, the political structure, and the economy in numerous formal and informal ways. Complex in certain aspects and baldly simple in others, his system assured that the RVN's destiny after 1968 would become synonymous with Thieu's ambitions, his power, and, ultimately, his weaknesses.

In an underdeveloped class structure traumatized by the effects of Diem's own power machine, the demography of the war, a subsidized war economy, and an enormous American presence, Thieu temporarily and partially remolded the elastic class system to suit his interests. He unified ambitious, essentially marginal class elements and the rich Chinese around only one common denominator: money and access to privilege. As a Rand Corporation summation of the views of twenty-seven high RVN officers and officials after the war said, "A central feature of the South Vietnamese regime . . . was corruption." His integrative effort encompassed a variety of approaches, ranging from a vast number of people brought into the RVN's employment to a higher elite which was incorporated into the war economy formally and informally, together sharing the main prerogatives of power. The fluid RVN power structure possessed intersecting economic, political, and military components in varying degrees, according to the people and elements involved, but it was never fully formalized before it collapsed both from its own contradictions and from the pressures the Revolution as well as the United States imposed on it.

The analysis of transitional and dependent social orders is potentially misleading if one attributes excess coherence and form to constantly evolving relationships. The task in Vietnam is made all the more difficult because the senior officers, Chinese capitalists, and civilian Vietnamese politicians were each internally divided, and only from 1969 to 1973 (but not later) did Nguyen Van Thieu sufficiently control power to make the structure susceptible to some generalizations. Thieu used his family as much as possible, of course, but his real strength was his ability to find and reward generals ready to cooperate with him loyally in running both the military and the civil administrations. Such a co-optive strategy was successful so long as there was enough to share. It was the sheer enormity of the American economic impact which defined the parameters of the RVN's class development and the political life intimately linked with it.

Both the Revolution and the U.S. government had a handful of analysts who tried to assess the structure of power within the RVN. Their work, as well as that of former RVN officials who have written postmortems, was remarkably parallel in both methods and conclusion. All assigned special significance to the Chinese capitalists in the running of the RVN system. Yet one cannot attribute causal power to them, because it was the French and later the Americans who ultimately controlled the collaborationist system. Without them, Thieu could not have undertaken so much, so well and so quickly. But while it is true that the Chinese by the 1960s were a traditional elite and the generals a distinctly new one, the political leverage the generals possessed made the Chinese highly dependent on their favors. A huge amount of money could be made in the economy and in the state's operations, and the Chinese obtained the major share in the former and a significant proportion of the latter. Opportunities for corruption available from direct control of state positions were vast, and officers and key bureaucrats dominated them.

Thieu was ultimately the functional master of the whole order during four years. His access to money was crucial to political cohesion in the military elite, and it kept most senior civil servants docile until 1973. The hybrid power structure which emerged was really a very personalized synthesis of Thieu and his coalition of loyal generals as well as a Chinese elite, and it is futile to try to determine their relative importance since each without the other was inconceivable. Getting rich was the common consensus which united them, and as Thieu manipulated their avarice, his machine possessed all of the subjective, arbitrary qualities one associates with the accumulation of capital by political means and corruption during a war which was sponsored entirely by a foreign power. Ultimately, the RVN's existence was improvised in an environment of chicanery, desperation, and tragedy which made absurdity and audacity common coin, with marginalized gangsters the mainstay of the social order the United States was attempting to keep in place.

A crucial aspect of America's funding for Thieu's system was mass employment and the perquisites that went with it. When Diem was overthrown, there were 121,000 civilian employees working for the RVN; by 1965 the number had grown to 179,000, increasing very slowly until 1968 (when Thieu took full command of the state administrative apparatus). From 208,000 government employees in 1968, the bureaucracy bounded to 337,000 in 1972 (the police composed 38 percent of this number), its share of the labor force having more than doubled since the early 1960s. The civil service had been fickle and inept in the stormy sea of post-Diemist politics, and Thieu sought to make it a reliable instrument of his power. Although their nominal salaries were low and kept falling, he allocated to them a whole panoply of corrupt practices to deepen his hold on their loyalties. The most common were bribes to obtain essential papers, ranging from normal legal transactions or identification documents to draft deferments, plus numerous petty forms of boodle. Corruption suffused and financially lubricated the state bureaucratic system at all levels.

The junior officer corps also became a major source of support for Thieu, for he satisfied their ambitions far more than any of his predecessors did. The regular military grew rapidly from 1961 to 1965, but the junior officer appointments failed to keep pace with it. When Thieu took power, he increased the number of first lieutenants from 8,764 in 1968 to 17,353 two years later and that of captains from 4,793 to 10,654, at a time when the regular military grew by less than a fifth. They too, of course, were allocated a share of condoned corruption as a supplement to their low salaries, and they often received their appointments because they were beholden to some senior officer for critical recommendations or, more simply, because they bought his favor. Their rackets were generally petty, ranging from the collecting of rice rations and salaries for dead or deserted soldiers to the funneling of military gasoline and supplies into the local markets, some of which the NLF purchased. Along with political officials, some participated in local usury, which during the Thieu period was 50 to 90 percent monthly. Together they could enforce their claims if necessary.

Higher-level officers were far more important, and their appointments were treated more seriously, since they alone could challenge Thieu's growing hegemony. Success in combat or purely military competence was increasingly ignored in senior appointments; political tendencies and personal ambition were far more critical. This made staff rather than combat officers ever-more preponderant at the upper ranks. Friends and relatives were very important. All appointments at the level of major or above had to be carefully approved by one of Thieu's closest allies in Saigon. He alone chose every general officer. There were only 40 generals in 1967, and 82 colonels, and it was to these men that Thieu turned his attention as he consolidated power. Shunting some of them off to powerless positions and avoiding any challenges to powerful generals' corruption, Thieu increased his control over the military apparatus by enlarging the number of generals to 73 and that of colonels to 200 in 1972, but the senior officer corps, in various degrees, remained seriously underbilleted after 1967, as Thieu cautiously filled the higher positions primarily with political appointees and assigned the lower officers duties which far exceeded both their rank and their abilities. Such a bottom-heavy officer corps was designed essentially to prevent a coup d'etat. Those at the top were repaid for their devotion with a significant share of the state's diverse economic resources, ranging from normal commerce to sanctioned corruption of every variety, from larceny and graft to import licenses. "We would be left with practically no one to fight the war," Thieu's vice-president, Tan Van Huong, admitted, "if all corrupt commanders were to be prosecuted and relieved." Thieu's genius was to deflect the ambitions of his select group of senior officers from a desire for real political power and to make them, as two former generals recalled, "motivated by money." By the most cautious estimates, fully two-thirds of all generals and colonels were corrupt. . . .

The RVN's military and political machinery increasingly merged in Thieu's hands and could not operate without him, and this fact was far more important to its eventual destiny than the issue whether it was trained to fight conventional or guerilla warfare. The military establishment's primary function was to maintain Thieu's power, and the United States' ability to fight a counterrevolutionary war depended on the durability of a regime which was, in the words of one of Thieu's generals after the war, "intrigue-ridden, dictatorial, and repressive." American officials knew by 1971 what was not fully revealed until spring 1975—that Thieu's talent as a military leader was mediocre at best. His role was political, and Washington supported him for this reason.

Thieu understood that by permitting corruption, indeed even encouraging it, he could win loyalty: "The best way of avoiding coups d'etat . . .," as one of his aides quoted him. But the fundamental dilemma of such an order for America's anti-Communist crusade remained. The various constituencies Thieu drew into his expanding system were usually linked to him informally rather than institutionally, a fact which somewhat disturbed U.S. officials, although not enough to alter their overwhelming wish to see stability maintained. Elections were, as Nguyen Cao Ky aptly phrased it from his own experience as the victorious vice-president in 1967, "a loss of time and money. They were a joke. They have served to install a regime that has nothing in common with the people—a useless, corrupt regime." The National Assembly, which Diem himself created, had no significant powers, and Thieu ignored it. Even the most sympathetic American analysts thought that at least one-third of its members were fortune seekers—and Thieu let them enjoy this search often. . . .

The general dilemma confronting the United States' efforts to expand the military's power and role in numerous underdeveloped nations since 1950 has been the senior officer class' utilization of American support to assume far greater political power. And given the weak economic elite in most nations, the military's political role quickly dominates and exploits the nation's economic development, which ultimately produces instability and crisis politics and thwarts genuine development. In the end, the militarization of the RVN not only monopolized politics but also catalyzed social and human transformations which gravely eroded the coherence and future of the non-Revolutionary ideologies and followers. Those strata of South Vietnamese society without political links could scarcely compete for a large share of the new riches, even though a small number of individuals, mainly Chinese, managed to succeed in the highly fluid context in one way or another. The urban masses lived on the narrowest margins, and even some brothels and bars belonged to the elite that was forming from officers, key bureaucrats, and the Vietnamese and Chinese elements directly allied to them.

American officials always saw clearly the role of the new RVN elite in making vast private gains from political power. They were often informed by various senior generals currying U.S. favor that "corruption exists everywhere, the rich get richer while the mass of the poor Vietnamese see little hope of improvement"—as Marshall Ky told American leaders in July 1965, while jockeying for a greater share of it himself. Far worse than corruption, in American eyes, was tension among the generals and political instability. This consideration caused Washington increasingly to support Thieu, until the officer corps rightly came to believe that he was their surest, perhaps only, link to the Yankee cornucopia. "Patterns of existent political alignments are greatly affected by corruption because of its endemic character in GVN and RVNAF functioning," the National Security Council's early 1969 review of the war concluded. Since reformers could only upset Thieu's cohesive and firmly managed dictatorship, American interest in reform never went beyond occasional subtle changes palatable to Thieu in the aid program.

In this sense, the Americans knew they were ultimately responsible for the Thieu regime, for without their money the RVN would not be able to buy allies who assured stability. The economic basis of its very existence would vanish. "Moreover," the NSC acknowledged in early 1969, "it is natural that many Vietnamese will hold the United States responsible for not controlling its aid so that corruption will not flourish." This relationship was the critical linkage in the social and class structure in the south after 1965, and all else would ultimately prove secondary. Conversely, since the United States now correctly saw that its entire mission was contingent on the RVN's stability, which only Thieu was able to provide, it in turn was wholly dependent on Thieu's remaining in power, a fact he perceived and exploited ruthlessly. Ironically, who was master and who was puppet was increasingly blurred with time.

Analyzed structurally, the apex of the Thieu system was a narrow clique of officers and key civilian officials, not more than several thousand. Immediately below them was a far more numerous set of lower-ranking officials and officers. Directly allied with this elite were various merchants, entrepreneurs in service industries, and businessmen, including a small group of landlords, who collectively channeled money to and from the higher levels via contracts, kickbacks, licenses for imports, and the like. While they never estimated its size, the AID's experts on the upper echelons of this system concluded, "Many of the larger industries in South Vietnam are currently controlled by a small number of coalitions of Chinese businessmen who are allied with strategic Vietnamese government personnel." The Fukienese, according to American officials, were by far the most powerful, Ly Luong Than was their most important leader, and they controlled or had major shares in textiles, scrap metal, construction, banking, insurance, food processing, and imports. Chinese from Swatow were congregated in banking, insurance, diverse manufacturing, and textiles.

All of the analyses of the dominating persons in this system number in the hundreds the officers and senior politicians and officials involved, and their capitalist allies—the large majority being Chinese—could not have been more than one or two thousand. This tiny but critical element accounted for the bulk of the accumulated capital and capital flight. Most of the capitalists had been wealthy before the war, but not on a remotely comparable scale. Directly beneath them was an altogether new group of largely politically based rich whose primary power lay in access to the state's largesse, and these were paralleled by entrepreneurs, mainly Chinese, but with a growing number of Vietnamese, who simply made money in conventional ways inevitable with the boom the American forces brought. . . .

Thieu, of course, never attempted seriously to create a broad class foundation for his regime, but the cumulative effect of Thieu's system was to create a congenial if fickle constituency out of those who were the direct or indirect beneficiaries of the American-funded society. There was never a class base for the Thieu regime in the true sense of class as an institutionally stable and broad element of society. The disintegration of the French legacy and the marginalization of the educated elements who had earlier been ideologically or economically predisposed to anti-Communist politics continued, inevitably conditioning a substantial portion of them for anti-

Thieu coalition politics with virtually anyone, including the NLF. The shallow privileged class residues inherited from the French era continued to narrow, especially as inflation after 1965 began to whittle away at the economic resources of all except the Chinese.

The very context in which Thieu's regime developed convinced most of its new elite that it could not endure, and this especially affected its Chinese members, who had traditionally been mobile, prone to keeping wealth highly liquid, and often linked to families and interests elsewhere in Southeast Asia. Between the Chinese and the officers, the basic paradox of the Thieu regime was the opportunism of its most powerful and favored supporters, which took the form of a vast flight of capital, an exodus of children, and a reluctance to invest in long-term economic development. The Chinese capitalists were by definition the weakest class on which the military elite could rely. And precisely because they knew that the generals were vulnerable and transitional, they tried to make certain that their options outside the country were always ready. The Chinese, American officials in Saigon accurately concluded in 1972, for the most part "do not consider themselves a part of the nation in which they live. For the large entrepreneurs, the business decision to invest here or transfer funds abroad is made on business calculations and not on any consideration of national need—exactly, in fact, like any foreign investor does."

The fragile class structure that the French had created and Diem eroded now became even weaker in the flotsam and jetsam of demography, social disintegration, and changes far too rapid to be absorbed coherently. The new lumpen element of war profiteers destroyed the final vestiges of the national and the petite bourgeoisies, plunging them into economic and moral crises which compromised some and radicalized others. And being wholly dependent on American money and support for the very existence of the RVN, the new profiteers had no nationalist or cultural legitimacy for their politics, a fact they could not alter. The underdevelopment of a possible conservative class characterized the pre-Revolutionary order until its end. Both the French and the American colonial legacies made this ephemeral, fluid class development inevitable by their reliance on the Chinese and on dependent, obsequious arriviste generals whose only loyalty in serving comprador roles was ultimately to their own, personal welfare.

Though South Vietnam's economy under Diem was wholly dependent on American aid, after 1964 it was far more fragile. The intensified war and the exponential growth of American GIs posed potentially catastrophic economic challenges to the United States' ambition. For agriculture was being uprooted and the population displaced into cities wholly unable to absorb them with local resources.

The purpose of American economic policy was to stanch the immense economic wounds the war was inflicting long enough to allow its vague military objectives to be attained at a time, as the Agency for International Development later ruefully admitted, when "no one thought the war would last ten years, let alone that we would lose it." The cost to the United States could, if its military assumptions were valid, remain tolerable only for a short period. But to cut its losses was tantamount to military surrender, which was unthinkable. Meanwhile, Washington's temporary economic solutions produced fabulous opportunities for growing corruption, becoming the key to Thieu's political consolidation and, to a lesser degree, the maintenance of more social stability among the masses than would otherwise have been possible. In effect, the RVN's very existence was linked to sufficient economic and military aid, surpassing in importance the outcome of battles or diplomacy, for the very artificiality of the economy and the war's impact left it vulnerable to countless potentially fatal problems.

In retrospect, the AID accurately concluded in 1975, the "period 1965–67 in Viet Nam was unlike anything ever experienced by an underdeveloped country." While the various mechanisms the United States employed may seem complicated to nonspecialists, in essence they were merely manifestations of a simple policy. An escalating war was destroying the existing economy, and Washington made the decision that it was vital to prevent inflation, which could only further radicalize the people and make defeat more certain. The Korean War, which was much smaller in terms both of troops and of areas affected at any one time, had created a runaway inflation, the memory of which was still fresh in Washington in 1964. To combat inflation, the United States decided to maximize imports, neutralizing the vast inflow of dollars accompanying its half a million soldiers, the American expansion of bases and military construction, and the ruination of South Vietnam's traditional productive economic sector. The RVN's seeming prosperity, so illusory for the majority of the nation, was based wholly on this strategy.

Agricultural production by 1968 was a quarter below the already low 1961–65 average. Not until 1970 did it finally surpass it, although per capita output never equaled it. Industrial production, mainly to service U.S. troop demands and provide supplies for construction, rose during 1964–67, dropping sharply in 1968. In 1964–67 imports increased over 100 percent, and imports during 1969–71 exceeded exports by a factor of over fifty-five. By 1967 about 40 percent of the RVN's gross national product was composed of imports entirely dependent on U.S. aid, and by 1970 nearly 50 percent was. Proportionately, the share of gross domestic product devoted to manufacturing dropped dramatically throughout this period—making South Vietnam the only major nation of Asia to experience this form of deindustrialization and leaving it with the lowest proportion in manufacturing of any of them. The South Vietnamese economy was sharply diverted from the production of goods, the only basis of real economic development, into the provision of services, making it structurally very weak and vulnerable to an economic crisis the moment the Americans started to withdraw.

A Viable State

BUI DIEM

Except for the special circumstances that put me close to the center stage of the war in Vietnam, and except for the sheer luck that spared me much of the suffering endured by others, I am not different from other Vietnamese of my generation. In terms of dreams and aspirations, frustrations and disappointments, my life story is essentially theirs.

Vietnamese of my generation came of age in the early forties with the hope that after almost a century as second-class citizens in their own country, they would have a chance to recover their dignity and achieve their independence from France. They dreamed also of peace and a decent life for themselves and their children. It was their misfortune that instead of independence, peace, and a decent life, they saw only revolution, war, and destruction. For three decades they existed in the maelstrom. And even now, when Vietnam no longer has to deal with foreign invaders, their misery continues. Theirs has been a tragedy of historic proportions.

In an interview with Walter Cronkite in 1963, President John Kennedy said, "In the final analysis, it's their war and they are the ones who will either win it or lose it." Much as we might like to, there is no getting away from Kennedy's judgment. The South Vietnamese people, and especially the South Vietnamese leaders, myself among them, bear the ultimate responsibility for the fate of their nation, and to be honest, they have much to regret and much to be ashamed of. But it is also true that the war's cast of characters operated within a matrix of larger forces that stood outside the common human inadequacies and failings. And it was these forces that shaped the landscape on which we all moved.

First among these root causes was the obduracy of France, which in the late forties insisted on retaining control of its former colony rather than conceding independence in good time to a people who hungered for it. Second was the ideological obsession of Vietnam's Communists. Not content with fighting to slough off a dying colonialism, they relentlessly sought to impose on the Vietnamese people their dogma of class warfare and proletarian dictatorship. Finally came the massive intervention by the United States, inserting into our struggle for independence and freedom its own overpowering dynamic. These three forces combined to distort the basic nature of Vietnam's emergence from colonialism, ensuring that the struggle would be more complex and bloodier than that of so many other colonies which achieved nationhood during mid-century.

Caught in the midst of these powerful forces, Vietnam's nationalists found themselves in a succession of precarious situations. In most cases they were forced to choose among unpalatable alternatives; often, indeed, they saw no choice at all. With their survival at stake, they were forced to take refuge in a series of uneasy and uncomfortable compromises that little

From *In the Jaws of History* by Bui Diem and David Chanoff, pp. 334–343. Copyright © 1987 by Bui Diem and David Chanoff. Reprinted by permission of Houghton Mifflin Company.

by little eroded their legitimacy. From one experience to another—first with the French and Bao Dai, then with Ngo Dinh Diem, then with the Americans and the military—they tried to carve out a role for themselves and establish their influence. But always they were pushed to the periphery, and the influence they wielded was never enough to affect the ultimate course of events. To myself and others, for a time it seemed we might be able to develop the nation's economy and build a functioning democracy, even while waging war. But eventually the room to make this kind of contribution diminished, and in the end, against a mechanized North Vietnamese invasion army equipped by the Soviets, all that remained was an alley fight for survival. By then Vietnam's nationalists had been forced to take their place alongside all the other Vietnamese who could only stand by and watch their fate unfold in front of them.

As I look back on the external forces that shaped our lives, it is the American intervention that stands out. French colonialism, after all, is dead and gone, a subject for historians who prefer the inert remains of the past to the passions of the present. As for Vietnamese communism, no one but the fervid or the blind any longer argues the merits of a system that has brought in its wake only war and deprivation and mass flight. (Not that having been right comforts us as we house our refugees and send what sustenance we can back to our families.) But American intervention is a living issue. In the train of failure in Vietnam, and in the face of hard choices elsewhere, the questions of its correctness and its morality still inform American foreign policy debates. Americans still seek to learn the lessons of intervention, and so do America's smaller allies, who cannot help but see in the fate of Vietnam intimations of their own possible futures.

For critics of the Vietnam War, the original decision to intervene was wrong, a result, as one of them put it, of a "steady string of misjudgments." It was wrong because American policymakers in the sixties failed to assess correctly the vital interests of the United States, because they exaggerated the geopolitical importance of Vietnam, and because they had an inflated concept of American capabilities.

Although it is neither my business nor within my competence to pass judgment on how the United States defined its interests at that time, it is my impression that such arguments are made on a distinctly *a posteriori* basis. I remember vividly the political atmosphere in the United States in the summer of 1964, the summer of the Tonkin resolution and Barry Goldwater's nomination, when I first visited this country. At that time the Johnson administration and practically the entire Congress were in favor of the commitment to defend Vietnam (the resolution passed in the Senate, 98 to 2, and in the House, 416 to 0). And so, *mirabile dictu,* were the national news media.

Moreover, the context of international affairs in that period provided good reasons for this nearly unanimous opinion, reasons that went beyond the specific perception of North Vietnamese aggressiveness. It was then the aftermath of the Communist attack in Korea, and China's Communist leaders were broadcasting the most belligerent and expansionistic views, even as they attempted to establish a Peking-Jakarta axis with Indonesia's pro-Communist President Sukarno. For the fragile governments of Southeast Asia the situation seemed serious indeed. Although twenty-five years later it became fashionable among some Americans to belittle Communist threats to the region's stability, among the responsible governments at the time there was deep anxiety.

Even for those South Vietnamese who thought they saw the inherent dangers in American intervention, there was still nothing illogical about it. The American interest in Vietnam, even its land intervention, seemed a natural extension of U.S. policies in Europe (the Marshall Plan, the Berlin airlift, Greece) and Asia (Korea) aimed at preventing the expansion of combined Soviet and Chinese power (at least until the early 1960s, no one could imagine that the two Communist giants would become antagonists). And for the Europeans who were able to rebuild their countries and save their democratic institutions, for the Germans in Berlin, for the Greeks, and for the South Koreans, those policies were not wrong. Nor were they based on misjudgments of geopolitical realities. In Vietnam the policy failed. But that is not to say that it was wrong there either. The disastrous mistakes that were made were mistakes in implementation rather than intention. But the thrust of the policy of containment and protection, that I do not think can be faulted. It is, on the contrary, something for Americans to be proud of.

The more vocal critics of the war in the sixties and seventies characterized the intervention, not just as wrong, but also as immoral. Their charge was based primarily on the theory that the war in Vietnam was a civil war, and that consequently American intervention was an act of aggression against people who were fighting to free themselves from an oppressive regime and unify their country in accord with the aspirations of the great majority of decent-minded Vietnamese.

It is my own belief that this theory held the field for so long primarily because it was a powerful attraction to the many Americans who were angry at their own government and society and were looking for issues to hang their anger on. Certainly, the facts that refuted it were readily available. From early on, both Saigon and Washington knew beyond a doubt that the National Liberation Front—the Vietcong—was a creation of the Communist party, and that without North Vietnamese organization, leadership, supplies, and, starting in 1964, without the North Vietnamese regular army, there would have been no revolution to speak of and no war. It was one of my greatest frustrations that our firm knowledge of this—both from widespread and incontrovertible evidence and also from personal experience among many of us of communist "front" techniques—made no impact on popular understanding in the West. Regardless of what was there to be seen, people saw only what they wished.

After the war, when propaganda no longer mattered, the party dropped its pretense. "Our Party," said Le Duan in his 1975 victory speech, "is the unique and single leader that organized, controlled, and governed the entire struggle of the Vietnamese people from the first day of the revolution." During the war, the North Vietnamese never openly admitted they had troops in South Vietnam. (Le Duc Tho even kept up the pretense with Henry Kissinger, although Kissinger knew the situation as well as he knew his own name, and Tho, of course, knew that he knew it.) But afterward the party treated this subterfuge simply as an excellent piece of public relations and its own role as a matter of intense pride. As the North Vietnamese general Vo Ban told French television interviewers in 1983, "In May 1959 I had the privilege of being designated by the Vietnamese Communist Party to unleash a military attack on the South in order to liberate the South and reunify the fatherland."

During the heyday of the antiwar movement, I marveled at the innocence of its spokesmen in believing something different from this. I wonder even now if they ever feel shame for their gullibility and for their contribution to the tragedy. But they are not heard from. It was, after all, only one chapter in their lives, as it was only a chapter in the book of American history.

The issue of morality, then, comes down to whether it was moral for the United States to have supported an admittedly flawed South Vietnamese regime in its attempt to survive against a totalitarian antagonist. Here, too, the answer seems to me self-evident. However unpalatable leaders like Nguyen Van Thieu might have been, South Vietnam was full of pluralistic ferment and possibilities for change and development. It was a place where good people could hope for something better to evolve, where they could even fight for it, as so many strong-minded opposition politicians, intellectuals, and writers did. None but ideologues can compare such a place with the chilling police state that destroyed it. And none, I think, can fairly question the morality of the effort to prevent its destruction.

To my mind, the lessons of American intervention in Vietnam have to do not so much with the geopolitical or moral underpinning of the war, but rather with the way the intervention was implemented. The real question was not whether to intervene, but how to intervene effectively.

. . . The salient feature of [the] confused and unclear process (as Bill Bundy characterized it) [by which the Johnson administration decided to bring an American land army to Vietnam] was not that it was ill planned and based on no comprehensive strategy. It was the startling attitude of American decision makers toward their ally. At the top levels of the administration, the State Department, and the Pentagon, there is no evidence to suggest that anyone considered the South Vietnamese as partners in the venture to save South Vietnam. In a mood that seemed mixed of idealism and naivete, impatience and overconfidence, the Americans simply came in and took over. It was an attitude that would endure throughout the remainder of the conflict. The message seemed to be that this was an American war, and the best thing the South Vietnamese could do was to keep from rocking the boat and let the Americans get on with their business.

The military consequences of this orientation were that the United States took the entire burden on itself instead of searching for ways to make a decisive impact while limiting its exposure. Had the South Vietnamese been consulted in early 1965, it is likely they would have preferred either no intervention or a limited effort sufficient to stabilize the military situation and block the infiltration routes from North Vietnam. An agreement among the United States, South Vietnam, and Laos, allowing U.S. troops to be stationed along the seventeenth parallel as a barrier, would have been quite feasible at the time. With that done. an immediate Vietnamization program could have been undertaken to strengthen and upgrade the South Vietnamese army.

Could such a simple strategy have worked? That is one of the "what if" questions with which the Vietnam War abounds. Colonel Harry Summers, in *On Strategy,* his uncompromising review of American military planning, concludes that it would have, that in fact, isolating the South Vietnamese battlefield from North Vietnamese reinforcement and resupply was the only logical objective for American arms. Whatever the imponderables of war, this approach would at least have had the virtue of establishing the United States as a peace-keeping force protecting South Vietnam from outside aggression. It would have reduced American casualties and precluded the involvement of American firepower in the disconcerting people's war that was such a nightmare for the GIs to fight and that created such powerful antagonism in the arena of international public opinion.

On the political level, too, this American failure to regard the South Vietnamese as people worthy of partnership had destructive results. It meant that the United States never pursued a consistent policy aimed at encouraging the development of a viable democracy in South Vietnam. Certainly, such a thing was possible. Between 1965 and 1967 the South Vietnamese drafted and adopted a constitution, elected a president, vice president, and legislature, and successfully held many local elections—all of this in the middle of a war. It was a substantial achievement, but it would not have happened except that during those years the impulse toward democracy in South Vietnam and the objectives of the Johnson administration coincided.

Unfortunately, thereafter "stability" became the American watchword. As long as the Saigon government demonstrated a modicum of equilibrium, that was all that was asked of it. Several years of progress toward decent government might erode, corruption and autocracy might swell, but these things were not a primary American concern. By 1969 Henry Kissinger and Richard Nixon had embarked on a complex chess game, manipulating big-power diplomacy, military force, and secret negotiations in an attempt to extricate the United States from its quagmire. Amidst this constellation of variables, they needed a government in Saigon that was stable and predictable. If Thieu provided them with that, then whatever else he might do was essentially irrelevant.

It was a fatal error on two counts. First, stigmatized as undemocratic and corrupt, South Vietnam was deemed unworthy of support by an ever-increasing percentage of the American public and Congress. Second, within South Vietnam itself, the unpopular nature of the regime produced apathy, cynicism, and finally, in the anticorruption movement, outrage. Charles Mohr, veteran correspondent of the *New York Times,* summed it up succinctly in a seminar at the American Enterprise Institute. "We lost the war in Vietnam," he said, "not because we did not bring enough pressure to bear on our enemy, but because we did not bring sufficient pressure on our ally." Admittedly, bringing pressure for reform and democracy is a delicate business. But in situations where the United States has significant leverage, the role of catalyst for change, of prodding contending factions toward consensus, beckons to American diplomacy.

To successfully play such a role, there are two prerequisites. One is the will to carry out a strong and consistent advocacy. The other is the determination to accept the consequences if in the end American pressure proves unavailing. The United States must find a way to say to a Ngo Dinh Diem or a Nguyen Van Thieu (or a Ferdinand Marcos or an Augusto Pinochet), "We have no alternative but to stand by our own values. If for your own reasons you find you cannot bring yourselves toward conforming with them, then we are very sorry, but we will have no choice but to leave you to your own devices." With all its power and prestige, the United States simply cannot allow itself to yield to the tyranny of the weak, to authoritarians who believe their importance is so vast that the United States cannot help but support them. If Vietnam has one single lesson to teach, it is that people cannot be saved in spite of themselves. Far better to get out and cut losses before ensnaring treasure, lives, prestige, and all in the service of those whose rule means violent discord and social breakdown.

In Vietnam I always believed that among decent and reasonable people there could be no disagreement about things like corruption, economic and social reforms, and democratic procedures. I believe the same is true elsewhere. Another *New York Times* man, A. M. Rosenthal, in reflecting on his decades of covering American diplomacy, had this to say: "What should our policy be? Simply to act in our belief and interest. Our belief is political freedom and our interest is political freedom. We will not be able to achieve them for others all of the time or even much of the time. But what we can do is stand up for what we believe in, all of the time. . . . That requires two things: vision and constancy. Haitians, Filipinos, Koreans, Afghans seem to have no great confusion about what they really seek from us. Neither do the Czechoslovaks or the Poles." Neither, he might have added, did the South Vietnamese.

The experience of Vietnam suggests that a policy such as Rosenthal recommends would not be simple idealism. After Vietnam it is natural to question the extent to which the United States can sustain any major commitment to a foreign nation unless that nation is capable of eliciting moral support from an idealistic and essentially antimilitaristic American public. The suggestion is that geopolitical considerations by themselves constitute an insufficient grounding for stable, long-term policy. From this perspective, a democratic commitment in foreign policy is not mere idealism; it is also pragmatic self-interest.

From 1965 through 1967, Lyndon Johnson's administration acted according to this concept of idealistic pragmatism. From time to time other administrations did too, but never consistently and never strongly. For all the rhetoric, the American commitment to democracy in South Vietnam was a timid and wavering and sometime thing. That is another way of saying that in South Vietnam American policy neglected the human dimension. It did not accord its allies their requisite dignity as human beings. (I am not speaking here of the thousands of Americans who worked devotedly alongside the Vietnamese.) At the decision-making level, Vietnam was regarded primarily as a geopolitical abstraction, a factor in the play of American global interests. That was true about the way the United States intervened in the war with its land army. It was true about the way the United States conducted the war. And it was especially true about how the United States left the war.

Of all the successive phases of U.S involvement—the intervention of 1965, the Americanization of the war, then its Vietnamization, and finally the disengagement—it is the disengagement that will stick longest in the minds of the South Vietnamese. Major mistakes were made during the war by everyone concerned. But the manner in which the United States took its leave was more than a mistake; it was an act unworthy of a great power, one that I believe will be remembered long after such unfortunate misconceptions as the search and destroy strategy have been consigned to footnotes.

It was not that the leave-taking itself was a disgrace. The United States fought long and hard in Vietnam, and if in the end circumstances required that it withdraw, it may be considered a tragedy but hardly an act of shame. The same cannot be said, however, for the manipulative and callous manner with which the American administration and the American Congress dealt with South Vietnam during the last years of the war. It was not one of America's finest hours, and there are plenty of lessons in it for both the United States and for other nations, particularly small ones that must rely on the United States for their defense.

As for Henry Kissinger, the architect of the Paris agreement, one can sympathize with his desire for "flexibility," that is, for control. Kissinger was in the middle, attempting to maneuver disparate and obstinate parties (including the North Vietnamese, South Vietnamese, Soviets, Chinese, even, on occasion, his own president) toward the same end. But he had taken on himself an awesome responsibility, negotiating not just for the global interests of the United States but for the existence of South Vietnam. In this context, he and Richard Nixon avoided holding frank discussions on common strategies with the South Vietnamese. They knew that Nguyen Van Thieu could do nothing without American support, yet they chose the unnecessary expedient of keeping developments to themselves until the last moment, then bringing to bear the heavy tactics of promises and threats. They treated a dependent ally of twenty years with finesse and then brutality, instead of with the openness the relationship required.

The fact that Kissinger and Nixon may have believed they had a viable agreement, or at least the best they could get, does not in my view justify their conduct toward South Vietnam. But at the same time, as unique as the Nixon administration's diplomatic style was, it was in effect just another aspect, another face of the American policy that had obtained in Vietnam

from the beginning, informed by worthy motives but without an understanding of the human beings who would be affected by its geopolitical
goals.

The congresses that in 1973, 1974, and 1975 washed their hands of
Vietnam shared fully in this same guilt. Although senators and representatives talked a good deal then about credibility and moral obligation, in fact
what they did was to make a geopolitical decision on the basis of what they
saw as American self-interest. They did so in callous disregard of the consequences their actions would have on a nation of twenty million people,
and they did so although it was no longer a matter of American blood, but
only of some hundreds of millions of dollars.

"Is it possible for a great nation to behave this way?" That was the
question an old friend of mine asked me in Saigon when news came in
August of 1974 that Congress had reduced the volume of aid. He was a
store owner whom I had gone to school with in North Vietnam, a totally
nonpolitical person. "You are an ambassador," he said. "Perhaps you understand these things better than I do. But can you explain this attitude of the
Americans? When they wanted to come, they came. And when they want to
leave, they leave. It's as if a neighbor came over and made a shambles of
your house, then all of a sudden he decides the whole thing is wrong, so he
calls it quits. How can they just do that?" It was a naive question from an
unsophisticated man. But I had no answer for it. Neither, I think, would
William Fulbright, or George McGovern, or the other antiwar congressmen.

In the end, though, the culpability is hardly theirs alone. So many
thought they knew the truth. The newsmen—as arrogant as any—Kissinger,
Thieu, Nixon, myself as well. But none of us knew the truth or, knowing it,
took it sufficiently to heart. Not we, and certainly not the implacable and
ruthless ideologues who were our enemies. The truth is in the millions of
Vietnamese families that have suffered the most horrible tragedies, people
who understood what was happening only in the vaguest way. The truth of
this war lies buried with its victims, with those who died, and with those
who are consigned to live in an oppressed silence, for now and for the coming generations—a silence the world calls peace.

✗ *F U R T H E R   R E A D I N G*

Denis Bloodworth, *An Eye for the Dragon* (1970)
Anthony Bouscaren, *The Last of the Mandarins: Diem of Vietnam* (1965)
Bernard B. Fall, *The Two Vietnams* (1967)
Frances FitzGerald, *Fire in the Lake* (1972)
Allan E. Goodman, *Politics in War: The Bases of Political Community in South
    Vietnam* (1973)
Lawrence E. Grinter, "Bargaining Between Saigon and Washington: Dilemmas of
    Linkage Politics During War," *Orbis,* 18 (1974), 837–67
George C. Herring, "'Peoples Quite Apart': Americans, South Vietnamese, and the
    War in Vietnam," *Diplomatic History,* 14 (1990), 1–23
Gerald C. Hickey, *Village in Vietnam* (1964)
George McT. Kahin and John W. Lewis, *The United States in Vietnam* (1969)

Robert W. Komer, *Bureaucracy Does Its Thing* (1972)
Jean Lacouture, *Vietnam Between Two Truces* (1966)
Donald Lancaster, *The Emancipation of French Indochina* (1961)
Jeffrey Race, *War Comes to Long An* (1972)
Robert Scigliano, *South Vietnam: Nation Under Stress* (1964)
Robert Scigliano and Guy Fox, *Technical Assistance in Vietnam* (1965)
Robert Shaplen, *The Road from War* (1970)
James Trullinger, *Village at War* (1980)
Nguyen Thai, *Is South Vietnam Viable?* (1962)
Denis Warner, *The Last Confucian* (1963)

CHAPTER

11

Richard M. Nixon's Strategy

for Withdrawal

Richard M. Nixon assumed the presidency in January 1969 with a clear mandate to end America's commitment to Vietnam. Convinced that a precipitous withdrawal of American troops would jeopardize South Vietnam's prospects for survival as well as America's global prestige and credibility, he opted for a strategy of Vietnamizing the war: withdrawing American forces gradually while turning over the conduct of the war to the South Vietnamese.

Twice Nixon widened the war, at least temporarily, in order, he believed, to hasten its end. In April 1970 he ordered U.S. and South Vietnamese troops into Cambodia in an effort to rout enemy bases there and buy time for Vietnamization. One of the most controversial moves of his presidency, the Cambodian incursion met with passionate opposition, especially on college campuses. Then in February 1971 he approved a major ground operation into Laos.

Nixon simultaneously moved on the diplomatic front. His special assistant for national security affairs, Henry A. Kissinger, began secret negotiations with Le Duc Tho, his North Vietnamese counterpart, in Paris early in 1969. After several years of talks, those efforts appeared ready to bear fruit toward the end of Nixon's first term in 1972. The president, however, considered it necessary to apply additional military pressure on Hanoi—the controversial "Christmas bombings" of 1972—in order to conclude a negotiated settlement. On January 27, 1973, a peace agreement was finally signed in Paris that allowed the total withdrawal of American combat forces.

Although much documentary evidence regarding the Nixon years remains closed to researchers, public and scholarly interest in the president's Vietnam policy has been strong. Interpreters of the Nixon record have differed over such critical matters as the underlying rationale for Vietnamization; the reasons for and consequences of the Cambodian invasion; the relationship between U.S. actions in Vietnam and a global strategy centered on détente with the Soviet Union and normalization of relations with China; and the nature of the Paris peace settlement. Critics on the left have

422

accused Nixon of needlessly prolonging the fighting for a settlement that
could have been achieved years earlier; critics on the right have charged him
with sacrificing an American ally on the altar of expediency and global
interests. The documents and essays in this chapter address these issues.

✗ D O C U M E N T S

In the opening document, Henry Kissinger offers his retrospective assessment
of the challenges that the continuing war in Vietnam posed for the Nixon
administration. He argues that the conflict remained a fundamental obstacle to
the administration's search for stability and order abroad—and at home. In
early January 1969 Kissinger's National Security Council staff circulated a
series of questions about Vietnam policy to concerned agencies within the
executive branch. The answers were summarized in National Security Study
Memorandum No. 1, dated January 21, from which extracts are printed as the
second document. In the next selection, Trinh Duc, a Vietcong guerrilla,
describes the difficulties that American firepower caused for the communist
insurgents during 1969 and 1970.

The fourth document is drawn from a nationwide address by Richard
Nixon, delivered on November 24, 1969, in which the president outlined his
Vietnamization strategy and appealed to the "silent majority" for support. In
the following document, reprinted from Nixon's televised national address of
May 11, 1970, the president explained and defended his decision to order U.S.
and South Vietnamese troops into Cambodia. The next document contains
extracts from Kissinger's news conference of January 26, 1972, in which he
discussed previously secret negotiations with North Vietnam, emphasizing the
remaining points of contention between the two sides. On September 11, 1972,
the Provisional Revolutionary Government (the title formally adopted by the
National Liberation Front in 1969) released a statement that laid out its negotiating position; it is reprinted as the final selection.

Henry A. Kissinger Reflects on the Nixon
Administration's Dilemma in Vietnam
(1969), 1979

In my view, Vietnam was not the cause of our difficulties but a symptom.
We were in a period of painful adjustment to a profound transformation of
global politics; we were being forced to come to grips with the tension
between our history and our new necessities. For two centuries America's
participation in the world seemed to oscillate between over involvement
and withdrawal, between expecting too much of our power and being
ashamed of it, between optimistic exuberance and frustration with the
ambiguities of an imperfect world. I was convinced that the deepest cause
of our national unease was the realization—as yet dimly perceived—that
we were becoming like other nations in the need to recognize that our
power, while vast, had limits. Our resources were no longer infinite in relation to our problems, instead we had to set priorities, both intellectual and

material. In the Fifties and Sixties we had attempted ultimate solutions to specific problems; now our challenge was to shape a world and an American role to which we were permanently committed, which could no longer be sustained by the illusion that our exertions had a terminal point.

Any Administration elected in 1968 would have faced this problem. It was a colossal task in the best of circumstances; the war in Vietnam turned it into a searing and anguishing enterprise. . . .

I cannot yet write about Vietnam except with pain and sadness.

When we came into office over a half-million Americans were fighting a war ten thousand miles away. Their numbers were still increasing on a schedule established by our predecessors. We found no plans for withdrawals. Thirty-one thousand had already died. Whatever our original war aims, by 1969 our credibility abroad, the reliability of our commitments, and our domestic cohesion were alike jeopardized by a struggle in a country as far away from the North American continent as our globe permits. Our invovlement had begun openly, and with nearly unanimous Congressional, public, and media approval. But by 1969 our country had been riven by protest and anguish, sometimes taking on a violent and ugly character. The comity by which a democratic society must live had broken down. No government can function without a minimum of trust. This was being dissipated under the harshness of our alternatives and the increasing rage of our domestic controversy.

Psychologists or sociologists may explain some day what it is about that distant monochromatic land, of green mountains and fields merging with an azure sea, that for millennia has acted as a magnet for foreigners who sought glory there and found frustration, who believed that in its rice fields and jungles some principle was to be established and entered them only to recede in disillusion. What has inspired its people to such flights of heroism and monomania that a succession of outsiders have looked there for a key to some riddle and then been expelled by a ferocious persistence that not only thwarted the foreigner's exertions but hazarded his own internal balance?

Our predecessors had entered in innocence, convinced that the cruel civil war represented the cutting edge of some global design. In four years of struggle they had been unable to develop a strategy to achieve victory—and for all one can know now such a strategy was not attainable. They had done enough to produce a major commitment of American power and credibility but not enough to bring it to a conclusion. In the last year of the Johnson Administration the Communists had launched a massive country-wide offensive. Few students of the subject question today that it was massively defeated. But its scale and sacrifice turned it into a psychological victory. Under the impact of the Tet offensive we first curtailed and then ended our bombing of the North for no return except the opening of negotiations which our implacable adversary immediately stalemated. Public support was ebbing for a war we would not win but also seemed unable to end.

And in our country, opposition grew. It was composed of many strands:

sincere pacifists who hated to see their country involved in killing thousands of miles away; pragmatists who could discern no plausible outcome; isolationists who wished to end American overseas involvement; idealists who saw no compatibility between our values and the horrors of a war literally brought home for the first time on television. And these groups were egged on by a small minority expressing the inchoate rage of the 1960s with shock tactics of obscenity and violence, expressing their hatred of America, its "system" and its "evil." All these groups had combined to produce the bitter chaos of the Democratic Convention of 1968, the campus violence, and the confusion and demoralization of the leadership groups that had sustained the great American postwar initiatives in foreign policy.

Richard Nixon inherited this cauldron. Of all choices he was probably the least suited for the act of grace that might have achieved reconciliation with the responsible members of the opposition. Seeing himself in any case the target of a liberal conspiracy to destroy him, he could never bring himself to regard the upheaval caused by the Vietnam war as anything other than a continuation of the long-lived assault on his political existence. Though he sympathized more with the anguish of the genuine protesters than they knew, he never mustered the self-confidence or the largeness of spirit to reach out to them. He accepted their premises that we faced a mortal domestic struggle; in the process he accelerated and compounded its bitterness.

Fairness compels the recognition that he had precious little help. After all, Hubert Humphrey, whose entire life was a reach for reconciliation, had been treated scarcely better during his campaign for the Presidency. And after Nixon took office those who had created our involvement in Vietnam moved first to neutrality and then to opposition, saddling Nixon with responsibility for a war he had inherited and attacking him in the name of solutions they themselves had neither advocated nor executed when they had the opportunity.

The Nixon Administration entered office determined to end our involvement in Vietnam. But it soon came up against the reality that had also bedeviled its predecessor. For nearly a generation the security and progress of free people had depended on confidence in America. We could not simply walk away from an enterprise involving two administrations, five allied countries, and thirty-one thousand dead as if we were switching a television channel. Many urged us to "emulate de Gaulle"; but they overlooked that it took even de Gaulle four years to extricate his country from Algeria because he, too, thought it important for France to emerge from its travails with its domestic cohesion and international stature intact. He extricated France from Algeria as an act of policy, not as a collapse, in a manner reflecting a national decision and not a rout.

Such an ending of the war was even more important for the United States. As the leader of democratic alliances we had to remember that scores of countries and millions of people relied for their security on our willingness to stand by allies, indeed on our confidence in ourselves. No serious policymaker could allow himself to succumb to the fashionable debunking of "prestige" or "honor" or "credibility." For a great power to abandon a small country to tyranny simply to obtain a respite from our own travail seemed to me—and still seems to me—profoundly immoral and destructive of our efforts to build a new and ultimately more peaceful pattern of international relations. We could not revitalize the Atlantic Alliance if its governments were assailed by doubt about American staying power. We would not be able to move the Soviet Union toward the imperative of mutual restraint against the background of capitulation in a major war. We might not achieve our opening to China if our value as a counterweight seemed nullified by a collapse that showed us irrelevant to Asian security. Our success in Middle East diplomacy would depend on convincing our ally of our reliability and its adversaries that we were impervious to threats of military pressure or blackmail. Clearly, the American people wanted to end the war, but every poll, and indeed Nixon's election (and the Wallace vote), made it equally evident that they saw their country's aims as honorable and did not relish America's humiliation. The new Administration had to respect the concerns of the opponents of the war but also the anguish of the families whose sons had suffered and died for their country and who did not want it determined—after the fact—that their sacrifice had been in vain.

National Security Study Memorandum No. 1, 1969

The responses to the questions posed regarding Vietnam show agreement on some matters as well as very substantial differences of opinion within the U.S. Government on many aspects of the Vietnam situation. While there are some divergencies on the facts, the sharpest differences arise in the interpretation of those facts, the relative weight to be given them, and the implications to be drawn. In addition, there remain certain areas where our information remains inadequate.

There is general agreement, assuming we follow our current strategy, on the following—

1. The GVN and allied position in Vietnam has been strengthened recently in many respects.

2. The GVN has improved its political position, but it is not certain that GVN and other non-communist groups will be able to survive a peaceful competition with the NLF for political power in South Vietnam.

3. The RVNAF alone cannot now, or in the foreseeable future, stand up to the current North Vietnamese-Viet Cong forces.

4. The enemy have suffered some reverses but they have not changed their essential objectives and they have sufficient strength to pursue these objectives. We are not attriting his forces faster than he can recruit or infiltrate.

5. The enemy is not in Paris primarily out of weakness.

The disagreements within these parameters are reflected in two schools in the government with generally consistent membership. The first school, which we will call Group A, usually includes MACV, CINCPAC, JCS and Embassy Saigon, and takes a hopeful view of current and future prospects in Vietnam within the parameters mentioned. The second school, Group B, usually includes OSD [Office of the Secretary of Defense], CIA and (to a lesser extent) State, and is decidedly more skeptical about the present and pessimistic about the future. There are, of course, disagreements within agencies across the board or on specific issues.

As illustration, these schools line up as follows on some of the broader questions:

In explaining reduced enemy military presence and activities, Group A gives greater relative weight to allied military pressure than does Group B.

The improvements in RVNAF are considered much more significant by Group A than Group B.

Group A underlines advancements in the pacification program, while Group B is skeptical both of the evaluation system used to measure progress and of the solidity of recent advances.

In looking at the political scene, Group A accents recent improvements while Group B highlights remaining obstacles and the relative strength of the NLF.

Group A assigns much greater effectiveness to bombing in Vietnam and Laos than Group B.

Following is a summary of the major conclusions and disagreements about each of six broad areas with regard to Vietnam: the negotiating environment, enemy capabilities, RVNAF capabilities, pacification, South Vietnamese politics, and U.S. military operations. . . .

Negotiating Environment

There is general U.S. government agreement that Hanoi is in Paris for a variety of motives but not primarily out of weakness; that Hanoi is charting a course independent of Moscow, which favors negotiations, and of Peking, which opposes them; and that our knowledge of possible political factions among North Vietnamese leaders is extremely imprecise. There continues wide disagreement about the impact on Southeast Asia of various outcomes in Vietnam.

Various possible North Vietnamese motives for negotiating are discussed, and there is agreement that the DRV is in Paris for mixed reasons. No U.S. agency responding to the questions believes that the primary reason the DRV is in Paris is weakness. All consider it unlikely that Hanoi came to Paris either to accept a face-saving formula for defeat or to give the U.S. a face-saving way to withdraw. There is agreement that Hanoi has been subject to heavy military pressure and that a desire to end the losses and costs of war was an element in Hanoi's decision. The consensus is that Hanoi believes that it can persist long enough to obtain a relatively favorable negotiated compromise. The respondents agree that the DRV is in Paris to negotiate withdrawal of U.S. forces, to undermine GVN and USG [U.S. government] relations and to provide a better chance for FV victory in the South. State believes that increased doubt about winning the war through continued military and international political pressure also played a major role. Hanoi's ultimate goal of a unified Vietnam under its control has not changed.

There continues to be a sharp debate between and within agencies about the effect of the outcome in Vietnam on other nations. The most recent NIE [National Intelligence Estimate] on this subject (NIE 50–58) tended to downgrade the so-called "domino theory." It states that a settlement which would permit the Communists to take control of the Government in South Viet-Nam, not immediately but within a year or two, would be likely to bring Cambodia and Laos into Hanoi's orbit at a fairly early state, but that these developments would not necessarily unhinge the rest of Asia.

The NIE dissenters believe that an unfavorable settlement would stimulate the Communists to become more active elsewhere and that it will be difficult to resist making some accommodation to the pressure than generated. They believe, in contrast to the Estimate, these adjustments would be relatively small and insensitive to subsequent U.S. policy.

Factors entering into the judgments are estimates of (1) Hanoi's and Peking's behavior after the settlement; (2) U.S. posture in the regions; (3) Asian leaders' estimates of future U.S. policy; (4) the reactions of the area's non-Communist leaders to the outcome in Viet-Nam; (5) vulnerabilities of the various governments to insurgency or subversion, and (6) the strengths of opposition groups within each state.

The assessments rest more on judgments and assumptions than on tangible and convincing evidence, and there are major disagreements within the same Department. Within the Defense Department, OSD and DIA [Defense Intelligence Agency] support the conclusions of the NIE, while Army, Navy and Air Force Intelligence dissent. Within State, the Bureau of Intelligence supports the NIE while the East Asian Bureau dissents.

Both the majority and the dissenters reject the view that an unfavorable settlement in Viet-Nam will inevitably be followed by Communist takeovers outside Indo China.

Indeed, even the dissenters, by phrasing the adverse results in terms such as "pragmatic adjustments" by the Thais and "some means of accommodation" leave it unclear how injurious the adverse effects would be to U.S. security. . . .

The Enemy

Analyses of various enemy tactics and capabilities reveal both significant agreements and sharp controversies within the Government. Among the major points of consensus:

A combination of military pressures and political tacts explains recent enemy withdrawals and lower levels of activity.

Under current rules of engagement, the enemy's manpower pool and infiltration capabilities can outlast allied attrition efforts indefinitely.

The enemy basically controls both side's casualty rates.

The enemy can still launch major offensives, although not at Tet levels, or, probably, with equally dramatic effect.

Major controversies include:

CIA and State assign much higher figures to the VC Order of Battle than MACV, and they include additional categories of VC/NLF organization.

MACV/JCS and Saigon consider Cambodia (and specifically Sihanoukville) an important enemy supply channel while CIA disagrees strongly. . . .

It is generally agreed that the NVN/VC manpower pool is sufficiently large to meet the enemy's replenishment needs over an extended period of time within the framework of current rules of engagement. According to the JCS, "The North Vietnamese and Viet Cong have access to sufficient manpower to meet their replenishment needs—even at the high 1968 loss rate of some 291,000—for at least the next several years. . . . Present operations are not outrunning the enemy's ability to replenish by recruitment or infiltration."

The South Vietnamese Armed Forces

The emphatic differences between U.S. agencies on the RVNAF outweigh the points of agreement. There is consensus that the RVNAF is getting larger, better equipped and somewhat more effective. And all agree that it could not now, or in the foreseeable future, handle both the VC and sizable NVA forces without U.S. combat support. On other major points there is vivid controversy. The military community gives much greater weight to RVNAF statistical improvements while OSD and CIA highlight remaining obstacles, with OSD being the most pessimistic. Paradoxically, MACV/CINPAC/JCS see RVNAF as being less capable against the VC alone than does CIA. . . .

Pacification

Two well-defined and divergent views emerged from the agencies on the pacification situation in South Vietnam. One view is held by MACV and Embassy Saigon and endorsed by CINCPAC and JCS. The other view is that of OSD, CIA and State. The two views are profoundly different in terms of factual interpretation and policy implications. Both views agree on the nature of the problem, that is, the obstacles to improvement and complete success. What distinguishes one view from the other is each's assessment of the magnitude of the problem, and the likelihood that obstacles will be overcome.

The first group, consisting of MACV JCS Saigon, maintains that "at the present time, the security situation is better than any time during period in question," i.e., 1961–1968. MACV cites a "dramatic change in the security situation," and finds that the GVN controls three-fourths of the population. JCS suggests that the GVN will control 90% of the population in 1969. The second group, OSD CIA State, on the other hand, is more cautious and pessimistic, their view is not inconsistent with another Tet-offensive-like-shock in the countryside, for example, wiping out the much-touted gains of the 1968 Accelerated Pacification Program, or with more gradual erosion. Representing the latter view, OSD arrives at the following conclusions:

(1) "The portions of the SVN rural population aligned with the VC and aligned with the GVN are apparently the same today as in 1962 [a discouraging year]: 5,000,000 GVN aligned and nearly 3,000,000 VC aligned.

(2) "At the present, it appears that at least 50% of the total rural population is subject to significant VC presence and influence."

CIA agrees, and State (INR) [Bureau of Intelligence and Research] goes even further, saying: "Our best estimate is that the VC have a significant effect on at least two-thirds of the rural population."

The Political Scene

This section on the political situation can be boiled down to three fundamental questions: (1) How strong is the GVN today? (2) What is being done to strengthen it for the coming political struggle with the NLF? (3) What are the prospects for continued non-Communist government in South Vietnam?

The essence of the replies from U.S. agencies is as follows: (1) Stronger recently than for many years but still very weak in certain areas and among various elites. (2) Some steps are being taken but these are inadequate. (3) Impossible to predict but chancy at best.

Within these broad thrusts of the responses there are decided differences of emphasis among the agencies. Thus MACV/JCS and Saigon, while acknowledging the problems, accent more the increasing stability of the Thieu regime and the overall political system; the significance of the moves being made by the GVN to bolster its strength; and the possibility of continued non-Communist rule in South Vietnam given sufficient U.S. support. CIA and OSD on the other hand, while acknowledging certain progress, are decidedly more skeptical and pessimistic. They note recent political improvements and GVN measures but they tend to deflate their relative impact and highlight the remaining obstacles. State's position, while not so consistent or clear-cut, generally steers closer to the bearishness of OSD and CIA. . . .

U.S. Military Operations

The only major points of agreement with the U.S. Government on these subjects are:

The description of recent U.S. deployment and tactics;

The difficulties of assessing the results of B-52 strikes, but their known effectiveness against known troop concentrations and in close support operations;

The fact that the Soviets and Chinese supply almost all war material to Hanoi and have enabled the North Vietnamese to carry on despite all our operations.

Otherwise there are fundamental disagreements running throughout this section, including the following:

OSD believes, the MACV/JCS deny, that there is a certain amount of "fat" in our current force levels that could be cut back without significant reduction in combat capability.

MACV/JCS and, somewhat more cautiously CIA ascribe much higher casualty estimates to our B-52 strikes.

MACV/JCS assign very much greater effectiveness to our past and current Laos and North Vietnam bombing campaigns than do OSD and CIA.

MACV/JCS believe that a vigorous bombing campaign could choke off enough supplies to Hanoi to make her stop fighting, while OSD and CIA see North Vietnam continuing the struggle even against unlimited bombing.

A Guerrilla Leader Remembers 1969 as "The Worst Year" (1969), 1986

Early in 1970 I was ambushed along with eight others in a jungle clearing. The nine of us were walking single file across a vegetable field that the villagers had carved out of the jungle, on our way from one hamlet to another. It was a cloudy night. The moon was partially covered over and no one could see much. I knew I should have taken the line around the clearing, keeping to the jungle, but I was in too much of a hurry. Toward the middle of the clearing there was a clump of banana trees. Just as I pulled even with them, I realized there were some shapes in the trees. They saw me at exactly the same instant, and instinctively I flattened to the ground.

Just at that moment claymore mines fired off on the path behind me, huge explosions. The instant they stopped I crawled back along the path right over where they had gone off. As I crawled I felt some of the bodies, then squirmed off at a right angle toward the jungle. Firing was going on all around. At least two bullets hit my backpack before I got to the tree line. I had to leave the bodies there in the field. I kept thinking how demoralizing it would be for the peasants when they came out in the morning.

So many killed in 1969 and 1970. There was no way we could stand up to the Americans. Every time they came in force we ran from them. Then when they turned back, we'd follow them. We practically lived on top of them, so they couldn't hit us with artillery and air strikes. During those years I had to reorganize my unit three times. Twice, the entire unit was killed. Each time I reorganized, the numbers were smaller. It was almost impossible to get new recruits.

Worse than the Americans were the Australians. The Americans' style was to hit us, then call for planes and artillery. Our response was to break contact and disappear if we could, but if we couldn't we'd move up right next to them so the planes couldn't get at us. The Australians were more

Nguyen Tan Thanh interview, from *Portrait of the Enemy* by David Chanoff and Doan Van Toai, pp. 107–109. Copyright © 1986 by David Chanoff and Doan Van Toai. Reprinted by permission of Random House Inc.

patient than the Americans, better guerrilla fighters, better at ambushes. They liked to stay with us instead of calling in the planes. We were more afraid of their style. . . .

There's no doubt that 1969 was the worst year we faced, at least the worst year I faced. There was no food, no future—nothing bright. But 1969 was also the time I was happiest. I destroyed several American tanks from the "Flying Horses" tank battalion that was stationed in Suoi Ram. I did it with pressure mines that our bomb makers made from unexploded American bombs. Each mine had seven kilos [fifteen pounds] of TNT. I was given an award as a champion tank killer.

The year 1969 was also the period when the true heroism of the peasants showed itself. Although we were isolated from the villagers, many of them risked their lives to get food to us. They devised all sorts of ingenious ways to get rice through the government checkpoints. Their feeling for us was one of the things that gave me courage to go on.

Another thing was the conviction the Americans couldn't last. In 1969 they began to pull out some of their troops. We believed that eventually they would have to withdraw altogether. We knew that even though we faced tremendous difficulties, so did they. They had terrible problems, especially at home. We didn't think their government could stand it in the long run. That gave me heart.

Richard M. Nixon on Vietnamization, 1969

Good evening, my fellow Americans: Tonight I want to talk to you on a subject of deep concern to all Americans and to many people in all parts of the world—the war in Viet-Nam.

I believe that one of the reasons for the deep division about Viet-Nam is that many Americans have lost confidence in what their Government has told them about our policy. The American people cannot and should not be asked to support a policy which involves the overriding issues of war and peace unless they know the truth about that policy.

Tonight, therefore, I would like to answer some of the questions that I know are on the minds of many of you listening to me.

How and why did America get involved in Viet-Nam in the first place?

How has this administration changed the policy of the previous administration?

What has really happened in the negotiations in Paris and on the battlefront in Viet-Nam?

What choices do we have if we are to end the war?

What are the prospects for peace?

Let me begin by describing the situation I found when I was inaugurated on January 20.

- The war had been going on for 4 years.
- 31,000 Americans had been killed in action.
- The training program for the South Vietnamese was behind schedule.

- 540,000 Americans were in Viet-Nam, with no plans to reduce the number.
- No progress had been made at the negotiations in Paris and the United States had not put forth a comprehensive peace proposal.
- The war was causing deep division at home and criticism from many of our friends, as well as our enemies, abroad.

In view of these circumstances there were some who urged that I end the war at once by ordering the immediate withdrawal of all American forces.

From a political standpoint this would have been a popular and easy course to follow. After all, we became involved in the war while my predecessor was in office. I could blame the defeat which would be the result of my action on him and come out as the peacemaker. Some put it to me quite bluntly: This was the only way to avoid allowing Johnson's war to become Nixon's war.

But I had a greater obligation than to think only of the years of my administration and the next election. I had to think of the effect of my decision on the next generation and on the future of peace and freedom in America and in the world.

Let us all understand that the question before us is not whether some Americans are for peace and some Americans are against peace. The question at issue is not whether Johnson's war becomes Nixon's war.

The great question is: How can we win America's peace?

Let us turn now to the fundamental issue. Why and how did the United States become involved in Viet-Nam in the first place?

Fifteen years ago North Viet-Nam, with the logistical support of Communist China and the Soviet Union, launched a campaign to impose a Communist government on South Viet-Nam by instigating and supporting a revolution.

In response to the request of the Government of South Viet-Nam, President Eisenhower sent economic aid and military equipment to assist the people of South Viet-Nam in their efforts to prevent a Communist takeover. Seven years ago President Kennedy sent 16,000 military personnel to Viet-Nam as combat advisers. Four years ago President Johnson sent American combat forces to South Viet-Nam.

Now, many believe that President Johnson's decision to send American combat forces to South Viet-Nam was wrong. And many others, I among them, have been strongly critical of the way the war has been conducted.

But the question facing us today is: Now that we are in the war, what is the best way to end it?

In January I could only conclude that the precipitate withdrawal of American forces from Viet-Nam would be a disaster not only for South Viet-Nam but for the United States and for the cause of peace.

For the South Vietnamese, our precipitate withdrawal would inevitably allow the Communists to repeat the massacres which followed their takeover in the North 15 years before.

- They then murdered more than 50,000 people, and hundreds of thousands more died in slave labor camps.

- We saw a prelude of what would happen in South Viet-Nam when the Communists entered the city of Hue last year. During their brief rule there, there was a bloody reign of terror in which 3,000 civilians were clubbed, shot to death, and buried in mass graves.
- With the sudden collapse of our support, these atrocities of Hue would become the nightmare of the entire nation—and particularly for the million and a half Catholic refugees who fled to South Viet-Nam when the Communists took over in the North.

For the United States, this first defeat in our nation's history would result in a collapse of confidence in American leadership not only in Asia but throughout the world.

Three American Presidents have recognized the great stakes involved in Viet-Nam and understood what had to be done.

In 1963 President Kennedy, with his characteristic eloquence and clarity, said:

> . . . we want to see a stable government there, carrying on a struggle to maintain its national independence.
>
> We believe strongly in that. We are not going to withdraw from that effort. In my opinion, for us to withdraw from that effort would mean a collapse not only of South Viet-Nam, but Southeast Asia. So we are going to stay there.

President Eisenhower and President Johnson expressed the same conclusion during their terms of office.

For the future of peace, precipitate withdrawal would thus be a disaster of immense magnitude.

- A nation cannot remain great if it betrays its allies and lets down its friends.
- Our defeat and humiliation in South Viet-Nam without question would promote recklessness in the councils of those great powers who have not yet abandoned their goals of world conquest.
- This would spark violence wherever our commitments help maintain the peace—in the Middle East, in Berlin, eventually even in the Western Hemisphere.

Ultimately, this would cost more lives. It would not bring peace; it would bring more war.

For these reasons I rejected the recommendation that I should end the war by immediately withdrawing all our forces. I chose instead to change American policy on both the negotiating front and the battlefront. . . .

It has become clear that the obstacle in negotiating an end to the war is not the President of the United States. It is not the South Vietnamese Government.

The obstacle is the other side's absolute refusal to show the least willingness to join us in seeking a just peace. It will not do so while it is convinced that all it has to do is to wait for our next concession, and our next concession after that one, until it gets everything it wants.

There can now be no longer any question that progress in negotiation depends only on Hanoi's deciding to negotiate, to negotiate seriously.

I realize that this report on our efforts on the diplomatic front is discouraging to the American people, but the American people are entitled to know the truth—the bad news as well as the good news—where the lives of our young men are involved.

Now let me turn, however, to a more encouraging report on another front.

At the time we launched our search for peace, I recognized we might not succeed in bringing an end to the war through negotiation.

I therefore put into effect another plan to bring peace—a plan which will bring the war to an end regardless of what happens on the negotiating front. It is in line with a major shift in U.S. foreign policy which I described in my press conference at Guam on July 25.

Let me briefly explain what has been described as the Nixon doctrine—a policy which not only will help end the war in Viet-Nam but which is an essential element of our program to prevent future Viet-Nams.

We Americans are a do-it-yourself people. We are an impatient people. Instead of teaching someone else to do a job, we like to do it ourselves. And this trait has been carried over into our foreign policy.

In Korea and again in Viet-Nam, the United States furnished most of the money, most of the arms, and most of the men to help the people of those countries defend their freedom against Communist aggression.

Before any American troops were committed to Viet-Nam, a leader of another Asian country expressed this opinion to me when I was traveling in Asia as a private citizen. He said: "When you are trying to assist another nation defend its freedom, U.S. policy should be to help them fight the war, but not to fight the war for them."

Well, in accordance with this wise counsel, I laid down in Guam three principles as guidelines for future American policy toward Asia:

- First, the United States will keep all of its treaty commitments.
- Second, we shall provide a shield if a nuclear power threatens the freedom of a nation allied with us or of a nation whose survival we consider vital to our security.
- Third, in cases involving other types of aggression, we shall furnish military and economic assistance when requested in accordance with our treaty commitments. But we shall look to the nation directly threatened to assume the primary responsibility of providing the manpower for its defense.

After I announced this policy, I found that the leaders of the Philippines, Thailand, Viet-Nam, South Korea, and other nations which might be threatened by Communist aggression welcomed this new direction in American foreign policy.

The defense of freedom is everybody's business—not just America's business. And it is particularly the responsibility of the people whose freedom is threatened. In the previous administration we Americanized the war in Viet-Nam. In this administration we are Vietnamizing the search for peace.

The policy of the previous administration not only resulted in our assuming the primary responsibility for fighting the war but, even more significantly did not adequately stress the goal of strengthening the South Vietnamese so that they could defend themselves when we left.

The Vietnamization plan was launched following Secretary [of Defense Melvin R.] Laird's visit to Viet-Nam in March. Under the plan, I ordered first a substantial increase in the training and equipment of South Vietnamese forces.

In July, on my visit to Viet-Nam, I changed General Abrams' orders so that they were consistent with the objectives of our new policies. Under the new orders, the primary mission of our troops is to enable the South Vietnamese forces to assume the full responsibility for the security of South Viet-Nam. . . .

We have adopted a plan which we have worked out in cooperation with the South Vietnamese for the complete withdrawal of all U.S. combat ground forces and their replacement by South Vietnamese forces on an orderly scheduled timetable. This withdrawal will be made from strength and not from weakness. As South Vietnamese forces become stronger, the rate of American withdrawal can become greater. . . .

If the level of infiltration or our casualties increase while we are trying to scale down the fighting, it will be the result of a conscious decision by the enemy.

Hanoi could make no greater mistake than to assume that an increase in violence will be to its advantage. If I conclude that increased enemy action jeopardizes our remaining forces in Viet-Nam, I shall not hesitate to take strong and effective measures to deal with that situation.

This is not a threat. This is a statement of policy which as Commander in Chief of our Armed Forces I am making in meeting my responsibility for the protection of American fighting men wherever they may be.

My fellow Americans, I am sure you can recognize from what I have said that we really only have two choices open to us if we want to end this war:

- I can order an immediate, precipitate withdrawal of all Americans from Viet-Nam without regard to the effects of that action.
- Or we can persist in our search for a just peace, through a negotiated settlement if possible or through continued implementation of our plan for Vietnamization if necessary—a plan in which we will withdraw all of our forces from Viet-Nam on a schedule in accordance with our program, as the South Vietnamese become strong enough to defend their own freedom.

I have chosen this second course. It is not the easy way. It is the right way. It is a plan which will end the war and serve the cause of peace, not just in Viet-Nam but in the Pacific and in the world.

In speaking of the consequences of a precipitate withdrawal, I mentioned that our allies would lose confidence in America.

Far more dangerous, we would lose confidence in ourselves. Oh, the immediate reaction would be a sense of relief that our men were coming home. But as we saw the consequences of what we had done, inevitable remorse and divisive recrimination would scar our spirit as a people. . . .

I have chosen a plan for peace. I believe it will succeed.

If it does succeed, what the critics say now won't matter.

If it does not succeed, anything I say then won't matter.

I know it may not be fashionable to speak of patriotism or national destiny these days. But I feel it is appropriate to do so on this occasion.

Two hundred years ago this nation was weak and poor. But even then, America was the hope of millions in the world. Today we have become the strongest and richest nation in the world. The wheel of destiny has turned so that any hope the world has for the survival of peace and freedom will be determined by whether the American people have the moral stamina and the courage to meet the challenge of free-world leadership.

Let historians not record that when America was the most powerful nation in the world we passed on the other side of the road and allowed the last hopes for peace and freedom of millions of people to be suffocated by the forces of totalitarianism.

And so tonight—to you, the great silent majority of my fellow Americans—I ask for your support.

I pledged in my campaign for the Presidency to end the war in a way that we could win the peace. I have initiated a plan of action which will enable me to keep that pledge.

The more support I can have from the American people, the sooner that pledge can be redeemed; for the more divided we are at home, the less likely the enemy is to negotiate at Paris.

Let us be united for peace. Let us also be united against defeat. Because let us understand: North Viet-Nam cannot defeat or humiliate the United States. Only Americans can do that.

Nixon Explains the Cambodian Incursion, 1970

Good evening, my fellow Americans. Ten days ago, in my report to the Nation on Viet-Nam, I announced a decision to withdraw an additional 150,000 Americans from Viet-Nam over the next year. I said then that I was making that decision despite our concern over increased enemy activity in Laos, in Cambodia, and in South Viet-Nam.

At that time, I warned that if I concluded that increased enemy activity in any of these areas endangered the lives of Americans remaining in Viet-Nam, I would not hesitate to take strong and effective measures to deal with that situation.

Despite that warning, North Viet-Nam has increased its military aggression in all these areas, and particularly in Cambodia.

After full consultation with the National Security Council, Ambassador Bunker, General Abrams, and my other advisers, I have concluded that the actions of the enemy in the last 10 days clearly endanger the lives of Americans who are in Viet-Nam now and would constitute an unacceptable risk to those who will be there after withdrawal of another 150,000.

To protect our men who are in Viet-Nam and to guarantee the continued success of our withdrawal and Vietnamization programs, I have concluded that the time has come for action.

Tonight I shall describe the actions of the enemy, the actions I have ordered to deal with that situation, and the reasons for my decision.

Cambodia, a small country of 7 million people, has been a neutral nation since the Geneva agreement of 1954—an agreement, incidentally, which was signed by the Government of North Viet-Nam.

American policy since then has been to scrupulously respect the neutrality of the Cambodian people. We have maintained a skeleton diplomatic mission of fewer than 15 in Cambodia's capital, and that only since last August. For the previous 4 years, from 1965 to 1969, we did not have any diplomatic mission whatever in Cambodia. And for the past 5 years, we have provided no military assistance whatever and no economic assistance to Cambodia.

North Viet-Nam, however, has not respected that neutrality.

For the past 5 years . . . North Viet-Nam has occupied military sanctuaries all along the Cambodian frontier with South Viet-Nam. Some of these extend up to 20 miles into Cambodia. The sanctuaries . . . are on both sides of the border. They are used for hit-and-run attacks on American and South Vietnamese forces in South Viet-Nam.

These Communist-occupied territories contain major base camps, training sites, logistics facilities, weapons and ammunition factories, airstrips, and prisoner of war compounds.

For 5 years neither the United States nor South Viet-Nam has moved against these enemy sanctuaries, because we did not wish to violate the territory of a neutral nation. Even after the Vietnamese Communists began to expand these sanctuaries 4 weeks ago, we counseled patience to our South Vietnamese allies and imposed restraints on our own commanders.

In contrast to our policy, the enemy in the past 2 weeks has stepped up his guerrilla actions, and he is concentrating his main forces in these sanctuaries . . . where they are building up to launch massive attacks on our forces and those of South Viet-Nam.

North Viet-Nam in the last 2 weeks has stripped away all pretense of respecting the sovereignty or the neutrality of Cambodia. Thousands of their soldiers are invading the country from the sanctuaries; they are encircling the Capital of Phnom Penh. Coming from these sanctuaries, . . . they have moved into Cambodia and are encircling the Capital.

Cambodia, as a result of this, has sent out a call to the United States, to a number of other nations, for assistance. Because if this enemy effort succeeds, Cambodia would become a vast enemy staging area and a springboard for attacks on South Viet-Nam along 600 miles of frontier, a refuge where enemy troops could return from combat without fear of retaliation.

North Vietnamese men and supplies could then be poured into that country, jeopardizing not only the lives of our own men but the people of South Viet-Nam as well. . . .

In cooperation with the armed forces of South Viet-Nam, attacks are being launched this week to clean out major enemy sanctuaries on the Cambodian-Viet-Nam border.

A major responsibility for the ground operations is being assumed by South Vietnamese forces. For example, the attacks in several areas, . . . are exclusively South Vietnamese ground operations under South Vietnamese command, with the United States providing air and logistical support.

There is one area, however, . . . where I have concluded that a combined American and South Vietnamese operation is necessary.

Tonight American and South Vietnamese units will attack the head-quarters for the entire Communist military operation in South Viet-Nam. This key control center has been occupied by the North Vietnamese and Viet Cong for 5 years in blatant violation of Cambodia's neutrality.

This is not an invasion of Cambodia. The areas in which these attacks will be launched are completely occupied and controlled by North Vietnamese forces. Our purpose is not to occupy the areas. Once enemy forces are driven out of these sanctuaries and once their military supplies are destroyed, we will withdraw.

These actions are in no way directed at the security interests of any nation. Any government that chooses to use these actions as a pretext for harming relations with the United States will be doing so on its own responsibility and on its own initiative, and we will draw the appropriate conclusions.

Now, let me give you the reasons for my decision.

A majority of the American people, a majority of you listening to me, are for the withdrawal of our forces from Viet-Nam. The action I have taken tonight is indispensable for the continuing success of that withdrawal program.

A majority of the American people want to end this war rather than to have it drag on interminably. The action I have taken tonight will serve that purpose.

A majority of the American people want to keep the casualties of our brave men in Viet-Nam at an absolute minimum. The action I take tonight is essential if we are to accomplish that goal.

We take this action not for the purpose of expanding the war into Cambodia, but for the purpose of ending the war in Viet-Nam and winning the just peace we all desire. We have made and we will continue to make every possible effort to end this war through negotiation at the conference table rather than through more fighting on the battlefield. . . .

My fellow Americans, we live in an age of anarchy, both abroad and at home. We see mindless attacks on all the great institutions which have been created by free civilizations in the last 500 years. Even here in the United States, great universities are being systematically destroyed. Small nations all over the world find themselves under attack from within and from without.

If, when the chips are down, the world's most powerful nation, the United States of America, acts like a pitiful, helpless giant, the forces of totalitarianism and anarchy will threaten free nations and free institutions throughout the world.

It is not our power but our will and character that is being tested tonight. The question all Americans must ask and answer tonight is this: Does the richest and strongest nation in the history of the world have the character to meet a direct challenge by a group which rejects every effort to win a just peace, ignores our warning, tramples on solemn agreements, violates the neutrality of an unarmed people, and uses our prisoners as hostages?

If we fail to meet this challenge, all other nations will be on notice that despite its overwhelming power the United States, when a real crisis comes, will be found wanting.

During my campaign for the Presidency, I pledged to bring Americans home from Viet-Nam. They are coming home.

I promised to end this war. I shall keep that promise.

I promised to win a just peace. I shall keep that promise.

We shall avoid a wider war. But we are also determined to put an end to this war. . . .

No one is more aware than I am of the political consequences of the action I have taken. It is tempting to take the easy political path: to blame this war on previous administrations and to bring all of our men home immediately, regardless of the consequences, even though that would mean defeat for the United States; to desert 18 million South Vietnamese people who have put their trust in us and to expose them to the same slaughter and savagery which the leaders of North Viet-Nam inflicted on hundreds of thousands of North Vietnamese who chose freedom when the Communists took over North Viet-Nam in 1954; to get peace at any price now, even though I know that a peace of humiliation for the United States would lead to a bigger war or surrender later.

I have rejected all political considerations in making this decision.

Whether my party gains in November is nothing compared to the lives of 400,000 brave Americans fighting for our country and for the cause of peace and freedom in Viet-Nam. Whether I may be a one-term President is insignificant compared to whether by our failure to act in this crisis the United States proves itself to be unworthy to lead the forces of freedom in this critical period in world history. I would rather be a one-term President and do what I believe is right than to be a two-term President at the cost of seeing America become a second-rate power and to see this nation accept the first defeat in its proud 190-year history.

Henry A. Kissinger Reveals the
U.S. Negotiating Position, 1972

As you remember from the many briefings that we have had on Viet-Nam, there has been no issue of greater concern to this administration than to end the war in Viet-Nam on a negotiated basis. We have done so because of what we felt the war was doing to us as a people and because we felt that it was essential that whatever differences that may have existed about how we entered the war and how we conducted the war, that we ended it in a way that showed that we had been fair, that we had been reasonable, and that all concerned people could support.

We have not approached these negotiations in order to score debating points. We have not conducted these negotiations in order to gain any domestic benefits. . . .

On the political evolution, our basic principle has been a principle we have been prepared to sign together with them, that we are not committed to any one political structure or government in South Viet-Nam. Our principle has been that we want a political evolution that gives the people of South Viet-Nam a genuine opportunity to express their preferences.

We have pointed out, in innumerable meetings, that we recognize that this is a tough problem. We have indicated with extraordinary repetitiveness, as those of you who have heard me will not challenge, with extraordinary repetitiveness, that we know that Vietnamese traditions are different and that we are prepared to listen to their version of what a free political process might be like.

We have searched our souls to try to come up with a proposal that seems free to us; and after all, the agreement by the existing government—to have a commission comprising the people that wish to overthrow them run, organize, and supervise the election, to put the election under international supervision, and to resign a month before the election—is not just a trivial proposal.

The North Vietnamese position has been that they want us to agree with them, first, on replacing the existing government and, secondly, on a structure in which the probability of their taking over is close to certainty.

They want us, in other words, to do in the political field the same thing that they are asking us to do in the military field, to negotiate the terms of the turnover to them, regardless of what the people may think. . . .

They have said that they want a government composed of people who stand for peace, neutrality, and independence. There is another magic word which eludes me at the moment. And Americans cannot object to this proposal. The only thing is, they are the only ones who know who stands for peace, neutrality, and independence.

Whenever in these negotiations we have said, "All right, you don't like Thieu. How about this fellow, or that fellow, or that fellow?" there is almost no one that we know who they believe stands for peace, neutrality, and independence.

So I would like to express this to you. The issue is to us: We are prepared, in all conscience and in all seriousness, to negotiate with them immediately any scheme that any reasonable person can say leaves open the political future of South Viet-Nam to the people of South Viet-Nam, just as we are not prepared to withdraw without knowing anything at all of what is going to happen next. So we are not prepared to end this war by turning over the Government of South Viet-Nam as part of a political deal.

We are prepared to have a political process in which they can have a chance of winning, which is not loaded in any direction. We have given our views of what this political process might be. We are prepared to listen to their views of what that political process might be. And we said in both notes of last fall, notes that were not intended for publication, at a time when we were hoping to be able to step before you with an agreement, that we are prepared to listen to their points.

Now, there has been some question of, "Did they ask us to replace or overthrow"—or whatever the word is—"the existing government in South Viet-Nam?"

We have every interest in stepping before you with total honesty. They have asked two things of us:

One, an indirect overthrow of the government; that is to say, that we have to withdraw. The way they phrase it, we would have to withdraw all American equipment, even that which the South Vietnamese Army has. They have asked us to withdraw all equipment, all future military aid, all future economic aid; and the practical consequence of that proposal, while they are receiving close to $1 billion worth of foreign aid, would be the indirect overthrow of the Government of South Viet-Nam, something about which there can be no question.

But they have further asked us, and we do not want to be forced to prove it, to change the government directly, generously leaving the method to us, and, therefore, the President's statement was true and is supportable.

We have no interest in engaging in a debate with the North Vietnamese that would force any more of this record into the open. We do have an interest that the American public understand exactly what is at issue today.

Negotiating Position of the
Provisional Revolutionary Government, 1972

The provisional Revolutionary Government of the Republic of South Vietnam solemnly declares as follows:

If a correct solution is to be found to the Vietnam problem, and a lasting peace ensured in Vietnam, the U.S. Government must meet the two following requirements:

1. To respect the Vietnamese people's right to true independence and the South Vietnamese people's right to effective self-determination; stop the U.S. war of aggression in Vietnam, the bombing, mining and blockade of the Democratic Republic of Vietnam; completely cease the "Vietnamization" policy; and all U.S. military activities in South Vietnam; rapidly and completely withdraw all U.S. troops, advisors, military personnel, technical personnel, weapons and war materials and those of the other foreign countries in the U.S. camp from South Vietnam; liquidate the U.S. military bases in South Vietnam; end all U.S. military involvement in Vietnam; and stop supporting the Nguyen Van Thieu stooge administration.

2. A solution to the internal problem of South Vietnam must proceed from the actual situation that there exist in South Vietnam two administrations, two armies, and other political forces. It is necessary to achieve national concord. The sides in South Vietnam must unite on the basis of equality, mutual respect and mutual nonelimination. Democratic freedoms must be guaranteed to the people. To this end, it is necessary to form in South Vietnam a provisional government of national concord with three

equal segments to take charge of the affairs in the period of transition and to organize truly free and democratic general elections.

✗ *E S S A Y S*

In the first essay, Arnold Isaacs, a journalist who covered the Vietnam War from 1972 to 1975 and traveled extensively throughout Indochina, presents a strong indictment of the Nixon policy. The Nixon administration's preoccupation with America's credibility led to a grievous exaggeration of the regional and global stakes involved in Vietnam. Isaacs suggests that a policy designed to cut U.S. losses by as speedy as possible a withdrawal would better have served American interests. He especially faults Nixon for expanding the war into Cambodia. In the next essay, Walter Isaacson, also a journalist, offers a less critical perspective. Although Isaacson, too, believes that Nixon and Kissinger magnified the extent to which America's credibility as a global power was being tested in Vietnam, he insists that the two men deserve substantial credit for inaugurating an irreversible process of U.S. troop withdrawals. By the end of 1972, Nixon and Kissinger had successfully negotiated a cease-fire that, for all its shortcomings, temporarily stopped the hostilities in Viet-nam while providing the Saigon regime with a decent opportunity to survive. Isaacson's essay also details some of the sharp policy differences and bitter bureaucratic infighting that surrounded the adoption of the Vietnamization strategy. This selection is drawn from Isaacson's biography of Henry Kissinger.

The Limits of Credibility

ARNOLD ISAACS

"It's time we recognized," declared Ronald Reagan, "that ours was, in truth, a noble cause." His campaign advisers had not wanted him to reawaken painful Vietnam memories. But the candidate personally penciled the phrase "noble cause" into his speech, it was said, to express his strong view that the nation should not reproach itself for the Vietnam conflict. "Let us tell those who fought in that war," he added, "that we will never again ask young men to fight and possibly die in a war our government is afraid to win." The 5,000 delegates at the Veterans of Foreign Wars 1980 convention—who had earlier broken their organization's long-standing precedent to endorse the Reagan candidacy—responded, one reporter wrote, with "sustained and boisterous cheers."

At the start of a new decade, the perception that American actions in Vietnam were a worthy effort, and that they failed not because they were misconceived but only because they were not carried out resolutely enough, seemed to respond to powerful needs in American life and institutions. It

Arnold R. Isaacs, *Without Honor: Defeat in Vietnam and Cambodia.* Copyright © 1983, pp. 488–498. Reprinted by permission of The Johns Hopkins University Press, Baltimore/London.

was a view that protected the reputations of the political leaders who shaped and executed those actions. It soothed military professionals who could not easily contemplate their own failure to achieve more decisive results on the Vietnamese battlefields. And by placing Vietnam in the same framework of conventional patriotic values in which Americans viewed their other wars, it reassured a troubled people that they had not, after all, forfeited the special moral standing America claimed for itself among the world's nations. Shaking off Vietnam guilt seemed essential, too, to officials and commentators who feared, not wholly without reason, that a post-Vietnam reaction was preventing the United States from acting effectively in the world.

Clearly, America could not remain forever immobilized by its memories of Vietnam. But to distort those memories was to risk equal policy errors in the future, arising from the same blindnesses that produced the Vietnam failure. For what the United States really lacked in Vietnam was not persistence but understanding—that, and the flexibility to change policies that had proven bankrupt. From start to finish, American leaders remained catastrophically ignorant of Vietnamese history, culture, values, motives, and abilities. Misperceiving both its enemy and its ally and imprisoned in the myopic conviction that sheer military force could somehow overcome adverse political circumstances, Washington stumbled from one failure to the next in the continuing delusion that success was always just ahead. This ignorance and false hope were mated, in successive administrations, with bureaucratic circumstances that inhibited admission of error and made it always seem safer to keep repeating the same mistakes rather than risk the unknown perils of a different policy.

The wounds of that experience were painful enough. With the war finally over, the revisionist belief that it was lost only because of Washington's timidity, rather than for Vietnamese reasons, was the self-infliction of still another wound—a refusal to learn the lesson that had been so expensively taught.

The delusion of Vietnam policy in the Johnson administration, at least until 1968, was that increasing American military force could not just prevent defeat of an anti-Communist regime in Saigon, but could in time discourage Hanoi from supporting the revolutionary movement in the South, and thus end the conflict. The Nixon administration's delusion was more remarkable. It was that exactly the same objective could be reached while American military force was diminishing.

A good deal of evidence suggests that when Nixon and Henry Kissinger moved into the White House in January 1969, they understood that they were inheriting a failure: that the enormous military effort in Vietnam had ballooned out of all proportion to any conceivable American interest there, and that the spectacle of a huge, expensively-armed U.S. expeditionary force thrashing about in an unavailing contest with a poor, middle-sized Asian Communist state was certainly not serving any American purpose. Vietnam was making the U.S. "look like a paper tiger," Nixon is reported to have acknowledged privately in early 1968, adding his private conclusion that "there's no way to win the war. But we can't say that, of course. In fact, we have to seem to say the opposite, just to keep some degree of bargaining leverage." Henry Kissinger too, by his own later account, believed when he took office that the war was "draining our national strength and had to be liquidated."

It is less clear how squarely Nixon or Kissinger faced the corollary of their logic: if the U.S. couldn't win, then Hanoi, presumably, couldn't lose. Kissinger left many acquaintances with the impression that he saw a Communist victory as tolerable, as long as it was suitably delayed to keep from openly humiliating the United States. Whether or not that was his real view, he certainly thought it useful for Hanoi—and Moscow—to be encouraged to believe so; the Vietnamese Communists, he evidently felt, would surely agree to a negotiated settlement once they understood that the U.S. would not actually seek to achieve its proclaimed goal of preserving a non-Communist regime in Saigon indefinitely. It would only be necessary for Hanoi to conclude, in other words, that Washington did not really mean what it said. To the administration's early offers of "serious talks," however, the North Vietnamese simply repeated their customary demands for total withdrawal of U.S. forces and removal of the Saigon "puppet administration."

Kissinger was shocked and angry at Hanoi's apparent lack of concern for American face. And he appears to have found completely unaccountable the fact that instead of saying one thing in public and something else in private, like the straightforward Americans, Ho Chi Minh and his colleagues kept saying the same unacceptable things no matter in which channel they were conveyed. Others might have considered that perhaps the Vietnamese Communists meant what they were saying. But to Kissinger, their refusal to be duplicitous was inexplicable, even suspect. It reflected a Vietnamese style of communication which he complained in his memoirs, "was indirect and, by American standards, devious or baffling."

Whoever was being devious, Nixon and Kissinger evidently continued to believe for some months that Hanoi would agree to what they saw as a reasonable, even generous, compromise. Journalists accompanying Nixon to his Midway Island summit with Nguyen Van Thieu in June 1969 were given the impression that he had "made up his mind to do whatever he has to do in order to extricate the United States" from the war; the president's and Kissinger's appraisal, newsmen were told, was that Hanoi and the Liberation Front were "just about ready for serious negotiations." Two months after Midway, when he began his secret meetings with North Vietnamese representatives, Kissinger "still half believed that rapid progress would be made" if the Communists could be convinced of American sincerity. As late as the end of September, Nixon expressed his hope publicly. "Once the enemy recognizes that it is not going to win its objectives by waiting us out," he told a press conference, "then the enemy will negotiate and we will end this war before the end of 1970. That is the objective we have."

In part, these expectations seem to have reflected a real belief in the generosity of their own proposals. Apparently, too, Nixon and Kissinger thought the Russians and Chinese could and would deliver a Vietnam settlement in return for American consideration on other matters. Both beliefs were wrong, and rooted in a profound misreading of the adversary U.S. forces had already fought for four frustrating years. Neither the president nor his adviser had yet grasped—possibly they never did—just how intensely the Vietnamese Communists' past had led them to mistrust diplomatic arrangements. ("Never Munich again, in whatever form," North Vietnam's Pham Van Dong vowed in 1966—a comment that not only suggested Hanoi's sense that it was duped in 1946 and 1954, but was also one of those stunning ironies so abundant in the history of the Vietnam conflict, since avoiding a new Munich was also a central theme of the American involvement there.) Nor did the new American president yet understand, apparently, the full measure of the Communists' stubborn belief in their own ultimate triumph. "I think the Americans greatly underestimate the determination of the Vietnamese people," Ho Chi Minh had said, while John F. Kennedy was still in the White House and only a few thousand American soldiers had yet been sent to Vietnam. "The Vietnamese people have always shown great determination when they were faced with a foreign invader."

Neither Kennedy nor Lyndon Johnson gave enough weight to that warning; President Nixon would prove no wiser.

When it finally dawned on Nixon and Kissinger that the North Vietnamese were not interested in a compromise on terms acceptable to the U.S., their first response was to threaten redoubled military pressure.

"Measures of great consequence and force" would be taken, Nixon warned Hanoi, if there were no significant progress in the peace talks by November 1, 1969—the anniversary of Johnson's bombing halt. Pentagon planners were assigned to prepare not just for resuming the bombing but for greatly intensifying it. But Hanoi ignored the threat, and there was no consensus within the American government either in favor of reescalation or that any thinkable military step would really prove decisive. The only certain result would be domestic political storms worse than any that had already occurred, and perhaps a split in the administration itself. As his self-imposed deadline neared, Nixon allowed himself—rather easily, it seems—to be talked out of following through on his ultimatum. Putting his hopes instead on the Vietnamization concept and on the possible helpful influence of China and the Soviet Union, he let November 1 pass with no dramatic gesture. The unilateral withdrawal of American troops, which had begun after the Midway summit in June, was now an irreversible policy.

Thereafter the administration's attempt was—in Kissinger's words—"to pursue a middle course between capitulation and the seemingly endless stalemate that we had inherited." That, surely, must be one of the most astonishing purposes ever advanced for continuing a large, costly war. What could lie "between" capitulation and stalemate, after all, except a sort of slow-motion defeat? If that was the implied object of the administration's policy, moreover, it could not be acknowledged. No American government could justify the deaths of 15,000 more American soldiers for such a purpose, not to mention the far larger loss of Asian lives. Perhaps for that reason, though Nixon and Kissinger had seemed to realize before taking office that the overriding U.S. interest was extrication from the war, once in power they seemed to shrink from the logic of their own perceptions.

There were, no doubt, varied personal and institutional reasons for this. Advocating a distasteful policy from outside the government was surely easier than actually beginning to carry it out. Too, once in the White House, Nixon and Kissinger were suddenly subject to a huge array of institutional pressures arising from a self-justifying system in which numerous reputations and bureaucratic interests could only be preserved by reaffirming existing policy. The information supplied by that system, while not entirely suppressing unwelcome truths, was certainly tilted toward justifying past decisions. As the settlement they had thought they could achieve kept eluding them, Nixon's and Kissinger's attitudes toward the North Vietnamese grew more baleful; it would have taken far more forgiving personalities than theirs not to begin wishing to punish those who denied them the political triumph both men thirsted for. Nixon and Kissinger were driven, also, by anger at domestic critics—particularly those who had participated in Johnson's war policies and thus seemed, to the new administration, outrageous hypocrites. And by temporizing, the new president and his adviser changed the choices before them perhaps more quickly than they had imagined would happen. Within less than a year of taking office, they no longer had the freedom to act as if undoing the mistakes of previous administrations; instead, they were compelled to vindicate the consequences of their own actions.

When their first hopeful overtures were rebuffed by Hanoi, Nixon and Kissinger spent the rest of their first year in office not disengaging from the war but imprisoning themselves in it, just as the Johnson administration had done. By the fall of 1969, Nixon's private comments no longer admitted the war was unwinnable or predicted its swift settlement. Instead, he was telling visitors, in words that could have been Lyndon Johnson's, "I will not be the first President of the United States to lose a war."

Like Johnson, too, Nixon came to see dissenters not as honorable critics but as witting or unwitting agents of treason. His administration soon began to recapitulate its predecessor's depressing descent into an intellectual and emotional state of siege. As criticism grew, his and Kissinger's differing insecurities seemed to bond, like two chemicals, into a new compound of angry, defensive rigidity. Within the fortress of their beliefs they listened, as the writer David Halberstam observed, "only to others who were believers." All doubts, whether arising from within the government or outside, were associated with weakness or disloyalty, and rejected.

Dissenting views were banished, too, as the result of Kissinger's bureaucratic style. Toward any possible competitors for power or influence, Kissinger's attitude was—no other word seems adequate—pathological. Through "incessant backbiting," as speechwriter Raymond Price called it, and by every other technique he could devise, some amazingly petty,

Kissinger maneuvered to keep all rivals out of foreign policy decisions. With respect to Vietnam, he was largely successful. Among those excluded, to the extent of Kissinger's considerable ability to do so, were Defense Secretary Melvin Laird and Secretary of State William Rogers, both of whom, for various reasons, hoped to reinforce Nixon's initial impulse to extricate himself and the country from the war. Instead, Laird and Rogers were largely shut out of Vietnam decision making. More than any other U.S. endeavor of such magnitude before or since, Vietnam policy in the Nixon administration came under the utter domination of only two men, who grew steadily more impervious to any perspectives that differed from their own.

If there was a single act by which the Nixon administration closed the trap on itself, it was the decision to send U.S. forces into Cambodia at the end of April 1970.

All else they had done in Indochina, Nixon and Kissinger could claim—and the American public could agree—was a matter of cleaning up someone else's mess. But Cambodia was their own. Americans knew the half-million man army flailing about in Vietnam was not sent there by Nixon, and they seemed willing to allow him a rather generous amount of time to extricate it in some fashion that would avoid national humiliation. They did want to see it extricated, though, and sending soldiers to fight in another Indochinese nation hardly seemed like the same thing. Neither did the strident, belligerent explanations from the White House. Cambodia could not be reconciled with Nixon's promise to end the war, and that, it seemed to me, was the real reason it generated such domestic outrage.

Anger at the Cambodian offensive was answered by an equal rage in the White House against its critics. But the more Nixon and Kissinger made the war theirs, the more damaging and painful failure appeared; and the more they had to defend their actions, the more they were compelled to assert illusory achievements and unreachable goals—like Lyndon Johnson, who was driven at last to lash out at Robert Kennedy, "We are going to win this war, and in six months all you doves will be politically dead." Nixon, too, especially after Cambodia, could only vindicate his decisions with success. That need nourished both the administration's wishful hope that Hanoi would somehow prove more flexible than it sounded and that it could be pressured into giving the U.S. an acceptable settlement, and its equally wishful overestimate of Saigon's effectiveness. Nixon's and Kissinger's expectations contradicted the realities that American influence on Vietnamese events was lessening as its military effort lessened and that there was no sustainable support for stronger measures; Hanoi, meanwhile, not the U.S., still controlled the pace and course of the war while remaining single-mindedly bent not on compromise, but victory.

Unable to resolve those contradictions, Nixon began to see the source of his frustrations in American, not Vietnamese, realities. Not Hanoi but the American antiwar movement "destroyed whatever small possibility may still have existed of ending the war in 1969," he wrote in his memoirs. His critics' motives were, in effect, treasonous. "North Vietnam cannot defeat or humiliate the United States. Only Americans can do that," he declared on November 3, 1969, in the "silent majority" speech he substituted for the military blows he had threatened. In that concept lay one significant origin of the domestic abuses that would destroy his presidency: against adversaries who sought the defeat of the United States, any tactic, however extreme, could be justified.

In Indochina, meanwhile, though he carried on the war as intensely as the domestic political environment allowed, its purposes grew steadily more indistinct. Thoughts of victory—Johnson's "coonskin on the wall"—vanished in 1968, with Tet, the bombing halt, and the start of peace talks. Thereafter the definition of American objectives vanished by degrees, like Alice's Cheshire cat.

The Nixon administration first offered mutual withdrawals of U.S. and North Vietnamese forces, but then undermined its own proposal by starting to pull American troops out unilaterally. The concept of mutual withdrawal remained in the peace plans but was blurred by an ambiguous ceasefire-in-place proposal in October 1970. Subsequently, the demand for removal of North Vietnamese troops was dropped altogether. What still prevented agreement was only Hanoi's insistence on unacceptable political terms. The U.S. had no prescription of its own for a political settlement, suggesting only that the future should be decided by problematic negotiations between the Communists and Saigon.

Thus, by 1972 the specific, concrete demands of the United States on Hanoi had been reduced to exactly one: American prisoners must be returned. Beyond that, for American purposes, the U.S. asked Hanoi only for restraint—that is, that it not take advantage of American disengagement to humiliate the United States. How much restraint, and for how long, would satisfy that condition was never clear. For South Vietnam, despite the rhetoric of alliance that was customarily used, declared U.S. objectives did not even specify the indefinite survival of a non-Communist government. Washington said only that the South Vietnamese people should choose their political future freely, and not under the threat of violence. That aim accorded with American values but unhappily not with Vietnamese conditions, or with the historical experience of civil conflicts anywhere else in the world, including America's own.

The disconnection of American objectives from Vietnamese realities was not incidental or accidental or the quirk of personality or circumstance. It was imbedded in the most fundamental strategic concepts of the nuclear age. For the overriding consideration of American actions in Vietnam was not to bring about any specific Vietnamese outcome, but to assist what had become known as "credibility," the impression that the United States was tough enough and effective enough to meet its responsibilities in the world, defend its interests, and use its nuclear weapons for those purposes if forced to that choice. Credibility was (and remains) the psychological component of the deterrence concept, which holds that the only way to avoid using nuclear arms is to possess them in enough quantity to discourage any other possessor from using them. Similarly, if the image of credibility could be sufficiently conveyed, its reality would never have to be demonstrated. Appearances, in other words, as the writer Jonathan Schell pointed out in his book *The Time of Illusion,* "were not merely important to deterrence—they were everything. If the deterrent was used, deterrence would have failed. If the image did not do its preventive work and there was a resort to action, the whole purpose of the policy would have been defeated."

Since credibility could never be proven, the only way to establish it was to demonstrate its attributes in all other American actions in the world, while also avoiding failures or irresolution that might contradict the desired image. Thus, once U.S. forces were committed in Vietnam, the original reasons quickly lost their primacy. What became necessary for the United States was not any given set of results that could be defined as a success, but rather a display of American determination, effectiveness, and reliability as an ally. Had this not been true, the stated U.S. war aims could not have shifted so greatly during the course of the conflict. American patience was exhausted by a war whose dominant impression was of soldiers fighting again and again over the identical terrain, without advancing or retreating or winning or losing, without any apparent relationship to any other battles before or afterward, and without visible movement toward a decisive result. But that image was an accurate metaphor for the policy. The result of the war was less important to Washington than the act of fighting it.

The U.S. intervened in Vietnam initially with ideas of defeating a Communist insurgency, containing what it then saw as a menacing and expansionist China, and disproving theories of liberation war, among other reasons. By the time the Nixon administration came to power, however, what mattered fundamentally to the U.S. leadership was not what happened to the Vietnamese, much less to the Lao or the Cambodians, but what happened to the world's—and particularly the Soviet Union's—impression of American capability and resolve. Nixon's rapprochement with the Chinese leadership made much of the war's original rationale meaningless and thus made its actual outcome a matter of even less concern to him or to the American government. If some form of settlement on America's minimum terms could be reached, so much the better. But even if there were no settlement, or one that failed, that would not be critically damaging either, as long as the United States was not perceived to weaken.

Defining goals in Vietnam with regard to the American image elsewhere was not invented by the Nixon administration, by any means. As long ago as the beginning of 1962 the Joint Chiefs of Staff had argued for intervention on the grounds that, along with the defense of Southeast Asia from Communism, "of equal importance" was the "psychological impact that a firm position by the United States will have on the countries of the world—both free and Communist." The real trap lay in the negative of that proposition: "A United States political and/or military withdrawal . . . would have an adverse psychological impact," the Chiefs also warned, "of even greater proportion." This, when only a few more than 2,500 American soldiers had been sent to Vietnam and only a dozen or so had been killed or wounded.

Three years later, with the Johnson administration poised to commit major ground forces to the conflict, a Defense Department official, John McNaughton, wrote what would become one of the most widely quoted passages in the *Pentagon Papers,* expressing U.S. aims in percentage terms: "70%—to avoid a humiliating U.S. defeat (to our reputation as a guarantor). 20%—to keep SVN (and the adjacent) territory from Chinese hands. 10%—to permit the people of SVN to enjoy a better, freer way of life."

Thus, when Nixon declared in 1969 that defeat in Vietnam "would result in a collapse of confidence in American leadership not only in Asia but throughout the world" and would "promote recklessness in the councils of those great powers who have not yet abandoned their goals of world conquest," he was not being at all inconsistent with previous American reasoning. The difference, though, was that by then all *other* goals of the intervention were vanishing. Thoughts of victory had evaporated, and nearly all specific demands on Hanoi were about to do the same.

Too, the more global-minded Nixon and Kissinger spun the credibility concept much farther from any local or regional circumstances than Johnson had. Though he was aware of more distant interests, Johnson normally focused on the classic assumptions of the domino theory: a failure of American resolve in Vietnam would endanger Thailand or Malaysia or, at a slightly greater distance, Indonesia and the Philippines. Nixon's and Kissinger's was a sort of super-domino theory. If America proved ineffectual in Vietnam, they thought, it would also be weakened—a "pitiful helpless giant"—in the Middle East, in strategic arms talks, everywhere on the globe, in fact, where important U.S. interests existed. Vietnam was part of a strategy in which everything was linked to the Soviet-American nuclear confrontation, and thus everything was also linked to everything else. The war there was limited, but to the extent that it was fought for the purpose of nuclear credibility, the stakes were unlimited. Vietnam was indivisible from preventing World III and saving the entire world, including the U.S., from possible nuclear blackmail and Communist totalitarianism. As Jonathan Schell put it, "the aim of upholding American credibility superseded any conclusions drawn from a simple accounting of tangible gains and tangible losses" in Vietnam.

Such an accounting would probably have dictated to most Americans—perhaps even Nixon and Kissinger—a policy of cutting losses and withdrawing. But, as Schell wrote, "The tangible objectives of limited war had been completely eclipsed by the psychological objective. The war had become an effort directed entirely toward building up a certain image by force of arms. It had become a piece of pure theatre."

For men who prided themselves on realism, Nixon and Kissinger were remarkably myopic about a world that was, inevitably, messier in reality than in strategists' theorizing. The issues of nuclear survival and their own balance-of-power design filled their vision so completely that they seemed not to grasp that other nations had other priorities. They acted as if they expected lesser nations to subordinate their own interests to superpower needs, on the ground that the safety of the entire world must override any narrow national goal.

The loss of superpower control, Nixon and Kissinger believed, was dangerous—as was explicitly spelled out by Kissinger when, speaking not of Southeast Asia but of the Mideast, he referred to the danger created when "two groups of countries with intense local rivalries . . . [are] backed by major countries, but not fully under the control of the major countries confronting each other." This, Kissinger said, "is the sort of situation that produced World War I." If world order was menaced when local rival states were "not fully under the control" of the major powers to whom they were allied, it followed that the superpowers were not only entitled but obliged to assert that control: the United States over nations under its influence and the Soviet Union over those in the Soviet orbit, in the name of the greater good of nuclear peace.

Obviously, this reasoning is not completely groundless, any more than is the concept of nuclear credibility. Regional disputes do raise the threat of possible superpower conflict. But Nixon and Kissinger characteristically saw *only* the Soviet-American dimension of all international issues. All other aspects were blotted out. On their mental map, the rest of the countries on the globe became blank spots, without individual character or history or motive, as lacking in feature and distinctive shape as squares on a chessboard.

Thus, though for years Vietnam preoccupied U.S. policy makers more than almost any other issue, the real Vietnam with all its particularities was hardly seen at all through Washington's lenses. The Vietnamese reasons for the conflict were irrelevant because they fell outside the circular logic of the American effort: the reason Americans had to prevail was because American troops and prestige were committed to doing so. Vietnam was vital because we had declared it vital, not for any attributes of its own. We were there, in a nutshell, because we were there. The war could have been anywhere else in the world and nearly all the issues and arguments, as far as Nixon and Kissinger were concerned, would have been the same. Their perspective almost demanded disregard of Vietnamese realities, in fact, for the Vietnamese circumstances so clearly failed to justify the size or cost of the American effort there. Rather than proceeding from an assessment of the actual events and the possible advantages or disadvantages of our intervention, American policy was stagecraft. Vietnam was an abstraction. And so, in the end, was the settlement that capped four excruciating years of Henry Kissinger's diplomacy.

The Paris agreement settled nothing but the issue of American involvement. The issue over which the war was fought—who would rule South Vietnam—was not resolved at all, but left to be negotiated along with other matters that all Vietnamese on both sides knew were not really negotiable. Even Secretary of State Rogers acknowledged that the political half of the agreement was "ambiguous, but deliberately ambiguous. We never pretended that it was definite and if we had attempted to work it out we would still be fighting."

The agreement was another illusion, detached from Vietnamese reality. Nor was it ever clear what Nixon or Kissinger really thought would be its outcome, except that presumably they believed it would meet their minimum condition of avoiding a clear American humiliation. The peace, in other words, was exactly what Schell called the war: a piece of theater, in which Vietnamese actors were expected to follow a script written not to resolve the conflict that was ravaging their country, but to make an American failure look like a success and thus preserve America's reputation elsewhere in the world.

Vietnam and the Nixon-Kissinger World Order

WALTER ISAACSON

Nixon inherited four major aberrations in American foreign policy:

• An ill-conceived war in Vietnam where victory was not feasible and withdrawal was difficult. More than 31,000 Americans had already died in a struggle as far away from Washington as the globe's geography permits. The U.S. had become involved because it viewed North Vietnam's actions as a manifestation of Chinese-Soviet expansionism. But by 1969, it was becoming clear that this was a misreading of the independent nationalism of the Vietnamese communists and of the relationship between China and the Soviet Union. In the U.S., the agony of the war was fomenting a new isolationism. A nation that began the decade with John Kennedy's pledge to bear any burden to assure the success of liberty around the world now had to adjust to an era of limits.

• The ostracism of China, home of one-fifth of the earth's people. America's notion of a monolithic communist threat had become outdated. Beginning in 1960, China had begun attacking Soviet "revisionism." The Soviets withdrew their advisers from China and stopped aid; old border disputes reignited. The U.S. faced the challenge, and opportunity, of playing a game of balance and maneuver. But entrenched attitudes about China made it difficult for Nixon's predecessors to see that its rift with the Soviet Union could be exploited.

• An escalating arms race between the U.S. and the Soviet Union that served the national interest of neither country. Throughout history, each addition to a nation's arsenal could readily be translated into increased global influence. But the 1960s brought the great irony of the nuclear age: the quantum leap in military force made incremental additions to each side's military power less meaningful. In addition, the rough parity between American and Soviet arsenals meant that the backbone of the containment policy—America's nuclear threat—was no longer believable. After twenty years of the nuclear arms race, the time had come for a new era in which superpower relations would be defined by an arcane arms control process.

• A stalemate in the Middle East marked by American impotence. After the Six-Day War of 1967, Washington's influence with Arab countries

From Walter Isaacson, *Kissinger: A Biography,* pp. 159–165, 234–239, 488–489.Copyright © 1992 by Walter Isaacson. Reprinted by permission of Simon & Schuster, Inc.

had dissipated while Moscow's grew. Egypt and Syria, in particular, became virtual clients of the Soviet Union. The situation did not serve U.S. interests, nor ultimately those of Israel or the cause of peace in the region.

Sometimes messily, sometimes brilliantly, Nixon and Kissinger would address all four of these aberrations. They would do so, however, in a manner that was relatively new in the conduct of American affairs: with a growing reliance on deception and secrecy and back channels to avoid having to deal with dissent in Congress, the public, or even within their own cabinet.

When Nixon and Kissinger took office, the U.S. had 536,000 troops in Vietnam. Americans were being killed at a rate of about two hundred a week. The cost of the war to U.S. taxpayers was running about $30 billion a year ($100 billion in 1990 dollars). Nor was the proverbial light visible at the end of the tunnel. "There is no plan for any reduction in our troop level," outgoing Defense Secretary Clark Clifford declared early in December 1968. Later that month he added: "The level of combat is such that we are building up our troops, not cutting them down."

The Hanoi communists considered Vietnam to be one nation, as decreed in the 1954 Geneva accords, and its division into two administrative units to be merely a temporary aberration imposed by outsiders—first the French, then the Americans. Washington, on the other hand, viewed the war as the invasion of the sovereign nation of South Vietnam by its communist neighbor to the north. Casting the struggle in a cold war context, it sought to prevent a communist takeover and, in the words of the official study known as the Pentagon Papers, "to keep South Vietnam from Chinese hands."

Though his later actions would seem to belie it, Nixon knew that an American military solution was not feasible. "There's no way to win this war," he told one of his speech writers, Richard Whalen, in March of 1968. "But we can't say that, of course. In fact, we have to seem to say just the opposite, just to keep some degree of bargaining leverage."

After FBI director J. Edgar Hoover came up to the [Hotel] Pierre to brief him on the recording equipment Lyndon Johnson used in the Oval Office, Nixon told [Chief of Staff H. R.] Haldeman: "I'm not going to end up like LBJ, Bob, holed up in the White House, afraid to show my face on the street. I'm going to stop that war. Fast." He ordered the recording equipment removed. He did not order his own bugging equipment installed until 1971, after the war had widened into Cambodia.

Kissinger had spelled out his views on Vietnam in an article for *Foreign Affairs,* which was released with great fanfare shortly after his appointment was announced. A "remarkable analysis . . . free from the myths and prejudices of the past," the *Washington Post* called it. "A powerful mind, rising above knowledge of the details to identify the way out," wrote columnist Joseph Kraft.

The article began with a tough critique of U.S. strategy. "We lost sight of one of the cardinal maxims of guerrilla war: the guerrilla wins, if he does not lose. The conventional army loses if it does not win." After the Tet offensive, it became clear the war was unwinnable, or to use Kissinger's more circumspect language, the U.S. "could no longer achieve its objectives within a period or with force levels politically acceptable to the American people."

Nevertheless, Kissinger contended, America could not simply cut its losses and withdraw. The reason, he said, was that the U.S. had to maintain its "credibility." This argument would be at the heart of his thinking on Vietnam and on every other global struggle for the rest of his career.

Even though the U.S. may not have been wise to get involved in Vietnam in the first place, Kissinger argued that it could not now withdraw without undermining its position throughout the world:

> The commitment of 500,000 Americans has settled the issue of the importance of Viet Nam. What is involved now is confidence in American promises. However fashionable it is to ridicule the terms "credibility" or "prestige," they are not empty phrases; other nations can gear their actions to ours only if they can count on our steadiness. . . . In many parts of the world—the Middle East, Europe, Latin America, even Japan—stability depends on confidence in American promises.

Kissinger's emphasis on credibility was a constant in his personal brand of realpolitik. There was some merit to the notion. As the world groped its way into the nuclear age, the traditional methods of asserting national power—such as controlling more territory, forging new alliances, and adding to arsenals—were becoming less meaningful. The main way that a nuclear power could enhance its global clout was to increase the *credibility* of its commitments. Power thus depended more on perception—about a nation's will and the believability of its threats—than on military might.

In the case of Vietnam, Kissinger's "credibility" argument was based on the dubious premise that if the U.S. pulled out, people around the world would respect it less. But in fact, by pursuing a futile embroilment, the U.S. squandered the true sources of its influence—and of its credibility—in the world: its moral authority, its sense of worthy purpose, and its reputation as a reasonable and sensible player.

"Why not withdraw?" Charles de Gaulle asked Kissinger during a fleeting conversation when Nixon visited Paris a month after his inauguration.

"A sudden withdrawal might give us a credibility problem," Kissinger replied.

"Where?" asked de Gaulle.

Kissinger cited the Middle East. "How very odd," said de Gaulle who had freed the French from the disastrous entanglement in Algeria. "It is precisely in the Middle East that I thought your enemies had a credibility problem."

An important corollary to Kissinger's credibility argument was left unstated. If preserving credibility was the main goal, then the U.S. did not have to save South Vietnam indefinitely. It merely had to achieve a "decent interval" between America's withdrawal and South Vietnam's collapse. Other justifications for the war, such as the domino theory favored by Lyndon Johnson, asserted that the U.S. had national security interests at stake in the wilds of Indochina that required the defeat of the communists. But Kissinger, according to both his friends and foes, felt otherwise. During 1968, he frequently said in private talks and seminars that the appropriate goal of U.S. policy was a "decent interval" of two or three years between the withdrawal of U.S. troops and a communist takeover in Vietnam.

In order to get a negotiated settlement that would preserve American credibility, Kissinger suggested in his *Foreign Affairs* article that the military issues be separated from the political ones. Washington should deal directly with Hanoi on the military questions, such as the withdrawal of troops from South Vietnam and the return of prisoners. Saigon would deal directly with the National Liberation Front on political questions, such as the type of government that would emerge in South Vietnam and the possibility of a coalition. "If we involve ourselves deeply in the issue of South Vietnam's internal arrangements," he wrote, "we shall find ourselves in a morass of complexities."

The problem with this proposal was that the communists were not willing to stop the military struggle without having achieved their political aims. As Kissinger himself later noted, "They had not fought for forty years to achieve a compromise." They fought in order to overthrow the regime in Saigon; for the U.S. to propose that there should be a military settlement that was divorced from the question of who got to rule the South clearly missed the point of the whole exercise. As the Hanoi Communist Party newspaper put it: "The military and political aspects of the issue are inseparable because the underlying cause of the Vietnam War is the American imposition of a stooge administration on the South Vietnamese people."

Shortly after his appointment, Kissinger called his old colleague and occasional critic Henry Rowen, president of the Rand Corporation, a Santa Monica think tank that specialized in military studies for the government. Kissinger had attended many seminars about Vietnam at Rand, and he knew the people there to be tough-minded skeptics about U.S. policy. What, Kissinger would ask, were the alternatives? Now he wanted to hire a team of Rand analysts to explore these alternatives and analyze the range of options.

To lead the team, Rowen picked what would seem, at least in retrospect, an odd couple: Daniel Ellsberg, Rand's foremost Vietnam expert, who later leaked the Pentagon Papers and became a hero to the Left; and Fred Ikle, head of Rand's social science division, who later became an advisor to Ronald Reagan and a hero to the Right. Ellsberg had known Kissinger since the late 1950s, had lectured at his defense policy seminar, and had given him advice when he visited Vietnam in the mid-1960s. Ikle had been a research associate under Kissinger at Harvard in the early

1960s. On Christmas Day of 1968, they flew with Rowen to New York, where for four days they met with Kissinger at the Pierre Hotel to discuss their report.

Their paper, which has never been made public, laid out seven options. At one extreme was "military escalation aimed at negotiated victory." Among the military actions that this could entail: "air and ground operations in Cambodia," "unrestricted bombing of North Vietnam including Hanoi," and the "mining of Haiphong." The goal, according to Option One, was "to destroy the will and capability of North Vietnam to support insurgency."

At the other extreme was "unilateral withdrawal of all U.S. forces." The discussion of this option began with an admission that it "has no advocates within the U.S. government." Indeed, it went further than the "peace plank" rejected at the Democratic convention as too dovish, and even Ellsberg was not in favor of it. Nevertheless, the arguments in its favor were explored, beginning with the premise that "the war is unwinnable" and that "we should therefore cut our losses." As for the credibility question, "other nations will accept our action because we have met our commitments by large investments of men and resources, and shown wisdom in accepting the situation."

On the first day of discussions, the unilateral withdrawal option was eliminated. "Henry said it was so far outside what was going to happen that it didn't help the options paper, and it would upset Nixon," Ikle later recalled.

As a result, the most dovish option was number six: "Substantial reduction in U.S. presence while seeking a compromise settlement." The idea involved obtaining Saigon's "approval" for regular withdrawals that would bring the U.S. troop level down to one hundred thousand by the end of 1971 while building up the South Vietnamese army to take over.

In between were other alternatives. But nowhere was there any suggestion—for the analysts that Christmas would surely have thought it absurd—that the U.S. could pursue a policy based on a mix of the two most extreme options, that is, military escalation as well as regular withdrawals. Both Ellsberg and Ikle later said that it would have seemed paradoxical to conceive of a policy based on trying to beat Hanoi into submission through unrestricted bombings and the invasion of Cambodia, on the one hand, while at the same time embarking on a policy of substantial unilateral troop withdrawals.

One reason that American policy would eventually turn into a crazy quilt of threats, bombing spasms, and inexorable withdrawals was because of what Nixon once dubbed "the madman theory." During the 1968 campaign, he and Haldeman were walking along a foggy California beach when Nixon began to explain that the key to a Vietnam solution was to get Hanoi to fear American threats. "I call it the madman theory, Bob. I want the North Vietnamese to believe I've reached the point where I might do *anything* to stop the war. We'll just slip the word to them that, 'for God's sake, you know Nixon is obsessed about Communism. We can't restrain him when he's angry—and he has his hand on the nuclear button'—and Ho Chi Minh will be in Paris in two days begging for peace."

"Henry bought into the madman theory," according to Haldeman. "He was eager to let the Soviets think that the president might at any moment take tough steps." Nixon later explained that, in his mind at least, it became a good-cop, bad-cop routine: Kissinger would come across as reasonable, but he would let it be known that he was having a difficult time controlling his president's warlike instincts.

Fundamental to Kissinger's philosophy—and to the realist political tradition—was that diplomacy must be backed by the threat of force. "Kissinger has a very strong ideological belief in the efficacy and legitimacy of the threat of violence as a tool of power," Daniel Ellsberg told Jann Wenner of *Rolling Stone* magazine in a 1973 interview. For example, during the war between the PLO and Jordan in 1970, Secretary of State Rogers would argue that, in order to facilitate diplomacy, the U.S. should pledge not to use force. On the contrary, argued Kissinger, diplomacy could work only if the threat remained.

The Rand paper noted that there were disagreements over basic facts within the U.S. government. So Ellsberg suggested that Kissinger put a series of questions to the different agencies, make them answer separately, and compare the discrepancies. Kissinger liked the idea, in part because it would swamp the bureaucracy and give him leeway to develop policy. Fritz Kraemer's son, Sven, who had become an aide to Kissinger, objected to the tenor of Ellsberg's questions. "Sven, you're completely right, but you don't understand what I'm doing." Kissinger replied. "I'm tying up the bureaucracy for a year and buying time for the new president."

The six pages, containing twenty-eight major topics and fifty-six questions, were issued as National Security Study Memorandum 1 on Inauguration Day. Through February and March, as the answers flowed in from the departments and agencies, Ellsberg worked secretly as a consultant collating them for Kissinger.

NSSM–1 did not serve to answer any questions. But it did give Kissinger an insight into the disagreements that were simmering within the bureaucracy. Was the "domino theory" correct that the fall of Vietnam might lead to a succession of neighboring revolutions? The CIA downplayed that possibility. The defense secretary's office did, too. But the intelligence units of the army, navy, and air force supported the domino theory. Within the State Department, the Bureau of Intelligence thought the theory was overblown, but the East Asian Bureau endorsed it.

Were B-52 strikes effective? The military thought so, the CIA and State Department did not. The CIA even argued that there was "substantial evidence" that the bombing made it easier for Hanoi to "mobilize people behind the Communist war effort." And on the key question (especially for those who might be considering whether to bomb or invade Cambodia) of how important the enemy supply routes through Cambodia were, the responses revealed that the U.S. military and the embassy in Saigon considered them very important, "while CIA disagrees strongly."

In general, the military and the Saigon embassy took optimistic views on most questions, asserting that the war was going rather well. The CIA, the civilians at the Pentagon, and most bureaus in the State Department were more pessimistic.

Kissinger believed that he would be able to reach a peace settlement quickly. "Give us six months," he told a group of protesting Quakers, "and if we haven't ended the war by then, you can come back and tear down the White House fence."

The young intellectuals on his staff believed him. "For the first time, I'm satisfied with the Vietnam policy of the U.S.," Morton Halperin told Daniel Ellsberg that spring. Looking back on that period, Anthony Lake, a young foreign service officer who would resign as Kissinger's assistant the next year after the invasion of Cambodia, recalled: "I believe that Henry was sincere in believing he could negotiate an end to the war, and do it sooner rather than later."

But Kissinger was not sympathetic to the idea of a quick withdrawal. "We could not simply walk away from an enterprise involving two administrations, five allied countries, and 31,000 dead as if we were switching a television channel," he later wrote.

So Kissinger embarked on what would be a four-year quest for a negotiated settlement. At the outset the U.S. had two major demands: North Vietnamese troops must be withdrawn from the South, and the government of Nguyen Van Thieu in Saigon must not be ousted other than by free elections. Hanoi demanded the opposite: that the U.S. must withdraw unilaterally, and the "American puppet" Thieu must be deposed. By the end of 1972, the U.S. would be ready to concede the first point, and Hanoi, at least for a decent interval of two years, would concede the second. . . .

The reason that the U.S. was mired in Vietnam was simple: the South Vietnamese army was not able to fend off the communists on its own. Until it could, there was no way to negotiate a withdrawal of American troops that would not lead to the overthrow of the Saigon government. For it is a reliable rule of diplomacy that you cannot win at the bargaining table something that you would be unable to win on the ground.

Spasms of bombings could, perhaps, delay the day of reckoning, but not change this reality. So unless the U.S. was willing to stay in Vietnam indefinitely, there could be no solution that assured Saigon's survival until the South Vietnamese army could take over the burden of fighting from the five hundred thousand U.S. troops there.

That was the military rationale behind Nixon's policy of beefing up the South Vietnamese army. "Although Kissinger didn't agree, it was clear to me that South Vietnam would not be able to survive a peace government unless it had the military forces to do so," said Nixon.

Building up Saigon's forces would permit the U.S. to reduce its own. In pursuing the war, the new administration realized that it was important to stay just ahead of the growing antiwar outcry, to buy time by keeping the public mollified through periodic withdrawals of U.S. troops. Taken together, these rationales led to a program that was originally called de-Americanization and that Defense Secretary Laird dubbed "Vietnami-zation," a more elegant but eerily callous term. It was a policy that Laird pushed, Nixon accepted, and Kissinger disparaged.

The idea was raised by Nixon in his 1968 campaign. "We need a mas-sive training program," Nixon said in an off-the-record talk to Southern convention delegates, "so that the South Vietnamese can be trained to take over the fighting, that they can be phased in as we phase out." On an October flight with the candidate from Bismarck to Boise, Laird told the press that up to ninety thousand U.S. troops could be pulled out in a year. (President Johnson's defense secretary Clark Clifford publicly rebutted Laird and pointed out that troop levels were still rising.)

Despite Laird's backing, the U.S. military was appalled by the notion of Vietnamization because they considered it tantamount to a slow surren-der. On June 7, Nixon scheduled a showdown in Honolulu with General Creighton Abrams, the U.S. commander in Vietnam, to be followed the next day by a meeting on Midway Island with South Vietnam's President Thieu.

Abrams seethed with contempt as he listened to Nixon's plan. The tight-lipped general realized that—however it was sugarcoated—the with-drawal proposal amounted to the end of the possibility that the U.S. would prevail and the beginning of a sad rearguard action by the American mili-tary. Kissinger later called Abrams's discomfort "painful to see."

The President's entourage—including Kissinger, Rogers, Laird, and five hundred other officials, reporters, and support staff—then descended on the two-square-mile American atoll of Midway, under the blank stares of the thousands of gooney birds that are its main inhabitants.

Nguyen Van Thieu, a proud military man who had risen from platoon commander to become Vietnam's president, was desperate to be treated as an equal, as the leader of an American ally rather than as a puppet or a sub-ordinate. Kissinger had asked that Thieu arrive first, so that Nixon would not have to wait for him. But Thieu had insisted that the American presi-dent was the host and thus should be there first to greet him. Kissinger acquiesced, but Nixon's plane nevertheless ended up arriving fifteen min-utes after Thieu's.

Thieu had also asked that he and Nixon meet alone; Nixon, through Kissinger, insisted that Kissinger be there. So Thieu brought along one of his assistants. When he arrived in the meeting room at the U.S. naval com-mander's house, he noticed that there was one big chair, apparently for Nixon, and three smaller chairs flanking it. Thieu turned around, walked silently into the dining room, found a chair the same size as Nixon's, car-ried it back, and placed it squarely facing Nixon's.

Thieu knew the size of troop withdrawals being planned—twenty-five thousand—because it had been well leaked beforehand. Displaying the dig-nity of a people used to the perfidies of foreigners, Thieu suggested the withdrawal on his own, saying that it should be called a "redeployment." The two men then walked to a sheet-metal Quonset hut to announce that they had jointly agreed that twenty-five thousand American soldiers were going to be redeployed back home.

It was clear to both presidents, as Nixon later recounted, that the announcement that day "would begin an irreversible process." Thieu later recalled a queasy feeling on that hot afternoon as he thought of an old Vietnamese saying: *dau xuoi duoi lot*—"if the head slides through easily, the tail will follow."

The moment was a historic coup for Nixon, and a political one as well. For the first time since the U.S. Marines' Ninth Expeditionary Brigade landed on "Red Beach Two" just north of Da Nang on March 8, 1965, American troops were withdrawing from Vietnam. He was jubilant.

Yet Nixon again showed his strange inclination, when given the choice of explaining the truth or engaging in deception, reflexively to opt for the latter, even if it served no purpose. The withdrawal decision, he declared to the press, was based on "Thieu's recommendation and the assessment of our own commander in the field." In fact, as every listener knew, Thieu and Abrams were the two people most opposed to the decision. It was a little lie, one that Nixon later called "a diplomatic exaggeration," but it was another indication of a larger syndrome: that Nixon, and to some extent Kissinger, felt that it was easier to deceive the American people than to nurture public understanding and support by being open about what they were doing.

In this case, however, Kissinger was more honest, perhaps because he was less pleased by the policy. In a background discussion with reporters on the way to Midway, Kissinger said that Vietnamization could help if it placed before Hanoi the specter of an opponent that would grow stronger. "If, however, we withdraw at a rate that gives Hanoi the feeling that we are really just looking for an excuse to get out, then it will thwart negotiations, because they will just sit there and wait." In that case, he added, Vietnamization would be no more than "an elegant bugout."

As it turned out, the withdrawals would continue at a painful rate: slow enough to drag out U.S. involvement for another three years amid glowing domestic anger, but fast enough to encourage Hanoi to sit and wait. When Clark Clifford publicly suggested later that month that one hundred thousand troops could be pulled out in 1969, Nixon bridled at the hypocrisy. This was the man who just six months earlier, when he was defense secretary, had been talking about the need for more of a buildup. But to Kissinger's dismay, Nixon added, "I would hope that we could beat Mr. Clifford's timetable."

For Kissinger, Vietnamization violated his cardinal rule of realism: military force and diplomacy must work together. In *Nuclear Weapons and Foreign Policy*, he had lambasted the U.S. decision to cease offensive operations in Korea while armistice talks were being held. His words in 1957 foreshadowed what he would face trying to negotiate a settlement in Vietnam: "By stopping military operations we removed the only Chinese incentive for a settlement; we produced the frustration of two years of inconclusive negotiations. In short, our insistence on divorcing force from diplomacy caused our power to lack purpose and our negotiations to lack force."

He later wrote strikingly similar words as he looked back on the policy of Vietnamization. It was unrealistic, he said, to have demanded a mutual withdrawal at the negotiating table while making unilateral withdrawals on the battlefield. "The more automatic our withdrawal, the less useful it was as a bargaining weapon; the demand for mutual withdrawal grew hollow as our unilateral withdrawal accelerated."

Laird continued to be the strongest advocate of Vietnamization. "I knew that time was running out for us because the public wasn't going to support the war any longer," he later said. "Henry didn't understand this because he wasn't a politician. Instead, all he worried about was that Vietnamization would undercut his diplomacy."

Whenever a withdrawal was due to be announced, Laird would go into a briefing frenzy, calling in reporters and favorite congressmen. "I felt I had to keep pressure on Kissinger and prevent him from getting Nixon to back away." One of these sessions produced a report on CBS News that "Laird has long since made up his mind we should be getting out faster"; on his news summary, Nixon underlined the phrase and scribbled a note to Kissinger: "His clever game!"

Laird also outflanked Kissinger in a bureaucratic coup a few weeks after they returned from Midway. In order for Vietnamization to work, Laird felt that it was necessary to change the "mission statement" that guided how U.S. troops were used. Instead of deploying them to confront enemy forces, Laird's new mission statement said their role should be to assist South Vietnam's army and to stake out a defensive rather than offensive posture of their own.

Without waiting for an NSC meeting or presidential decision, Laird sent out this significant change. "I informed Kissinger and the president I had done it on the same day I issued the orders," he recalled. Kissinger tried to convince Nixon to reject the change. But since Laird had already sent it out, it stood. "Kissinger was upset and called me deceitful," says Laird, "but you have to be willing to play the other guy's game now and then."

During Nixon's long vacation in San Clemente at the end of that August, [NSC staff member] Tony Lake was visiting Kissinger to discuss Vietnam. "I said that the problem with Vietnamization was that it was like salted peanuts: once the public got a taste for it, there was no stopping it." It was therefore important, Lake continued, to get the best possible deal right away while the U.S. position was strongest.

Kissinger asked him to turn his thoughts into a memo. Lake wrote three pages. Kissinger took the memo, praised the part about how Vietnamization weakened the U.S. bargaining position, but then eliminated the conclusion that it therefore made sense to go for a deal immediately. He included it in a longer, pessimistic memo of his own to Nixon. "The more troops are withdrawn," Kissinger wrote, "the more Hanoi will be encouraged."

That week Kissinger won his first (and last) skirmish against Vietnamization. Nixon had decreed that each round of troop withdrawals would depend on three criteria: a reduction in enemy activity, progress at the negotiating table, and improvement in South Vietnam's capabilities. But in mid-August, after an eight-week lull in the fighting, communist forces launched surprise attacks on Cam Ranh Bay and more than a hundred other targets in South Vietnam. At Kissinger's urging, Nixon responded by post-poning the next phase of U.S. troop withdrawals that had been scheduled by Laird for late August.

In a private background briefing for a few journalists in San Clemente, Kissinger explained that the delay proved that the U.S. was not a prisoner of the withdrawal bandwagon. "We have to impress Hanoi with our staying power or we won't have flexibility," he said. "It is important that Hanoi understands—and the American people understand—that the three criteria do apply and that we are not just engaged in a mechanical exercise."

Nevertheless, the three criteria were soon ignored and the withdrawals did in fact become mechanical. Just two weeks later, Nixon decided to pro-ceed with another withdrawal of 40,500 troops. At a meeting in the Oval Office, as [White House adviser] Ehrlichman scribbled notes (and doodled a remarkably good likeness of Nixon's nose), Kissinger suffered his final defeat. When Nixon commented that Vietnamization was going well, Kissinger asked, "But how are we going to turn it off if necessary later?" The real problem, Nixon replied, was that the withdrawals were "not fast enough." Never again would he delay a withdrawal announcement, no mat-ter how bad the news from the battlefield or grim the tidings from the bar-gaining table. . . .

In the end, it is hard to argue that the strategic interests at stake for the U.S. in pursuing the Vietnam War for another four years were worth the human, financial, moral, and spiritual costs. In all, 58,022 Americans lost their lives. Of these, 20,552 were now dead who had been alive when Nixon and Kissinger took office, including 4,278 who were killed in the last year of fighting. The direct cost of the war to the taxpayer was about $140 billion, or approximately $1,900 for each American household.

The moral principle of proportionality decrees that in fighting a war a nation should do no worse than the evil it seeks to prevent. The total amount of bombs the U.S. dropped on Indochina, at a cost of $6 billion, was 7,975,000 tons, about four times the tonnage used in all theaters dur-ing World War II. All told, 924,048 communist soldiers and 185,528 South Vietnamese soldiers were reported killed.

From the standpoint of American foreign policy, the war did more to deflect the nation from its important interests than it did to preserve its "credibility." When Kissinger had his bitter showdown with a recalcitrant Thieu in October 1972, he snapped that "for four years we have mortgaged our whole foreign policy to the defense of one country." To a realist such as Kissinger, such a distortion of national interest should have seemed idiotic. For he knew Bismarck's dictum: "Woe to the statesman whose reasons for entering a war do not appear so plausible at its end as at its beginning."

When America first entered the war, the reason was to counter the men-ace of a monolithic communism directed from Moscow and Beijing. By 1969, Kissinger and Nixon knew that this was not the situation. Another reason for entering the war was to contain China. Kissinger's 1971 trip to Beijing made this strategic interest less compelling.

Finally, the reason for American involvement came down to preventing a pro-communist nationalist revolution from imposing its system on a reluctant people. That was a moral, decent goal. But if the South Vietnamese people and its rickety regime could not protect themselves after eight years of massive U.S. support—if they could not fight off the threat without American boys dying for them indefinitely—then the U.S. involvement served only to postpone the inevitable. This was hardly a goal worthy of great sacrifice.

Nevertheless, the criticism must be put in perspective. By the beginning of 1973, Kissinger and Nixon had brought the nation's military misadventure in Vietnam to an end. Instead of slinking away as the Vietnamese factions continued the war, Kissinger had secured a cease-fire that, at least for the moment, curtailed the killing. In addition, America's ally had been given a decent chance to survive.

Officials in the previous two administrations, many of whom became preening doves as soon as their responsibility ended, had overseen a foolish deployment of close to 550,000 American troops over eight years. The Nixon administration immediately reversed the process and began withdrawing. It had all troops and POWs home in just over four years. It would have been wiser to do it more quickly and cleanly, but at least it was done. "We found more than half a million American troops in Vietnam when we came into office, and we got them home without destroying those who had relied on us," Kissinger said.

The Paris agreement was the final element of a reshaped American foreign policy that—rather amazingly—provided the nation with the chance to play as influential a role in the world as it had before the paralyzing despair of its Vietnam involvement. By engineering the end of that war along with the opening to China and the détente with the Soviet Union, Kissinger had helped create a triangular structure for global stability that was beyond the imaginations of the Kennedy and Johnson administrations as well as the inert bureaucracy of the foreign policy establishment.

✗ *F U R T H E R   R E A D I N G*

Jonathan Aitken, *Nixon: A Life* (1994)
Stephen E. Ambrose, *Nixon* (vols. 1–3) (1987–1991)
Henry Brandon, *The Retreat of American Power* (1974)
Dan Caldwell, ed., *Henry Kissinger* (1983)
Jeffrey J. Clarke, *Advice and Support: The Final Years, 1965–1973* (1988)
Raymond Garthoff, *Détente and Confrontation* (1985)
J. W. Garver, "Sino-Vietnamese Conflict and Sino-American Rapprochement,"
    Political Science Quarterly, 96 (1981), 445–61
Allan E. Goodman, *The Lost Peace* (1978)
Seymour M. Hersh, *The Price of Power* (1983)
Marvin and Bernard Kalb, *Kissinger* (1974)
Henry Kissinger, *Diplomacy* (1994)
———, "The Vietnam Negotiations." *Foreign Affairs,* 47 (1969) 211–34

————, *Years of Upheaval* (1983)

Robert S. Litwak, *Détente and the Nixon Doctrine* (1984)

Roger Morris, *Uncertain Greatness: Henry Kissinger and American Foreign Policy* (1977)

Richard M. Nixon, "Asia After Vietnam," *Foreign Affairs,* 46 (1967), 111–25

————, *RN: The Memoirs of Richard Nixon* (1978)

Robert E. Osgood. *Retreat from Empire?* (1973)

Herbert S. Parmet, *Richard Nixon and His America* (1990)

Jonathan Schell, *The Time of Illusion* (1975)

Robert D. Schulzinger, *Henry Kissinger* (1989)

William Shawcross, *Sideshow: Kissinger, Nixon and the Destruction of Cambodia* (1979)

John Stoessinger, *Kissinger: The Anguish of Power* (1976)

Tad Szulc, *The Illusion of Peace* (1978)

G. H. Turley, *The Easter Offensive* (1985)

CHAPTER

12

The Antiwar Movement

and Public Opinion

The American people overwhelmingly supported government policy in Vietnam during the early years of the U.S. military buildup, much as they had other post-World War II foreign policy commitments. Even after Johnson's major escalation of 1965, dissent remained muted, with the exception of vocal protests by a handful of isolated student and intellectual groups. But as the war dragged on inconclusively and American casualties mounted throughout 1966 and 1967, protest marches and demonstrations proliferated. A symbolic march on the Pentagon in the fall of 1967 drew tens of thousands of antiwar protesters. Following the Tet offensive of early 1968, the ranks of the antiwar movement swelled.

Despite the persistence of stereotypes perpetuated in part by the media, antiwar dissidents were not confined to the young, radicals, intellectuals, and the disaffected. Indeed if one defines the antiwar movement more broadly to encompass all who came to question the efficacy of the U.S. commitment to Vietnam, by 1968 it included many powerful individuals within the business and financial communities, the media, and the government itself. Public-opinion polls conducted during the late 1960s and early 1970s revealed a steady erosion of popular support for U.S. policy. Many observers at the time noted that the war had polarized American society more than any other event since the Civil War.

The nature of the antiwar movement—its origins, purposes, and ultimate impact on policy—has long been a subject of heated controversy. Perhaps of equal importance, albeit less frequently studied, is the aggregate domestic response to Vietnam, measurable by public-opinion surveys. Who opposed the war? Why did they oppose it? What impact did antiwar activities, or changes in levels of public support, have on the actions of the Johnson and Nixon administrations?

X *D O C U M E N T S*

Students for a Democratic Society (SDS), an organization that by the mid-1960s had become a leading voice for the student protest movement and the New Left, announced its opposition to the war in 1965. A public statement explaining its position, issued to the press in October 1965, is the first document. The next selection gives excerpts from a speech by SDS president Carl Oglesby during a protest march in Washington, D.C., on November 27 of that year. Widely circulated, the address reproached not only the war but the system that had produced it. Martin Luther King, Jr., the preeminent civil-rights leader and Nobel Peace Prize recipient, declared his opposition to America's involvement in Vietnam on April 4, 1967. Portions of King's controversial speech, delivered as a sermon at New York's Riverside Church, are printed as the third document.

The military draft quickly emerged as a focus of antiwar activity. The next document, issued in the fall of 1967 by the Antidraft Resistance, led to federal prosecution of five of its signers, including famed pediatrician Benjamin Spock and Yale University chaplain William Sloane Coffin, Jr. In the following selection, author and former White House speechwriter James Fallows reflects on the class inequities of the draft. The sixth document features a veteran's anguished memories of how antiwar civilians mistreated him upon his return from service in Vietnam.

Former student activist Todd Gitlin, now a sociology professor at the University of California, Berkeley, in the next document recalls the New Left's infatuation with the Vietcong and other Third World revolutionary movements. In the last document, John Kerry, a leader of Vietnam Veterans Against the War, bitterly attacks government policy. Now a Democratic senator from Massachusetts, Kerry condemned the duplicity that underlay American policy at a congressional hearing on April 22, 1971.

SDS States Opposition to the War, 1965

Students for a Democratic Society wishes to reiterate emphatically its intention to pursue its opposition to the war in Vietnam, undeterred by the diversionary tactics of the administration.

We feel that the war is immoral at its root, that it is fought alongside a regime with no claim to represent its people, and that *it is foreclosing the hope of making America a decent and truly democratic society.*

The commitment of SDS, and of the whole generation we represent, is clear: we are anxious to build villages; we refuse to burn them. We are anxious to help and to change our country; we refuse to destroy someone else's country. We are anxious to advance the cause of democracy; we do not believe that cause can be advanced by torture and terror.

We are fully prepared to volunteer for service to our country and to democracy. We volunteer to go into Watts to work with the people of Watts to rebuild that neighborhood to be the kind of place that the people of Watts want it to be—and when we say "rebuild," we mean socially as well as physically. We volunteer to help the Peace Corps learn, as we have been learning in the slums and in Mississippi, how to energize the hungry and desperate and defeated of the world to make the big decisions. We volunteer to serve in hospitals and schools in the slums, in the Job Corps and VISTA, in the new Teachers Corps—and to do so in such a way as to strengthen democracy at its grass-roots. And in order to make our volunteering possible, we propose to the President that all those Americans who seek so vigorously to build instead of burn be given their chance to do so. We propose that he test the young people of America: if they had a free choice, would they want to burn and torture in Vietnam or to build a democracy at home and overseas? There is only one way to make the choice real: let us see what happens if service to democracy is made grounds for exemption from the military draft. I predict that almost every member of my generation would choose to build, not to burn; to teach, not to torture; to help, not to kill. And I am sure that the overwhelming majority of our brothers and cousins in the army in Vietnam, would make the same choice if they could—to serve and build, not kill and destroy. . . .

Until the President agrees to our proposal, we have only one choice: we do in conscience object, utterly and wholeheartedly, to this war; and we will encourage every member of our generation to object, and to file his objection through the Form 150 provided by the law for conscientious objection.

Carl Oglesby Denounces the "Liberals' War," 1965

Seven months ago at the April March on Washington, Paul Potter, then President of Students for a Democratic Society, stood in approximately this spot and said that we must name the system that creates and sustains the war in Vietnam—name it, describe it, analyze it, understand it, and change it.

Today I will try to name it—to suggest an analysis which, to be quite frank, may disturb some of you—and to suggest what changing it may require of us.

We are here again to protest against a growing war. Since it is a very bad war, we acquire the habit of thinking that it must be caused by very bad men. But we only conceal reality, I think, to denounce on such grounds the menacing coalition of industrial and military power, or the brutality of the blitzkrieg we are waging against Vietnam, or the ominous signs around us that heresy may soon no longer be permitted. We must simply observe, and quite plainly say, that this coalition, this blitzkrieg, and this demand for acquiescence are creatures, all of them, of a government that since 1932 has considered itself to be fundamentally *liberal*.

The original commitment in Vietnam was made by President Truman, a mainstream liberal. It was seconded by President Eisenhower, a moderate liberal. It was intensified by the late President Kennedy, a flaming liberal. Think of the men who now engineer that war—those who study the maps, give the commands, push the buttons, and tally the dead: Bundy, McNamara, Rusk, Lodge, Goldberg, the President himself.

They are not moral monsters.

They are all honorable men.

They are all liberals.

But so, I'm sure, are many of us who are here today in protest. To understand the war, then, it seems necessary to take a closer look at this American liberalism. Maybe we are in for some surprises. Maybe we have here two quite different liberalisms: one authentically humanist, the other not so human at all.

Not long ago, I considered myself a liberal. And if someone had asked me what I meant by that, I'd perhaps have quoted Thomas Jefferson or Thomas Paine, who first made plain our nation's unprovisional commitment to human rights. But what do you think would happen if these two heroes could sit down now for a chat with President Johnson and McGeorge Bundy?

They would surely talk of the Vietnam war. Our dead revolutionaries would soon wonder why their country was fighting against what appeared to be a revolution. The living liberals would hotly deny that it is one: there are troops coming in from outside, the rebels get arms from other countries, most of the people are not on their side, and they practice terror against their own. Therefore, *not* a revolution.

What would our dead revolutionaries answer? They might say: "What fools and bandits, sirs, you make then of us. Outside help? Do you remember Lafayette? Or the 3,000 British freighters the French navy sunk for our side? Or the arms and men we got from France and Spain? And what's this about terror? Did you never hear what we did to our own loyalists? Or about the thousands of rich American Tories who fled for their lives to Canada? And as for popular support, do you not know that we had less than one third of our people with us? That, in fact, the colony of New York recruited more troops for the British than for the revolution? Should we give it all back?"

Revolutions do not take place in velvet boxes. They never have. It is only the poets who make them lovely. What the National Liberation Front is fighting in Vietnam is a complex and vicious war. This war is also a revolution, as honest a revolution as you can find anywhere in history. And this is a fact which all our intricate official denials will never change.

But it doesn't make any difference to our leaders anyway. Their aim in Vietnam is really much simpler than this implies. It is to safeguard what they take to be American interests around the world against revolution or revolutionary change, which they always call Communism—as if that were that. In the case of Vietnam, this interest is, first, the principle that revolution shall not be tolerated anywhere, and second, that South Vietnam shall never sell its rice to China—or even to North Vietnam.

There is simply no such thing now, for us, as a just revolution—never mind that for two thirds of the world's people the twentieth century might as well be the Stone Age; never mind the terrible poverty and hopelessness that are the basic facts of life for most modern men; and never mind that for these millions there is now an increasingly perceptible relationship between their sorrow and our contentment.

Can we understand why the Negroes of Watts rebelled? Then why do we need a devil theory to explain the rebellion of the South Vietnamese? Can we understand the oppression in Mississippi, or the anguish that our Northern ghettos make epidemic? Then why can't we see that our proper human struggle is not with Communism or revolutionaries, but with the social desperation that drives good men to violence, both here and abroad? . . .

Let's stare our situation coldly in the face. All of us are born to the colossus of history, our American corporate system—in many ways, an awesome organism. There is one fact that describes it: with about 5 percent of the world's people, we consume about half the world's goods. We take a richness that is in good part not our own, and we put it in our pockets, our garages, our split-levels, our bellies, and our futures.

On the *face* of it, it is a crime that so few should have so much at the expense of so many. Where is the moral imagination so abused as to call this just? Perhaps many of us feel a bit uneasy in our sleep. We are not, after all, a cruel people. And perhaps we don't really need this super dominance that deforms others. But what can we do? The investments are made. The financial ties are established. The plants abroad are built. Our system *exists*. One is swept up into it. How intolerable—to be born moral, but addicted to a stolen and maybe surplus luxury. Our goodness threatens to become counterfeit before our eyes—unless we change. But change threatens us with uncertainty—at least.

Martin Luther King, Jr., Declares His Opposition to the War, 1967

Since I am a preacher by trade, I suppose it is not surprising that I have seven major reasons for bringing Vietnam into the field of my moral vision. There is at the outset a very obvious and almost facile connection between the war in Vietnam and the struggle I, and others, have been waging in America. A few years ago there was a shining moment in that struggle. It seemed as if there was a real promise of hope for the poor—both black and white—through the Poverty Program. Then came the build-up in Vietnam, and I watched the program broken and eviscerated as if it were some idle political plaything of a society gone mad on war, and I knew that America would never invest the necessary funds or energies in rehabilitation of its poor so long as Vietnam continued to draw men and skills and money like some demonic, destructive suction tube. So I was increasingly compelled to see the war as an enemy of the poor and to attack it as such.

Perhaps the more tragic recognition of reality took place when it became clear to me that the war was doing far more than devastating the hopes of the poor at home. It was sending their sons and their brothers and their husbands to fight and to die in extraordinarily high proportions relative to the rest of the population. We were taking the young black men who had been crippled by our society and sending them 8000 miles away to guarantee liberties in Southeast Asia which they had not found in

Southwest Georgia and East Harlem. So we have been repeatedly faced with the cruel irony of watching Negro and white boys on TV screens as they kill and die together for a nation that has been unable to seat them together in the same schools. So we watch them in brutal solidarity burning the huts of a poor village, but we realize that they would never live on the same block in Detroit. I could not be silent in the face of such cruel manipulation of the poor.

My third reason grows out of my experience in the ghettos of the North over the last three years—especially the last three summers. As I have walked among the desperate, rejected and angry young men, I have told them that Molotov cocktails and rifles would not solve their problems. I have tried to offer them my deepest compassion while maintaining my conviction that social change comes most meaningfully through non-violent action. But, they asked, what about Vietnam? They asked if our own nation wasn't using massive doses of violence to solve its problems, to bring about the changes it wanted. Their questions hit home, and I knew that I could never again raise my voice against the violence of the oppressed in the ghettos without having first spoken clearly to the greatest purveyor of violence in the world today—my own government.

For those who ask the question, "Aren't you a Civil Rights leader?" and thereby mean to exclude me from the movement for peace, I have this further answer. In 1957 when a group of us formed the Southern Christian Leadership Conference, we chose as our motto: "To save the soul of America." We were convinced that we could not limit our vision to certain rights for black people, but instead affirmed the conviction that America would never be free or saved from itself unless the descendants of its slaves were loosed from the shackles they still wear.

Now, it should be incandescently clear that no one who has any concern for the integrity and life of America today can ignore the present war. If America's soul becomes totally poisoned, part of the autopsy must read "Vietnam." It can never be saved so long as it destroys the deepest hopes of men the world over.

As if the weight of such a commitment to the life and health of America were not enough, another burden of responsibility was placed upon me in 1964; and I cannot forget that the Nobel Prize for Peace was also a commission—a commission to work harder than I had ever worked before for the "brotherhood of man." This is a calling that takes me beyond national allegiances, but even if it were not present I would yet have to live with the meaning of my commitment to the ministry of Jesus Christ. To me the relationship of this ministry to the making of peace is so obvious that I sometimes marvel at those who ask me why I am speaking against the war. Could it be that they do not know that the good news was meant for all men—for communist and capitalist, for their children and ours, for black and white, for revolutionary and conservative? Have they forgotten that my ministry is in obedience to the One who loved His enemies so fully that He died for them? What then can I say to the Viet Cong or to Castro or to Mao as a faithful minister of this One? Can I threaten them with death, or must I not share with them my life?

And as I ponder the madness of Vietnam, my mind goes constantly to the people of that peninsula. I speak now not of the soldiers of each side, not of the junta in Saigon, but simply of the people who have been living under the curse of war for almost three continuous decades. I think of them, too, because it is clear to me that there will be no meaningful solution there until some attempt is made to know them and their broken cries.

They must see Americans as strange liberators. The Vietnamese proclaimed their own independence in 1945 after a combined French and Japanese occupation and before the communist revolution in China. Even though they quoted the American Declaration of Independence in their own document of freedom, we refused to recognize them. Instead, we decided to support France in its re-conquest of her former colony.

Our government felt then that the Vietnamese people were not "ready" for independence, and we again fell victim to the deadly Western arrogance that has poisoned the international atmosphere for so long. With that tragic decision, we rejected a revolutionary government seeking self-determination, and a government that had been established not by China (for whom the Vietnamese have no great love) but by clearly indigenous forces that included some communists. For the peasants, this new government meant real land reform, one of the most important needs in their lives.

For nine years following 1945 we denied the people of Vietnam the right of independence. For nine years we vigorously supported the French in their abortive effort to re-colonize Vietnam.

Before the end of the war we were meeting 80 per cent of the French war costs. Even before the French were defeated at Dien Bien Phu, they began to despair of their reckless action, but we did not. We encouraged them with our huge financial and military supplies to continue the war even after they had lost the will to do so.

After the French were defeated it looked as if independence and land reform would come again through the Geneva agreements. But instead there came the United States, determined that Ho should not unify the temporarily divided nation, and the peasants watched again as we supported one of the most vicious modern dictators—our chosen man, Premier Diem. The peasants watched and cringed as Diem ruthlessly routed out all opposition, supported their extortionist landlords and refused even to discuss reunification with the North. The peasants watched as all this was presided over by U.S. influence and then by increasing numbers of U.S. troops who came to help quell the insurgency that Diem's methods had aroused. When Diem was overthrown they may have been happy, but the long line of military dictatorships seemed to offer no real change—especially in terms of their need for land and peace.

The only change came from America as we increased our troop commitments in support of governments which were singularly corrupt, inept and without popular support. All the while, the people read our leaflets and received regular promises of peace and democracy—and land reform. Now they languish under our bombs and consider us—not their fellow Vietnamese—the real enemy. They move sadly and apathetically as we herd them off the land of their fathers into concentration camps where minimal social needs are rarely met. They know they must move or be destroyed by our bombs. So they go.

They watch as we poison their water, as we kill a million acres of their crops. They must weep as the bulldozers destroy their precious trees. They wander into the hospitals, with at least 20 casualties from American firepower for each Viet Cong-inflicted injury. So far we may have killed a million of them—mostly children.

What do the peasants think as we ally ourselves with the landlords and as we refuse to put any action into our many words concerning land reform? What do they think as we test out our latest weapons on them, just as the Germans tested out new medicine and new tortures in the concentration camps of Europe? Where are the roots of the independent Vietnam we claim to be building?

Now there is little left to build on—save bitterness. Soon the only solid physical foundations remaining will be found at our military bases and in the concrete of the concentration camps we call "fortified hamlets." The peasants may well wonder if we plan to build our new Vietnam on such grounds as these. Could we blame them for such thoughts? We must speak for them and raise the questions they cannot raise. These too are our brothers.

Perhaps the more difficult but no less necessary task is to speak for those who have been designated as our enemies. What of the NLF—that strangely anonymous group we call VC or communists? What must they think of us in America when they realize that we permitted the repression and cruelty of Diem which helped to bring them into being as a resistance group in the South? How can they believe in our integrity when now we speak of "aggression from the North" as if there were nothing more essential to the war? How can they trust us when now we charge *them* with violence after the murderous reign of Diem, and charge *them* with violence while we pour new weapons of death into their land?

How do they judge us when our officials know that their membership is less than 25 per cent communist and yet insist on giving them the blanket name? What must they be thinking when they know that we are aware of their control of major sections of Vietnam and yet we appear ready to allow national elections in which this highly organized political parallel government will have no part? They ask how we can speak of free elections when the Saigon press is censored and controlled by the military junta. And they are surely right to wonder what kind of new government we plan to help form without them—the only party in real touch with the peasants. They question our political goals and they deny the reality of a peace settlement from which they will be excluded. Their questions are frighteningly relevant.

Here is the true meaning and value of compassion and non-violence—when it helps us to see the enemy's point of view, to hear his questions, to know of his assessment of ourselves. For from his view we may indeed see the basic weaknesses of our own condition, and if we are mature, we may learn and grow and profit from the wisdom of the brothers who are called the opposition. . . .

Somehow this madness must cease. I speak as a child of God and brother to the suffering poor of Vietnam and the poor of America who are paying the double price of smashed hopes at home and death and corruption in Vietnam. I speak as a citizen of the world, for the world as it stands aghast at the path we have taken. I speak as an American to the leaders of my own nation. The great initiative in this war is ours. The initiative to stop must be ours.

This is the message of the great Buddhist leaders of Vietnam. Recently, one of them wrote these words: "Each day the war goes on the hatred increases in the hearts of the Vietnamese and in the hearts of those of humanitarian instinct. The Americans are forcing even their friends into becoming their enemies. It is curious that the Americans, who calculate so carefully on the possibilities of military victory, do not realize that in the process they are incurring deep psychological and political defeat. The image of America will never again be the image of revolution, freedom and democracy, but the image of violence and militarism."

If we continue, there will be no doubt in my mind and in the mind of the world that we have no honorable intentions in Vietnam. It will become clear that our minimal expectation is to occupy it as an American colony, and men will not refrain from thinking that our maximum hope is to goad China into a war so that we may bomb her nuclear installations.

The world now demands a maturity of America that we may not be able to achieve. It demands that we admit that we have been wrong from the beginning of our adventure in Vietnam, that we have been detrimental to the life of her people.

In order to atone for our sins and errors in Vietnam, we should take the initiative in bringing the war to a halt. I would like to suggest five concrete things that our government should do immediately to begin the long and difficult process of extricating ourselves from this nightmare:

1. End all bombing in North and South Vietnam.
2. Declare a unilateral cease-fire in the hope that such action will create the atmosphere for negotiation.
3. Take immediate steps to prevent other battlegrounds in Southeast Asia by curtailing our military build-up in Thailand and our interference in Laos.
4. Realistically accept the fact that the National Liberation Front has substantial support in South Vietnam and must thereby play a role in any meaningful negotiations and in any future Vietnam government.
5. Set a date on which we will remove all foreign troops from Vietnam in accordance with the 1954 Geneva Agreement.

Part of our ongoing commitment might well express itself in an offer to grant asylum to any Vietnamese who fears for his life under a new regime which included the NLF. Then we must make what reparations we can for the damage we have done. We must provide the medical aid that is badly needed, in this country if necessary.

Meanwhile, we in the churches and synagogues have a continuing task while we urge our government to disengage itself from a disgraceful commitment. We must be prepared to match actions with words by seeking out every creative means of protest possible.

As we counsel young men concerning military service we must clarify for them our nation's role in Vietnam and challenge them with the alternative of conscientious objection. I am pleased to say that this is the path now being chosen by more than 70 students at my own Alma Mater, Morehouse College, and I recommend it to all who find the American course in Vietnam a dishonorable and unjust one. Moreover, I would encourage all ministers of draft age to give up their ministerial exemptions and seek status as conscientious objectors. Every man of humane convictions must decide on the protest that best suits his convictions, but we must all protest.

There is something seductively tempting about stopping there and sending us all off on what in some circles has become a popular crusade against the war in Vietnam. I say we must enter that struggle, but I wish to go on now to say something even more disturbing. The war in Vietnam is but a symptom of a far deeper malady within the American spirit, and if we ignore this sobering reality we will find ourselves organizing clergy- and laymen-concerned committees for the next generation. We will be marching and attending rallies without end unless there is a significant and profound change in American life and policy.

In 1957 a sensitive American official overseas said that it seemed to him that our nation was on the wrong side of a world revolution. During the past ten years we have seen emerge a pattern of suppression which now has justified the presence of U.S. military "advisors" in Venezuela. The need to maintain social stability for our investments accounts for the counterrevolutionary action of American forces in Guatemala. It tells why American helicopters are being used against guerrillas in Colombia and why American napalm and green beret forces have already been active against rebels in Peru. With such activity in mind, the words of John F. Kennedy come back to haunt us. Five years ago he said, "Those who make peaceful revolution impossible will make violent revolution inevitable."

Increasingly, by choice or by accident, this is the role our nation has taken—by refusing to give up the privileges and the pleasures that come from the immense profits of overseas investment.

I am convinced that if we are to get on the right side of the world revolution, we as a nation must undergo a radical revolution of values. When machines and computers, profit and property rights are considered more important than people, the giant triplets of racism, materialism, and militarism are incapable of being conquered.

A true revolution of values will soon cause us to question the fairness and justice of many of our past and present policies.

Proclamation of the Antidraft Resistance, 1967

To the young men of America, to the whole of the American people, and to all men of goodwill everywhere:

1. An ever growing number of young American men are finding that the American war in Vietnam so outrages their deepest moral and religious sense that they cannot contribute to it in any way. We share their moral outrage.

2. We further believe that the war is unconstitutional and illegal. Congress has not declared a war as required by the Constitution. Moreover, under the Constitution, treaties signed by the President and ratified by the Senate have the same force as the Constitution itself. The Charter of the United Nations is such a treaty. The Charter specifically obligates the United States to refrain from force or the threat of force in international relations. It requires member states to exhaust every peaceful means of settling disputes and to submit disputes which cannot be settled peacefully to the Security Council. The United States has systematically violated all of these Charter provisions for thirteen years.

3. Moreover, this war violates international agreements, treaties and principles of law which the United States Government has solemnly endorsed. The combat role of the United States troops in Vietnam violates the Geneva Accords of 1954 which our government pledged to support but has since subverted. The destruction of rice, crops and livestock; the burning and bulldozing of entire villages consisting exclusively of civilian structures; the interning of civilian non-combatants in concentration camps; the summary executions of civilians in captured villages who could not produce satisfactory evidence of their loyalties or did not wish to be removed to concentration camps; the slaughter of peasants who dared to stand up in their fields and shake their fists at American helicopters;—these are all actions of the kind which the United States and the other victorious powers of World War II declared to be crimes against humanity for which individuals were to be held personally responsible even when acting under the orders of their governments and for which Germans were sentenced at Nuremberg to long prison terms and death. The prohibition of such acts as war crimes was incorporated in treaty law by the Geneva Conventions of 1949, ratified by the United States. These are commitments to other countries and to Mankind, and they would claim our allegiance even if Congress should declare war.

4. We also believe it is an unconstitutional denial of religious liberty and equal protection of the laws to withhold draft exemption from men whose religious or profound philosophical beliefs are opposed to what in the Western religious tradition have been long known as unjust wars.

5. Therefore, we believe on all these grounds that every free man has a legal right and a moral duty to exert every effort to end this war, to avoid collusion with it, and to encourage others to do the same. Young men in the armed forces or threatened with the draft face the most excruciating choices. For them various forms of resistance risk separation from their families and their country, destruction of their careers, loss of their freedom

and loss of their lives. Each must choose the course of resistance dictated by his conscience and circumstances. Among those already in the armed forces some are refusing to obey specific illegal and immoral orders, some are attempting to educate their fellow servicemen on the murderous and barbarous nature of the war, some are absenting themselves without official leave. Among those not in the armed forces some are applying for status as conscientious objectors to American aggression in Vietnam, some are refusing to be inducted. Among both groups some are resisting openly and paying a heavy penalty, some are organizing more resistance within the United States and some have sought sanctuary in other countries.

6. We believe that each of these forms of resistance against illegitimate authority is courageous and justified. Many of us believe that open resistance to the war and the draft is the course of action most likely to strengthen the moral resolve with which all of us can oppose the war and most likely to bring an end to the war.

7. We will continue to lend our support to those who undertake resistance to this war. We will raise funds to organize draft resistance unions, to supply legal defense and bail, to support families and otherwise aid resistance to the war in whatever ways may seem appropriate.

8. We firmly believe that our statement is the sort of speech that under the First Amendment must be free, and that the actions we will undertake are as legal as is the war resistance of the young men themselves. But we recognize that the courts may find otherwise, and that if so we might all be liable to prosecution and severe punishment. In any case, we feel that we cannot shrink from fulfilling our responsibilities to the youth whom many of us teach, to the country whose freedom we cherish, and to the ancient traditions of religion and philosophy which we strive to preserve in this generation.

9. We call upon all men of good will to join us in this confrontation with immoral authority. Especially we call upon the universities to fulfill their mission of enlightenment and religious organizations to honor their heritage of brotherhood. Now is the time to resist.

James Fallows Reflects on the Draft's Inequities (1969), 1975

Many people think that the worst scars of the war years have healed. I don't. Vietnam has left us with a heritage rich in possibilities for class warfare, and I would like to start telling about it with this story:

In the fall of 1969, I was beginning my final year in college. As the months went by, the rock on which I had unthinkingly anchored my hopes—the certainty that the war in Vietnam would be over before I could possibly fight—began to crumble. It shattered altogether on Thanksgiving

"What did You do in the Class War Daddy?" by James Fallows from *The Washington Monthly,* October, 1975. Reprinted with permission from *The Washington Monthly.* Copyright by The Washington Monthly Company, 1611 Connecticut Avenue, NW, Washington, D.C. 20009.

weekend when, while riding back to Boston from a visit with my relatives, I heard that the draft lottery had been held and my birthdate had come up number 45. I recognized for the first time that, inflexibly, I must either be drafted or consciously find a way to prevent it.

In the atmosphere of that time, each possible choice came equipped with barbs. To answer the call was unthinkable, not only because, in my heart, I was desperately afraid of being killed, but also because, among my friends, it was axiomatic that one should not be "complicit" in the immoral war effort. Draft resistance, the course chosen by a few noble heroes of the movement, meant going to prison or leaving the country. With much the same intensity with which I wanted to stay alive, I did not want those things either. What I wanted was to go to graduate school, to get married, and to enjoy those bright prospects I had been taught that life owed me.

I learned quickly enough that there was only one way to get what I wanted. A physical deferment would restore things to the happy state I had known during four undergraduate years. The barbed alternatives would be put off. By the impartial dictates of public policy I would be free to pursue the better side of life.

Like many of my friends whose numbers had come up wrong in the lottery, I set about securing my salvation. When I was not participating in anti-war rallies, I was poring over the Army's code of physical regulations. During the winter and early spring, seminars were held in the college common rooms. There, sympathetic medical students helped us search for disqualifying conditions that we, in our many years of good health, might have overlooked. Although, on the doctors' advice, I made a half-hearted try at fainting spells, my only real possibility was beating the height and weight regulations. My normal weight was close to the cut-off point for an "underweight" disqualification, and, with a diligence born of panic, I made sure I would have a margin. I was six-feet-one-inch tall at the time. On the morning of the draft physical I weighed 120 pounds.

Before sunrise that morning I rode the subway to the Cambridge city hall, where we had been told to gather for shipment to the examination at the Boston Navy Yard. The examinations were administered on a rotating basis, one or two days each month for each of the draft boards in the area. Virtually everyone who showed up on Cambridge day at the Navy Yard was a student from Harvard or MIT.

There was no mistaking the political temperament of our group. Many of my friends wore red arm bands and stop-the-war buttons. Most chanted the familiar words, "Ho, Ho, Ho Chi Minh/NLF is Gonna Win." One of the things we had learned from the draft counselors was that disruptive behavior at the examination was a worthwhile political goal, not only because it obstructed the smooth operation of the criminal war machine, but also because it might impress the examiners with our undesirable character traits. As we climbed into the buses and as they rolled toward the Navy Yard, about half of the young men brought the chants to a crescendo. The rest of us sat rigid and silent, clutching x-rays and letters from our doctors at home.

Inside the Navy Yard, we were first confronted by a young sergeant from Long Beach, a former surfer boy no older than the rest of us and seemingly unaware that he had an unusual situation on his hands. He started reading out instructions for the intelligence tests when he was hooted down. He went out to collect his lieutenant, who clearly had been through a Cambridge day before. "We've got all the time in the world," he said, and let the chanting go on for two or three minutes. "When we're finished with you, you can go, and not a minute before."

From that point on the disruption became more purposeful and individual, largely confined to those whose deferment strategies were based on anti-authoritarian psychiatric traits. Twice I saw students walk up to young orderlies—whose hands were extended to receive the required cup of urine—and throw the vial in the orderlies' faces. The orderlies looked up, initially more astonished than angry, and went back to towel themselves off. Most of the rest of us trod quietly through the paces, waiting for the moment of confrontation when the final examiner would give his verdict. I had stepped on the scales at the very beginning of the examination. Desperate at seeing the orderly write down 122 pounds, I hopped back on and made sure that he lowered it to 120. I walked in a trance through the rest of the examination, until the final meeting with the fatherly physician who ruled on marginal cases such as mine. I stood there in socks and underwear, arms wrapped around me in the chilly building. I knew as I looked at the doctor's face that he understood exactly what I was doing.

"Have you ever contemplated suicide?" he asked after he finished looking over my chart. My eyes darted up to his. "Oh, suicide—yes, I've been feeling very unstable and unreliable recently." He looked at me, staring until I returned my eyes to the ground. He wrote "unqualified" on my folder, turned on his heel, and left. I was overcome by a wave of relief, which for the first time revealed to me how great my terror had been, and by the beginning of the sense of shame which remains with me to this day.

It was, initially, a generalized shame at having gotten away with my deception, but it came into sharper focus later in the day. Even as the last of the Cambridge contingent was throwing its urine and deliberately failing its color-blindness tests, buses from the next board began to arrive. These bore the boys from Chelsea, thick, dark-haired young men, the white proles of Boston. Most of them were younger than us, since they had just left high school, and it had clearly never occurred to them that there might be a way around the draft. They walked through the examination lines like so many cattle off to slaughter. I tried to avoid noticing, but the results were inescapable. While perhaps four out of five of my friends from Harvard were being deferred, just the opposite was happening to the Chelsea boys.

We returned to Cambridge that afternoon, not in government buses but as free individuals, liberated and victorious. The talk was high-spirited, but there was something close to the surface that none of us wanted to mention. We knew now who would be killed.

As other memories of the war years have faded, it is that day in the Navy Yard that will not leave my mind. . . .

We have not, however, learned the lesson of the day at the Navy Yard, or the thousands of similar scenes all across the country through all the years of the war. Five years later, two questions have yet to be faced, let alone answered. The first is why, when so many of the bright young college men opposed the war, so few were willing to resist the draft, rather than simply evade it. The second is why all the well-educated presumably humane young men, whether they opposed the war or were thinking fondly of A-bombs on Hanoi, so willingly took advantage of this most brutal form of class discrimination—what it signifies that we let the boys from Chelsea be sent off to die.

The "we" that I refer to are the mainly-white, mainly-well-educated children of mainly-comfortable parents, who are now mainly embarked on promising careers in law, medicine, business, academics. What makes them a class is that they all avoided the draft by taking one of the thinking-man's routes to escape. These included the physical deferment, by far the smartest and least painful of all; the long technical appeals through the legal jungles of the Selective Service System; the more disingenuous resorts to conscientious objector status; and, one degree further down the scale of personal inconvenience, joining the Reserves or the National Guard.

A Veteran Remembers His Bitter Homecoming, 1981

The day I got discharged, I flew into Philadelphia Airport. I got two and a half rows of ribbons. I'm very proud. I'm a meritorious sergeant and I got an honorable discharge. How do you like that shit?

I got off the plane and I went into a bar. The only thing I knew how to do was drink. I order a shot of CC and a beer and I'm standing there with a big smile on my face. There was a guy over at a table with two kids and a woman. The kids were about my age—nineteen or twenty.

"Home on leave, are you," the guy says to me.

"Nope, just got discharged."

"You just got back from where," one of the kids says.

"Vietnam."

"How do you feel about killing all of those innocent people?" the woman asks me out of nowhere.

I didn't know what to say. The bartender got a little uptight. But, I didn't say anything. They told me when I got discharged that I was going to get this shit. But, I didn't believe them.

"Excuse me," I called the bartender over. "Could I buy them all a drink?" I felt guilty. I *did* kill. I tried to make amends somehow.

"We don't accept any drinks from killers," the girl says to me. Now I'm pissed. The bartender tells me to take it easy and goes over and chews out this girl. She says, "How does it feel being in the Army?"

From *Nam: The Vietnam War in the Words of the Men and Women Who Fought There.* Copyright © 1981 by Mark Baker. By permission of William Morrow & Co., Inc.

"He's not in the Army, he's a Marine," the bartender said.

"You bet your fucking ass, I'm a Marine."

"Oh, you going to get nasty now?" They were harassing me right in the fucking bar. I paid for my drinks, left the bartender a tip and walked out. Forgot all about it. I got in the car with my brother and his wife and I was just too happy being home to let that bother me. But now it does.

Later when we got home, my brother said, "Don't wear your uniform." What kind of shit was that? I wanted to wear the fucking thing. I had my ribbons. I was proud of what I'd done. I'm a king. That didn't hurt me then, but it hurts me now.

Todd Gitlin Recalls the New Left's Revolutionary Romanticism, 1987

As the war became more militant, so did the antiwar movement—in demands, in spirit, in tactics. Between 1965 and 1967, as American troops in Vietnam doubled and redoubled and redoubled twice more, most antiwar movers and shakers shook off their leftover faith in negotiations and endorsed immediate withdrawal. When doubters asked, "How can we get out of Vietnam?" the quick answer was: on boats. But the New Left wing, young and sick at heart at what it reasonably took to be empire flexing its muscles, moved beyond rebellion against American foreign policy. Much of the leadership, and some of the rank and file—it is hard to say exactly how many—slid into romance with the other side. To wear a button calling for "Victory to the National Liberation Front," to wave an NLF flag or shout, "Ho, Ho, Ho Chi Minh/The NLF is gonna win," meant more than believing that the NLF was the most popular force in South Vietnam, or that Vietnamese had flocked to it for compelling reasons, or that it represented the least bad practical alternative for Vietnam—all defensible propositions. It meant feeling the passion of the alignment and placing it at the heart of one's political identity. It meant finding heroes where the American super-state found villains and pointed its guns. It meant imagining comrades riding to *our* rescue.

This was *a* tendency, not the only one, not final or unopposed even in SDS [Students for a Democratic Society]. Its significance was certainly inflated by the prowar Right and by the attentions of a demagogic press. Although almost always greatly outnumbered by American flags turned to patriotic antiwar use, NLF flags seized a disproportionate share of the media spotlight at the giant antiwar marches. And so a too-uncomplicated endorsement of Third World revolutions—and revolutionary organiza-tions—built a firebreak around the New Left part of the antiwar movement, sealing it off from the underbrush sympathy of the unconvinced. Surely those NLF flags were part of the explanation for one of the stunning political facts of the decade: that as the war steadily lost popularity in the

From *The Sixties* by Todd Gitlin, pp. 261–263. Copyright © 1987 by Todd Gitlin. Used by permission of Bantam Books, a division of Bantam Doubleday Dell Publishing Group, Inc.

late Sixties, *so did the antiwar movement.* At the growing edge of the New Left, it was as if there had to be a loyalty oath for working against the war, or American dominion in general. The napalm had to be stopped for the correct reasons. Strategy-minded antiwar liberals rudely reminded us that we were forfeiting the respect of Americans who were turning against the war but were unwilling to do so at the price of their own sense of patriotism. But the hell with them! Which side were they on, anyway?

The consequence of the New Left's Third World turn—both product and impetus of our isolation—was yet more isolation. But the reporters had not invented those NLF flags out of proverbial whole cloth. Desperate for moral companionship—America having forfeited our love—a part of ourselves looked with respect, even awe, even love, on an ideal version of ourselves who we thought existed—*had* to exist—out there in the hot climates. We needed to feel that someone, somewhere in the world, was fighting the good fight and winning. Better: that the world's good guys formed a solid front. Even better: that out of the rubble, someone, somewhere, might be constructing a good society, at least one that was decent to the impoverished and colonized. If the United States was no longer humanity's beacon—and if the movement was not building a new society itself—the light had to be found outside. The melodrama of American innocence was alive and well in the anti-American left. Henry Luce [of *Time-Life*] had been deluded when he anticipated "the American Century"; we thought this was going to be the *anti*-American Century, just as pure, just as irresistible, with a different although equivalently happy ending.

And always there was the war, which we took to be the definitive moral test of America's intentions toward the vast poor and dark-skinned world. The Third Worldist movement route began in McComb, Mississippi, and led to the Mekong Delta. With the United States pulverizing and bullying small countries, it seemed the most natural thing in the world to go prospecting among them for heroes. Their resistance was so brave, their enemies so implacable, their nationalism so noble, we could take their passions, even their slogans and styles of speech, even—in fantasy—their forms of organization for our own. And so we identified with victims who were in the process of repossessing their homelands, as we were straining to overcome our own sense of homelessness. We loved them for what we took to be their struggle for independence, as we were struggling—no mere hackneyed word—for our own. We started out feeling the suffering of peasants, defending their right to rebel, and ended up taking sides with the organizations and leaders who commanded the rebellion—all the while knowing, in anguish, that guerrilla organizations usurp the freedom which rebels are willing to die for, yet also knowing, also in anguish, that without organization (even, often, the wrong organization: dictatorship in embryo) all the bravery in the world is squandered. Some of us took seriously the dreadful histories that Communist groups had imposed, and some didn't, but the New Left tendency was to agree that American occupation was so clear and present an evil—a *homegrown* evil—that the other side would have to be forgiven its crimes. Even the movement's antiutopians thought the future of "the other side," and the morality of guerrilla war, were questions to be left until later, luxuries, or, worst of all, potential weapons in the hands of the napalmers, the question for the present being simply whether the guerrillas, or the enemy nation (the two were often confused), were entitled to have any future of their own. The issue became *how we felt* more than *what would end the war.* We would settle for nothing less than a cleaning of the historical slate.

And so, increasingly, we found our exemplars and heroes in Cuba, in China, in the Third World guerrilla movements, in Mao and Frantz Fanon and Che and Debray, most of all—decisively—in Vietnam. It no longer felt sufficient—sufficiently estranged, sufficiently furious—to say no to aggressive war; we felt driven to say yes to revolt, and unless we were careful, that yes could easily be transferred onto the Marxism-Leninism which had commandeered the revolt in the interest of practicality. Apocalypse was outfitted with a bright side. If the American flag was dripping napalm, the NLF flag was clean. If the deluded make-Vietnam-safe-for-democracy barbarism of the war could be glibly equated with the deliberate slaughter of millions in Nazi gas chambers—if the American Christ turned out to look like the Antichrist—then by this cramped either-or logic the Communist Antichrist must really have been Christ. America had betrayed us; the war, Carl Oglesby movingly said in 1965, "broke my American heart." Only true-blue believers in the promise of America could have felt so anti-American. Ours was the fury of a lover spurned. But a fury so intense, left to itself, would have consumed us. "Don't you want somebody to love?" as the Jefferson Airplane sang. So we turned where romantics have traditionally turned: to the hot-blooded peoples of the subtropics and the mysterious East. The Manichaean all-or-nothing logic of the Cold War was conserved, though inverted, as if costumes from Central Wardrobe had been rotated.

A Vietnam Veteran Opposes the War, 1971

Thank you very much, Senator Fulbright, Senator Javits, Senator Symington, Senator Pell. I would like to say for the record, and also for the men behind me who are also wearing the uniform and their medals, that my sitting here is really symbolic. I am not here as John Kerry. I am here as one member of the group of 1,000 which is a small representation of a very much larger group of veterans in this country, and were it possible for all of them to sit at this table they would be here and have the same kind of testimony. . . .

I would like to talk on behalf of all those veterans and say that several months ago in Detroit we had an investigation at which over 150 honorably discharged, and many very highly decorated, veterans testified to war crimes committed in Southeast Asia. These were not isolated incidents but crimes committed on a day to day basis with the full awareness of officers at all levels of command.

It is impossible to describe to you exactly what did happen in Detroit—

the emotions in the room and the feelings of the men who were reliving their experiences in Vietnam. They relived the absolute horror of what this country, in a sense, made them do.

They told stories that at times they had personally raped, cut off ears, cut off heads, taped wires from portable telephones to human genitals and turned up the power, cut off limbs, blown up bodies, randomly shot at civilians, razed villages in fashion reminiscent of Genghis Khan, shot cattle and dogs for fun, poisoned food stocks, and generally ravaged the countryside of South Vietnam in addition to the normal ravage of war and the normal and very particular ravaging which is done by the applied bombing power of this country.

We call this investigation the Winter Soldier Investigation. The term Winter Soldier is a play on words of Thomas Paine's in 1776 when he spoke of the Sunshine Patriots and summer time soldiers who deserted at Valley Forge because the going was rough.

We who have come here to Washington have come here because we feel we have to be winter soldiers now. We could come back to this country, we could be quiet, we could hold our silence, we could not tell what went on in Vietnam, but we feel because of what threatens this country, not the reds, but the crimes which we are committing that threaten it, that we have to speak out.

I would like to talk to you a little bit about what the result is of the feelings these men carry with them after coming back from Vietnam. The country doesn't know it yet but it has created a monster, a monster in the form of millions of men who have been taught to deal and to trade in violence and who are given the chance to die for the biggest nothing in history; men who have returned with a sense of anger and a sense of betrayal which no one has yet grasped.

As a veteran and one who feels this anger I would like to talk about it. We are angry because we feel we have been used in the worst fashion by the administration of this country.

In 1970 at West Point Vice President Agnew said "some glamorize the criminal misfits of society while our best men die in Asian rice paddies to preserve the freedom which most of those misfits abuse," and this was used as a rallying point for our effort in Vietnam.

But for us, as boys in Asia whom the country was supposed to support, his statement is a terrible distortion from which we can only draw a very deep sense of revulsion, and hence the anger of some of the men who are here in Washington today. It is a distortion because we in no way consider ourselves the best men of this country; because those he calls misfits were standing up for us in a way that nobody else in this country dared to; because so many who have died would have returned to this country to join the misfits in their efforts to ask for an immediate withdrawal from South Vietnam; because so many of those best men have returned as quadriplegics and amputees—and they lie forgotten in Veterans Administration Hospitals in this country which fly the flag which so many have chosen as their own personal symbol—and we cannot consider ourselves America's best men when we are ashamed of and hated for what we were called on to do in Southeast Asia.

In our opinion, and from our experience, there is nothing in South Vietnam which could happen that realistically threatens the United States of America. And to attempt to justify the loss of one American life in Vietnam, Cambodia or Laos by linking such loss to the preservation of freedom, which those misfits supposedly abuse, is to us the height of criminal hypocrisy, and it is that kind of hypocrisy which we feel has torn this country apart.

We are probably much more angry than that, but I don't want to go into the foreign policy aspects because I am outclassed here. I know that all of you talk about every possible alternative for getting out of Vietnam. We understand that. We know you have considered the seriousness of the aspects to the utmost level and I am not going to try to dwell on that. But I want to relate to you the feeling that many of the men who have returned to this country express because we are probably angriest about all that we were told about Vietnam and about the mystical war against communism.

We found that not only was it a civil war, an effort by a people who had for years been seeking their liberation from any colonial influence whatsoever, but also we found that the Vietnamese whom we had enthusiastically molded after our own image were hard put to take up the fight against the threat we were supposedly saving them from.

We found most people didn't even know the difference between communism and democracy. They only wanted to work in rice paddies without helicopters strafing them and bombs with napalm burning their villages and tearing their country apart. They wanted everything to do with the war, particularly with this foreign presence of the United States of America, to leave them alone in peace, and they practiced the art of survival by siding with whichever military force was present at a particular time, be it Viet Cong, North Vietnamese or American.

We found also that all too often American men were dying in those rice paddies for want of support from their allies. We saw first hand how monies from American taxes were used for a corrupt dictatorial regime. We saw that many people in this country had a one-sided idea of who was kept free by our flag, and blacks provided the highest percentage of casualties. We saw Vietnam ravaged equally by American bombs and search and destroy missions, as well as by Viet Cong terrorism, and yet we listened while this country tried to blame all of the havoc on the Viet Cong.

We rationalized destroying villages in order to save them. We saw America lose her sense of morality as she accepted very coolly a My Lai and refused to give up the image of American soldiers who hand out chocolate bars and chewing gum.

We learned the meaning of free fire zones, shooting anything that moves, and we watched while America placed a cheapness on the lives of orientals.

We watched the United States falsification of body counts, in fact the glorification of body counts. We listened while month after month we were told the back of the enemy was about to break. We fought using weapons against "oriental human beings." We fought using weapons against those people which I do not believe this country would dream of using were we fighting in the European theater. We watched while men charged up hills because a general said that hill has to be taken, and after losing one platoon or two platoons they marched away to leave the hill for reoccupation by the North Vietnamese. We watched pride allow the most unimportant battles to be blown into extravaganzas, because we couldn't lose, and we couldn't retreat, and because it didn't matter how many American bodies were lost to prove that point, and so there were Hamburger Hills and Khe Sanhs and Hill 81s and Fire Base 6s, and so many others.

Now we are told that the men who fought there must watch quietly while American lives are lost so that we can exercise the incredible arrogance of Vietnamizing the Vietnamese.

Each day to facilitate the process by which the United States washes her hands of Vietnam someone has to give up his life so that the United States doesn't have to admit something that the entire world already knows, so that we can't say that we have made a mistake. Someone has to die so that President Nixon won't be, and these are his words, "the first President to lose a war."

We are asking Americans to think about that because how do you ask a man to be the last man to die in Vietnam? How do you ask a man to be the last man to die for a mistake? But we are trying to do that, and we are doing it with thousands of rationalizations, and if you read carefully the President's last speech to the people of this country, you can see that he says, and says clearly, "but the issue, gentlemen, is communism, and the question is whether or not we will leave that country to the communists or whether or not we will try to give it hope to be a free people." But the point is they are not a free people now under us. They are not a free people, and we cannot fight communism all over the world. I think we should have learned that lesson by now. . . .

We wish that a merciful God could wipe away our own memories of that service as easily as this administration has wiped away their memories of us. But all that they have done and all that they can do by this denial is to make more clear than ever our own determination to undertake one last mission—to search out and destroy the last vestige of this barbaric war, to pacify our own hearts, to conquer the hate and the fear that have driven this country these last ten years and more, so when 30 years from now our brothers go down the street without a leg, without an arm, or a face, and small boys ask why, we will be able to say "Vietnam" and not mean a desert, not a filthy obscene memory, but mean instead the place where America finally turned and where soldiers like us helped it in the turning.

Thank you.

✗ *E S S A Y S*

In the opening essay, Melvin Small of Wayne State University explores the influence of the antiwar movement on Lyndon B. Johnson and Richard M. Nixon. He contends that the protesters succeeded in capturing the attention of both presidents and in affecting their policies in Vietnam to a far greater extent than most observers have thought. The middle essay considers the evolution of the antiwar movement from the mid-1950s to the mid-1970s. In it, Charles DeBenedetti, a professor of history at the University of Toledo until his death in 1987, and Charles Chatfield, a professor of history at Wittenberg University, locate the origins of the movement in the earlier opposition of a small group of liberal protesters to atmospheric nuclear testing. The ranks of the antiwar activists expanded exponentially with the escalation of America's involvement in Vietnam after 1965. DeBenedetti and Chatfield examine the shifting composition, amazing diversity, tactical differences, and ever expanding social, political, and cultural agenda of the antiwar movement. They emphasize that, although it failed to achieve many of its stated purposes, the peace movement of the Vietnam era both challenged and changed American society in fundamental ways.

In the last essay, Christian G. Appy of the Massachusetts Institute of Technology analyzes the underlying reasons behind the negative reaction that so many returning combat veterans had toward the antiwar movement. The backgrounds, values, and life experiences of the predominantly working-class veterans diverged sharply from those of the largely middle-class peace activists, creating what Appy describes as a class gulf between the two groups. Not only did that gulf hamper mutual understanding between veterans and protesters, but it also led many veterans to view antiwar demonstrations as personal attacks.

The Impact of the Antiwar Movement

MELVIN SMALL

As I was leaving [former White House counsel] Leonard Garment's office after an interview, he asked me whether I thought antiwar dissenters had affected the decision makers. I replied that I did not know yet, as my research was incomplete. "But surely," the lawyer responded, "you must have a theory of the case."

At that time, midway through my research, I was pursuing many theories. Among the most plausible were that the movement (1) exerted pressures directly on Johnson and Nixon that contributed to their deescalation policies; (2) exerted pressures indirectly by turning the public against the war; (3) encouraged the North Vietnamese to fight on long enough to the point that Americans demanded a withdrawal from Southeast Asia; (4) influenced American political and military strategies, since Johnson and Nixon were convinced that Hanoi counted on the movement; (5) retarded

From *Johnson, Nixon, and the Doves* by Melvin Small. Copyright © 1988 by Rutgers, the State University of New Jersey. Reprinted by permission of Rutgers University Press.

the growth of general antiwar sentiment because the public perceived the protesters as unpatriotic; and (6) combinations of these theories.

Although I still cannot answer Garment's question categorically, it is clear to me now that the antiwar movement and antiwar criticism in the media and Congress had a significant impact on the Vietnam policies of both Johnson and Nixon. At two key points at least—October 1967 and October 1969—mass demonstrations affected American foreign policy. The March on the Pentagon shocked many in the Johnson administration and produced the public relations campaign that contributed to public shock after Tet. The Moratorium helped to convince Nixon that Americans would not accept the savage blows envisaged in Operation Duck Hook [a contingency plan for the massive bombing of North Vietnam's cities and blockade of its ports]. On many other occasions, involving such issues as bombing pauses, diplomatic and military initiatives, and major speeches, antiwar activities and dissent were important factors for the decision makers. Even more dramatically, the movement played a role in Lyndon Johnson's decisions not to seek a second term and to wind down the war and played a major, if latent, role in restraining Richard Nixon from reescalating. In addition, many of the Watergate crimes were related to Nixon's attempt to crush the movement. Thus, the movement played an indirect role in the first resignation of a president in American history.

The extent of the impact of the movement on decision makers cannot be gauged through an empirical approach. The most ingenious attempt, which correlated policy and opinion changes with mass demonstrations, came up with inconclusive and unconvincing findings. The historian must rely instead on traditional tools to flesh out the often impressionistic evidence that allows one to make educated guesses about policymaking.

It is never easy to determine the motivations behind any public policy. The motivations behind foreign policies are even more difficult to determine than the motivations behind domestic policies, if only because officials try to obscure the role of sordid domestic politics when they defend national security. Irrespective of the stated and attributed rationales for foreign policies, one can identify the factors that attracted the attention of the decision makers as they considered their options. Archival and published records reveal the external events that worried them enough to be taken into account as they decided what and when to bomb in Vietnam, how many soldiers to call up or send home, and what sorts of diplomatic initiatives to undertake. Further, one can assess the importance of the antiwar movement to Washington by the energies expended in monitoring and suppressing its activities. If, as the key figures often said, the movement had no impact on their foreign policies, why was it that they spent so much of their time and attention on it?

Even those who downplay the importance of the movement concede that public opinion was a crucial variable in the construction of Vietnam policies. It is in their links to public opinion that the movement and antiwar critics exercised their most profound influence on those policies. To be sure, throughout the terms of both presidents, public opinion polls revealed considerable support for whatever the military did in Vietnam. On the other hand, in both administrations, support for escalation tended to decrease as the war dragged on and as first Johnson and then Nixon proved incapable of terminating it with dispatch.

Antiwar activities helped convince more and more Americans to oppose the war, or at least begin to feel uncomfortable about the nation's involvement in Vietnam. At times, some of their activities, as framed by sensation-seeking media, may have produced a patriotic backlash. Overall, however, the movement eroded support for Johnson and Nixon, especially among college students at the best universities, their parents, and members of the attentive and informed public. Some groups of people in the United States count for more than others. The loss of Yale and the *New York Times* to Johnson and even Nixon meant more than the retention of support from state colleges in Texas and the Scripps-Howard chain of newspapers. Through their constant and often publicized attacks, experts in the movement, the media, and on the campuses helped to destroy the knee-jerk notion that "they in Washington know." This was a very important development. For the first time since 1945, major reference figures in the bipartisan establishment began to speak out against an American cold war policy and led many citizens to question the judgment and wisdom of their presidents.

From the start, it was clear that the longer the war went on, the more likely Americans would tire of their increasingly costly involvement. If the United States could not win, in the absence of a strong initial and sustained commitment to wait out the patient and dedicated enemy in Vietnam, pressures for withdrawal had to increase over time. Dean Rusk, who sees opposition rising at home because of Tet and other policy failures, irrespective of previous criticism from the antiwar movement, emphasizes this approach.

Yet that previous criticism had to be important for several reasons. First, movement activities and elite opposition in the media helped to keep the war "on the front burner" from 1965 through 1971. With the war an object of almost constant attention, presidents found it difficult to pursue military policies that the public would find objectionable. In addition, the critics presented arguments and information that provided a framework for those who did not know how to articulate their general opposition to what was becoming an endless war. The existence of any opposition helped to reinforce other opposition. Senator [Wayne] Morse's lonely stand against the war in 1964 encouraged some citizens in their opposition, as did Senator [J. William] Fulbright's hearings in early 1966, which had been encouraged by the rising opposition on elite campuses during the previous year. That opposition was legitimized to some degree when congressmen read its letters and petitions into the *Congressional Record*.

The movement's impact on the public and on the administration was enhanced by the way the antiwar argument was presented. As one critic of the movement has argued, those who opposed the war stole the moral issue from the administration early on. That issue, simplistic and naive from a

Realpolitik perspective, was understood more easily than the incompetently presented limited war argument. The moral argument, with the bombing and destruction of peasant society as its cornerstone, was echoed in Western Europe as well as in neutral nations. As the war continued, the argument received "disproportionate media attention," according to Walt Rostow.

The antiwar movement plus the course of events affected the intellectual and opinion-making community, which in turn encouraged the activists and weakened the administration. Much of the nation's intellectual elite was associated with the prestigious universities where mass protests began and were nurtured. Both Johnson and Nixon blamed pied-piper professors on those campuses, more than students, for their problems there.

Whether their animosity was properly targeted, Johnson and Nixon should have expected the criticism from those opinion leaders. Irving Kristol contends that "no modern nation ever constructed a foreign policy acceptable to its intellectuals." Perhaps, but American intellectuals were not especially dovish in 1964 and 1965. By 1970, however, according to one survey, intellectuals were overwhelmingly antiwar, with more than two-thirds changing their views during the preceding years. Their favorite journals, the *New York Times,* the *New Yorker,* and the *New York Review of Books,* influenced them, and the journals, in turn, were influenced by many of the intellectuals themselves.

The alienation of the American intellectual elite did not affect the policymakers directly, in part because there was little contact between that elite and the Oval Office. That was to be expected. At the same time, the desertion of the intellectuals had an indirect impact on government officials. In a trickle-down effect, Democratic party leaders, as well as those members of the public who took their lead from favorite writers and professors, were influenced by the desertion from the cold war foreign policy consensus of many liberal intellectuals. "Trickle down" is even too vague a term to describe the relationship between intellectual discontent and the rise of the [Robert] Kennedy opposition faction within the party after 1965.

Kristol may have been correct about intellectuals generally disapproving of a nation's foreign policy, especially a policy that appears to be amoral or immoral, but it is the extent of that disapproval and the passion with which it was held that is important on the Vietnam issue. It is difficult for a democracy to operate effectively in the international sphere without the support of its intellectual leadership.

It is also clear that the disaffection of intellectuals and elite college students affected establishment types outside of government who feared for the future of their country. Respected leaders such as Dean Acheson and Clark Clifford, who worried about the establishment in the next generation, ultimately urged the administration to cut its losses before the country fell apart.

Antiwar protests, among others, in a period that witnessed unprecedented rowdy demonstrations, took a physical and emotional toll on the occupants of the White House. Neither Johnson nor Nixon could tolerate criticism, even when they expected it from the media or from liberals. Both were subjected to the most extensive and abusive criticism of any twentieth century president. On occasion, they and their advisers went to great lengths to avoid the demonstrators, who nevertheless managed to appear almost every time the presidents stepped out of the White House. Johnson, in particular, was irritated by the incessant public manifestations of displeasure with his policies and that irritation may have been a background variable in his decision to leave Washington for the peace of his ranch.

Both Johnson and Nixon developed offensives against their critics, especially in the movement, which included the mobilization of the CIA and FBI to monitor and harass them. Both claimed that such activities were not a product of their own concern with demonstrations but their fear that Hanoi would misinterpret them. Further, both believed that some, if not most, of the antiwar movement was foreign inspired and financed; the government had to devote considerable energies to defend the country against subversion.

On the latter charge, they were mistaken. The intelligence agencies concluded in report after report that foreign influences in the antiwar movement were marginal. On the other hand, their major contention that the movement and all of its manifestations encouraged Hanoi is no doubt true. The key question, and an imponderable one at that, is whether that encouragement prolonged the war.

Without a strong antiwar movement that limited the administration's abilities to pursue a tougher military policy, goes the prolongation argument, the North Vietnamese would have accepted a half a loaf and the war would have ended much sooner. The antiwar movement here is linked to the general development of antiwar attitudes among the public.

The contest for the public's support between the government and its opponents was an important element in the making of Vietnam policy. For example, when Richard Nixon committed Washington to a Vietnamization program, domestic opinion was one "crucial variable." Vietnamization would convince the public that the war was not endless; the American commitment would decrease gradually. Domestic support would be maintained that would convince the North Vietnamese not to count on the American people to force Nixon's negotiating hand. There was a "logical flaw" in this position. If Vietnamization cooled dovish fervor in the United States, it also revealed the light at the end of the tunnel for Hanoi. Why negotiate when the last American soldier would depart Vietnam in the foreseeable future?

Moreover, the prolongation-of-the-war argument deemphasizes the commitment of Hanoi to fight on virtually forever for its goal of an independent communist Vietnam. Further, one of the major reasons Johnson and Nixon did not use tougher tactics was their fear that the Russians and Chinese might be compelled to intervene to rescue their socialist ally.

The ability to employ tougher military tactics was not just crippled by an alert antiwar movement. It is likely that the population in general, with or without the leadership of antiwar critics, would not have countenanced the bombing of the dikes in the North or the use or threatened use of tactical nuclear weapons. Americans would not have needed the movement to express their strong displeasure over the employment of such drastic means in a limited war. Here, the administrations caused their own problems. By never explaining in a convincing fashion why the war was so important, Johnson and Nixon found it impossible to escalate in a manner that would only be justified in a full-scale war vital to America's very survival. Johnson kept a low theoretical profile in the years from 1965 through 1967, in part to avoid encouraging the growth of the antiwar movement. We have come full circle. Although only strong presidential leadership and a declaration of national emergency would have given the presidents the backing to employ tougher tactics, one of the reasons they eschewed that approach was the fear of arousing the antiwar movement.

It is true that once Nixon talked and acted tougher in 1972, the communists accepted less than the whole loaf at the bargaining table. Whether that would have been the case before détente neutralized the Soviet Union, as well as before the destruction and the disbanding of the antiwar movement, is a difficult question.

Irrespective of the validity of the argument that the movement prolonged the war by encouraging Hanoi, Johnson and Nixon *believed* that the North Vietnamese counted on American opinion, influenced by the movement, as one of its main allies. Both administrations considered this alleged factor as they constructed their political and military strategies. Here, then, is irrefutable evidence of the impact of the movement on policymaking during the war, if only indirect impact.

Some critics ignore the movement and opinion and point to the media, where dissenters and dissenting commentators turned the nation around on the war. Unfair to both Johnson and Nixon, the media allegedly created the movement and undermined both administrations. George Christian thinks the press was lost by 1967. Hubert Humphrey saw the media in 1968, the crucial year of decision, as "viscerally and intellectually" anti-Johnson. In a similar vein, Edith Efron described television network news on Vietnam in the fall of 1969 as reflecting an antiadministration bias. Finally, the media were undoubtedly important in the popular understanding of Tet.

Former antiwar leader and sociologist Todd Gitlin, who does not agree with such criticism, nevertheless points out that movement ideas and activities were publicized by the media. One of his old colleagues, David Dellinger, has written that the movement had three explicit targets—the government, the public, and the activists themselves. Especially in the early days, when the public and government were not listening, media attention provided gratification for the foot soldiers who continued to turn out for the demonstrations. As the movement picked up steam, the media helped to legitimize dissent.

For the most part, however, experts do not agree with the theory of an "oppositional" media. In a study comparable to but more sophisticated than Efron's, Daniel Hallin concluded that at least as far as the *New York Times* and television news were concerned, both administrations received more than a fair break from the media. Another expert, Herbert Gans, demonstrated how, early in the war, Lyndon Johnson dominated the airwaves. Even when critical reports came in from the field through 1967, editors in New York and elsewhere either did not print them or toned them down.

Presidents' views dominate the media until major reference figures from the establishment begin to disagree with them and appear in such numbers that the media are forced to cover their criticism. Both Johnson and Nixon began with overwhelming support in the media, which declined over time. Their slowly developing criticism was legitimate and generally without malice. The presidents' failing and controversial policies, as well as their own growing antagonism to the media, led to an entirely understandable decrease in media support. Johnson, for example, blamed the media for creating the credibility gap, when in fact it was his invention.

Even the Tet argument used by the media critics can be turned around to support the notion that the press and television were more than fair to Johnson. One reason for widespread public concern over Tet was the failure of the media to prepare the nation for such an event because it accepted so uncritically the light-at-the-end-of-the-tunnel pronouncements from Washington.

The relationships between the media, the movement, public opinion, and foreign policy are complicated. They are far too complicated to blame the media for the decline of support over time for the Johnson and Nixon policies.

The antiwar movement succeeded in capturing the attention of Johnson and Nixon and affecting their policies in Vietnam. One of the important lessons one can learn from studies such as this is that government officials do not always behave the way they should according to the neat academic models of opinion formation and policymaking. Johnson and Nixon simply did not behave rationally on many occasions when they confronted media criticism and antiwar demonstrations. Surprisingly thin-skinned for professional politicians, they overreacted to criticism in unpredictable and unstructured manners. One never knew when a few demonstrators in front of the White House, or a speech on a college campus, or an editorial in the *Washington Post* might set off one or the other, even at times when they enjoyed the support of the vast majority of their constituents.

It might well be that there is less to learn here than one might suspect. Johnson and Nixon were unusual residents of the Oval Office. Both were among the most volatile, unstable, and maybe even pathological of recent presidents. Comparing their behavior and personalities to those of Roosevelt, Truman, Eisenhower, Kennedy, Ford, Carter, and Reagan, one must be leery about generalizing from Johnson and Nixon to all presidents.

Yet, as I was told time and again by such experienced presidential counselors and observers as Bryce Harlow, George Reedy, and Jack Valenti, much of the time, *all* presidents are just like everyone else. They react to criticism and challenges, even from a minority of their constituents, quite often from the gut and not from the brain. What this means is that those who exercise their rights as citizens to gather, protest, and petition in

494   *Major Problems in the History of the Vietnam War*

comparatively small numbers have more of an impact on their leaders than one would expect. Such a conclusion might help to sustain others who question present and future foreign policies.

The Antiwar Movement and American Society

CHARLES DEBENEDETTI AND CHARLES CHATFIELD

A darkening cloud of war gathered almost imperceptibly in the decade after 1955, and the storm broke before its magnitude was recognized. Its center was in Indochina, but it engulfed America. For ten years more it churned across the nation, charging every internal conflict with high tension and obscuring the issues which defined national identity. In the roiling darkness a Catholic priest wrote from hiding that America was "hard to find."

The priest was part of the antiwar movement, an amorphous and pervasive social current that connected the war in Vietnam to domestic struggles. The movement was both a cultural and a political phenomenon, and in that duality lay its central paradox: its cultural power compromised its political effectiveness. It gave cultural dissonance a political import more surely than it affected public policy. Nonetheless, it was part of the political process, for it was locked in a struggle with the government over how the people would define their values, institutions, and destiny.

. . . As a whole more antiwar than peace-seeking, [this] movement was a loose alignment of elements which changed in style, tactics, and thrust during the era. It altered partly in response to political and international circumstances and partly in relation to the personal ethos of its participants as they wrestled with the meaning of the war and the society.

The movement involved only a few dozen organizations in 1960, over twelve hundred a decade later. Most of them were local and ephemeral. Numbers never were an accurate index of the antiwar movement, either in organizations or in demonstrations. Although antiwar dissent gained continuity from a core of activists, insofar as it was organized at all, its components were not primarily membership organizations. There never was a single directing agency, common leadership, or ideology. Only at a few points was there even a formal coalition, and then it was but partial. Highly eclectic, protesters employed tactics ranging from letter writing to bombings, from prayer vigils to self-immolations. Improvisational, they experimented with organized lobbying, electoral politics, mass demonstrations, teach-ins, vigils, and nonviolent civil disobedience. The measure of the movement was its influence, not the number of its adherents. Probably the very diversity of dissent increased its outreach, for its leadership permeated the society from the most elite and conventional to the most antisocial elements.

From Charles DeBenedetti and Charles Chatfield *An American Ordeal: The Antiwar Movement of the Vietnam Era.* (Syracuse: Syracuse University Press, 1990), pp. 1–5, 388–99, 401–405, 408. By permission of the publisher.

The American antiwar movement was at once a product of history and a process that made history. As a process, the movement was a highly charged force for change that galvanized some American citizens to challenge their government's nuclear weapons testing and then its policy in Southeast Asia. As a product, the movement was the latest expression of a long tradition of citizen peace activism that was organized around issues such as international disarmament and opposition to great-power interventionism. The Vietnam War was the catalyst for changes in peace advocacy, as well as in the nation, but in order to appreciate this fact it is necessary to locate the movement's prewar sources and to follow its course beyond the formal termination of war in 1973. Otherwise, we are left with only the stereotypes formed in the period of most intense conflict—images that obscure the continuity between seeking peace and confronting war.

In 1955 the movement appeared as a fresh form of peace advocacy familiar in American history. Seizing on the perceived threat from nuclear testing in order to advocate alternatives to Cold War confrontation, a coalition of liberal internationalists and radical pacifists developed new organizations and tactics. By the time of the nuclear test-ban treaty of 1963, the coalition had been influenced also by a revitalized radicalism, identified in the North with the New Left and in the South with civil rights activists. By then it had acquired the internal differences and the distinctive ethos which would characterize opposition to war in Indochina.

With the government's escalation of military involvement in Vietnam in the first half of the 1960s, the coalition was gradually transformed into an antiwar movement. It defined the issues on which policy would be debated for a decade. It provided a focus for citizens who felt uneasy about the war, and it attracted new constituencies of discontent which strengthened the movement's left-wing cast. When President Lyndon Johnson definitively committed the nation to war in 1965, he faced a loosely organized opposition ready to contest him for the support of the nation's political center.

As the war expanded in scope, intensity, and cost over the next two years, antiwar dissidents improvised a wide range of actions which forced the war issue into the public arena, generated organized opposition to intervention, pressed the administration to make ever-larger claims for the war, and fragmented the movement itself. Protest moved into the streets. Early in 1968 the ferocity of the communist Tet offensive triggered a change of war strategy and imposed limits on U.S. military commitment. In the midst of mounting domestic disorder, antiwar liberals pressed the war issue in electoral politics; but their chosen vehicles, the McCarthy and Kennedy campaigns, collapsed and left them on the political margin. About the same time, radicalism as a driving force of organized protest began to wane, and militant extremism spun off on the periphery.

The antiwar movement declined early in the Nixon presidency, but it regrouped to mount massive demonstrations in the fall of 1969. Exhausted and fragmented, though, it was unable to capture or mobilize the widespread public protest evoked by the administration's invasion of Cambodia the following spring. The politics of confrontation seemed to have played out, despite a brief resurgence in the spring of 1971. Although war dissenters still challenged government policy, they increasingly worked within established political institutions responding to war-weariness among the public.

Gradually leadership returned to political liberals until, with the 1972 presidential campaign of George McGovern, the war issue was brought fully within the political system. By the end of the year, Congress itself appeared ready to confront the Nixon administration. That contest was preempted by the Paris peace accord of January 1973, but shortly afterward the issue of presidential authority emerged as the Watergate syndrome. Antiwar dissidents linked the constitutional issue to the war, first on behalf of withdrawal from military engagement and, after the peace agreement, in opposition to a widening air war over Indochina and continued aid to the regime in Saigon.

The shifts in the emphasis and tactics of antiwar protest were largely a result of its intersection with political institutions. In particular, stridency and militancy in protest were related to the obduracy of the Johnson and Nixon administrations: confrontation was a product of the interaction of committed dissent and an unresponsive government. Insofar as the political system accommodated criticism in electoral and congressional politics, protest tended to flow within established channels.

Rapid transformations in organized protest were also a product of its relationship to American society. Like the larger culture of which it was a part, the antiwar movement of 1955–1975 was a diverse and dynamic enterprise that changed dramatically in its composition, assumptions, and purposes. Especially in the 1960s the United States experienced sharp challenges to important cultural norms—traditional religious beliefs, scientific objectivity, white and male dominance, adult standards of behavior, the assumption that poverty was a normal part of society, the notion of a Cold War mission, and the liberalism of consensus. As each of these became organized, it added to a plethora of social movements which were related to one another only tenuously, if at all. The demand to end the war and the concomitant challenge to established authority aligned several of these dissident elements.

On the one hand, the vision of a broad coalition for social change provided the antiwar movement with an incisive, radical cutting edge. Leading activists believed that national values and institutions had been distorted by a Cold War emphasis on maintaining order by force, which in turn was repressing pressures for social justice, whether in the Third World or in the United States. It was in this sense that the antiwar movement was related to other social and cultural protests of the decade. On the other hand, the eclecticism of antiwar protest made it especially vulnerable to fragmentation. Its leaders disagreed over whether to pursue a single-minded challenge to war or to develop a broad coalition for social change. They were divided by the eddies of controversy carried in the cultural currents that fed into the antiwar movement. They were burdened by stereotypes grounded in the reality of their uneasy association with radicals and counterculture figures, fixed in popular mythology by the media, and exploited by the supporters of administration policy. Thus, the organized movement developed a dual identity that was the source of its strength as well as its weakness. As a cultural force it vibrated with resilience and adaptability, energizing people with ideas, criticisms, political alternatives, and values. As a political force it remained embarrassingly weak, and this contributed to its disillusionment and despair. In spite of its appeal among church people, organized women, traditional peace workers, intellectuals, students, and assorted leftists, it remained largely on the political periphery. Movement leaders helped to rally a shattering cultural rebellion that altered the course of American politics and foreign policy; but the society for which many of them yearned remained "hard to find."

Fundamentally, the war was always about America. From start to finish in the arguments over intervention, the welfare of the Vietnamese people was secondary. Pro-war citizens maintained that the war was necessary to contain Asian communism far from America's shores. Policymakers referred to Vietnam as a "showcase" of nation building, a "proving ground" of successful counterinsurgency, or a "test" of America's will to prevail in the greater Cold War. Although critics of the war, on the other hand, argued that intervention thwarted the emergence of an independent Third World and many of them showed a poignant concern for the people of Indochina, even they argued mainly that the war effort hurt the United States. Antiwar activists habitually charged that the war weakened prospects for Soviet-American détente, destabilized the international order, smeared the nation's image as a positive force, wasted chances for domestic reform, and subverted national values and institutions. The war was in Indochina, but the ordeal for the antiwar movement and the citizens it sought to mobilize was in and over America. . . .

Bernard Fall once observed that there were many wars in Vietnam—multiple dimensions to the conflict. Similarly, there were many antiwar movements in America. Protest had many masks, so different that some observers contended that there was no such thing as an antiwar movement. William Stringfellow doubted its existence in 1969, and he opposed the war. Shortly after the November Mobilization, he wrote in *Christianity and Crisis* that "the war protests of the past few years have been spasmodic, haphazard, frustrated, fatigued and incoherent." They were all of that. Antiwar activists did not establish a single directing organization, coordinated leadership, or ideology. They drew on varied constituencies. They offered contradictory critiques of American society and foreign policy. They argued among themselves almost as bitterly as they excoriated those they held responsible for the war. As Stringfellow knew, however, his observation was a reflection of the character of the peace and antiwar movement rather than a denial of its existence.

There was after 1955, in fact, a definable body of Americans who sought new initiatives in disarmament and the international order that would reverse the nuclear arms race and reduce Soviet-American tensions. Drawing on established peace societies such as the American Friends Service Committee, the Fellowship of Reconciliation, the Women's International League for Peace and Freedom, and the War Resisters League, peace advocates added specialized campaigns such as SANE [National Committee for Sane Nuclear Policy] and CNVA [Committee for Non-Violent Action] (and also Women Strike for Peace and the Student Peace Union), whose primary achievement was to draw attention to the issue of atmospheric nuclear testing. After 1965 many of these same people sought to reverse Washington's military involvement in Vietnam. Few foreign policy dissidents dared hope at the outset to assemble a massive campaign against intervention. They were joined nonetheless by countless citizens who improvised an identifiable antiwar movement of disparate groups, leaders, followers, and tendencies. It was more assembled than it was organized. It functioned as a movement of movements.

Its constituent organizations were national, regional, and local, with only loose connections among the levels or the groups. Many of them were nuclei of people within professional or civic bodies. Most were ephemeral, leaving only traces of their activity. The size of the movement is very difficult to estimate, since only a few national organizations had definable memberships. Their combined known membership probably was between forty and eighty thousand people in 1962 and increased to three or four hundred thousand a decade later. Most of that growth came from the addition of new organizations such as Vietnam Veterans Against the War, Clergy and Laity Concerned [CALC], and Another Mother for Peace [AMP]. The figure does not include coalitions, covert groups such as the Resistance, or political ones like the Socialist Workers Party. Moreover, the total number includes groups as different as CALC and AMP: the former was a network for specific projects, the latter a largely nominal grouping. The memberships themselves were not particularly significant (although changes in any definable group were instructive) because dissent grew at mostly local levels, often spontaneously, and faded there. In this broad sense, probably several million citizens were involved in antiwar activity. The assembling of increasingly large crowds through 1969 was impressive, but even so, the impact of public demonstrations depended more on media coverage than on mere numbers. Most important, especially after 1971, dissatisfaction with war policy was multiplied and channeled through a labyrinth of citizen networks.

Liberals and leftists, men and women, blacks and whites, students and established intellectuals, clergy and laity: countless citizens passed in and out of the antiwar movement. Its core was indelibly middle class and well educated. It was a typically American reform effort—a voluntary crusade attracting adherents and impelling them to act out of a felt personal responsibility for social wrongs. The tendency to define political obligation in terms of personal morality, and the assumed value of action per se, contributed to the movement's persisting problems with poor organization, lack of discipline, and intermittent participation. It proved very difficult to mount sustained political pressure, and the temptation to attribute frustration in this regard to the system itself or to the government only exacerbated a sense of moral isolation from society. On the other hand, this same personal and moral quality gave the movement the fluidity, adaptability, and irrepressibility that enabled it to survive and metamorphose in a struggle that none of the dissidents had anticipated.

Building on small, established groups, the resurgent peace movement of 1955–1963 was essentially a form of public advocacy. It focused attention on atmospheric testing, and it organized through a liberal coalition. Political liberals in SANE, for instance, sponsored conferences, developed newspaper advertisements, popularized expert testimony, and organized letter-writing campaigns. Even the radical pacifists in the CNVA applied non-violent direct action mainly for its symbolic value in dramatizing the nuclear arms issue. The great majority of actions were low-key and informational, although gradually the movement became more aggressive and turned to mass demonstrations, prayer vigils, and nonviolent civil disobedience. Then, with the signing of the 1963 test-ban treaty, the coalition began to dissolve.

By that time, intensified civil rights campaigns, heightened sensibility to the Third World, and the rise of a new and youthful left began to shift the weight of elements in the peace movement, motivating activists to put themselves on the line for their beliefs. Some peace advocates joined early critics among the articulate elite to criticize U.S. intervention in Vietnam, but the movement did not undergo a significant change until 1965. Then the sudden escalation of military involvement in Vietnam precipitated an abrupt change in focus from the generalized Cold War to the specific conflict. As American intervention assumed massive proportions, the peace movement rapidly evolved an antiwar thrust and offered leverage to the gathering dissent.

The tactics of the movement changed, but not suddenly. At the outset they represented an extension of the antinuclear campaign, emphasizing persuasion (as in teach-ins) and political pressure. Between 1965 and 1967 protest remained largely respectful, its tactics designed to build an antiwar consensus. Facing hostile prowar majorities, most activists talked, taught, and marched without disruption. A few burned their draft cards—or, in extreme cases, themselves—in symbolic demonstrations of their willingness to atone for their country's alleged wrongdoing.

Almost from the outset, however, there was a sharp note of disillusionment with Lyndon Johnson, who had campaigned against Goldwater on a peace platform and had identified himself with the social programs of the Great Society. Congressional reluctance to confront the issues in Vietnam and evidence of official dissimulation served to heighten the frustration. In the face of a war escalating indefinitely and an apparently unresponsive political system, dissidents challenged the credibility and implacability of the government. The tone of protest became sharper, even theatrical, like that of the concurrent civil rights and black power movements. The emphasis of dissident strategy turned from an attempt to influence key policy-shapers to the mobilizing of massive demonstrations.

By 1967 the weight and initiative in the antiwar movement had shifted to the left. It was attracted there by the social turbulence that now swirled around the war issue, and it was driven there by the apparent inflexibility of national policy. By the fall of 1968, opponents of the war were afflicted with despair (encouraged by political responses in the spring, they felt disillusioned in the summer). Anguish deepened through the next two years. There seemed to be no recourse, nothing that had not been tried. The dissenting judgment on the war appeared to have been vindicated—Vietnamization was a response to popular disaffection—and yet the devastation continued, even expanded, with no indication that the United States was about to abandon its original political objectives. Distorted judgment in that period was not limited to antiwar activists; it was a national malaise.

Between 1967 and 1971 dissidents aligned sporadically in attempts to reverse U.S. military policy in Vietnam, but they could not agree on what that implied. Their purpose was clear; their direction was not. The war and the protest against it alike became tokens of what was wrong in America. Public policy debate was freighted with symbolism, and rising disaffection was diffused. The antiwar movement reacted, expanded, or contracted in intensity as U.S. policy in Indochina varied. It appeared to abandon its function as an advocate to alternative policy and emerged in an adversarial role.

There was a self-conscious shift "from protest to resistance," although it was never as aggressive as it was portrayed. The overwhelming majority of antiwar actions remained peaceable and restrained. Dissidents mainly petitioned, prayed, marched, picketed, published, and worked through the political system. Quite plainly, however, a notable minority of activists escalated their protest in nonviolent sit-ins, occupation of draft boards and ROTC installations, and organized draft resistance. The number of draft-card burnings rose to a few thousand, and there were a few dozen recorded instances of flag-burning. Nonetheless, tactics remained in general both nonviolent and symbolic.

With the country trapped between a racial crisis at home and military failure abroad, a relatively small number of extremists resorted to physical attacks on the institutions and representatives of domestic authority. Infatuated with the romantic anarchism of yippies or the rebel mystique of the Weathermen, some militants called for mass disorder and street actions, and a few argued for outright violence. Whenever possible, they attached themselves to the periphery of the antiwar movement. Such was the air of moral crisis that a few radical pacifists courted confrontation on the assumption that it could be kept nonviolent. To a surprising degree it was, but the exceptions made the media—notably in Chicago in 1968 and at the MayDays of 1971. Although the great majority of antiwar activists condemned violence and continued to pray and petition, a very small number of extremists sought to "bring the war home," detonating bombs, attacking police, and committing vandalism. The pseudorevolutionary fantasy played itself out, but not before it had been attached to the public image of the antiwar movement.

The revolutionary rhetoric of radical leftists, the actions of militant

extremists, a counterculture fringe, nonviolent civil disobedience, and organized draft resistance: protesting the war increasingly meant resisting
authority, and it was portrayed as being more confrontational than it actually was. In particular, the Nixon White House deliberately heightened and
exploited confrontation. The administration's carefully crafted strategy of
attacking critics while withdrawing troops, combined with the exhaustion
of the radical left—and the nation—seemed to brake the momentum of
opposition. Countless dissidents drifted off into other reform endeavors or
became passive. Ironically, the dispersal of street dissidence facilitated
antiwar efforts within Congress and the Democratic party, even though it
left many protesters with a sense of failure.

The movement never regarded itself as exclusively adversarial, of
course. The ADA, SANE, and Allard Lowenstein's campaign to dump
Johnson functioned within the political system. Even as confrontation
reached its apogee in the streets of Chicago in 1968, critics within the
Democratic convention hall challenged the war through conventional
strategies of persuasion and electoral politics. Nixon's winning campaign
that year was predicated on his achieving peace, and Humphrey's loss
intensified efforts to reform the Democratic party. The Moratorium of the
following year was an essentially liberal strategy. By that time a broad
grouping of antiwar liberals and elite policy critics was in a position to
bring the movement more fully into the political mainstream. It was not
only that radicalism had disintegrated; the political system had become
more responsive.

This could be seen throughout the country, where independent local
groups were organized on political lines. They were not tabulated in the
declining memberships that so distressed national peace organizations.
Rather, they reflected pervasive discontent with the war. Gradually, this
was directed into congressional politics. Through the McGovern candidacy
it was normalized in the Democratic party. With the demand for withdrawal
by a specific date, it was pursued in the legislature. In 1973 activists on the
national level developed a systematic lobbying effort around the issue of
military assistance for Saigon. They helped to link war-related corruption
and arbitrary policies such as the bombing of Cambodia to the issue of
presidential unaccountability, which reached its nadir in the Watergate
scandal. So enmeshed with other national issues was the war, and so integrated with other advocacy groups were Vietnam dissidents, that the antiwar movement became all but invisible.

These shifts in composition and approach were matters of emphasis.
The personalized and heterogeneous peace and antiwar movements of
1955–1975 encompassed a wide range of tactics, from polite letter-writing
to terrorist bombings, from quiet prayer vigils to horrific self-immolations,
from reasoned analysis to fiery rhetoric. Lacking any central direction or
agreed-upon strategy, the choice of action was determined mostly by personal impulses; but it was strongly influenced by the political conduct of
the war and the degree to which the political system itself accommodated
protest.

Antiwar activists contributed to the growth of public disaffection with the war and helped to give it focus, but they were unable to harness it. At least prior to the 1973 peace accord, they did not establish themselves as a positive reference point for the many politicians and millions of people whose early support of the war turned into resentful neutrality. The opportunity certainly seemed to be there. According to public opinion polls, domestic opposition to Washington's Vietnam policies consistently spread through parts of American society. On the one hand, there existed a small but vibrant antiwar movement, extremely articulate and politically active. On the other hand, there was a much larger body of people (some analysts estimated that it was sixty times the organized antiwar movement) who opposed U.S. military engagement but refused to make their dissent public.

The two groups differed with respect to class and culture. Organized opposition to the war came mainly from middle-class, college-educated whites, materially comfortable and motivated by largely moral considerations. Politically liberal and sympathetic to social justice causes, antiwar activists were also tolerant of changes in popular culture, sexual mores, and race relations. In contrast, the great majority of Americans favoring disengagement from Vietnam were a people apart. According to public opinion analysts, the greatest number of them were in the lower economic class, often women and blacks, with grade-school educations and low-prestige jobs. Politically inarticulate and generally isolationist, these disaffected citizens opposed the war as a waste of men and money and had little confidence in the democratic sensibilities of the Vietnamese people, North or South. Suspicious of most authority, they seemed ambivalent in the face of cultural change, but they made no secret of their dislike for active protesters and street demonstrators.

The connection with civil rights groups was a special case. It antedated and stimulated the organized antiwar movement. In the early 1960s, SNCC [Student Nonviolent Coordinating Committee] inspired radical activists; but it was ruptured by an internal crisis, and the emphasis on black power precluded any real cooperation with that organization. Martin Luther King, Jr., briefly became a cementing force in the movement, but the connection was very much weakened by his assassination. In any case, civil rights groups had political problems and agendas of their own.

Middle-class antiwar activists made some lackluster attempts to rally working-class Americans to their side. Although they repeatedly tried to organize around the idea of a coalition of the disaffected, radical sectarianism and self-interest invariably proved to be disruptive, and in any case cooperation was limited to specific antiwar actions. Some of the SDS militants who, like Tom Hayden, migrated into northern urban ghettoes in a sincere attempt to facilitate community organization carried with them opposition to the war. Some radical pacifists marched into marginal neighborhoods to mobilize people there against exploitation and war. The Socialist Workers party worked hardest to draw supporters from the trade unions into demonstrations, and with some success. For the most part, however, there were few serious attempts to convert lower-class dissent into an active antiwar force. Although radicals tended to romanticize blacks and poor whites, for the most part working-class Americans were regarded as inert and inaccessible.

Potential supporters of the antiwar movement may have been alienated by qualities they associated with militant radicals who, although not representative, got much media exposure: a kind of romantic egoism, political indiscipline, an orientation toward action regardless of consequences, argumentative sectarianism, and disdain for venerated national symbols. The movement was most visible between 1967 and 1971 when it was least conventional and, therefore, least acceptable to many Americans. Antiwar activists took to the streets in impressive numbers then. They even penetrated government offices and corporate boardrooms, but they failed to mobilize the American laboring class or even the middle class.

According to contemporary opinion analysts, most people responded to the Vietnam War as they did to other foreign policy developments—not out of a knowledge of the situation, but rather in response to cues issued by respected reference groups. Normally, political guidance is provided by political parties or religious and social affiliations. During the war years, however, the country's traditional reference groups divided, the leadership of consensual policy was fragmented, and public opinion on the war issue became ambivalent. Theoretically, the breakup of traditional reference groups should have provided antiwar activists with an extraordinary opportunity to establish their own movement as a respected opinion-shaping base, but its organizational style and cultural image appear to have fixed it in popular thought as a deviant force on the margin of national life. Antiwar tactics specifically addressed the political mainstream after 1971, but they were perforce less visible and could not reshape the popular mythology surrounding war-related activism. In various ways, organized protest was affected by the pervasive discontent on which it fed.

By 1973 there was general consensus among activists that earlier, radical attempts to form coalitions around domestic issues had been a serious distraction. The liberal wing of the movement was dominant then, among pacifists as well as in its traditional bastions such as SANE and Americans for Democratic Action. These activists were inclined to concentrate on their basic middle-class constituency, to work through the established political system, and to regard earlier anxiety about their class orientation as another diversion from the peace effort. They concluded that the movement had left itself vulnerable in other ways as well, notably its stereotyped association with so-called anti-Americanism and the counterculture.

Abuse of revered national symbols did accompany opposition to the war, although it occurred mainly on the periphery of organized activity and was misunderstood. It took forms such as street theater, unfurling Vietcong flags, spilling blood on Selective Service files, burning draft cards, and even some violence against war-related public property. Predictably, this cultural agitprop infuriated large numbers of Americans and antagonized some elements of the movement. It was counterproductive insofar as it did not take seriously the myths and symbols that defined America, doubtless conveying a sense that the war and the national ordeal were not taken seriously either. That was deeply offensive to many people who anguished over Vietnam.

In a more profound and almost certainly more usual sense, the denigration of popular symbols reflected the activists' own indignation—even anger—that patriotism was draped around an unjust war. If so-called Americanism itself had not been used a cultural weapon, it could have been put in quotation marks to describe antiwar rhetoric: anti-"Americanism." Draft-card burning clearly had this force, particularly after it was made a federal offense. The connotation was similar to the occasional inversion of the flag, an international signal of distress.

Unfortunately for activists, distress was generic in the 1960s. Symbolism was used to challenge social and cultural conformity in general, and it offered no distinction between rejection of a dominant, even if oppressive, lifestyle and a specific, if repressive, foreign policy. This left the antiwar movement vulnerable to extraneous attack, since the contest over the war was waged more on the level of symbols than on issues. The recognizable peace sign itself was subjected to tortuous exegesis designed to convert it from an affirmative to a negative image. Moreover, it proved very difficult to condemn the war as immoral without impugning the morality of the nation, or the leadership as distinct from the people. The problem was aggravated by activists' pervasive concern with popular anomie (the motif of moral numbness) and complicity (the Eichmann motif). "Madness is an infection in the air," Daniel Berrigan wrote, and it obscured all distinctions.

Negative images were indiscriminately associated with dissent itself, especially those of violence and disorder. In reality, violence was seldom employed in antiwar protests. In was used mostly by local right-wing activists or police, especially prior to 1967. In that year disruptive street actions and attacks on draft board property began to increase in frequency and, more important, in notoriety. Concurrently the country experienced worsening racial crisis and campus unrest. Governing authorities, growing apprehensive about the relation of domestic violence and Vietnam, made serious attempts to infiltrate security agents in the antiwar movement, both for surveillance and harassment. Not until 1968–1971 did the connection between violence and the antiwar movement become salient in American politics. Militancy did increase then. With the disintegration of the radical left and the rise of groups such as the Weathermen, some dissidents detonated bombs, set fire to buildings, and attacked police. Still, it is difficult to correlate the actual growth of antiwar violence with the sharp rise in official concern at the time. According to a 1970 study conducted by Treasury Department officials Eugene Rossides and G. Gordon Liddy, there were 4,358 bombings in the United States from January 1969 to April 1970, of which 36 percent could be attributed to specific sources and 20 percent to antiwar dissidents. Otherwise, there are no federal figures which attribute violence to the war issue.

In spite of lacking concrete evidence, the Nixon administration consistently identified antiwar protest with domestic violence and terrorism, particularly after it failed to link the movement to communism. Ironically, some administration officials used agents provocateurs to incite antiwar activists to violence or encouraged prowar enthusiasts to inspire citizen attacks on dissidents. The Nixon White House made a determined effort to discredit and destroy the antiwar movement, and it identified dissent with violence so effectively that it made the legitimacy of protest itself a political issue.

Government officials and prowar partisans also routinely attacked antiwar activists as being either communist-inspired or a source of encouragement to Vietnamese communists and, thus, a force prolonging the war. Doubtless some radical leaders naïvely romanticized Hanoi (as the White House knowingly romanticized Saigon); but despite their most energetic efforts, investigative agencies failed to find any evidence to the charge that dissenters were either inspired or manipulated by communists. Exhaustive studies prepared for both Johnson and Nixon concluded instead that even radical elements in the movement were indigenous American idealists, however perverse they might seem. Indeed, by the 1970s the word "commie" conveyed cultural and social deviance more than political subversion.

Similarly, there is no evidence that protest prolonged the war. Certainly the war continued despite dissident attempts to end it. The fact that Vietnamese communists periodically proclaimed their appreciation of the antiwar movement does not mean that they depended on it. To suppose so is to confuse cause-and-effect with parallel causes and to perpetuate the underestimation of Vietnamese will and capacity which itself contributed to American defeat. The charge that the movement prolonged the war rests on the assumption that it sapped the will of the nation to fight (or that the Vietnamese thought it did) and that the contest could otherwise have been won. In fact, it seems likely that most Americans concluded that the effort was futile and counterproductive, and withdrew their support accordingly. In this sense, it was the people themselves who were "no longer so naïve" about the war.

Nonetheless, the antiwar movement was vulnerable to unwarranted charges of abetting violence and communism. It was extraordinarily large and diverse. It was organized to attract dissidents, not to discriminate among them. Included in its number were a relatively few who were prepared to emulate the violent acts of what Fred Halstead aptly called "plate glass revolutionaries" and others who proffered a romantic version of Maoist revolution. Moreover, its public image was formed when those elements were most visible and domestic confrontation most intense.

Much of the difficulty in defining the movement's image was a consequence of its association with suspect causes. This challenge antedated the war in SANE's experience, and it surfaced repeatedly in the coalition politics of the movement. The notion of excluding anyone from demonstrations on the basis of ideology could be interpreted as accommodating the "we-they" polarization that underlay the war itself. Moreover, the intensely personal morality of many activists made the exclusion of any form of witness ethically tenuous. On the other hand, inclusiveness carried practical penalties. The association of radical, countercultural, and anti-"American" images with antiwar demonstrations aggravated divisiveness and made the movement vulnerable to attack.

The major peace groups adapted to their dilemma in three ways. First, they tried to distinguish between slogans and behavior, accepting demonstrators under any banner as long as they conducted themselves in an orderly manner. Second, they developed elaborate crowd controls, including thousands of specially trained marshals, in order to impose a measure of discipline and to intercede between demonstrators and their detractors. Third, they tried to sequence events so as to make alternatives available to people whether they chose to express their views, conduct nonviolent civil disobedience, or court nonviolent confrontation. Throughout the period both activists and security forces learned a great deal about controlling large popular demonstrations, but movement leaders could not preclude all violence or offensiveness. Nor could they insure that the media would accurately convey their cause. In fact, theirs was not purely an antiwar movement. It was connected—partly in reality and certainly in the popular mind—with other domestic change movements, and that relationship determined in a large measure both its vulnerability and its force.

The significance of the antiwar movement depends upon what it is measured against, of course, and evaluation is laden with anomalies. Leading activists never believed that they could literally stop the war, and yet they did not relent in their struggle to do so. Indeed, they even cultivated the impression that public opposition could reverse official policy. The Johnson and Nixon administrations insisted that they would not respond to protest, and yet both adapted their policies to pressure from dissenters. Public opinion surveys indicated that the American people consistently resented the antiwar movement but increasingly agreed with its arguments and conclusions.

The very contradictions in the movement and in reactions to it suggest dissonance. Probably it helped to transform the war in Southeast Asia into a protracted domestic struggle which, when compounded by related social turmoil, produced a crisis in the American social and political order. Certainly antiwar activists confronted their people and leaders with fundamental questions about democratic politics and national interest. . . .

From 1955 on, more and more citizens were learning from related experiments in social change. By the early 1960s a resurgent peace movement converged with political liberalism, radicalism revitalized in a New Left, and a civil rights movement imbued with an interfaith revival of the social gospel. Reform efforts created a base of material resources, adaptable ideas, experienced organizers, and networks of supporters. Together they animated a lively sense of idealism: they contributed to the range, tone, energy, and momentum of the opposition which crystalized around escalating intervention in Vietnam.

Although interaction with other social reform impulses contributed synergistic power to the antiwar movement, it also aggravated an inherent division there. Nominally, the split was between liberals and radicals, but those labels do not convey a sense of the issues because both wings were in flux, and neither was fixed by a governing ideology or stable constituency. Still, there was an irreducible difference in the ways they approached the Vietnam War. Some activists fresh from peace and civil rights campaigns viewed American intervention in Indochina as a mistake, an aberration that had to be corrected through public education and electoral action so that the United States could resume its quest for international order and domestic reform. They were in this measure liberals. Other activists, especially from the Old and New Left, viewed Vietnam as a counterrevolutionary war of American aggression that sprang from the elitist and self-interested culture of American capitalism, which they wanted to transform for the sake of social and international justice. Their approach was at least in this sense radical.

Together, antiwar liberals and radicals believed that American military intervention in Vietnam was wrong and that Washington bore the principal responsibility for effecting a peace settlement. Beyond that basic agreement they divided. Often their difference was expressed in strategic quarrels on the relative merits of immediate or negotiated withdrawal, of organization around the single issue of the war or on multiple social issues, and of various techniques for effecting change, such as persuasion, conventional politics, mass demonstrations, or confrontation. Prolonged and often esoteric quarrels over strategy only obscured the main line of division. Antiwar liberals saw the war as a policy issue, antiwar radicals as a means toward revolutionary social change. The former tried to de-escalate and then end U.S. military involvement, while the latter challenged intervention in an attempt to transform the distribution of power and privilege in America. One side saw Vietnam as a crisis in a democracy that it wanted to save; the other viewed the war issue as an opportunity to redeem society from falseness and corruption. The lines were not neat (there were liberals, after all, who also wanted to redistribute power and privilege), the alternatives not necessarily exclusive. Nonetheless, antiwar rhetoric often masked a debate over America.

For the most part, that division was understood only by a small core of activists. The antiwar movement provided a focal point for large numbers of Americans who for one reason or another opposed the war but were not involved in protest organizations. Organized activism related millions of otherwise disconnected people to a single issue. This was its raison d'être: to mobilize public opposition to the war.

The opposition to this war was also linked to the liberalization of popular culture. Wars tend to breed cultural conformity and conservative politics, but the Vietnam War was different. In varying measure, the antiwar movement aligned the organized disaffection of blacks, women, and students. It also competed with these groups and others, such as environmentalists. It included a few activists who thought themselves the harbingers of a counterculture, many who emphasized individual autonomy and alternative group loyalties, and a majority that questioned authority at a root level.

These social demands and cultural trends were part of what Ronald Lora, in *America in the '60s,* has aptly called "a revolt against traditional cultural authorities." They included challenges to conventional wisdom about religion, scientific objectivity, national security, the sources of poverty, the infinite durability of the environment, and adult, white, and male dominance. Some of these causes enlisted specific groups—increasingly blacks, established intellectuals, students, and women. They sprang up independently before the war and perhaps would have run their courses without it, becoming more or less institutionalized in the normal process of social change. They were tenuously related to Vietnam by activists who perceived the effort to end the war as part of the struggle for a more open society. The pursuit of that social and cultural goal led to confusion and severe tension, and it also corroded the ethic of authority, whether in protest organizations, in delegated civic responsibility, or in the military chain of command.

What is liberation to some is disintegration to others, however. By 1971 a plurality of Americans agreed that domestic disunity was a greater problem than the war itself. Insofar as protest contributed to domestic strife (or the impression of it), it contributed to that war-weariness which ultimately impelled the nation to withdraw. The alignment of antiwar activism with other social and cultural change likely reinforced a popular impression that protest itself was a social problem. Therefore the antiwar movement and the war were resented for the same reason: they were eroding familiar values and institutions. Ironically, then, Vietnam threatened the quite different social values of both activists and traditional citizens. Given the perception that the antiwar movement was contributing to social dissonance, it was understandable that a public impatient with Vietnam declined to endorse demonstrative protest.

The most distinctive quality of organized opposition to the war was its moral thrust. Vietnam intensified the dissatisfaction with pragmatic liberal realism and the anxiety over moral numbness which had surfaced with respect to nuclear arms. The war was widely condemned as immoral, not only on the universal grounds of pacifism but in terms of "just war" ethics—by Reinhold Niebuhr as much as A. J. Muste, by Hans Morgenthau as well as Daniel Berrigan. Policy was challenged on moral grounds, especially after 1968 when military victory was implicitly abandoned. As American troops were withdrawn, Indochinese became the only combatants—and civilians—at risk. For those who followed events, the question was more clearly what U.S. policy was doing to others. The issue of war-related public morality was brought home in the latter years of the Nixon administration when the events surrounding Watergate joined it to the issue of accountability. Throughout the period the moral criterion was the only common denominator in the antiwar movement, where it was pressed incessantly.

Calling the war "immoral" was a form of rhetoric—an abstract shorthand for "terribly wrong." The administration countered that the conflict was a matter of honor and obligation: hence moral. Offsetting ethical claims tended to undercut the force of abstractions. To that extent the nation lost familiar value-laden reference points. Words such as communism, containment, democratic government, free world, peace, and victory became too obviously manipulative, and too often contradicted by reports from Southeast Asia. Notions such as patriotism, loyalty, and national honor were imbued with ambivalence as the antiwar movement associated them with dissent. It was little wonder, then, that the public was benumbed by abstract words naming alternative moralities. In this environment it was hardly ironic that skepticism about war was extended to exhortations for peace. It was appropriate for *Commonweal* to advise the graduating class of 1975 that its fight would be against cynicism.

The obverse of public ethics was the morality of personal responsibility. Whatever its sources in American culture, this was a strong current in the 1960s. Early in the decade it impelled black students to take repression upon their own shoulders, and some white students perceived racism as a shared responsibility. The sense of personal accountability for social injustice surfaced in the Peace Corps and community service. It was extended to Vietnam. Especially among the pacifist and youthful elements of the antiwar movement, it was joined to an ethics of action: the notion that belief must find expression in behavior, that decision is the epitome of morality, that to witness outweighs results.

This attitude was characteristic of the so-called romantic radicalism of the period. Its attraction was felt mainly among young people, although it was also inherent in radical pacifism. Doubtless it was profoundly therapeutic when activists were oppressed by the apparent futility of their efforts. Apparently relegated to the periphery of their society and alienated from their government, they could at least witness to the truth as they knew it: "*at least it was something to do.*" Still, the emphasis on personal morality aggravated the problems of already isolated activists. It could not only motivate activism but also rationalize withdrawal from politics. To the extent that action justified itself, the test of political impact was eroded. To the extent that the transformation of character became an all-absorbing goal, the organizational bonds required for sustained public action were snapped.

Such moralism never dominated the antiwar movement as a whole. Liberals, including leading pacifists, and even radicals in the Communist party and Socialist Workers party did try to mount politically effective campaigns, although they might rely on mass demonstrations to do so. Again they faced the difficulty of coalition politics. Theirs was a hydra-headed movement. The established peace groups had to reconcile differences not only among themselves but also with a series of ephemeral groupings, each with its own floating constituency. More or less together, they reacted to whatever crisis promised to unify them and give them access to the public. Under circumstances beyond their control, activists often appeared to be leaderless, their movement politically unstable. Nonetheless, at the core there was staying power and remarkable persistence, due in part to a coterie of dedicated, even professional, organizers and in part to the intractable fact of the war itself.

The problems associated with building a coalition against the war thus derived partially from the diversity and intensity with which individuals gathered in the hope of improving the quality of American society. In the midst of a despondent reflection on the fragility of the movement in 1973, an activist noted that someone had counted seven hundred volunteer groups in Massachusetts that were dedicated to various causes. What a dynamic society, she thought! The antiwar movement was a part of that dynamism.

The fabric of American society was dramatically rewoven in the two decades after 1955. Racism was at least mitigated. Student life-styles and curricula were altered. The status of women was reexamined. The Democratic and Republican coalitions began to realign. The executive branch was constrained by the 1973 War Powers Act. A large number of new peace organizations were formed which continued after the war, such as SANE, the Council for a Livable World, the World Without War Council, the Center for War/Peace Studies, the Fund for Peace and its project centers, and the Campaign to Stop Funding the War (under various names). Those concerned themselves mainly with foreign policy. Clergy and Laity Concerned and Common Cause bridged over to domestic issues. A number of other organizations stimulated peace research and education, or international exchange. All of them were complemented by a plethora of associations addressing civil rights, environmental, and feminist issues, or by cells of socially concerned professionals—civil servants, business people, physicians, psychologists, scientists, entertainers, educators, historians. Throughout the period there seemed to be a cycle of social consciousness, protest, campaigns, and long-term organization for concrete goals. The process was accompanied by turbulence, as old social patterns were rent and refashioned.

Whatever forces were acting elsewhere in American society, the war had at least two major effects on it. First, the war touched all domestic conflicts, charging them with high tension and obscuring the issues around which national identity was being redefined. Second, the antiwar movement interacted with the process of social reconstruction. Voluntarism in opposition to the war mushroomed, especially on the local level. Often it was only loosely connected to national organizations—perhaps to receive information, raise funds, or send demonstrators to a mobilization. Indeed, local activists sometimes resented the fact that their resources were drained to support national actions. All this citizen activity suggests that the movement in the broadest sense was not so peripheral to the American mainstream as its leaders feared. Its history on the national level reflected efforts in the American interior—in church meetings, college teach-ins, congressional offices, city street actions, curbside vigils, and divided families—where most Americans struggled among themselves over Vietnam. . . .

Martin Luther King, Jr., and many other activists observed, when confronted with allegations of protest violence, that in objective terms the

United States was employing devastating and indiscriminate violence in Indochina. It was imposing its will as though that were a goal in itself: this was the point of their opposition to the war. But those were not objective times, and it still is difficult to reflect on King's words without raising extremely painful questions that go to the heart of national identity and purpose. It was, and perhaps still is, easier to pretend that dissent was merely the rhetorical expression of malcontents whose tactics contradicted or obscured their plea for peace—to treat the challenge of antiwar dissidents as willful or trivial rather than to answer it.

There gathered in the United States between 1955 and 1975 the largest domestic opposition to a warring government in the history of modern industrial society. Originating in a small-scale protest against Washington's Cold War policies, specifically against the atmospheric testing of nuclear weapons, it exploded after 1965 into a sustained challenge to military intervention in Indochina. Overwhelmingly, antiwar dissidents regarded the decision on Vietnam as a definition of American purpose. They were idealists, and they identified their ideals with their nation. This is why they tried so desperately to reach the public. It is also why they were so vulnerable to popular rejection and apathy. They felt intensely that they shared the ordeal of the war—for the nation. They argued that the core issue was not the future of democracy in Vietnam: that they insisted, was beyond the purview of the United States. The critical issue was the purpose of the American people. The antiwar movement did not force the United States to quit the war. Its political significance was, instead, that it persistently identified that choice as the essential issue of American foreign policy and national identity.

American Veterans and the Antiwar Movement

CHRISTIAN G. APPY

To many veterans, the protests of college students felt like moral and social putdowns, expressions not of principle and commitment but simply of class privilege and arrogance. These feelings often come out most explicitly in long interviews. Steve Harper, a veteran from Akron, Ohio, was one of the nine subjects of Murray Polner's valuable book *No Victory Parades* (1971). Harper told Polner: "The critics are picking on us, just 'cause we had to fight this war. Where were their sons? In fancy colleges? Where were the sons of all the big shots who supported the war? Not in my platoon. Our guys' people were workers and things like that. . . . Still, we did things that made me sore. Like stopping the bombing—and maybe even putting us in Vietnam in the first place. If the war was so important, why didn't our leaders put everyone's son in there, why only us?" For Harper, debate about the war often seemed like a personal attack because so much of it was carried

Reprinted from *Working Class War: American Combat Soldiers and Vietnam* by Christian G. Appy. Copyright © 1993 by The University of North Carolina Press. Used by permission of author and the publisher.

on by "big shots" who did not have to fight the war. The critics and architects of the war did the talking, while the sons of workers did the fighting. Surely, he concluded, whatever the privileged might say about the war, they must be against grunts like him.

Harper's own views about the war, as he readily conceded, were confused. In the same breath he could denounce limitations on American bombing and the initial U.S. intervention in Vietnam. That is not necessarily a contradictory position. In effect he said, we should have won the war or stayed out. A simple enough argument to state, but one that evades the questions of whether the war could have been won or whether it was worth winning (that is, a just cause) and the further question of why it would be right to continue trying to win a war in which the original intervention was wrong or misguided. When those questions are broached, Harper's conflicted feelings and those of many veterans are drawn to the surface. A 1979 Harris survey found that a vast majority of veterans (89 percent) agreed with the statement, "The trouble in Vietnam was that our troops were asked to fight in a war which our political leaders in Washington would not let them win." Yet a clear majority of veterans (59 percent) also agreed with a completely contrary viewpoint: "The trouble in Vietnam was that our troops were asked to fight in a war we could never win." The general public shared this contradictory view (73 and 65 percent agreeing with each statement, respectively). Of course, both formulations have a common appeal: they put the onus of responsibility for the war and its outcome on American leaders, not on ordinary soldiers and civilians. They also pose the same attractive alternatives suggested by Harper: win or stay out.

As for the moral legitimacy of the war, Steve Harper struggled to defend U.S. intervention. The United States, he said, was helping the people of Vietnam, people who "wanted us there" and who "wanted their freedom." Hard as he tried to sustain that view, however, his memories of the war kept contradicting it. He could not forget how the Vietnamese almost always seemed to be helping the Viet Cong ("they take all the Americans have to offer and give us nothin' and give the VC all they have"). Nor did he try to disguise his disdain for the Vietnamese military and government, which he saw as riddled with corruption and unable and unwilling to fight successfully against the Viet Cong ("they'd turn and run, from their officers on down"). Finally, Harper could only resolve the contradictions between his faith in the American mission and the realities he experienced by arguing, "We were there to help but Vietnamese are so stupid they can't understand that a great people want to help a weak people."

In the end, Harper's defense of the war came down to a simple affirmation that American soldiers were right to go to Vietnam, that they were doing their duty. Perhaps because his own testimony about the war punched gaping holes in official justifications of American intervention, Harper returned repeatedly to a defense, not of U.S. policy, but of soldiers like himself. "We were soldiers, doing our jobs. We didn't want to bring disgrace on ourselves and our folks. We were right in being there." So much self-worth and dignity depended on his belief that his own actions were right. That is the crucial point. Harper's defense of American intervention was not insincere, but in defending the war, he expressed his stronger need to defend himself. At times he entertained the possibility that the United States was wrong to involve itself in Vietnam. Yet, he could not fully embrace that position because it suggested to him that simply doing his duty might also have been wrong. Clinging to the idea that he was right in being there, he felt he must also conclude that the nation was right to send him.

Harper's effort to link the moral integrity of individual soldiers and the justice of the war was shaken by his knowledge of the class inequalities of military service. If the war were really so important, truly a just war, he was sure the leaders would ask everyone to fight. While he insisted that he had done the right thing by going to Vietnam, he could not ignore the obvious presence of millions of young Americans who thought it was their duty, not to fight in the war, but actively to resist it.

> Last week, I had to be in Chicago; I ran into a "Resist the Draft" rally on the street. At first I smile: kids at it again, just a fad. Then I started getting sore. About how I had to go and they could stay out. Cosco went in and he was the straightest guy I ever knew. My Negro buddy didn't like the war, but he went in too. I just stood there and got sore at those rich kids telling people to "resist the draft." What about us poor people? For every guy who resists the draft one of us gotta go and he gets sent out into the boonies to get his backside shot at. One of their signs read "We've Already Given Enough." And I thought, "What *have* they given?"

Because of the class gulf between most protesters and veterans, the specific political message of the antiwar demonstrators was mostly inconsequential to veterans like Harper. "We've Already Given Enough" or "Bring the Boys Home" were slogans intended to support the lives of soldiers and surely offended him less than the waving of Viet Cong flags or the chant "Ho Ho Ho Chi Minh, the NLF is going to win." To many veterans, however, all protest seemed like yet another class privilege enjoyed by wealthier peers, and even moderate objections to the war, if made by draft-immune college students, were often read as personal attacks. Student protests put into bold relief the contrast between the experiences of the two groups. Watching protest marches reminded some veterans of their own marches in Vietnam—those endless, exhausting, and dangerous humps. While they were enduring the hardship and danger of war, college students were—in the eyes of many soldiers—frolicking on campus in a blissful round of sex, drugs, and rock 'n roll *and* getting the credentials necessary to gain high-paying jobs. Then, too, simply the physical appearance of protesters, their long hair and shaggy dress, could anger veterans. Of course, soldiers in Vietnam also stretched conventional military rules related to dress and hair, so much so that by 1968 it was not uncommon to find men in the boonies wearing unofficial medallions, beads, and headgear and displaying wild graffiti ("eat the apple, fuck the Corps") on their flak jackets and helmet liners. Vets, however, had the perception that their own assertions had been harder won, that the kids on campus seemed to get away with everything. Then, too, they were especially irritated by nonveterans who dressed up in military uniforms, a popular fashion of the time. It was not so much that the old uniforms mocked the military; few people were as scornful of the military as most vets, but they felt you had to earn the right to wear the uniform in a casual way and that nonvets who did it were insulting those who had worn them in combat.

The resentment and jealousy vets felt toward protesters were based on more than anger that those at home seemed to have such a wonderful, safe time while those in Vietnam faced such danger. They also resented and envied the pride and conviction protesters took in their activism. For veterans torn by confusion about the war they had fought, and struggling to feel some pride in what they had done, the protesters' passion, self-assurance, and sense of purpose could generate a nagging—if unspoken—envy. Faced with people so sure the war was wrong, vets were convinced their own morality was under siege.

Victor Belloti, a captain in the Boston Fire Department, went to Vietnam in 1965 as a combat medic. He was the first of three generations to graduate from high school, and after the war he earned a college degree at the University of Massachusetts in Boston. He was reminded of his strong feelings about college students while talking about the attitude of combat soldiers toward men who served in rear areas. He laughed about all the ribbing the grunts used to give men in the rear, how they called them office pogies and "Remington Raiders," and how he would say things to them like, "You ought to come out in the field with us sometime and see the real war." When asked how deep the antagonism was between the two groups of soldiers, Belloti said that while there was some tension, most of his complaints were made in fun. By way of comparison he thought of his feelings for college students who demonstrated against the war.

> I didn't have anywhere near the contempt or resentment for people in the rear that I had for the university students I met after the war. To me most of them were the arch-liberals from suburban communities, having never really worked in their lives. They were kids who had never had anything go wrong with them and they went on "marches" and they protested the Vietnam War. They didn't have the slightest idea what was going on over there. Politically they were right, I'm not saying they weren't. But this shit about baby-killers. I know guys who sacrificed a lot for women and children in ambush situations and going through villages. The political rightness or wrongness of the situation? We weren't wanted there. We knew that when we were over there.

Belloti's contempt for campus protesters clearly draws on a keenly felt sense of class inequality, but what was "this shit about baby-killers"? The line, so crucial to his claim that protesters did not understand the reality of Vietnam (however right they might be about the "politics") is tossed into the account with an offhandedness that assumes we know precisely what he means, that the point is beyond dispute, and that no further explanation is necessary. In fact, understanding its significance is a complicated but essential way of getting at one of the central moral legacies of military service in Vietnam.

Among most veterans, Belloti's reference to "baby-killers" would be accepted with a knowing nod of recognition. Many take it as axiomatic that the antiwar movement regarded them as immoral killers. Stories certifying that commonplace were passed around among veterans with a frequency and resonance that imbued them with a mythic quality. David Chambers, interviewed in the late 1960s, reported: "At Travis Air Force Base an incident occurred which—true or not—spread like wildfire in Nam, and I think was believed by the guys. It seemed very possible to me, too. A vet, just back, was in the men's room when a hippie came up to him. He asked the vet if he had just returned from Nam and when he said yes, he had, the guy shot him in the arm." Chambers makes a key point. Though the story is dubious (how, for one thing, would a hippie even make it onto the base?), it seemed plausible to many veterans. Even before returning home, these men anticipated rejection. Stories like this gained such currency that they were quickly generalized beyond individual anecdotes to statements such as "The protesters are calling us baby-killers" or "Hippies are spitting at veterans." By the 1980s, these images became widely accepted throughout American culture as literal representations of the homecoming received by most veterans. The archetypal story featured a returning veteran arriving at an airport (usually in California). He is wearing his dress uniform with campaign ribbons. As the vet walks through the terminal, a hippie, often a girl, approaches, calls him a baby-killer, and spits at him.

Were veterans really spit upon by hippies or protesters? In the late 1980s journalist Bob Greene posed this question in his syndicated column and received more than a thousand letters, some of which he collected in a book (*Homecoming*). Greene was persuaded that spittings had indeed occurred and devoted the first third of his collection to letters from men claiming it had happened to them. However, Greene concedes that there is an "apparent sameness" to these letters, a sameness that should, I think, make one wary of their literal truthfulness. Here is a typical sample: "I arrived at Los Angeles International Airport. . . . On my way to the taxis, I passed two young women in the waiting area. One of these young women approached me and, in a low voice, called me a 'baby killer' and spat on my ribbons. I was in uniform and wearing the Vietnamese Service Medal, the Vietnamese Campaign Medal, an Air Force Commendation Medal, and the Purple Heart." The remainder of the letters in Greene's book are from veterans who either express deep skepticism about the spitting allegations or who believe being spit at was an uncommon experience. Many even testify to acts of great kindness from strangers upon returning home. The most commonplace letters were in many respects the most poignant. They came from men simply struggling to express the pain, confusion, and isolation they felt upon returning to the United States, how uncomfortable people seemed to be around them, or how little people seemed to want to know about their experience.

Alongside the stories of war protesters standing guard at airports to taunt returning veterans should be placed a surprising survey. In 1979 Harris pollsters used a "feeling thermometer" to measure public attitudes toward Vietnam veterans. On a scale of 1 to 10, with 10 being the warmest possible feeling and 1 the coolest, a sample of 237 "antiwar activists" rated Vietnam veterans 8.9, far above their rating of military leaders (4.7) and congressional representatives (5.0), and even higher than their ranking of "people who demonstrated against the war in Vietnam" (7.7—not all anti-war activists endorsed public demonstrations as a useful tactic to end the war). Though the attitudes of antiwar activists may have been cooler toward veterans during the war years (the poll came several years later), a total reversal in feeling seems unlikely.

While antiwar activists claimed warmer feelings toward Vietnam vets than the "baby-killer" stories suggest, the Harris survey found that veterans had a very low opinion of protesters. The sample of 1,179 Vietnam veterans ranked protesters at 3.3, a response pollsters consider "very cool." Veterans gave an even lower score (1.9) to people who left the country to avoid the draft. Antiwar activists had much more respect for draft evaders, ranking them at 7.1.

Granting that most people in the peace movement did not hate veterans and did not abuse them, many veterans certainly perceived the antiwar movement as a personal rejection. A key reason, as discussed, was that Vietnam was a working-class war wealthier students had the best chance of avoiding. Moreover, protesters were not always careful to distinguish between the managers of the war and the workers who did the fighting. The antiwar movement openly and fervently attacked not only the political decision to intervene in Vietnam but the conduct of the war as well. How else, activists might argue, could they make Americans aware of the discrepancy between official justifications of the war and its reality? The war's injustice could not be fully demonstrated unless it was shown that the military was burning down Vietnamese villages, killing civilians, and supporting corrupt, dictatorial regimes. How could those realities be exposed without making soldiers feel morally suspect? Furthermore, some protesters simply did not make a clear distinction between the war and those who fought it, and they regarded American soldiers as ready and willing killers or ignorant dupes.

When Gene Holiday returned from Vietnam, he was curious to meet some people on "the hippie side." "They never really called me a baby-killer, but they said I was a marine and I was one of those kind of people." He got especially upset the day he saw an antiwar demonstration in 1971. "I got real angry at a couple people for carrying the North Vietnamese flag. [I told them]: 'You're 18, you don't even know what the hell went on. What are you carrying that thing for?' I took the flag and started ripping it up." The argument quickly escalated into a brutal fight between Gene and three demonstrators. It ended when all four were arrested.

By the late 1960s, moreover, a minority within the antiwar movement wanted not simply an end to American intervention but a victory for Vietnamese left-wing revolutionary nationalism. As Todd Gitlin has pointed out, among the New Left wing of the peace movement, at least among its late 1960s leadership, there was a strong tendency to romanticize

Third World revolutionaries: "With the United States pulverizing and bullying small countries, it seemed the most natural thing in the world to go prospecting among them for heroes. Their resistance was so brave, their enemies so implacable, their nationalism so noble, we could take their passions, even their slogans and styles of speech . . . for our own. . . . It no longer felt sufficient . . . to say no to aggressive war; we felt driven to say yes to revolt."

Gitlin, an important New Left figure, recalls that American flags almost always outnumbered NLF flags at antiwar demonstrations. However, the NLF flags received "a disproportionate share of the media spotlight." Student activists who championed the NLF comprised a rather small portion of American college students. In the late 1960s about 7 to 10 percent of college students described themselves as radicals, and of these, probably only a fraction sided with the Vietnamese Revolutionary Forces. However, those who did embrace America's official enemy contributed to the isolation of the antiwar movement. As Gitlin writes, "Surely those NLF flags were part of the explanation for one of the stunning political facts of the decade: that as the war steadily lost popularity in the late Sixties, *so did the antiwar movement.*" Of course the movement's loss of support was largely fueled by the attacks of government officials like President Nixon and Vice-President Agnew who tried to persuade the public that the entire movement sided with the enemy. While many veterans were receptive to this wildly distorted claim, they were by no means alone.

While the antiwar movement has been branded with far too much blame for the mistreatment of Vietnam veterans, society as a whole was certainly unable and unwilling to receive these men with the support and understanding they needed. The most common experiences of rejection were not explicit acts of hostility but quieter, sometimes more devastating forms of withdrawal, suspicion, and indifference. When veterans told new acquaintances that they had served in Vietnam, it was not uncommon for people to treat them warily. Veterans could feel themselves making other people nervous and uneasy. They often wondered if they were just being paranoid or if others were in fact being remote and detached, keeping them at arm's length. Some veterans began to expect such behavior and their expectation of tension helped to create it. For some, all contact with nonveterans became uncomfortable, even intolerable.

Tony Almeida, son of a firefighter, returned from Vietnam in 1969. At an outdoor rock concert he struck up a conversation with a young woman and some of her friends:

> They were my own age but they were college kids—definitely not from the type of upbringing I'd come from, for sure. One thing led to another and to get to the point I ended up in bed with this girl. We were about to make love and some question she asked me—I don't remember the question but I remember responding, "Yeah, I was in the marines."
>
> She looked at me and she said, "Then you were in Vietnam?"
>
> I said, "Yeah, I just came back from Vietnam, in fact, not too long ago."

She just completely withdrew and sat up on one elbow and said, "Sorry." No, wait, she didn't say she was sorry, she just said, "You have to leave now."

I could have punched her right in the face at that point. That's when I started to feel guilty, I guess, about participating in the war. That's when I started to realize that there was this whole *other* set of experiences that had happened with other people and there must have been some reason why they were making those connections. I don't know what stopped me from saying "Who the fuck are you?" But I just took it, got up and got dressed and left. I didn't talk about Vietnam again with anybody except other vets until 1978.

Faced with society's indifference, uneasiness, and outright rejection and gripped by their own troubled memories of the war, thousands of veterans lapsed into the sort of silence reported by Tony Almeida. For years—a full decade, sometimes longer—a startling number of men who fought in Vietnam—who knows how many—would not talk about their experience with nonveterans, would not even volunteer that they had been in a war. . . .

✗ *F U R T H E R   R E A D I N G*

Edward J. Bacciocco, *The New Left in America* (1974)

Lawrence M. Baskir and William A. Strauss, *Chance and Circumstance* (1978) (on the draft)

William C. Berman, *William Fulbright and the Vietnam War* (1988)

Paul Burstein and William Fredenberg, "Changing Public Policy: The Impact of Public Opinion, Anti-War Demonstrations, and War Costs on Senate Voting on Vietnam War Motions," *American Journal of Sociology,* 84 (1978), 99–122

Charles DeBenedetti, *The Peace Reform in American History* (1980)

———, "On the Significance of Citizen Peace Activism: America, 1961–1975," *Peace and Change,* 9 (1983), 6–20

David Dellinger, *From Yale to Jail* (1993)

Mitchell K. Hall, *Because of Their Faith: CALCAV and Religious Opposition to the Vietnam War* (1990)

Fred Halstead, *Out Now* (1978)

Patrick Lloyd Hatcher, *The Suicide of an Elite: American Internationalists and Vietnam* (1990)

Tom Hayden, *Reunion* (1988)

Kenneth H. Heineman, *Campus Wars: The Peace Movement at American State Universities in the Vietnam Era* (1993)

Godfrey Hodgson, *America in Our Time* (1976)

Milton S. Katz, "Peace Liberals and Vietnam: SANE and the Politics of 'Responsible' Protest," *Peace and Change,* 9 (1983), 21–39

Alexander Kendrick, *The Wound Within* (1974)

David W. Levy, *The Debate over Vietnam* (1991)

William L. Lunch and Peter W. Sperlich, "American Public Opinion and the War in Vietnam," *Western Political Quarterly,* 32 (1979), 21–44

Allen J. Matusow, *The Unraveling of America* (1984)

James Miller, *"Democracy is in the Streets"* (on SDS) (1987)

Thomas Powers, *Vietnam: The War at Home* (1973)

W. J. Rorabaugh, *Berkeley at War: The University of California in the 1960s* (1989)
Milton Rosenberg, Sidney Verba, and Phillip Converse, *Vietnam and the Silent Majority* (1970)
Kirkpatrick Sale, *SDS* (1973)
David L. Schalk, *War and the Ivory Tower: Algeria and Vietnam* (1991)
Melvin Small and William D. Hoover , eds., *Give Peace a Chance: Exploring the Vietnam Antiwar Movement* (1992)
George R. Vickers, *The Formation of the New Left: The Early Years* (1975)
Milton Viorst, *Fire in the Streets* (1979)
Sandy Vogelgesang, T*he Long Dark Night of the Soul: The American Intellectual Left and the Vietnam War* (1974)
James Weinstein, *Ambiguous Legacy: The Left in American Politics* (1975)
Tom Wells, *The War Within* (1994)
Nigel Young, *An Infantile Disorder?: The Crisis and Decline of the New Left* (1977)
Nancy Zaroulis and Gerald Sullivan, *Who Spoke Up?* (1984)

CHAPTER

13

The Media and the War

✗

Often referred to as the first media war, the Vietnam conflict was subjected to unprecedented saturation coverage by print and broadcast journalists. Most specialists agree that the stories presented and the images projected by the American media exerted a profound effect on popular attitudes toward the war. Beyond that broad generalization, however, there is little consensus among analysts with regard to the media's influence.

The following questions are among those most frequently and most intensely debated: Were American correspondents unduly critical of government policy? Did their reports deceive—or inform—the American people? Did the media have its own hidden antiwar agenda? Why, if press and television reporters initially favored U.S. involvement in Vietnam, did some turn against that policy? How did they use their influence? Was their reporting fair or biased? probing or superficial? Did the grisly images of war projected daily on American television screens help spark opposition to the conflict? And finally, how great are the power and influence of the media within American society? Toward what ends, and in whose interests, are they used?

✗ DOCUMENTS

In the first document, an editorial published on February 14, 1962, the *New York Times* offers support for American policy while acknowledging that Vietnam might well escalate into a major conflict. In the next document, former UPI and *New York Times* correspondent Neil Sheehan recalls that nearly all members of the press in the early 1960s shared the government's desire to rout the communists. The selection is drawn from his prize-winning study of U.S. adviser John Paul Vann.

The documents that follow the Sheehan excerpt reflect growing doubts within the media about the war. Walter Lippmann, one of the most influential journalists of his generation, denounced LBJ's approach to the war in his widely read column on January 16, 1967, reprinted as the third document. The fourth document is from the July 10, 1967, issue of *Newsweek* magazine, noting that the war was beginning to make its mark on nearly every facet of American life, raising some troubling questions about the course of the conflict. Following the Tet offensive, CBS television anchorman Walter Cronkite hosted a report from Vietnam; parts of it appear as the fifth document. In the program, which aired on February 27, 1968, he characterized American policy as one "mired in stalemate." *Life* magazine, in its issue of June 27, 1969, took the extraordinary action of publishing photographs of every American killed in action between May 28 and June 3 of that year—a week, it emphasized, of no special significance. The accompanying text is reprinted here as the sixth selection; the 242 photographs are not.

In the next document, Vice President Spiro T. Agnew blasts the television networks for what he says is a highly biased coverage of the Nixon administration's Vietnam policy. The speech, which is excerpted here, was delivered in Des Moines, Iowa, on November 13, 1969. Finally, Don Oberdorfer, who covered the war for the Knight-Ridder newspapers and the *Washington Post*, calls charges of media bias during the war simplistic and unfair.

The *New York Times* Supports American Policy, 1962

The question of how to portray the growing American military role in South Vietnam is facing the Administration with a delicate problem.

There are now, news reports say, some 4,000 uniformed Americans in South Vietnam. They are engaged in such activities as training Vietnamese—often in combat situations flying Vietnamese troops into and out of combat and carrying out air reconnaissance and other dangerous intelligence missions. United States ships are patrolling the Vietnamese coast against military infiltration by sea from North to South Vietnam. If Americans are shot at during the course of these activities they are shooting back, and there have already been American combat casualties. Gen. Paul D. Harkins has been appointed to command the expanding American military operations in South Vietnam.

The Administration has been trying to depict the scope of this extensive American involvement in South Vietnam with as much restraint as possible. Some curbs have been put on news coverage of American activities in South Vietnam. The American role in South Vietnam is still primarily confined to assistance to the Vietnamese. American units are not independently engaged in combat. Undue publicity might well inflate the American role beyond its true proportions, and this could compromise Washington's efforts to keep the South Vietnam struggle a limited war.

There should, however, be no concealment of the possibility that what we are doing in South Vietnam may escalate into a major conflict. Whether it does will depend on just how extensively and openly Communist North

"The Truth About Vietnam," editorial, February 14, 1962. Copyright © 1962 by The New York Times Company. Reprinted by permission.

Vietnam and its supporters, Communist China and Russia, choose to intervene in South Vietnam. The United States would find it difficult, if not impossible, to withdraw from the fight if they do decide to throw in major forces. There is reason to believe they will not do this, that they are also interested in keeping the conflict a limited one. But the possibility of a major war is still there, and the situation is one about which American officials ought to be candid.

Neil Sheehan Recalls Initial Press Attitudes Toward the War (1962–1963), 1988

Once a reporter had demonstrated that he would endure discomfort and expose himself to danger by marching through the paddies and spending nights in the field—that he would take this soldier's baptism—he was accepted by these amiable and sincere men, and frank discussion followed. On his next trip the exchange was freer. The advisors also noticed, from wire service dispatches printed in *Pacific Stars & Stripes,* the armed forces newspaper in the Far East, and from clippings mailed by their wives and families, that the reporters protected them by quoting anonymously or otherwise disguising the source when the remark or information was derogatory. By the time of [the battle of] Ap Bac [January 1963], I and the half dozen other American correspondents had been out on numerous operations with the 7th Division and were friendly with [U.S. Army adviser John Paul] Vann and his men. (Nick Turner of Reuters, and Peter Arnett, a New Zealander who worked for the Associated Press, counted as Americans because they held essentially the same attitude as their American colleagues.) The American reporters shared the advisors' sense of commitment to this war. Our ideological prism and cultural biases were in no way different. We regarded the conflict as our war too. We believed in what our government said it was trying to accomplish in Vietnam, and we wanted our country to win this war just as passionately as Vann and his captains did. . . .

Ho and his followers were not alone in seizing on Ap Bac. The resident newsmen in South Vietnam also seized on it. We reacted as if we had been waiting for it because, beleaguered as we felt, we *had* been waiting for it. The contradiction between the press reporting of the war and the official version being propounded by [MAAG Chief General Paul D.] Harkins and Ambassador [Frederick] Nolting had grown into an embittered confrontation.

The controversy was another issue of these years that had its origin in World War II. There had been little to argue about once the shooting had

From *A Bright Shining Lie: John Paul Vann and America in Vietnam,* by Neil Sheehan, pp. 270–271, 314–315. Copyright © 1988 by Neil Sheehan. Reprinted by permission of Random House, Inc.

started in that war. The threat to national survival was beyond question, and the generals and admirals were sometimes brilliant and normally capable— or they were dismissed. Reporters became habituated to a role that was characterized more by support than skepticism. With some exceptions, the ability to stand aside and exercise independent and critical judgment of basic policy and of authority was lost as a result. In the postwar period the American press remained the most vigorous on earth, but where foreign affairs was concerned the reporting, while often gifted, was weighted toward the furthering of the anti-Communist crusade. When the press did cause trouble the argument was over detail, not substance. The news media were also being manipulated by government to an extent they did not realize.

At the outset of the 1960s, the relationship was essentially unchanged. The military institutions, and those associated with the military in the running of American overseas interests like the State Department, were continuing to receive credit for a competence and perspicacity they no longer possessed. The reporters of the period were not accustomed to thinking of their military leaders and diplomats as deluded men, and the military leaders and diplomats were not accustomed to reporters who said that they were consistently wrong. The secrecy that shielded the meetings and written communications of the men at the top helped to perpetuate the false impression that they sought and weighed facts in their discussions. The secrecy that in the 1940s had protected the nation was by the 1960s concealing the fact that the system was no longer rational.

The resident correspondents in Vietnam were also questioning detail, not substance. We thought it our duty to help win the war by reporting the truth of what was happening in order both to inform the public and to put the facts before those in power so that they could make correct decisions. (Our ignorance and our American ideology kept us from discerning the larger truths of Vietnam beneath the surface reality we could see. Professionally, we were fortunate in our ignorance. Had any reporter been sufficiently knowledgeable and open-minded to have questioned the justice and good sense of U.S. intervention in those years, he would have been fired as a "subversive.") The confrontation had occurred because of the unprecedented consistency with which we were questioning details.

Our critical faculty did not come from any genius. One of the regular complaints Harkins and Nolting made about us was that we were "immature and inexperienced." Our youth and inexperience made it possible for us to acquire what critical faculty we were displaying. Vietnam was our first war. What we saw and what we were told by the men we most respected and most closely identified with—the advisors in the field like Vann—contradicted what we were told by higher authority. We were being forced at the beginning of our professional lives to come to grips with a constant disparity between our perception of reality and higher authority's version of it, the opposite of the experience of the World War II generation of journalists.

Walter Lippmann on a "Limited War" with "Unlimited Aims," 1967

As regards credibility about the progress of the war in Vietnam, no one in high place has been more candid and informative than Senator [John] Stennis of Mississippi. About a month ago he made a speech describing how poorly we are succeeding, saying that "under existing circumstances, the American people must be prepared for a long-drawn-out and bloody war of attrition in Vietnam . . . which . . . may result in our being tied down in those steaming jungles for ten years or more." This estimate agrees substantially with that of General Westmoreland who, in a TV interview with CBS on Dec. 27, told Charles Collingwood, who had asked how long the war would last, that "it will be several years. I cannot be any more precise than that."

There is, however, a critical difference in their views. Senator Stennis believes the war could and should be shortened by escalating it without limit. General Westmoreland accepts the official doctrine of the Johnson Administration that he must fight a limited war. But he warns us that this will mean an indefinitely long war.

There is now under way a hard debate on whether to go beyond or to hold fast to the official doctrine of a limited war. That means a war in which the civilian population and the civilian economy of North Vietnam are in principle immune from attack, a war in which American troops are not committed to the occupation of the whole of South Vietnam and the suppression of the rebellion.

These limitations on our military action are the reason, Senator Stennis believes, why—in spite of 6,000 dead, 35,000 wounded, more than 30 billions spent—the United States is not yet in sight of winning the war. Senator Stennis cites "as an example, in the area of responsibility of one United States division there are some 131 villages. In April 1966, only ten of those villages were considered to be secure. Today . . . despite intensive efforts, only eighteen are secure."

Senator Stennis speaks for a growing number when he argues that, if this is the best that can be done with limited war, then the only choice before us is to withdraw dishonorably or to quit using "half measures," and to use any means necessary to compel the enemy to give up the fight. This is the issue which confronts the President and how he deals with it will have enormous consequences.

To hold to the present course will almost certainly mean that in order to appease Senator Stennis and the Chiefs of Staff the President will authorize some escalation, enough to wound but not enough to kill. The war will still be long, hopeless, inconclusive, cruel. And increasingly it will be an offense to the moral conscience of the American people. If, on the other hand, the President goes beyond limited war, and follows Chairman

From Walter Lippmann column, *Newsweek,* 70, July 16, 1967, pp. 16–17. Reprinted by permission.

[Mendell] Rivers of the House Armed Services Committee who wants to "flatten Hanoi if necessary and let world opinion go fly a kite," there is every reason for thinking that, having adopted genocide as a national policy, the country will find itself isolated in an increasingly angry and hostile world. That would mean more than watching world opinion fly a kite. It would mean that we would be suspected and hated not only in the Communist and neutral world but in very large sections of the nations with which we are most closely allied. We would come to be regarded as the most dangerous nation in the world, and the great powers of the world would align themselves accordingly to contain us.

It would be a comfort to be able to believe that the President is still in control of the war and that he is still able and willing to review and revise his thinking. He wants so much to fight only a limited war. Why does he now find himself confronted with the agonizing fact that limited war has not worked'? *Because limited war can be effective only for limited objectives.* The reason why the President is confronted with the demand for unlimited war is that he has escalated his objectives in Vietnam to an unlimited degree.

The President does not seem to understand that he has done this and that in doing it he has broken with the policy set by President Eisenhower and President Kennedy. The Johnson objectives in Vietnam are radically different from what they were under his two predecessors. Both of them insisted, as President Kennedy put it, "in the final analysis, it is their war. They are the ones who have to win it or lose it. We can help them, we can give them equipment, we can send our men out there as advisers, but they have to win it, the people of Vietnam." President Johnson has made it an American war.

In escalating his objectives he runs the danger of having to authorize unlimited escalation and the unlimited expenditure of American lives and resources to create a new Vietnamese society, one which has never existed before. The objectives which the President has pushed upon the American people are unlimited and no one should be astonished that they cannot be, that they are not being, achieved by limited means.

Newsweek Editorializes About "A Nation at Odds," 1967

The Fourth of July is a metaphor of the American dream—a sacred, self-conscious re-enactment of innocent days not quite beyond recall. All across America this week, the great pageant is being played out for the 191st time. On big-city boulevards and small-town Main Streets, the children will line the curbs waving their American flags at the marching bands, the papier-mâché floats depicting the Liberty Bell, the out-of-step Boy Scouts, the

From "A Nation at Odds," *Newsweek*, 70, July 10, 1967, pp. 16–17, 20. Reprinted by permission.

wizened Spanish-American War veterans hunched in the back-seats of gleaming convertibles lent by the local auto agency, the clangorous fire engines. Rhetoric as old as the Republic will boom from thousands of platforms bedecked with familiar bunting. Everything is as it has always been—yet a bittersweet air clings to the festivities. Cleft by doubts and tormented by frustration, the nation this Independence Day is haunted by its most corrosively ambiguous foreign adventure—a bloody, costly jungle war half a world away that has etched the tragedy of Vietnam into the American soul.

Few scars show on the surface. A stranger watching the holiday fireworks show in Detroit, the McLuhanesque march of the "transistor band" in Atlanta (50 teen-agers brandishing portable radios all tuned to the same station playing martial music), the flag-raising in the dusty, historic plaza of Sonoma (where the California Bear Republic was proclaimed 121 years ago) could easily mistake America for an omnipotent, blessedly prosperous land at peace. No war fever grips the countryside, no gasoline ration stamps dot the car windshields, no Gold Stars decorate picture windows. The casualty lists run inconspicuously on the inside pages of newspapers; wounded veterans are kept mostly out of sight, remain mostly out of mind. Save on the otherworldly mosaic of the TV screen, the war is almost invisible on the home-front. But, like a slow-spreading blight, it is inexorably making its mark on nearly every facet of American life.

The obvious costs of Vietnam are easy enough to compute: 11,373 American dead, 68,341 wounded, treasure now spent at the rate of $38,052 a minute, swelling the war's price by more than $25 billion in two years. Indeed, never have Americans been subject to such a barrage of military statistics—and never have they been so hopelessly confused by them. There are no statistics to tot up Vietnam's hidden price, but its calculus is clear: a wartime divisiveness all but unknown in America since the Blue bloodied the Gray.

In the new world's citadel of democracy, men now accuse each other of an arrogance of power and of complicity in genocide, of cowardice and disloyalty. So incendiary have feelings become that close-knit families have had to agree not to disagree about Vietnam at table. Ministers have become alienated from their flocks, parents from their children, teachers from their students and from each other, blacks from whites, hawks from doves. The crisis of conscience has spilled out into the streets—in mammoth antiwar marches like last April's big parade in New York and the "Support Our Boys" countermarch a month later. It obsesses the nation's intellectuals, spawning a bookshelf of some of the most sophisticated political analysis ever produced in America rubbing bindings with cheap charades like "MacBird!"

More than anything, Vietnam has made Americans question their fundamental assumptions about themselves and their country. In the jargony shorthand of the mid-1960s, the problem is distilled into a single, cryptic phrase: the credibility gap. For all its righteous pretensions, has America in fact stumbled into the discredited imperialist role? Are Americans henceforth doomed to fight the kind of distant, painful wars the British waged against the intractable Boers a half-century ago? Is America really in Vietnam to honor its inviolable commitments? To contain Communist China at relatively small cost? To shoulder the white man's burden of bringing democracy to the benighted? Does the military-industrial complex Dwight Eisenhower evoked in his farewell address seven years ago actually call the tune on U.S. policy? If right is on our side, Americans ask themselves, why don't *our* Vietnamese fight as well as *their* Vietnamese? Is Vietnam a colossal blunder? Or, in the hard reality of the nuclear age, are Lyndon Johnson and his advisers right after all? . . .

. . . Not since the 1930s has an American President been subjected to such scurrilous attack as has Lyndon Johnson. And rarely in American history have draft-dodging and flag-burning been so openly exalted as acts of conscience against the "immorality" of the nation's duly elected leaders. As for the thunder on the right—the eggs and red paint hurled at antiwar marchers, the Birchite muttering about Washington's "no-win" policy—it has only intensified the apocalyptic atmosphere.

The excesses of the extremists are only the frosting on the iceberg. The stubborn enigma of Vietnam has confronted reasonable men with a Hobson's choice that erodes the underpinnings of responsible politics—a cruel selection of priorities that intensifies domestic frictions, particularly in the ghettos, even as it pre-empts the resources that might soothe them. And the nation has become so committed to seeing Vietnam through to an honorable conclusion that repudiation of that commitment would unleash shock waves that would rock the country.

Thus, like a neurotic clinging desperately to set patterns of behavior, America is likely to submerge its anxieties in a brave show of business-as-usual unless the war dramatically escalates. Deep in their hearts, most Americans cherish the idea that somehow the nightmare will turn out to have a silver lining—that the U.S. will in the end achieve its limited and honorable goals in Vietnam. After all, have Americans ever failed before? Significantly though, it is the most articulate fraction of the population that has had the most profound misgivings about America's Vietnam adventure. Right or wrong, these thinkers, artists and clerics influence U.S. opinion, however slowly, and the patterns they pioneer will be felt for years.

Here, in fact, lies what may prove the most important long-range consequence of the war in Vietnam. Whatever sorrow or salvation it brings to the Vietnamese, its impact on America is almost certain to be stronger still. Almost surely, the war cannot be mastered without still greater sacrifice on the part of the American people—the latest speculation centers on an increase of 100,000 U.S. troops. And it cannot be lost or abandoned without incalculable cost to the nation's self-esteem.

The day of reckoning could come at the polls in 1968. But more likely it will come later on, after the generation of GI's and dissenters—the heroes and the hippies—take their places at the console of power. Then, the heritage of Vietnam will become visible. The danger is that it will take the form of an excruciating hunt for a scapegoat. The hope is that it will mark the birth of a cathartic realism about the true dimensions of America's world authority and its concept of itself.

Walter Cronkite Criticizes a Policy
"Mired in Stalemate," 1968

Walter Cronkite: These ruins are in Saigon, capital and largest city of South Vietnam. They were left here by an act of war, Vietnamese against Vietnamese. Hundreds died here. Here in these ruins can be seen physical evidence of the Vietcong's Tet offensive, but far less tangible is what those ruins mean, and like everything else in this burned and blasted and weary land, they mean success or setback, victory or defeat, depending upon whom you talk to.

President Nguyen Van Thieu: I believe it gives to the VC, it shows first to the VC that the—the Vietnamese people from whom they hoped to have a general uprising, and to welcome the VC in the cities, this is a very bad test for them.

Nguyen Xuan Oanh (critic of government): I think the people have realized now that there [are] no secure areas. Your own home in the heart of the city is not secure. I am stunned myself when I see that the Vietcong can come to your door and open the door and just kill you instantly, without any warning, and without any protection from the government.

Cronkite: There are doubts about the measure of success or setback, but even more, there are doubts about the exact measure of the disaster itself. All that is known with certainty is that on the first two nights of the Tet Lunar New Year, the Vietcong and North Vietnamese Regular Forces, violating the truce agreed on for that holiday, struck across the entire length of South Vietnam, hitting the largest 35 cities, towns, and provincial capitals. How many died and how much damage was done, however, are still but approximations, despite the official figures.

The very preciseness of the figures brings them under suspicion. Anyone who has wandered through these ruins knows that an exact count is impossible. Why, just a short while ago a little old man came and told us that two VC were buried in a hastily dug grave up at the end of the block. Had they been counted? And what about these ruins? Have they gone through all of them for buried civilians and soldiers? And what about those 14 VC we found in the courtyard behind the post office at Hue? Had they been counted and tabulated? They certainly hadn't been buried.

We came to Vietnam to try to determine what all this means to the future of the war here. We talked to officials, top officials, civilian and military, Vietnamese and American. We toured damaged areas like this, and refugee centers. We paid a visit to the Battle at Hue, and to the men manning the northernmost provinces, where the next big communist offensive is expected. All of this is the subject of our report. . . .

We'd like to sum up our findings in Vietnam, an analysis that must be speculative, personal, subjective. Who won and who lost in the great Tet offensive against the cities? I'm not sure. The Vietcong did not win by a

Text by Walter Cronkite found in Peter Braestrup, *Big Story: How the American Press and Television Reported and Interpreted the Crisis of Tet 1968 in Vietnam and Washington,* 1977, Vol. II.

knockout, but neither did we. The referees of history may make it a draw. Another stand-off may be coming in the big battles expected south of the Demilitarized Zone. Khe Sanh could well fall, with a terrible loss in American lives, prestige, and morale, and this is a tragedy of our stubbornness there; but the bastion no longer is a key to the rest of the northern regions, and it is doubtful that the American forces can be defeated across the breadth of the DMZ with any substantial loss of ground. Another standoff. On the political front, past performance gives no confidence that the Vietnamese government can cope with its problems, now compounded by the attack on the cities. It may not fall, it may hold on, but it probably won't show the dynamic qualities demanded of this young nation. Another stand-off.

We have been too often disappointed by the optimism of the American leaders, both in Vietnam and Washington, to have faith any longer in the silver linings they find in the darkest clouds. They may be right, that Hanoi's winter-spring offensive has been forced by the communist realization that they could not win the longer war of attrition, and that the communists hope that any success in the offensive will improve their position for eventual negotiations. It would improve their position, and it would also require our realization, that we should have had all along, that any negotiations must be that—negotiations, not the dictation of peace terms. For it seems now more certain than ever that the bloody experience of Vietnam is to end in a stalemate. This summer's almost certain stand-off will either end in real give-and-take negotiations or terrible escalation; and for every means we have to escalate, the enemy can match us. and that applies to invasion of the North, the use of nuclear weapons, or the mere commitment of 100-, or 200-, or 300,000 more American troops to the battle. And with each escalation, the world comes closer to the brink of cosmic disaster.

To say that we are closer to victory today is to believe, in the face of the evidence, the optimists who have been wrong in the past. To suggest we are on the edge of defeat is to yield to unreasonable pessimism. To say that we are mired in stalemate seems the only realistic, yet unsatisfactory, conclusion. On the off chance that military and political analysts are right, in the next few months we must test the enemy's intentions, in case this is indeed his last gasp before negotiations. But it is increasingly clear to this reporter that the only rational way out then will be to negotiate, not as victors, but as an honorable people who lived up to their pledge to defend democracy, and did the best they could.

Life Publicizes One Week's Dead in Vietnam, 1969

The faces shown on the next pages are the faces of American men killed—in the words of the official announcement of their deaths—"in connection with the conflict in Vietnam." The names, 242 of them, were released by the

From *Life,* 66 (June 27, 1969). Copyright © Time Warner. Reprinted with permission.

Pentagon during the week of May 28 through June 3, a span of no special significance except that it includes Memorial Day. The numbers of the dead are average for any seven-day period during this stage of the war.

It is not the intention of this article to speak for the dead. We cannot tell with any precision what they thought of the political currents which drew them across the world. From the letters of some, it is possible to tell they felt strongly that they should be in Vietnam, that they had great sympathy for the Vietnamese people and were appalled at their enormous suffering. Some had voluntarily extended their tours of combat duty; some were desperate to come home. Their families provided most of these photographs, and many expressed their own feelings that their sons and husbands died in a necessary cause. Yet in a time when the numbers of Americans killed in this war—36,000—though far less than the Vietnamese losses, have exceeded the dead in the Korean War, when the nation continues week after week to be numbed by a three-digit statistic which is translated to direct anguish in hundreds of homes all over the country, we must pause to look into the faces. More than we must know *how many,* we must know *who.* The faces of one week's dead, unknown but to families and friends, are suddenly recognized by·all in this gallery of young American eyes. . . .

On the back of a picture he sent home shortly before his death near Saigon, Sgt. William Anderson, 18, of Templeton, Pa., jotted a wry note: "Plain of Reeds, May 12, 1969. Here's a picture of a 2-star general awarding me my Silver Star. I didn't do anything. They just had some extra ones." His family has a few other recent photographs of the boy, including one showing him this past February helping to put a beam into place on his town's new church. His was the first military funeral held there.

Such fragments on film, in letters, in clippings and in recollection comprise the legacies of virtually every man shown in these pages. To study the smallest portion of them, even without reference to their names, is to glimpse the scope of a much broader tragedy. Writing his family just before the time he was scheduled to return to the U.S., a California man said, "I could be standing on the doorstep on the 8th [of June]. . . . As you can see from my shakey printing, the strain of getting 'short' is getting to me, so I'll close now." The ironies and sad coincidences of time hang everywhere. One Pfc. from the 101st Airborne was killed on his 21st birthday. A waiting bride had just bought her own wedding ring. A mother got flowers ordered by her son and then learned he had died the day before they arrived. A Texan had just signed up for a second two-year tour of duty when he was killed, and his ROTC instructor back home remembered with great affection that the boy, a flag-bearer, had stumbled a lot. In the state of Oregon a soldier was buried in a grave shared by the body of his brother, who had died in Vietnam two years earlier. A lieutenant was killed serving the battalion his father had commanded two years ago. A man from Colorado noted in his last letter that the Marines preferred captured North Vietnamese mortars to their own because they were lighter and much more accurate. At four that afternoon he was killed by enemy mortar fire.

Premonitions gripped many of the men. One wrote, "I have given my life as have many others for a cause in which I firmly believe." Another, writing from Hamburger Hill, said, "You may not be able to read this. I am writing it in a hurry. I see death coming up the hill." One more, who had come home on leave from Vietnam in January and had told his father he did not want to go back and was considering going AWOL, wrote last month, "Everyone's dying, they're all ripped apart. Dad, there's no one left." "I wish now I had told him to jump," the boy's father recalled. "I wish I had, but I couldn't."

Such despair was not everywhere. A lieutenant, a Notre Dame graduate, wrote home in some mild annoyance that he had not been given command of a company ("I would have jumped at the chance but there are too many Capts. floating around") and then reported with a certain pleasure that he was looking forward to his new assignment, which was leader of a reconnaissance platoon. In an entirely cheerful letter to his mother a young man from Georgia wrote, "I guess by now you are having some nice weather. Do you have tomatoes in the garden? 'A' Co. found an NVA farm two days ago with bananas, tomatoes and corn. This is real good land here. You can see why the North wants it."

There is a catalogue of fact for every face. One boy had customized his 13-year-old car and planned to buy a ranch. Another man, a combat veteran of the Korean War, leaves seven children. A third had been an organist in his church and wanted to be a singer. One had been sending his pay home to contribute to his brother's college expenses. The mother of one of the dead, whose son was the third of four to serve in the Army, insists with deep pride, "We are a patriotic family willing to pay that price." An aunt who had raised her nephew said of him, "He was really and truly a conscientious objector. He told me it was a terrible thought going into the Army and winding up in Vietnam and shooting people who hadn't done anything to him. . . . Such a waste. Such a shame."

Every photograph, every face carries its own simple and powerful message. The inscription on one boy's picture to his girl reads:

To Miss Shirley Nash
We shall let no Love come between Love.
Only peace and happiness from Heaven Above.
Love always.
                                        Perpetually yours,
                                        Joseph

Spiro T. Agnew Assails the Television Networks for Biased Coverage, 1969

Tonight I want to discuss the importance of the television news medium to the American people. No nation depends more on the intelligent judgment

Transcript of Spiro Agnew's address in Des Moines, Iowa, November 14, 1969. Copyright © 1969 by The New York Times Company. Reprinted by permission.

of its citizens. No medium has more profound influence over public opinion. Nowhere in our system are there fewer checks on vast power. So, nowhere should there be more conscientious responsibility exercised than by the news media. The question is, Are we demanding enough of our television news presentations? And are the men of this medium demanding enough of themselves?

Monday night a week ago, President Nixon delivered the most important address of his Administration, one of the most important of our decade. His subject was Vietnam. His hope was to rally the American people to see the conflict through to a lasting and just peace in the Pacific. For 32 minutes, he reasoned with a nation that has suffered almost a third of a million casualties in the longest war in its history.

When the President completed his address—an address, incidentally, that he spent weeks in the preparation of—his words and policies were subjected to instant analysis and querulous criticism. The audience of 70 million Americans gathered to hear the President of the United States was inherited by a small band of network commentators and self-appointed analysts, the majority of whom expressed in one way or another their hostility to what he had to say.

It was obvious that their minds were made up in advance. . . .

Now every American has a right to disagree with the President of the United States and to express publicly that disagreement. But the President of the United States has a right to communicate directly with the people who elected him, and the people of this country have the right to make up their own minds and form their own opinions about a Presidential address without having a President's words and thoughts characterized through the prejudices of hostile critics before they can even be digested.

When Winston Churchill rallied public opinion to stay the course against Hitler's Germany, he didn't have to contend with a gaggle of commentators raising doubts about whether he was reading public opinion right, or whether Britain had the stamina to see the war through.

When President Kennedy rallied the nation in the Cuban missile crisis, his address to the people was not chewed over by a roundtable of critics who disparaged the course of action he'd asked America to follow.

The purpose of my remarks tonight is to focus your attention on this little group of men who not only enjoy a right of instant rebuttal to every Presidential address, but, more importantly, wield a free hand in selecting, presenting and interpreting the great issues in our nation.

First, let's define that power. At least 40 million Americans every night, it's estimated, watch the network news. Seven million of them view A.B.C., the remainder being divided between N.B.C. and C.B.S.

According to Harris polls and other studies, for millions of Americans the networks are the sole source of national and world news. In Will Rogers's observation, what you knew was what you read in the newspaper.

Today for growing millions of Americans, it's what they see and hear on their television sets.

Now how is this network news determined? A small group of men, numbering perhaps no more than a dozen anchormen, commentators and executive producers, settle upon the 20 minutes or so of film and commentary that's to reach the public. This selection is made from the 90 to 180 minutes that may be available. Their powers of choice are broad.

They decide what 40 to 50 million Americans will learn of the day's events in the nation and in the world.

We cannot measure this power and influence by the traditional democratic standards, for these men can create national issues overnight.

They can make or break by their coverage and commentary a moratorium on the war.

They can elevate men from obscurity to national prominence within a week. They can reward some politicians with national exposure and ignore others. . . .

Nor is their power confined to the substantive. A raised eyebrow, an inflection of the voice, a caustic remark dropped in the middle of a broadcast can raise doubts in a million minds about the veracity of a public official or the wisdom of a Government policy.

One Federal Communications Commissioner considers the powers of the networks equal to that of local, state and Federal Governments all combined. Certainly it represents a concentration of power over American public opinion unknown in history.

Now what do Americans know of the men who wield this power? Of the men who produce and direct the network news the nation knows practically nothing. Of the commentators, most Americans know little other than that they reflect an urbane and assured presence seemingly well-informed on every important matter.

We do know that to a man these commentators and producers live and work in the geographical and intellectual confines of Washington, D.C., or New York City, the latter of which James Reston terms the most unrepresentative community in the entire United States.

Both communities bask in their own provincialism, their own parochialism.

We can deduce that these men read the same newspapers. They draw their political and social views from the same sources. Worse, they talk constantly to one another, thereby providing artificial reinforcement to their shared viewpoints.

Do they allow their biases to influence the selection and presentation of the news? David Brinkley states objectivity is impossible to normal human behavior. Rather, he says, we should strive for fairness.

Another anchorman on a network news show contends, and I quote: "You can't expunge all your private convictions just because you sit in a seat like this and a camera starts to stare at you. I think your program has to reflect what your basic feelings are. I'll plead guilty to that."

Less than a week before the 1968 election, this same commentator charged that President Nixon's campaign commitments were no more durable than campaign balloons. He claimed that, were it not for the fear of hostile reaction, Richard Nixon would be giving into, and I quote him exactly, "his natural instinct to smash the enemy with a club or go after him with a meat axe."

Had this slander been made by one political candidate about another, it would have been dismissed by most commentators as a partisan attack. But this attack emanated from the privileged sanctuary of a network studio and therefore had the apparent dignity of an objective statement.

The American people would rightly not tolerate this concentration of power in Government.

Is it not fair and relevant to question its concentration in the hands of a tiny enclosed fraternity of privileged men elected by no one and enjoying a monopoly sanctioned and licensed by Government?

The views of the majority of this fraternity do not—and I repeat, not—represent the views of America.

That is why such a great gulf existed between how the nation received the President's address and how the networks reviewed it.

Don Oberdorfer on Charges of Media Bias, 1987

Was the press biased in Vietnam?

Not in the simple use of the word. The coverage of Vietnam was a complicated subject, most of which is conveniently forgotten by one side or the other in the debate. For the American press, Vietnam was a learning experience—much as it was for the rest of the country and the government. We knew very little at the beginning, but as the war progressed people in the press, along with people in the government who were our sources after all, began to get this very hazy, fuzzy situation into focus. And this picture was not the same picture that was being portrayed in the official reports. We know now, because of the Pentagon Papers, people's memoirs, and other things that the picture portrayed in the official reports was not the one that was believed by many of the policymakers.

One of the things that happened was that the consensus within the government broke down and suddenly instead of having one monolithic viewpoint presented to the press, you had conflicting viewpoints and therefore conflicting sets of sources. And if you look at the stories, it's quite clear that many of the things in Vietnam that were taken as press enterprise [came] from military or civilian officials who knew what was going on and communicated it by the back channels to the press. And they did it because they objected to the policy or objected to the deception about the policy, and also because some of them saw the press as the way to advance ideas which had been rejected from the top of the American government.

Kim Willenson et al., *The Bad War: An Oral History of the Vietnam War,* pp. 193–194. Copyright © 1987, Newsweek, Inc. Reprinted with permission.

✗ *E S S A Y S*

In the first essay, Robert Elegant blasts his former colleagues in the media for biased reporting. A former reporter who covered Vietnam for the *Los Angeles Times,* he argues that, for the first time in modern history, the outcome of a war was determined by written and, especially, televised coverage. The next essay, by Peter Braestrup of the Woodrow Wilson International Center for Scholars in Washington, focuses on press and television accounts of the Tet offensive and its aftermath. A former Vietnam correspondent with the *Washington Post* and the *New York Times,* Braestrup also accuses the press of distortion and superficiality, although his attack is less biting than Elegant's. In the last essay, Daniel C. Hallin, a professor of political science and communication at the University of California, San Diego, offers a different perspective. Hallin faults the media for their largely uncritical stance toward the war for most of its duration and argues that they never probed into the underlying causes of the conflict or of U.S. policy. He sees the media as a key component of the modern state, not its critic.

How to Lose a War

ROBERT ELEGANT

In the early 1960s, when the Viet Nam War became a big story, most foreign correspondents assigned to cover the story wrote primarily to win the approbation of the crowd, above all their own crowd. As a result, in my view, the self-proving system of reporting they created became ever further detached from political and military realities because it instinctively concentrated on its own self-justification. The American press, naturally dominant in an "American war," somehow felt obliged to be less objective than partisan, to take sides, for it was inspired by the *engagé* "investigative" reporting that burgeoned in the US in these impassioned years. The press was instinctively "agin the Government"—and, at least reflexively, for Saigon's enemies.

During the latter half of the 15-year American involvement in Viet Nam the media became the primary battlefield. Illusory events reported *by* the press as well as real events *within* the press corps were more decisive than the clash of arms or the contention of ideologies. For the first time in modern history, the outcome of a war was determined not on the battlefield, but on the printed page and, above all, on the television screen. Looking back coolly, I believe it can be said (surprising as it may still sound) that South Vietnamese and American forces actually won the limited military struggle. They virtually crushed the Viet Cong in the South, the "native" guerrillas who were directed, reinforced, and equipped from Hanoi; and thereafter they threw back the invasion by regular North Vietnamese divisions. None the less, the War was finally lost to the invaders *after* the US disengagement because the political pressures built up by the media had made it quite

From Robert Elegant, "How to Lose a War," *Encounter* LVII (August 1981), excerpts from pp. 73–90. Reprinted by permission of *Encounter.*

impossible for Washington to maintain even the minimal material and moral support that would have enabled the Saigon régime to continue effective resistance.

Since I am considering causes rather than effects, the demoralization of the West, particularly the United States, that preceded and followed the fall of South Viet Nam is beyond the scope of this article. It is, however, interesting to wonder whether Angola, Afghanistan, and Iran would have occurred *if* Saigon had not fallen amid nearly universal odium—that is to say, *if* the "Viet Nam Syndrome," for which the press (in my view) was largely responsible, had not afflicted the Carter Administration and paralyzed American will. On the credit side, largely despite the press, the People's Republic of China would almost certainly not have purged itself of the Maoist doctrine of "worldwide liberation through people's war" and, later, would not have come to blows with Hanoi if the defense of South Viet Nam had not been maintained for so long.

"You could be hard about it and deny that there was a brotherhood working there, but what else could you call it?" This is a question that Michael Herr asked in his *Dispatches,* a personally honest, but basically deceptive book.

> But . . . all you ever talked about was the war, and they could come to seem like two different wars at the same time. Because who but another correspondent could talk the kind of *mythical* war you *wanted* to hear described?

I have added the italics; for in the words "mythical" and "wanted" the essential truth is laid bare. In my own personal experience most correspondents *wanted* to talk chiefly to other correspondents to confirm their own *mythical* vision of the war. Even newcomers were pre-committed, as the American jargon has it, to the collective position most of their colleagues had already taken. What I can only call surrealistic reporting constantly fed on itself; and did not diminish thereby, but swelled into ever more grotesque shapes. I found the process equally reprehensible for being in no small part unwitting.

John le Carré (whose extravagant encomium adorns the cover of the Pan edition of *Dispatches:* "The best book I have ever read on men and war in our times") is, I feel, too clever a writer to believe he painted an even proximately accurate picture of South-east Asia in *The Honourable Schoolboy* (1972). But he brilliantly depicted the press corps and the correspondents' Asia, an encapsulated, self-defining world whirling in its own eccentric orbit. Correspondents, briefly set down in the brutally alienating milieu called Viet Nam, turned to each other for professional sustenance and emotional comfort. After all, there was nowhere else to turn, certainly not to stark reality, which was both elusive and repellent.

Most correspondents were isolated from the Vietnamese by ignorance of their language and culture, as well as by a measure of race estrangement. Most were isolated from the quixotic American Army establishment, itself often as confused as they themselves were, by their moralistic attitudes and their political prejudices. It was inevitable, in the circumstances, that they came to write, in the first instance, for each other.

To be sure, the approbation of his own crowd gave a certain fullness to the correspondent's life in exile that reached beyond the irksome routine of reporting and writing. The disapprobation of his peers could transform him into a bitterly defensive misanthrope (I think here of one industrious radio and newspaper stringer who was reputed to be the richest correspondent in Viet Nam, except, of course, for the television stars). Even the experienced correspondents, to whom Asia was "home" rather than a hostile temporary environment, formed their own little self-defensive world within the larger world of the newcomers.

It was no wonder that correspondents writing to win the approbation of other correspondents in that insidiously collegial atmosphere produced reporting that was remarkably homogeneous. After each other, correspondents wrote to win the approbation of their editors. who controlled their professional lives and who were closely linked with the intellectual community at home. The consensus of that third circle, the domestic intelligentsia, derived largely from correspondents' reports and in turn served to determine the nature of those reports. If dispatches did not accord with that consensus, approbation was withheld. Only in the last instance did correspondents address themselves to the general public, the mass of lay readers and viewers.

It was my impression that most correspondents were, in one respect, very much like the ambitious soldiers they derided. A tour in Viet Nam was almost essential to promotion for a US Regular Army officer, and a combat command was the best road to rapid advancement. Covering the biggest continuing story in the world was not absolutely essential to a correspondent's rise, but it was an invaluable cachet. Quick careers were made by spectacular reporting of the obvious fact that men, women, and children were being killed; fame or at least notoriety rewarded the correspondent who became part of the action—rather than a mere observer—by influencing events directly.

Journalists, particularly those serving in television, were therefore, like soldiers, "rotated" to Viet Nam. Few were given time to develop the knowledge, and indeed the intellectual instincts, necessary to report the War in the round. Only a few remained "in country" for years, though the experienced Far Eastern correspondents visited regularly from Hong Kong, Singapore, and Tokyo. Not surprisingly, one found that most reporting veered farther and farther from the fundamental political, economic, and military realities of the War, for these were usually *not* spectacular. Reporting Viet Nam became a closed, self-generating system sustained largely by the acclaim the participants lavished on each other in almost equal measure to the opprobrium they heaped on "the Establishment," a fashionable and very vulnerable target.

For some journalists, perhaps most, a moment of truth through self-examination was never to come. The farther they were from the real conflict, the more smugly self-approving they now remain as commentators who led the public to expect a brave new world when the North Vietnamese finally "liberated" South Viet Nam. Even those correspondents who today gingerly confess to some errors or distortions usually insist that the true fault was not theirs at all, but Washington's. The enormity of having helped in one way or another to bring tens of millions under grinding totalitarian rule—and having tilted the global balance of power—appears too great to acknowledge. It is easier to absolve one's self by blaming exclusively Johnson, Nixon, and Kissinger. . . .

Journalistic institutions are, of course, rarely afflicted by false modesty. They have not disclaimed credit for the outcome of the war, and their representatives have taken public bows for their successful intervention. The multitude of professional prizes bestowed upon the "big-story" coverage of Viet Nam certainly implied approval of the general effort.

However, the media have been rather coy; they have not declared that they played a *key* role in the conflict. They have not proudly trumpeted Hanoi's repeated expressions of gratitude to the mass media of the non-Communist world, although Hanoi has indeed affirmed that it could not have won "without the Western press." The Western press appears either unaware of the direct connection between cause (its reporting) and effect (the Western defeat in Viet Nam), or strangely reluctant to proclaim that the pen and the camera proved decisively mightier than the bayonet and ultramodern weapons.

Nor have the media dwelt upon the glaring inconsistency between the expectation they raised of peaceful, prosperous development after Saigon's collapse and the present post-War circumstances in Indo-China. . . .

. . . Any searching analysis of fundamental premises has remained as unthinkable to "the critics" as it was during the fighting. They have remained committed to the proposition that the American role in Indo-China was totally reprehensible and inexcusable, while the North Vietnamese role—and, by extension, the roles of the Khmer Rouge in Cambodia and the Pathet Lao in Laos—was righteous, magnanimous, and just. Even the growing number who finally deplored the repressive consequences of the totalitarian victory could not bring themselves to re-examine the premises that led them to contribute so decisively to those victories. Thus William Shawcross, before his sententious book, *Sideshow,* wrote of the Communists' reshaping of Cambodian society: "The process is atrociously brutal." Although "the Khmer people are suffering horribly under their new rulers," this is how Shawcross unhesitatingly assigned the ultimate blame:

> They have suffered every day of the last six years—ever since the beginning of one of the most destructive foreign policies the United States has ever pursued: the "Nixon-Kissinger doctrine" in its purest form. . . .

Most correspondents on the scene were not quite as vehement. But they were moved by the same conviction of American guilt, which was so fixed that it resisted all the evidence pointing to a much more complex reality. Employed in the service of that crusading fervor was, for the first time, the most emotionally moving medium of all.

Television, its thrusting and simplistic character shaping its message, was most shocking because it was most immediate. The Viet Nam War was a presence in homes throughout the world. Who could seriously doubt the veracity of so plausible and so moving a witness in one's own living room?

At any given moment, a million images were available to the camera's lens in Saigon alone—and hundreds of millions throughout Indo-China. But TV crews naturally preferred the most dramatic. That, after all, was their business—show business. It was not news to film farmers peacefully tilling their rice-fields, though it might have been argued that nothing happening *was* news when the American public had been led to believe that almost every Vietnamese farmer was regularly threatened by the Viet Cong, constantly imperiled by battle, and rarely safe from indiscriminate US bombing.

A few hard, documented instances. A burning village was news, even though it was a deserted village used in a Marine training exercise—even though the television correspondent had handed his Zippo lighter to a non-commissioned officer with the suggestion that he set fire to an abandoned house. American soldiers cutting ears off a Viet Cong corpse was news—even if the cameraman had offered the soldiers his knife and "dared" them to take those grisly souvenirs. (Since the antics of the media were definitely *not* news, the network refrained from apologizing for the contrived "event" when a special investigation called the facts to its attention.) Cargo-nets full of dead South Vietnamese soldiers being lowered by helicopters were news—even if that image implicitly contradicted the prevailing conviction that the South Vietnamese never fought, but invariably threw away their weapons and ran. . . .

Equally lamentable was the failure of the Western press to cover with any thoroughness the Army of the Republic of South Viet Nam, which over the long run was doing most of the fighting. Correspondents were reluctant to commit their safety to units whose resolution they distrusted—sometimes for good reason, more often because of a kind of racist contempt—in order to get stories that interested their editors so little. Coverage of Vietnamese politics, as well as social and economic developments, was sporadic—except for military coups and political crises, and those were often misreported.

Examples of misdirected or distorted reporting could be amassed almost indefinitely. The War, after all, lasted some twenty years. A former *Washington Post* and *New York Times* correspondent, Peter Braestrup, has published a two-volume study of the coverage of the Tet Offensive of 1968. Quite significantly, it attracted little interest compared to, say, William Shawcross's *Sideshow* or Michael Herr's *Dispatches*.

Nowadays, Jean Lacouture, Anthony Lewis, and William Shawcross (among some other "Viet Nam veterans") clearly feel deceived or even betrayed by the Communists of Indo-China; yet surely, they voluntarily adopted the ideological bias that allowed Hanoi to deceive them. The Vietnamese Communists—unlike their Cambodian confréres—had, after all, openly *declared* their intention of imposing totalitarian rule upon the South. Why, then, were the "critics of the American war" so genuinely

surprised by the consequences? More crucially, why did a virtual generation of Western journalists deceive itself so consistently as to the nature of
the "liberation" in Indo-China? Why did the correspondents *want* to believe
in the good faith of the Communists? Why did they so *want* to disbelieve
the avowed motives of the United States? Why did so much of their presumably factual reporting regularly reflect their ideological bias?

The obvious explanation is not as ingenuous as it may appear: the
majority of Western correspondents and commentators adopted their idio-
syncratic approach to the Indo-China War precisely because other journalists had already adopted that approach. To put it more directly, it was
fashionable (this was, after all, the age of Radical Chic) to be "a critic of
the American war."

Decisive in the case of the Americans, who set the tone, was the normally healthy adversary relationship between the US press and the US government. American newspapermen have often felt, with some justification,
that if an Administration affirmed a controversial fact, that fact—if not
prima facie false—was at the least suspect. As the lies of successive
Administrations regarding Indo-China escalated, that conviction became
the credo of the press. The psychological process that began with the
unfounded optimism of President John F. Kennedy's ebullient "New
Frontiersmen," who were by and large believed, ended with the disastrous
last stand of Richard Nixon's dour palace guard, who were believed by no
one.

The reaction against official mendacity was initially healthy, but later
became distorted, self-serving, and self-perpetuating. A faulty syllogism
was unconsciously accepted: Washington was lying consistently; Hanoi
contradicted Washington; therefore Hanoi was telling the truth.

The initial inclination to look upon Hanoi as a fount of pure truth was
intelligently fostered by the Communists, who selectively rewarded "critics
of the American war" with visas to North Viet Nam. A number of influential journalists and public figures (ranging from former cabinet officers to
film actresses) were fêted in North Viet Nam. They were flattered not only
by the attention and the presumed inside information proffered by the
North Vietnamese, but by their access to a land closed to most Americans.
The favored few—and the aspiring many—helped establish a climate in
which it was not only fashionable but, somehow, an act of courage to follow the critical crowd in Saigon and Washington while praising Hanoi. The
skeptical correspondent risked ostracism by his peers and conflicts with his
editors if he did not run with "the herd of independent minds," if he did not
support the consensus.

The larger reason for the tenacity of the consensus went much deeper.
It welled from a new view of *this* War, which was quite different from the
press's view of other wars—and from a new messianic approach to the role
of the press in wartime.

The main question persists. Why was the press—whether in favor of
official policy at the beginning or vehemently against the War at the end—
so superficial and so biased?

Chief among many reasons was, I believe, the politicization of correspondents by the constantly intensifying clamor over Viet Nam in Europe and America. Amateur (and professional) propagandists served both sides of the question, but the champions of Hanoi were spectacularly more effective. They created an atmosphere of high pressure that made it exceedingly difficult to be objective.

In Korea, senior officers who were incensed by unfavorable reports would sometimes demand: "Who are you for—the Communists or us?" Most correspondents were detached and could answer honestly: "Personally for the UN and the US, but professionally for neither side. Just trying to tell the true story. . . ." In Viet Nam that response was virtually impossible amid growing Western horror at the "dirty, immoral war." Correspondents were almost compelled to become partisans, and most became partisans for Hanoi, or, at least, *against* Saigon and Washington.

Revulsion in Europe and America sprang as much from the nature of the correspondents' reporting as it did from the belligerents' direct manipulation of public opinion. Some of my senior colleagues had learned wisdom on a hundred battlefields, having covered World War II, the Chinese Civil War, the Viet Minh campaign against the French, and the Indonesian revolt against the Dutch. I had at least been through Korea, the Malayan "Emergency," and the fighting between Chinese Nationalists and Chinese Communists for Quemoy. But most correspondents had never seen war before their arrival in Indo-China. Many confused the beastliness of all war with the particular war in Indo-China, which they unthinkingly concluded was unique in human history because it was new to them.

This much must be said: the best of their reporting accurately conveyed the horror of war—all war. Yet it presented the suffering, barbarism, and devastation as somehow peculiar to Indo-China. It almost made it appear that other wars had been fought by mailed champions on fields remote from human habitation, while in Indo-China, for the first time, carnage brutally involved both massed military formations and the civilian populace. Since a guerrilla war is inherently not as destructive as a conventional war, human suffering and material devastation had, in reality, been markedly greater in Korea than in Viet Nam—and much, much greater on both Asian and European fronts in World War II.

Because Viet Nam did not attract many senior correspondents for extended tours, at any given time a majority of the correspondents were new to the complexities of Indo-China. Some could not even look after themselves in combat, the *sine qua non* of a successful—and surviving—war correspondent.

One afternoon in May 1968, when the Viet Cong were attacking the outskirts of Saigon, six young correspondents piled into a single mini taxi to drive to the shifting "front." They were startled when advised to take two or three taxis so that they could get out faster if they came under fire. A tall, rotund neophyte wearing a scarlet shirt paraded up and down the road the Viet Cong were attacking. He was dismayed by the pained abhorrence with which South Vietnamese paratroops regarded him, until it was explained that he was drawing rocket fire. The six clustered around a 24-year-old US 1st lieutenant, just out of the Military Academy at West Point, who was struggling to communicate with the Vietnamese major commanding and, simultaneously, to direct the gunships that swooped low, firing their machine-guns. While shells burst around them, the correspondents tried to interrogate the lieutenant on the morality of the US presence in Indo-China. . . .

The "Viet Nam Syndrome" is compounded of a variety of symptoms, none unique in itself, but unprecedented in combination and devastating in their totality. Wars have been badly reported in the past. Facts have been mis-stated, and their interpretation has been biased. Emotions have been deliberately inflamed, and reporters have ridden to fame on waves of mis-representation. But never before Viet Nam had the collective policy of the media—no less stringent term will serve—sought by graphic and unremit-ting distortion the victory of the enemies of the correspondents' own side. Television coverage was, of course, new in its intensity and repetitiveness; it was crucial in shifting the emphasis from fact to emotion. And television will play the same role in future conflicts—on the Western side, of course. It will not and cannot expose the crimes of an enemy who is too shrewd to allow the cameras free play.

As long as the "Viet Nam Syndrome" afflicts the media, it seems to me that it will be virtually impossible for the West to conduct an effective for-eign policy. It is apparently irrelevant that the expectations of paradise after Hanoi's victory evoked by "the critics of the American war" became the purgatory the Indo-Chinese people have suffered. Just as many denizens of the ante-bellum American South did not know that "*Damnyankee*" was really two words, an entire generation in Europe and the United States behaves as if "the dirty, immoral war in Viet Nam" were an irrefutable and inseparable dogma. Merely equate El Salvador (or any other American intervention) to Viet Nam—and not only the American public, but all "lib-eral" Europeans will condemn it without reservation. That is all they need to know. In its final effect—what has over the last decade been called "the paralysis of political will"—it will make it especially difficult for the US to honor any political commitment anywhere in the world where small and threatened nations may expect American support for their independent exis-tence. Before they fall to an aggressor, they will have been victimized by "the Viet Nam Syndrome."

It has long appeared to me that the medical and legal professions enjoy one enormous advantage. If they err, doctors and lawyers may be blamed. Yet, except in the most flagrant cases, the client or the patient pays them again for correcting their mistakes—if they can, and if he can. But the media on Viet Nam, it has become blatantly obvious, have enjoyed even greater advantages. Even in the most flagrant cases, they have not been blamed. They have, rather, been acclaimed for their errors. Who can, ulti-mately, prove it otherwise? The peoples of the non-Communist world have paid dearly for these errors—and may well continue to pay.

Missing the "Big Story"

PETER BRAESTRUP

In overall terms, the performance by the major American television and print news organizations during February and March 1968 constitutes an extreme case. Rarely has contemporary crisis journalism turned out, in retrospect, to have veered so widely from reality. Essentially, the dominant themes of the words and film from Vietnam (rebroadcast in commentary, editorials, and much political rhetoric at home) added up to a portrait of defeat for the allies. Historians, on the contrary, have concluded that the Tet offensive resulted in a severe military-political setback for Hanoi in the South. To have portrayed such a setback for one side as a defeat for the other—in a major crisis abroad—cannot be counted as a triumph for American journalism.

Why did the media perform so unsatisfactorily? I have come to this general conclusion: The special circumstances of Tet impacted to a rare degree on modern American journalism's special susceptibilities and limitations. This peculiar conjuncture overwhelmed reporters, commentators, and their superiors alike. And it could happen again.

In most American foreign policy crises since World War II, there have been objective factors that assuaged journalistic needs and curbed journalistic excess. One thinks in particular of the 1962 Cuban missile crisis and Hanoi's 1972 offensive, the latter a far stronger military effort than Tet. In both cases, 1962 and 1972, there were perceived forewarnings of trouble, a well-defined geographical arena, a widely shared sense of the relative strengths and capabilities of the opposing sides, a conventional confrontation remote from journalistic havens, and a coherent Presidential response. None of these reassuring elements was fully present at Tet-1968. In Vietnam, the sudden penetration of downtown Saigon by Vietcong sapper teams impacted personally on correspondents' lives. The geographical dispersion of the concurrent communist attacks elsewhere in the country led to uncertainty among newsmen about the enemy's intent, strength, and degree of success in the countryside. Journalists' unfamiliarity both with the South Vietnamese and with the relative military capabilities of each side increased this uncertainty.

Inevitably, then, the overall pattern of events in Vietnam in February 1968 was for a time obscure. But commentators and many reporters did not wait. By the time the fog of war began to lift later that month, the collective emanations of the major media were producing a kind of continuous black fog of their own, a vague conventional "disaster" image, which few newsmen attempted to reexamine and which few news managers at home sought to question. Indeed, in the case of *Newsweek,* NBC, and CBS, and

Peter Braestrup, *Big Story: How the American Press and Television Reported and Interpreted the Crisis of Tet 1968 in Vietnam and Washington,* 1977, Vol. II, pp. 705–709, 711–717, 724–727. Reprinted by permission of the author. © Peter Braestrup, 1977.

of photo displays by others, the disaster theme seemed to be exploited for its own sake. The journalistic fog had thinned to a patchy haze by the time of President Johnson's March 31 speech, but it had not been penetrated by a cold, retrospective light. The record was not set straight. The hasty assumptions and judgments of February and early March were simply allowed to stand.

Was this thematic persistence due to a sudden seizure of "antiwar" feeling among newsmen, an ideological media conspiracy against Johnson Administration war policy?

One must rely for the answer on contemporary impressions and interviews obtained 18 months to two years after the fact—when time and a new set of perceptions had clouded memories. What seems fairly clear is that, in January 1968, there was little optimism among newsmen, as among congressmen, with regard to the Vietnam venture. Many, as we have indicated, were simply skeptical of any success; a few were hostile to the military and sympathetic to the academicians and senators active in the peace movement; others hoped for a negotiated settlement. Hawks were few, except on *Time*. Outspoken doves were rare, except on the *Times*. At CBS and NBC, it appears, there was both impatience with the war's length and revulsion at its horrors. In Vietnam, there was little conversation about war policy; instead, newsmen exchanged anecdotes about the war's various aspects. Overall, there seems to have been no ideological consensus *prior* to Tet that could serve as an explanation for media treatment of the crisis.

It is true that, after the attacks broke, *Newsweek* became explicit in its political stance, citing the "utter inadequacy" of Administration war policy and calling for a negotiated settlement. . . . (That magazine's Vietnam news coverage was more negative than that of the other print media.) However, *Newsweek*'s editors may have been equally concerned about keeping up with political fashion, with the much more vocal antiwar opinion, with the pessimism of Walter Cronkite and the New York *Times*'s editorial page.

Thus, out of his own experience, and interviews with his colleagues, this writer is convinced that ideology, per se, played a relatively minor role in the media treatment of the Tet crisis. The big problems lay elsewhere, and persist to this day.

Yet, downgrading the ideological factor in Tet media coverage—a factor so heavily stressed by Nixon Administration spokesmen in 1969–72 in their attacks on the "Eastern establishment press"—should not be taken to mean that newsmen, especially those in Washington and New York, were neutral with respect to the Johnson Administration. They were suspicious and resentful, on personal-professional grounds. As was noted at the beginning of this study, the credibility among newsmen of President Johnson, Secretary McNamara, and senior officialdom by 1968 was low. Johnson, starting with his first public budget discussions in 1964, had gained a reputation in Washington for manipulation and half-truths. The public utterances of generals and civilian officials alike concerning the war had seldom been distinguished by brutal candor. And Tet . . . came after an Administration propaganda campaign intended to shore up support for a long-term limited war policy that embraced neither a decisive military strategy nor a plausible diplomatic ending. The policy satisfied neither hawks nor doves. Yet, this 1967 "progress" campaign had, in effect, made implicit promises that no unpleasant surprises were in store.

Although they voiced misgivings, newsmen in Vietnam (or Washington) could not *prove* in 1967 that the Administration's professed optimism was overblown. They had to report what the Administration said. But there was an underlying journalistic resentment, especially in Washington, at being thus used, and, when the crisis came, Johnson was not given the benefit of the doubt, as Presidents usually are. As several Washington reporters later noted, the primary reaction of many newsmen in the capital after Tet was to indulge in retribution for prior manipulation by the Administration. Thus, while formal ideology did not heavily flavor media treatment of Tet, to a rare degree the initial coverage reflected subjective reactions by newsmen—not only to the sights and circumstances of Tet itself, but also to the Administration's past conduct.

This coverage was also shaped by habit and convention. The press, and, most strikingly, television news since the early 1960s, have sought "themes" and "story lines" to routinize major developments and to make events intelligible. "Keep it simple," is the deskman's warning to reporters, as much for his own sake as for the reader's. Election campaigns are portrayed as horse races (with front runners and dark horses); votes on major issues in Congress are often defined as "defeats" or "victories" for the President; and, for a long time in the 1950s and 1960s, local struggles in Africa and Latin America were simplified as contests between "procommunists" and "anticommunists." These ingrained professional habits left newsmen ill-equipped to cope with the unusual ambiguities and uncertainties surrounding Tet. In Washington, the assault on the U.S. Embassy in Saigon came as a crisis piled on top of another (apparent) crisis—the dramatic seizure of the *Pueblo* by the North Koreans—which had preoccupied news managers for a week. Moreover, . . . President Johnson did not seize the initiative in terms of information or decision-making; and although Washington newsmen do not like to admit it, their dependence on the White House for a "news agenda" and a "frame of reference," especially in crisis, is considerable. When the President is vague, or delegates the discussion of bad news to subordinates (as Johnson largely did at Tet), without demonstrably responding to the crisis himself, the government seems incoherent, the future filled with uncertainty.

We have seen that in Vietnam, too, the circumstances for newsmen were at first ambiguous and uncertain. There was the personally threatening combat in Saigon, the looming drama of Khe Sanh, the destructive urban battle in Hue. There were the fragmentary reports of action in other towns and cities. And there was Westmoreland himself predicting a second wave. To newsmen accustomed to the relatively brief, localized rural battles that characterized the war until Tet, the very persistence of communist effort in Saigon, Hue, and Khe Sanh and along the highways was unsettling. The fate of the initially inaccessible countryside, the state of the long-neglected ARVN (suddenly a key actor), the intentions and capabilities of the foe were all question marks throughout much of February. . . .

In retrospect, after all is said and done, the problem for the major bureaus in Vietnam was not lack of *opportunity* to piece together the over-all picture and dispel some confusion as time went on. It lay in their initial reactions to the Tet crisis, and in the subsequent preoccupation of most reporters and their managers with more compelling matters, such as Khe Sanh and upcoming enemy moves.

Faced with ambiguities and uncertainty, the major bureaus in Saigon, for the most part, reacted in two ways. The first generalized tendency was to follow standard Vietnam operating procedure, which in turn was condi-tioned by standard perceptions of "news." For newspapers and AP and UPI, this meant mining and processing the most dramatic elements out of the daily communiqués and briefings in Saigon. For everyone, it meant deploy-ing reporters to the most dramatic action elsewhere. This approach through-out an episodic war had yielded both "hard news" and vivid human interest "features" for print, and a steady flow of filmed vignettes, oftentimes film clichés, for television. The tendency to head for "the action" (which notice-ably faded among newsmen in Saigon in later years) was by no means uni-versal in 1965–68. But it was common to the reporters most respected by their peers. Going to "the action" served the obvious professional require-ments of seeing and experiencing the war one had been sent to cover; and it sustained a proud tradition in U.S. journalism. In the case of television, it also satisfied superiors' demands for GI combat stories. On another level, it legitimized (or seemed to legitimize) a newsman's claim to speak with authority on the war; it gave him a certain status. And the risks of brief exposure to danger justified his relative comfort amid so much courage and suffering.

Most newsmen in Vietnam, in their late twenties and thirties, sought the opportunity to witness a prolonged life-and-death drama of major impor-tance to America. But their time horizons were short. Their focus was nar-row. By temperament or training they were not "experts," systematic researchers, writers skilled in synthesis; they were adventurers and, to some extent, voyeurs; at their best, on some occasions, they were also shrewd observers and interrogators, and perceptive tellers of tales. To them and their superiors, the inherent drama—and importance—of Saigon, Hue, and Khe Sanh were compelling, and obviously "news." And the concentra-tion of journalistic manpower on these dramatic but isolated stories insured that they were treated at home as the significant "news." What else was worthy of sustained firsthand attention was less obvious; and the media in Vietnam committed major sins of omission as time went on.

The second generalized reaction by the major news bureaus in Saigon was in keeping with the more ambitious, more "intellectual" journalism of the late 1950s and 1960s. It was to "explain" or "interpret" what had hap-pened and, implicitly or explicitly, to forecast the future, especially as the fighting at Hue and Khe Sanh dragged on.

The wire services were relatively constrained in this regard; in passing, to enliven their war wrap-ups, they dwelled on the possibilities of renewed anti-cities attacks or the prospect of a second Dienbienphu at Khe Sanh. Far less constrained were *Time,* and especially *Newsweek,* where "projecting the story" was a standard technique. And on television, similar projection was used to lend added "significance" to reporters' comments (e.g., "The war is no closer to an end tonight than it was this morning").

On the *Times* and, more markedly, the [*Washington*] *Post,* some license had been given since the early 1950s to ordinary reporters (as opposed to columnists, whose independence was generally accepted) to "explain" events within the confines of conventional hard-news stories. Here, selected opinions and interpretations were often vaguely attributed to anonymous "officials," "insiders," "observers," or "senior officers," as in *Time* or *Newsweek.* Greater freedom was allowed to reporters when they wrote under the rubric of "news analysis" or "commentary." Foreign correspondents, faced with the task of explaining far-off events to American readers, were allowed the most leeway. They often went beyond observable events, attributed information, and quoted opinion to interpret developments on their own authority.

Such interpretative reporting had long been characteristic of the *Post*'s Washington coverage, occasionally to the point, in the early 1960s, where the analysis got more space and "play" than the hard news being analyzed. "News analysis" came to the *Times* in the 1950s, with James Reston among the first practitioners. The form caused early misgivings on the paper despite Reston's reputation for finding the facts, taking no sides, and eschewing the temptation to supply all the answers. But such fears eased. By Tet-1968, news analysis by *Times* reporters, especially in the Sunday "News of the Week in Review" section, was commonplace.

In the careful hands of Reston, Hanson Baldwin, Edwin Dale (the *Times* economist), and a few other specialists, the technique added considerably to reader understanding of complex matters. But no comparable competence existed among newsmen with regard to Vietnam. Indeed, as we have noted, both the war's circumstances and the media's own various organizational incentives worked against the acquisition of such competence in Vietnam (and Washington). Moreover, the problem in February 1968 for all would-be news analysts was that the Tet battlefields provided an insufficient "data base" from which to draw broad independent conclusions or to "project the story" in many areas. "Herd journalism" and the news focus on enemy threats and localized fighting in Saigon, Hue, and Khe Sanh—however important those battles might be—left many other crucial matters unexplored firsthand. Yet, the very existence of great uncertainty, added to the subjective responses noted earlier, appears to have impelled editors to publish, and reporters (and pundits) to compose, "analyses" of the crisis that would fill the vacuum. It proved a serious lapse of self-discipline. As we have seen, most analyses were the hasty reactions of the half-informed. Fewer than 15 percent of the *Times* and *Post* items about Vietnam were in explicit "commentary" categories, yet this segment of the coverage, often prominently displayed and "rebroadcast," accounted for a disproportionate share of both papers' sins of commission. And the "projection-analysis" technique, used so heavily on television and in *Newsweek,* produced more pervasive distortions.

These two immediate professional responses by major Vietnam news bureaus and their superiors back home—a focus of firsthand reporting on a few dramatic events, plus undisciplined "analysis" and "projection"— underlay the overall failure of the press and TV to cope with the formidable circumstances of February-March 1968. As often happens, these initial journalistic reactions set the tone and supplied the themes assigned to the crisis over the entire period.

The chronically short attention span of the media—four to six weeks in 1968—insured a feast-and-famine flow of information, aggravated by space and time limitations. As is usually the case in crisis, most space and "play" went to the Tet story early, when the least solid information was available. There was no institutional system within the media for keeping track of what the public had been told, no internal priority on updating initial impressions. As usual, the few catch-up or corrective stories later on were buried on back pages. This practice in turn gave Saigon correspondents little incentive to produce such stories. The *Post* was the most obvious example: On eight days in March, no story from Vietnam made page one. The networks cut their "Vietnam-related" weekday evening film reports: ABC went from 42 in the January 30-February 29 period to 24 in March; CBS, 28 to 17; NBC, 38 to 28. . . . For film reports out of Vietnam only, the networks dropped from 105 to 49. *Time* went from a weekly February average of 99.85 column inches of text on Vietnam at home and abroad to 71.87 in March; *Newsweek,* from 126.10 to 107.50.

The result was that the media tended to leave the shock and confusion of early February, *as then perceived,* "fixed" as the final impression of Tet, and thus as a framework for news judgment and public debate at home. At Tet, the press shouted that the patient was dying, then weeks later began to whisper that he somehow seemed to be recovering—whispers apparently not heard amid the clamorous domestic reaction to the initial shouts.

There is little disagreement among historians or even journalists that the dramatic Tet surprises of late January were indeed shocking—to official Washington and the public at home, and to the U.S. Embassy and the Presidential Palace in Saigon, to say nothing of urban South Vietnamese and U.S. newsmen caught in the fighting. But drama or shock does not automatically mean a decisive turn of events, in this case "defeat" or "demoralization" on the ground. At Tet, the media managers hastily assumed it did, and led their readers to do the same. A mind-set—most obvious in the selection of page-one stories, TV film, and newspaper photographs—quickly developed: Tet was a *disaster,* not only for the highly visible 10 percent of the South Vietnamese population caught up in the urban fighting, but, actually or imminently, for the allied armies, the pacification effort, the Thieu government. Tet, belying the Johnson Administration's "progress" campaign, *thereby* showed that the war was being "lost." Tet proved that the North Vietnamese were the "winners" and their foes the "losers." Tet was a triumph for the wily Giap—in South Vietnam.

Was anything other than allied "defeat" discernible to newsmen in February-March 1968 on the ground? The answer is: Yes, starting about late

February. Earlier, the newsmen in Saigon called into question MACV's hasty cumulative totals of enemy losses, and noted contradictions between the first optimistic communiqués and the realities at Hue and on Saigon's outskirts. They were skeptical of Ambassador [Ellsworth] Bunker's early (but ultimately accurate) accounting of enemy failures (no procommunist uprisings, few ARVN defections). But they neglected to echo General [Frederick C.] Weyand's sensible warning in early February that it was premature to add up the final Tet score, good or bad; and, with the "disaster" mindset, they pressed officials for predictions of future enemy initiatives—forgetting to keep posted on what was already happening as February ended.

Yet, after the recapture of Hue on February 24, the manpower was available, at least in the larger bureaus (AP, UPI, *Time,* the networks, the *Times*), to travel about for a systematic "second look." Moreover, the reporters were enormously helped by freedom from censorship—a freedom not enjoyed by their counterparts in both World Wars and Korea, or in coverage of the Arab-Israeli wars. Thanks to official cooperation and U.S. air mobility, they had unprecedented access to the battlefield. And they had facilities for relatively rapid transmission of film and prose. By March 1, it would have been possible to observe and to report that: (1) enemy military pressure had slackened, except at Khe Sanh; (2) the fighting was shifting back to the countryside; (3) ARVN, despite its 50 percent strength level and some extraordinarily incompetent senior leadership, had held together and fought back; (4) pacification, although hit hard, was not "dead"; and (5), amid many problems and much human suffering, urban recovery was beginning here and there. In short, it was a mixed picture, but clearly neither a military nor a psychological "disaster."

Time made a good effort to catch up. The other big organizations did not. Most of the scattered *Post* and *Times* catch-up stories—dealing with localized recovery—missed page one and landed inside the paper. In mid-March, *Newsweek,* CBS, and NBC were still portraying North Vietnamese troops as holding the "initiative," if only because of a fixation with Khe Sanh. Drama was perpetuated at the expense of information.

Competition did not make for more sophisticated journalism. The fierce rivalry between UPI and AP (with the outcomes judged on the basis of clients' choices of competing agency stories) and among networks (judged on the basis of news program audience "ratings") did not lead to breadth of coverage, and hence to a comprehensive countrywide portrait of a countrywide war. It led, as often happens, to clustering of rival newsmen at the same places, so that each agency "matched" the other on the same story. The wire services put out Saigon war wrap-ups competing for "impact" back home. Competition between NBC and CBS seemed at times a contest over who could shout the same words more loudly.

But in other media, where short-range competitive success was harder to quantify—and where *Time* and the *Times* clearly outgunned their putative rivals in Vietnam—the pressures were less severe, and duplication less frequent. Indeed, in terms of *staff*-written reports from Vietnam outside

Saigon, the *Times* and *Post* overlapped relatively little after the first three
weeks of February.

Traditional American journalistic skills—notably in reporting what can
be seen or heard—served the print media well at Da Nang, Hue, in the
Delta, and in some of the Saigon street fighting. AP's John Wheeler and
others reported accurately from Khe Sanh, during the early stages of the
siege of that base. But the newsmen, by and large, did not *see* very much of
the countrywide Tet offensive or its aftermath. There were many gaps in
their information (as in that initially available to officialdom). Yet, most
news managers at home were apparently willing, even eager, to supply their
audiences with quick, imaginative descriptions of the strategy of the "wily
Giap," the psychological impact of Tet on South Vietnamese morale, the
future of the Thieu regime. the "death throes" of pacification, the enemy's
"awesome" weaponry—all mostly based on guesswork and secondhand
sources in Saigon or Washington.

Most important, throughout Tet, the great bulk of the wire-service output (and its refined versions in network scripts) and of the newspapers'
page-one Vietnam material did not come from eyewitness reports. It was
secondhand or third-hand information—reprocessed, as we have seen, several times over. To produce its war wrap-ups, the UPI, in particular, added
color and spice—"words that pop out at you"—to the bare fragments. The
Saigon rewrite man sought a specific—a bombing raid, a downed aircraft,
a montage of enemy mortar attacks, a "Dienbienphu angle"—to give his
lead paragraphs eye appeal for jaded stateside deskmen. All this was conventional journalistic technique, but the accent on such specifics first exaggerated and then belittled the tempo of the war during February and March,
since no context was provided. It was "news," but not information. It did
not tell us how the war, overall, was going.

Even if one excludes the first week of Tet fighting (which heavily
involved Saigon), the preponderance of Saigon stories is striking: 80 percent of all wire-service output (war wrap-ups, official statements, etc.), 80
percent of all *Times* and *Post* staff-written stories—but only 20 percent of
TV film reports. (The network anchorman's nightly script, on the other
hand, was largely based on wire-service Saigon war wrap-ups, and this
script supplied two-thirds of all TV "reports" about Vietnam.) In the print
media, news managers did indeed like eyewitness action stories, but unless
it was Khe Sanh or Hue, the Saigon "headquarters" dateline got the page-
one play. . . .

The Tet experience makes clear the requirement for maximum candor
on the part of the President and his spokesmen *before* crisis and for
Presidential coherence *during* crisis: Congress and the public cannot rely
only on the specialized reactions of the press and TV to threatening events.
But, ultimately, the remedies for most of the chronic flaws evident in the
1968 performance of the major news organizations lie with the media managers. Reporters and sub-editors, the myths of the craft notwithstanding,
are highly responsive to firm managerial direction, either implicit or
explicit. To be sure, reporters may fasten on some events and neglect

others; department heads engage in bureaucratic bargaining; habits and conventions of deskmen ("gatekeepers") are strong. Budgets and owner predilection may limit managerial initiatives. Sensitivity to competitive audience ratings (in TV) and to the pattern of client response (in the wire services) may influence news selection. But, particularly in newspapers and news magazines, news policies are what the top editor and his senior editors say they are.

The February-March 1968 experience reflected in good measure a number of management policy failures persisting into the troubled 1970s. There were—and are—no universally accepted "objective standards" in the news business. However, already at Tet, there was a notable lack of management insistence on the "balance," professional discipline, and respect for the "naked facts" so often invoked as journalistic virtues. There was also a curious lack of imagination and common sense.

What did the media manager at home know when the first AP bulletins came off the ticker on January 31? He was not an "expert" on the war. But he knew, or should have known from harsh experience, that in the first days of any battle, any crisis, no one (including his staffers in Saigon in this instance) has a clear picture; that most reactions will be partisan and off-the-cuff; that political Washington, like Wall Street, tends to overreact to big news, especially big bad news. Especially in crisis, even the most authoritative sources speaking in all objectivity may be victims of the fog of war or of sheer distance from the action—a gap in perception and communication which always separates headquarters from field. The manager should have reacted with wariness to first reports—especially in terms of initial "play" and receptivity to "instant analysis"—expecting the situation to clarify, and pressing his correspondents in Vietnam for such clarification, as time went on.

Yet, we found few examples of such calls for clarification to newsmen in Saigon or Washington. By all accounts, queries on substance were rare (except in the *Time* and *Newsweek* system) and largely reflected the conventional instant wisdom at home: Wasn't the Administration covering up something? Wasn't Khe Sanh the important story, a potential Dienbienphu? Most managers did not exercise the traditional newspaper city editor's function of questioning a reporter's more sweeping assertions (a function painstakingly revived, for example, by prudent *Post* senior editors during much of the dogged 1972–73 Watergate reporting by Carl Bernstein and Bob Woodward). Instead, it would appear, some managers joined in the overreaction to Tet, and even exploited it, perhaps because they no longer felt that the Administration could supply them with a reliable context or agenda for Vietnam "news," and they had no coherent framework of their own. Amid the uncertainty and clamor at home, consciously or unconsciously, many managers simply adopted the "disaster" scenario, and thus encouraged subordinates to do the same

We saw at Tet the first show of the more volatile journalistic style—spurred by managerial exhortation or complaisance—that has become so popular since the late 1960s. With this style came an often mindless readiness to seek out conflict, to believe the worst of the government or of authority in general, and on that basis to divide up the actors on any issue into the "good" and the "bad." It was a predilection shared by much of academia. The Army in Vietnam, then the "military-industrial complex," then the Central Intelligence Agency, among others, became the targets; their flaws were simplified, highlighted, but rarely explored in depth, and then largely forgotten. Harassment of newsmen by the Nixon Administration, followed by the monumental Watergate scandal of 1972–74, seemed abundantly to justify any "adversary" posture. But adversary journalism is, increasingly, as difficult to apply to the complexities of present-day social problems, energy crises, economic vicissitudes, and foreign policy as it was to Vietnam.

For lack of coherent managerial concepts, issues open and close swiftly in the media, like bad plays on Broadway. Only compelling dramas like Watergate and Presidential election campaigns enjoy a sustained run. It would seem that even the managers of serious newspapers and magazines have come to see television, with its emotive appeal and its fads, as a threatening rival worthy of closer emulation. At Tet, the short managerial attention span brought down the curtain while the play was still going on.

Increasingly painful limitations of time, space, and money, and the competitive quest for audiences seem to preclude easy recipes for better performance. As critics often forget, the major media do not constitute an organized, unified information conglomerate, but an array of relatively small, disparate, rival commercial organizations engaged in hurriedly assembling, variously processing, and distributing "news" which, as Walter Lippmann pointed out, is not—and cannot be—the same commodity as "truth." This "system" is easily overloaded in crisis, and tilted, and it was overloaded and tilted at Tet. Yet, some compensatory remedies emerge from examination of the Tet experience. In crisis, the major media manager can remind his producers or deskmen—those harassed gatekeepers—of the need for skepticism, of the likelihood that the "facts" will change and need explicit correction. He can underline the difference between "drama" and "significance," and allocate space or time accordingly. He can discourage instant analysis and prediction. He can order his dispersed reporters to inform one another on the state of current knowledge and to remember the need for a future overview. He can insist on intense questioning of all actors in domestic debate. On television, he can see that a minimum of context is supplied to film reports ("no microcosms" is a good rule). He can order that a running summary be kept of his organization's pertinent news output, in order to detect gaps which need filling in or initial impressions which require fresh investigation.

In slack periods, the manager often must spur his subordinates on. But in times of crisis, the audience is hungry, and journalistic adrenalin flows freely; the leader's duty then is to challenge hasty judgments, while stressing dispassionate inquiry and persistent legwork. In short, he should reinforce the proclaimed journalistic virtues.

A Critique of the Oppositional Media Thesis

DANIEL C. HALLIN

In December 1968 the *CBS Evening News* included an unusual two-part special report on the pacification program. CBS had chosen its topic well. "Pacification" involved the struggle for political support or hegemony in the villages of South Vietnam, and this was what the war was ultimately about—or at least had been when it started. So here was an opportunity, at an important point of transition between two administrations, to pause and take another look at the roots and implications of the war. The report was unusually long for television, a total of thirteen minutes, and it included a long interview with a critic of administration policy (Senator John Tunney of California), a sign that perhaps the old tendency simply to report how official policy was being carried out might be giving way at last to a real discussion of what American policy should be.

How did CBS pose the issues raised by pacification? Here are Walter Cronkite's introduction to the report and correspondent Murray Fromson's wrap-ups to the two segments:

> *Cronkite.* American officials in Saigon came up with their most optimistic pacification report of the war today. They said that almost three-fourths of South Vietnam's seventeen million people now live in relatively secure areas controlled by the Saigon government. . . . Tonight we look at one of [the] contested areas.

> *Fromson (concluding Part I.)* So pacification does not stand still. It moves forward, it moves back. But what is the balance? What is the trend. . . . ? An effort is being made to measure this, and we'll look at the measurements in our next report.

> *Fromson (concluding Part II).* Another offensive by the Communists would undermine the program. . . . But the momentum seems to be in the other direction. Since the November 1 bombing halt government and U.S. troops have taken over nearly 800 hamlets. . . . The goal is to occupy another 300 of these hamlets by the anniversary of the Tet offensive.

There was no great debate here, nor any reexamination of the roots of the war. The story was structured from beginning to end around the question of the *effectiveness* of existing policy. Reporting on the deaths of two civilians, killed when an American tank fired into the village, Fromson said, "What may be regarded as a military necessity also creates problems for the pacification team." The whole of Part II was devoted to the computerized Hamlet Evaluation System (HES), which produced the official figures on the progress of pacification. That was where Senator Tunney came in: he was not there to debate the wisdom of the justice of American policy in Vietnam, but simply to offer an opposing view on the accuracy of the fig-

From *The "Uncensored War": The Media and Vietnam* by Daniel C. Hallin. Copyright © 1986 by Daniel C. Hallin. Reprinted by permission of Oxford University Press, Inc.

ures produced by HES. At one point Fromson broached the important question of why the peasants of the village chose sides as they did—and not always as Americans assumed they should. "Out of fear or perhaps genuine disbelief in the government," he said, "well over half the people in Ku Chi are still influenced by the Communists." But he quickly dropped the issue, and canceled the doubts potentially raised by the phrase "genuine disbelief in the government": "The hope of winning them over depends on security," he continued, and went on to discuss the effectiveness of the local militias being organized by the government to help "break the grip" of the Vietcong.

Why this purely "technical" approach to a story that could so easily have served as a vehicle to explore more fundamental issues? Surely one reason is simply that it is easier. It is undeniably difficult for a reporter to go into a culture very different from his or her own, in a situation of political conflict vastly different from the American experience, and say anything very substantial about the causes of the conflict or its meaning to the people involved. Add to this the fact that—Vietnam being a limited war for Americans—reporters, like soldiers, served limited tours (television correspondents often served only six months, rarely much more than a year), and that almost none spoke Vietnamese (though at least one member of a three-man television crew almost always would), and it is not surprising that journalists fell back on simpler issues.

But the tendency to analyze events in terms of strategy and tactics, success and failure, "momentum" and lack of momentum is not confined to situations where the reporters are relatively ignorant outsiders. It is a general characteristic of news analysis in American journalism, most evident, in fact, in the reporting of the story reporters know best, that of the presidential election. The focus on tactics and effectiveness in coverage of the antiwar movement is another example. It is related to objectivity, and brings us around to a last look at the political consequences of the conventions of objective journalism.

Here is one final way of posing the dilemma of objectivity: on the one hand the journalist is supposed to adopt, as Lippmann put it, an attitude of "disinterested realism"; on the other hand the journalist is expected to explain the news at least to some degree, to provide background and context, and this expectation is strongest in a period like the post-Tet period of the Vietnam War, when political elites are at odds and the world seems out of joint. So the journalist has to provide interpretation and analysis without appearing to depart from objectivity. And the easiest way to accomplish this is to focus on "technical" questions that do not embroil the journalist in the conflicts of interest, perspective, and value that are the dangerous stuff of political life. It is much easier to discuss with an attitude of "disinterested realism" the accuracy of the HES than, for example, the question of whether American intervention in Vietnam was ultimately good or bad for the Vietnamese peasant.

Journalists do not, of course, only report and analyze events. They also report what people of various kinds say about events. But the debate over the war, as it appeared on television, was also very narrow in focus. No doubt this was due both to the quality of the debate itself and to the journalists' standards of newsworthiness. It was, as we have seen, the debate in Washington that dominated news coverage, at least as far as substantial discussion of the war is concerned. There were periods when this debate burst the normal bounds of political discussion; at the 1968 Democratic Convention there was a debate over the origins of the war and the question of whether the United States should have gotten into it to begin with. Later on there were periods when the relative power of Congress and the presidency in foreign policy were debated. But the day-to-day discussion of the war that dominated most television coverage was narrowly focused on immediate policy issues: would the invasion of Cambodia get the country into another "quagmire"? Would the Laotian operation destroy Vietnamization? Did that operation violate congressional limitations on the use of U.S. troops? Should the president announce a timetable for withdrawal?

The routines of what I have called objective journalism had particularly contradictory consequences in the later period on the war. On the one hand they continued often to be a source of power to an administration which knew how to use them to manage the news. On the other, when the morale of the troops was collapsing or Washington officials were at odds, the journalist began to look much more like the independent "watchdog" his critics and champions so often fancy him to be. The journalist clearly responded to the shifting of political boundaries, extending to a wider range of political views the right to a hearing; at the same time journalistic conventions also set bounds on the range of issues that would be seriously discussed. Many aspects of objective journalism contributed to this narrowing of the bounds of discourse. Two have been mentioned: the tendency to analyze events in technical terms and the emphasis on official Washington as the locus of political discussion. To these might be added the focus of most news on specific, day-to-day events: the issue was, "How is the war going today?" not, "What is this war about?" "How did it happen?" "What can we learn from it?"

This limiting of the focus of the news had two interrelated consequences. First, it meant that the dominant political ideology of American society was to a large extent protected from the threat Vietnam could potentially have posed; here is one more important sense in which the modern American press must be seen as an integral part, not an adversary of the state. For certain parts of the American public, mostly among the college-educated young, Vietnam led not only to dissatisfaction with certain policies or incumbent politicians, but to a questioning of basic assumptions about the character of the American political system and the American role in world politics. There was, for one thing, a questioning of the legitimacy of the foreign policy decision-making process, which resulted in large part from the revelations of the official "management" of opinion. . . . And there was a questioning of the benevolence of American power: many came to see Vietnam not merely as a "tragic miscalculation," but as an aggressive war motivated by power, comparable to the Soviet intervention in

Czechoslovakia, which happened to coincide with the deepening of American divisions over Vietnam. Some of these issues are now beginning to be debated, and this is no doubt a delayed effect of Vietnam, resulting in part from the fact that the generation socialized to politics during the war is now coming into positions of power. In the reporting of Central America, for instance, there has sometimes been open discussion of the appropriateness of the Cold War perspective that has dominated U.S. foreign policy in the postwar period; there has even been discussion of whether the American role in the region has been a benevolent or an imperialistic one.

But during the Vietnam War issues of this sort were simply not on the news agenda. Never, for example, did I hear an American utter the word *imperialism* on television. On those rare occasions (rare, that is, after Tet) when the underlying reasons for American intervention were discussed explicitly, what journalists did was to defend the honorableness of American motives.

As for the legitimacy of the foreign policy decision-making process, . . . television continued to accord the administration most of the trappings and privileges of authority that previous administrations had enjoyed. There was, of course, considerable discussion of the "credibility gap" as well as debate over the power of the presidency. But the limits of discussion in this area can be seen in the fact that only seven stories in the sample contained any references—and this includes reporting of statements by domestic critics—to deliberate government deception of the public. The most substantial of these was a brief story on the *Pentagon Papers,* mentioning what the documents revealed about Johnson's 1964 statement that he would not send American boys to Asia. Very little of the substance of the *Pentagon Papers,* however, got into television coverage. The controversy over the leaking and publication of the Papers, on the other hand, being "hard news" rather than "mere history," was covered very extensively.

Vietnam fits a pattern that has often been observed in situations of political crisis: the media in such periods typically distance themselves from incumbent officials and their policies, moving in the direction of an "adversary" conception of their role. But they do not make the "system"— or its core beliefs—an issue, and if these are questioned, usually rise to their defense; this happened with Watergate as well.

More broadly, the narrow immediacy of television meant that none of the larger questions posed by the war was raised in any substantial way in the news. There was no discussion of the origins of revolution ("Guerrilla war, like hives, can break out any time, any place," one correspondent explained). There was no second look at the doctrine of containment or its application to a conflict like Vietnam: should such a conflict be treated as one "front" in a global struggle? There was no discussion of why this war eventually seemed to contradict so drastically the image of war and the image of themselves Americans held when they went into it: Why the violence that came to be symbolized by My Lai? Why the collapse of morale? Why the hostility of so many of those we thought we were saving, even the ones fighting with us?

The reply television people usually give to this sort of criticism is that lack of time makes it impossible for television to do more than deal with daily headlines, and that that function is performed by other elements of the news media: by documentaries, news magazines, "op-ed" articles, and the like. To this I would make several responses. First, a large part of the public learns of world affairs only from daily journalism; the typical television documentary is shown in a low-rating slot, seen by only a small fraction of the audience for the evening news. The levels of American journalism that are supposed to provide deeper reporting, moreover, including the television documentary, share many of the characteristics that limit the ability of daily news to deal with wider issues, including the focus on Washington's agenda and the technical angle in news analysis.

Finally, though it is certainly true that the time constraints imposed on television journalism by the commercial nature of the medium limit what it can do, the limits that result from ideology, culture, and journalistic routines seem much more fundamental. Television covered Vietnam nearly every day for more than seven years, producing hours of reporting on the war. Some of that reporting concerned events of great immediate significance. But the majority did not: it was taken up with routine battle coverage (several days old because most film was shipped by air); reports on technology; human-interest vignettes about the troops; occasional "light" stories about such trivia as what it is like to parachute out of an airplane; and many speeches and press conferences, relatively few of which were of real historical significance. When one looks at it all in a concentrated period of time, it is clear that a great deal of television's coverage had no significant value as information about the war. The problem with Vietnam coverage was quality, not quantity.

The media probably bear a good deal of the responsibility for the political troubles they have had in the post-Vietnam era. Americans went into Vietnam believing it was a replay on a smaller scale of World War II: a struggle to defend democracy against aggression, which we would surely win, not only because we were more powerful but because the right was clearly on our side. Television held this view strongly, perhaps more strongly than the public itself. It didn't work out that way, and eventually television brought the bad news. But it never explained why: it never reexamined the assumptions about the nature of the war it had helped to propagate in the early years. So to the public, the bad news must have seemed nearly as incomprehensible as an earlier "American defeat" in Asia: the "loss" of China. The Chinese revolution triumphed just when the Cold War consensus was becoming solidified, and only a few unhappy souls were so foolish as to suggest some historical development might be taking place in China that could not be reduced to the global struggle between democracy and totalitarianism. Add to this the fact that the United States had clear military superiority at the time, and it is hardly surprising that a great deal of the public should have accepted the notion that treason was the only reasonable explanation for defeat. In the same way, it is hardly surprising that Americans should gravitate toward the view that "loss of Vietnam" resulted simply from a lack of American will, which leads easily to the conclusion that the media were to blame: no more sophisticated explanations were put before them.

Did the media "lose Vietnam"? I shall argue that this is not the most important question to ask about the media's role in that war. But it is worth taking up initially, in more precise and less sensational formulation. Could American power have been used more effectively in Vietnam if officials had had more control over the media? Perhaps. But the case is by no means as strong as often supposed.

. . . Voluntary guidelines for the protection of military information worked well. There were only a handful of violations of those guidelines by the press, and there is no evidence that the military considered the press a source of significant damage to military operations. As a strictly military problem press coverage was entirely trivial compared with, say, interservice rivalries, which resulted—to name only one of many inefficiencies— in predictable American air traffic over North Vietnam.

Officials sometimes complained of diplomatic damage done by press coverage. But again there is little evidence that this was extensive. The bombing of Cambodia in 1969, for example, was kept secret, as officials have later told the story, not only to prevent opposition in the United States, but because it was believed that Sihanouk and the North Vietnamese would be more likely to protest if the bombing were officially acknowledged. They were therefore furious when the *New York Times,* using official sources, disclosed it; aside from the *Pentagon Papers* case, in which the courts concluded the government had been unable to show evidence of harm to national security, this is the episode most often cited as evidence press leaks were harming American diplomacy. But it is not obvious that it would have been of enormous significance if these protests had occurred, unless perhaps protests from Sihanouk made the bombing an issue in the United States (the bombing of Cambodia did not become a political issue until years later). And, in any case, it turned out that neither Sihanouk nor the North Vietnamese did protest. The most significant diplomatic secret of the war was Kissinger's meetings in Paris with Le Duc Tho—and this secret was kept.

So the case would seem to come down to the impact of the press on the "home front." This case can be made in a number of different ways. At times, for example, officials believed that if only the United States could send a clear enough "signal" of its resolve to the North Vietnamese, the latter could be expected to back down. And the ability to project an image of unity at home was seen as crucial to the communication of this signal. But the notion that "signaling" by itself would have induced the North Vietnamese and NLF to give up a goal they had been pursuing for decades seems very dubious—an illusion born of the assumption that the Vietnamese revolutionaries were merely proxies for the Soviet Union and China, and that Vietnam was a limited war for them just as it was for us.

The military generally believed that the war could have been won if the United States had escalated more rapidly and with fewer political limits. And it is certainly true that considerations of public opinion were in part responsible for some of the limitations placed on the use of U.S. military power. Bombing targets were limited, for instance, in part because extensive civilian casualties were seen as politically damaging. And yet it seems very likely that if Johnson had chosen to go "all out" in Southeast Asia, he could have sold that policy to the public, perhaps more easily, in fact, than the policy of limited war. Limitations on the bombing, after all, were at least as controversial a political issue as civilian casualties in the North. The *New York Times* would not have liked it if Johnson had given the military free reign, nor would the *St. Louis Post-Dispatch* or Walter Lippmann. But the *Daily News* (which was calling in 1964–65 for an invasion of China) and the *Chicago Tribune* would have been ecstatic; and my own guess is that the media in general would have been swept uneasily but powerfully into war fever. Indeed, it was in part the fear that the public would respond too vigorously to an unrestrained call to arms, pushing the country into precisely the kind of confrontation favored by the *Daily News,* that motivated the decision to keep the war limited. The Johnson administration chose to fight a limited war not so much because it felt political opposition gave it no choice, but because it was unwilling to sacrifice other political priorities to an all-out war effort, because it feared the war could grow out of control, and because many officials—an increasing number as time went on—were not convinced the expanded measures advocated by the military would bring victory at reasonable cost.

Eventually public opinion did become a powerful constraint on U.S. policy. After Tet (or, perhaps correctly, after the Johnson administration declined to take the final opportunity Tet provided to mobilize the country for all-out war) political divisions made it impossible for the United States to persist even in a limited war. So in the end one could say that public opinion was indeed decisive, as Ho Chi Minh and many others had predicted it would be.

But it is not clear that it would have been much different if the news had been censored, or television excluded, or the journalists more inclined to defer to presidential authority. It should not be forgotten that public support for the shorter and less costly limited war in Korea also dropped as its costs rose, despite the fact that television was in its infancy, censorship was tight, and the World War II ethic of the journalist serving the war effort remained strong.

A comment Dean Rusk made to reporters on the subject of censorship is revealing. "Unless we are in a formal state of war," he said, "with censorship here [in Washington], there is no point in having censorship [in Vietnam]. . . . Here is where most of the leaks come." Republicans in Washington were questioning the president's credibility on the war long before most television correspondents were. At least a year before Cronkite called the war a "bloody stalemate" and urged negotiation, the secretary of defense had reached essentially the same conclusion. The collapse of America's "will" to fight in Vietnam resulted from a political process of which the media were only one part. And that process was deeply rooted in the nature and course of the war—the fact that it was a limited war, not only in its tactics but in its relevance to vital American interests; and also the fact that it was an unsuccessful limited war, which expanded well beyond the level of commitment most policymakers would have considered rational at the outset.

The behavior of the media . . . is intimately related to the unity and clarity of the government itself, as well as to the degree of consensus in the society at large. This is not to say that the role of the press is purely reactive. Surely it made a difference, for instance, that many journalists were shocked both by the brutality of the war and by the gap between what they were told by top officials and what they saw and heard in the field, and were free to report all this. But it is also clear that the administration's problems with the "fourth branch of government" resulted in large part from political divisions at home, including those within the administration itself, which had dynamics of their own. In a sense, what is really remarkable, as [McGeorge] Bundy observed, is that the press and the public went as far with American policy in Vietnam as they did. And it is hard to see how, short of a real turn to authoritarian government, political doubt and controversy could have been contained much longer. Perhaps even a shift to authoritarian government would not have changed the outcome. It remains to be seen whether the Soviet Union will have the "will" to persist to a clear-cut victory in Afghanistan, even though Afghanistan is more comparable to Mexico than Vietnam in its relevance to Soviet security. Maybe the lesson of Vietnam is not that it is difficult for an open society to fight a limited war, but that it is difficult to fight a limited war against an enemy for whom it is not a limited war.

I have put the word *will* in quotation marks because its use implicitly begs another, more basic question: Should the United States have wanted to persist in Indochina, or to intervene there to begin with? The answer to that question of course depends on a number of others. Could the United States have won at any reasonable cost? How substantial a national interest did the United States have in the outcome of the various political struggles of Indochina? What possibilities of political compromise existed? And, finally (a question which did not in fact affect policy, but should have), what outcome was best for the people of Indochina? My own view is that the United States could not have defeated the Vietnamese revolution at any reasonable cost, to itself or to the Indochinese, and had little real national interest there, the hostility of the Vietnamese Communists to the United States being no more inevitable in the long run than that of the Chinese. I also suspect that while an early Communist government in South Vietnam might have been harsh, as revolutionary regimes usually are for some period, it would eventually, like the Chinese, have moderated and set out on a course of serious modernization within a socialist framework, probably more rapidly if it had come to power while it still had political roots and alliances in the South—before the NLF was destroyed—and through political rather than military means.

These issues . . . were never seriously discussed in news coverage of the war, not, at any rate, in *New York Times* coverage during the years when the decision was made to intervene, or in television coverage in subsequent years. They were not discussed because the constraints of ideology and of journalistic routines tying news coverage to Washington perspectives excluded them from the news agenda. From this angle the implications of government control over the media looks very different.

There is no doubt that control of images and information is central to the exercise of political power. Once a set of goals is decided upon, there are often, for example, important tactical advantages in secrecy; this is obvious to anyone who has engaged in negotiations. (There are also important advantages in publicity and credibility; this is one of the dilemmas of modern politics.) But if we learned from Machiavelli that deception is honorable in the conduct of war, we learned from Thucydides that it is prudent for a world power to consider the justice and larger political wisdom of its actions. Politics is not a football game: winning is not the only thing that counts. The wise use of power is as central to the art of politics as its effective use.

I would not be so foolish as to suggest that an open political process will always produce wise political results. Perhaps if political systems were to move in the direction of more sustained active discussion of political affairs, and a major process of political education were to take place, that would be true, at least when conflicts of interest were not sharp. But that kind of democracy is a long way off. Still, in the case of Vietnam, it seems likely that greater openness would have produced a better decision. Those who imagine that political elites would govern better without the press and the public looking over their shoulders should look back to the decision-making process of the early 1960s that led to American intervention in Vietnam; the foreign policy decision-making of that period is probably as close as the United States can come in peacetime to the ideal expressed by much of the political science of the 1950s, and, now again, by conservatives of the 1970s and 1980s, that after elections "the ordinary citizen must turn over power to elites and let them rule." It is true enough, as conservatives have argued, that every society must maintain a balance between democracy and authority. But in the case of Vietnam excessive authority looks more like the source of imbalance than excessive democracy.

FURTHER READING

Michael Arlen, *Living-Room War* (1982)
Peter Arnett, *Live from the Battlefield: From Vietnam to Baghdad* (1994)
George Bailey, "Television War: Trends in Network Coverage of Vietnam, 1965–1970," *Journal of Broadcasting,* 20 (1976), 147–158
Malcolm W. Browne, *Muddy Boots and Red Socks: A Reporter's Life* (1994)
Todd Gitlin, *The Whole World Is Watching* (1980)
David Halberstam, *The Powers that Be* (1979)
William M. Hammond, *Public Affairs: The Military and the Media* (1988)
Michael Herr, *Dispatches* (1977)

Martin F. Herz, *The Prestige Press and the Christmas Bombing* (1980)

Montague Kern, Patricia W. Levering, and Ralph B. Levering, *The Kennedy Crises: The Press, the Presidency, and Foreign Policy* (1983)

Lawrence W. Lichty, "The War We Watched on Television," *American Film Institute Report,* 4 (1973), 30–37

Michael Mandelbaum, "Vietnam: The Television War," *Daedalus,* 111 (1982), 157–168

John E. Mueller, *War, Presidents and Public Opinion* (1973)

Harrison E. Salisbury, *A Time of Change* (1988)

Jonathan Schell, *The Real War* (1988)

Kathleen J. Turner, *Lyndon Johnson's Dual War* (1985) (on the press)

Sidney Verba et al., "Public Opinion and the War in Vietnam," *American Political Science Review,* 61 (June 1967), 317–333

The Paris Peace Accords of 1973 and the Fall of South Vietnam

✕

The Paris Peace Accords left many fundamental problems unresolved. North Vietnam had not abandoned its long-held objective of unifying the country under its direction. Nor had South Vietnam abandoned its goal of maintaining a government free of communist influence. Given those irreconcilable ambitions, it should not be surprising that the Paris agreements never brought peace to Vietnam. In fact, in the weeks immediately following the signing ceremony in January 1973, both sides were guilty of flagrant truce violations, which worsened throughout 1973 and 1974.

The United States continued to provide massive economic and military support to the Thieu regime. But with the spreading Watergate scandal, Congress reasserted its constitutional role in foreign affairs, denying or limiting many Nixon administration requests for aid to South Vietnam. Congress's hand was strengthened when the Watergate revelations forced Richard M. Nixon to resign as president in August 1974. His successor, Gerald R. Ford, faced an increasingly activist Congress that was reluctant to undertake any new commitments in Vietnam.

When North Vietnam launched a major military offensive in the spring of 1975, officials in Hanoi were evidently as stunned as those in Washington by the rapidity of South Vietnam's disintegration. Congress refused to comply with the Ford administration's last-minute request for emergency aid. On April 30, the South Vietnamese government formally capitulated. Ten years after the introduction of U.S. combat forces, and nearly thirty years after Ho Chi Minh's declaration of independence, the struggle for Vietnam was over. The triumphant northerners quickly gave Saigon a new name— Ho Chi Minh City.

This final phase of the Vietnam War has sparked much political and scholarly controversy. Why did the peace agreement break down so quickly? Which side bears primary responsibility for failing to fulfill its provisions? Why did South Vietnam collapse so swiftly in the face of North Vietnam's offensive? What role did the United States play in these events? Did Washington abandon its ally at a critical moment? Might additional American aid or military support have enabled Saigon to survive? And finally, how is the communist victory best explained?

✗ D O C U M E N T S

In a letter of January 5, 1973, Richard M. Nixon tried to reassure Nguyen Van Thieu about the future of his regime. One of a series of letters exchanged between the two leaders before the signing of the Paris Peace Accords, it is reprinted here as the first document. Key sections of the multilateral part of those accords follow. They were signed in Paris on January 27, 1973, by representatives of the United States, North Vietnam, South Vietnam, and the Provisional Revolutionary Government. On April 15, 1975, Secretary of State Henry A. Kissinger appealed to Congress to provide emergency aid to South Vietnam, then reeling from North Vietnam's military offensive; his request is reprinted as the third selection.

The remaining documents are reminiscences. Secretary of Defense James R. Schlesinger, Jr., recalls the advice that he gave President Ford as South Vietnam appeared on the verge of collapse. Next, a member of the South Vietnamese air force and a sixteen-year-old civilian give their personal recollections of South Vietnam's final days. Then, General Van Tien Dung offers a North Vietnamese perspective on the fall of Saigon. Finally, in the last document, excerpted from his memoirs, Nixon places the blame for South Vietnam's fall on Congress.

Richard M. Nixon Reassures Nguyen Van Thieu, 1973

This will acknowledge your letter of December 20, 1972.

There is nothing substantial that I can add to my many previous messages, including my December 17 letter, which clearly stated my opinions and intentions. With respect to the question of North Vietnamese troops, we will again present your views to the Communists as we have done vigorously at every other opportunity in the negotiations. The result is certain to be once more the rejection of our position. We have explained to you repeatedly why we believe the problem of North Vietnamese troops is manageable under the agreement, and I see no reason to repeat all the arguments.

We will proceed next week in Paris along the lines that General [Alexander] Haig explained to you. Accordingly, if the North Vietnamese meet our concerns on the two outstanding substantive issues in the agreement, concerning the DMZ and the method of signing, and if we can arrange acceptable supervisory machinery, we will proceed to conclude the settlement. The gravest consequences would then ensue if your government chose to reject the agreement and split off from the United States. As I said in my December 17 letter, "I am convinced that your refusal to join us would be an invitation to disaster—to the loss of all that we together have fought for over the past decade. It would be inexcusable above all because we will have lost a just and honorable alternative."

As we enter this new round of talks, I hope that our countries will now show a united front. It is imperative for our common objectives that your government take no further actions that complicate our task and would make more difficult the acceptance of the settlement by all parties. We will keep you informed of the negotiations in Paris through daily briefings of Ambassador Lam.

I can only repeat what I have so often said: The best guarantee for the survival of South Vietnam is the unity of our two countries which would be gravely jeopardized if you persist in your present course. The actions of our Congress since its return have clearly borne out the many warnings we have made.

Should you decide, as I trust you will, to go with us, you have my assurance of continued assistance in the post-settlement period and that we will respond with full force should the settlement be violated by North Vietnam. So once more I conclude with an appeal to you to close ranks with us.

The Paris Peace Accords, 1973

The Parties participating in the Paris Conference on Viet-Nam,

With a view to ending the war and restoring peace in Viet-Nam on the basis of respect for the Vietnamese people's fundamental national rights and the South Vietnamese people's right to self-determination, and to contributing to the consolidation of peace in Asia and the world.

Have agreed on the following provisions and undertake to respect and to implement them:

Chapter I The Vietnamese People's Fundamental National Rights

Article 1. The United States and all other countries respect the independence, sovereignty, unity, and territorial integrity of Viet-Nam as recognized by the 1954 Geneva Agreements on Viet-Nam.

Chapter II Cessation of Hostilities—Withdrawal of Troops

Article 2. A cease-fire shall be observed throughout South Viet-Nam as of 2400 hours G.M.T., on January 27, 1973.

At the same hour, the United States will stop all its military activities against the territory of the Democratic Republic of Viet-Nam by ground, air and naval forces, wherever they may be based, and end the mining of the territorial waters, ports, harbors, and waterways of the Democratic Republic of Viet-Nam. The United States will remove, permanently deactivate or destroy all the mines in the territorial waters, ports, harbors, and waterways of North Viet-Nam as soon as this Agreement goes into effect.

The complete cessation of hostilities mentioned in this Article shall be durable and without limit of time.

Article 3.   The parties undertake to maintain the cease-fire and to ensure a lasting and stable peace.

As soon as the cease-fire goes into effect:

a. The United States forces and those of the other foreign countries allied with the United States and the Republic of Viet-Nam shall remain in-place pending the implementation of the plan of troop withdrawal. The Four-Party Joint Military Commission described in Article 16 shall determine the modalities.

b. The armed forces of the two South Vietnamese parties shall remain in-place. The Two-Party Joint Military Commission described in Article 17 [not included here] shall determine the areas controlled by each party and the modalities of stationing.

c. The regular forces of all services and arms and the irregular forces of the parties in South Viet-Nam shall stop all offensive activities against each other and shall strictly abide by the following stipulations:

• All acts of force on the ground, in the air, and on the sea shall be prohibited;

• All hostile acts, terrorism and reprisals by both sides will be banned.

Article 4.   The United States will not continue its military involvement or intervene in the internal affairs of South Viet-Nam.

Article 5.   Within sixty days of the signing of this Agreement, there will be a total withdrawal from South Viet-Nam of troops, military advisers, and military personnel, including technical military personnel and military personnel associated with the pacification program, armaments, munitions, and war material of the United States and those of the other foreign countries mentioned in Article 3 (a). Advisers from the above-mentioned countries to all paramilitary organizations and the police force will also be withdrawn within the same period of time.

Article 6.   The dismantlement of all military bases in South Viet-Nam of the United States and of the other foreign countries mentioned in Article 3 (a) shall be completed within sixty days of the signing of this Agreement.

Article 7.   From the enforcement of the cease-fire to the formation of the government provided for in Article 9 (b) and 14 of this Agreement, the two South Vietnamese parties shall not accept the introduction of troops, military advisers, and military personnel including technical military personnel, armaments, munitions, and war material into South Viet-Nam.

The two South Vietnamese parties shall be permitted to make periodic replacement of armaments, munitions and war material which have been destroyed, damaged, worn out or used up after the cease-fire, on the basis of piece-for-piece, of the same characteristics and properties, under the supervision of the Joint Military Commission of the two South Vietnamese parties and of the International Commission of Control and Supervision.

Chapter III The Return of Captured Military Personnel and Foreign Civilians, and Captured and Detained Vietnamese Civilian Personnel

Article 8

a. The return of captured military personnel and foreign civilians of the parties shall be carried out simultaneously with and completed not later than the same day as the troop withdrawal mentioned in Article 5. The parties shall exchange complete lists of the above-mentioned captured military personnel and foreign civilians on the day of the signing of this Agreement.

b. The Parties shall help each other to get information about those military personnel and foreign civilians of the parties missing in action, to determine the location and take care of the graves of the dead so as to facilitate the exhumation and repatriation of the remains, and to take any such other measures as may be required to get information about those still considered missing in action.

c. The question of the return of Vietnamese civilian personnel captured and detailed in South Viet-Nam will be resolved by the two South Vietnamese parties on the basis of the principles of Article 21 (b) of the Agreement on the Cessation of Hostilities in Viet-Nam of July 20, 1954. The two South Vietnamese parties will do so in a spirit of national reconciliation and concord, with a view to ending hatred and enmity, in order to ease suffering and to reunite families. The two South Vietnamese parties will do their utmost to resolve this question within ninety days after the cease-fire comes into effect.

Chapter IV The Exercise of the South Vietnamese People's Right to Self-Determination

Article 9. The Government of the United States of America and the Government of the Democratic Republic of Viet-Nam undertake to respect the following principles for the exercise of the South Vietnamese people's right to self-determination:

a. The South Vietnamese people's right to self-determination is sacred, inalienable, and shall be respected by all countries.

b. The South Vietnamese people shall decide themselves the political future of South Viet-Nam through genuinely free and democratic general elections under international supervision.

c. Foreign countries shall not impose any political tendency or personality on the South Vietnamese people.

Article 10. The two South Vietnamese parties undertake to respect the cease-fire and maintain peace in South Viet-Nam, settle all matters of contention through negotiations, and avoid all armed conflict.

Article 11. Immediately after the cease-fire, the two South Vietnamese parties will:

• achieve national reconciliation and concord, end hatred and enmity, prohibit all acts of reprisal and discrimination against individuals or organizations that have collaborated with one side or the other;

- ensure the democratic liberties of the people: personal freedom, freedom of speech, freedom of the press, freedom of meeting, freedom of organization, freedom of political activities, freedom of belief, freedom of movement, freedom of residence, freedom of work, right to property ownership, and right to free enterprise.

Article 12

a. Immediately after the cease-fire, the two South Vietnamese parties shall hold consultations in a spirit of national reconciliation and concord, mutual respect, and mutual non-elimination to set up a National Council of National Reconciliation and Concord of three equal segments. The Council shall operate on the principle of unanimity. After the National Council of National Reconciliation and Concord has assumed its functions, the two South Vietnamese parties will consult about the formation of councils at lower levels. The two South Vietnamese parties shall sign an agreement on the internal matters of South Viet-Nam as soon as possible and do their utmost to accomplish this within ninety days after the cease-fire comes into effect, in keeping with the South Vietnamese people's aspirations for peace, independence and democracy.

b. The National Council of National Reconciliation and Concord shall have the task of promoting the two South Vietnamese parties' implementation of this Agreement, achievement of national reconciliation and concord and ensurance of democratic liberties. The National Council of National Reconciliation and Concord will organize the free and democratic general elections provided for in Article 9 (b) and decide the procedures and modalities of these general elections. The institutions for which the general elections are to be held will be agreed upon through consultations between the two South Vietnamese parties. The National Council of National Reconciliation and Concord will also decide the procedures and modalities of such local elections as the two South Vietnamese parties agree upon.

Article 13.   The question of Vietnamese armed forces in South Viet-Nam shall be settled by the two South Vietnamese parties in a spirit of national reconciliation and concord, equality and mutual respect, without foreign interference, in accordance with the postwar situation. Among the questions to be discussed by the two South Vietnamese parties are steps to reduce their military effectives and to demobilize the troops being reduced. The two South Vietnamese parties will accomplish this as soon as possible.

Article 14.   South Viet-Nam will pursue a foreign policy of peace and independence. It will be prepared to establish relations with all countries irrespective of their political and social systems on the basis of mutual respect for independence and sovereignty and accept economic and technical aid from any country with no political conditions attached. The acceptance of military aid by South Viet-Nam in the future shall come under the authority of the government set up after the general elections in South Viet-Nam provided for in Article 9 (b).

Chapter V The Reunification of Viet-Nam and the Relationship Between North and South Viet-Nam

Article 15. The reunification of Viet-Nam shall be carried out step by step through peaceful means on the basis of discussions and agreements between North and South Viet-Nam, without coercion or annexation by either party, and without foreign interference. The time for reunification will be agreed upon by North and South Viet-Nam.

Pending reunification:

a. The military demarcation line between the two zones at the 17th parallel is only provisional and not a political or territorial boundary, as provided for in paragraph 6 of the Final Declaration of the 1954 Geneva Conference.

b. North and South Viet-Nam shall respect the Demilitarized Zone on either side of the Provisional Military Demarcation Line.

c. North and South Viet-Nam shall promptly start negotiations with a view to reestablishing normal relations in various fields. Among the questions to be negotiated are the modalities of civilian movement across the Provisional Military Demarcation Line.

d. North and South Viet-Nam shall not join any military alliance or military bloc and shall not allow foreign powers to maintain military bases, troops, military advisers, and military personnel on their respective territories, as stipulated in the 1954 Geneva Agreements on Viet-Nam.

Henry A. Kissinger Appeals to Congress for Emergency Aid, 1975

The long and agonizing conflict in Indochina has reached a tragic stage. The events of the past month have been discussed at great length before the Congress and require little additional elaboration. In Viet-Nam President Thieu ordered a strategic withdrawal from a number of areas he regarded as militarily untenable. However, the withdrawal took place in great haste, without adequate advance planning, and with insufficient coordination. It was further complicated by a massive flow of civilian refugees seeking to escape the advancing North Vietnamese Army. Disorganization engendered confusion; fear led to panic. The results, as we all know, were tragic losses—of territory, of population, of material, and of morale.

But to fully understand what has happened, it is necessary to have an appreciation of all that went before. The North Vietnamese offensive, and the South Vietnamese response, did not come about by chance—although chance is always an element in warfare. The origins of these events are complex, and I believe it would be useful to review them briefly.

Since January 1973, Hanoi has violated—continuously, systematically, and energetically—the most fundamental provisions of the Paris agreement. It steadily increased the numbers of its troops in the South. It improved and expanded its logistics system in the South. It increased the armaments and ammunition of its forces in the South. And as you know, it blocked all efforts to account for personnel missing in action. These are facts, and they are indisputable. All of these actions were of course in total violation of the agreement. Parallel to these efforts, Hanoi attempted—with considerable success—to immobilize the various mechanisms established by the agreement to monitor and curtail violations of the cease-fire. Thus, it assiduously prepared the way for further military actions.

South Viet-Nam's record of adherence to the agreement has not been perfect. It is, however, qualitatively and quantitatively far better than Hanoi's. South Viet-Nam did not build up its armed forces. It undertook no major offensive actions—although it traded thrusts and probes with the Communists. It cooperated fully in establishing and supporting the cease-fire control mechanisms provided for in the agreement. And it sought, as did the United States, full implementation of those provisions of the agreement calling for an accounting of soldiers missing in action.

But perhaps more relevant to an understanding of recent events are the following factors.

While North Viet-Nam had available several reserve divisions which it could commit to battle at times and places of its choosing, the South had no strategic reserves. Its forces were stretched thin, defending lines of communication and population centers throughout the country.

While North Viet-Nam, by early this year, had accumulated in South Viet-Nam enough ammunition for two years of intensive combat, South Vietnamese commanders had to ration ammunition as their stocks declined and were not replenished.

While North Viet-Nam had enough fuel in the South to operate its tanks and armored vehicles for at least 18 months, South Viet-Nam faced stringent shortages.

In sum, while Hanoi was strengthening its army in the South, the combat effectiveness of South Viet-Nam's army gradually grew weaker. While Hanoi built up its reserve divisions and accumulated ammunition, fuel, and other military supplies, U.S. aid levels to Viet-Nam were cut—first by half in 1973 and then by another third in 1974. This coincided with a worldwide inflation and a fourfold increase in fuel prices. As a result almost all of our military aid had to be devoted to ammunition and fuel. Very little was available for spare parts, and none for new equipment.

These imbalances became painfully evident when the offensive broke full force, and they contributed to the tragedy which unfolded. Moreover, the steady diminution in the resources available to the Army of South Viet-Nam unquestionably affected the morale of its officers and men. South Vietnamese units in the northern and central provinces knew full well that they faced an enemy superior both in numbers and in firepower. They knew that reinforcements and resupply would not be forthcoming. When the fighting began they also knew, as they had begun to suspect, that the United States would not respond. I would suggest that all of these factors added significantly to the sense of helplessness, despair, and, eventually, panic which we witnessed in late March and early April.

I would add that it is both inaccurate and unfair to hold South Viet-Nam responsible for blocking progress toward a political solution to the conflict. Saigon's proposals in its conversations with PRG [Provisional Revolutionary Government] representatives in Paris were in general constructive and conciliatory. There was no progress toward a compromise political settlement because Hanoi intended that there should not be. Instead, North Viet-Nam's strategy was to lay the groundwork for an eventual military offensive, one which would either bring outright victory or at least allow Hanoi to dictate the terms of a political solution.

Neither the United States nor South Viet-Nam entered into the Paris agreement with the expectation that Hanoi would abide by it in every respect. We did believe, however, that the agreement was sufficiently equitable to both sides that its major provisions could be accepted and acted upon by Hanoi and that the contest could be shifted thereby from a military to a political track. However, our two governments also recognized that, since the agreement manifestly was not self-enforcing, Hanoi's adherence depended heavily on maintaining a military parity in South Viet-Nam. So long as North Viet-Nam confronted a strong South Vietnamese army and so long as the possibility existed of U.S. intervention to offset the strategic advantages of the North, Hanoi could be expected to forgo major military action. Both of those essential conditions were dissipated over the past two years. Hanoi attained a clear military superiority, and it became increasingly convinced that U.S. intervention could be ruled out. It therefore returned to a military course, with the results we have seen.

The present situation in Viet-Nam is ominous. North Viet-Nam's combat forces far outnumber those of the South, and they are better armed. Perhaps more important, they enjoy a psychological momentum which can be as decisive as armaments in battle. South Viet-Nam must reorganize and reequip its forces, and it must restore the morale of its army and its people. These tasks will be difficult, and they can be performed only by the South Vietnamese. However, a successful defense will also require resources—arms, fuel, ammunition, and medical supplies—and these can come only from the United States.

Large quantities of equipment and supplies, totaling perhaps $800 million, were lost in South Viet-Nam's precipitous retreat from the northern and central areas. Much of this should not have been lost, and we regret that it happened. But South Viet-Nam is now faced with a different strategic and tactical situation and different military requirements. Although the amount of military assistance the President has requested is of the same general magnitude as the value of the equipment lost, we are not attempting simply to replace those losses. The President's request, based on General Weyand's [Gen. Frederick C. Weyand, Chief of Staff, United States Army] assessment, represents our best judgment as to what is needed now, in this new situation, to defend what is left of South Viet-Nam. Weapons, ammunition, and supplies to reequip four divisions, to form a number of ranger groups into divisional units, and to upgrade some territorial forces into infantry regiments will require some $326 million. The balance of our request is for ammunition, fuel, spare parts, and medical supplies to sustain up to 60 days of intensive combat and to pay for the cost of transporting those items. These are minimum requirements, and they are needed urgently.

The human tragedy of Viet-Nam has never been more acute than it now is. Hundreds of thousands of South Vietnamese have sought to flee Communist control and are homeless refugees. They have our compassion, and they must also have our help. Despite commendable efforts by the South Vietnamese Government, the burden of caring for these innocent victims is beyond its capacity. The United States has already done much to assist these people, but many remain without adequate food, shelter, or medical care. The President has asked that additional efforts and additional resources be devoted to this humanitarian effort. I ask that the Congress respond generously and quickly.

The objectives of the United States in this immensely difficult situation remain as they were when the Paris agreement was signed—to end the military conflict and establish conditions which will allow a fair political solution to be achieved. We believe that despite the tragic experience to date, the Paris agreement remains a valid framework within which to proceed toward such a solution. However, today, as in 1973, battlefield conditions will affect political perceptions and the outcome of negotiations. We therefore believe that in order for a political settlement to be reached which preserves any degree of self-determination for the people of South Viet-Nam, the present military situation must be stabilized. It is for these reasons that the President has asked Congress to appropriate urgently additional funds for military assistance for Viet-Nam.

I am acutely aware of the emotions aroused in this country by our long and difficult involvement in Viet-Nam. I understand what the cost has been for this nation and why frustration and anger continue to dominate our national debate. Many will argue that we have done more than enough for the Government and the people of South Viet-Nam. I do not agree with that proposition, however, nor do I believe that to review endlessly the wisdom of our original involvement serves a useful purpose now. For despite the agony of this nation's experience in Indochina and the substantial reappraisal which has taken place concerning our proper role there, few would deny that we are still involved or that what we do—or fail to do—will still weigh heavily in the outcome. We cannot by our actions alone insure the survival of South Viet-Nam. But we can, alone, by our inaction assure its demise.

The United States has no legal obligation to the Government and the people of South Viet-Nam of which the Congress is not aware. But we do have a deep moral obligation—rooted in the history of our involvement and sustained by the continuing efforts of our friends. We cannot easily set it aside. In addition to the obvious consequences for the people of Viet-Nam, our failure to act in accordance with that obligation would inevitably influence other nations' perceptions of our constancy and our determination. American credibility would not collapse, and American honor would not be destroyed. But both would be weakened, to the detriment of this nation and of the peaceful world order we have sought to build.

James R. Schlesinger, Jr., Recalls the Collapse of South Vietnam (1975), 1987

My first inkling that we had lost came when the North Vietnamese began to make maneuvers toward the end of 1974 and in January of 1975 and we did not respond. They were testing us. They did not really believe that they were getting away with what they were getting away with. But given the constraints under which we had to operate, I knew they were going to get away with it. Then of course came the attack in the Central Highlands and the total collapse of the ARVN divisions. At that point it was all over. I had been making menacing sounds in public whenever the subject of North Vietnam had come up—they'd just better beware, and so forth. But the congressional restraints that had been established in the summer of '73 wouldn't permit our taking effective countermeasures.

Now, many of the people who were with me were people who had served there, and they had emotional ties to the country, and they just could not—and I understand it, and I'm not criticizing them—back off and say "We did our best, but it is now hopeless." They kept seeing hope where hope did not exist. [General] Fred Weyand, for example, whom Ford had sent out to Southeast Asia, was tied to Thieu and to the Vietnamese with bonds of loyalty. He came back and reported to the President, that six hundred and fifty million bucks is needed.

Before Mr. Ford asked for additional assistance in Vietnam we had a meeting of the NSC, and I said "Mr. President, it's all over." He was kind of rankled by that, quite indignant. I got sort of the Michigan fight song. And I said "Mr. President, you should go up to the Hill tomorrow and say we have suffered a severe setback, call for blood, sweat, and tears, and a national effort to deal with the consequences, but there's no way that you can persuade anybody that Vietnam is salvageable."

A South Vietnamese Pilot Reflects on His Country's Defeat (1975), 1990

My parents moved to the South in 1954, when the country was partitioned and the Communists took over the North. I was just one year old at the time. My parents knew the Communists and did not want to live under their government. So they came south to freedom.

I joined the Air Force and went to flight school. I got out of flight school in early April of 1975. By that time, when pilots flew they never had enough fuel. We had to take some planes apart in order to get parts for other planes. And we never had enough bullets. We had to count the bullets for the planes. We wanted to fight. But how could we fight without weapons?

Excerpted from *Tears Before Rain: An Oral History of the Fall of South Vietnam* by Larry Engelmann. Copyright © 1990 by Larry Engelmann. Reprinted by permission of Oxford University Press, Inc.

Some of us in the Air Force talked to each other about the possibility of losing the war. But when we talked like that we were afraid because we thought maybe we had heard too much Communist propaganda. We knew that we had good generals at the top. As long as we had good generals, how could we lose?

I was at Tan Son Nhut on April 28 when North Vietnamese pilots bombed us. They came over in A-37s and dropped bombs on us. It didn't frighten me at all. In 1968 during Tet, the Communists had come into the city, too, and we pushed them out. So this was nothing new to us. But then, on April 29, we heard that our generals had run away. We couldn't believe it. We—the young ones—we expected to continue fighting. But how could we fight when there were no generals to lead us any more?

On the morning of April 30 all of the pilots were talking about a message they had heard on the emergency radio channel. They said that the American fleet had told all Vietnamese pilots to bring their aircraft out to the ships so that they would not fall into Communist hands. Many of the pilots took helicopters filled with people out to the American fleet after they heard that message.

I wasn't yet sure that I wanted to leave. So I didn't go out on a helicopter. I knew that there were still soldiers fighting in the Delta. So I thought maybe I would go south and join them. But then, late in the morning, I heard that the government had already surrendered to the Communists. Only then did I decide to leave.

I went with a friend down to the Saigon River. There was a boat that was just leaving, so we decided to get on it. We were feeling bad about leaving, but when the government surrendered, there was no more hope. People in Saigon were celebrating because they had been fooled by the Communists. They thought that when the Communists took over there would be no more war. But now they would have to learn.

When our boat went down the Saigon River no one fired at us. There were more than 3,000 people on the boat—men, women and children. We had no food or water on board and we did not know what would happen once we got into the South China Sea. But we believed that we could not stay and live under Communism.

We all looked at Vietnam for the last time as we left. The last thing we saw was the beautiful beach at Vung Tau. It was a nice day. The sun was shining. And everyone was crying.

After we saw Vung Tau for the last time, a soldier on the boat took his own gun and put it under his chin and shot himself to death. And some people jumped over the side of the ship and disappeared in the sea. I watched two men jump over the side.

We were in the South China Sea for three days without food or water. On the third day a Danish ship found us. They took the women and children off and took them to Hong Kong. Then they gave us food and water so we wouldn't die at sea and they told us how to get to Hong Kong. During the rest of the journey we didn't talk to each other because we were so sad about losing our country.

A South Vietnamese Civilian Remembers His Last Days in Saigon (1975), 1990

Every night I cry for Vietnam. I remember and I cry. In the darkness my memories turn into tears. There are tears for my dad and my mom and for my brother and my sisters, and for all of the people who ran away from Vietnam and for all of those who could not run away. I don't want my memories to be lost, like tears in the rain. . . .

I was sixteen in the spring of 1975. At that time in school kids were starting to worry about the Communists taking over. Some of them talked about leaving the country. Some days, on the way home from school, I saw long lines of people trying to get papers or trying to change their money so they could leave the country.

My brother came home from college. My dad told my brother and me that he wanted us to leave the country for a while. "You are young," he said. "You have a future. And when everything is safe again you can come back." He thought we should go to the United States to study. Then when we returned to Vietnam we would have a better future. But it was very difficult to get out of Vietnam, and for a long time we did not believe we would be able to leave.

My best friend's name was Nguyen Quang. His sister, Nguyen Huong, worked as a clerk at the American Embassy. He told us that she might be able to get us out of the country. The Americans told her that they would fly her and her relatives out of Vietnam. All she had to do was type our names on a list. So we said that would be all right. She told her boss—who was also Vietnamese—that she had two young men who wanted to get out of Vietnam and that they were not relatives. But she said she wanted to put the two names on her list. And her boss said that was okay.

After our names were on the list she called us and said that we had to be ready to leave at any time, day or night. She said she would tell us where to go when we were scheduled to leave.

Then at ten in the morning on April 28, she came to our house and said, "Sonny, you had better get ready, because you will be leaving in one hour." She told us where we were supposed to go. A bus was going to pick us up there and take us to the airport. We could only bring one bag each for clothes. We did not have much time to say goodbye. I only had time to say, "Dad, I love you. I have to leave now." Mom and Dad cried a lot that morning. They told my brother, "Take good care of Ut."

Dad then drove us to where a bus was to pick us up. We had no special papers and we really didn't know if we would be asked for any. We drove to a big building that had a fence around it. We knocked on the gate and a man let us in. He had a list of names. Our names were on his list. When we got inside the fence I was surprised because there was a large courtyard and it was filled with people who were waiting. The people had come from all

Excerpted from *Tears Before Rain: An Oral History of the Fall of South Vietnam* by Larry Engelman. Copyright © 1990 by Larry Engelman. Reprinted by permission of Oxford University Press, Inc.

over the country—from central Vietnam and from the northern cities. There were about a thousand people there. I asked some of them, "Where did you come from?" I didn't see anybody I knew. And they told me, "We came from Danang," or, "We came from Nha Trang." So many people from so many different cities. And there seemed to be nobody there from Saigon but my brother and me.

I felt happy at that moment. I was young and I would not have to live under the Communists. I could go to school in the United States and then when the Communists had been driven out I could come back to Saigon.

We had not been in the courtyard of the building very long when they called our names. My brother and I went to the gate again and a bus driver was standing there with a list and he checked off our names. We got on the bus. I could hardly believe it. We were the first ones to leave the courtyard. We were each carrying just one bag. My brother and I had no money. My dad told us to call him when we got to the U.S. and then he would send us some money. We were going to stay with a friend in California.

We were driven to the airport. It was really crowded. We had to get off the bus and stand outside. There was a big field with people in it and the sun was very hot. There were loud-speakers paging people and vendors trying to sell food and drinks and trying to exchange money. Lots of people were crying and lots of them were shocked because they didn't really know what was happening or where they were going.

We really didn't know what would happen. Then all of a sudden they called our names over the loudspeaker. I was very surprised because I had asked some of the other people, "How long have you been waiting here?" and some of them said, "One week already." Others had been waiting two or three days. I thought at first that my brother and I would never get on a plane, but then they called our names. We were taken into the terminal with other people. They searched us there and searched our luggage. Then they asked us to stand in a long line. After a little time they led us out to an airplane. Outside the plane there were two Vietnamese MPs standing and watching the people. They wanted to prevent deserters from leaving the country. They looked at everyone carefully. They didn't stop us or question us and we got on the plane.

I thought it would be a nice airplane. It was a big C-130. We walked up the back ramp. When we got inside we saw that there were no seats. We just had to get in and sit on the floor—like sardines. When I saw that I thought, "Oh, my God, are we going to take this all the way to the United States without seats? And packed so close together?" But nobody was saying anything so I didn't say anything about it, either. I just thought that thought.

As they were loading us—it was very late in the afternoon—all of a sudden I heard a lot of explosions outside, around the plane. And thought, "Oh, my God, what is happening out there?" The door was still open and I saw an explosion right behind the plane. A big explosion. Then the airplane started to move with the door still open. I was looking out the door and I saw people running around in all directions shooting crazily into the air. They seemed to be in a panic. People all around me on the airplane started screaming and crying. Some of them started praying very loudly. I grabbed my brother and I said, "I hope we don't crash."

They didn't even have time to close the door. They just went down the runway with the door open. As we took off, all of us could see out the back, and on the ground it looked like there were hundreds of explosions and fires and people were running in all directions. It looked like the whole airport was going crazy.

Then right behind us another C-130 came up—it took off on another runway only a few seconds after we did. I think we were the last two planes to take off from Tan Son Nhut. We were very lucky.

As we left Saigon, there was an American soldier standing at the back door of the plane, and he was shooting at the ground. He just kept shooting as we pulled away. And people were still crying inside the plane. I watched the soldier shooting and I wondered what he was shooting at. I think he was just trying to show American power one last time. I think he was trying to say with his gun, "Don't shoot at our airplane. Don't mess around with this airplane. We've got guns on board. We're Americans. Stay away. Leave us alone." But I can only guess. I don't think he knew what was happening, either. We were all confused.

Anyway, that was my last look at my country. I saw Vietnam as we flew away and at the back door of the plane was a soldier with a gun shooting at it.

We landed in the Philippines at Clark Field. We were taken to a big warehouse. The Americans had everything very well organized for us. We were surprised. They put us all in a big waiting area. We had televisions and beds. The next day they told us that the Communists had taken over Saigon. We were shocked. We did not know what would happen. "What about our family?" we asked. "What about Mom and Dad? What will happen to us now when we get to the United States?" We had nothing but questions.

We watched the news on television. We saw the Communists in Saigon. A lot of people cried when they saw that. My brother and I cried, too. Our family was still in Vietnam. And we looked at each other and asked, "What will happen to us tomorrow?"

A North Vietnamese Commander Celebrates the "Great Spring Victory" (1975), 1977

When it was almost light, the American news services reported that [U.S. Ambassador Graham] Martin had cleared out of Saigon in a helicopter. This viceregal mandarin, the final American plenipotentiary in South Vietnam, beat a most hasty and pitiful retreat. As it happened, up until the day he left Saigon, Martin still felt certain that the quisling administration could be preserved, and that a ceasefire could be arranged, so he was halfhearted

Van Tien Dung, *Our Great Spring Victory: An Account of the Liberation of South Vietnam,* translated by John Spragens, Jr. Copyright © 1977 by Cora Weiss. Reprinted by permission of Monthly Review Foundation.

about the evacuation, waiting and watching. He went all the way out to Tan Son Nhut airfield to observe the situation. Our barrage of bombs and our fierce shelling had nearly paralyzed this vital airfield, and the fixed-wing aircraft they had intended to use for their evacuation could no longer operate. The encirclement of Saigon was growing tighter by the day. The Duong Van Minh card which they had played far too late proved useless. When Martin reported this to Washington, President Ford issued orders to begin a helicopter evacuation. Coming in waves for eighteen hours straight, they carried more than 1,000 Americans and over 5,000 of their Vietnamese retainers, along with their families, out of the South. Ford also ordered Martin to evacuate immediately "without a minute's delay."

The American evacuation was carried out from the tops of thirteen tall buildings chosen as landing pads for their helicopters. The number of these landing pads shrank gradually as tongues of fire from our advancing troops came closer. At the American embassy, the boarding point for the evacuation copters was a scene of monumental confusion, with the Americans' flunkies fighting their way in, smashing doors, climbing walls, climbing each other's backs, tussling, brawling, and trampling each other as they sought to flee. It reached the point where Martin, who wanted to return to his own house for his suitcase before he fled, had to take a back street, using the rear gate of the embassy. When "Code 2," Martin's code name, and "Lady 09," the name of the helicopter carrying him, left the embassy for the East Sea, it signaled the shameful defeat of U.S. imperialism after thirty years of intervention and military adventures in Vietnam. At the height of their invasion of Vietnam, the U.S. had used 60 percent of their total infantry, 58 percent of their marines, 32 percent of their tactical air force, 50 percent of their strategic air force, fifteen of their eighteen aircraft carriers, 800,000 American troops (counting those stationed in satellite countries who were taking part in the Vietnam war), and more than 1 million Saigon troops. They mobilized as many as 6 million American soldiers in rotation, dropped over 10 million tons of bombs, and spent over $300 billion, but in the end the U.S. ambassador had to crawl up to the helicopter pad looking for a way to flee. Today, looking back on the gigantic force the enemy had mobilized, recalling the malicious designs they admitted, and thinking about the extreme difficulties and complexities which our revolutionary sampan had had to pass through, we were all the more aware how immeasurably great this campaign to liberate Saigon and liberate the South was. . . .

The most extraordinary thing about this historic campaign was what had sprouted in the souls of our cadres and fighters. Why were our soldiers so heroic and determined during this campaign? What had given all of them this clear understanding of the great resolution of the party and of the nation, this clear understanding of our immeasurably precious opportunity, and this clear understanding of our unprecedented manner of fighting? What had made them so extraordinarily courageous and intense, so outstanding in their political acumen in this final phase of the war?

The will and competence of our soldiers were not achieved in a day, but were the result of a continuous process of carrying out the party's ideological and organizational work in the armed forces. And throughout our thirty years of struggle, there had been no campaign in which Uncle Ho had not gone into the operation with our soldiers. Going out to battle this time, our whole army had been given singular, unprecedented strength because this strategically decisive battle bore his name: Ho Chi Minh, for every one of our cadres and fighters, was faith, strength, and life. Among the myriad troops in all the advancing wings, every one of our fighters carried toward Ho Chi Minh City the hopes of the nation and a love for our land. Today each fighter could see with his own eyes the resiliency which the Fatherland had built up during these many years, and given his own resiliency there was nothing, no enemy scheme that could stop him.

Our troops advanced rapidly to the five primary objectives, and then spread out from there. Wherever they went, a forest of revolutionary flags appeared, and people poured out to cheer them, turning the streets of Saigon into a giant festival. From the Binh Phoc bridge to Quan Tre, people carrying flags, beating drums and hollow wooden fish, and calling through megaphones, chased down the enemy, disarmed enemy soldiers, neutralized traitors and spies, and guided our soldiers. In Hoc Mon on Route 1, the people all came out into the road to greet the soldiers, guide them, and point out the hiding places of enemy thugs. Everywhere people used megaphones to call on Saigon soldiers to take off their uniforms and lay down their guns. The people of the city, especially the workers, protected factories and warehouses and turned them over to our soldiers. In all the districts bordering the city—Binh Hoa, Thanh My Tay, Phu Nhuan, Go Vap, and Thu Duc—members of the revolutionary infrastructure and other people distributed leaflets, raised flags, called on enemy soldiers to drop their guns, and supplied and guided our soldiers. Before this great army entered the city, the great cause of our nation and the policies of our revolution had entered the hearts of the people.

We were very pleased to hear that the people of the city rose up when the military attacks, going one step ahead, had given them the leverage. The masses had entered this decisive battle at just the right time, not too early, but not too late. The patriotic actions of the people created a revolutionary atmosphere of vast strength on all the city's streets. This was the most precious aspect of the mass movement in Saigon-Gia Dinh, the result of many years of propaganda, education, organizing, and training by the municipal party branch. When the opportune moment arrived, those political troops had risen up with a vanguard spirit, and advanced in giant strides along with our powerful main-force divisions, resolutely, intelligently, and courageously. The people of the city not only carried flags and food and drink for the troops, but helped disperse large numbers of enemy soldiers, forced many to surrender, chased and captured many of those who were hiding out, and preserved order and security in the streets. And we will never forget the widespread and moving images of thousands, of tens of thousands of people enthusiastically giving directions to our soldiers and guiding them as they entered the city, and helping all the wings of troops strike quickly and unexpectedly at enemy positions. Those nameless heroes of Saigon-Gia Dinh brought into the general offensive the fresh and beautiful features of people's war.

As we looked at the combat operations map, the five wings of our troops seemed like five lotuses blossoming out from our five major objectives. The First Army Corps had captured Saigon's General Staff headquarters and the command compounds of all the enemy armed services. When the Third Army Corps captured Tan Son Nhat they met one wing of troops already encamped there—our military delegation at Camp Davis; it was an amazing and moving meeting. The Fourth Army Corps captured Saigon's Ministry of Defense, the Bach Dang port, and the radio station. The 232nd force took the Special Capital Zone headquarters and the Directorate-General of Police. The Second Army Corps seized "Independence Palace," the place where the quisling leaders, those hirelings of the United States, had sold our independence, traded in human blood, and carried on their smuggling. Our soldiers immediately rushed upstairs to the place where the quisling cabinet was meeting, and arrested the whole central leadership of the Saigon administration, including their president, right on the spot. Our soldiers' vigorous actions and firm declarations revealed the spirit of a victorious army. By 11:30 A.M. on April 30 the revolutionary flag flew from "Independence Palace"; this became the meeting point for all the wings of liberating troops.

At the front headquarters, we turned on our radios to listen. The voice of the quisling president called on his troops to put down their weapons and surrender unconditionally to our troops. Saigon was completely liberated! Total victory! We were completely victorious! All of us at headquarters jumped up and shouted, embraced and carried each other around on our shoulders. The sound of applause, laughter, and happy, noisy, chattering speech was as festive as if spring had just burst upon us. It was an indescribably joyous scene. Le Duc Tho and Pham Hung embraced me and all the cadres and fighters present. We were all so happy we were choked with emotion. I lit a cigarette and smoked. Dinh Duc Thien, his eyes somewhat red, said, "Now if these eyes close, my heart will be at rest." This historic and sacred, intoxicating and completely satisfying moment was one that comes once in a generation, once in many generations. Our generation had known many victorious mornings, but there had been no morning so fresh and beautiful, so radiant, so clear and cool, so sweet-scented as this morning of total victory, a morning which made babes older than their years and made old men young again.

Nixon Blames Congress for the Fall of South Vietnam (1975), 1978

For more than two years after the peace agreement the South Vietnamese had held their own against the Communists. This proved the will and mettle of the South Vietnamese people and their desire to live in freedom. It also proved that Vietnamization had succeeded. When Congress reneged on our obligations under the agreements, the Communists predictably rushed in to fill the gap. The congressional bombing cutoff, coupled with the limitation placed on the President by the War Powers Resolution in November 1973, set off a string of events that led to the Communist takeover in Cambodia and, on April 30, 1975, the North Vietnamese conquest of South Vietnam.

Congress denied first to me, and then to President Ford, the means to enforce the Paris agreement at a time when the North Vietnamese were openly violating it. Even more devastating and inexcusable, in 1974 Congress began cutting back on military aid for South Vietnam at a time when the Soviets were increasing their aid to North Vietnam. As a result, when the North Vietnamese launched their all-out invasion of the South in the spring of 1975, they had an advantage in arms, and the threat of American action to enforce the agreement was totally removed. A year after the collapse of South Vietnam, the field commander in charge of Hanoi's final offensive cited the cutback in American aid as a major factor in North Vietnam's victory. He remarked that Thieu "was then forced to fight a poor man's war," with his firepower reduced by 60 percent and his mobility reduced by half because of lack of aircraft, vehicles, and fuel.

The war and the peace in Indochina that America had won at such cost over twelve years of sacrifice and fighting were lost within a matter of months once Congress refused to fulfill our obligations. And it is Congress that must bear the responsibility for the tragic results. Hundreds of thousands of anti-Communist South Vietnamese and Cambodians have been murdered or starved to death by their conquerors, and the bloodbath continues.

✗ *E S S A Y S*

Allan E. Goodman, a political scientist at Georgetown University, examines the breakdown of the Paris Peace Accords in the opening essay. A former State Department official who spent several years in Vietnam, he contends that the agreement collapsed not because of any flaws in its terms or in the negotiating process but because the Saigon government proved incapable of ending the war—either through accommodation with the PRG or victory over it. In the second essay, William J. Duiker of Pennsylvania State University discusses the final communist offensive and explores the broader question of why the communists ultimately prevailed. He argues that of all the great revolutions, the Vietnamese revolution, more than any other, was above all an act of human will. Duiker emphasizes the communists' superior organizational strengths and strategic vision, which he contrasts with the chronic weaknesses of their nationalist rivals.

What Went Wrong?

ALLAN E. GOODMAN

Through the Vietnam negotiations the United States sought to legitimize the way it ended its decade of direct involvement in the war. To Henry Kissinger, what happened thereafter depended on whether the military stalemate that had made the Paris Agreement possible would last. As he observed in a press conference a year after the agreement had been signed:

> No settlement is self-enforcing. It is not possible to write an agreement whose terms, in themselves, guarantee its performance. Any agreement will last if the hostility of the parties is thereby lessened, if the parties have an incentive to observe it, and/or if the parties pay a penalty for breaking it.
>
> If those three conditions are not met, no matter what the terms of the agreement, there is a tendency toward erosion.
>
> In Viet Nam, in civil war conditions, the hostility of the parties does not significantly lessen.
>
> The incentives and penalties have been affected by many events of the past year [especially the U.S. Congress's cutoff of funds for the air war in Cambodia].
>
> So, at this moment, a great deal depends on the perception of the two sides of the existing military balance.

What had Kissinger initially expected? He initialed the Paris Agreement believing that he had achieved understandings with Le Duc Tho about the following: the future level of warfare in the south, that détente would involve a tapering off of Communist-country aid to Hanoi, that follow-up negotiations would occur if the ambiguities of the agreement created problems, and that U.S.-DRV relations would be normalized. But in mid-February 1973, when he visited Hanoi on what he called "an exploratory mission to determine how to move from hostility to normalization" of relations with the DRV, Kissinger had a disturbing meeting with North Vietnamese premier Pham Van Dong. Pham suggested that most of the DRV's Politburo saw the Paris Agreement as little more than a face-saving instrument that permitted U.S. withdrawal. He called the NCRC [National Council of Reconciliation and Concord] a transitional coalition and said that the cease-fire was primarily with the Americans. As Pham put it, the cease-fire-in-place definitely would not be permitted to evolve into another way of partitioning Vietnam.

Nevertheless, Kissinger hoped that the Paris Agreement would eventually lead to a peaceful political settlement. After his Hanoi trip, for example, he told the press:

Reprinted from *The Lost Peace: America's Search for a Negotiated Settlement of the Vietnam War* by Allan E. Goodman with permission of Hoover Institution Press, pp. 165–180. © 1978 by the Board of Trustees of the Leland Stanford Jr. University.

The big problem is whether Indochina can be moved from a condition of guerrilla war or even open warfare to a condition in which the energies of the peoples of that region are concentrated on constructive purposes.

If that objective can be achieved, if that process can start for a period of three or four years, then any decision to resume the conflict by any of the parties will have to be taken in an environment of peace and against the experience of the population in [war-like] tasks with which they have become almost totally unfamiliar.

However, in a war in which time was a weapon and negotiation a tactic, the Paris Agreement proved neither a substitute for a military victory by Saigon nor a deterrent to the continued pursuit of military victory by Hanoi.

For Saigon, as one high GVN official remarked, the agreement permitted "continuing the war and improving our position on the battlefield with American help. The fact that there was an agreement took the edge off our American critics for a time." Saigon never believed that the causes of the war were negotiable, or that Hanoi would compromise unless it was defeated militarily in the south. Just as the war itself had seemed more important to the Americans fighting it than it did to the GVN in 1966 and 1967, so also the negotiations and the Paris Agreement were regarded by South Vietnamese officials as something far more desirable from Washington's standpoint than from Saigon's.

Throughout the negotiations, Thieu used them as a means of demonstrating his independence from the Americans and a chance to show his critics on the right, as well as the Communists, that he was no U.S. puppet. Thieu's intransigence delayed the start of substantive talks, accounted in part for the three-month delay that occurred after Henry Kissinger announced that peace was at hand, and necessitated the invention of a complicated signing ceremony in which, at Thieu's insistence, neither the GVN nor the PRG formally acknowledged the other's existence. The terms of the agreement were also not surprising to Saigon; by mid-1972 the GVN was prepared to continue the war regardless of what was agreed on in Paris. So, for Saigon, the negotiations provided time and the maximum amount of U.S. assistance possible to improve its position on the battlefield.

For Hanoi and the PRG, the negotiations provided a means to sustain the fighting, and the agreement provided a means eventually to win the war. By 1969, the kind of war Hanoi wanted to fight required a secure and uninterrupted flow of supplies from its Communist allies into the north, and thence into the south via the Ho Chi Minh trail. The bombing suspension that accompanied the negotiations provided security for the NVA's rear bases. But, as a Hanoi radio commentary pointed out on August 13, 1972: ". . . in solving the South Vietnam problem one cannot deal only with the military problem. . . . To cease-fire or to release the captured soldiers are only concrete acts; the political objective is the only problem of decisive significance. Such a cease-fire cannot eliminate the cause of the war. Instead, such a cease-fire will permanently maintain the factors for waging war again at any time." And this is precisely what the Paris Agreement did.

Indeed, as one high-level U.S. official observed in a January 1975 interview in Saigon, "Hanoi basically saw the Paris Agreement as a generous and face-saving way for the United States to end its Vietnam involvement. They then expected Thieu to be ousted, PRG territorial control to be consolidated, and the National Council of Reconciliation and Concord to be established. They still expect this. They still expect the GVN to collapse. They feel the military balance is in their favor, that Saigon's soldiers know this, and that sooner or later Thieu and his generals will blunder into a defeat."

As President Nixon wrote in his 1973 state of the world report, the Paris Agreement made it possible for the U.S. prisoners of war to be returned, and it provided Saigon with a "decent interval" of two years, in which "to demonstrate inherent strength." But the Paris Agreement did not end the war—and neither Washington, nor Saigon, nor Hanoi expected that it would. However, Kissinger did believe that the Paris Agreement would precipitate movement toward a political settlement. Speaking to newsmen shortly before the agreement was signed, he observed. ". . . it is not easy to achieve through negotiations what has not been achieved on the battlefield, and if you look at the settlements that have been made in the postwar period, the lines of demarcation have almost always followed the lines of actual control. . . . we have taken the position throughout that the agreement cannot be analyzed in terms of any one of its provisions, but it has to be seen in its totality and in terms of the evolution that it starts."

But, since neither Saigon nor Hanoi gained in Paris all that they had gained on the battlefield, both believed that further fighting was essential to achieving their basic goals. For Saigon, continuing the war would prove to the north that it could not impose a military solution once U.S. forces left Vietnam. As President Thieu declared in a speech in June 1974:

> We will . . . not allow the Communists to use military means in lieu of the already agreed-to peaceful solution—the one provided for by the Paris Agreement, which calls for a cease-fire and an election. We will not let the Communists resort to war to solve the Vietnam problem. We must prove to them that they shall fail in their attempt to resort to military means, that their renewed aggression shall take them nowhere, and they had better sit down and negotiate seriously so that an election may soon be organized. All that we have done in reaction to Communist truce violations is only aimed at making the Communists realize the pointlessness of their use of force.

For Hanoi, continued fighting was essential to eliminating the "leopard spots" created by a cease-fire-in-place. As the lead editorial in the Hanoi journal *Vietnam Courier* declared in September 1973:

> The Paris Agreement recognizes the existence in South Viet Nam of two administrations, two armed forces, and two zones of control. Does this entail the threat of a new and permanent partition of Viet Nam, now split into three parts? Drawing lessons from their experiences of 1954, the Vietnamese negotiators dismissed all U.S.-Saigon proposals for regroup-

ing belligerent forces into a number of well-defined areas: such an operation would facilitate the execution of Nguyen Van Thieu's plan to liquidate
"Viet Cong pockets" at a given moment with the support of the U.S.A. or,
if need be, to perpetuate the division of South Viet Nam. On insistence of
the DRVN and PRC, the U.S.A. had finally to agree that the cease-fire be
carried out on the spot, which makes the map of South Viet Nam look like
a "leopard skin." But this very "leopard skin" must disappear within the
shortest time. The existence of two zones, the recognition of which is
imperative in the present phase in order to achieve a solution to South Viet
Nam's internal problems, is not intended to last indefinitely.

Certainly it is not a *complete* victory and this is also a question of the relation of forces reflecting itself in the Agreement concluded: the PRG . . .
will have to coexist for a certain time with the puppet regime. . . . As
shown by the events since January 1973, the situation "half-war, half-
peace" will be the backcloth for a multisided struggle on the ground in
South Viet Nam with its political, economic, and also its military aspects.

But as 1973 began, both sides were ill-prepared to expand their political support beyond areas they had controlled for decades. Much of the
PRG's infrastructure was still weak: the prestige of, and latent sympathy
for, the Communist movement had been much reduced by the brutality and
the terrorist tactics used during and since the 1968 Tet offensive. For the
non-Communists, political mobilization was still largely a product of the
antagonisms among them, not a common cause designed to prepare the
GVN for a political struggle with the PRG. When U.S. forces were removed
from the equation, the countryside reverted to the patterns of control that
each side had maintained rather consistently since the war began. It was in
these areas that, the "postwar war," as my Vietnamese friends referred to it,
was fought.

From the first speculations over the possibility of an agreement leading
to a cease-fire-in-place through the end of the 1973 dry season (that is,
from early October 1972 through spring 1973), both the PRG and the GVN
concentrated on expanding the territory they controlled. Each accused the
other of capturing key access points to South Vietnam, populated areas of
the countryside adjacent or strategic to the defense of those areas, and certain provincial and district capitals. For the PRG, such land-grabbing made
good sense; for the GVN, it was suicide.

In the first year after the Paris Agreement, Saigon alleged that it had
been violated 35,673 times. The PRG charged Saigon with 301,000 violations: 34,266 land-grabbing operations, 35,532 artillery shellings, 14,749
aerial bombardments and reconnaissances, and 216,550 police and pacification operations. The initial intent of both sides was to take territory that
would later have to be adjudicated by the Two Party Joint Military
Commission (TPJMC) as provided for in Article 3(b) of the Paris
Agreement. . . . When the TPJMC proved unable even to inspect contested
areas, let alone to determine "the areas controlled by each party and modalities of [troop] stationing," both sides fought to regain the territory they had
lost.

In the first eighteen months after the agreement, the PRG withdrew from more than 90 hamlets in which it had maintained a long-term presence and from some 300 others that had been seized during land-grabbing operations in January 1973. Through deploying its forces more thinly, the GVN claimed it had increased its control over nearly 1000 hamlets. The lack of Communist aggressiveness in the land-grabbing war had long-range tactical value: in attempting to assert control over areas long ruled by the PRG, the GVN was encouraged to overextend its forces. The more the government pursued this war, the more vulnerable it became. The more it appeared to be an aggressor, the less military aid it would receive from a rebellious U.S. Congress, and the less it appeared to the population of South Vietnam to be working toward peace. "If we attack our enemies," one captured Communist directive noted, "we will suffer politically. . . . If we permit them to move into our areas, then counterattack, our political image will remain intact." Reporting from such contested areas in 1973 and 1974, U.S. journalists pointed out that GVN control was increasingly restricted to the daytime hours—a pattern reminiscent of that prevailing during most of the 1960s.

On the GVN side, what was needed was both expansion of governmental services and effective security forces that would assure the government twenty-four-hour control and, thereby, a chance for its propaganda, pacification, and economic development programs to take root. Thieu sought to accomplish this through an official administrative revolution begun in mid-spring of 1973. This involved the centralization of all program management and decision-making in the hands of officials personally chosen by Thieu. As Ngo Dinh Diem had used the government structure as a substitute for popular political mobilization, so Thieu now tried to use it as an alternative both to accommodation with the PRG and to mobilization of the popular support that would be essential if the NCRC should be established. But territory seized by the South Vietnamese government in the last moments of the 1972 war did not prove to be fertile ground for "reforms." In this respect, Thieu imitated his predecessors: Saigon governments consistently tended to apply new programs and concepts to areas in which problems were the most acute, or to launch nationwide efforts that spread resources so thinly that the population was frequently alienated from the government rather than mobilized by it.

It was a familiar pattern. Hanoi had always used lulls in the war to consolidate and strengthen the bases of its support in the south. The Saigon government used these lulls to expand its territory rather than to bring competent administration and effective security to the areas already under its control.

Along with the land-grabbing war came the struggle over a series of besieged strategic military bases. These bases alternated as tempting targets for the NVA and as strategic outposts from which the GVN could harass and occasionally interdict infiltration from the Ho Chi Minh trail into the central and northern regions of South Vietnam. They had been the scene of heavy conventional fighting in the past. One such base, Tong le Chanh, was under attack for 411 days before it fell to the North Vietnamese. Most of these bases, beginning with the fall of Le Minh base in western Pleiku on September 24, 1973, were lost to the North Vietnamese several times by the end of 1974. From the North Vietnamese viewpoint, attacks against these bases were designed as much to relieve pressure on supply routes as they were to test GVN morale and to produce in the average GVN soldier's mind the expectation of defeat.

The most intense fighting over these bases—more than 8000 soldiers on both sides were reported killed—occurred from early March through April 1974. By the first week in April, five GVN bases, many of them former U.S. Green Beret outposts, had fallen to NVA assaults. Communist spokesmen hailed the attacks as "a necessary act in order to prevent and stop Saigon land-grabbing operations." The outposts taken secured infiltration routes from Cambodia and NVA use of a newly built road extending from the demilitarized zone to the Parrot's Beak. . . .

As fighting over the strategic fire bases continued in northern and central South Vietnam, the PRG and the GVN were also fighting over the Mekong Delta's rice. There were no front lines in the rice war because the boundaries between zones of government and Communist control in the delta depended on the time of day and the season. Early in 1973, the GVN declared it would deny rice to PRG zones. That August, local GVN officials confiscated all rice in excess of a week's supply from each farming household in territory adjacent to PRG areas. Families were then given weekly withdrawal privileges from provincial storehouses. The excess rice of each household was sold to the government at prices averaging 10 to 50 percent below the market price.

The government's blockade proved ineffective: by paying two to three times the market price, the PRG retained unhindered access to all the rice it needed. Local officials meanwhile used their confiscation powers to increase their exactions from the farmers. Cash values of crops were downgraded arbitrarily, and payments were delayed for from one to several weeks. The net result of these developments was that Saigon, not the PRG, was denied access to rice. By early 1975, GVN officials estimated that fully 20 percent of the 1974 crop had been lost in this manner.

By the fall of 1974, the military balance began shifting to Hanoi's favor. . . . There were then more North Vietnamese Army (NVA) regular combat forces in South Vietnam than at any time during the past decade. Estimates of total Communist troop strength ranged from 285,000 (preferred by most U.S. analysts) to 387,000 (suggested by GVN officials). Considerably more than half of these troops were deployed in regular infantry divisions in the area extending from the central highlands northward to the DMZ. U.S. officials feared that, if North Vietnam committed any of its estimated four to six reserve divisions to an offensive in the central highlands, or to a drive against the coastal cities of Hue or Danang, the GVN would have a less than equal chance of containing the attack. Communist artillery and armor equaled that of the GVN in number, while more than 10 percent of this inventory included weapons that could be fired completely out of the range of the ARVN's field guns. Enough ordnance had been stockpiled by the NVA to sustain an offensive at the 1972 level for a year.

Ranged against the North Vietnamese and PRG forces were 1.1 million GVN regular and paramilitary defense forces. While fully one-half to two-thirds of Saigon's forces were engaged in static defense missions, no more than 10 percent of the NVA forces were similarly deployed. Some ARVN commanders suggested that, as long as their troops had both to defend 90 percent of the population and to fight the North Vietnamese, even a delicate balance of forces no longer existed. They were right.

By 1974, both Hanoi and Saigon declared that military action was necessary to save the Paris Agreement. Their cease-fire had never been more than a less-fire. The International Commission for Control and Supervision (ICCS), and the Joint Military Commissions responsible for the maintenance of the cease-fire, were never permitted to determine which contested areas were controlled by the GVN and which by the PRG. The cease-fire and resupply inspection mechanisms were hamstrung from the start by the noncooperation of the PRG and Hanoi. The activities of the inspection forces ceased altogether after one unarmed U.S. member of the FPJMT, investigating, with the consent of the PRG, an air crash site where remains of MIAs were reported, stepped from his clearly marked helicopter and was shot dead.

Hanoi charged that it had been misled by the United States into thinking that all U.S. military installations in South Vietnam would be dismantled within sixty days of the agreement. The United States, instead, had transferred to the GVN title to all of its facilities before it signed the Paris Agreement. The North Vietnamese infiltrated additional military personnel into South Vietnam and introduced entirely new weapon systems into the south, while the United States provided Saigon with a few new F5-E fighter aircraft to replace and augment its force of F5-As. According to the terms of the agreement, both sides were permitted only to replace "armaments, munition, and war materiel which have been destroyed, damaged, worn-out or used up . . . on the basis of piece-for-piece, of the same characteristics and properties. . . ."

The agreement provided for the return of all POWs, the release of political prisoners, and a full accounting for all soldiers listed as missing in action (MIA). Only the U.S. POWs were returned to the last man. There has never been a complete accounting by Hanoi of the U.S. MIAs. The GVN charged Hanoi with imprisoning 60,000 soldiers and civilians, while political prisoners in GVN jails were released only in April 1975 when the PRG captured Saigon.

The neutrality of Cambodia and Laos was not respected, nor was an Indochina-wide cease-fire realized. Hostilities in Laos stopped for a time, but this was largely because the United States no longer needed the upcountry communications complex to guide bombers to targets in North Vietnam. The Laotian forces of the right, center, and left proclaimed a cease-fire on February 21, 1973, and fourteen months later formed a coalition government. The coalition was soon dominated by the Communist Pathet Lao. Hostilities were resumed shortly thereafter, and the coalition collapsed in the wake of the fall of Phnom Penh and Saigon in the spring of 1975.

The Paris Agreement (Article 12[a]) had also provided that "the two South Vietnamese parties shall sign an agreement on the internal matters of South Vietnam as soon as possible and do their utmost to accomplish this within ninety days after the cease-fire comes into effect, in keeping with the South Vietnamese people's aspiration for peace, independence and democracy." Talks between the two parties began in late March 1973. Over a period of two years, the always acrimonious, sometimes stalled, and ultimately boycotted (after April 16, 1974) discussions revealed only that the GVN and the PRG favored establishing a National Council of Reconciliation and Concord. However, Saigon objected, as it had for the better part of a decade, to the provision in Article 12[a] that the council be composed "of three equal segments." Thieu saw this as giving the Communists undue advantage, even though the council was to function on the basis of unanimity. He argued that the third segment—called the third political tendency by its adherents in Saigon—would be dominated by the Communists, and he worked steadily to isolate, imprison, and generally weaken those associated with it. . . .

In essence, what the agreement had left up to the two South Vietnamese parties to negotiate was not negotiable. The question of who was to have power in the south, both the GVN and the PRG concluded, could only be resolved on the battlefield, not at the conference table. Hoping that international pressure might prevent any resumption of large-scale warfare, the United States arranged a conference for February 26 to March 2, 1973, . . . at which twelve countries were to guarantee the provisions of the Paris Agreement. When these signatories were later asked by the United States to urge Hanoi to halt its 1975 offensive in South Vietnam, not one agreed to do so. Kissinger's expectation that the level of military assistance reaching North Vietnam would decline also was not vindicated. By the end of 1974, Hanoi was receiving approximately twice as much aid as it had during the previous years of the war, twice what the United States was then authorized to provide Saigon.

Throughout the spring and early summer of 1973, U.S. and North Vietnamese representatives held talks on the creation of a Joint Economic Commission through which the U.S. would implement its pledge to contribute to the postwar reconstruction of the DRV. For the most part, negotiations were technical; they avoided charges and countercharges about violations of the agreement. The negotiators went relatively far in terms of talking about specific amounts and projects that would be appropriate for U.S. support. But in the fall of 1973, the U.S. Congress passed a law prohibiting any funds being given to Hanoi until Hanoi accounted for all of the U.S. MIAs. This Hanoi refused to do.

For nearly a week in June, Kissinger and Tho negotiated what they characterized as an amplification and consolidation of the original agreement. Kissinger explained to the press why such follow-up negotiation had become necessary:

> . . . during the course of March and April the United States became quite concerned about the manner in which the cease-fire agreement was being implemented. We were specifically concerned about the following points:
>
> One, the inadequate implementation of the cease-fire.
>
> Secondly, the continued infiltration into South Viet-Nam and the continued utilization of Laos and Cambodia as corridors for that infiltration.
>
> Three, we were concerned about the inadequate accounting for the missing in action.
>
> Fourth, we were concerned about the violations of the demilitarized zone.
>
> Fifth, we were concerned about the inadequate cooperation with the international control commission and the slow staffing of the two-party military commission.
>
> Sixth, we were concerned about the violations of Article 20 requiring the withdrawal of foreign troops from Laos and Cambodia.

But the resulting June communiqué . . . read like the Paris Agreement's obituary. Kissinger and Tho had met nine times that week and the communiqué was the result of more than forty hours of their work. But the hopelessness of the situation was evident: throughout the June talks both Saigon and Hanoi continued to insist on many of the very issues that had stymied the negotiations in October, November, and December 1972. At the conclusion of the June negotiations, Kissinger said that he hoped "to be able to reduce my own participation in this process [of follow-up negotiations] in order to preserve my emotional stability." In late June, the U.S. Congress voted to end all funds for U.S. air operations in Indochina on August 15, 1973. Throughout July, former White House counsel John Dean captured the nation's attention with his side of the Watergate story; by fall, the Nixon administration was under siege domestically, just as its foreign policy of détente was to face a challenge in the Middle East.

With the Cambodian bombing cut off, the president and Kissinger realized that the United States had lost its only means of enforcing the Paris Agreement. There had been debate within the administration in April 1973 over whether a resumption of the bombing of North Vietnam would be an appropriate response to, as Kissinger later put it, Hanoi's "flagrant violations of the agreements." But, Kissinger later said, "President Nixon . . . never made a final decision . . ." Many U.S. officials believe that, when it did become clear that U.S. air power would no longer be used in Indochina, the last obstacle to an all-out Communist offensive was removed. Kissinger and Tho met once more in December, with little result. Their talks on December 20, 1973, were designed, from Hanoi's perspective, to see if further progress could be made toward implementing U.S. postwar assistance to the DRV. Kissinger reportedly took the position that one part of the agreement could not be implemented as long as other parts of it were being violated. He stressed the need for the level of military activity in South Vietnam to be reduced, for Hanoi to account for all of the American MIAs, and for the North Vietnamese troops to withdraw from Cambodia and Laos.

With the Paris Agreement moribund, Kissinger's most difficult negotiations were those he had with Congress over future aid to Vietnam. Both he and Nixon had assured Thieu that the United States would not stand idly by in the face of continuing pressure from the NVA and that U.S. aid to Saigon would continue at appropriate levels. In November and December 1972, and again during his state visit in 1973, Thieu pressed Nixon for a specific pledge, but Nixon continually responded by saying that only Congress could make such pledges. As late as the fall of 1974, however, senior U.S. officials were still telling their South Vietnamese counterparts that Saigon would get its aid.

But the U.S. Congress ultimately proved impervious to the pleadings of many that military assistance for the 1974–1975 fiscal year be appropriated, even at the authorized level. Administration spokesmen argued that Saigon spent at the level of the actual authorization ($1 billion) and geared its defense program to that ceiling rather than to the $700 million that was appropriated in September 1974 after a surprise cut was made during House debate. And of the $700 million then available for military aid, more than $400 million were charged off for shipping costs. At the end of the pipeline was less than $300 million in military assistance. Exclusive of their shipping costs, Moscow and Peking provided Hanoi nearly $400 million in war materiel. Interviews with a variety of GVN officials acknowledged that the U.S. cut, coupled with worldwide inflation, gravely affected Saigon's capability to respond to a North Vietnamese offensive. To these pleadings and assessments congressional leaders tended to respond as did Senator Hubert Humphrey, floor manager of the Foreign Assistance Act, in a speech he gave at the time:

After millions of words about the lessons of Vietnam, we ignore the most important lesson, that political battles cannot be resolved by force of arms.

We learned this lesson at great sacrifice to our nation. Yet our policymakers now are engaged in a course of action which does not recognize this basic reality of Indochina. The United States has embarked upon a course of encouraging the funding of maximum military confrontation, hoping that somehow those we are supporting can prevail.

. . . How can the policy of military confrontation be sustained when it is clear that neither the Congress nor the American public is willing to fund the wars in Vietnam and Cambodia at high levels for the indefinite future?

Kissinger later told Barbara Walters, in an interview on the May 5, 1975, "Today Show," that he would never have negotiated the Paris Agreement if he had thought the U.S. Congress would have proved so difficult. Because of the restrictions placed on the use of American air power and the reluctance of Congress in 1974 to appropriate adequate aid for

Saigon, Kissinger said he believed the resumption of the war by North Vietnam was inevitable. Ultimately, in the face of that prospect Saigon's army, and then its government, collapsed.

I originally thought it would be possible to end this study of the Vietnam negotiations with a prediction of how an eventual political settlement between the Communists and the non-Communists in South Vietnam could evolve. Such a settlement, I thought, was likely on the one hand, because of the strong anticommunism of substantial segments of Vietnamese religious and social forces, and on the other, because it was difficult for me to imagine the GVN collapsing overnight. But with a political settlement, I did expect the creation of a government not unlike the tripartite one hinted at in the Paris Agreement. Thereafter, I expected the gradual emergence of the PRG as the dominant political force in the south, just as, in 1945 and 1946, the Viet Minh—even though a minority in the north—came to dominate all other nationalist forces in the coalition government established there after World War II.

In retrospect I underestimated the PRG's prediction that the "internal contradictions" in the GVN would cause it to collapse, eliminating the need for Saigon's army to be defeated militarily. Such internal contradictions were abundant, even to the most casual observers: proclaiming an economic and social revolution, the GVN depended on the very elites who stood to lose the most from change. The peasant soldier was still led by ill-trained, urban-born scions of the elite, and army officer assignments were still largely determined by bribery. In 1975, nationalist political forces were as unprepared and unorganized for a political struggle with the PRG as they had been in 1965.

Yet, to my mind, each year that the GVN managed to survive made its collapse a little less likely. Moreover, the political opposition that Thieu faced in the fall of 1974 hardly compared with that against Diem in 1963, and the ARVN appeared to be equal to the military challenge it expected from the NVA in 1975. As one high U.S. embassy official put it that January: "We are talking about well-equipped experienced [ARVN] soldiers who know we won't do their fighting for them. The NVA is going to launch another offensive but all our indicators show that it will be nothing compared to what the ARVN withstood and pushed back at Tet 1968 or in the 1972 Easter offensive." With respect to the strength of the 1975 NVA offensive, the embassy official was right.

I traveled to Saigon in early January 1975 to conduct one last series of interviews for this book. Another dry season had begun in Vietnam and with it, the postwar war resumed against the backdrop of the breakdown of the Paris Agreement. I arrived on the eve of the fall of the provincial capital of Phuoc Long, although its loss was not confirmed by the GVN for several days. But the next day, a Vietnamese friend told me that when he saw the street banners go up proclaiming: "All compatriots support the heroic defenders of Phuoc Long," he knew the end was at hand. What I learned during the next three weeks convinced me that he was right.

After three weeks of interviewing Vietnamese officials and opposition political leaders, I concluded that the most well-organized segments of the South Vietnamese population actually expected a Communist victory. Their leaders began to use the word *accommodation* synonymously with *adaptation*. *Accommodation* had once referred to "live and let live" arrangements whereby GVN supporters coexisted with the NLF. But by January 1975, *adaptation* meant surviving while living under communism. Cabinet level GVN officials believed that Phuoc Long was only the beginning. As one cabinet minister put it, "Much more of our territory will now be lost." I was repeatedly told that the boundary between North and South Vietnam was now, de facto, south of the seventeenth parallel and that there was to be a line drawn inside South Vietnam dividing it into eastern and western (Communist) regions.

The political opposition was equally pessimistic about both prospects for further partitioning of Vietnam and accommodation with the PRG. Consequently, the opposition was leaderless by January 1975 and no longer willing either to struggle for an alternative to Thieu or to participate in politics. The active opposition leaders who two years earlier were rarely in their offices due to their political activities in the countryside now were never in their offices due to having returned to private life. No one was coming forward to take their place.

When a strategic retreat was ordered from the central highlands in mid-March, the South Vietnamese soldiers panicked and in domino fashion abandoned outpost after outpost. They were reacting as much to the prospect of a fight with the NVA as to their future under the GVN. ARVN soldiers no longer believed (if they ever did) that they would eventually win against the NVA, and they no longer wanted war. As one U.S. embassy official put it in April 1975:

> We should have asked ourselves long ago how an army can go on functioning when it is simply a business organization in which everything is for sale, from what you eat to a transfer or a promotion. We never encouraged the Vietnamese forces to fight aggressively, to take the offensive. We fought the war for them and made them over dependent on air support. We prepared them for conventional war when the Communists were fighting unconventionally, and then, when the Communists finally adopted conventional tactics, the South Vietnamese didn't know what to do. The fact they have no leadership is largely our fault; we made them followers, so successfully that even the soldiers who were willing to fight got killed or wounded as a result of incompetence, or lost by default. . . .

From Ban Me Thuot in the central highlands, to Danang on the northern coast, and to the Mekong Delta in the south, retreating ARVN soldiers refused to believe that the future promised to them could be achieved by the government that the United States had supported in Saigon. America's lost peace in Vietnam came not only because of what was negotiated, but also because neither the process of negotiations nor the agreement itself produced a Saigon government that could end the war—through accommodation with the PRG or through victory over it.

I have not written this . . . with a view to apportioning responsibility for the whole chapter for history labeled "The Vietnam War." But such an accounting would certainly have to come to terms not only with what made a meaningful negotiated settlement unlikely, but also with the wisdom of the decision by successive American presidents to seek such a settlement, and the implications that this decision had for the strategy by which the war was fought. In retrospect, to be incremental in our military strategy and conciliatory in our negotiating strategy with an adversary who, from the outset, equated restraint with weakness, and to whom compromise was inconceivable, had the effect of obscuring what the costs of intervention in Vietnam were likely to be and, equally important, what the ultimate gains there might look like. But when U.S. policy-makers suddenly faced the end of the proverbial tunnel in Vietnam and witnessed the Saigon army fleeing the countryside—abandoning in a matter of days what it had taken a decade to secure and "pacify"—they realized there was no realistic option open that would have justified the investment. Probably there never was. Thus are the lives of men and women and the spirit of great nations wasted in adventures that ultimately bring neither the peace intended nor honor.

Why the Communists Won

WILLIAM J. DUIKER

The 1975 campaign had progressed with truly lightning speed, stunning the Saigon regime and even surpassing the expectations of the Party leadership in Hanoi. In three weeks, eight provinces had fallen to the Communists. Virtually all forces in Saigon's I and II Corps were wiped out. ARVN had lost almost half its main force units, and more than half its aircraft. The capital was in a state of evident panic, while Washington appeared impotent. On the final day of March, two days after the fall of Da Nang, the Politburo met again and concluded that the war had entered a stage of massive development. Van Tien Dung was instructed to prepare to launch a general offensive against Saigon with the objective of seizing total victory within four weeks: "Not only has the revolutionary war in the South entered a period of developing by leaps and bounds, but the time is ripe for carrying the general offensive and general uprising to the enemy's lair. From this moment, the final decisive battle of our army and people has begun; its aim is to complete the people's national democratic revolution in the South and bring peace and the reunification of the Fatherland."

On April 2, Van Tien Dung ordered most North Vietnamese main force units to turn south. With seaports along the northern and central coast now open and ARVN prisoners pressed into service as truck drivers, war materiel began to flow south in vast quantities, while an air shuttle was set up from the D.R.V. to Kontum and Da Nang. Two more reserve divisions were sent south and a new military headquarters was set up near Saigon to

From William J. Duiker, *The Communist Road to Power in Vietnam,* excerpts from pp. 314–329. Reprinted by permission of the author.

replace COSVN. Van Tien Dung was named chairman, with Pham Hung as his chief political officer. Le Duc Tho was on hand to provide a direct link with the Politburo. After several days of intensive consultation, the new military command agreed on a basic strategy for the final assault, to be labeled the "Ho Chi Minh Campaign" because of Hanoi's intention to rename Saigon for the founder of the Party. According to Dung's account, the plan was to set up a strategic encirclement of the city by cutting Route 4 from the delta and Route 1 from Tay Ninh, while main force units marching down from the north would concentrate for a major thrust on the provincial capital of Xuan Loc, east of Saigon, where the crucial Eighteenth Division was located. As those main force units prepared for the final assault on Saigon, local forces would seize suburban areas, and the Party's suicide and guerrilla units in the city would prepare to surface to incite a general uprising.

In Saigon, hopes that the situation could be stabilized were rapidly evaporating. With the earlier plan to set up a defense line anchored at Tay Ninh and Nha Trang outdated by the swift pace of events, Thieu moved to set up a line from the city of Tay Ninh, still under siege, to Phan Rang on the coast, anchored at Xuan Loc, where the Eighteenth Division formed the last major bulwark against total collapse. Even this position might soon become untenable. With half of the ARVN gone, Saigon had only about six divisions plus a few brigades and ranger groups remaining, a total of less than 100,000 troops. Prospects for U.S. support appeared dim. The Ford administration was attempting to push through Congress a $1 billion aid package, but congressional resistance to any further aid to the Saigon regime had increased and approval appeared unlikely.

With military stabilization apparently out of the question, there was increasing talk of a compromise settlement. There had been hints from various diplomatic sources that Hanoi might accept a negotiated settlement. Hanoi's presumed price for peace was the departure of President Thieu and the immediate end of any further U.S. involvement in South Vietnam. Opposition politicians in Saigon clamored for the resignation of Nguyen Van Thieu and began to explore the possibility of a peace candidate such as the popular but enigmatic general Duong Van Minh. There had been some encouragement of this line from the PRG, when on April 2 Foreign Minister Nguyen Thi Binh had expressed a willingness to talk to Minh. Even top officials in the U.S. Embassy were cautiously optimistic that a compromise agreement could be worked out.

It is doubtful, however, that Hanoi was interested in a political settlement. With military victory now within easy reach and little likelihood of a U.S. response, there seemed no persuasive reason to compromise. As intelligence reports showed, Party leaders had decided at the end of March to settle for nothing less than total victory. A diplomatic settlement was hinted at probably to increase divisiveness in Saigon.

By the third week of April, North Vietnamese divisions had occupied Phan Rang and were beginning to encircle Xuan Loc, moving in on the highway leading to Bien Hoa, site of a major GVN airbase and weapons arsenal. From the delta, Communist units were moving north toward Saigon. All of Tay Ninh Province had been occupied except the capital, which was still under siege. As the campaign neared its climax, Saigon's resistance briefly flared. At Xuan Loc, the Eighteenth Division dug in and proved tougher than expected, slowing down the Communist blitzkrieg and stimulating a brief flurry of optimism in Saigon that total defeat could yet be averted. But the odds were too great and, after a few days of stiff resistance, ARVN units began to withdraw southward toward Vung Tau, while Communist forces bypassed Xuan Loc and began to move directly on Bien Hao and to shell its air base.

It was by now no secret that Hanoi intended to carry its offensive directly to the heart of enemy rule. The plan called for wearing down the five remaining ARVN divisions on the outskirts of the city and then launching a massive assault with main force and armored units directly into the city before government units in the suburbs could respond. The attack would be led by North Vietnamese mechanized forces, which would advance directly on the main highways into the heart of Saigon. There they would attempt to seize five major targets—the presidential palace, the headquarters of the Saigon city military command, the general police directorate, Tan Son Nhut Airport in the north-western suburbs, and the nearby headquarters of the general staff. As described by Dung, the plan was

> to use whatever forces necessary from each direction to encircle enemy forces, isolating them and preventing them from pulling back to Saigon; to wipe out and disperse the enemy main-force infantry divisions in the outer defense perimeter right on the spot; and to save the greatest number of forces to thrust in quickly and capture key positions in the outskirts. This would open the way for mechanized and tightly organized assault units to advance rapidly along the main roads and strike directly at the five chosen objectives inside the city.

The attacks in the suburbs went on schedule, as company or battalion-sized units in Go Vap, Nha Be, Binh Chanh, Hoc Mon, Thu Duc, and Cu Chi rose on April 27 and, with the aid of regular forces in the area, began to overrun military and government installations in the vicinity and to seize key bridges and guide the main force units into the city. Others were to eliminate traitors and call on ARVN soldiers to desert their units.

Meanwhile, within the city the Party's municipal apparatus activated its special action squads and sapper units and prepared to seize key government installations, while propaganda units prepared to distribute leaflets and set up loudspeakers at key points to arouse the populace to support the invading revolutionary forces. Special sapper units were organized at Nha Be and Long Tau to sabotage GVN shipping and to cut the river route to the sea. Others were active in Long Binh and Bien Hoa, while a few were infiltrated into the city to supplement the sixty special action cells and 300 armed civilians directed by the Party's municipal leadership. By the twenty-ninth, main force units were well established in key positions around the capital. In the east, routes to the south and west were cut and

Bien Hoa Air Base and Vung Tau had been isolated. At command head-quarters, Pham Hung and Le Duc Tho made preparations for forming a transitional revolutionary administration in the capital.

In Saigon, the situation raced to a climax. Phnom Penh had fallen to Communist forces on April 17. On the eighteenth the Ford administration, despite Ambassador Graham Martin's objections, ordered a gradual pullout of nonessential Americans. On the twenty-third President Ford announced that the war was finished as far as the United States was concerned. The South Vietnamese, he said, must confront whatever fate awaited them. Under considerable pressure, Thieu finally resigned on the twenty-first and was replaced by Tran Van Huong, a veteran Saigon politician who had achieved a moment of fame during a brief stint as prime minister in 1965. The change was futile, for the Communists refused to deal with him. Van Tien Dung described him as just a "very crafty civilian traitor" replacing a "savage military traitor." Huong resigned on the twenty-seventh and was replaced by Duong Van Minh. Minh quickly formed a new cabinet and ordered the United States to remove its personnel from the GVN in twenty-four hours. The demand had little significance, for current plans called for total evacuation by the twenty-ninth in any case. Nor had it any useful results, for the PRG contemptuously rejected negotiations with the new president.

On April 26, as the first rains began in the delta, Van Tien Dung and his subordinates had moved by car to their advance campaign headquarters near Ben Cat. That afternoon the final campaign began with an artillery barrage on the outskirts of Saigon. From all directions, North Vietnamese forces advanced toward the city and relentlessly scattered resistance from the remaining ARVN forces on the outskirts of the capital. By the evening of the twenty-ninth, Saigon was surrounded as by a vise and Hanoi's main force units, in the words of Van Tien Dung, were poised like a "divine hammer" held aloft, awaiting the word to launch the direct assault on the city of Saigon.

At 2:00 A.M. on April 30, as the last Americans were preparing to leave Vietnam from helicopter pads around the city, the PRG indicated its final refusal to the appeal for negotiations from the Saigon government. During the early morning, Hanoi's "deep strike units" began to move slowly down the major highways toward the city. Armored vehicles advanced in columns straight into the city, followed by infantry. As they entered without meeting resistance, special action squads occupied bridges while propaganda units passed out leaflets and revolutionary flags and called on the populace to welcome the revolutionary forces. There was some evidence of enthusiasm, particularly in working-class neighborhoods, but for the most part the advance was observed in silence. The attacking troops were supposed to be guided by revolutionary squads, but in at least one case, a tank commander lost his way and had to ask directions from ARVN troops standing by the side of the road.

President Duong Van Minh had met with his ministers at Independence Palace in the heart of the city and at 10:00 A.M. issued an appeal for a cease-fire. The appeal was ignored. In an indirect response, the Politburo issued a directive to its troops advancing into Saigon: "Continue the attack on Saigon according to plan, advancing in the most powerful spirit, liberate and take over the whole city, disarm enemy troops, dissolve the enemy administration at all levels, and thoroughly smash all enemy resistance." Shortly before noon, the lead tank of the Second Army Corps rumbled up Thong Nhut Boulevard and rolled onto the green lawn of the Independence Palace. Troops arrested the government ministers inside the building and raised the revolutionary flag of the PRG over the palace. Two hours later, Duong Van Minh called on all ARVN forces to lay down their arms. The war, the long bitter struggle that had lasted in one form or another for an entire generation, was finally at an end.

The predominantly military character of the final campaign has led some observers to downgrade the political significance of the Communist victory and assert that the takeover of the South was a military conquest, pure and simple. A number of high Saigon civilian and military officials echo this contention by complaining that the war was lost primarily because of the failure of the Ford administration to provide adequate military assistance to the ARVN forces in the final months. The charge is understandable. Although the 1975 campaign was described by Party spokesmen as a combined general offensive and uprising, an attack by revolutionary armed forces in rural areas coordinated with a popular uprising in the cities in the tradition of the Tet Offensive and the great August Revolution of 1945, the reality is somewhat different. The bulk of the fighting was undertaken by regular force units of the PAVN. Although the PLAF undoubtedly participated in attacks at the local level, the most damaging blows were inflicted by North Vietnamese troops. And what the Party lauded as a mass popular uprising in the cities consisted in the main of the mobilization of the Party's small municipal apparatus to welcome the North Vietnamese troops—the *bo doi*—as they entered the cities from the suburbs. While there was some organized jubilation in a few working-class areas, there was relatively little spontaneous enthusiasm among the general urban populace. It is not surprising that Hanoi would dress up the final stage of the conflict as a popular upsurge against an unpopular regime. In fact, however, the final triumph was achieved primarily by force of arms.

But the fact that the 1975 campaign was primarily a military offensive should not obscure the fundamental reality that the Party's success over a generation was attributable, above all, to nonmilitary factors. Hanoi's ability to organize and direct the insurgency and to exploit the chronic weaknesses of its adversary in Saigon were the cardinal factors in its success. Even at the end, the defeat of the GVN was probably caused less by a shortage of aircraft and ammunition than by a lack of nerve in Saigon and by the pervasive sense of malaise throughout South Vietnamese society, itself the legacy of a generation of failure by successive governments to build the foundations of a viable non-Communist society. Not least, the defeat was caused by serious deficiencies in the strategic planning of the Thieu regime. Thieu's hasty last-minute decision to abandon most of the northern provinces and the Central Highlands was ill-conceived and created a disastrous sense of confusion among top military officers as well as within the government. It contributed in no small measure to the completeness of the final collapse.

The U.S. failure to provide adequate military support in the final weeks, although not one of Washington's prouder moments, was not a decisive factor in the outcome of the war. For years the Communists had done better with less. Despite President John F. Kennedy's insistence that, in the last analysis, the war had to be waged and won by the Vietnamese, Washington's clients had come to depend heavily on U.S. largesse. It was a fatal flaw, for when the military shield represented by the power of the United States was withdrawn, the many weaknesses of the Saigon regime quickly surfaced and proved decisive.

All great revolutions are the product of multiple causes. They result from the convergence of several factors, some of them related directly to the overall political and cultural environment, others the consequence of individual human action. Marxist theory reflects this reality by locating the sources of revolution in both objective and subjective conditions. Objective conditions determine whether or not a mature revolutionary situation has arisen in a given society. Subjective conditions reflect the degree of preparedness and astute leadership provided by a revolutionary party. Revolution rarely succeeds unless both factors are present. The Marxist viewpoint is thus not simply a handy heuristic device, but a practical and often effective approach to the problem of waging revolution in human society.

But although all great revolutions share elements of both spontaneity and human will, the relative importance of these two factors has varied greatly over the years. Many of the classical revolutions in modern history—the French Revolution of 1789, the Russian Revolution of 1917, and, more recently, the revolution in Iran in the late 1970s—grew out of a relatively spontaneous eruption of popular discontent. Only after the initial stage of popular uprising did a revolutionary organization begin to manipulate these conditions to promote a final and total overthrow of existing authority.

The modern phenomenon of people's war has added a new dimension to the revolutionary process. Spontaneity has been replaced with calculation, the popular uprising with the concept of a protracted conflict. Although the presence of objective conditions favoring revolt is still considered to be ultimately essential, this factor is increasingly subordinated to the existence of a dedicated revolutionary organization whose duty it is to exacerbate the political and social tensions in societies undergoing the stress of change. The revolutionary party must serve as the catalyst to activate the latent revolutionary conditions in such societies and then take advantage of the resultant ferment to bring about a violent upheaval against the status quo and the formation of a revolutionary regime.

Although Lenin, because of his stress on the importance of individual human action in the revolutionary process, may claim partial credit for the liberation of the Marxist dialectic from the "iron laws" of history, it was Mao Tse-tung who carried Lenin's idea to its logical conclusion and, in the form of people's war, put it into practice. The Vietnamese carried on the Maoist tradition and set out deliberately to create revolutionary conditions that would topple the government and bring communism to power. Discontent against French colonial rule and later against the failures of the Saigon regime was undeniably a factor in creating the objective conditions underlying the Vietnamese revolution. But the Communist Party mobilized the inchoate frustration and anger of the mass of the Vietnamese population and fashioned it into a fierce and relentless weapon of revolutionary war.

Of all the great revolutions, then, the Vietnamese revolution was, above all, an act of human will. That does not mean that it took place in a vacuum. Even the Vietnamese Party leadership conceded that a revolutionary upsurge could not take place unless the proper opportunity—the semimystical *thoi co*—had arisen. Some of the conditions that are necessary are the classical symptoms that characterize the emergence of a prerevolutionary situation in any human society—widespread poverty, economic disorder, social inequality and unrest, an unpopular or incompetent government, and a "transfer of allegiance" on the part of the urban middle class. Such conditions, of course, do not necessarily lead to revolt. But without them, revolution is difficult, if not impossible.

At various times in its modern history, Vietnam has exhibited a number of these symptoms, and they were clearly a factor in the growth of the revolutionary movement. But it was characteristic of the situation in Vietnam that the Communists did not passively await the emergence of an economic and social crisis before launching their bid for power, but deliberately attempted to bring it about through exacerbating latent tensions in society and bringing the existing government to the point of collapse. Even in the late 1950s, when Diem's own actions had led to widespread discontent in South Vietnamese society, it was the Communists, above all, who set a match to the powder keg and thus inaugurated the revolutionary war.

In such conditions, the comparative political ability of revolutionaries and ruling elites becomes a crucial issue. And this was what was most extraordinary about the situation in Vietnam—the contrast between the chronic weakness and political ineptitude of the Saigon governing elite and the political genius of the Communist Party. The underlying reasons for the weakness of non-Communist nationalism have been the subject of scholarly analysis for decades, but satisfactory answers have been elusive. Was it merely an accident of history that could be rectified by time and effort? A generation of policymakers in Washington took this view, and based U.S. strategy on the assumption that with adequate military and economic assistance, a regime would eventually emerge that could establish an aura of political legitimacy and a popular base among the population at large. The Communists, of course, thought otherwise. They were convinced that Saigon's weaknesses were endemic and would eventually become the decisive factor in the war.

In retrospect, it appears that the Communists had a clearer view. A generation of U.S. technology and advice was unable to remedy the manifold deficiencies of the GVN. And although the mistakes of the United States may have contributed to the failure in Saigon, it seems probable that the key to the problem lay in Vietnam. The ineffectiveness of the Vietnamese nationalism during the colonial period is a matter of record. It consistently failed to produce a challenge to French rule or to provide a nucleus for a mass movement of national proportions such as those formed in a number of other colonial or semicolonial societies in the region. It is surely significant that the first non-Communist government in Vietnam did not come to power as a result of its own efforts, but was imposed from above, by the French. The governments that arose in Saigon after the Geneva settlement bore the mark of that heritage. They were concerned over the need to overcome the chronic factionalism that had characterized nationalist behavior during the colonial period, but they failed to resolve the problem or to build a constituency among the mass of the population. To the end, the only real source of Saigon's authority was the U.S. military presence.

Why were the moderate forces in Vietnam less able than their counterparts elsewhere to emerge as the central force in the struggle for independence? Over the years, a number of hypotheses have been advanced. Some observers have suggested that the root cause lay in the stifling effects of French policy, that the brutal repression of the Vietnamese nationalist movement by the colonial regime left a vacuum that was filled by the Communists. This explanation may be emotionally satisfying to critics of French colonial policy, but it is not very persuasive. On the whole, moderate nationalist forces in Vietnam received little worse treatment than they did elsewhere in colonial Southeast Asia. Only those avowedly determined to root out French rule by force, such as the VNQDD [Vietnam Nam Quoc Dan Dang, or Vietnamese Nationalist Party], were exposed to systematic persecution. Although moderate political parties in Vietnam were seldom allowed to enjoy a legal existence, they were given tacit permission to operate during the late 1930s, with no visible effects on their capabilities. A few nationalist figures were arrested and condemned to terms in prison, but most, including such fervent critics of French rule as Nguyen An Ninh and Ta Thu Thau, were soon back on the streets as the result of periodic amnesties declared in Paris. In fact, a non-Communist nationalist movement based on quasi-legal action and mass support, such as the Indian Congress Party, failed to develop in Vietnam not solely because the French prevented it, but primarily because no one attempted to form one.

It can hardly be said, then, that French brutality repressed moderate nationalists, thus leaving the field, by elimination, to the Communists. To the contrary, released documents in the French archives show that the Sûreté had become concerned about the Communists as early as 1929 and throughout much of the following decade devoted the greater part of its efforts to relentlessly pursuing the Party and preventing it from spreading its roots throughout the country. If anything, it is likely that French harassment served to toughen the Communists for the generation of struggle that lay ahead.

Party historians have a different explanation for the weakness of their rivals. Predictably, they view the issue through the prism of Marxist class analysis, and explain it as a consequence of the belated development of the Vietnamese bourgeoisie under colonial rule and its resultant failure to assume an active role in the Vietnamese revolution. By contrast, the Vietnamese working class developed early, in the mines, plantations, and factories run by French colonial interests, and was thus able to take the lead in the struggle for independence after the defeat of the VNQDD at Yen Bay in early 1930. This is an interesting hypothesis, but it lacks sufficient corroborative evidence based on a comparative analysis with other colonial societies in Southeast Asia, where similar conditions apparently existed without leading to a Communist victory. Moreover, it does not account for the fact that the Communist movement itself did not emerge directly from the Vietnamese proletariat but from among discontented members of the traditional ruling class, the sons and daughters of the patriotic scholar-gentry.

The question thus needs to be reformulated. The point is not that the Vietnamese middle class failed to assert its leadership over the nationalist movement, thereby leaving a vacuum to be filled by the proletariat. It is that such a high percentage of the most politically active elements within the educated elite chose to follow the Communists rather than their nationalist rivals, thus providing the Party with its early leadership and a significant advantage in the struggle to determine the course of the Vietnamese revolution. If such is the case, the cultural argument referred to earlier seems a more plausible hypothesis. Marxism exerted a peculiar attraction among the educated scholar-elite in Vietnam. Logical in its portrayal of the historical forces at work in the world, activist in its call for the formation of a disciplined revolutionary organization devoted to the struggle for change, ethical in its vision of a future utopia based on economic and social equality, it offered a persuasive alternative to the now discredited Confucian world view and provided patriotic Vietnamese with a basis on which to struggle for independence and build a new sense of national identity.

The fact that Marxism appealed particularly to the young generation of patriotic scholar-elites is crucial. This was the traditional ruling class in Vietnamese society. It had a heritage of educational leadership and service to society, and an equally strong awareness of the concept of Vietnamese nationhood. It was thus the logical class to lead the struggle against colonial rule. Many alienated members of this class were attracted to Marxism, giving the Party a momentum that it never relinquished. This must be recognized as one of the most significant facts in the history of modern Vietnam.

The weakness of their nationalist rivals was, of course, no guarantee that the Communists themselves would succeed. Economic and military support from Western powers provided non-Communist elites with a bulwark against social and political deterioration and a measure of protection against the spontaneous forces of popular discontent. The Communists could not wait for the proper conditions to arise. They must themselves bring them about by an act of will. Here, of course, was the challenge of people's war in South Vietnam—to hone the disparate sources of revolt into a well-oiled and highly disciplined instrument of revolutionary war. Only through the application of relentless pressure by the insurgency could the latent structural flaws in South Vietnamese society be magnified into yawning cracks that would eventually bring the entire structure to the ground. In Vietnam, there is little doubt that the Party met that challenge. If some revolutions are essentially a collapse of the old order, and others are the product of individual human action, the Vietnamese revolution is quintessentially an example of the latter.

The reasons for the Party's success have attracted considerable attention among scholars in recent years. Certainly one major factor was its comprehensive strategy of people's war. [My] primary theme . . . is the gradual evolution of that strategy from the early years of the Communist movement down to the final triumph in 1975. The strategy began as a rather unquestioning application of Bolshevik doctrine, as passed on by the Comintern in Moscow. The Russian model had little relevance to Vietnam, however, and during World War II the Party replaced it with a new strategy designed to reflect local conditions. This new strategy owed a debt to the Chinese theory and practice of people's war, but above all it was a product of the fertile mind of Ho Chi Minh. Its major components were put into practice during the revolt that took place at the end of the Pacific War. The success of the August Revolution is adequate testimony to the genius of the concept.

The strategy used during the August uprising could not be applied successfully against a highly armed adversary, and during the Franco-Vietminh conflict the Party turned more explicitly to the Chinese model of three-stage war. The strategy was generally successful, but it had certain weaknesses, among which was the excessive reliance on military factors in the later stages of the war, thus matching the Party's major area of weakness (firepower) against the primary strength of its adversary. After Geneva, then, the Party leadership returned to the strategy used during the August Revolution. But with escalation in the early 1960s, the Party was forced once again to resort to the military option. Now, however, it appeared to recognize the limited relevance of the Maoist model and attempted to combine it with key elements from the Vietnamese approach. Specifically, it attempted to make greater use of the "political force of the masses" in an effort to achieve a better balance of political and military struggle than had obtained during the previous conflict. It also returned to the August Revolution model by seeking to use the revolutionary force of urban radicalism through the concept of a coordinated military offensive and general uprising. Finally, it now made deliberate use of diplomacy as a means of achieving a psychological advantage over the United States and eventually maneuvering it out of the war.

There is, then, a coherent pattern in the development of Vietnamese revolutionary doctrine. Clearly, however, it would be foolhardy to suggest that it had emerged full-blown from the minds of Party leaders in the mid-1940s. On the contrary, Vietnamese revolutionary strategy, in its mature form, was the product of trial and error, of a series of pragmatic decisions taken over a period of several decades and based on real contemporary situations. In the process, it periodically ran into serious difficulties. On several occasions, Party leaders miscalculated enemy intentions and capabilities. On others, they overestimated (or underestimated) the force of the masses and their degree of support for the revolutionary cause. Not surprisingly, problems were encountered in attempting to cope with the challenges of foreign involvement. In particular, U.S. escalation in the mid-1960s presented Party strategists with a dilemma, and for a while they appeared to grope almost in desperation for a solution.

It should also be kept in mind that under the carefully cultivated impression of unity there was frequently dissension over policy within the Party leadership. Virtually every major decision was accompanied by hesitation, vacillation, and internal controversy over the strategy to be applied. There was disagreement over timing, over the relationship between political and military struggle, and over the relative priority to be assigned to revolutionary war in the South and socialist construction in the North. It would be misleading to see in such dissent indications of serious factionalism within the Party leadership. It is noteworthy that the Leninist tradition of democratic centralism was maintained throughout the struggle. But disagreement did exist. A clearer appreciation of the nature of such inner-Party tension, and the identity of the individuals involved, must await additional evidence.

Despite such problems, on the whole the strategy was effective. This must be ascribed to several factors. In the first place Party leaders possessed a clear view of the power relationships among and the security interests of the various forces involved. They correctly assessed the chronic weakness of their rivals within the nationalist camp; they correctly predicted that a significant proportion of the population could be motivated to serve the revolutionary cause in a long and difficult struggle; and they realized that France and the United States had neither the patience nor national interests sufficient to justify a protracted conflict in Indochina. In such calculations, strategists in Hanoi proved to be more clear-sighted than their counterparts in Paris and Washington.

A key factor in the Party's ability to mobilize support within Vietnam was the success of its effort to link the force of nationalism with that of social reform. The essentials of that strategy had been drawn up in 1941 with the formation of the Vietminh Front. As this study has attempted to show, this linkage was not easily achieved. Radical programs of benefit to the poor undermined the effort to win the support of moderate nationalists. But a neglect of the issue of land reform left poor peasants indifferent and difficult to mobilize for the war effort. In the late 1940s, Party strategy had placed heavier emphasis on the anti-imperialist than on the antifeudal cause. This was rectified in the early 1950s, and during the war against the United States Hanoi attempted to place relatively equal weight on both factors—the national liberation struggle and the land revolution.

How successful was the Party's effort to "walk on two legs," to construct a strategy on the dual issues of patriotism and social revolution? A definitive judgment must await further study, but available information suggests that the policy was reasonably successful. At some stages (the early years of the Party and during the first stages of the Franco-Vietminh conflict) the national issue predominated; at other times (the Nghe-Tinh revolt, the August Revolution, just prior to the 1954 settlement, and during the late 1950s) economic issues played a crucial role. During the struggle in the South, both issues contributed to support for the revolutionary cause. Interviews with prisoners and defectors show that those who joined the NLF did so for a variety of reasons. The majority were poor peasants or members of the rural proletariat, but urban volunteers were by no means rare. Most cited patriotism or personal motives as their reasons for joining, although social pressure undoubtedly played a role and there is evidence of compulsion in some instances. Members who joined before 1954 frequently mentioned patriotism as the primary reason. Those who joined after Geneva seemed to offer a wider variety of motives—a desire for adventure or for land, hopes for career advancement, a desire to avoid government conscription or to escape from personal problems. In his study of the movement in Long An Province, Jeffrey Race alluded to the importance of the NLF's ability to provide an alternate road to personal identity and upward mobility for those discontented with life under the GVN.

It is worthy to note that idealism—resentment against government corruption and injustice, or a wish to evict the U.S. imperialists—was often cited as a major factor in recruitment. Virtually all mentioned the idea of the "just cause," the "righteous war" against foreign control and the reactionary government in Saigon. It is particularly significant that patriotic motives played a part in recruitment in rural areas, a sign that nationalism had taken root among the village population. This concept of the "just war" was not just a passing enthusiasm, or one that would be easily undermined as a result of sacrifice and hardship. A surprising number of deserters gave personal reasons for leaving the movement and continued to believe that the revolutionary cause was a righteous one.

In general, then, the Party's propaganda had a fairly broad appeal within the population, and in both urban and rural areas. Still, Party leaders must have been somewhat disappointed by their failure to operate more effectively in the cities. Active support in urban areas never reached the levels apparently expected by the party. This failure was generally ascribed in internal documents to organizational weaknesses, or to the influence of the "noxious weeds" of bourgeois attitudes in the cities of South Vietnam. Whatever the reason, the failure to build a more dynamic movement in Saigon, Da Nang, and Hue was undoubtedly a factor in compelling the Party to turn to a more military approach. That in turn led to increasing reliance on troops from the North, thus diluting somewhat the issue of nationalism. Whatever the case, the concept of the popular uprising steadily lost force in Hanoi's strategy and at the end had become more the ritualistic perpetuation of a myth than a building block of victory. In the final analysis, the Communist takeover did not differ substantially from the Maoist dictum of surrounding the cities from the countryside. This was not a crucial weakness, in China or in Vietnam. In both instances Communist policy was aided by errors committed by the enemy and was thus able to prevent the urban population from committing itself wholeheartedly to the government's cause. That, in itself, was a solid achievement, and an important factor in revolutionary success.

It has been observed that the Party's achievement was a triumph of organization rather than spirit. Certainly organization, indoctrination, and the application of pressure and the threat or use of force played a major role in realizing and maintaining commitment to the revolutionary cause. The nature of the Party's organizational genius has been competently explored in previous studies, and need not detain us here. Suffice it to say that the Communists had striking success in mobilizing all available human and material resources in a total and concentrated effort to seize power. Women, children, and even the aged were put to use so that young males could be released for combat. But the effectiveness of the Party's organizational efforts should not lead us to underestimate the emotional appeal of the cause. In fact, as one American researcher reported, as late as 1964 nearly 90 percent of all members of the PLAF were volunteers.

One final factor remains to be explored. A paramount feature in almost all modern revolutions has been the existence of dynamic and charismatic leadership. It is difficult to imagine the revolts in Russia, China, or Cuba, for example, without reference to the roles played by Lenin, Mao Tse-tung, and Fidel Castro. Curiously, this factor is frequently overlooked in Vietnam. Because Ho Chi Minh lacked theoretical inclinations, his role in shaping revolutionary strategy has often been ignored; because his style of leadership was quiet rather than forceful, conciliatory rather than aggressive, his influence in the decision-making process has frequently seemed ambiguous; and because his part in directing Party strategy probably diminished in the final years of his life, the importance of his influence in the latter stages of the war is difficult to substantiate. Still, over the course of the Vietnamese revolution as a whole, his influence towers. He is best known, of course, as the living symbol of the Vietnamese revolution. For more than a generation his personality, embodying the qualities of virtue, integrity, dedication, and revolutionary asceticism, transcended issues of party and ideology and came to represent, in an Eriksonian sense, the struggle for the independence and self-realization of the Vietnamese nation. Nikita Khrushchev alluded to this trait in his memoirs, when he referred to the Vietnamese leader as a "holy apostle" of the revolution, a man whose sincerity, conviction, and incorruptibility could win anyone over to belief in his cause.

But if Ho Chi Minh is best remembered as the spiritual leader of the Vietnamese revolution, his practical contributions should not be ignored. The key building blocks in the Party's revolutionary strategy bear the stamp of his genius. His fine hand can be seen in the careful attention to organization and detail, in the concern for unity (both internal and within the socialist camp as a whole), and in the delicate structure of the united front. It is perhaps most obvious in the Party's astute handling of the international situation and in its use of diplomacy as a cardinal feature of its revolutionary strategy. In an age when many of the leaders of newly independent nations in Asia lacked the administrative and organizational abilities to match their personal charisma (Sukarno and U Nu come immediately to mind), Ho Chi Minh was an unusual composite of moral leader and organizational genius, half Gandhi, half Lenin. It was a dynamic combination. It is not too much to say that, without Ho Chi Minh, there might not have been a Vietnamese revolution, at least in the form we know.

X *FURTHER READING*

Weldon A. Brown, *The Last Chopper* (1976)
Wilfred Burchett, *Grasshoppers and Elephants: Why Vietnam Fell* (1977)
David Butler, *The Fall of Saigon* (1985)
Alan Dawson, *55 Days: The Fall of South Vietnam* (1977)
Gerald R. Ford, *A Time to Heal* (1979)
P. Edward Haley, *Congress and the Fall of South Vietnam and Cambodia* (1982)
Stuart A. Herrington, *Peace with Honor?* (1983)
Stephen T. Hosmer et al., *The Fall of South Vietnam* (1980)
Nguyen Tien Hung and Jerrold L. Schecter, *The Palace File* (1986)
William E. LeGro, *Vietnam from Cease-Fire to Capitulation* (1981)
John Pilzer, *The Last Day* (1976)
Gareth Porter, *A Peace Denied* (1975)
Frank Snepp, *A Decent Interval* (1977)
Tad Szulc, "How Kissinger Did It: Behind the Vietnam Cease-Fire Agreement," *Foreign Policy,* No. 15 (1974), 21–61
Tiziano Terzani, *Giai Phong! The Fall and Liberation of South Vietnam* (1976)
Tran Van Tra, *Ending the Thirty Years' War* (1982)
Joseph J. Zasloff and MacAlister Brown, eds., *Communism in Indochina* (1975)

C H A P T E R

15

Consequences and Lessons

of the War

✗

Although twenty years have elapsed since the conclusion of the Vietnam War, the debate over the war's meaning continues to rage. The proliferation of novels, memoirs, films, and television programs about Vietnam testifies to the war's continuing hold on the American people. A veritable explosion of scholarly and political accounts of the Vietnam conflict has paralleled the remarkably diverse outpourings of popular culture. Yet the picture that emerges from those diverse efforts remains hazy.

What have been the war's consequences—on America, on Asia, and on the rest of the world? How should we read the lessons of the war? Those fundamental questions have inspired a variety of conflicting answers. The documents and essays in this chapter explore those issues, continuing the debate introduced in Chapter 1 about the broader meaning of the war.

✗ D O C U M E N T S

In the first document, an excerpt from a presidential press conference of June 9, 1975, President Gerald R. Ford responds to questions about the lessons he has learned from America's experience. In the next document, Ford's successor, President Jimmy Carter, describes the profound moral crisis that he believes the war created for America. His comments formed part of a major foreign-policy address delivered at Notre Dame University on May 22, 1977. In a book published in 1985, part of which is reprinted as the third selection, Richard M. Nixon reflected on the lessons of Vietnam, charging that Saigon's fall represented one of the Soviet Union's greatest victories. In the next document, William Sullivan, a career foreign-service officer and former U.S. ambassador to Iran, sees some very different consequences of the war. Acknowledging its tragic nature, he argues that the war nonetheless helped to bring about a strategic balance in Asia favorable to the United States. The fifth document is an address delivered by President Ronald Reagan at the 1988

608

Veterans' Day ceremony. He made his remarks, celebrating the nobility and sacrifice of Vietnam veterans, at the Vietnam Veterans' Memorial in Washington. The following selection includes excerpts from President Bill Clinton's public remarks after announcing the end of the U.S. trade embargo against Vietnam on February 3, 1994.

The final three documents comprise personal reflections from American veterans deeply affected by the war. First, John Ketwig explains the powerful emotions that the unveiling of the Vietnam War memorial stirred in him. Then Stephen A. Howard, an African-American draftee, explains why his experiences in Vietnam have left such painful psychological scars. Finally, Lily Adams, an Army nurse in Vietnam, describes her own troubled adjustment after the war, concluding with a personal assessment of the war's contradictory legacy.

Gerald R. Ford on the Lessons of Vietnam, 1975

The President. I think . . . there are a number of lessons that we can learn from Vietnam. One, that we have to work with other governments that feel as we do—that freedom is vitally important. We cannot, however, fight their battles for them. Those countries who believe in freedom as we do must carry the burden. We can help them, not with U.S. military personnel but with arms and economic aid, so that they can protect their own national interest and protect the freedom of their citizens.

I think we also may have learned some lessons concerning how we would conduct a military operation. There was, of course, from the period of 1961 or 1962 through the end of our military involvement in Vietnam, a great deal of controversy whether the military operations in Vietnam were carried out in the proper way, some dispute between civilian and military leaders as to the proper prosecution of a military engagement. I think we can learn something from those differences, and if we ever become engaged in any military operation in the future—and I hope we don't—I trust we've learned something about how we should handle such an operation.

Q. Does that mean that you would not conduct a limited war again with a certain amount of restraint on the part of our bombers and so forth?

The President. I wouldn't want to pass judgment at this time on any hypothetical situation. I simply am indicating that from that unfortunate experience in Vietnam, we ought to be able to be in a better position to judge how we should conduct ourselves in the future.

Jimmy Carter Sees a "Profound Moral Crisis," 1977

For too many years, we've been willing to adopt the flawed and erroneous principles and tactics of our adversaries, sometimes abandoning our own values for theirs. We've fought fire with fire, never thinking that fire is better quenched with water. This approach failed, with Vietnam the best example of its intellectual and moral poverty. But through failure we have now found our way back to our own principles and values, and we have regained our lost confidence.

By the measure of history, our nation's 200 years are very brief, and our rise to world eminence is briefer still. It dates from 1945, when Europe and the old international order lay in ruins. Before then, America was largely on the periphery of world affairs, but since then, we have inescapably been at the center of world affairs.

Our policy during this period was guided by two principles: a belief that Soviet expansion was almost inevitable but that it must be contained, and the corresponding belief in the importance of an almost exclusive alliance among non-Communist nations on both sides of the Atlantic. That system could not last forever unchanged. Historical trends have weakened its foundation. The unifying threat of conflict with the Soviet Union has become less intensive, even though the competition has become more extensive.

The Vietnamese war produced a profound moral crisis, sapping world-wide faith in our own policy and our system of life, a crisis of confidence made even more grave by the covert pessimism of some of our leaders.

In less than a generation, we've seen the world change dramatically. The daily lives and aspirations of most human beings have been transformed. Colonialism is nearly gone. A new sense of national identity now exists in almost 100 new countries that have been formed in the last generation. Knowledge has become more widespread. Aspirations are higher. As more people have been freed from traditional constraints, more have been determined to achieve, for the first time in their lives, social justice.

The world is still divided by ideological disputes, dominated by regional conflicts, and threatened by danger that we will not resolve the differences of race and wealth without violence or without drawing into combat the major military powers. We can no longer separate the traditional issues of war and peace from the new global questions of justice, equity, and human rights.

It is a new world, but America should not fear it. It is a new world, and we should help to shape it. It is a new world that calls for a new American foreign policy—a policy based on constant decency in its values and on optimism in our historical vision.

Richard M. Nixon Reads Vietnam's Lessons, 1985

Today, after Communist governments have killed over a half million Vietnamese and over 2 million Cambodians, the conclusive moral judgment has been rendered on our effort to save Cambodia and South Vietnam: We have never fought in a more moral cause. Assertions in the antiwar news media that life in Indochina would be better after our withdrawal served to highlight in a tragic way the abysmally poor level of their reporting throughout the war. But of all their blatantly inaccurate statements over the years, none was more hideously wrong than that one.

From Richard M. Nixon *No More Vietnams*. Copyright © 1985 by Richard M. Nixon. By permission of William Morrow & Co., Inc.

"If wise men give up the use of power," de Gaulle once said, "what madmen will seize it, what fanatics?"

When we abandoned the use of power in Indochina, we also abandoned its people to grim fate. When the American ambassador to Cambodia, John Gunther Dean, was about to be evacuated from Phnom Penh, he offered Lon Nol's closest colleague, Sirik Matak, asylum in the United States. The former Premier responded in a letter:

Dear Excellency and Friend,

I thank you very sincerely for your letter and for your offer to transport me toward freedom. I cannot, alas, leave in such a cowardly fashion. As for you, and in particular your great country, I never believed for a moment that you would have this sentiment of abandoning a people which has chosen liberty. You have refused us your protection, and we can do nothing about it.

You leave and my wish is that you and your country will find happiness under this sky. But mark it well, that if I shall die here on the spot and in the country I love, it is too bad, because we are all born and must die one day. I have only committed this mistake of believing you.

Sisowath Sirik Matak

It was a fittingly noble, if tragically sad, epitaph for his country, his people, and himself. He was among the first whom the Khmer Rouge executed.

After we abandoned the use of power, it was seized by the North Vietnamese and Khmer Rouge Communists. Our defeat was so great a tragedy because after the peace agreement of January 1973 it was so easily avoidable. Consolidating our gains would not have taken much to accomplish—a credible threat to enforce the peace agreement through retaliatory strikes against North Vietnam and a sufficient flow of aid to Cambodia and South Vietnam. But Congress legislated an end to our involvement. It also legislated the defeat of our friends in the same stroke.

A lesson that our adversaries should learn from our intervention in Vietnam is that the United States, under resolute and strong leadership, will go to great lengths and endure great sacrifices to defend its allies and interests. We fought in Vietnam because there were important strategic interests involved. But we also fought because our idealism was at stake. If not the United States, what nation would have helped defend South Vietnam? The fact is that no other country would have fought for over a decade in a war half a world away at great cost to itself in order to save the people of a small country from Communist enslavement.

One lesson we must learn from Vietnam is that if we do not exercise power for the good, there are plenty of men like Ho Chi Minh, Le Duan, Khieu Samphan, and Pol Pot who will gladly exercise it for evil purposes. Our armed intervention in the Vietnam War was not a brutal and immoral action. That we came to the defense of innocent people under attack by totalitarian thugs is no moral indictment. That we mishandled it at times in no way taints the cause. South Vietnam and Cambodia were worthy of our help—and the 3 million people who were killed in the war's aftermath deserved to be saved. Our abandonment of them in their moment of greatest need was not worthy of our country.

Another lesson we must learn is that in the real world peace is inseparable from power. Our country has had the good fortune of being separated from our enemies by two oceans. Others, like our friends in Indochina, did not enjoy that luxury. Their enemies lived just a few miles away up the Ho Chi Minh Trail. Our mistake was not that we did too much and imposed an inhumane war on peace-loving peoples. It was that in the end we did too little to prevent totalitarians from imposing their inhumane rule on freedom-loving peoples. Our cause must be peace. But we must recognize that greater evils exist than war.

Communist troops brought peace to South Vietnam and Cambodia—but it was the peace of the grave.

The Third World war began before World War II ended. Saigon's fall ten years ago was the Soviet Union's greatest victory in one of the key battles of the Third World war. No Soviet soldiers fought in Vietnam, but it was a victory for Moscow nonetheless because its ally and client, North Vietnam, won and South Vietnam and the United States lost. After we failed to prevent Communist conquest in Vietnam, it became accepted dogma that we would fail everywhere. For six years after Vietnam, the new isolationists chanted "No more Vietnams" as the dominoes fell one by one: Laos, Cambodia, and Mozambique in 1975; Angola in 1976; Ethiopia in 1977; South Yemen in 1978; Nicaragua in 1979.

William Sullivan Identifies Some Positive Consequences, 1987

This may sound Panglossian, but a Vietnam had to happen to us sometime. This war was a very tragic event. It tore the country apart. It had consequences politically, socially, and economically from which we are still suffering. But it did draw a line under the prevailing sense of omnipotence and omniscience that the United States postwar generation had developed. When we came out of World War II we were artificially strong. We had a monopoly on nuclear weapons, the strongest conventional military forces, the most resilient economy, a vibrant political system. The rest of the world was in ruins, but it was bound to come back.

And, of course, this is the thing that is so hard to explain to the rednecks. I sometimes do lectures for the Council on Foreign Relations in places like Wichita. Why, they want to know. "Why can't it be like it was then? Goddamnit, we could snap shit and people would pay attention!" A lot of yahoos in this country never accepted that things had inevitably changed. And eventually, just by sheer force of decibels, they got us around to the point that we were prepared to behave like John Wayne and sort of

Kim Willenson et al., *The Bad War: An Oral History of the Vietnam War,* pp. 385–387. Copyright © 1987, Newsweek, Inc. Reprinted with permission.

knock their teeth out, knock 'em back, put 'em back in their box, blow 'em back to the Stone Age, whatever phrase you want to use. Sooner or later we were going to run into a place where we tried to do that and it didn't work.

So the Panglossian part is that just in terms of not having suffered the ruination of the country, we were damned lucky it happened in a place that didn't really matter all that much, like Indochina. Had we taken a stand in a place like Hungary, it could have blown up the world, including the United States. Fifty-eight thousand lives is too many to pay for a lesson, but it's probably smaller than we might have paid had we gone into Czechoslovakia in '68, or done something else that would have led to a direct confrontation with the Soviets or with the Chinese. So Vietnam was a tragedy but it may have been the tragic price that American hubris needed somewhere along the line to get back to reality.

Looking back on Vietnam, the supreme irony of it is that four Presidents took the United States into combat in Vietnam because they were convinced that the strategic balance in Asia was shifting against us and our friends. It wasn't just the Lao Dong [Vietnam Workers' party] moving down into South Vietnam; it was also the Chinese operations in Thailand and Malaysia and the Philippines and above all in Indonesia. What they saw was a vise tightening across the sea-lanes connecting Japan to its energy sources, isolating Australia and New Zealand, and the whole of Southeast Asia becoming Communist.

Now, that didn't happen, but I think the point that all the commentaries that were written on the tenth anniversary missed is that while we didn't win the war, *had* we won, we would have had to keep troops in South Vietnam. And had we kept troops in South Vietnam, the North Vietnamese and the Chinese would have had to patch up their differences to some extent, and the Soviets and the Chinese would have had to give them logistic support. The whole thing would have stayed glued together even though it was palpably inconsistent. Once we pulled out, everything changed. The Chinese were able then to vent their true feelings about the Vietnamese. The Soviets moved in with the Vietnamese in a way that's concerned the hell out of the Chinese. And what you got was the Chinese making this enormous change and reaching an accommodation with the United States.

And the consequence was a cosmic shift in the geostrategic position. Although the Chinese are not our allies, they act in concert with us, in intelligence and other things. We've changed our whole outlook as a result. We no longer think in terms of fighting two and a half wars; we think in terms of one and a half wars. The *Soviets* have to think about two and a half wars. It's the Chinese who keep pounding on the Soviets and the Vietnamese in Southeast Asia, and it's the Vietnamese and Soviets who keep the Chinese in check. Had we plotted it and planned it this way as Machiavellians, it couldn't have come out better.

The fact is, we stumbled into it by what turned out to be an enormously costly, traumatic national experience for the United States—not only fifty-eight thousand people killed, but also the disruption in our own society. Now I think that disruption in some milder form would have come anyway.

Vietnam was not a catalyst so much as an accelerator of changes that were inevitable in our society: the civil rights movement in the South, the women's revolution, the youth revolution, the black revolution. Because it all came at once it was somehow or other in our minds associated with Vietnam. But all those things, it seems to me, have obscured the fact that in its own unintended way, the Vietnam operation turned out to be one of the master strategic strokes of the century. Lyndon Johnson would never believe it in his grave but this is so. And when the historians finally get around to it, I think a lot of the pain and the trauma that went with the sixties will be put in another perspective.

It's very easy, particularly for those who philosophically oppose these changes, to attribute them all to Vietnam and to, essentially, a failure of American will. The great right-wing myth is that the military had that war won, but the damn civilians and the press and the fuzzy intellectuals snatched defeat from the jaws of victory. You know damn well we didn't have that war won and the supreme irony is, aren't we lucky we didn't, because we've now got an equilibrium in the Pacific which is probably the best that has prevailed there since the sixteenth century.

Ronald Reagan Calls Vietnam a Noble and Just Cause, 1988

We're gathered today, just as we have gathered before, to remember those who served, those who fought, those still missing, and those who gave their last full measure of devotion for our country. We're gathered at a monument on which the names of our fallen friends and loved ones are engraved, and with crosses instead of diamonds beside them, the names of those whose fate we do not yet know. One of those who fell wrote, shortly before his death, these words: "Take what they have left and what they have taught you with their dying and keep it with your own. And take one moment to embrace those gentle heroes you left behind."

Well, today, Veterans Day, as we do every year, we take that moment to embrace the gentle heroes of Vietnam and of all our wars. We remember those who were called upon to give all a person can give, and we remember those who were prepared to make that sacrifice if it were demanded of them in the line of duty, though it never was. Most of all, we remember the devotion and gallantry with which all of them ennobled their nation as they became champions of a noble cause.

I'm not speaking provocatively here. Unlike the other wars of this century, of course, there were deep divisions about the wisdom and rightness of the Vietnam war. Both sides spoke with honesty and fervor. And what more can we ask in our democracy? And yet after more than a decade of desperate boat people, after the killing fields of Cambodia, after all that has happened in that unhappy part of the world, who can doubt that the cause for which our men fought was just? It was, after all, however imperfectly pursued, the cause of freedom; and they showed uncommon courage in its service. Perhaps at this late date we can all agree that we've learned one lesson: that young Americans must never again be sent to fight and die unless we are prepared to let them win.

But beyond that, we remember today that all our gentle heroes of Vietnam have given us a lesson in something more: a lesson in living love. Yes, for all of them, those who came back and those who did not, their love for their families lives. Their love for their buddies on the battlefields and friends back home lives. Their love of their country lives.

This memorial has become a monument to that living love. The thousands who come to see the names testify to a love that endures. The messages and mementos they leave speak with a whispering voice that passes gently through the surrounding trees and out across the breast of our peaceful nation. A childhood teddy bear, a photograph of the son or daughter born too late to know his or her father, a battle ribbon, a note—there are so many of these, and all are testimony to our living love for them. And our nation itself is testimony to the love our veterans have had for it and for us. Our liberties, our values, all for which America stands is safe today because brave men and women have been ready to face the fire at freedom's front. And we thank God for them.

Yes, gentle heroes and living love and our memories of a time when we faced great divisions here at home. And yet if this place recalls all this, both sweet and sad, it also reminds us of a great and profound truth about our nation: that from all our divisions we have always eventually emerged strengthened. Perhaps we are finding that new strength today, and if so, much of it comes from the forgiveness and healing love that our Vietnam veterans have shown.

For too long a time, they stood in a chill wind, as if on a winter night's watch. And in that night, their deeds spoke to us, but we knew them not. And their voices called to us, but we heard them not. Yet in this land that God has blessed, the dawn always at last follows the dark, and now morning has come. The night is over. We see these men and know them once again—and know how much we owe them, how much they have given us, and how much we can never fully repay. And not just as individuals but as a nation, we say we love you.

President Bill Clinton Lifts the Trade Embargo on Vietnam, 1994

From the beginning of my Administration, I have said that any decisions about our relationships with Vietnam should be guided by one factor and one factor only—gaining the fullest possible accounting for our prisoners of war and our missing in action. We owe that to all who served in Vietnam and to the families of those whose fate remains unknown.

Today I am lifting the trade embargo against Vietnam because I am

"President Clinton Lifts the Trade Embargo on Vietnam," February 4, 1994. Copyright © 1994 by The New York Times Company. Reprinted by permission.

absolutely convinced it offers the best way to resolve the fate of those who remain missing and about whom we are not sure.

We've worked hard over the last year to achieve progress. On Memorial Day, I pledged to declassify and make available virtually all government documents related to our P.O.W.s and M.I.A.s. On Veterans Day, I announced that we had fulfilled that pledge.

Last April, and again in July, I sent two presidential delegations to Vietnam to expand our search for remains and documents. We intensified our diplomatic efforts. We have devoted more resources to this effort than any previous Administration. Today more than 500 dedicated military and civilian personnel are involved in this effort under the leadership of General Shalikashvili, Secretary Aspin, and our commander in the Pacific, Admiral Larson. Many worked daily in the fields, the jungles, the mountains of Vietnam, Cambodia and Laos, often braving very dangerous conditions, trying to find the truth about those about whom we are not sure.

Last July, I said any improvement in our relations with Vietnam would depend on tangible progress in four specific areas: first, the recovery and return of remains of our P.O.W.s and M.I.A.s; second, the continued resolution of discrepancy cases, cases in which there is reason to believe individuals could have survived the incident in which they were lost; third, further assistance from Vietnam and Laos on investigations along their common border, an area where many U.S. servicemen were lost and pilots downed; and fourth, accelerated efforts to provide all relevant P.O.W.-M.I.A.-related documents. Today I can report that significant tangible progress has been made in all these four areas.

First, on remains. Since the beginning of this Administration, we have recovered the remains of 67 American servicemen. In the seven months since July, we've recovered 39 sets of remains, more than during all of 1992.

Second, on the discrepancy cases. Since the beginning of the Administration, we've reduced the number of these cases from 135 to 73. Since last July, we've confirmed the deaths of 19 servicemen who were on the list. A special United States team in Vietnam continues to investigate the remaining cases.

Third, on cooperation with Laos. As a direct result of the conditions set out in July, the Government of Vietnam and Laos agreed to work with us to investigate their common border. The first such investigation took place in December and located new remains as well as crash sites that will soon be excavated.

Fourth, on the documents. Since July we have received important wartime documents from Vietnam's military archives that provide leads on unresolved P.O.W.-M.I.A. cases. . . .

I have made the judgment that the best way to insure cooperation from Vietnam and to continue getting the information Americans want on P.O.W.s and M.I.A.s is to end the trade embargo. I've also decided to establish a liaison office in Vietnam to provide service for Americans there and help us to pursue a human rights dialogue with the Vietnamese Government.

I want to be clear: These actions do not constitute a normalization of our relationships.

Earlier today, I met with the leaders of our nation's veterans organizations. I deeply respect their views.

I talked with them about my decision, and I explained the reasons for that decision. Some of them, in all candor, do not agree with the action I am taking today, but I believe we all agree on the ultimate goal: to secure the fullest possible accounting of those who remain missing. And I was pleased that they committed to continue working with us toward that goal.

Whatever the Vietnam War may have done in dividing our country in the past, today our nation is one in honoring those who served and pressing for answers about all those who did not return. This decision today, I believe, renews that commitment and our constant, constant effort never to forget those until our job is done.

An American Veteran Helps to Dedicate the Vietnam War Memorial (1982), 1985

November of 1982 brought a tidal wave of emotions and long-suppressed memories into my life, all centered around a shaded corner of the mall in Washington, D.C., where a Vietnam Memorial was being constructed. A television camera scanned the vast wall of names, my eyes recognized a ghost from the past, and I burst into tears. I didn't know he hadn't made it. The children were upset at the sight of their daddy crying. We hustled them into the car and drove to Washington. The memorial was surrounded by snow fence and security guards, waiting quietly to be dedicated the following weekend. Television hadn't prepared me for the power of those huge, black walls; it takes a lot of space to print 57,939 names. We stood on a small knoll beneath the naked branches of hickories in winter dress. Perhaps a hundred strangers were scattered around us, many sobbing, none ashamed. My eyes were watering uncontrollably when the children spotted a squirrel and rescued me with their delighted chatter. . . .

The parade started at ten. We stood on the curb, hunched against the wind. Not long ago, I swore I would never come to the memorial, let alone a parade. Now I needed to be there, to see it and be a part of it, but from a distance. State by state, the waves of veterans came. Phalanxes of wheelchairs, ragged clusters out for a stroll, paunchy, nearing middle age, often irreverent. Clad in three-piece suits, jungle fatigues, green berets, and Indian war bonnets. Jeans and T-shirts. On crutches and canes. There was a disproportionate amount of long hair, as if overcompensating. Orange banners defying America to admit to Agent Orange, and black banners

Reprinted with the permission of Macmillan Publishing Company from . . . *And a Hard Rain Fell: A GI's True Story of the War in Vietnam* by John Ketwig, pp. 299, 301–303. Copyright © 1985 by John Ketwig.

remembering POWs and MIAs. Too often, someone broke ranks to rush to the curb and share a hug and a tear with a ghost come to life. I strained my eyes when the Ohio contingent passed. Perhaps it's best I didn't recognize the barrel chest and wavy blonde hair I had known for less than a day. I called Archie's name, and no one answered.

I was expecting the end of the parade when I saw an approaching solution to years of regret. They looked like all the others, except some carried outrageous signs.

> I am a Vietnam Veteran.
> I like the memorial.
> And if it makes it difficult
> To send people into battle again . . .
> I'll like it even more!

I could hear them now, chanting as they must have chanted in 1969 when I had stayed home. "HELL NO, OUR KIDS WON'T GO!" I hesitated, as I had hesitated in 1969. No, I couldn't wait another thirteen years! I pulled Carolynn off the curb and into the midst of them. I added my voice to theirs, fighting back years of emotion and frustration that threatened to crack my throat. I was amazed as people stepped from the curb to shake our hands or slap our backs.

Someone thrust a cassette recorder to my face and asked what I was feeling. I was too emotional. "We can't allow this to be the end of it. The war isn't over. We can't allow Vietnam to be swept under the rug as past history, because many of the men responsible for Vietnam are right over there," I pointed to the Pentagon, "hard at work, trying to involve us in Nicaragua, or El Salvador, or Libya, or Angola, or anywhere they can try out their terrible toys. It's not past history. It's a terrible, terrible threat, and we have children of our own now. We don't want to raise them to die in some swamp for no reason!" The recorder disappeared, and Carolynn worried that it might have been some form of government surveillance. I didn't care; I had an American right to my opinion, and to voice it. It was a free and glorious feeling, and we followed along to the memorial amid overwhelming joy and sadness. Rain had left the lawn a shambles. Behind us, a pathetic voice declared, "Nice of them to provide all this mud to make us feel at home." A worn guitar hung neck-down from a backpack. A wrinkled old man welcomed us home, his World War I uniform immaculate and proud.

I didn't need speeches to remember The Nam. Carolynn and I lunched on crepes and wine at the Smithsonian Associates' restaurant, enjoying a rare meal without bibs or potty breaks. By the time we returned to the memorial, it was dedicated. The crowd was enormous, and I tugged Carolynn into the midst of it. These were my peers, my generation. I didn't know them, but I wanted to soak up their company. Just being here, I was making a statement I had been unable to make for many years.

Finally the sun faded, the November chill returned, and we headed home. We walked hand in hand under Lincoln's stony gaze, through the trees where the antiwar protesters had been beaten and teargassed. To our right the bronze image of Thomas Jefferson watched us retreat; to our left the White House glowed in the glare of electric lights. Carolynn asked if I was okay.

Behind us, there were no proud sabers or prancing horses. There was only a black wall with 57,939 terrible reminders of the American blood shed in The Nam. Every morning, members of Congress would see it, feel it. It stood out, black and somber, and it couldn't be ignored. I was fine.

In early January of 1983, a group of "scholars and analysts," many from the Defense Department and the Army War College, met at the Smithsonian Institution in Washington, D.C. Officially known as The Smithsonian Institution's Wilson International Center For Scholars, they hoped to define "the lessons of Vietnam." The conference lasted two days. The Baltimore Sun reported, "There was disagreement and criticism, but little in the way of raw emotion." Half a mile away, a veteran stood before a black wall and shivered . . . and a hard rain fell.

An African-American Draftee Reflects on the War's Impact, 1984

When I got out, I applied for disability. But they didn't give me 10, 20, 30, 90 percent. Nothin'. They said I was physically fit for service. But for years I had to exercise, exercise to tone back the stomach and pelvic muscles. And even today, if I don't follow a perfect game plan eating proper foods, I get congestion in my intestines. And, at first, sex was a problem, but then it became a mental thing. At least there is no more of that to worry about.

I started to free-lance. And I was rolling in this industrial photography, doing the whole deal when they were building the Washington subway. But the contracts dried up. I am a highly skilled photographer, but I can't get a job. And my art is becoming more and more sophisticated, becomin' computerized. And I'm still on the outside looking in. I know that if I go someplace and I tell this employer I'm a Vietnam vet, it don't mean shit. Pardon the expression.

You know, I was sitting in my apartment with Carolyn. We weren't married yet. And I picked up the Washington *Post,* and it said Saigon had fell. I said, "What the F was I there for?" I mean what was the whole purpose? All of a sudden you—your—your mechanism said, Hey, you don't have to worry about it. It cuts off. You don't think about Vietnam. That's the way it was.

Then about two years ago, one day, I decided that I'm not out to lunch. I'm null and void. I am not getting up today for no reason. And not getting up today for any reason is not justifiable in our society. See, you can't quit our society.

I don't have the flashbacks and the nightmares. It's the depression. And

From *Bloods: An Oral History of the Vietnam War by Black Veterans* by Wallace Terry. Copyright © 1984 by Wallace Terry. Reprinted by permission of Random House Inc.

you can't identify what the depression is. Plenty of times I just wouldn't come home. All day, you know. And 30 minutes not coming home in my house is a long time. Or you walk into your house one night, take all the clothes out of your closet, and stack 'em up on the floor.

We came back totally fucked up in the head. But it took ten years for our bodies to catch up to where our heads were. All of a sudden you feel this psychological pain become physical pain. Then if you're lucky, which I was, somebody come up and pull your coat and say, "Hey, you need some help." 'Cause if my old lady hadn't decided I needed some help, I would probably either be dead or in jail today.

I went to Walter Reed first. They put me in a situation with about 34 people in a room. How in the hell are you gonna talk to me about my problems with 34 other problems in your face? I went to the VA hospital in Baltimore, and they gave me two aspirins and told me to go to bed and call in the morning. By my wife havin' a job that she could have Blue Cross and Blue Shield, I got a private shrink gettin' me through the moment. But I don't understand why we gotta pay this guy $90 an hour when I gave you three years, four months, five days, and twelve hours of the best of my life.

This psychological thing, we try to suppress it. But it kills us quicker than if somebody just walked up to you and put a bullet in your head. 'Cause it eats away at your inner being. It eats away at everything that you ever learned in life. Your integrity. Your word. See, that's all you have.

Vietnam taught you to be a liar. To be a thief. To be dishonest. To go against everything you ever learned. It taught you everything you did not need to know, because you were livin' a lie. And the lie was you ain't have no business bein' there in the first place. You wasn't here for democracy. You wasn't protecting your homeland. And that was what wear you down. We were programmed for the fact as American fighting men that we were still fighting a civilized war. And you don't fight a civilized war. It's nothing civilized about—about war.

Like this day, they took this water buffalo from the farmers. Either paid them off or killed them. It didn't matter. Whichever was best.

They lifted it with the Huey about 300 feet. Nobody paid much attention. 'Cause you on a chopper base. You see helicopters liftin' off with all kinds of strange things.

So he flew the chopper up, just outside Bien Hao. The game plan was to drop it. And when you drop a water buffalo 300 feet, it has a tendency to splatter. So that meant the farmers around knew that you were almighty. That you would take their prized possession. That we'll come and get your shit.

So we dropped it in the middle of a minefield. Set off a whole bunch of 'em.

I know the Vietnamese saw it. They watched everything we did.

I think we were the last generation to believe, you know, in the honor of war. There is no honor in war.

My mama still thinks that I did my part for my country, 'cause she's a very patriotic person.

I don't.

A Former Army Nurse Considers the War's Impact, 1987

I get on the bus [after returning from Vietnam]. Everyone is staring at me. I mean, they're looking at me like I just killed somebody. I'm sitting there thinking something must be wrong with my uniform, that they're critical of me because I'm not shipshape—I really did not have any idea what it was all about. So I get off the bus. People are giving me dirty looks all over the place. Still, I can't figure it out. I had heard in Vietnam from letters back that people in the World were negative about us, only it didn't make any sense to me. Why would they be negative about us when we're saving lives backward and forward? Anyhow, I go inside, change into my jeans, and go down to my friend's house. When I get there I take my uniform out of my bag, throw it on the floor and say, "Burn it!" "You sure you don't want to save this? Just look at all the medals! What did you get the medals for?" "I don't want to talk about it—just burn it!"

So I moved into an apartment in San Francisco, on the edge of Chinatown. I lived alone and was very angry and very hostile, only I didn't know what I was angry and hostile about. I didn't know if I was angry at the country for being angry at me. I didn't know if I was angry because all that work in Vietnam was for nothing—I mean, I was very, very confused. That's why I ended up going to bars looking for Vietnam vets. . . .

What do I tell my kids about Vietnam? The truth. The confusion. I've explained to Erika about one kid who had one leg missing, one arm missing, and one eye missing. When he came in to us he yelled, "You bitches leave me alone!" The captain got on his case, said, "You don't talk to them like that—they're women and you don't say those words to them!" Well, the kid had been hanging around with GIs and didn't know *bitch* was a bad word. He was a toughie, a real toughie, that kid. He ended up getting very attached to me and used to cry whenever I'd leave him. Well, I resisted getting attached to him—I resisted and resisted and felt real guilty for not allowing myself to give him what I wanted to give him. Because I didn't want to get attached, not to anybody. So I explained to Erika that this kid haunted me. That I did everything I should have done, that there was no way I could have adopted him—yet he got to me. That kid really got to my defenses.

Yeah, I had problems with children. Last Christmas is the first one I survived without going totally bananas at the sight of crowds of children. And that's because I'm really very well healed. I went to Salute One [the dedication ceremonies for the Vietnam Veterans Memorial in Washington], dealt with my grief at the Wall, and left a hundred pounds lighter.

Vietnam taught me a lot. It taught me that war is not the practical way of dealing with disagreements among countries, and it taught me that the men and women who served in Vietnam are very special people.

From *In the Combat Zone* by Kathryn Marshall. Copyright © 1987 by Kathryn Marshall. By permission of Little, Brown and Company.

When I discuss Vietnam I find myself discussing the negative stuff. War is negative, and most of the time Vietnam was negative. But I want to emphasize that, as a nurse in a war zone, I found myself performing beyond my limits—as a result, I have more self-confidence, know that I can tackle any task, that nothing is impossible if you want it bad enough. I'm really proud to have served in Vietnam. No one can take that away from me or from the other vets.

I was lucky enough to witness the special friendship between men that you rarely see in so-called real life. I learned that men can be gentle, tender, and loving with each other. I learned that men and women can work together with mutual respect and admiration. But no matter what positive experiences we had over there, I know war is not the answer to anything. That's why I'll continue to work on peace issues for the rest of my life.

Soldiers aren't the only ones who die in wars. Like I tell my kids, grandmas, grandpas, mommies, daddies, and babies die in wars, too.

X *E S S A Y S*

In the first essay, Paul Kennedy, a Yale University historian, assesses the Vietnam War's impact on the international power system. The author of a highly acclaimed book on the rise and fall of the great powers over the past five hundred years, from which this selection is drawn, Kennedy argues that the war's practical and symbolic consequences have been profound for the United States and for the rest of the world. Eric M. Bergerud of Lincoln University critically considers the broader lessons of the war in the middle essay. He disagrees strongly with those who have held that the United States could have won the war if only it had adopted different tactics. Finally, historian Marilyn B. Young of New York University explains why the Vietnam War has become a political and cultural touchstone for Americans, despite their inability to reach a consensus on the conflict's meaning. Indeed, she argues that it will likely remain indefinitely "a zone of contested meaning." Young also probes why the war in Vietnam has left such a powerful—and often tragic—imprint on the men and women who served there.

The Impact of Vietnam on America's World Role

PAUL KENNEDY

In so many ways, symbolic as well as practical, it would be difficult to exaggerate the impacts of the lengthy American campaign in Vietnam and other parts of Southeast Asia upon the international power system—or upon the national psyche of the American people themselves, most of whose perceptions of their country's role in the world still remain strongly influenced by that conflict, albeit in different ways. The fact that this was a war fought

From *The Rise and Fall of the Great Powers* by Paul Kennedy, pp. 404–409. Copyright © 1987 by Paul Kennedy. Reprinted by permission of Random House, Inc.

by an "open society"—and made the more open because of revelations like the Pentagon Papers, and by the daily television and press reportage of the carnage and apparent futility of it all; that this was the first war which the United States had unequivocally lost, that it confounded the victorious experiences of the Second World War and destroyed a whole array of reputations, from those of four-star generals to those of "brightest and best" intellectuals; that it coincided with, and in no small measure helped to cause, the fissuring of a consensus in American society about the nation's goals and priorities, was attended by inflation, unprecedented student protests and inner city disturbances, and was followed in turn by the Watergate crisis, which discredited the presidency itself for a time; that it seemed to many to stand in bitter and ironic contradiction to everything which the Founding Fathers had taught, and made the United States unpopular across most of the globe; and finally that the shamefaced and uncaring treatment of the GIs who came back from Vietnam would produce its own reaction a decade later and thus ensure that the memory of this conflict would continue to prey upon the public consciousness, in war memorials, books, television documentaries, and personal tragedies—all of this meant that the Vietnam War, although far smaller in terms of casualties, impacted upon the American people somewhat as had the First World War upon Europeans. The effects were seen, overwhelmingly, at the *personal* and *psychological* levels; more broadly, they were interpreted as a crisis in American civilization and in its constitutional arrangements. As such, they would continue to have significance quite independent of the strategical and Great Power dimensions of this conflict.

But the latter aspects are the most important ones for our survey, and require further mention here. To begin with, it provided a useful and sobering reminder that a vast superiority in military hardware and economic productivity will not always and automatically translate into military *effectiveness.* . . . Economically, the United States may have been fifty to one hundred times more productive than North Vietnam; militarily, it possessed the firepower to (as some hawks urged) bomb the enemy back into the stone age—indeed, with nuclear weapons, it had the capacity to obliterate Southeast Asia altogether. But this was *not* a war in which those superiorities could be made properly effective. Fear of domestic opinion, and of world reaction, prevented the use of atomic weapons against a foe who could never be a *vital* threat to the United States itself. Worries about the American public's opposition to heavy casualties in a conflict whose legitimacy and efficacy came increasingly under question had similarly constrained the administration's use of the conventional methods of warfare; restrictions were placed on the bombing campaign; the Ho Chi Minh Trail through neutral Laos could not be occupied; Russian vessels bearing arms to Haiphong harbor could not be seized. It was important not to provoke the two major Communist states into joining the war. This essentially reduced the fighting to a series of small-scale encounters in jungles and paddy fields, terrain which blunted the advantages of American firepower and (helicopter-borne) mobility, and instead placed an emphasis upon jungle-warfare techniques and unit cohesion—which was much less of a problem for the crack forces than for the rapidly turning over contingents of draftees. Although Johnson followed Kennedy's lead in sending more and more troops to Vietnam (it peaked at 542,000, in 1969), it was never enough to meet General Westmoreland's demands; clinging to the view that this was still a limited conflict, the government refused to mobilize the reserves, or indeed to put the economy on a war footing.

The difficulties of fighting the war on terms disadvantageous to the United States' real military strengths reflected a larger political problem— the discrepancy between means and ends (as Clausewitz might have put it). The North Vietnamese and the Vietcong were fighting for what they believed in very strongly; those who were not were undoubtedly subject to the discipline of a totalitarian, passionately nationalistic regime. The South Vietnamese governing system, by contrast, appeared corrupt, unpopular, and in a distinct minority, opposed by the Buddhist monks, unsupported by a frightened, exploited, and war-weary peasantry; those native units loyal to the regime and who often fought well were not sufficient to compensate for this inner corrosion. As the war escalated, more and more Americans questioned the efficacy of fighting for the regime in Saigon, and worried at the way in which all this was corrupting the American armed forces them-selves—in the decline in morale, the rise in cynicism, indiscipline, drug-taking, prostitution, the increasing racial sneers at the "gooks," and atrocities in the field, not to mention the corrosion of the United States' own currency or of its larger strategic posture. Ho Chi Minh had declared that his forces were willing to lose men at the rate of ten to one—and when they were rash enough to emerge from the jungles to attack the cities, as in the 1968 Tet offensive, they often did; but, he continued, despite those losses they would still fight on. That sort of willpower was not evident in South Vietnam. Nor was American society itself, increasingly disturbed by the war's contradictions, willing to sacrifice everything for victory. While the latter feeling was quite understandable, given what was at stake for each side, the fact was that it proved impossible for an open democracy to wage a halfhearted war successfully. This was the fundamental contradiction, which neither [Secretary of Defense Robert] McNamara's systems analysis nor the B-52 bombers based on Guam could alter.

More than a decade after the fall of Saigon (April 1975), and with books upon all aspects of that conflict still flooding from the presses, it still remains difficult to assess clearly how it may have affected the U.S. posi-tion in the world. Viewed from a longer perspective, say, backward from the year 2000 or 2020, it might be seen as having produced a salutory shock to American global hubris (or to what Senator [J. William] Fulbright called "the arrogance of power"), and thus compelled the country to think more deeply about its political and strategical priorities and to readjust more sen-sibly to a world already much changed since 1945—in other words, rather like the shock which the Russians received in the Crimean War, or the British received in the Boer War, producing in their turn beneficial reforms and reassessments.

At the time, however, the short-term effects of the war could not be other than deleterious. The vast boom in spending on the war, precisely at a time when domestic expenditures upon Johnson's "Great Society" were also leaping upward, badly affected the American economy. . . . Moreover, while the United States was pouring money into Vietnam, the USSR was devoting steadily larger sums to its nuclear forces—so that it achieved a rough strategic parity—and to its navy, which in these years emerged as a major force in global gunboat diplomacy; and this increasing imbalance was worsened by the American electorate's turn against military expenditures for most of the 1970s. In 1978, "national security expenditures" were only 5 percent of GNP, lower than they had been for thirty years. Morale in the armed services plummeted, in consequence both of the war itself and of the postwar cuts. Shakeups in the CIA and other agencies, however necessary to check abuses, undoubtedly cramped their effectiveness. The American concentration upon Vietnam worried even sympathetic allies; its methods of fighting in support of a corrupt regime alienated public opinion, in western Europe as much as in the Third World, and was a major factor in what some writers have termed American "estrangement" from much of the rest of the planet. It led to a neglect of American attention toward Latin America—and a tendency to replace Kennedy's hoped-for "Alliance for Progress" with military support for undemocratic regimes and with counterrevolutionary actions (like the 1965 intervention in the Dominican Republic). The—inevitably—open post-Vietnam War debate over the regions of the globe for which the United States would or *would not* fight in the future disturbed existing allies, doubtless encouraged its foes, and caused wobbling neutrals to consider re-insuring themselves with the other side. At the United Nations debates, the American delegate appeared increasingly beleaguered and isolated. Things had come a long way since Henry Luce's assertion that the United States would be the elder brother of nations in the brotherhood of man.

The other power-political consequence of the Vietnam War was that it obscured, by perhaps as much as a decade, Washington's recognition of the extent of the Sino-Soviet split—and thus its chance to evolve a policy to handle it. It was therefore the more striking that this neglect should be put right so swiftly after the entry into the presidency of that bitter foe of Communism, Richard Nixon, in January 1969. But Nixon possessed, to use Professor [John Lewis] Gaddis's phrase, a "unique combination of ideological rigidity with political pragmatism"—and the latter was especially manifest in his dealings with foreign Great Powers. Despite Nixon's dislike of domestic radicals and animosity toward, say, Allende's Chile for its socialist policies, the president claimed to be unideological when it came to global diplomacy. To him, there was no great contradiction between ordering a massive increase in the bombing of North Vietnam in 1972—to compel Hanoi to come closer to the American bargaining position for withdrawal from the South—and journeying to China to bury the hatchet with Mao Tse-tung in the same year. Even more significant was to be his choice of Henry Kissinger as his national security adviser (and later secretary of state). Kissinger's approach to world affairs was historicist and relativistic: events had to be seen in their larger context, and related to each other; Great Powers should be judged on what they did, not on their domestic ideology; an absolutist search for security was utopian, since that would make everyone else absolutely insecure—all that one could hope to achieve was relative security, based upon a reasonable balance of forces in world affairs, a mature recognition that the world scene would never be completely harmonious, and a willingness to bargain. Like the statesmen he had written about (Metternich, Castlereagh, Bismarck), Kissinger felt that "the beginning of wisdom in human as well as international affairs was knowing when to stop." His aphorisms were Palmerstonian ("We have no permanent enemies") and Bismarckian ("The hostility between China and the Soviet Union served our purposes best if we maintained closer relations with each side than they did with each other"), and were unlike anything in American diplomacy since [George] Kennan. But Kissinger had a much greater chance to direct policy than his fellow admirer of nineteenth-century European statesmen ever possessed.

Finally, Kissinger recognized the limitations upon American power, not only in the sense that the United States could not afford to fight a protracted war in the jungles of Southeast Asia *and* to maintain its other, more vital interests, but also because both he and Nixon could perceive that the world's balances were altering, and new forces were undermining the hitherto unchallenged domination of the two superpowers. The latter were still far ahead in terms of strictly military power, but in other respects the world had become more of a multipolar place: "In economic terms," he noted in 1973, "there are at least five major groupings. Politically, many more centers of influence have emerged. . . ." With echoes of (and amendments to) Kennan, he identified five important regions, the United States, the USSR, China, Japan, and western Europe; and unlike many in Washington and (perhaps) everyone in Moscow, he welcomed this change. A *concert* of large powers, balancing each other off and with no one dominating another, would be "a safer world and a better world" than a bipolar situation in which "a gain for one side appears as an absolute loss for the other." Confident in his own abilities to defend American interests in such a pluralistic world, Kissinger was urging a fundamental reshaping of American diplomacy in the largest sense of that word.

The diplomatic revolution caused by the steady Sino-American *rapprochement* after 1971 had a profound effect on the "global correlation of forces." Although taken by surprise at Washington's move, Japan felt that it at last was able to establish relations with the People's Republic of China, which thus gave a further boost to its booming Asian trade. The Cold War in Asia, it appeared, was over—or perhaps it would be better to say that it had become more complicated: Pakistan, which had been a diplomatic conduit for secret messages between Washington and Peking, received the support of both those Powers during its clash with India in 1971; Moscow, predictably, gave strong support to New Delhi. In Europe, too, the balances had been altered. Alarmed by China's hostility and taken aback by

Kissinger's diplomacy, the Kremlin deemed it prudent to conclude the SALT [Strategic Arms Limitations Talks] I treaty and to encourage the various other attempts to improve relations across the Iron Curtain. It also held back when, following its tense confrontation with the United States at the time of the 1973 Arab-Israeli war, Kissinger commenced his "shuttle diplomacy" to reconcile Egypt and Israel, effectively freezing Russia out of any meaningful role.

It is difficult to know how long Kissinger could have kept up his Bismarck-style juggling act had the Watergate scandal not swept Nixon from the White House in August 1974 and made so many Americans even more suspicious of their government. As it was, the secretary of state remained in his post during Ford's tenure of the presidency, but with increasingly less freedom for maneuver. Defense budget requisitions were frequently slashed by Congress. All further aid was cut off to South Vietnam, Cambodia, and Laos in February 1975, a few months before those states were overrun. The War Powers Act sharply pared the president's capacity to commit American troops overseas. Soviet-Cuban interventions in Angola could not, Congress had voted, be countered by sending CIA funds and weapons to the pro-western factions there. With the Republican right growing restive at this decline in American power abroad and blaming Kissinger for ceding away national interests (the Panama Canal) and old friends (Taiwan), the secretary of state's position was beginning to crumble even before Ford was swept out of power in the 1976 election.

Lessons of an Intractable Conflict

ERIC M. BERGERUD

Although war continues in Southeast Asia at the time of this writing, the American role in it ended in 1975. Not surprisingly, given the magnitude of our defeat, participants in the war and a large number of scholars have come forward—and will continue to do so—with various views of the catastrophe. Because the issues raised are both painful and recent, nothing like a consensus is possible. In addition, many issues pertaining to the American conduct of the war are difficult to approach for solid data is not yet available. The fine volumes currently being produced by the Center for Military History will undoubtedly help future research by creating a basic, detailed, and reliable narrative framework. From the Vietnamese side, there is even more to be learned. Unfortunately, unless the political situation changes fundamentally, any history coming from Vietnam will have to be treated with great caution. The Republic of Vietnam, so difficult to understand while it existed, remains an analytical enigma and badly needs a historian. Nevertheless, for Americans the war is over, the outcome clear, and some start has to be made to analyze the greatest debacle in our history since the American Civil War.

Reprinted from Eric M. Bergerud, *The Dynamics of Defeat: The Vietnam War in Hau Nghia Province*, 1991, pp. 323–332, 335, by permission of Westview Press, Boulder, Colorado.

A large number of interesting books and articles have appeared since 1975 concerning the American conduct of the Vietnam War. Some of the authors are former participants in the struggle; others are historians, political scientists, and journalists. Many of the authors argue that a different strategy or method of operation in Vietnam might have led to success. People holding this view do not necessarily believe that success would have been worth the cost, but many do. In general, those believing that the United States lost a war that it could have won fall into three groups.

A first group consists of former policymakers or their apologists, including Richard Nixon, Henry Kissinger, and General Westmoreland. They argue that, even though leaders (never themselves of course) made some strategic mistakes and accepted unwise political constraints, the American effort had been largely successful by 1973. The Front was crushed, and the NVA was contained. The real failure, these men maintain, took place when Congress, stampeded by a shallow and uninformed press and a woefully misguided antiwar movement, abandoned a sovereign ally well on the way to victory. The betrayal resulted from an evil brew of domestic politics, war weariness, and the Watergate scandal. It is further argued that, had Nixon remained in power and had Congress not been so perfidious, a stronger South Vietnam, potentially aided by American air power, would have either deterred attack in 1975 or defeated one if it came. The fact that the NVA fought the final battle singlehandedly is offered as evidence that the United States had been victorious against the Front. These individuals prove their contention that the South could have prevailed by focusing on NVA defeats during the Easter Offensive of 1972.

A second group exemplifies a near-consensus in the American military today. Most notably represented by Harry Summers, these people maintain that once the decision to use force is made (a political decision to be sure) it should be applied quickly and decisively. Pure firepower, sophisticated weaponry, and tactical refinement must never substitute for strategy. Force should never be employed unless the political will exists to support it. Vietnam is cited as a perfect example of how not to fight a war. According to this argument, the political constraints placed on the joint chiefs by President Johnson and other civilians forced General Westmoreland into a "no-win" strategy of attrition. Johnson's decision to raise the level of violence in small increments was a naive, academic, and politically cowardly response. It also allowed the enemy to dictate the tempo of the war. Many officers holding this view are quick to grant that it may have been a mistake to get involved in Vietnam in the first place. However, they contend that, once the decision to intervene was made, a rational conduct of the war would have included a mobilization of the reserves, a declaration of war, unrestricted bombing of the North, a naval blockade of North Vietnam, and a ground campaign aggressive enough to cut the Ho Chi Minh Trail and eject PAVN from South Vietnam. An ideal campaign would have involved ground operations in Cambodia, Laos and across the DMZ into North Vietnam. These measures, so this argument goes, should have been implemented as quickly as possible, and this relentless pressure should have stopped only when Hanoi agreed to a genuine, rather than a cosmetic, peace agreement.

A third argument is more popular with many academics and former participants in the village war. William Colby, Robert Komer, Guenter Lewy, and Andrew Krepinevich take this position. This group contends that U.S. policymakers did not understand the "political" nature of the Vietnam War and thus allowed General Westmoreland to follow a futile strategy of attrition. Consequently, Americans neglected the key political and social issues, such as rural poverty, corruption, and administrative inefficiency, that fueled the insurgency. To compound the difficulty, these men maintain, MACV created a top-heavy, overly complicated, and unwieldy ARVN in the mirror image of the U.S. Army. Both American forces and their ARVN progeny misused military force by an unnecessary reliance on firepower, which brought politically counterproductive violence in civilian areas. Forces were also poorly deployed to fight the critical "other war." The insurgency was in the hamlets, not in the hinterlands, it is argued; therefore, the bulk of American forces should have been deployed to reflect this reality. Instead of wasting resources on the "big battalion" war, MACV should have concentrated on rebuilding GVN forces and gaining security for the rural population. Furthermore, these men echo the stand of John Vann, arguing that the United States could have forced the GVN to "harness the revolution" through sweeping reform. According to this argument, a more sophisticated political strategy could have been created that would have appealed to non-Communist elements within the Front and led to the isolation of the Party.

Advocates of the third group share some common assumptions concerning the insurgency. First of all, they assume that control of the countryside by either player was thin: Most Vietnamese peasants, even in Front areas, were, in truth, neutral. Second, they argue that the problems facing the GVN stemmed from a government apparatus that was not responsive to the desires of the rural population—a major problem, no doubt, but one that Americans could have remedied by increasing aid and, more importantly, demanding reform. However, the Party's defects, the argument proceeds, were structural and beyond change. Party control was based on cynical propaganda, coercion, and terror. These analysts assume that communism per se was a bad thing for Vietnam, Asia, and the United States. The allies could have countered propaganda with reform, good deeds, and good example, and the Americans and the GVN could have broken the cycle of terror and coercion through proper force deployments and by giving the peasantry the military means to help protect themselves. In other words, if U.S. assistance had provided a credible promise of security and a better life, the people would have turned on their real enemy. The remaining "hard-core" remnant of dedicated Party members then could have been hunted down. Lastly, implicit in this argument is the contention that a more appropriate policy in the countryside, including a redeployment of ground forces to heavily populated areas and a general increase of resources allocated to the pacification campaign, would have led to a less violent war, allowing

American participation to continue long enough to obtain victory over the Front. A revitalized GVN, supported by its own people, would then have been strong enough, with continued U.S. aid, to prevail over the long haul. Such arguments should sound familiar by now for they were the "party line" at CORDS.

Hau Nghia province was quite a small political entity, more likely to be of interest to an anthropologist than to a military historian. Yet, the sad history of Hau Nghia illustrates very well the enormous problems facing Americans as they attempted to do battle, physically and psychologically, with a powerful and determined enemy. Both sides, even if sometimes mistaken in strategy or tactics, used all their possible energy to prevail in this strategically important place. Furthermore, although the course of the war differed to some degree from province to province, Hau Nghia had certain characteristics that make possible some important generalizations concerning the wider war in Vietnam. It was quite typical of the entire upper Mekong Delta, the heartland of the insurgency, in terms of ethnic makeup, social structure, and economic base. Densely populated, ethnically Vietnamese, and primarily agricultural, it was exactly the type of province within which the Americans and the GVN had to prevail, within a reasonable amount of time, in order to be victorious. Ultimately, of course, despite an extraordinary military and political effort, victory eluded the allies. And regrettably, the factors that led to failure in Hau Nghia province cast serious doubt on each of the three arguments summarized above that suggest an alternative conduct of war would have led to the continued independence of a non-Communist South Vietnam.

One central conclusion, made clear by the war in Hau Nghia province, bears directly on each of the assertions that a change in policy would have led to success: The Party's analysis of the situation in rural Vietnam in 1965 was correct and ours was wrong. Recall for a moment that Party cadres believed that the GVN never had nor ever could obtain legitimacy because of structural factors that could not be changed. The Party viewed the inefficiency and wholesale corruption that characterized the GVN at every level as the inevitable result of social contradictions. An urban, Westernized, and largely Catholic elite, the Party maintained, could never create a just society—or one viewed as just by the peasantry—in a poor, rural Asian country. The Party argued, with considerable justification, that Diem and his successors had kept intact the French colonial apparatus, with the Americans assuming the role of protector.

It does not require a Marxist analysis to confirm these assumptions, and a goodly number of Americans, such as John Vann, agreed with most of them. Where Vann and others parted company with the Party was on their belief that the GVN, if pressured sufficiently by the Americans, could have reformed and revitalized itself and attracted non-Communist progressives away from the Front. Such prospects did not worry Party cadres, believing as they did that revolution—a fundamental redistribution of wealth and power—was sought by enough of the peasantry to neutralize any reform efforts by the GVN. In addition, if any reform was identified with the

Americans, this could only justify the Party's contention that the GVN was a "puppet" of the foreigners and add fuel to the most widely heralded and supported goal of the Front—expulsion of the United States from Vietnam.

So, it did not really matter whether or not the Front had the support of a majority of the peasantry. It is very possible that Vann and others were right when they claimed that most peasants did not care who ruled in Saigon and just wanted to be left alone. The Party had what it needed, the support of the most politically aware and most determined segment of the peasantry. There can be no doubt that, in Hau Nghia and several other provinces, the Front had a virtual lock on the "best and brightest" of the rural youth. The revolutionary movement that had demolished the GVN in Hau Nghia by 1965, although controlled from the outside, was locally recruited and self-sustaining. To be sure, as charged by the Americans, the Front was ruthless in its tactics, unquestionably more so than the GVN. Yet, no revolutionary movement has ever succeeded on terrorism alone. Enough people in Hau Nghia accepted the ideas of the Front to provide the social and political base for a legitimate government. The situation facing the GVN in Hau Nghia at the time of U.S. intervention was just the opposite— the only support it could find came from a few Catholic hamlets and ARVN artillery. This is not to argue that the Front was more virtuous than the GVN; it was, however, much stronger. These were facts of life in Hau Nghia and several other provinces, and they would have faced the Americans regardless of what course of action was adopted.

Three consequences followed from the fact that the Front and not the GVN possessed legitimacy in much of rural Vietnam. In the first place by 1965 (and probably much earlier), the Front had gained moral ascendancy over the GVN. Once again, this is not to argue that, in absolute terms, the Front was morally superior to the GVN. At present, Vietnam is a sad, oppressed, and destitute country. No doubt, many people in rural Vietnam deeply regret the outcome of the war. However, while the war was on, as confirmed by scores of reports and interrogations received by the Americans at Hau Nghia in every phase of the conflict, peasants perceived the followers of the Front as honest, efficient, and genuinely concerned about the people's welfare. They perceived GVN officials, on the other hand, as aloof and corrupt. The dedication and courage of enemy fighting men, compared with the listless performance that characterized most GVN forces, was widely acknowledged and admired by U.S. troops. No matter how hard and terrifying the war was for American or South Vietnamese soldiers, fighters for the Front led an absolutely hellish existence. They lived in holes, regularly faced hunger and disease, were subjected to air strikes, napalm and artillery bombardment, and lacked decent medical care. Whatever the actual validity of the "body count" figures, there can be no doubt that joining the Front was the most dangerous choice by far that could have been made by young people in Vietnam. Yet, enough Front cadres remained totally convinced that they would prevail to keep the general population's perceptions concerning the outcome of the war very much in doubt. Put another way, the GVN, even with massive American support, could never create the essential foundation for strong and resilient morale—the perception that it could win. The collapse in 1975 is very intelligible in this light.

From this situation follows the second consequence of the lack of legitimacy that faced the GVN: A genuine revival of government support or an actual change in allegiance on the part of the rural population could not have taken place while the war was in progress. As we have seen, any progress the GVN achieved in the countryside was due to measures that weakened the Front, chiefly through military attrition. All efforts to change the fundamental attitudes of the people of Hau Nghia toward the GVN failed, if American records are accurate. An undetermined but substantial number of peasants always either supported the Front or were sympathetic toward it. An even larger number of people were in doubt over the eventual outcome of the struggle, an attitude that encouraged neutrality. To be sure, the GVN did have its supporters in Hau Nghia and many more elsewhere. There were good commanders, good soldiers, good officials, and even a few good policemen—but never enough of them. Recall that the Hau Nghia Popular Forces, the units most responsible for hamlet security, were next to worthless, a very good indication that a great many people felt little reason to take major risks to protect the state. In this regard, Americans usually missed the point. When they constructed a political equation for Vietnam, it always resembled a hypothetical public opinion poll that asked whether most people in South Vietnam supported the GVN or the Front. The question they should have asked was which side were more people willing to die for. Had they asked the second question, they would not have liked the answer.

Last, if it is correct to assume that no real possibility existed to change the political allegiance of the rural population to one of genuine support of the GVN, it must follow that the only way for the GVN and the Americans to have prevailed was to have crushed the Front militarily. As has been seen, this very nearly occurred. Indeed, had South Vietnam been an island, the GVN undoubtedly would have survived. But South Vietnam, of course, was not an island. Consequently, considering the geography and terrain of Vietnam and the great strength of the Front in much of the country by 1965 (especially in provinces like Hau Nghia), crushing the Front inevitably would have been a very time-consuming process, regardless of the means chosen to do so.

More specific conclusions drawn from Hau Nghia also bear on the matter of alternative strategies. In the first place, Nixon and Westmoreland are wrong to maintain that Congress sabotaged a basically successful war effort after 1973. On the contrary, if the situation in Hau Nghia province at the time of the cease-fire is any guide, the GVN was in a nearly hopeless situation. Although the insurgency in Hau Nghia and throughout Vietnam had been seriously weakened by 1973, it was still intact, and, as we have seen, the Front had halted its downward spiral. At the time of the 1975 NVA offensive, Americans estimated that about 40,000 guerrillas were active in South Vietnam. Some, but not all, were northerners. During the Easter

Offensive in 1972, it will be recalled, local force units in Hau Nghia were greatly strengthened due to desertions from territorial units and the PSDF. Furthermore, during that offensive, the NVA, with some Front aid, had seized a third of the country, mostly in the Central Highlands. Called Third Vietnam, this area was sparsely populated and contained less than 10 percent of the population. However, hamlets in this area, including some in Hau Nghia, were fully mobilized for revolutionary warfare. The continued existence of the insurgency had serious consequences for the GVN. As long as the Front existed, the spell of fear and possible doom continued to blanket the countryside. Weariness generated by years of unending war threatened to bring exhaustion and psychological collapse at any moment. Equally important, the bulk of the military manpower available to the GVN was tied down by the insurgency until the very end. In January 1975, there were nearly 500,000 men in the RF/PF, mostly involved with the pacification campaign. In addition, fifteen ARVN regiments were deployed in the Mekong Delta, far from areas of strategic importance. The drain on the South Vietnamese finances from such a military establishment was severe, and, by 1975, the economy had started to collapse and the political system disintegrate.

Also, the strategic situation was positively dreadful from the point of view of the GVN even before 1975, particularly in the Central Highlands. Although the 1972 fighting is sometimes portrayed as an ARVN victory, the reality was more complex and far less favorable. Despite the recapture of Quang Tri in September 1972 (ARVN's last success), the GVN, even with the help of American air power, was unable to regain most of the territory lost. In 1974 the NVA was victorious in a series of middle-sized battles. It was just such a series of encounters that led to the loss of Phuoc Long province in northwestern III CTZ during January 1975. It is difficult to believe that, had he still been in power, President Nixon would have chosen to reopen hostilities to counter gradual aggression. Even if he had done so, massive air support of the type employed in 1972 would have taken some time to deliver because many of the air assets were no longer in Asia. In addition, the NVA had studied its defeats during 1972 and had instituted several tactical refinements. So, whereas the threat of U.S. air power might have deterred a massive attack in 1975, the North could have responded by finding the threshold at which the Americans would intervene and then exerting pressure just below it. Above all, most ARVN units could match PAVN only through greatly superior firepower. Fighting in Hau Nghia showed that, at every level and despite numerous tactical blunders, PAVN and Front military forces were superior to their GVN counterparts in morale and determination. They were, after all, ultimately able to defeat a sizable army without any friendly air support whatsoever, an impressive military achievement. Unfortunately for the GVN, by 1975, the NVA for the first time had reached at least parity in most fields of land weaponry. There is nothing the United States could have done to prevent the DRV from strengthening its armed forces. Furthermore, it is difficult to believe that a few extra billions of dollars in military aid for the GVN would have made a fundamental difference. Consequently, particularly considering the total and wretched nature of the rout during 1975, more U.S. aid and even the reintroduction of American air power could have, at most, delayed the collapse.

The U.S. military's claim that a rapid and decisive use of force would have led to victory is more plausible, but it, too, has difficulties. As the experience in Hau Nghia province made very clear, the Front was highly dependent upon aid from the DRV once it decided to emphasize main force operations after 1964. Supplies from the DRV, particularly in the field of heavier armament, were required if the Front were to finish off ARVN. They were even more necessary if the Front main force units had any hopes of engaging American units in pitched battle. The sanctuaries in Cambodia offered an excellent place to rest and prepare units. They also frustrated, to a large degree, American efforts in 1966–1967 to trap large enemy units. As we have seen, the temporary loss of the sanctuaries, along with the permanent loss of the Sihanoukville supply line, injured the Front in Hau Nghia quite seriously. Furthermore, there is little doubt that the U.S. Army had the capabilities, especially if reinforced, to have cut the Ho Chi Minh Trail, neutralized the sanctuaries, and isolated Front forces from outside aid.

If the DRV would have been sufficiently frightened by more vigorous bombing, such actions might possibly have led the North to end direct aid to the insurgency and withdraw PAVN. It does not necessarily follow, however, that the North could have or would have tried to end hostilities in South Vietnam. The Front was nominally independent. Had necessity demanded, its political apparatus could have operated without guidance or assistance. It is inconceivable that the Front would have laid down its arms without a fight and yielded the huge portion of rural Vietnam, including Hau Nghia province, that it controlled and administered by 1965. Had the Front chosen to fight on alone, it would have faced serious problems. American units could have operated at squad and company levels at a much earlier date than they, in fact, felt safe to do so, and large offensives would not have been possible. This last point, however, might have been a blessing in disguise for the Front. Had the insurgency been forced to stand on the defensive, the manpower and cadres squandered during the two Tet Offensives would have been saved. It is possible, although not at all certain, that a massive show of force by the Americans might have shaken the conviction held by Front followers that victory was inevitable. However, no increase of military effort against the North in 1965–1966 would have altered the weakness of the GVN in the countryside. The U.S. military still would have had to assist GVN forces in an interminable pacification campaign. Above all, it would have been very difficult to counter a decision by the Front to lower the level of the war, conserve strength, and wait out the Americans no matter how long it took.

Had the United States chosen to go all-out militarily, more serious difficulties would have faced Washington if the DRV had chosen to fight. This wouldn't have been a very likely decision (unless vetoed by both Peking and Moscow), particularly if American forces had invaded the North above the DMZ, as urged by the joint chiefs. A land campaign in any part of North Vietnam would have presented daunting problems to the United States. North Vietnamese villages, to varying degrees, were all organized for a "people's war." Front-controlled villages and hamlets in Hau Nghia province were painful and frustrating to deal with for American forces, even with indigenous assistance from the South Vietnamese. In the North, Americans would have faced alone the tactical nightmares created by guerrilla warfare.

Americans would have faced a more serious problem in the strategic realm. The only way U.S. forces could have forced the NVA into a set-piece battle would have been to threaten geographic objectives absolutely vital to the DRV. Yet, not even the most ambitious contingency plans advocated an all-out invasion of the DRV. Consequently, PAVN divisions, unless they chose to fight to the end for the Ho Chi Minh Trail itself, would have been free to withdraw. As fighting in Hau Nghia province showed time and again, enemy units could be bombed, shelled, and bludgeoned but almost never trapped. Therefore, at some point, both sides would have formed a line, creating a situation similar to that in Korea during 1952–1953. Had such a situation developed, American forces would have faced a war of attrition with a much higher level of casualties than actually were endured. As soon as U.S. divisions stood in place, the tactical initiative would have passed to the NVA. The enemy would not have been compelled to either destroy American forces or seize territorial objectives. Rather, they would have concentrated on killing Americans with selective assaults, sapper attacks, and artillery bombardment. Recall that, except for 1969, the marines facing PAVN near the DMZ suffered the highest level of American casualties by a wide margin. . . .

Of course, NVA losses would have been very painful and perhaps might have led to an acceptable settlement. On the other hand, grim tenacity marked every phrase of the enemy's war effort. And North Vietnam would not have lacked moral support from the outside world. As it was, except for some very good clients like South Korea, America's closest friends refused to strongly support the war; the Canadian government even provided sanctuary to young men evading the draft. An all-out "aggressive" war against the DRV would have caused the United States to be treated like an international leper. In addition, it is reasonable to conjecture that a massive American military effort, which would have required higher draft calls, the cancellation of student draft deferments, and mobilization of reserves, could not have been made unless accompanied by political efforts within the United States to justify the action as absolutely vital to national security. In the resulting atmosphere, it would have been extremely difficult for American forces to sit behind a human Maginot Line in the Vietnamese and Laotian jungle, regardless of tactical wisdom. On the contrary, great pressure would have existed to push on ever deeper into North Vietnam in an attempt to break the enemy's will as quickly as possible. Had the United States yielded to this pressure, a very explosive situation would have developed, including the very real possibility of Chinese intervention that, in turn, could have led to general war. Consequently, although a much more vigorous military effort as early as possible would have offered some prospects for eventual success, we must conclude that these prospects were not bright and may well have entailed a debacle far greater than the one suffered.

The American experience in Hau Nghia province also illustrates why a different approach toward fighting the "village war" or the "people's war" would probably not have led to a successful conclusion. If anything, the case that the United States needlessly lost the war in the countryside is more difficult to support than the one that advocated increased military activity as the path to victory. Indeed, the "other way" argument is based upon a major historical distortion and fundamentally wrong assumptions on the nature of U.S. forces available and the nature of revolutionary war in Vietnam.

In the first place, it is often claimed that American leaders, particularly in the military, did not understand the need for a vigorous pacification campaign and were interested only in big battles leading to higher "body counts." This was never true in either practice or theory. As we have seen, the pacification campaign was theoretically crucial for the success of Westmoreland's strategy. And the whole rationale for fighting Front main force and NVA units in their base areas was to provide a "shield" behind which the GVN could rebuild its forces, which had been nearly shattered in 1965, and to allow it to reestablish a basic presence in the countryside. Although it is true that Westmoreland and others underestimated the difficulties involved and ordered some operations, such as CEDAR FALLS, that probably were not worth the effort, the enemy was hurt, ARVN was saved, and the GVN was able to reenter large areas of rural Vietnam.

American arms temporarily rescued the GVN in 1965, but our intervention coincided with a massive intervention on the part of the NVA at a rate initially faster than the U.S. buildup. Immediate operations against the guerrillas in the countryside throughout Vietnam either would have required a far greater number of American troops than anyone envisioned (a number that would have taken a long time to build up anyway) or it would have required spreading American resources very thin—a strategy that MACV, given enemy main force strength, considered much too risky. With the number of serious moments faced by the 25th Division, such as the attack on Company A in April 1966, caution was most understandable. MACV also realized the disastrous propaganda implications of even a small-scale American Dien Bien Phu, further intensifying Westmoreland's desire to operate in strength. It is also necessary to consider that some of the safe zones that were the targets of the "big-unit war" were in direct proximity to heavily populated areas and crucial allied bases. We shall never know how the enemy would have reacted had the big battles not been fought, but it is reasonable to assume that they would have found targets of opportunity. The Party's great strength gave it a large number of options.

Furthermore, even Westmoreland, archvillain in the eyes of the "other warriors," authorized a large number of pacification operations by American units from the very beginning of the war. . . .

Above all, those arguing that a more concentrated effort on the hamlet and village level would have brought success are in error because they implicitly assume that South Vietnamese society was as malleable as clay. As shown over and over again during the war in Hau Nghia province, the best that the GVN could do was attempt to crush the Front. With the aid of U.S. forces, it very nearly succeeded. Yet, all American efforts, as best exemplified by the RD Cadre Program, failed to bring about a fundamental change in political attitudes in the rural population. The most difficult idea to accept for many Americans in Vietnam was that the GVN was inefficient and corrupt because it was inefficient and corrupt. It is no doubt true that many governments around the world are and have been far more corrupt and repressive than the GVN. It is even probable that many people serving the GVN genuinely believed that they had something of value to offer the people they governed. However, because of the accident of geography, the GVN was faced with an insurgency that could lay claim to a great victory over colonialism, that was extremely strong politically, and that was guided by a determined and powerful ally controlling every inch of land bordering the country. In such circumstances, despite intense effort and great dedication (not to mention the blood and treasure expended), any American hope of "harnessing the revolution" and making a weak society strong was doomed. All that remained was force, coercion, and violence, and, however successfully used, it was not enough.

So we come, at last, full circle. The value of the history of the war in a small place like Hau Nghia province lies in pointing out that the military and political situation facing the United States and the government of South Vietnam in the larger arena was intractable, given the realities existing in those nations and in the world. The United States did not fail in Vietnam because of tactical errors that were open to remedy. The errors made were on a much higher level. The American military seriously underestimated the difficulties involved in dealing with enemy forces. And the civilian leadership, particularly under Johnson, underestimated the strength and tenacity of the enemy and overestimated the willingness of its own people and soldiers to continue the struggle indefinitely. In short, American leaders, both civilian and military, committed a strategic blunder that has brought many a general to grief: They chose the wrong battlefield. Tragically, this error brought violent consequences that Americans must contemplate for a very long time, indeed.

The War's Tragic Legacy

MARILYN B. YOUNG

The course of the Vietnam War challenged all the axioms of the post-World War II world, and the ideological conviction the United States needs to

Text from *The Vietnam Wars, 1945–1990* by Marilyn B. Young. Reprinted by permission of HarperCollins Publishers, Inc.

pursue its global domination has yet to be recovered, if it ever can be. The Vietnam War remains today and is likely to remain for the foreseeable future a zone of contested meaning; and the struggle over its interpretation is central to contemporary American politics, foreign and domestic, and of American culture as well.

A fundamental axiom of U.S. foreign policy had been that this nation is always on the side of freedom and justice. "When I got to Saigon I was twenty-two," Richard Holbrooke remembered, "and I believed everything I had been told by the United States government. I believed that the commitment was correct—freedom of choice, self-determination, save the country from Communism—and that we were doing the right thing because the U.S. government *did* the right thing. In those days you didn't question it." Vietnam seriously weakened that automatic response for Holbrooke and for much of his generation; many Americans born during the decade of the war grew up not believing *anything* their government told them.

If axiomatic American goodness was brought into question by the war, so too was the axiomatic evil of the government's designated enemies. Everything that had been used to characterize the enemy—his indifference to human life, his duplicity, his ruthlessness—had at various times during the war been seen to characterize the United States as well. And while this might have been a surmountable problem in the name of a cause fervently embraced by a majority of Americans, it had become a very serious problem in the absence of such a cause.

Nor have American policymakers been able to appeal to the experience of Munich quite as confidently as in the past, although the Bush administration repeatedly did so during the Iraq crisis. For the post-World War II generation of voters, Vietnam has replaced Munich as their foreign policy paradigm.

Popular revulsion from the Vietnam War has been a sufficiently serious constraint on foreign policy to merit special designation by pro-war publicists and politicians: "the Vietnam syndrome." Thus pathologized, its symptoms—grave reluctance to send American troops abroad, close questioning of administration interventionist appeals, consistent poll results indicating that an overwhelming majority judge the Vietnam War to have been not simply a mistake but fundamentally wrong—require a cure, a pacification program. As in Vietnam itself, pacification is both military and civilian. Reagan's 1983 invasion of the tiny island of Grenada—in which 6,000 elite troops won 8,700 medals in the course of an exceedingly brief war against the Grenadian militia and a small group of Cuban advisers— was designed to make Americans "stand tall" again, confident in their capacity to exercise force when their government deems it necessary. Similarly, in 1986 Reagan met the problem of international terrorism by terror-bombing Muammer el-Qadaffi's headquarters in Libya. And in 1989, the Bush administration invaded Panama to remove a former ally who had fallen out of favor. In the summer of 1990, President Bush's rapid military buildup in Saudi Arabia seemed directed not only at Iraq but also at a war-phobic American public.

Militarists, both civilian and in the armed forces, took comfort from the positive response of the public to these actions. But Pentagon analysts were also quick to note the speed and secrecy with which these interventions were launched and, more to the point, terminated. Reagan administration efforts to enlist popular support for American armed intervention in Nicaragua, on the other hand, received little encouragement.

On the civilian front, postwar pacification addresses itself to the restoration of the belief in the essential benevolence of U.S. actions, or, if not always its actions, then certainly its intentions. Jimmy Carter's human rights policy was an effort to achieve the restoration of America's good name, to give the world, in [National Security Adviser Zbigniew] Brzezinski's words, "greater respect for the moral meaning of America . . . and for the President himself as the personal expression of the fundamentally spiritual message of America." The policy required certification of good behavior before congressional appropriations could be approved for regimes whose human rights violations had reached a sufficient level of abuse to come to general international attention. The policy was more rhetorical than real, for whenever serious policy choices had to be made, human rights invariably took second place. In El Salvador in 1979 and 1980, for example, tens of thousands of citizens were being killed by U.S.-trained and -funded military death squads (30,000 between 1979 and 1981; double that number by 1985). Shortly before his assassination, in February 1980, Archbishop Oscar Romero appealed to Carter to end military aid to El Salvador, and he was ignored.

Ronald Reagan jettisoned Carter's human rights policy and set out on a more direct and less expensive approach to healing spiritual wounds: he renamed them. The United States invasion of Vietnam was a "noble cause," the American-paid mercenaries in Nicaragua were "freedom fighters." In one press conference, he rewrote the history of Vietnam itself, informing reporters that it had always been two countries that France had liberated after World War II and whose possible reunification was disrupted by Ho Chi Minh's refusal to participate in elections.

Another postwar necessity has been the development of a satisfactory approach to popular insurgencies or governments in the Third World, a task both complicated and made urgent by the ongoing impact of Vietnam on the United States: "Our failure in Vietnam still casts a shadow over U.S. intervention anywhere," a Reagan administration report warned. Unless the pessimism engendered by Vietnam is overcome and an interventionist policy restored, "America's ability to defend its interest in the most vital regions, in the Persian Gulf, the Mediterranean and the Western Pacific" will be undermined. In this area too there has been renaming, from the "counterinsurgency" of the 1960s to "low intensity conflict."

The phrase "low intensity conflict" may do more than rename, however. As Michael Klare has pointed out, "for U.S. policymakers and war planners . . . low-intensity conflict . . . represents a strategic reorientation of the U.S. military establishment, and a renewed commitment to employ force in a global crusade against Third World revolutionary movements and governments." It is a "broad concept that spans the spectrum of conflict from relative peace to conventional war." Perhaps this is the major departure from the past: low-intensity conflict frankly embraces a policy of permanent war.

The Reagan report identified a monolithic Third World forever poised on the brink of change as the permanent enemy in this permanent war. Communist-led or not, change uncontrolled by the United States endangers its interests. In the report, all the countries of the Third World look alike, all peasants are either passive or terrorized into support for guerrilla movements, and all guerrillas are the same: outsiders supported by the Soviet Union or its regional surrogates. On the other side, all legitimate governments are also alike: modernizing elites, prevented from achieving reasonable reforms by the need to first defeat Communist-inspired popular movements from below, while all revolutionary governments are also the same: totalitarian minorities kept in power by force and Soviet support.

None of the above was true. But acting as if it were sometimes made it so, or effectively so—self-fulfilling prophecies, which exacted a terrible cost on the countries involved. Nicaragua, Angola, Mozambique, have each been blocked from exploring the larger possibilities of their revolutions in order to defend their countries against U.S.-funded mercenary armies. In this way, insurgencies were punished, their example tarnished, and American interests, as recent administrations have defined them, safe-guarded. . . .

Over 26 million American men came of draft age during the Vietnam War; 2.15 million of them went to Vietnam, 1.6 million were in combat. Those who fought the war and died in it were disproportionately poor, badly educated, and black. (A high school dropout who enlisted had a 70 percent chance of being sent to Vietnam, a college graduate only 42 percent; until 1971, student deferments protected the majority of students from the draft altogether.) It was also a teen-aged army—over 60 percent of those who died in Vietnam were between the ages of seventeen and twenty-one, and the average age of those who served was nineteen, five to seven years younger than in other American wars.

Between 1966 and 1972, a special Great Society program—Project 100,000—scooped up over 300,000 young men previously considered ineligible for the military because of their low test scores. Project 100,000, Secretary of Defense Robert McNamara declared, was the "world's largest education of skilled men." With lower admissions scores, the "subterranean poor" would have an opportunity to serve their country in Vietnam; simultaneously, the program had the advantage of avoiding the politically unpleasant alternative of requiring students or reservists to do the same. The benefits, especially to young black men, were said to be especially striking. As Daniel Patrick Moynihan pointed out, the military was "an utterly masculine world. Given the strains of disordered and matrifocal family life in which so many Negro youth come of age, the armed forces are a dramatic and desperately needed change, a world away from women, a world run by strong men and unquestioned authority, where discipline, if harsh, is nonetheless orderly and predictable, and where rewards, if limited, are granted on the basis of performance." In its first two years of operation, 41 percent of those brought into the military through Project 100,000 were black, 80 percent had dropped out of high school, 40 percent could read at less than sixth-grade level, and 37 percent were put directly into combat. Court-martialed at double the usual rate, over eighty thousand of these veterans left the military without the skills and opportunities McNamara assured them would be theirs, and many of them with service records that would make civilian life far more difficult than if they had never served at all.

Each young man who went to war had an individual tour of duty, 365 days, and then home, on his own, with no effort on anyone's part to prepare for the shock of return, to help make the transition from war to peace, from the privileging of violence to its prohibition, from the sharp edge death brings to the life of a soldier to the ordinary daily life of a civilian, which denies death altogether. They had spoken always of coming back "to the world," counting each day "in country" which brought them closer to the end of their tour. But the homecoming was harder than any of them had expected. Later, many veterans would tell stories of having been spat upon by anti-war protesters, or having heard of veterans who were spat on. It doesn't matter how often this happened or whether it happened at all. Veterans *felt* spat upon, stigmatized, contaminated. In television dramas, veterans were not heroes welcomed back into the bosom of loving families, admiring neighborhoods, and the arms of girls who loved uniforms; they were psychotic killers, crazies with automatic weapons. It was as if the country assumed that anyone coming back from Vietnam would, even should, feel a murderous rage against the society that had sent him there. The actual veteran—tired, confused, jet-propelled from combat to domestic airport—disappeared. Or rather, he became a kind of living hologram, an image projected by conflicting interpretations of the war: a victim or an executioner, a soldier who had lost a war, a killer who should never have fought it at all.

Of course there were also just the daily bread-and-butter problems of finding work in an economy far less open than it had been when the war was young. Today, from one quarter to one third of the homeless (between one quarter and three quarters of a million men) are Vietnam-era veterans. Without training or skills, without any public sense that the country owed them anything at all, many Vietnam veterans found themselves not only unrewarded but even disadvantaged by their service records. The war had begun to unravel even as it was being fought, so that by 1971 dissent and disobedience within the armed forces were endemic. The result was a tremendous increase in the number of less than honorable discharges— "bad paper"—which have followed the 500,000 to 750,000 men who received them ever since, making it difficult for them to get and keep jobs, and depriving them of educational and even medical benefits.

The lack of skills, the bad service records, the war wounds, have been only part of the difficulty many veterans face. At first, the widespread appearance of psychological problems was named "postwar trauma" and assimilated to the literature on the problems of veterans of other wars. It soon became clear, however, that Vietnam veterans were not like veterans of other wars. As early as 1970, Vietnam Veterans Against the War organized "rap sessions," sometimes attended by sympathetic psychiatrists, to help returning soldiers deal with their experiences. Even the Veterans Administration, obviously reluctant to single out Vietnam veterans as having any particular difficulties (especially in the light of the meager benefits accorded them), reported a "greater distrust of institutions" and a "bitterness, disgust and suspicion of those in positions of authority and responsibility."

More disturbing was the persistence—or sudden onset ten or even fifteen years after the war—of symptoms of acute distress, accompanied by flashbacks, severe sleep problems, depression, and rage. "Postwar trauma" was renamed "post-traumatic stress disorder" and assimilated not to battle fatigue or shell shock but to what people experience as survivors of floods or earthquakes. A V. A. doctor estimates that as many as 700,000 veterans suffer from some form of "post-traumatic stress disorder" (or PTSD). A massive study of Vietnam-era veterans revealed that those who had been "exposed to significant amounts of combat and/or witnessed or were participants in abusive violence [against prisoners, civilians, etc.] demonstrate long term problems" with disabling memories of the war.

Veterans of other American wars, Robert Jay Lifton argued in his book *Home from the War,* had come to terms with the absurdity and evil of war by believing that *their* war "had purpose and significance beyond the immediate horrors [they] witnessed." But "the central fact of the Vietnam War," Lifton wrote in 1973 while it was still going on, "is that no one really believes in it." Although it is possible to challenge Lifton and demonstrate that soldiers in World War II also had difficulty discerning significance beyond the immediate horror of their situation, it is nevertheless true that when they got home, the purpose and significance of what they had done was universally affirmed and most were able to accept it. This was not the situation of Vietnam veterans, for even those who came home to families or communities who approved of the war were aware of those who protested against it. Moreover, the announced goals of the war—to repel an outside invader, to give the people of South Vietnam the chance to choose their own government—were daily contradicted by the soldier's sense that in fact he was himself the invader, and that "the government he had come to defend [was] hated by the people and that he [was] hated most of all."

"What kind of a war is it?" Larry Rottman, poet and veteran, asked in a poem written during the war,

> where you can be pinned down
> all day in a muddy rice paddy
> while your buddies are being shot
> and a close-support Phantom jet

who has been napalming the enemy
wraps itself around a tree and explodes
and you cheer inside.

"To have been in a war does not mean you understand the memories of it," Gloria Emerson has written. In published and unpublished novels, memoirs, poems, Vietnam veterans have tried to understand their memories.

For women veterans the problem was compounded by the initial inability of anyone, including themselves, to acknowledge that they too were combat veterans. No one seems to have kept close count of their numbers. The Department of Defense says 7,500 women were on active military service in Vietnam during the war; the Veterans Administration lists 11,000 women as having served there. Together with civilians working for the Red Cross or other voluntary services, the general estimate is that a total of between 33,000 and 55,000 women worked in Vietnam during the war. Like the young men who fought the war, the young women who nursed their wounds, or tried to "take their minds off the war," were confused, often defensive, almost always pained by their memories. "Our job was to look them [wounded soldiers] in the eye and convince them that everything was all right." It took practice, but "you finally built up a facade and could literally look at somebody dying and smile like Miss America or whatever we personified to them." The war gave many women responsibilities and a sense of power actually denied them in civilian life. But this new status too was confusing and even distressing in that there was no way to extricate it from the death and dehumanization that were its occasion. One nurse resisted having to treat wounded Vietnamese until one day she was forced to take care of an infant and broke down: "How, I wondered, could I ever come to believe I hated a baby?"

Lynda Van Devanter tried to join a VVAW demonstration when she returned from Vietnam, but was told, "This demonstration is only for vets." "I am a vet," she explained. "I was in Pleiku and Qui Nhon. . . ." "I . . . don't think you're supposed to march," came the answer. "But you told me it was for vets." "It is. . . . But you're not a vet."

In 1982, the Veterans Administration acknowledged that women were truly Vietnam vets: for the first time groups were established for women suffering from post-traumatic stress disorder. "She is afraid to trust again," Marilyn McMahon says in her poem "Wounds of War":

Her days are haunted
    by the texture of blood
    the odor of burns
    the face of senseless death;
friends known and loved
    vanished
    abandoned.
She sits alone in the darkened room
    scotch her only hope.

"The war is never over," one homeless man explained to a reporter in

1987. "You drink one too many beers and it pops up. . . . Sometimes, I hope to settle down somewhere where I won't be reminded of what I've seen. But I really don't see a future for myself." Being unable to imagine a future often precludes having one. More veterans have committed suicide since the war than died in it—at least sixty thousand. Nor is the connection between their war experience and their death at all obscure. Steven L. Anderson's parents, for example, found this note next to the body of their dead son: "When I was in Vietnam, we came across a North Vietnamese soldier with a man, a woman and a three- or four-year old girl. We had to shoot them all, I can't get the little girl's face out of my mind. I hope that God will forgive me."

In May 1971, Medal of Honor winner Dwight W. Johnson was shot dead by the owner of a store he was attempting to rob. In Vietnam, Johnson killed "five to 20 enemy soldiers, nobody knows for sure," when the tank crew he was trying to rescue blew up in front of his eyes. "When he ran out of ammunition," his obituary continues, "he killed one with the stock of his machine gun." Unskilled and jobless in Detroit, Skip Johnson's fortunes turned when he was awarded the Medal of Honor for his heroism that day. Civic notables showered him with gifts and the Army persuaded him to return to the service as a recruiter in Detroit's predominantly black high schools. But his wife noticed some changes in him, as she had in other veterans she knew: "They get quiet. It's like they don't have too much to say about what it was like over there. Maybe it's because they've killed people and they don't really know why they've killed them."

Eventually Skip Johnson went AWOL from his recruiter's job and ended up in Valley Forge VA Hospital, where the head psychiatrist reached a preliminary diagnosis: "Depression caused by post-Vietnam adjustment problem." Later, the doctor observed Johnson's guilt over having survived the tank ambush and over "winning a high honor for the one time in his life when he lost complete control of himself. He asked: 'What would happen if I lost control of myself in Detroit and behaved like I did in Vietnam?' The prospect of such an event apparently was deeply disturbing to him." The psychiatrist refrained from answering Johnson's question; but a store manager in the western end of Detroit was more forthcoming: " I first hit him with two bullets," the manager . . . said later. "But he just stood there, with the gun in his hand, and said, 'I'm going to kill you. . . .' I kept pulling the trigger until my gun was empty."

Johnson's mother, thinking about her son's life and death after he was buried at Arlington National Cemetery with full military honors, wondered whether he had simply "tired of this life and needed someone else to pull the trigger."

And many of those who have not tired of their lives, nor suffered from "post-traumatic stress disorder," who have homes, jobs, families, ambitions, nevertheless find the war somehow remains central to their lives. . . .

After the Korean War, the poet Thomas McGrath memorialized the American war dead—"brave: ignorant: amazed: Dead in the rice paddies, dead on the nameless hills." In November 1982, the brave, ignorant, amazed dead of Vietnam were remembered at the dedication of a Vietnam Veterans Memorial. Money for the memorial had been raised by the veterans themselves; the winning design, by Maya Ying Lin, provided for two black granite walls bearing the names of the Americans who died in Vietnam. There was a protest by those who deemed the design insufficiently patriotic, and so a life-size statue of three GIs, two white, one black, was added to the original conception. Maya Ying Lin protested that it was like "drawing a moustache" on her design, but in the event, the statues have a different impact, as unpredictable as that of the wall itself.

Unlike the commemoration of the flag raising at Iwo Jima, these soldiers are flagless and exhausted. They seem to be waiting for something, but the only thing visible in the direction in which they look are the giant slabs with the names of their dead comrades. At first Bruce Weigl wondered why he had come to the dedication ceremony in Washington on Veterans Day, 1982. "I think we came," he wrote later,

> without really knowing it, to make the memorial our wailing wall. We came to find the names of those we lost in the war, as if by tracing the letters cut into the granite we could find what was left of ourselves. It turns out that, beyond all the petty debates over the monument, no veteran could turn his back on the terrible grace of Maya Lin's wall and the names of the 57,939 who died or disappeared in Vietnam from July 1959 to May 1975: America's longest most vicious sin.

What militarists deplore as the Vietnam syndrome can better be understood as a relatively unique event in American history: an inability to forget, a resistance to the everyday workings of historical amnesia, despite the serious and coordinated efforts of the government and much of the press to "heal the wounds" of the war by encouraging such forgetting, or what comes to the same thing, firm instructions on how to remember. At the dedication of the Vietnam Memorial, President Reagan announced that the time had come to move on, "in unity and with resolve, with the resolve to always stand for freedom, as those who fought did, and to always try to protect and preserve the peace." Harry Haines, a Vietnam veteran, terms Reagan's call the "administrative version of Vietnam memory." According to Reagan, in Vietnam Americans stood for freedom "as Americans have always stood— *and still do.*" The Vietnam War, Haines observes, is thus "normalized, the deaths are made rational, and the veterans are whole once again, stronger for their expiated burden."

To Harry Haines, the design of the memorial is ambiguous, able to contain Weigl's meaning but also that of a veteran who shouted at a group that attempted to hold a vigil for peace at the memorial: "No, not here. . . . These people died fighting against communism and for freedom. Those people [the vigil group] have no right. It's the same thing that went on with Vietnam, saying we don't belong in El Salvador." How the memorial is interpreted is part of an *ongoing* political struggle. Its meaning, Haines insists, lies "not so much in how the dead are remembered by those of us who survived Vietnam at home or abroad, but in how that remembrance is used by power to explain—to justify—sacrifices in future Vietnams."

What distinguishes many Vietnam veterans from those who fought in other U.S. wars, Peter Marin has written, is their exceptional "moral seriousness," emerging from a "direct confrontation not only with the capacity of others for violence and brutality but also with their own culpability, their sense of their own capacity for error and excess." When a friend asked Marin, as those faced with the morally serious so often do, "Well, what is it [the veterans] really want?" Marin found himself answering spontaneously, "'Justice.' That is what they want, but it is not justice for themselves—though they would like that too. They simply want justice to exist for there to be justice in the world. . . ." Which is why, perhaps, Tim O'Brien insists that a "true war story is never moral. It does not instruct, nor encourage virtue, nor suggest models of proper human behavior. . . . If a story seems moral do not believe it. If at the end of a war story you feel uplifted, or if you feel that some small bit of rectitude has been salvaged from the larger waste, then you have been made the victim of a very old and terrible lie. There is no rectitude whatsoever. There is no virtue."

Michael Herr, a reporter who breathed the war in as deeply as any combat soldier, wrote that it "took the war to teach it, that you were as responsible for everything you saw as you were for everything you did. The problem was that you didn't always know what you were seeing until later, maybe years later, that a lot of it never made it in at all, it just stayed stored there in your eyes." Vietnam has remained stored in the eyes of America; very slowly it is becoming possible to know what we have seen. To figure out what it might mean, to accept responsibility for it, will take much longer.

✗ *F U R T H E R   R E A D I N G*

Douglas Allen and Ngo Vinh Long, eds., *Coming to Terms: Indochina, the United States, and the War* (1991)

T. Louise Brown, *War and Aftermath in Vietnam* (1991)

Nguyen Van Canh, *Vietnam Under Communism, 1975–1982* (1983)

Walter H. Capps, *The Unfinished War* (1982)

Nayan Chanda, *Brother Enemy: The War After the War* (1986)

William J. Duiker, *Vietnam Since the Fall of Saigon* (1980)

H. Bruce Franklin, *M.I.A. or Mythmaking in America* (1993)

Peter Goldman, *Charlie Company: What Vietnam Did to Us* (1980)

Bob Greene, *Homecoming* (1989)

John Hellman, *American Myth and the Legacy of Vietnam* (1986)

Herbert Hendin and Ann P. Haas, *Wounds of War: The Psychological Aftermath of Combat in Vietnam* (1985)

Stanley Hoffman et al., "Vietnam Reappraised," *International Security,* 6 (1981), 3–26

Ole Holsti and James N. Rosenau, *American Leadership in World Affairs: Vietnam and the Breakdown of Consensus* (1984)

David E. Kaiser, "Vietnam: Was the System the Solution?" *International Security,* 4 (1980), 199–218

Walter LaFeber, "The Last War, the Next War, and the New Revisionists," *Democracy,* 1 (1981), 93–103

Anthony Lake, ed., *The Vietnam Legacy* (1976)

Robert Jay Lifton, *Home from the War* (1973)

Myra MacPherson, *Long Time Passing: Vietnam and the Haunted Generation* (1984)

Terry Nardin and Jerome Slater, "Vietnam Revised," *World Politics,* 33 (1981), 436–448

Thomas G. Paterson, "Historical Memory and Illusive Victories: Vietnam and Central America," *Diplomatic History,* 12 (1988).

Norman Podhoretz, *Why We Were in Vietnam* (1982)

Earl C. Ravenal, *Never Again* (1978)

John Carlos Rowe and Rick Berg, eds., *The Vietnam War and American Culture* (1991)

Harrison E. Salisbury, *Vietnam Reconsidered: Lessons from a War* (1984)

Neil Sheehan, *After the War Was Over* (1991)

Robert Warren Stevens, *Vain Hopes, Grim Realities: The Economic Consequences of the Vietnam War* (1976)

W. Scott Thompson and Donaldson D. Frizzell, eds., *The Lessons of Vietnam* (1977)

John Wheeler, *Touched with Fire: The Future of the Vietnam Generation* (1984)

Marilyn B. Young, "Revisionists Revised: The Case of Vietnam," *The Society for Historians of American Foreign Relations Newsletter,* 10 (1979), 1–10